Landscape

416 Chambers Street, Peterborough,
Ontario K9H 3V1   (705) 745-3623

SITE PLANNING ● LANDSCAPE ARCHITECTURE ● URBAN DESIGN

SITE PLANNING ● LANDSCAPE ARCHITECTURE ● URBAN DESIGN

Landscape Design
With Plants

British Embassy, Bangkok. *(Maurice Lee)*

Landscape Design With Plants

Edited by
BRIAN CLOUSTON

VAN NOSTRAND REINHOLD COMPANY
New York   Cincinnati   Toronto   London   Melbourne

Library of Congress Catalog Card Number 79-16732

ISBN 0-442-26197-7

Printed in Great Britain

Published in 1979 by Van Nostrand Reinhold Company
A division of Litton Educational Publishing, Inc.
135 West 50th Street, New York, NY 10020, U.S.A.

Van Nostrand Reinhold Limited
1410 Birchmount Road
Scarborough, Ontario M1P 2E7, Canada

1 3 5 7 9 11 13 15 16 14 12 10 8 6 4 2

Library of Congress Cataloging in Publication Data
Main entry under title:

Landscape design with plants.

Includes bibliographies and indexes.
1. Landscape architecture. 2. Landscape gardening.
3. Plants, Ornamental. I. Clouston, Brian.
SB472.L37   1979   712   79-16732
ISBN 0-442-26197-7

FOREWORD

Landscape Design With Plants complements *Techniques of Landscape Architecture*, which was first published in 1967 under the auspices of the Institute of Landscape Architects, as a guide to architectural and land form. Since then, the Institute has been incorporated within the new Landscape Institute, with broader terms of reference and increased value placed on ecology. This publication is intended to give guidance in a world of immeasurable complexity that is only just beginning to be explored and understood. Some years ago it was estimated that there were 250,000–350,000 known plant species and subspecies available, habitat permitting, to the landscape designer. To this encyclopaedic florilegium must now be added the study of the relationship of one plant to another, and of plant life to animal life.

Obviously, such a vast field must be narrowed down and made comprehensible. This book sets out to do just that, and represents the collective experience and judgment of practitioners and theorists distinguished in their own spheres. It is comprehensive enough to provide a basis of knowledge from which each individual can set out on his own adventures, but not so comprehensive as to be overwhelming. As many of the authors emphasize, technique is only a means to an end, and that end is the creation of a humanistic as opposed to an animal environment.

At first, therefore, keep your palette to a minimum and be master of it. It will be a long time before you can attain the heights reached by J. Landwehr, the Director of Parks at Amstelveen in Holland, whose knowledge, acquired over a lifetime, 'extends to a use of over 500 species of native plant material, with detailed information regarding their germination, establishment, rate of growth and stability. These are used in the park aesthetically to create what Landwehr calls landscape pictures, which are of great beauty' (*see* page 120). But this book could be the first rung in a long ladder.

GEOFFREY JELLICOE

Autumn mood. *(Maurice Nimmo)*

PREFACE

Landscape Design With Plants was commissioned by the Institute of Landscape Architects. Many chapters were specially commissioned for the book, others being based on a series of articles specially written by eminent members of the profession for the Institute's journal, *Landscape Design*.

Much valuable information published in the journal will thus be available to a wider audience, presented in a form which has given the authors the opportunity to extend the scope of their original contributions.

The book is divided into three parts, the first being concerned mainly with design, the second with techniques and the third providing information sheets on plants and trees.

By combining theoretical and practical aspects of landscape design with plants together in one book, landscape architects and others concerned with the creation of new landscapes and the rehabilitation of degraded landscape, will have to hand, for the first time, a comprehensive handbook.

Each generation leaves behind visible evidence of its character. We, who are privileged to inherit some of the world's finest man-made landscape, need to reflect from time to time on our contribution to our art. In most, though not all landscapes, plants form the major embellishment. It is vital, therefore, that our knowledge and understanding of the use of plants in landscape design is sound.

It is only by combining the art, practice and management of landscape that we can hope to pass on to future generations a landscape as beautiful as that which our predecessors created.

Part I deals with the use of plants in landscape design. The subject is introduced with a discussion of design in relation to landscape and the importance of the fourth dimension—time. Six chapters follow, each covering a different aspect of the use of plants in landscape—designing with trees; forest planting; trees in urban areas; shrubs and groundcover; herbaceous plants and bulbs, and finally water plants.

Part II is concerned with the practical difficulties and technical aspects of planting, the choice of species to combat particular problems and the grouping of plants to create special habitats. The book does not attempt to give absolute answers. The emphasis is on the need for a sound practical approach to some of the commonly encountered problems facing landscape architects and others in the design and establishment of landscapes. Where possible actual examples are described.

A two-part chapter deals with the use of native plants, providing a useful link with the first part of the book. The subject matter is philosophical and theoretical in part, but also gives practical advice and examples. This is followed by a chapter concerned with planting design and management to encourage wildlife.

The following six chapters deal with planting and plant establishment in difficult situations. These include planting in artificial conditions; transplanting semi-mature trees; planting on spoiled land; the landscape treatment of reservoir margins; planting and air pollution; and planting to stabilize steep slopes. It is perhaps this part of the book which best illustrates the depth of research now being undertaken into the practical application of planting techniques.

Two chapters are included on planting in arid climates and tropical lowland areas. With the growing demand by developing countries for the skills of the landscape designer, knowledge of the problems of planting in adverse climatic conditions and familiarity with the plants of hot countries is becoming increasingly important.

The final chapter discusses the management and maintenance of landscape. It is an appropriate subject with which to conclude, as the publication of the book coincides with the introduction of a new management class into the ranks of the profession.

Part III consists of information sheets on plants and trees, giving concise illustrated data on species commonly used in landscape projects.

This book could not have been produced without the

vii

enthusiasm and generosity of the chapter authors, many of whom have been called upon to make a double effort in first preparing material for an article, and secondly in taking the original material and updating and adapting it to form part of a composite publication. Nor could it have been accomplished without the co-operation of the Institute of Landscape Architects' journal, *Landscape Design*, and its editor, Geoffrey Collens, who provided much of the material.

Our thanks to all the individuals and organizations who have been kind enough to supply us with the many illustrations used in the book. Special thanks should go to Judy Snaith, and to James Ridell Ltd of Newcastle who made black and white prints from colour slides and reproduced many of the plans and drawings.

My thanks are due also to two members of my staff, Kathy Stansfield and Richard Sturdy. Without their extraordinary and unstinting help the book would have been impossible to achieve. I can only hope that *Landscape Design With Plants* is in a small way a reward for their efforts.

BRIAN CLOUSTON

CONTENTS

THE AUTHORS

Brenda Colvin, CBE, PPILA
Landscape architect in private practice since 1925. Currently in partnership with Hal Moggridge, AILA, ARIBA involved mainly in rural planning, such as reservoirs and agricultural problems in England and Wales, and work overseas. Founder member of ILA and IFLA. Landscape consultant to CEGB, Birmingham Water Board, new towns, universities, and various other educational establishments. Author of *Land and Landscape* and *Trees for Town and Country*.

Sylvia Crowe, DBE, PPILA, Hon. FRIBA, Hon. MRTPI
Landscape architect in private practice since 1945. Landscape consultant to Forestry Commission until 1974; CEGB, new towns, water authorities and many local authorities. Chairman of the Tree Council. Author of many books and papers including *Tomorrow's Landscape; Landscape of Power; Landscape of Roads; Forestry in the Landscape; Forests in Relation to Landscape and Amenity* (paper to The Royal Society).

Gordon Patterson, Dip LA (Reading), AILA
Senior Partner, Gordon Patterson & Partners, Landscape Architects. Principal work includes landscape of Stevenage New Town, various health authorities and government agencies. Formerly in charge of Landscape Department at the School of Architecture and Landscape, Gloucestershire College of Art and Design. Vice Chairman of the Editorial Committee of the ILA journal *Landscape Design*. Co-author of *Mughal Gardens of India*.

Preben Jakobsen, RA Dip (Copenhagen), DH (Kew)
Landscape architect in private practice since 1969. Experience includes landscape work for various government bodies, local authorities and industrial concerns, consultant to new towns, hospitals, universities, and projects in Europe and the Middle East. Formerly part-time lecturer and studio instructor at Thames Polytechnic Landscape Architecture diploma course. Has given lectures and papers on landscape design to various courses and professional groups, and written reports, articles and reviews in professional journals and magazines.

A. du Gard Pasley, FILA
Landscape architect in private practice. Author and lecturer on various aspects of landscape design.

Allan Hart, AILA, AIPRA (Dipl.), DH (Kew)
Landscape architect in own private practice since 1968. Experience includes landscape work with commercial firms, local authorities and central government, including extensive projects, design and management in Cyprus, Gibraltar, Libya and Hong Kong. Author of *Use of Plant Material—Handbook of Urban Landscape*; co-author of *Select List of Plants Suitable for Landscape Work in Hong Kong* (Department of the Environment).

Richard M. R. Hoyle
Studied Landscape Architecture at Gloucestershire College of Art and Design, Cheltenham. Landscape architect with Brian Clouston and Partners working on large-scale schemes involving habitat creation. Thesis on 'A Guide to the Use of British Native Plants in Landscape Work, With Particular Reference to Urban Areas'. Experience with a major landscape contractor. Set up Native Plant Consultancy in 1974 as an advisory service on the use, conservation and supply of native plants.

Allan Ruff, DH (Edin), Dip LD (Newcastle), AILA
Lecturer in Landscape Design to Postgraduate Landscape Design Course, Department of Town Planning, Manchester University. Previous experience as landscape architect at Scottish Special Housing Association, in private practice and as a lecturer at Leeds Polytechnic Department of Architectural Studies. Published 'Ideas for the Future Management of Native Areas', Report of Symposium 'Nature in Cities' (Landscape Research Group 1974).

Anne E. Yarrow, BA (Geography, Cantab), MSc (Conservation, London)

Senior Planner to Countryside Section, East Sussex County Planning Department. Experience in private practice with Land Use Consultants London, in countryside planning and landscape design projects throughout Britain.

Richard Baker, Dip. Arch. (PNL), RIBA
Architect in the Department of Architecture and Planning, Corporation of London. Fourteen years' experience in private practice and public offices.

Kathryn Stansfield, BA, (Town Planning, Manchester), MA (Manchester)
Research and Editorial Assistant for Brian Clouston and Partners. MA thesis, 'The Poetry of Planning', covered the visual aspects of the urban and rural environment, as seen through the work of Dr Thomas Sharp. Member of History of Planning Group. Student member of RTPI.

Richard Sturdy, BSc (Hortic, London), Dip LD (Manchester)
Landscape architect with Brian Clouston and Partners. Six years' experience in private practice covering a wide range of projects, including courtyard designs and urban landscaping, in Britain and abroad. Short-term project with UN in Nepal. Practical nursery experience.

Ronald L. Hebblethwaite, BSc, FILA
Principal Landscape Architect to CEGB. Considerable experience in the United States of America; former Landscape Architect to Hampshire County Council. Former ILA Council Member and Chairman of the ILA Research Committee. Still very active in research, and has represented the ILA on a number of committees.

Raymond P. Gemmell, BSc (Agricultural Botany, Leeds), MI Biol, FLS, Ph D (Wales)
Ecologist to Greater Manchester Council. Attached to Joint Reclamation Team of Greater Manchester and Lancashire County Councils working on establishment of vegetation on colliery and toxic chemical wastes. Ph D research on revegetation of Lower Swansea Valley.

Christopher J. Gill, MA (Agricultural Sciences, Cambridge), PhD (Liverpool)
Associate with Clouston Cobham and Partners, Ph D thesis on 'The Revegetation of Reservoir Margins' at Liverpool University Botany Department and continued research in same field at Cambridge for four years. Involved in planting schemes for Empingham, Brenig and CEGB reservoirs.

Professor A. D. Bradshaw, MA (Botany, Cantab), PhD (Wales)
Has taken part in many studies in evolutionary and ecological genetics at Aberystwyth and Bangor Universities. Professor of Botany at Liverpool University since 1968. Instrumental with Sir Norman Rowntree and Sir Duncan Poore in starting the reservoir margin work.

P. J. W. Saunders, BSc, Ph D (Exeter)
Member of Science Division of the Headquarters of the Natural Environment Research Council since 1973, concerned with management of pollution research. Research Fellowship in Pollution Research Unit, Manchester University 1970. Ph D in Plant Pathology (1968) followed by research at the National Institute of Agricultural Botany, Cambridge. Author of *The Estimation of Pollution Damage* (Manchester University Press Environment Pollution Series, 1976).

Christopher M. Wood, BSc (Chemistry), Dip TP, MA (Town Planning), MRTPI
Lecturer in Town and Country Planning, Manchester University. Formerly Associate of Land Use Consultants, London. Research Fellowship in Pollution Research Unit, Manchester University 1970. Author of *Town Planning and Pollution Control* (Manchester University Press Environmental Pollution Series) 1976.

Jill Foister, BSc (Geography, Hull), Dip LD (Manchester)
Landscape architect with Brian Clouston and Partners. Experience in private practice, following two years as a Landscape Research Assistant at Newcastle University working on a Landscape Reclamation Project.

William Bowen
Horticultural Officer, Bath University. Experience in commercial horticulture, and in design, construction and maintenance of amenity grounds and landscape features for hospitals, embassies, sports grounds and other large undertakings. Trained at Monmouthshire (Gwent) College of Agriculture and Horticulture. Several years as Assistant Curator of Grounds and Gardens, University of Ghana, W. Africa; has worked for University of London Botanical Supply Unit, Department of the Environment, and Leeds University.

B. T. Siedlecki, Dip LA (Reading), FILA
Principal Landscape Architect in the Landscape Branch of Property Services Agency, Department of the Environment; work includes projects abroad. Experience with private landscape contractors, LCC, Corby New Town, N. Riding of Yorkshire, Transmission Project Group of CEGB in Guildford. Spent three years in Zambia under contract to government, working on presidential residences, airports, hospitals, schools, residential and office projects.

Trevor Walker, BSc, Ph D, FLS
Senior Lecturer, Department of Plant Biology, University of Newcastle upon Tyne. Special interest in tropical vegetation, particularly ferns and cytology. Plant collecting expeditions to Sri Lanka, Java, Sulawesi (Celebes), Bali, Papua New Guinea, New Britain, Trinidad, and Jamaica. Prolonged visits to India, Malaya, Singapore and South Africa.

Anne Willens, BSc (Horticulture). Student member ILA
Independent consultant, worked for Landscape Branch

of Birmingham City Architects Office, Agricultural Research Council, and in private practice with landscape architects Robert Adams; Derek Lovejoy. Experience abroad in Abu Dhabi and UAE with Agricultural Planning Associates; also Oman, Jordan, North Africa, and South America, including research into salinity problems. Now involved in landscape work, nursery propagation, silviculture and ecological surveys.

Ralph Cobham, BA Agr. B, Dip Agr. Econ., MSc Principal Partner, Clouston Cobham and Partners, Rural Development, Landscape Management and Environmental Consultants. Previously Lecturer in Agricultural Economics and Farm Management at Trinity College, Dublin. Involved in several multi-disciplinary rural developments in UK and overseas, including assisting the establishment of a landscape labour force and associated maintenance facilities for the Village Association of New Ash Green Village. Landscape, irrigation and rural settlement developments have been undertaken in Iran, Saudi Arabia and along the Trucial Coast. Presently the Project Officer for ten Demonstration Farms being established by the Countryside Commission throughout England and Wales. Member of British Institute of Agricultural Consultants.

Snowdrop in winter. *(Dick Hoyle)*

Overleaf: **St Dunstan's in the East, London.** *(John Chitty)*

Part I

DESIGN

Design: Introduction

BRENDA COLVIN

1. WHAT THE EYE WILL SEE, THE IMAGINATION FORESEES

Design implies purpose: the adaptation of means to an intended objective. It implies change from that which has been to that which will be under new circumstances.

All man-made changes to our environment involve design—whether with or without artistry—often almost unconsciously. Today much of our too-hasty design is influenced only by necessity, short-term economy or greed. In the landscape, the lack of thoughtful, sensitive design leads to lowering of civilized standards and to degradation of human life.

Landscape architecture seeks to apply design in its fullest sense: in order to ensure the best possible adaptation of the means to an intended, carefully considered end in the new scene, we find that artistry, or visual appreciation, must act in unison with the sciences of the earth. Humanity, using the earth both as a palette and a means of livelihood, comes to see the necessity of designing creatively, not only in three dimensions but in the progression of time and change—the dynamic necessity of landscape change—depending, like evolution itself, on movement in time. Landscape growth is a long slow process: those who profess to design it need patience and experience. They have to develop a four-dimensional imagination.

In three dimensions, the artist expresses design through the mediums of form, colour and texture, in varying proportions related to his objective and his materials.

All these apply equally to landscape design and though these, like the re-grouping, the contrasts of light and shadow, the punctuation and the materials used, are of a different scale, the artist's individual style and his power of appreciation influence all his work as in any three-dimensional design.

2. RELATING FUTURE TO PAST—A FUNCTION OF DESIGN

The time dimension is an additional problem, more critical perhaps in this than in the traditional arts, because our material constantly undergoes change. The seasonal changes, the growth and ageing of plants, the effects of climate and erosion, provide problems more critical and immediate for us than for designers in other fields.

In landscape design, past and future must be related. We think not just of an area or region as now seen, but of how it came to be so: what has been its history, and how it will develop when it passes out of the designer's hands. The present is the link between past and future. Good design should ensure a stable link in the time chain so that the theme or pattern of the intention influences the whole concept and relates the new movement to its origins and general objective. The continuity of the theme, from the former changing pattern to that which will follow, and to the total heritage of civilized life, depends on the link our design forges in the chain.

Landscape design differs from other arts in that after implementation in three dimensions, the design is still immature and can only develop its full potential in course of time. The project when completed is new-born, requiring parental care to ensure its survival and development. Our designs must be adapted to the future use of the site and to the system of maintenance responsible for its care.

Design and after-care are complementary in a sense different from that of inorganic structures, because change begins inevitably from the time of planting. This time factor influences landscape design from the earliest stage, since we have to foresee not only the vegetation changes, due to season and age, but also the effects of erosion and sedimentation of land form. The future use

3

(Photograph by Richard Bryant)

of a landscape must determine the new form, just as much as the future use of a building determines the architecture. The vague specification 'restoration of landscape' sometimes given in planning consents is as meaningless as if an architect were required to build a structure without a brief. Is it to be a hospital, a school or a cathedral? Is the landscape to be a farm, a forest or a mountain?

3. THE EARTHY PATH TO TRUTH

The skills of landscape design are largely concerned with what our eyes can see, but our work is of the Earth, earthy. Throughout the centuries of western civilization, artists have been inspired by the belief that beauty is a means of approaching truth:

'Phaedrus learnt what beauty is from
Socrates beneath the tree:
Beauty is the only form
Of spirit that the eyes can see
So brings to the outcast soul
Reflections of Divinity.'[1]

Sir Kenneth Clark in his personal view of civilization (quoting Bishop Sugar, one time Regent of France) said: 'The dull mind rises to truth through that which is material', and noted that this idea, whose western origins are seen in early Greece, is the philosophy on which our civilization was nourished.[2]

This concept is consoling for landscape architects, whose art can only be expressed in material things with definite limitations of climate and soil conditions. Other designers today may be able (and content) to express *themselves*, seeking above all originality. Instead of seeking truth in the mysterious outer world, it is being sought in the even more mysterious sub-conscious mind, which may be far from that 'beauty which our eyes can see'. By overstressing individuality and originality, the natural standard of appreciation of nature, by which truth was judged, is lost and new standards are sought.

But for all artists, including landscape architects, it is essential to find the relationship of the part to the whole: to express the truth that the whole is greater than the sum of the parts. The successful solution of this problem is, I believe, the quality above all others to which our emotions respond in any great work of art.

Landscape design recognizes in the science of ecology—that is, in the relationship of living things to their surroundings, to the other forms of life depending on the same air, soil, food and water which support all of us—the essential need to relate ourselves and our work to that greater whole. We have learnt that 'Man is one among other groups of living things, each equally important in an integrated system'. We can think of the biosphere as a single entity. That envelope of soil, air, water and all the life it supports is the flesh on the earth's rocky crust, without which the planet would be a dry skeleton like the moon; its parts, its molecules, atoms and protoplasm are interchangeable in time—and all living forms are literally in actual fact 'members one of another'.[3]

Man is a late-comer whose demise or extinction would scarcely be missed in the slow processes of evolution.

4. INDIVIDUAL RESPONSIBILITY AND TEAMWORK

Dr. Bronowski has pointed out, however, that man is the only animal that is faced with a dilemma between his wishes and his integrity. We now have the power, through modern technology, to destroy ourselves and perhaps much other life in the process, if we so wish. The question we face now is: can technology be relied upon to steer us between our wishes and our integrity to safe survival? Could it be that man's future depends more than we like to admit on the quality of work and the integrity of individual decisions in every field? I believe that Clifford Tandy's presidential address to the Institute of Landscape Architects on 8 October 1973 put this same question less bluntly and with far greater artistry.[4]

We are apt to leave too much to 'them'—to the technologists and politicians—but surely it is true that each has responsibility in some degree and that at least amongst landscape architects, individuals who advise on the design and use of land, however small or however extensive, can contribute to future quality of life by creating fine and healthy landscape in the areas they influence, aiming so far as possible to conserve and promote vegetation and other forms of life. We know that animal life depends on plant life. The trees and plants we use serve to purify the air, the crops serve to provide food, but the total scene should serve not only to ensure survival, but also to bring to humanity those 'reflections of Divinity' and the consolations and joy of nature.

Although this book deals with vegetation rather than land form and all the human artefacts and other things composing the total landscape, it is essential at the start to consider landscape design 'in the round' because landscape is the setting for our lives.

Now that we are realizing this, and the rate at which the scene is being changed by human action, whether for new use or for restoration after past misuse, all changes under our control should be done as a process of conscious design, using to the full our appreciation of art as well as the best available scientific knowledge. Those of us in the land-based professions can contribute much from our various fields to the teamwork—the multiple skills of design and after-care needed to ensure development of the intention, founded on the designer's imaginative foresight.

The principles and philosophy underlying our task should be dwelt on and understood by all, whether designers, scientists or managers, however specialized their own contribution.

Unlike most other expressions of art, the basic material of design in this case is the *land* as it exists beneath our feet and on which our subsistence depends. Full appreciation of its character and needs and conditions is the foundation of our studies, as its capacity affects the future potential use.

The artist's eye can often see beneath the superficial and so sense, instinctively, further than the intellect can as yet analyse. While we make use of all that can be learnt from scientific studies, inborn instincts of balance and beauty are still the artist's lodestar.

REFERENCES

1. Piper, M. Libretto for *Death in Venice*, opera by Benjamin Britten (London; Faber Music Ltd., 1973)
2. Clark, K. *Civilisation—A Personal View* (British Broadcasting Corporation and John Murray, 1969)
3. *The Bible*—Romans Ch. 12. v.5
4. Tandy, C. R. V. 'Presidential Address to the Institute of Landscape Architects', 8 October 1973. *Landscape Design*—Issue No. 104, November 1973

Asian Institute of Technology, Bangkok. *(Maurice Lee)*

CHAPTER 1

DESIGN WITH TREES

BRENDA COLVIN

1.1 ADAPTATION TO LOCALITY

The landscape architect's choice of tree species must in all cases be influenced by ecological facts. The plantsman has either to limit the choice to species naturally adapted to the site, or else adapt the site to the species required for some other reason, whether it be aesthetic or functional. Adaptation of the site to the selected vegetation is suitable only for small plantations, usually in urban situations or closely related to buildings. It may involve the provision of special soil, irrigation and drainage, all to be recognized as artificial, and therefore requiring constant attention and care. The former choice, that of choosing species adapted to the situation, is applicable on the broad scale and is visually better suited to large scale projects, especially in open countryside. Maintenance of natural planting in the short term is less demanding and in the long term can be reduced to the minimum. Here we are concerned mainly with the latter choice and refer to it as ecological planting.

In the past, most conscious design of gardens and landscape was on a scale very small by comparison with the needs of the present day. The tendency to design in harmony with local conditions rather than impose a conception based on our power to dominate nature is not just a modern fashion; rather it is the result of working on this large scale. The designer may have to decide between ecological and artifical planting according to the circumstances of each project, but as our understanding of the relationships between the plant and its environment grows, so we come to a greater appreciation of the visual value of the diversity indicated by ecology. It is perhaps inevitable that public taste in this matter lags behind that of professional designers. Horticulturalists and owner gardeners in this country seem slow to see that garden-type planting overlays and masks nature's own scheme of diversity and interest. For that reason, if for no other, it is appropriate only on a small scale in artificial surroundings. It is to be hoped that the public generally is coming to see the national importance of conserving the wonder-ful diversity of character in the wider landscape which is founded on the ecological facts of our land.

1.2 LET THE HISTORY OF THE LAND BE SEEN

The landscape of this island, to all who trouble to read the signs, reflects its geological structure and history. We can help to preserve the record in our new creative work just as much as we can by simple preservation of existing features. On all large sites, especially those in or adjoining rural scenery, the outer plantations, seen from roads, rail and water, and generally from local views, can be planted according to ecological principles even if, in the interior details, concessions to popular taste are required. A graduation from 'pop planting' near the buildings to classic ecological truth on the fringes is a reasonable compromise. The function of horticultural flamboyance is to provide decoration pleasing to clients and users of the site and perhaps to inspire the designer and test his horticultural skill. All planting should in some degree be functional, and artificially decorative planting of a garden type is an interesting challenge which can stimulate us to demonstrate the need for good design in any medium.

In every case we should be clear in our own minds as to which function we are serving, and of the reasons for our choice, so that the long-term intention can be understood by clients and maintenance staff and followed accordingly. Verbal expression of this intention should also be stated, either in the form of a report, or in the plans, which will serve as a record and guide for those responsible for maintenance as the scheme matures.

Tree cover is the normal condition for most of the British Isles. Any area below the five hundred metres contour, left to itself and protected from vandalism, grazing or other biotic factors, will revert to forest unless exposed to high gales or salt spray. It is not sufficiently recognized that trees grown thus under natural conditions mature faster and are more securely rooted than transplants. The only maintenance required to produce

7

good specimens from self-sown seedlings or sucker growths is protection from damage and undue competition. Adequate protection in the early years is usually essential until the trees are well established. Self-propagated groups of this type, protected and thinned to selected specimens, give excellent and natural-looking spinneys and woodland. The Forestry Commission and other landowners are realizing the advantages of the system: under suitable circumstances, timber of economic value can be produced, but for amenity and landscape values where timber is of secondary importance, natural regeneration has a greater potential which has too often been overlooked.

1.3 SELF-SOWN VEGETATION

The general public and others such as architects, developers, engineers and even planners, tend to regard all young growth as scrub to be cleared before starting new work. Amenity societies often advise planting new trees in places where unnoticed existing saplings would serve their purpose better. Many of our older hedgerows contain thousands of young elm, field maple, oak or other saplings which could develop into fine tree groups if not

PLATE 1.1 **Natural regeneration of beech woods showing two different stages of growth.** *(Forestry Commission)*

fine timber. Disused waste ground, when closely examined, often contains enough seedling trees to form effective woodland without further planting; old railways, parade grounds and marshalling yards harbour saplings capable of fine maturity if protected and cared for. These natural growths do not transplant well, and they can only survive if ground levels remain unchanged, but their existence should be recorded in preliminary site investigation and appraisal. Existing features can in many cases influence the design and treatment of new developments. Given due care and attention, undisturbed areas with their ability to regenerate can speed up the establishment of new landscape and reduce planting costs.

Young trees adapt more easily than old trees to changed conditions of drainage and irrigation. Much trouble taken to preserve old established trees is sometimes wasted if the tree is unable to adapt to drier conditions due to change of drainage levels in the course of development: where any such risk is apparent, understudy planting of similar species is advisable. In many cases it would be wise to adapt the layout of the design to existing young saplings rather than to the older mature trees. For the short-term effect, we can add large nursery-grown trees, remembering that even these would be outstripped by self-sown or sucker growths in, say, about fifteen years.

1.4 DESIGN FOR BOTH SHORT- AND LONG-TERM EFFECT

For the sake of ensuring quick effects as well as long-term growth, we can use more than one method to start with (such as a mixture of large stock and forest seedlings), on the assumption that time will prove which is best and that those responsible for maintenance will decide on the correct thinning to bring about the designer's intention. Maintenance schedules indicating this are essential in such cases, but so long as even our most detailed instructions cannot ensure the development of long-term intentions, designers tend to rely on permanent planting of semi-mature trees at the outset. Improved training of landscape managers and closer co-operation between these and designers should advance the art of landscape design in the future. Designers could make much better use of mixed systems of planting if they could feel sure that their final intention is understood and likely to be correctly developed by the maintenance system. As an example of past failures in this respect, the case of a war memorial garden on Wimbledon Common can be quoted. Miss Madeline Agar, commissioned in the 1920s to design the grounds around a First World War memorial, planned for its long-term objective, concentric rings of English oak, with much undisturbed ground between, but for short-term public use she superimposed over the long-term plan an additional scheme of winding paths with flowering trees and shrubs to make immediate

PLATE 1.2 **Trimpley Reservoir. New use of previous farmland on the River Severn, combining industry and recreation in what can still appear as a clearing in a forest. Public footpaths do not conflict with sheep grazing so that some agricultural use continues, and the cost of maintenance of the land is reduced.** *(Severn-Trent Water Authority)*

effect. That was before the days of semi-mature tree planting. The short-term scheme was intended to be temporary, and should have been removed when the oaks were nearing maturity. Instead the small oaks were sacrificed as soon as they began to threaten the lilacs and laburnums, although sensitive thinning could have preserved both until the oaks, nearing maturity, could have proved the long-term value of her choice.

Moisture conditions are a governing factor, often of more importance than soil types. Species such as willow, alder and poplar, commonly found along the banks of rivers and streams, create the character of many valley regions. Their appearance suggests the lush fertility of waterborne soils, deep, moist and rich in humus and minerals, just as the appearance of gorse and pine suggest the sandy uplands, thin soils which are periodically dry. Their use in design conveys a mood and sets the scenic character of an area. Even if for special reasons we do not keep strictly to native species, the character can be retained by the use of introduced species which harmonize so well with the native plants that they do not appear intrusive. This, however, calls for experience and sensitive judgment on the part of the designer.

1.5 LOCAL CHARACTER

There are obvious advantages in keeping to the local species in many cases: they blend well with the scenery and help to give new projects the appearance of belonging to their setting, and they are more likely in many instances to suit local conditions better than introduced species. But it is not a rule to be applied under all circumstances: there may be excellent reasons for preferring exotics in special cases, where their appearance does not strike a discordant note and when they have become adapted to the local ecosystem. Many species (like the sycamore), though probably introduced by man, have become firmly established in our countryside and are quite capable of competing with species which are strictly indigenous. Many introduced trees and shrubs endure sea gales as well as, or better than, natives. Several introduced pines are invaluable for shelter, as also is the evergreen oak, *Quercus ilex*, in coastal areas not liable to very severe frosts, and providing these are types which will not dominate or eliminate the local vegetation, our mild interference with an ecosystem is no more than a normal biotic factor.

9

It may be more useful to study the natural habit of growth of local vegetation than to note the particular species of which it is composed. The grouping, and the way groups are shaped by wind gives us clear indications of the spacing, sizes of plants needed, and the width of plantations in windswept sites. In windy sites it is also important to note the extent and direction of shelter provided by plantations. Local observations of this sort are usually a better indication of which to plant and how to adjust to special sites than all the books and scientific research on the subject, as every site has individuality and special circumstances which must influence our designs and choice of species. These circumstances are often well known to local inhabitants, and their opinions can thus be of great value.

Some general characteristics of native vegetation are generally applicable, however, being the result of the climate and soils of our land. For example, the fringes of woods and open glades harbour a richer variety of smaller trees, shrubs and herbs than the forest interior which may be composed mainly of tall timber trees without shrubby undergrowth. In this case the woodland fringe provides the chosen home for the great majority of wild life, birds, insects and mammals. It also provides shelter for the ground inside and encourages the growth of seedling trees. The close compact grouping of these fringes provides an example we do well to follow when possible, especially where wind shelter is needed. It helps to deter trespass, to encourage the establishment of songbirds, butterflies and all the rest of the wild life now threatened with extinction, and in many cases it enables the designer to give pleasing definition to the shapes of open spaces such as playing fields and community grounds whose pragmatic outlines are apt to be visually boring and monotonous. Our open spaces can be designed as the equivalent of the glades formed in the forest under natural conditions by decay of ancient tree groups or changes of ground water level, gales and other natural events.

Another characteristic of natural grouping which we do well to study is the interrelation and mixture of species, usually found in groups which have become self-established. Pure stands or monocultures, as we have seen, are rare in nature: yet the mixture is usually formed of groups rather than of individuals. The groups may show strong contrasts and diversity, depending on small-scale local differences of land form, soil type, drainage, temperature, etc. Such ecological guidelines are an excellent example worth studying for application in our designs.

1.6 ECOLOGICAL PLANTING

Our reasons for ecological planting, especially in the case of trees, may be summed up as follows:
1. Conservation
2. Appearance
3. Diversity

4. Economy (capital cost and long-term maintenance).

These four reasons are closely linked, but while for the purposes of future maintenance the first and fourth are to be stressed, all four are to be related in the design.

1.61 Conservation

In landscape, conservation implies the design and maintenance of a self-perpetuating environment—not changeless, since all life implies change, but in perpetual balance as it exists in nature. *Homo sapiens* evolved along with other forms of life in the primitive environment which nature provided: the species has recently acquired the power to disturb the balance of nature. Arrogant in our power, we forget that our race was cradled in that natural setting and that while life could continue to exist without our 'sapience' we cannot survive alone. We can destroy in a few years the conditions which through untold millennia adapted nature to our existence.

1.62 Appearance

The link between conservation and visual appearance is the fact that the human ambition to dominate nature can only partly be indulged by working with natural forces. The most successful landscape creations, whether they be the gardens of Buddhist temples, the parks of Le Nôtre or the English landscape gardens of Kent, Brown and Repton, are capable of survival in so far as they were designed with understanding of the forces of nature and obeyed nature's laws: that is to say on an ecological basis.

The more we learn about the working of the life cycle, the greater grows our appreciation of the visual results in the landscape. With greater understanding, we come to feel more deeply the meaning of the natural grouping. Realization of the relationship between vegetation and ground formation to the structure and nature of the underlying rocks, and to climatic influences, reinforces and develops our natural appreciation. It appears that many intuitive responses are based on our physical relationship to all that lives and breathes, and to human dependence on the same material things and unchanging laws that govern the rest of life.

1.63 Diversity

The third reason for ecological planting is the need for broad scale diversity. Diversity is not the least important of nature's laws. Its relationship to scale is perhaps the most difficult problem for man to master. We know that monoculture is unhealthy, but how large an area do we regard as monoculture? Nature's diversity is not a haphazard mixture, all is organized in a cellular pattern, but there is no tiresome repetition: no two crystals are alike. The perpetuation of natural forest depends on constant variation in the size and shape of the open glades and fringes, lakes and river valleys in a long slow cycle of alternating mass and void. The human eye responds instinctively to this natural fact but our minds are still struggling to learn how it can be applied in planting design. We are aware that monotonous repetition of a form, of a sound, of any unit, however beautiful in itself, becomes unbearable to our senses if endlessly repeated. Yet our slums, our housing estates, our factories (urban and rural) prove our present inability to design diversity on the scale of natural laws. Painters, sculptors and other artists make full use of diversity within a whole conception on that scale: the difficulty arises when the scale of the whole gets beyond their experience. Then we reach the scale of natural landscape and find that a new approach, a new art is needed and that the future of our race depends on our ability to adapt our creative faculty to nature's laws in the development of that art. Our diversification must not be haphazard: each unit must have clear relationship to a whole, but unlike the edge of a canvas, or the mass of sculpted stone, the boundaries and limitations and scale of the whole are often indeterminate or controversial.

One of the limitations is the passage of time, and here the aesthetic design is linked to the down-to-earth and our fourth reason for ecological planting, namely economy.

1.64 Economy

This fourth reason depends on those given above. If our objective, for the other reasons listed, is that of a self-perpetuating environment, economy can reinforce and strengthen the reasons for ecological planting in the long term, if not in capital cost, though both should play a part. In the longer cycles economy in landscape maintenance far outweighs capital cost and though as yet proof of this statement may be lacking, those experienced in the field cannot doubt that research could provide and will be available, to give authentic figures to illustrate its truth.

In the wild, nature ensures a self-perpetuating system through reproduction by seed or suckers from parent plants. Of course the system works only if the parent plants are suited to the soil and other environmental factors. Evolution through countless generations has brought this about and each local ecosystem is a balanced continuum with flora, fauna and all forms of life adapted to its soil and climate and to each other's survival. Human needs for changes of land use disrupt this balance and, impatient for quick results, we often fail to see the need to preserve or reinstate it even where that would be an economic possibility. We could make much better use than we do of nature's extravagance by following the local ecosystem as far as other circumstances of the project permit.

The shapes resulting from existing local differences, so different from the geometric shapes of human habit and habitation, are typical of new attitudes towards landscape design. Approaching the problem with a realization of the advantages of working with, rather than against nature, a more humble view of our relationship with nature opens to us a vast field of new discovery and endeavour.

Vegetation relates closely to ground shape. Even half a metre of vertical difference may indicate a change of planting in low-lying land. The interesting curve of a contour line may be emphasized by a change of vege-

PLATE 1.3 **View from Chiltern escarpment. On the slopes the typical chalkland vegetation is seen, including juniper on the left. In the distance, the lines of hedgerow and roadside verge link spinneys and shelter groups, forming a green network which favours wild life of all kinds and creates a lovely scene. This valley has now sadly been sacrificed to the M40.** *(Forestry Commission)*

tation, and such effects can be purposely designed to suit the pragmatic requirements of the plan. As an example of this kind I would mention a site where the ground level of a car park was so close to a saline water table that shrubs and trees could only thrive planted on raised ground. The screening required for the car park indicated modelling of surrounding banks to give enough dry root run to suit the shrubs and trees needed.

1.7 PLANT ASSOCIATIONS

The typical plant associations found on most of our British landscape types have a characteristic charm so differentiated that one can judge most soil types by their vegetation, and even assess fairly closely the pH value of a given area. The lovely mixture of yew and whitebeam, accompanied by wayfaring tree, spindle, blackthorn, etc. occurs typically on the shallow soils of chalk hillsides, just as pine and heather typify thin acid soils and podsols, while oak, holly and hazel thrive on the heavier clays. The field maple occurs most abundantly on various limestones, with crab-apples and honeysuckle. The valleys and water courses, the marshes, fens and commons, each have their typical trees and shrubs accompanied by herbaceous species and ground flora associated with the familiar trees. This aspect of the subject cannot be covered in depth in a brief chapter. We can all learn from the landscape we see, and by reading the work of ecologists such as Tansley, whose *The British Islands and their Vegetation* is a mine of information invaluable for the landscape plantsman. Ian McHarg's book *Design with Nature* is a thought-provoking inspiration for landscape architects and points the way to improvement of our professional work.

1.8 HEDGE HISTORY

Much new knowledge available recently, particularly in regard to the historic associations and relics of former forest vegetation, enables us to date the hedges and, through them, the land tenure and parish boundaries of former settlements. A whole new range of knowledge on these matters is opening up which may influence our thinking on matters of design. Of the former forest once covering the British Isles, these relics in the form of hedges, shelter belts, woods and parks remain, and are a last refuge for the wild life of the old forests. We now know that the older a hedge is, the greater its wealth of native vegetation and fauna. Hedges and verges of road, rail and waterways are important links in a web enabling

the movement and migration of many living species which are unable to cross large unbroken tracts of urban development or cultivated areas. The continuity of a web or network of vegetation, connecting town and country, from coast to coast, has great conservation value. In many areas the fields are too small and the hedges too many for modern needs. Often larger enclosures may be visually preferable, but to destroy the whole pattern is a ruthless and unnecessary extreme which the future will surely regret: the broad national implications of conservation are not at variance with fine landscape. Farmers, planners and landscape designers can seek the proper balance in their individual areas, respecting the economic sizes of enclosures, but aiming to keep the older historic hedges as links in the web of conservation. The green lines of shelter belt, hedge or towpath, linking spinneys, woodlands and parks, give a more pleasing composition than unrelated scattered items.

This is a case where experience and study reinforce the artist's intuitive response. Intellect and intuition are not always so clearly in step, but this checking of the relationship between art and science is inherent in the discipline of landscape design.

FURTHER READING

Bonham-Carter, V. *The Survival of the English Countryside* (London: Hodder and Stoughton, 1971)

Colvin, B. *Land and Landscape* (London: John Murray, 2nd edition 1970)

Colvin, B. *Trees for Town and Country* (London: Lund Humphries, 4th edition 1972)

Fairbrother, N. *The Nature of Landscape Design* (London: Architectural Press, 1974)

Haywood, S. M. *Quarries and the Landscape* (London: The British Quarrying and Slag Federation Ltd., November 1974)

Holliman, J. *Consumers Guide to the Protection of the Environment* (London: Pan/Ballantine 1971)

Jellicoe, G. *Studies in Landscape Design* (Oxford: University Press, 1960, 1966, 1970)

Lovejoy, D. (Ed.) *Land Use and Landscape Planning* (Aylesbury: Leonard Hill, 1973)

McHarg, I. L. *Design with Nature* (New York: The Natural History Press, Garden City, 1969)

Mitchell, A. *A Field Guide to the Trees of Britain and Northern Europe* (London: Collins, 1974)

Tansley, A. G. *British Islands and their Vegetation* (Cambridge: University Press, 1939)

CHAPTER 2

Planting for Forestry

DAME SYLVIA CROWE

Forests are no exception to the rule that landscape beauty and ecological health go hand in hand. Their contribution in both respects can be very great, provided that planting and maintenance are directed to these ends.

2.1 THE NEED FOR AFFORESTATION

In the present man-eroded landscape of Britain, strong positive action is needed to reverse the impoverishment of what was once a well-forested country.

Under favourable and stable conditions, forests are self-perpetuating and will develop and retain the climax vegetation for their particular situation. However, even without direct human action, this climax may be arrested, or regeneration prevented, by some outside intervention; for instance grazing animals, usually but not necessarily introduced by man, may prevent regeneration. There may be climatic changes or other natural hazards; for instance, certain forests in the western United States, whose true climax species is spruce, remain permanently at the arrested climax of Lodgepole pine (*Pinus contorta*) owing to naturally-generated fires.

It cannot therefore be assumed that a forest will necessarily either perpetuate itself or develop into its climax vegetation even in a state of nature. When the effects of human intervention are taken into account, the prospects of regeneration are much reduced and man must often take steps to counteract the effects of his past

PLATE 2.1 **Different species drifting into each other. Aberfoyle.** *(Sylvia Crowe)*

PLATE 2.2 **Indigenous silver birch giving light to a conifer crop. The effect would be still better if the birch had been allowed to drift into the forest on the far side of the road. Allen Forest, Perthshire.** *(Forestry Commission)*

actions. A typical case is that of the Scottish Highlands, where regeneration is prevented both by grazing of sheep and deer and by the degraded condition of the soil, caused by generations of over-grazing and over-burning. Forest planting must therefore be seen as a means of repairing past ecological impoverishment as well as maintaining and increasing the biological richness and landscape quality of such woodlands as still exist.

2.2 THE FOREST HABITAT

Forests provide a greater range of habitats than any other type of plant association. Their vertical range extends from deep into the soil up to one hundred feet above ground level. Within this territory, dependent life-forms range from organisms on the roots to birds roosting in the tree-tops.

The main divisions of the forest habitat are classified by Tansley in his book *Britain's Green Mantle* as the canopy, the shrub layer, the field layer and the ground layer. To this should be added the root system, which, functioning at varying depths, plays a vital part in recycling the water and nutrients upon which all growth depends. The ecological richness of woodlands depends on their composition both in species and age. The variation in this respect between different species is considerable. The oak has by far the most associated species. It is host to a great

many insects (and hence to birds), its leaf-fall is rich and its open canopy encourages the growth of shrub and field layer. Ash is less prolific in the organisms it supports directly, but its light foliage also encourages growth on the forest floor.

Beech scores only moderately as a host and its deep shade excludes all but a few shrubs and forest flowers. Its leaf-fall, while enriching alkaline soils, does less to improve acid soils. Spruce is even more inhibiting to undergrowth since its shade persists through the year and also contributes little to soil improvement. Larch on the other hand, with its deciduous nature, lighter foliage and softer needles, is far more hospitable and produces a richer field layer and greater soil improvement.

Diversity in the age of trees adds to the richness of the forest's ecology. Some wild life favours young trees in the thicket stage, birds nest high in the branches of tall trees and some, such as the woodpecker, need old dead wood. Shrub layer and the edge bordering open glades are favoured by a great variety of birds.

The wide range of habitats provided by a mixed-age natural forest, or by one managed on a system of selective felling, may be equalled or even exceeded by a timber forest managed on a system of clear fellings, provided these fellings are planned in size and shape on a basis of conservation. A maximum of edge can be provided by well-contrived felling coupes, and the clear-felled areas will produce a spectacular flush of forest flowers.

14

2.3 THE SCALE OF THE FOREST MOSAIC

A mosaic of different-aged stands of trees gives great beauty as well as the widest range of habitats. This mosaic, however, can work on varying scales, and it is in the interests of the landscape that it should do so. The smallest scale is one of mixed-aged, mixed-species, woodland, on a fertile soil which will support a wide range of plant species which, in their turn, will support a wide range of fauna. Visually, such a woodland will be interesting and pleasant and will almost certainly fit easily into its surroundings. But if all forests were of this type we should lose some of our most satisfying landscapes, and certain bird and animal species might lose the particular type of habitat they need. Pure, or almost pure stands of a single species can have a beauty and character of their own. A beech wood may have a limited range of associated species, but it is surpassingly beautiful, seen both from within and without. The clear statement of beech climax forest could only be lessened by introducing mixed planting. The occasional sub-dominant gean (*Cerasus avium*), however, is insufficient to break the unity of the beech canopy, and can be an added spring delight. On chalklands, whitebeam and yew will often colonize the edge of the beechwood, giving a perfect transition to the surrounding landscape.

A closed canopy of oak may be less spectacular than beech, but it has great character in texture and colour. Sessile oakwoods, clothing steep hillsides, can be a vital part of a strong hill landscape, which would be weakened by breaking up the closely patterned texture of the oak canopy. The same clear statement, which needs no blurring, can be found within a stand of mature Douglas fir or spruce.

These pure stands are still part of a mosaic, but in larger units than that of a mixed forest. The precise scale of the mosaic in every case needs to be studied from both the visual and ecological angle. Close attention to change of soil and micro-climate will often provide the guide.

PLATE 2.3 **Indigenous species adding conservation value to a forest. Soudly Ponds, Forest of Dean.** *(Forestry Commission)*

PLATE 2.4 **A single species forest has a different type of beauty from one of mixed species.** *(Forestry Commission)*

2.4 THE DIFFERING ROLES OF FORESTS

Whether planting new woodlands or managing and re-stocking old ones, the particular contribution which they can make to the landscape, the community and to conservation should be decided. Soil improvement, shelter, wild life conservation and appearance can and should be served by all woodlands whatever their other functions. Additional values will usually include timber production and often recreation. The relative weight given to these objectives will vary, and will influence forest planting and management. A natural forest managed as a nature reserve will require very different treatment from that appropriate to a timber-producing forest.

2.41 Timber-producing forests

In forests planted and managed primarily for timber there are obviously constraints which do not arise if the prime objects are landscape beauty and conservation. The degree of these constraints will vary according to the species of the timber crop. It is much easier to achieve a richly varied woodland, fitting naturally into the British landscape, in those areas where oak can be grown as the timber crop, rather than where spruce is the only viable choice. Nevertheless some practices are applicable to all forests. The varied age group and carefully designed felling coupes are cases in point. (A large square area of thicket-stage oak is no more beautiful than one of thicket-stage spruce.) The admission of light to edges, thinning trees at the sides of rides, giving space and light to stream-sides, leaving certain topographical features unplanted, encouraging the 'volunteer species' which may appear such as rowan or birch, are all practices which add to the landscape and conservation values of forests, whatever the timber crop may be.

But since a species such as spruce will not by itself encourage the diversity, or, to most eyes, provide the beauty of a deciduous forest, more positive action needs to be taken to ensure changes of species to give visual and ecological diversity. Birch and rowan on the poorer outcrops, alders in the wet hollows, larch on bracken-covered hillsides, can transform a monotonous spruce forest into a place of interest and bring the landscape to life by responding to the changing seasons instead of maintaining the same general tone throughout the year.

PLATE 2.5 **Forests provide an interior landscape. New Forest, ancient and ornamental.** *(Forestry Commission)*

The deciduous leaf-fall will enrich the degraded soil and there are other ecological advantages in diversity, as well as the obvious reduction in fire and pest risk. For instance it has been found that clearings, forming deer lawns and planted with alder and willow, provide browse for the deer, thereby diverting them from the young crop trees.

2.5 WOODLANDS AS VISUAL ELEMENTS IN THE LANDSCAPE

There are two visual aspects of woodland: one is the interior, to be experienced by walking within the canopy of trees; the other is external, seeing the woodland as part of a wider landscape. Forests are the only type of landscape, except perhaps canyons, which can be enjoyed from within, giving the same sense of containment as the interior of a great building. The closed, high canopy of trees nearing maturity gives this sensation to the full. This interior view is looked after almost entirely by following the precepts of sound conservation and providing the varied experiences given by the mosaic patterns previously mentioned.

Passing from the enclosure of high forest to open views over unplanted land or young crops is an aesthetic experience of high quality. The external view requires, in addition, careful attention to the siting, shape and composition of the wood. Since woodlands form a positive, three-dimensional element in the landscape, they are a dominant feature and need to be related sympathetically to the land form and the general landscape pattern. Their colour and texture is almost as important as their shape.

Deciduous woodlands in an agricultural landscape, similar in texture to the network of hedges in which they stand, form nodal points in a unified pattern. The continuing loss of hedgerows in agricultural land is eroding this network and node pattern. But in some parts of the country an enlarged alternative can be seen, with belts of trees and scrub drifting out from small woodlands, along gullies or on thin-soiled ridges. If the nodal woodlands in either pattern are of conifers they will form a strongly accented and less restful pattern. Alternatively there may be a pattern formed by drifting the deciduous trees into the mainly coniferous heart of the woodlands. In a landscape predominantly of hardwoods, a group of Scots pine on a hilltop can form the strongest feature for miles around. An almost equal accentuation of topography can be given by a drift of dark Douglas fir in the re-entrant of a valley. In conifer country, the deciduous relief of larch drifting over the breast of a hill can lighten a whole landscape, as can the native birch and rowan clothing the rocky knolls on a mountainside.

Examples of this blending of timber crop and native vegetation can be seen on some Scottish hillsides, such as those flanking Loch Garvie, a welcome contrast to other hillsides completely blanketed by conifer crops.

There are, however, some strong, hard, landscapes such as the Border country, where clean-cut windbreaks of conifers, provided they are well-placed and shaped, are as much in character with their surroundings as are the deciduous small woodlands of southern England with their softer landscape.

2.6 PLANTING MIXTURES

The object of planting in mixtures may either be to produce a mixed woodland, or to raise the climax tree within a nurse crop which will subsequently be removed. A nurse crop is desirable for many hardwoods, and necessary for beech. The silvicultural reason for the nurse crop is to protect and draw up the main crop. The economic reason is to provide a short-term timber crop by felling the nurse trees when they have achieved their silvicultural purpose.

Various methods of mixture by lines or groups are practised. The worst from a landscape point of view is the vertical 'pyjama stripe', which should never be used and is particularly unfortunate when seen on steep hillsides. In a permanently mixed forest, there may be either an overall mixture of species, or separate areas of each species. Either method can form a good landscape, but in the case of separate blocks the shapes need to be well related to the topography and landscape pattern, and the species drifted into each other as would occur in natural woodland. Separate hard-outlined compartments of different species never look natural, and when the shapes fail to accord with the land form they can be positively ugly.

Where a secondary species is planted to improve the appearance and ecological diversity of the main timber crop, the secondary species should be carefully sited for maximum effect. A narrow fringe of hardwoods round a conifer plantation should be avoided. Drifts breaking into the main crop from the edge will be more effective. These drifts should relate to topography, accentuating ridges, valleys, stream-sides and other natural features.

Planting should thin out at the edge of plantations, allowing indigenous species to establish themselves and give a natural transition to the surrounding landscape. This practice also helps to establish a wind-firm edge and a very rich wild-life habitat. A forest managed for timber on a felling and replanting regime can incorporate a network of permanent cover along exposed margins, the sides of rides, steep valleys and rocky ridges. This ecologically rich network will serve equally the interests of conservation and good landscape.

2.7 NATIVE SPECIES

The list of native trees commonly planted in forests is very short: oak (*Quercus* species), beech (*Fagus sylvatica*), ash (*Fraxinus excelsior*), Scots pine (*Pinus sylvestris*), to which may be added the old-established aliens, sycamore (*Acer pseudoplatanus*) and sweet chestnut (*Castanea*

PLATE 2.6 **Interior landscape: the Lime Avenue, Santon Downham, Thetford.** *(Forestry Commission)*

sativa). If dutch elm disease dies out, elm can be added to the list of native timbers, while aspen and lime are grown locally.

There is, however, a far wider range of native forest shrubs and smaller trees which forms the associated plant communities of the climax trees and which can be introduced and encouraged in new plantations. Many of these are both beautiful and very rich providers for wild life.

Alder (*Alnus glutinosa*) will colonize stream-sides and damp hollows over a wide range of soil and climate. It is a soil improver and a source of food for wild fowl and deer. The flat-topped growth of the mature tree and the pattern of its catkins have the quality of Chinese painting. *Salix caprea*, often its companion in the damp valleys, is spectacular in the spring and an attraction to bees. It is also the food plant of the Purple Emperor butterfly. *Viburnum opulus*, a native of damp oakwoods, is equally attractive. Where light penetrates the forest edge will be found hawthorn, wild rose and blackthorn, while throughout the oak forest may be found hazel and the occasional wild crab, both important sources of wild-life food.

While these attractive native shrubs can easily be recognized as desirable plants for the forest, it should also be realized that plants often regarded as weeds are vital to wild life. The common bramble is one of the richest sources of food, including the provision of winter browse for deer.

In the highland regions, birch (which is second only to the oak in richness of associated species) and the beautiful rowan will colonize the poorest ground. Given time and helpful management, a newly planted forest will develop the shrub and field layer and associated trees natural to the soil and climate. In the case of birch and rowan, if seed parents are present, the colonization will be so speedy that it is only necessary to leave appropriate areas free from the crop-tree and protected from grazing. Any unplanted area within the forest fence will quickly be colonized. In other cases, where seed parents are absent or propagation of the species by seed is less prolific, the plant associations can be planted to hasten the establishment of a whole and balanced forest ecology.

19

2.8 INTRODUCED SPECIES

Great Britain has an unusually short list of native species. This is due to severance from the European land-mass before species driven south by the last ice-age had time to recolonize in the wake of the retreating ice. On the other hand the temperate climate and great variety of soil types provide favourable conditions for growing a very wide range of species from other parts of the world. Under these circumstances it is inevitable that many species from overseas have been introduced. A right decision on when and where to plant the introductions is not always easy. The arguments against introductions can be both visual and ecological.

Established native ecosystems may be thrown out of balance by introduced species. One example is the introduction of *Rhododendron ponticum* into woodland where it has become an invasive weed, stifling forest flora and preventing natural regeneration of the trees. Other introductions have been assimilated without detriment to the ecology and with benefit to the landscape. We would be sorry to lose the sweet chestnut or the walnut.

For visual as well as scientific reasons, there is advantage in retaining different types of native woodland in different situations, thus ensuring the survival of special ecosystems and giving a sense of place to different parts of the world. Introductions can blur these distinct characteristics and end by creating a dull similarity everywhere. This has happened to a large extent over the last few decades in Great Britain by the 'enrichment' of lowland hardwood forests with introduced conifers and it must be hoped that this trend will now cease and that the typical hardwoods will be given pride of place.

There are, however, situations where introduced species will serve some specific purpose for which no native plant is suitable. *Robinia pseudoacacia* is a valuable tree for restoring lost fertility and Corsican pine is usually a better species for stabilizing sand dunes than the Scots pine, and better withstands pollution in industrial areas. Over-grazed and over-burnt areas in the Highlands will not allow the species which once grew there to develop into timber trees but these lands can be far more easily colonized by species from the Pacific coast of America, notably Sitka spruce on wet peat and Lodgepole pine on harder ground. *Nothofagus* in the Welsh hills, red oak (*Quercus rubra*) on drier soils or Norway maple (*Acer platanoides*) on alkaline soils, have all been found capable of producing better timber than native hardwoods in similar situations, and all can be considered welcome additions to our forest trees.

In all these cases where a new need or changed growing conditions make introduced species more suitable than natives, it is reasonable to plant them, and indeed to search out any new source of supply which may fill a genuine need. But where the native species will flourish they should be given preference and allowed to form the characteristic landscapes of the countryside, otherwise there is danger that our whole landscape will merge into one huge, muddled arboretum. Where there is a valid reason for using exotics, their effect on the soil and the ecological systems should be carefully watched so that any harmful side effects may be counteracted.

The few remaining natural woodlands should certainly be conserved, although to achieve this re-planting may be necessary. In the case of the Caledonian pine forests, the degeneration of the ground and depredations of deer have prevented regeneration, and seedlings have to be raised in a nursery and planted out.

A truly natural condition scarcely exists in the British Isles. Our choice is either to work with our inherited forest ecology or, where necessary, deliberately to change it. We have not the option of doing nothing. Our intervention in the past has given us the responsibility to plant and manage forests in a way which will increase the ecological richness and stability of the land, while adding to its beauty.

PLATE 2.7 **Sheep and deer grazing have prevented natural regeneration of the old Caledonian Pine Forest. They can be restored by protection and re-planting.**
(Forestry Commission)

PLATE 2.8 **Pine tree over Maddum Lake, North Jutland, Denmark.** *(Preben Jakobsen)*

FURTHER READING

Crowe, Sylvia. *Forestry in the Landscape* (London: HMSO, 1966; third impression with amendments, 1972)

Steele, R. C. *Wildlife conservation in woodlands* (London: HMSO, 1972)

Tansley, A. G. (Ed. Proctor, M. C. F.). *Britain's Green Mantle* (London: George Allen and Unwin Ltd., 2nd edition, 1968)

CHAPTER 3

Trees in Urban Areas

GORDON PATTERSON

3.1 INTRODUCTION

Most of us gladly accept the tree as part of the urban scene. Many of our cities, towns and especially our villages, owe much of their character to the incidental use of vegetation in their midst. Trees are an important part of the townscape, and one of the most interesting and effective design elements which the landscape architect has at his disposal. Perhaps this happy acceptance of something seemingly so inessential to a basic mode of living (although many of us have enjoyed tree houses in our time) stems from some deep desire within all of us, if not to get back to the primeval forests, at least to identify with the natural order of things. We all feel the need to be made aware from time to time of the way the seasons alter, contrasting with the otherwise dull repetition of the everyday routine and scene. How often we hear the city dweller praising the virtues of a tree-lined boulevard or the seclusion and privacy afforded by a tree-bound square. Such delights should be regarded not as the privilege of the few but as a universal necessity to be found in all parts of our towns and cities.

Many of our ideas about the place of trees in the urban environment stem from the traditions of the past, and in this respect England has a particularly rich heritage. The open quality of Cambridge and Bath or the London parks immediately springs to mind and the great tract of river and downland which runs into the heart of the city of

PLATE 3.1 **Single, splendid specimens of birch and cedar make an effective landscape for private flats in Croydon.** (Landscape Architects: *Derek Lovejoy and Partners, London. A. Court Photographers Limited*)

PLATE 3.2 **Heavy shade provided by lime trees in Tivoli Gardens, Copenhagen, contrasts with the bright sunlight of the space around the fountain, and frames the view.** *(K. Stansfield)*

Bristol is an inspiring example of the integration of town and countryside.

Not all our towns have been so fortunate, but most exhibit some feature of landscaping with trees, whether it be in the form of the tree-lined avenues once so popular in our towns that streets were lined to the horizon, or whether it is in the one fair-sized park which served the whole of an industrial town. In this way the patterns of open space in our towns have been created. Changing fashions and opinions limit the extent to which the past can provide inspiration for the future, but we should not ignore the many historical examples which owed their creation to a vision and a genius which has stood the test of time.

3.2 THE EFFECT OF TREES ON THE URBAN ENVIRONMENT

There are, of course, purely visual pleasures to be derived from looking at individual trees. But in urban scenes it is more often the visual play of a mass of natural foliage when contrasted with built forms which is important and which adds up to a sum that in total is greater than that of its parts.

Trees provide contrasts of colour, texture and form in a built environment, introducing the shapes and colours of nature into the man-made geometric patterns of roads and buildings.

Changing colour with the passing of the seasons, trees provide endless variety and delight; fresh greenery and gay blossoms in spring; swollen globes of green casting heavy shade in summer; ripening fruit and seed and vivid autumn colours. Even in winter, those which shed their leaves still provide visual pleasure in the delicate sculpture of naked branches casting intricate shadows on brick or concrete walls and pavings.

Trees often have particularly evocative qualities or associations: noble trees like the oak and beech remind us of deep forests; tall uncompromising poplars echo the columnar structures of surrounding buildings; willows, traditionally associated with water, create an impression of softly falling rain from their light-coloured pendulous foliage.

Trees have more than simply a visual appeal. The wind rustling through leaves is a sound evocative of the countryside, and a welcome diversion from city noises. The smell of blossom, ripening fruit or dying leaves all have their associations with nature, and temper the

23

PLATE 3.3 **A specimen weeping beech planted in paving at Southrow, Blackheath, in London.** (Landscape architects: *Eric Lyons Cunningham Partnership. Sam Lambert photographs*)

artificiality of urban surroundings.

There is another aspect of considerable importance, and partly psychological in its effect. Trees contribute to the well-being and comfort of the town dweller in replacing oxygen, recycling water and improving the soil. They are capable of absorbing large quantities of dust from the atmosphere; some species, notably conifers and evergreens, trap it on the surface area of their leaves (*see* Chapter 13, Plants and Air Pollution). Although the residue is washed off during rainy periods, the ground beneath the canopy benefits during the long dry spells.

Some benefit is claimed both from the cooling effect of trees on their surroundings by the shade they afford and by the temperature reduction produced as the result of evapo-transpiration. This is of particular importance in hot climates. There can also be no doubt that in general terms the surrounding soil is improved. This benefit can be gained more especially where the ground is open and the recycling process provided by leaf fall is completed. It is, however, likely to prove unimportant in most fully urban conditions, where it is usually necessary to provide a good soil at the outset.

To a limited extent, depending upon the amount of planting relative to built areas, trees can provide a valuable habitat for wildlife, linking open spaces and parks within the urban framework (*see* Chapter 8).

There are certain disadvantages to planting trees within urban areas which must be taken into account in

PLATE 3.4 **The value of existing trees, both as specimens and groups is illustrated by this Old People's Home where the spinney or woodland in the background enhances the setting, and the existing single Black Pine has been incorporated into the landscape design.** (Landscape Architects: *Gordon Patterson & Partners*)

landscape schemes. Those who have responsibility for clearing streets, gulleys or gutters of leaves may well feel that many of these counter-considerations are paramount. Nor does it stop at the annual leaf-fall. Roots can get into drains and foundations, while certain trees such as some species of lime exude sticky substances which can be dangerous in causing nuisance and even accidents to passers-by. Trees in an unsafe condition can fall and even those that look in good health can sometimes do the unexpected. All this should not, however, deter us or detract from the very tangible advantages which trees can bring to an everyday scene. The disadvantages can be avoided by careful selection of species to suit the particular requirements of the site.

3.3 REQUIREMENTS

Trees in urban areas exist in a largely artificial environment, and their physiological needs must be met if planting is to be successful. These include soil, water, microclimate (shade and shelter), supply of nutrients and drainage, all of which are considered in Chapter 9. The particular needs and problems associated with transplanting semi-mature trees are the subject of Chapter 10.

Trees require space. Not only do they require room enough to grow upwards, but usually a certain freedom to expand downwards and outwards. The spread of a mature tree may be 20 m or more. Planting in accordance with minimum space recommendations is seldom advisable, for if a tree outgrows the space provided it may cause damage to buildings and have to be felled.

3.4 TREES AND THE TOWNSCAPE

Trees should be seen as an integral part of the total three-dimensional urban structure, giving definition and meaning to the spaces between buildings, and enhancing the buildings themselves. There is an endless variety of tree-forms which can be used to define spaces, to provide a natural focal point to a view, or to soften the impact of built forms—as individual specimens, in small groups, or massed to form green swathes. The selection of tree species should reflect the designer's understanding of the purpose of the site and its architectural character, the trees being of the appropriate scale, shape, texture and colour. Trees may be required simply to enhance urban developments, or for more functional purposes:
i) to block out undesirable features such as industrial areas or car parks;
ii) to indicate changes in use, e.g. the demarcation line between traffic and pedestrian routes;
iii) for emphasis and direction as in avenue planting, for enclosure of seating areas, children's play areas, etc.;

FIGURES 3.1 & 3.2
Artist's impression of the effectiveness of tree planting to replace an unsightly dump, and screen the houses from traffic. I.C.I. Blakeley. (Landscape Architects: *Donaldson/Edwards Partnership*)

25

PLATE 3.5 **Some trees owe their character to their form and none perhaps more so than this pine growing from an island in the courtyard of a Technical College in Copenhagen. It is, of course, a highly contrived situation, but is none the less attractive.** (Photographers: *Gordon Patterson and Partners*)

iv) individual specimens, or trees with special character, can be used for more formal ornamental purposes, as living sculptural elements in town squares or courtyards.

Trees have a time scale of their own; they are part and parcel of a naturally recurring cycle and should always be seen as dynamic rather than static entities. Growth and change-over time should be anticipated by the designer if he is to make the most of trees in a landscape scheme. Trees should be regarded as part of a continuing process of planting, growth to maturity, and removal, otherwise there will be a lack of succession, and possibly even total disappearance of trees in some parts of our towns. In some urban situations, arboriculture has been looked at in crop rotational terms and this technique, perfected in many Dutch towns, can often give very satisfactory results.

Trees in cities need to be kept under continuing surveillance. The recent scourge of elm disease has brought this fact home to many, since virtually overnight a useful and beautiful feature has become a liability. The occurrence of the attack pinpoints the desirability of having on hand a continuous brief of stewardship and husbandry and the need for planting younger trees to replace those which have to be felled. Only in this way can we hope to predict with any reliability what the state of either individual trees or the overall system is likely to be at any point in time.

It is very important to see tree planting in our towns and housing estates as an organic process. With such an emphasis, planting design can take on something of the expanding quality of town building itself and be seen as an integral part of the townscape rather than merely as a decorative addition to the urban form. This does not necessarily exclude the placing of individual specimens, but for cultural and visual reasons trees in an urban setting may have the greatest impact when seen as a collective mass against the façades of bricks and mortar, or running through and against the more open fabric of townscape. Where space permits, groups of trees can be allowed to coalesce into quite significant knots of foliage, taking on the appearance of small plantations or spinneys. When linked visually with associated clumps these strands of green can form the basis of that cellular structure so important to the successful townscape pattern.

This approach of course is not new. It owes its origins to the early landscape traditions 'of joining willing woods', so effectively begun by Earl Bathurst at Cirencester in the early eighteenth century. It is a technique of design, however, which has had a fair measure of success in its application in many of the early new towns where small scale and repetitive units have been effectively landscaped. Some of these town sites were fortunate in embracing tracts of existing woodland and these in turn have helped to form the nucleus of an extended series of belts of tree planting which now run right through the middle of many housing areas. These plantations give an overall green structure to the town, and also provide compartments in which varied development can often take place without wrecking the total picture. Such estates enjoy a very satisfactory measure of landscape enclosure. When trees start to override the roof ridges, the whole housing landscape immediately benefits from a sense of containment.

Trees should be selected for the effect or use desired; too wide a range of species should be avoided as the different shapes, textures and colours are likely to result in

PLATES 3.6 & 3.7 **Proposals and plan for West Ham Park incorporating a water area and golf course. Continuity of the tree pattern enclosing and enveloping parcels of land creates a cellular landscape structure.** (Landscape Architects: *Gordon Patterson and Partners*)

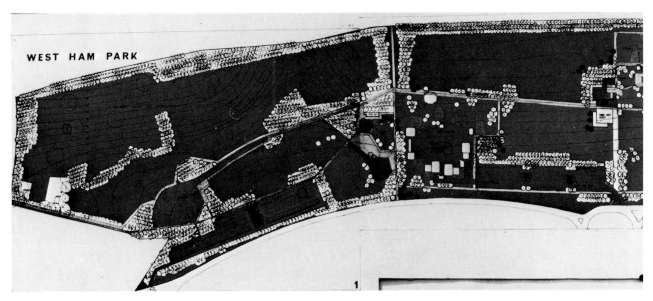

WEST HAM PARK

27

PLATE 3.8 **Shadow effect of existing birch trees retained close to new flats at Croydon. The trees give some shade on an open site, a degree of privacy to large windows and a feeling of maturity until new planting is established.** (Landscape Architects: *Derek Lovejoy and Partners, London. A. Court Photographers Ltd*)

a restless composition. The best effects are generally achieved with boldness and simplicity, as in mass planting of a single species, closely spaced, or of a few species with similar texture, form and colour. Some trees may be selected to act as foils to existing buildings, enhancing rather than obscuring the architecture, or as elements in a formal design. It is necessary to consider the seasonal variation in order to design a scheme which will be effective and harmonious throughout the year. Evergreens will provide colour and strongly defined natural forms during the winter, which may be of particular value in areas where buildings lack variety. Trees with colourful foliage or blossom will generally be more effective planted in groups, provided that the range of colours is limited to those which blend well together and are appropriate for the site.

The landscape architect must compose a design which works in both time and space, trees being so placed that they achieve the desired effect from all angles. This can often only be achieved by working on the site as the trees

are being planted and viewing them critically as they are placed. The views of the pedestrian should be taken into account so that the design reflects an understanding of progression through spaces, from light to shade, unfolding and concealing views, enclosing and opening up spaces.

3.5 TREES IN HOUSING AREAS

3.51 Existing trees

Existing trees have many advantages if carefully incorporated within housing layouts. The retention of the trees can add immeasurably to the sense of establishment of the place and give it a quality that would have taken many years to develop otherwise, although there are problems concerning the use of large trees in housing layouts. Much depends on the physical condition as well as upon the nature of the particular tree involved. Elms

28

for example although handsome adjuncts in housing are notoriously undependable. They can shed branches without warning and their roots can be troublesome in relation to drains and footings. On the other hand a mature oak, provided it is not affected by change in water relation, drainage or water table will often grow quite happily beside a road or building.

The existing trees on the site should be carefully identified and surveyed before a final selection of those to be retained is made. This appraisal should include the condition of the tree, its probable life expectancy, susceptibility to disease, and maintenance requirements. The position of existing trees relative to new buildings, roads etc., should be most carefully assessed so that those trees retained are of maximum value to the overall design

and are allowed to continue to grow as freely as possible. Whilst existing beautiful trees can form the focal point of a new design, it is useless to expect them to survive alterations in water table and civil engineering works unscathed, unless adequate protection is provided during building operations. Trees must be protected against damage, by fencing off groups or cladding single specimens prior to any work on site. The roots should be protected from pollutants, vehicles and building materials. All construction activities, storage etc. should be kept a safe distance beyond the spread of the crown. Trees vary considerably in their reaction to changes in surrounding soil levels and professional advice should be taken in each case; deep rooting trees are generally more tolerant of a lowering in soil levels than shallow-rooted

PLATE 3.9 **Young elm trees which have grown out from an old hedge furnish these early New Town houses with a foil and screen in scale with the layout. They will, however, need to be carefully thinned and pruned.** (Landscape Architects: *Gordon Patterson and Partners*)

FIGURE 3.3 **Artist's impression of domestic landscaped areas with trees, for new housing in London.**
(*Andrew Donaldson*)

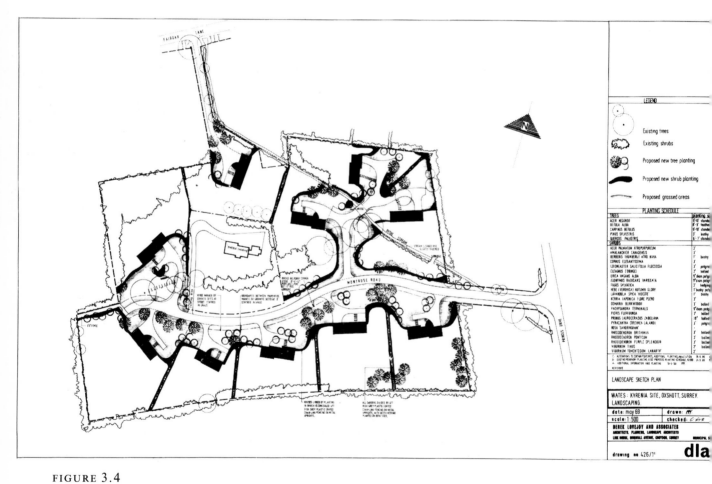

FIGURE 3.4

Design for exclusive housing scheme in Surrey. Large houses in a parkland setting at very low density with private hedged back gardens. Strong linking shrubberies screen the gardens creating a sense of 'baroque' movement in the landscape. The fronts were planted only with trees and bulbs, with stone blocks in the grass to define legal boundaries.

(Landscape Architects: *Derek Lovejoy and Partners*. Architects: *Wates Limited Architects Department*)

species. As far as possible soil levels around the tree boles should be maintained and the level of water table kept constant by using revetments or retaining walls (which should be at least 3 m away from the tree). As a last resort, if the soil level has to be raised, this should be done only with light sandy soil or ballast at a rate of between 80–150 mm per annum. Alternatively the soil can be held back with revetments or retaining walls.

3.52 Density and building types

The density and type of building will determine how much land is available for tree planting—mostly in areas of common open space. For instance in low density developments there may be scope for forest trees; in medium density layouts, lines or groups and massed belts of trees may be planted. In high density schemes with high rise buildings single trees of forest dimensions will be more effective as a foil than smaller trees.

The scale and character of the trees must be related to the scale of buildings and spaces. A tree which eventually grows above the roof line gives a most satisfying effect; and if small trees are used they are generally more effective in groups.

The purpose of the spaces may determine the type of tree planting. In play areas within residential development, groups of trees which can withstand more than average interference are most likely to survive. In sitting areas, shade and protection from wind will be important; the seating, paths and tree layout are inter-dependent and should be designed together. Pedestrian movement should be kept a safe distance from the boles of trees.

Tree planting in private gardens will depend very much on the space available, but there is a considerable amount of choice, even for smaller gardens. Trees with open, light foliage or narrow spread are generally suitable, as well as small fruit and blossom trees, though the latter are perhaps too highly favoured in many areas.

3.53 Proximity to buildings

Trees continuously change in shape and size both above and below ground, and sufficient space must be allowed for the likely spread of roots and branches. Roots may cause contraction of the soil by extracting soil moisture, and this in turn may cause cracks to appear in nearby buildings, particularly on heavy clay soils. Elm, poplar, willow and ash are the most likely offenders and should be planted at least as far away from a building as their estimated height. Other trees can be planted up to about two-thirds of their height away, or closer if the foundations reach to a depth of 2 m or more, or other precautions are taken such as an underground wall barrier or raft foundations. Roots may deflect or grow into pipes which should be protected by concrete casting or made of cast iron if near to trees. In addition root

PLATE 3.10 **This housing scheme provides small scale intimate spaces, with generous provision for private gardens. Robust quick growing shrubs and trees have been used, planted in raised beds where possible. They include species of** *Robinia, Rhus* **and** *Cotoneaster*. **Mozart housing for Westminster C.C.** (Landscape Architects: *Michael Brown Partnership*. Photographer: *Anthony Blake*)

suckers may penetrate soil and grass, and break up hard surfaces—particularly poplars and elms. Thus sucker species should be avoided.

Trees which are to be sited close to buildings should be selected for their light foliage, or carefully sited away from windows. Where mature trees have blocked out the light, a tree surgeon can be called in to solve the problem while maintaining the shape and character of the tree by careful pruning.

FIGURE 3.5
Artist's impression of trees used to frame views along pedestrian ways in new housing in London. *(Andrew Donaldson)*

PLATE 3.11 **Silver birch form an attractive feature of the Town Square at Stevenage, set at intervals along a paved pedestrian street.** *(Cement and Concrete Association)*

PLATE 3.12 **Young trees and shrubs as part of a car park design for new blocks of flats, Delft, Holland. The scheme was designed using native species.** *(Ian Laurie)*

3.6 TREES IN STREETS AND SHOPPING AREAS

There are limited opportunities for tree planting along existing streets and as this is rarely considered at the design stage, planting is generally confined to specimen trees in odd corners, with formal avenues or group planting where space allows, for example on roundabouts. Tree planting along streets can accomplish more than any other planting in visually breaking up the hard lines of road surfaces and buildings and dividing pedestrian footpaths from the traffic flow. Suitable trees should be planted far enough from the kerb to allow them to spread without too much pruning, and be kept clear of overhead wires and underground services. In avenue planting, single trees interspersed with groups will often achieve more satisfying informal results than even spacing, and trees can be used to great effect in framing views or buildings. Variation of species and scale can help relieve the monotony of city and suburban streets and emphasize a particular building or space. The opportunities are greater in pedestrian areas such as shopping streets where little or no traffic is permitted, or precincts which have been designed for pedestrian use only. In Stevenage New Town shopping centre, trees are an integral part of the design, affording shade and shelter in sitting areas and enriching the scene for pedestrians.

City conditions are generally unfavourable for tree growth, and species must be selected which can tolerate air pollution, dry conditions, limited light, glare from pavements etc. It is essential to maintain the balance between water absorbed into the root system and that evaporated from the leaves. This can be done by pruning to remove excess leaf growth or cutting back the branches each year. Trees will require annual application of fertilizers in late autumn or early spring, and protection against pests. (*See* Chapter 9 for details of planting in paved areas.)

3.7 TREES IN CAR PARKS

Car parks impose a particular set of restrictive conditions in their design which are not always fully appreciated at the outset. Although they can provide a useful space within the urban framework in which to plant trees, the task of accommodating trees in these surroundings is not always as straightforward as it may seem. The difficulty experienced in establishing individual trees or groups, especially in large areas of unrelieved hard surfacing, is often due to the dry conditions, lack of air, and the intensity of the light which is thrown up from ground to tree, which can cause leaf scorch and abnormal transpiration.

Even after satisfying the minimum loss of parking

33

PLATE 3.13
Detail of winter branches of the plane tree. *(Dick Hoyle)*

PLATE 3.14
Detail of plane tree bark. *(Dick Hoyle)*

spaces (usually a prerequisite in urban space planning), a disjointed fashion of planting often results, failing to provide a satisfactory visual flow to a scheme. Damage may be caused to tree boles (and lower branches) by vehicles backing into them, and tree roots may be poisoned if fuel run-off gets into the water supply. To avoid this it is usually suggested they should be planted between raised kerbs or in elevated boxes. Here again, however, discontinuity of the ground surface can lead to an artificial appearance and it will usually be found that trees look better and more natural if the base of the tree is visible. Therefore whilst hazard fencing at bumper height can go some way to meeting practicalities, it is more frequently the careful siting of trees in relation to the overall car park design which gives the best solution, rather than the *ad hoc* filling with trees so commonly practised.

34

3.8 TREE SELECTION

Local soil and water characteristics should be thoroughly investigated, e.g. type and depth of soil and sub-soil, and level of water table. The site may be prone to frost or air pollution or other micro-climatic influences which will affect tree selection.

The size of the trees relative to the space available and rates of growth must be taken into account. It is misleading to show the mature size of the tree on a landscape plan, particularly if it is very slow growing.

The general appearance and character of the tree is important whether individual specimens or groups are being considered. Tall narrow trees may be appropriate in restricted spaces such as central road reserves where spreading trees could be dangerous. Weeping or pendulous species provide contrast and movement; small scale trees would be useful where a limited space is available, e.g. if trees are to be planted in small scale residential areas. The effect of seasonal change can be very important where colour and variety is lacking in the built environment: the winter effect of bare branches and bark texture or evergreen leaves; autumn colouring, fruit and seeds; summer leaf shade and density; and new spring leaves and blossom.

Length of life and availability are important factors in tree selection. For instance birch, willow and poplar will grow quickly but for long lasting effects, in parks perhaps, slow growing long-lived species may be more appropriate.

In the past urban tree planting has probably embraced, if anything, too wide a choice of specimens with the result that planting schemes have often lacked an overriding sense of unity. The common desire has been to include one of everything, and this approach is unlikely to lead to the best results, at least in visual terms. This way of thinking has arisen in part from a gardenesque approach; that is, identifying the solution in terms of what we recognize in our own back gardens. In fact, there are relatively few trees which meet all the design criteria for truly satisfactory urban growth, in much the same way as there are relatively few tree species which form the climax of our deciduous semi-natural English woodlands. This is why so much of our countryside takes on its characteristic, much admired, unified appearance.

There are, in addition, many other reasons, cultural, technical and traditional, for limiting the number of species within urban planting schemes. If the quest for variety has to be satisfied then this particular problem would best be met in the context of the wider issue of a truly ecological selection. Seen in this particular way there are again relatively few trees which meet the rather stringent requirements of cities and towns. The success of the London plane (*Platanus hispanica*) in meeting the very rigorous demands made upon it is a fine example of a tree well adapted to urban conditions. The Norway maple (*Acer platanoides*), though it cannot claim the stature of the plane, adapts well to urban surroundings. It is not particularly demanding regarding water conditions or as a feeder, and so far has remained relatively free from pests and diseases. It is a tree with a considerable degree of natural variety in its form and colours, as well as creating interest because of its dumpy massing, branching and autumn colour. It is also decorative during its flowering period. It can therefore lay some claim to being seen as a ready alternative dominant for general purposes in urban areas.

The common lime (*Tilia × vulgaris*) has some claim to precedent in use as a town tree. Certainly its size and grace as well as the delicate green of its foliage and flowers do much to commend it in this respect. It does, however, have a number of serious disadvantages; some trees will sucker profusely or encourage aphids and drop sticky substances and nectar from their flowers. They are tolerant of a wide variety of soils, though less likely to adapt to particularly dry conditions than maples and planes. They also have a tendency to die back in the head, particularly after they have attained a considerable size. *Tilia × euchlora* is possibly the most suitable lime for urban planting as it has none of these disadvantages.

These trees, along with a handful of others such as the

PLATE 3.15

The stature of one tree can often support a whole scene so long as it survives. This plane tree, although isolated, acts as a pivotal point between the lake and library, bringing unity to the whole scene. Elsinore, North Zealand, Denmark.
(Photographers: *Gordon Patterson and Partners*)

tree of heaven (*Ailanthus altissima*), native cherry (*Prunus avium*) and black pine (*Pinus nigra*) and in some places the sycamore (*Acer pseudoplatanus*) can be relied upon to provide a good backbone to urban planting.

Table 3.1 lists trees suitable for planting in urban areas, with their main characteristics. It contains many specimens described in further detail and illustrated in the Tree Information Sheets at the end of the book.

TABLE 3.1
Trees suitable for urban use

Latin and common name	Use, tolerance, qualities	Latin and common name	Use, tolerance, qualities
Acer platanoides* Norway maple	Streets and parks. Tolerates polluted atmosphere. Early spring flowers and good autumn colour.	*Fagus sylvatica* beech	Groups, park—requires large space. Shelterbelt. Hardy; wind firm, forest tree. Delicate green, spring; gold autumn. Interesting varieties for shape and colour.
Acer pseudoplatanus* sycamore	Difficult urban conditions. Wind and salt resistant. Fast growth, free seeding. Excessive fertility can be a nuisance. Coarse foliage can attract pests in summer.	*Fraxinus excelsior** common ash	Cold urban sites; where subtle effects required. Withstands smoke and exposed sites. Light shade, hardy. Graceful and decorative. Winter, sculptural effect. Keep away from buildings.
Aesculus hippocastanum horse chestnut	Ornamental; parks and avenues. Impressive spring flowers and autumn colour.		
Ailanthus altissima tree of heaven	Urban squares and streets. Smoke resistant; grows on poor soils. Bold foliage; open forked branches.	*Ilex aquifolium* holly	Understorey planting; hedges, ornamental. Withstands smoke and wind. Evergreen; winter colour.
Alnus glutinosa common alder	Urban river and lakeside; slag heaps; group/coppice planting. Spring catkins.	*Picea omorika*	Groups, specimen—parks and open spaces. All year round interest. Good form and colour near buildings.
Betula verrucosa silver birch	Groups. Domestic areas; near buildings, in limited space Small scale; quick growth, short-lived. Needs plenty of light; moist or dry conditions; all year round interest. Slender branches, light leaves, attractive bark. Spring catkins.	*Platanus hybrida** × *acerifolia*, × *hispanica* London plane	Industrial sites; street tree. Tolerates polluted atmosphere, cold winds, compacted soil and heavy pruning. Large leaves, dappled bark, globular seeds remain all year. Forest stature. Open leaf, branch network. Decorative and elegant.
Carpinus betulus hornbeam	Cold exposed sites; streets; shelterbelt. Hardy. Winter colour; retains brown leaves.	*Populus* 'Serotina' black Italian poplar	Quick screening for tall buildings, industries. Tolerates polluted atmosphere. Fast growth. Red-brown leaves early. Keep away from buildings.
Crataegus monogyna* common hawthorn	Street, park, development schemes. Interest all year round, flowers, fruit.		

36

*Prunus avium** wild cherry	Parks, open spaces, streets. Attractive blossom, bark and autumn colour.		winter stem colour. Wind movement. Many varieties.
Quercus robur oak	Park—specimen, small group, avenue. Requires large space. Traditional; very decorative; light shade. Interesting leaf shape and acorns.	*Sorbus aria** whitebeam	Street, restricted sites, near buildings. Upright, wind resistant. Attractive foliage especially in wind.
Robinia pseudoacacia false acacia	Paved courtyards, streets. Hardy, smoke resistant. Open, light attractive foliage and flowers. Shallow roots. Brittle branches.	*Sorbus aucuparia** rowan; mountain ash	Small scale—good for small spaces. Attractive pinnate leaves; winter berries; white flowers in spring.
Salix × chrysocoma weeping willow	Specimen, waterside. Requires large space. Urban lakes and riversides. Quick growth. Good	*Tilia × euchlora** common lime	Parks and open spaces. Requires large space. Magnificent specimen tree; groups and avenues. Fresh pale green leaves, yellow in autumn. Long-lived; tolerates pruning.

* Most commonly planted species.

3.9 MAINTENANCE AND MANAGEMENT

The long-term success of tree planting in urban areas, as in any landscape scheme, depends on the quality of the ongoing maintenance and management. Trees planted in urban areas require more care than in rural or natural conditions if they are to survive, develop, and grow to full stature. It is important, therefore, that the appropriate size and species of tree be selected to fulfil the designer's requirements and the site conditions, so that the tree has the best possible chance to develop from the start. The larger the size of the tree on planting, the less prone it will be to damage by vandals, which is generally a hazard in urban areas. A semi-mature tree will, therefore, be more likely to survive attacks by vandals, although it will require a considerable amount of care and attention if it is to be transplanted successfully (*see* Chapter 10).

3.10 CONCLUSION

It takes years, sometimes generations, to replace a mature tree, and a complete change of heart to prevent un-necessary felling and vandalism. Our present urban environment would benefit from the planting of many thousands of trees, some to replace mature specimens, others to create beauty in newly-built developments. The importance of trees as supremely useful elements in planting schemes for urban areas cannot be over-emphasized. No other form of planting brings the presence of nature so forcefully into our man-made environment, or does so much to conceal the ugliness and enhance the beauty of our urban surroundings.

FURTHER READING

Colvin, B. *Trees for Town and Country* (London: Lund Humphries, 4th edition 1972)

Fairbrother, N. *New Lives, New Landscapes* (London: The Architectural Press, 3rd impression 1971)

Johnson, H. *The International Book of Trees* (London: Mitchell Beazley Ltd., 1973)

Morling, R. J. *Trees* (London: Estates Gazette Ltd., revised edition, 1963)

Zion, R. L. *Trees for Architecture and Landscape* (New York: Van Nostrand Rheinhold Company, 1968)

CHAPTER 4

Shrubs and Groundcover

PREBEN JAKOBSEN

4.1 INTRODUCTION

The terms shrubs and groundcover may mean different things to different people. In the widest sense groundcover can be of any height, depending upon the vantage points. The common characteristic, whatever the height, is that the plant covers the soil with its leaves. The more rigorous definitions given below, however, should serve to indicate how they relate in height to other plant material and to clarify their meanings in the context of this chapter.

The *Oxford Dictionary* defines a shrub as a woody plant of less size than a tree and usually divided into separate stems from near the ground (OE *scrybb* brushwood).

Webster's Dictionary defines groundcover as: the small plants in a forest except young trees; a low plant (as ivy) that covers the ground in place of turf; a plant adapted for use as groundcover.

Professor R. W. Curtis of Cornell University gives the following range of heights for shrubs and groundcover:

Groundcover	150–300 mm (6–12 in.)
Low shrub	450–1000 mm (18–36 in.)
Small shrub	1–1·5 m (approx. 4–5 ft)
Medium shrub	1·5–2·5 m (approx. 6–8 ft)
Large shrub/small tree	3–7·5 m (10–25 ft)

4.2 HISTORICAL BACKGROUND

A traditionally popular form of planting in England can be described as mixed or *mélange* planting where different varieties of natural and exotic groundcovers and shrubs are combined. The late Margery Fish was one of the greatest popularizers of this type of planting, which, it should be stressed, includes a high proportion of native plant material or selected forms therefrom.

Another type of groundcover planting in the United Kingdom can be traced from the period between the wars, when Michael Haworth Booth coined the word *boscage* planting, and put this into effect in his own nursery near Haslemere and later in his clients' gardens. This method did not become generally recognized until after the Second World War. He became an authority on and exponent of a type of planting which can best be described as anti-bare earth policy, where the plant material totally covers the ground. The majority of material used consisted of Japanese Kurume azaleas with hummock forming plants such as various species of genista, cytisus, hebe, hydrangea and viburnum, all being allowed to 'knit' together.

A third form of planting is woodland—paradise planting, which uses an exuberance of plant material and is a combination of boscage and *mélange* traditions of which the Savill Garden in Windsor Great Park is an outstanding example. There are also many National Trust properties and private estate gardens where this form of planting is accepted as the norm. Successful as these plantings may be, however, there are signs that this style has passed its peak.

Cyclical movements can be discerned in the design and use of different types of shrubs and groundcovers in landscape design. There is currently a commonly held view that much of the inspiration in Britain during the last twenty years has been derived from America and the Continent. Looking back into the past, however, similar movements can be discerned in England in Victorian times and during the earlier part of the twentieth century. The use of ivy as a groundcover can be seen as an example of this cyclical change. Ever since the Victorian writer Shirley Hibberd first published his monograph on the ivy, the gardeners of the British Isles have led the world in the use of groundcover. Perhaps no other individual plant is better suited to this climate as a groundcover. From Victorian times to the late 1920s saw the heyday of its use and from this stems the popularization of ivy in the United States. The ivy including its variants and foreign counterparts is perhaps the archetype of all native groundcovers; it is heartening to note the renaissance in its use which is now occurring.

Landscape design is influenced by movements in architecture and art. The influence of cubism, for example (by such notable artists as Mondrian and Klee in particular) on the use of shrubs and groundcovers, is

PLATE 4.1
A carefully controlled composition using shrubs and groundcover for exhibition purposes. Det Kongelige Haveselskabs Have, Frederiksberg, Copenhagen. *(Preben Jakobsen)*

PLATE 4.2
Order. Stylized design overemphasizing natural forms. Local park in Kingston, London. *(Preben Jakobsen)*

PLATE 4.3
Chaos. Small groups have form and harmony, but the total effect is chaotic. Victorian park, Bristol. *(Preben Jakobsen)*

PLATE 4.4
Landscape cell, Lutyens house, with herbaceous planting within enclosed space. *(Preben Jakobsen)*

particularly obvious when one analyses the work of the renowned Brazilian landscape architect Burle Marx, who paints great brushstrokes with groundcovers on which a limited amount of statuesque accent and emphasis planting is carefully displayed.

4.3 DESIGN DISCIPLINE

No one part of planting design can be viewed in isolation. Shrubs and groundcover form an integral part of the overall design in which trees, by virtue of their size, are often considered to be dominant features. The lower planting levels with which we are primarily concerned in this chapter and the two following chapters on Herbaceous Plants and Bulbs and Water Plants, complement the design. They form linking areas of focal elements, and create diversity and kinetic impact (*see* 4.43).

Landscape architecture is an art form in which planting design plays a major role. The great challenge is to make effective use of such ephemeral material within a disciplined design framework. The supreme quality in most art forms is self-restraint and purity of design intent. It is well to bear in mind at the outset Mies van der Rohe's comment 'less is more' and guard against a natural inclination towards artistic self-indulgence.

The good designer will be the first to acknowledge and seek to use to effect the individual design characteristics of the plant material with which he is working. The dogmas and rules associated with landscape design, however, are not so rigid that they must remain unbroken and a design may benefit from an ingenious or daring departure from conventional principles. The application of creative thought processes will help to provide inspiration.

4.4 DESIGN PRINCIPLES

The importance of creating a structured skeleton for the design cannot be overstressed. This provides a framework for the planting composition and space definition, by means of open and closed hierarchical landscape cells.

When composing a design one is essentially juxtaposing one or several volumes against each other, creating positive and negative volumes, or solid and void spatial compartments or cells.

The architect Sir Edwin Lutyens was a great exponent of the compartmentalization of external spaces relative to his buildings. He created cells of yew hedges which in essence are outdoor rooms forming a continuation of the building into the landscape, thus skilfully containing the excesses of Gertrude Jekyll's colourful herbaceous borders (*see* 4.7).

If one analyses the landscape of the British Isles it will be found that it consists of a structured network of cells, based on boundaries of field ownership, roads, railways, rivers, canals, geological formations, etc. Therefore in landscape design terms one is working with a hierarchy of cells: the cell enclosure can consist of shelterbelts, hedgerows, edges of woodland and so on. Buildings sited within these cells form nuclei within more refined cells, and more obvious segmentation is formed by the cell

PLATE 4.5
Tension and bridging point and line movement. There is an element of expectation as a result of the obstructed through view. Audley End, near Cambridge. *(Preben Jakobsen)*

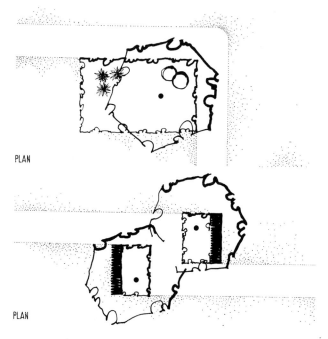

PLAN

PLAN

FIGURE 4.1 **Pivot point, illustrating physical and visual change of direction.**

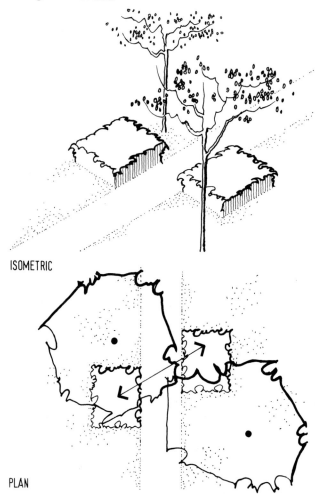

ISOMETRIC

PLAN

FIGURE 4.2 **Bridging point. The balanced tension is created simultaneously at different levels forming a harmonious whole.**

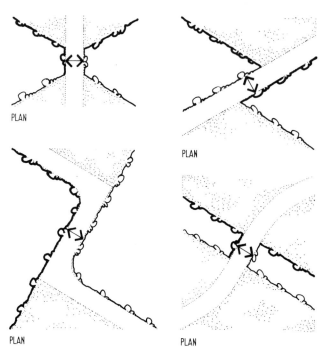

PLAN

PLAN

PLAN

PLAN

FIGURE 4.3 **Tension points. The figure shows the simplest solution; an offset view, a deflected view and a tension point created by opposing areas of planting. The principle also applies to roads.**

enclosing elements—hedges, borders and other delineating distinctive plant material which is more carefully maintained.

Apart from the visual containment of plants, the formation of cells can be seen as a self-perpetuating need for improved microclimatic conditions.

It follows that space and volume are closely related. This concept, sometimes termed *volumetrics*, can be applied both in the early stages of the design, to create the framework and spatial relations, and at later stages when plant material is being selected. All plant material can be seen as positive volumes, as can architectural elements such as buildings or walls. Spaces can be described as negative volumes, although if one tries to imagine a cube of air, it becomes positive as soon as the space is enclosed or surrounded by plant material. Certain plant material, depending on the density of foliage and branch system, can be a combination of both positive and negative volume—that is, solid organic matter and air.

4.41 Design dynamics

Architectural theories concerning the relationship between the moving observer and his immediate environment have equal application to landscape design. Plant material can be effectively used to create a kinetic relationship between the pedestrian observer and the landscape, unfolding views and enclosing spaces along

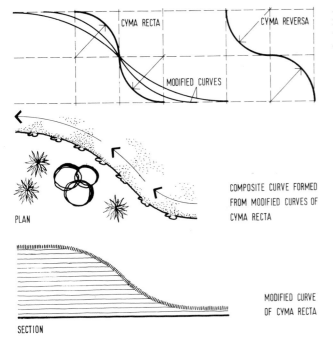

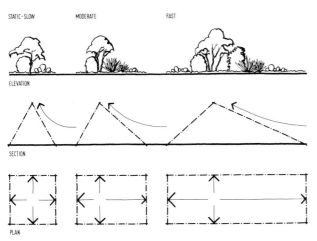

COMPOSITE CURVE FORMED FROM MODIFIED CURVES OF CYMA RECTA

MODIFIED CURVE OF CYMA RECTA

SECTION

FIGURE 4.4 **The ogee is a double continuous curve (cyma recta and cyma reversa), concave below, passing into convex above. It can be used in plan or sectional form.**

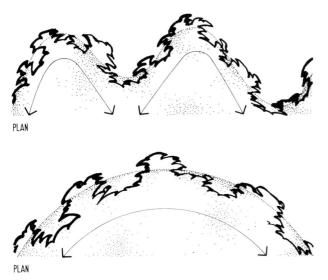

FIGURE 4.5 **Design speeds. In terms of volumes, the more extended the shape of the triangle and the square, the faster the design speed. The principle still applies to circular or informally shaped beds.**

paths in a carefully designed sequence, or applied on a larger scale to the movement of people in cars, such as the design of motorway planting for viewing at high speeds.

Unlike architecture, landscape design is concerned with living material which not only grows and changes during the seasons and over time, but moves in response to wind or to the touch. Thus the kinetic experience is enriched and made more intimate and varied.

The movement of the observer can be influenced by the positioning of groups of planting relative to the path. Where a change of direction is desired, groundcovers as well as trees and accent shrubs can be used to create pivot points at which one is physically and visually forced to change direction. Pivot points can be extended to form bridging points across paths and roads (*see* Figures 4.1 and 4.2). If the bridging points are sited close together, these in turn create tension points in the design where the space is narrowed down or constricted before opening up and expanding into another space (*see* Figure 4.3).

When composing and making design statements with groundcovers and shrubs, certain rules governing artistic line movements may be considered. Classic lines of beauty still hold true. They are largely based on the historical orders of Greek and Roman architecture and most are applicable to planting design. Examples of ogee curves, more correctly known as cyma recta and cyma reversa, shown in Figure 4.4 indicate how they are most commonly used in landscape architecture.

Using the idea of line movement, the design can be given a momentum of its own which can be described as a 'design speed'. This can be static, slow, moderate or fast. The inherent design force built into any line movement is self-expressive, as is shown in Figure 4.5.

Certain misconceptions exist relating to design line movement. All too often designers seek to create line movement by giving a wavy outline to planting beds. Tree and shrub planting will itself create all the wavy line movement at a higher level as it grows.

Plant material junctions should not be too acute. Where the design line movement abuts a building, or two converging paved areas meet grass areas, the acute point formed results in an awkward space for planting, and should be avoided where possible.

A landscape designer's flair may be judged in part by his attention to detail—in particular how he separates, defines and juxtaposes the different hard and soft landscape materials. Certain designs require sharp edge delineation and definition, which will either mean high maintenance or raising the paved plane considerably above the planting area. Some rampant groundcovers such as *Rubus tricolor* will produce a serrated edge. Ascending ones such as *Lonicera pileata* and *Prunus laurocerasus* 'Otto Luyken' or neat but prolific *Stephanandra incisa* 'Crispa' will cover the edge of paved spaces, producing an irregular but constant delineation.

Care should be taken when showing edge definition on plan. A neat drawing with straight lines to indicate

FIGURE 4.6 **The planting beds are given bold, free flowing continuous curves, respecting free growth of plant material.**

PLATE 4.6

The edge definition is subtle because of the use of small setts which allows the groundcover *Cotula squalida* to penetrate into the gaps. Also illustrated is *Festuca ursinum* a hummock forming grass which is useful on its own for large areas. Glostrup Hospital, Denmark. *(Preben Jakobsen)*

PLATE 4.7

A charming composition illustrating the principle of enframement using large shrubs and the gateway to draw the observer towards the summerhouse. In the foreground meadow grasses; note the use of grass for the path. Lutyens House. *(Preben Jakobsen)*

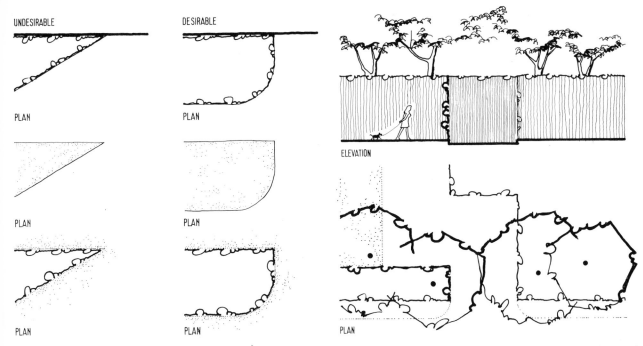

FIGURE 4.7 **Avoidance of acute plant material junctions. The diagram shows a paving to wall situation, paving to paving or grass to grass.**

FIGURE 4.8 **Concealed access; the bridging point at the site entrance completely obscures the view into the site.**

overhanging paved edges may be wrongly interpreted.

Lawn mowing strips and groundcover separation are clearly defined directional line movements. Their inclusion is often deemed desirable when easier and more economical maintenance is envisaged, but should be avoided if possible because of the unpleasant effects of parallelism. In tropical climates, however, they may be necessary to prevent two different species from becoming too entangled. Rough cut grass affords a more romantic edge definition with an appropriately slow design speed, when allowed to define its co-existence with groundcover and shrubs of its own accord.

4.42 Access, vistas and enframement

The point of entry into any given space is always of crucial importance in the design. For instance, one may choose to make it discreet or emphasize it by enframement. A drive or access road into a site may have predominantly vista-like qualities which can be reinforced with banks of tall and medium shrub and groundcover planting flanking each side. The long accepted tradition that when one entered a site, part of the building was first seen and then lost from view, to re-emerge later, still remains an effective design technique. Surprise and expectation have been important design concepts in landscape since the days of such well-known exponents as Brown, Repton, Puckler, Andrée, Kemp, Miller and Mawson.

The principle of enframement can be used effectively to draw attention to specifically desirable views and possibly

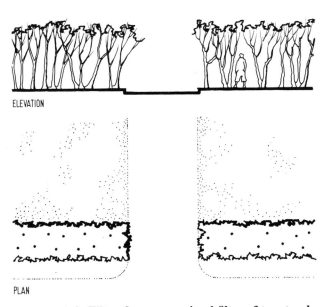

FIGURE 4.9 **Filtered access; a visual filter of tree trunks allows a partial view.**

to block out the less desirable elements. For instance, massed foreground planting may be used to screen the near view, larger framing plants placing the emphasis on the distant view.

Enframement of certain views in connection with doorways or atrium courtyards can best be achieved by the use of large vertical shrubs or small trees with a horizontal

45

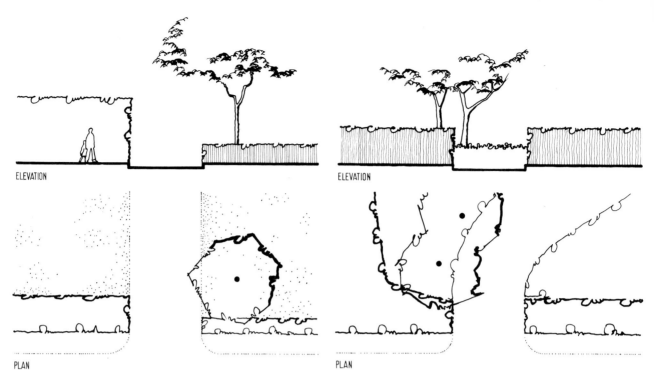

FIGURE 4.10 **Semi-closed access provides a screen at one side and partial vision at the other.**

FIGURE 4.11 **Deflected access: the planting exerts a directional influence.**

ELEVATION

PLAN

ELEVATION

PLAN

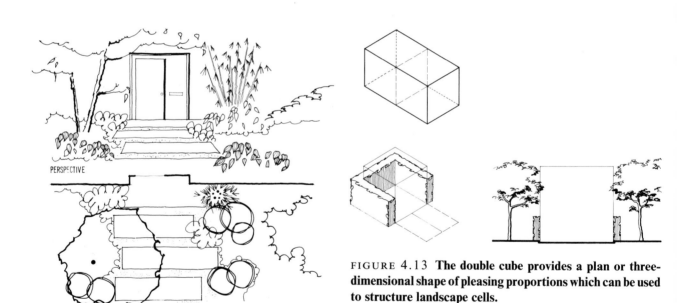

PERSPECTIVE

PLAN

FIGURE 4.12 **Enframement of an entrance using plants of different heights.**

FIGURE 4.13 **The double cube provides a plan or three-dimensional shape of pleasing proportions which can be used to structure landscape cells.**

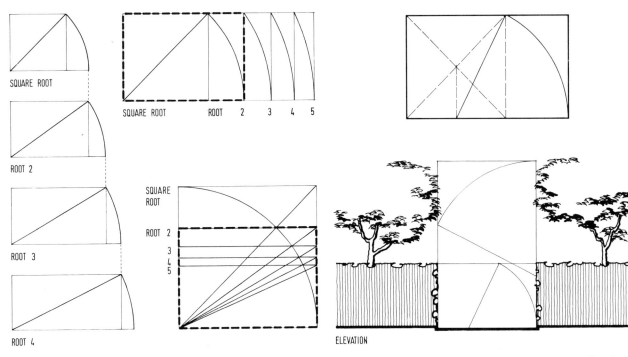

FIGURE 4.14 **The sequential formation from the square root.**

FIGURE 4.15 **The golden section and its application in landscape architecture.**

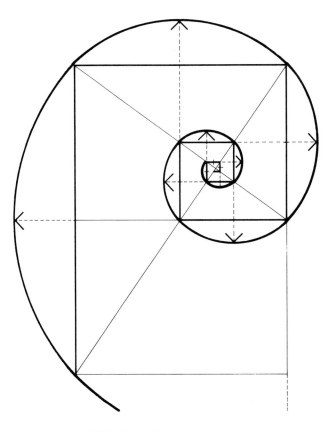

FIGURE 4.16 **The logarithmic spiral.**

branch structure such as *Cornus controversa, Cercis canadensis*, etc. Anchoring as a design technique is akin to enframement in so far as it has a similar design purpose, that is, to control corners and portions of the design which need reinforcement. The planting of dome-shaped shrubs at the base of a small sculptural tree or shrub is another form of anchoring.

4.43 Scale, proportion and balance

Once more a comparison with architectural design is useful. In interior spaces the proportion of room height to area is important, and the architect works with geometric principles such as double cubes, root cubes, the golden section, and the logarithmic spiral. This has application in landscape architecture in the creation of spaces, many of which are literally outdoor rooms or cells. For example, in a courtyard the proportion of floor space should be relative to wall height.

Scale and proportion together constitute perhaps the most abused and misunderstood aspects of planting design. The failure to assess the proportion of one groundcover such as grass against other groundcovers and shrubs often results in unbalanced planting. Sometimes the landscape architect has little choice in the matter; for example, on housing estates where the roadway and footpath layouts are often determined

47

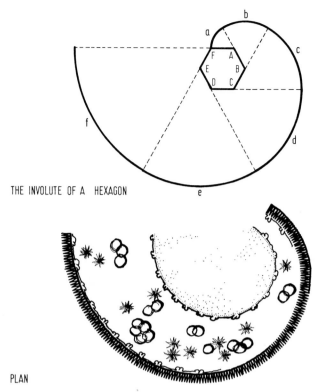

THE INVOLUTE OF A HEXAGON

PLAN

FIGURE 4.17 **Involute of a hexagon demonstrating use of logarithmic spiral.**

without prior consultation, it may be difficult to harmonize the planting of the disproportionate left-over spaces.

Equal proportions may be acceptable in a formal design, but in informal schemes the normal rule of thumb proportion of shrubs and groundcover to grass would be between 1:5 and 1:7. For reasons of economy, the designer may be forced to accept a larger area of grass to groundcover and shrubs than desired. Where there is some doubt, as when road and footpath layouts create left-over cells, then these should be fully planted to give visual cohesion and facilitate maintenance. Initial design concepts can sometimes be maintained in these cases by compromising on planting distances and cheaper plant material. There are limits, however, to how far one can go without prejudicing the scheme.

4.44 Juxtapositioning

Juxtapositioning is the essence of all planting design. The principles already described relating to bridging and tension points, pivot points and enframement are in effect a large scale form of juxtaposition. Where two or more kinds of the same planting material are used repetitively across a footpath or road or diagonally across a viewpoint etc, a sequential rhythm is set up, but the designer should beware of overstating and overbalancing volume relationships.

ELEVATION

PLAN

FIGURE 4.18 **Accents and emphasis 1:2:3 relationship.**

ELEVATION

PLAN

FIGURE 4.19 **Accents and emphasis 1:2:3 relationship.**

48

FIGURE 4.20 **Accents and emphasis. A single dominant, two co-dominants and five subservient shapes on the horizontal plane.**

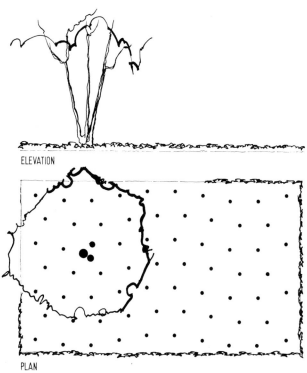

FIGURE 4.21 **Accents and emphasis. A single multi-stemmed tree or shrub with low level groundcover. Note proportional stagger of setting out.**

The dynarhythmic force described in 4.43 is created by the art of juxtapositioning. Basic plant compositions of different design speeds may be based on Euclidian geometric shapes—the circle, square, and triangle (used by the Bauhaus which so impressed many designers). A dynamic design speed can be built up in three dimensions by increasing the number of accent plants and the way they are sited (*see* Figure 4.5).

Different accents and emphasis can be created by the ways in which shrubs and trees are placed in relation to each other and the ground plane. Some examples are shown in Figures 4.18–4.21. In each case the base plane is the groundcover. Figure 4.18 shows a simple 1:2 relationship; Figure 4.19 indicates the well-known 1:2:3 relationship, where the tree is the dominant and the lower shrubs are co-dominants. The remaining two figures show variations on this theme. A basic triad plant composition could consist of a sculptural, multi-stemmed *Aralia elata*, a dome shape or hummock of *Hebe rakaiensis* and a spiky linear form such as *Phormium tenax*.

Accent planting may consist largely of distinct bold planting, which may be linear and spiky in form yet with an hemispherical outline, such as *Cortaderia argentea*, *Yucca gloriosa* and *Phormium tenax*. The most dominant accent may be a large sculptural foliage shrub such as *Fatsia japonica* which together with the spiky accents acts as a pivotal point.

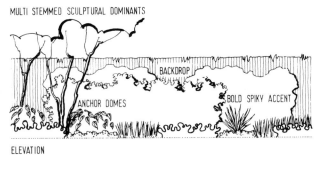

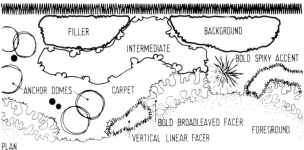

FIGURE 4.22 **General illustration of basic planting terminology.**

49

PLATE 4.8
Plant shapes showing an harmonious 1:2:3 relationship—low horizontal foreground plants, dome shaped *Senecio greyi* **and spikey** *Phormium tenax. (Preben Jakobsen)*

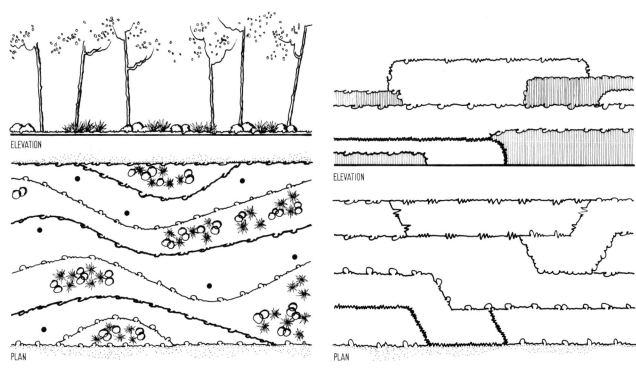

FIGURE 4.23 **Drift planting.**

FIGURE 4.24 **Interlocking and overlapping planting.**

When working with long, linear groundcover and shrub borders, the use of distinct 'facers' and foreground plant material is necessary. This may be linear vertical such as *Libertia* spp, *Iris* spp or linear foliage of bold outline such as *Hosta* spp and *Viburnum davidii*. (The latter is useful as both an individual dome shape, or used *en masse*.) The 'facer' may have rotund foliage such as *Senecio greyi*, or crisp, ferny leaves such as *Stephanandra incisa* 'Crispa'.

'Fillers' is the term used to describe background plant material which plays a subservient role, in a position where it is obscured to a large extent, and where bold and distinctive planting material of quality (often expensive) would be wasted. Invariably the designer will select cheap easily propagated plant material for this situation, for example *Spiraea* spp.

Drift planting. This is a type of planting where a distinct linear flow is aimed at, contrasting linear carpets of groundcover with each other. Drift planting can be used with or without accent planting and emphasis and may be of varied height (*see* Figure 4.23). Interlocking and overlapping planting is similar in many respects to drift planting, usually the material is of higher stature and there is a greater change of textures (*see* Figure 4.24).

4.45 Functional use

The functional requirements of landscape design can be met by relating the planting and arrangement of spaces back to the average size of the user and the objects brought into any given space. From Leonardo da Vinci and the Renaissance to Corbusier and the twentieth century, this has been of major importance in making analytical assessments in design terms. The designer is thus able to influence the movements of the user. The following list indicates the ways in which plants can be used for different functions:

i)   channelling and directing traffic;
ii)   protection against vandalism;
iii) emphasizing desire lines;

PLATE 4.9

Use of hedges to segregate pedestrians and traffic. The view is foreshortened and the large area of tarmacadam is camouflaged. Templemere, Span Estate, London. *(Preben Jakobsen)*

51

iv) prevention of short cuts;

v) specific spatial requirements—especially enclosure;

vi) curtailment of access and vision;

vii) positive camouflage—used to improve the design;

viii) negative camouflage—less acceptable when used to cover up errors which come to light when buildings are constructed etc.;

ix) deliberate emphasis or distortion of space;

x) containment, compartmentalization and creation of landscape cells with a large structural framework, be it organic or not. For example, in plan diagrammatic form a cellular network of footpaths will create islands which need not necessarily be enclosed by shrubs and other forms of planting, groundcover being ideal.

When shrubs and groundcover are related to the heights of the human figure, the design possibilities for different plant heights become clearer (*see* Figure 4.27).

i) *Ground level.* Groundcover is primarily used to create a ground plane or carpet which links and defines spaces without impeding views, and as a base or platform on which to display accent planting. It may also be used to prevent access. In some cases groundcovers can be effectively used as climbers as well, being continued from the horizontal to the vertical plane and thus masking the meeting point between a building or wall and the ground (*see* Figure 4.39).

ii) *Knee height.* Medium to large scale groundcovers are generally used where a taller and more positive definition of space is required. They can be used as part of a gradual build up of planting from lower to higher levels.

iii) *Waist height.* Plants of this height can be used more directionally for distinction and edge definition. The height begins to impede the view, depending on the distribution and the observation point. This group can be used to prevent short cuts being taken and may provide a protective barrier against vandals. They can be used as part of a gradual build up, as described in (i).

iv) *Eye level.* Medium to large shrubs are used largely to give direction, provide enclosure and privacy and to obstruct or frame a view. Thorny material can be a useful access barrier or boundary definition and a deterrent to vandals.

v) *Above eye level.* Large shrubs and small trees are chiefly used to create landscape cells, to give direction and provide screens for shelter and privacy. Really tall plants and trees can be used for emphasis, enframement and special effects, such as reflections in water.

4.46 Planting centres and setting out

This subject is always controversial. German speaking landscape architects refer to plant material as the *lebende Baustoffe*, literally 'living (organic) building material'. This is an appropriate analogy as the designer needs to be just as aware of the behavioural patterns and perfor-

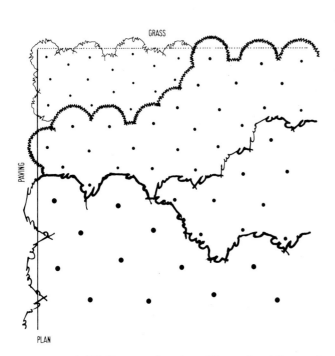

FIGURE 4.25 **Progressive transition of setting out. Spacing between different plant groups equals 1·5 × planting centres of the smaller species.**

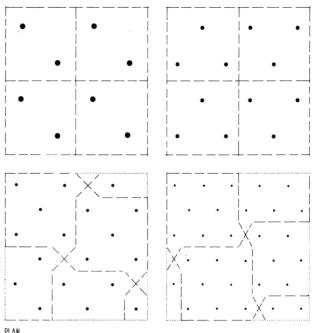

FIGURE 4.26 **Allocation of specific number of plants per square metre.**

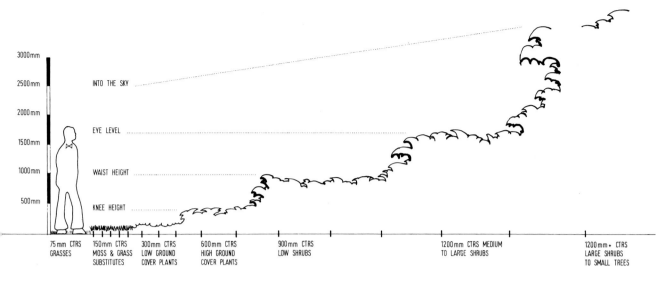

FIGURE 4.27 **Shrubs and groundcover related to the human figure.**

mance of organic material as of inert material, particularly spread and growth rate. These become extremely important when selecting suitable planting centres. The spread of the plant material needs to be considered, and whether it will 'knit' sufficiently to conceal all patches of bare earth between the plants.

Most landscape architects develop their own system of spacing and setting out. Richard Sudell maintained that a good rule of thumb is to plant at the same distance as ultimate height. Thus if the mature height is 1 m, the planting centres should be 1 m apart; this is presumably on the basis that most shrubs and groundcovers are slightly wider than tall.

Another concept which has been developed over the years is that when forming planting associations where the span coverage of two shrubs and groundcovers differ, say a 2 m and 1 m diameter, then the following equation should be applied:

$$\frac{2\,m + 1\,m}{2} = 1\cdot5\,m \text{ planting centres}$$

When dealing with herbaceous and mat-forming groundcovers, the method of allocating a specific number of plants per m² is useful, but demands a good knowledge of plant material. This method would involve categorizing plants in broad groups, such as weak, moderate and fast growers. The weaker the plant's growth rate and mature state, the higher number per m², and conversely the bulkier, coarser and faster growing the plants, the less number per m².

Fortunately most groundcovers and shrubs can be classified into groups as far as planting centres are concerned. For general working purposes the doubling of centres for setting out seems practical. Figure 4.27 shows the planting centres generally used and gives the height of each group relative to the human figure. Note that the proportional distance increases between plant groups, relative to size. Examples are given below:

i) 150 mm planting centres
    Within this group falls *Cotula squalida*, and species of *Festuca* and *Sagina*.
ii) 300 mm planting centres
    The basic distance for mat-forming groundcovers such as *Vinca minor, Hypericum calycinum, Euonymus gracilis, Erica vagans, Hebe propinquum, Pachysandra terminalis*, etc.
iii) 600 mm planting centres
    Examples include *Vinca major, Viburnum davidii, Stephanandra incisa* 'Crispa', *Lonicera pileata* and *Symphoricarpos x chenaultii* 'Hancock'.
iv) 900 mm planting centres
    Examples include species of *Cotoneaster, Berberis, Spiraea, Cornus* and *Viburnum*.
v) 1 200 mm planting centres
    This group includes taller species of those in (iv) and species of *Pyracantha, Ligustrum, Syringa, Buddleia*.

The above method of spacing will give a close-knit appearance in about three to five years. By compromising on wider spacing, an equally good groundcover will be obtained over a longer period.

It is difficult, however, to generalize about plant material, because growth patterns are so varied. *Cotoneaster* 'Herbst Feur', for example, will spread at least 2 m from the planting centre, rooting as it grows, and is self-layering while certain types of leggy and spindly shrubs with a vertical emphasis, such as *Rubus cockburnianus, Hippophae rhamnoides, Philadelphus* and *Rosa* spp require a secondary mat-forming groundcover underneath to be effective. These are not suitable where

53

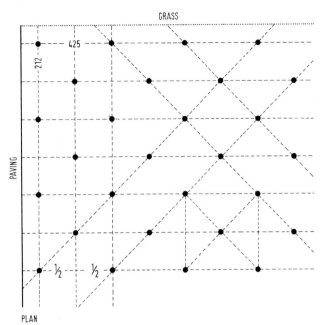

GRASS

PAVING

PLAN

FIGURE 4.28 **Setting out: quincunx (an arrangement of five objects in a square, one at each corner and one in the middle).**

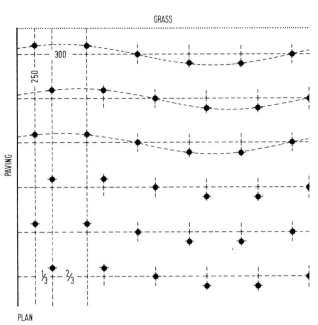

GRASS

PAVING

PLAN

FIGURE 4.29 **Setting out at average 300 mm centres: asymmetrical stagger.**

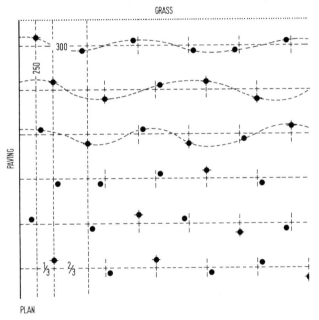

GRASS

PAVING

PLAN

FIGURE 4.30 **Setting out: asymmetrical stagger.**

economies are desirable as one has to pay twice to cover the same area of ground.

A very common practice consists of laying out the plants in straight rows, or on a grid known as the quincunx, as in an orchard or using forestry planting techniques. A common layout is shown in Figure 4.28; this is not to be recommended except where a formal layout is intended. Much more subtle effects can be created with a little time and effort, which are closer to the patterns and structures found in nature. Using equidistant lines on paper (strings along the ground) as a base, the distance of the plant from the lines can be varied according to a predetermined pattern. The simplest method is shown in Figure 4.29 where the planting along the first row ranges between 0–50 mm on each side of the base line, and that along the second follows the same layout with planting commencing a third of the way between the first two plants on the first row. Figure 4.30 shows more complex variations of which there are an infinite number.

Planting centres chosen for climbers along walls and fences will depend on the design effect required from the inert materials, such as brick or timber. If planting against a given length of fence or wall, for example, or the end elevation of a building, one-third planting to two-thirds wall from corner or end creates a harmonious asymmetric composition. The golden rule when planting climbers is to plant in twos (one extra as an insurance policy), no closer than 1·2 m.

Harmonious sequential rhythms are necessary in order to achieve a natural look when selecting planting centres for accent groups of plant material used with or without mat-forming groundcover. In Japanese garden design the ratio of 2:3:5:7 is always discernible. Even numbers tend to appear regimented. Another useful concept to apply when grouping plant material and selecting planting positions is to stipulate that no three plants, shrubs or trees should be planted in a line. This is particularly applicable to trees where it shows most with tree trunks, but also applies to any distinct plant material which is compact or vertical.

A 'natural' asymmetric effect can be obtained particularly when planting bulbs in grass by simply scattering them by hand, and planting them where they fall. A handful of pebbles could be substituted to locate groups of other plants.

4.5 DETAILED DESIGN CONSIDERATIONS AND PLANT SELECTION

In this section more detailed consideration is given to aspects of design, and the ways in which these will affect plant selection.

To ensure that the planting design will work and that a good effect can be achieved, plants must be chosen which suit the site conditions—the soil characteristics, light, degree of shelter or exposure, and so forth.

Having analysed the site conditions and determined the design skeleton, the designer will be in a position to select the plants which will meet his needs.

Understanding of the natural biodynamic processes and ecological inter-relationships between different plants and plant communities will provide valuable information and inspiration for the landscape architect (*see* Chapter 7). It is useful, perhaps, to recall the Shakespearian quotation used by William Robinson to preface every issue of his renowned magazine *The Garden*: 'This is an art which does not mend nature: change it rather: but the art itself is nature.'

The designer may wish to impart symbolic or stylistic expressionism in the choice of material. On occasions he may arbitrarily choose plant material from another country or continent to meet his requirements, providing that the ecological acceptability of plant species selected relative to the location is ascertained. Without wishing to add to the existing controversy between some designers and co-professionals in allied fields of botany, ecology, forestry, and so forth, it is perhaps worth pointing out that much alien plant material is visually indistinguishable from indigenous plant material, while many native plants look distinctly exotic and foreign. This is shown in Frederick Law Olmsted's experiment with apparent 'exotics', in actual fact hardy native plants with striking foliage, in Central Park, New York.

It is well known that the bulk of shrubs and groundcovers in general use in North America and Northern Europe originated from South East Asia. While one country's weeds may be used as another country's groundcover, there is a danger in introducing alien species. Some have become so adept in naturalizing themselves, like Japanese Knotweed, *Polygonum cuspidatum*, that they have become pernicious weeds which have proved almost impossible to eradicate and have spread uncontrollably in parts of the British Isles.

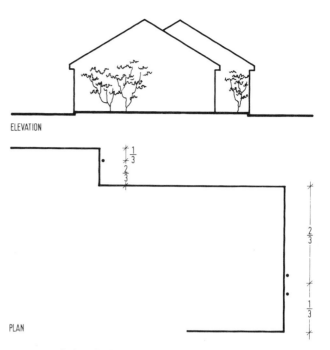

ELEVATION

PLAN

FIGURE 4.31 **Siting climbers.**

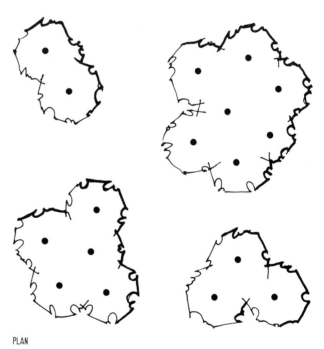

PLAN

FIGURE 4.32 **Plant grouping 2:3:5:7 for harmonious sequential rhythm.**

4.51 Size, life span and growth rate

When designing with shrubs and groundcover an effect of maturity and permanence can be achieved in a relatively short time; the minimum is one year but more often will be three to five years. It is worth stressing that in planting

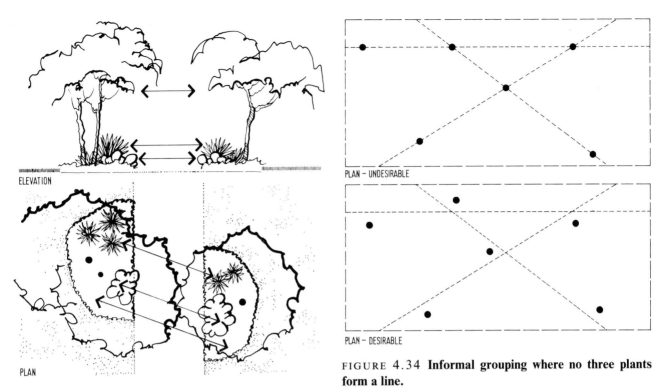

ELEVATION

PLAN

FIGURE 4.33 **Balanced bridging point using 2:3:5:7 ratio.**

PLAN – UNDESIRABLE

PLAN – DESIRABLE

FIGURE 4.34 **Informal grouping where no three plants form a line.**

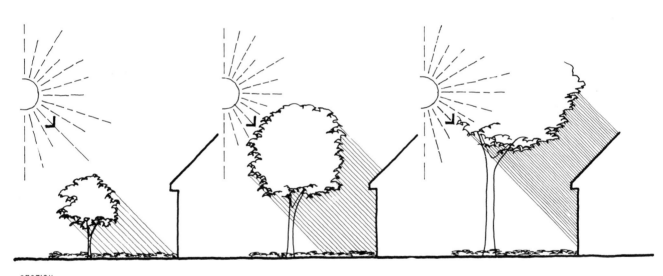

SECTION

FIGURE 4.35 **Growth rate of tree on groundcover affecting light penetration.**

design forward planning on the basis of what the design will look like in five, ten and twenty-five or more years is desirable.

The growth rate of groundcover and shrubs should never be considered out of context to the growth rate of trees. In the formative years the growth rates are out of step; groundcover planting under a young tree has plenty of light, but as the tree grows this will gradually change to deep shade. In maturity, light may once more penetrate beneath the tree, as shown in Figure 4.35. It is important therefore to choose plants which will grow in the changing conditions, unless replanting with different species is anticipated. Suitably tolerant groundcovers are *Vinca minor, Hypericum calycinum* and *Epimedium*.

Inexperienced designers often rely on nurserymen's descriptions relative to height and this can cause some nasty surprises. Take for example a shrub like *Cotoneaster serotinus*, often described by nurserymen as 2×2 m

56

high. At Highdown, Goring-by-sea it is approximately 13 × 13 m, enough to cover an average housing unit of today, including its patio garden. Another example is the now widely planted groundcover *Prunus laurocerasus* 'Zabeliana' of which there is a specimen at Nymans in Sussex, approximately 3 × 3 m and still remaining horizontal. It is as well to have access to several authoritative sources of written information in order to have as many comparisons as possible, but there is no real substitute for practical experience.

Planting for immediate effect can be acceptable when working on major exhibition projects or landscape areas to be laid out for temporary use, or where the required plant material cannot readily be obtained. Some of the best rapid growing groundcovers and shrubs are listed below:

Euonymus fortunei 'Emerald Gaiety'
Hypericum calycinum
Rosa virginiana 'Harvest Fire'
Rubus tricolor
Stephanandra incisa 'Crispa'
Symphoricarpos × chenaultii 'Hancock'

In Scandinavia, fast growing and often short-lived shrubby, multi-stemmed willows or other plants are used on major landscape projects as temporary 'fillers', sometimes along the outer row of a shelter belt, until the slow-growing plant material becomes established.

4.52 Characteristics and habit

The shape and growth characteristics of plants under the ground is as important as that above ground. The underground spread of plant roots, for instance, may be very considerable.

An understanding of the shape or form in which the plants grow and spread will help the designer not only in selection, but in layout. When choosing a groundcover, for instance, the plant's ability to colonize and spread over an area relative to its centre of planting will be important.

The compatibility of the plant material to be used should be ascertained. Certain plants need to cohabit and become entangled with each other in order to flourish satisfactorily, whereas other plants have a detrimental effect on each other, to the extent that the other species is severely weakened and in some cases completely destroyed. The foliage of *Artemisia*, for example, contains absinthium which, when deposited on the ground near adjoining plants, will severely weaken certain species, such as *Hypericum*, when it rains.

In temperate climates the marked differences between the seasons will influence the selection of plants to a considerable degree. The ideal plant will provide interest throughout the year—flowers in spring; foliage in summer; colour and berries in autumn; and branches, bark and evergreen foliage in winter. Flowers are the least

TABLE 4.1
Examples of different structure and branch forms

1. Vertical linear	*Cytisus*
	Ephedra
	Phormium
	Salix purpurea 'Nana'
2. Horizontal tabulate	*Cornus controversa* and other variegated spp
	Emmenopterys henryi
	Enkianthus campanulatus
	Trochodendron aralioides
	Viburnum plicatum 'Mariesii'
3. Ascending horizontal	*Lonicera pileata*
	Prunus laurocerasus 'Otto Luyken'
4. Bizarre and sculptural	*Acanthopanax sieboldianus*
	Aralia elata
	Colletia cruciata
	Corylus avellana 'Contorta'
	Euonymus alatus
	Fatsia japonica
	Poncirus trifoliata
	Rosa omeiensis pteracantha
5. Hummock, dome shaped	*Hebe anomala*
	H. rakaiensis
	Picea abies 'Nidiformis'
	Rhododendron williamsianum
	Salix lanata
	Stephanandra incisa 'Crispa'
	Viburnum davidii
6. Pendulous	*Buddleia alternifolia*
	Genista aetnensis

important in design terms—plant form and foliage having a greater impact for a longer period.

In tropical climates the seasons are less clearly distinguished, and flowering seasons may be much longer, thus the selection of plants for seasonal variation and characteristics may not be so important.

Many groundcovers are exceptionally hardy, and will withstand average wear and tear, once established. Greater advantage should be taken of this fact, allowing planting design compositions to be made more serviceable. The amount of wear that a groundcover exposed to walking can stand varies enormously, depending on the species. The Arnold Arboretum in America has for several years been conducting trial plots of both cultivated and specie groundcovers, including lawn substitutes, which will withstand close cutting and

57

trampling without harm. A serious attempt to institute similar trial plots should be instigated by some of the horticultural establishments in this country.

Most shrubs and groundcovers, like trees, possess a distinctive form and branch structure, some examples of which are given in Table 4.1. The way in which this is perceived will vary according to the season, and the distance from which the plant is viewed. The clearest effect will be that of deciduous material in winter. Shrub forms may be part hazy and part solid where there is a mixture of evergreen and deciduous material, becoming more distinct during the spring and summer. An example will serve to show the variety in structure and outline in a single species. A large group of ghost brambles during the summer can be likened to a nimbus cloud formation. In winter their elegant, multi-stemmed arching, bluish-white branches will have a lighter but none the less distinct volume, despite the loss of foliage, allowing a *clair voyée* through to the groundcover beneath and beyond. From middle distance the ferny texture of the foliage billowing in the wind will be very apparent; close up it has a strong impact, with its heavily indented foliage elegantly drooping down in cascading plumes.

The time of day and light conditions will also affect the way in which a plant appears to the observer. At twilight, the outline becomes black and more rounded, depending on viewing distance. *Contrajour* effects (against the light) may be particularly noticeable in stormy weather, or where light coloured foliage is displayed against dark hedges, trees or a building.

Bold and architectural plants have in recent years had an unparalleled vogue, for obvious reasons; they are distinct and lend themselves to use for accent and emphasis. William Robinson was perhaps the first great exponent of foliage planting design. Although he abhorred architectural design and carpet bedding, he was one of the first to select bold, statuesque architectural plants and to introduce them into the countryside and woodland to afford naturalization.

All plant material can be graded according to texture of foliage, branches and bark. Leaves may be rotund, cordate, oval, oblong, or acuminate and so forth in shape with smooth, glossy or hairy surfaces; branches and bark may be rough or smooth, thin or thick, etc.

The range of opposing textures should be sufficiently distinct to obtain the desired contrast, which may be reinforced by the overall shape of the plant and its colour.

Colour is of great importance to the planting scheme, but should form part of a carefully considered design in which the form, structure, texture and density all play their part. Shrubs and groundcover dissimilar in shape may not be so in colour, and this may result in a blurring of the design if not considered. Similarly plants having dominant characteristics may be far from dominant in colour.

Colour in plant material is not an inert pigment. It is a culmination of the light-reflective and light-absorptive qualities of the foliage, the former being seen to particular effect in shiny foliaged evergreens such as *Prunus laurocerasus*, or *Ilex* spp where the foliage may appear silvery and metallic. Another good example is *Nothofagus cliffortioides* which, when sited in the sun against a dark background or shaded area, looks like floating, horizontally stratified, sparkling silver coins.

When using colour in a design, spottiness should be avoided by providing sufficiently large units of colour. Gertrude Jekyll affirmed that colour in the garden should not consist of mere dabs set out on a palette. To use plants correctly they should form 'beautiful pictures'.

The most common colours of indigenous plant material in the country concerned will form a guide to the range which may be suitable. In Britain, for example, a large percentage of the native flora is predominantly white or near white, followed by yellow and blue. In tropical climates the range of colours will be far greater and the strong sunlight will display vibrant colour to great effect.

Strong colours should be used with care: red, for example, although a complementary colour of green, can completely destroy a spatial composition by overpowering the greens. Neutral white or cream is a useful transition element from light to dark blue, or yellow to orange and red. Strong plant colours may have limited uses except in urban situations where bold colours are used to enliven the exterior of buildings. Similarly colourful groundcovers can be used to form large-scale abstract patterns, akin to Victorian carpet bedding adapted to the use of permanent groundcovers.

When using colour in planting design one is able to accentuate three-dimensional volumes by over- and under-stressing their visual impact, but a balance in the choice of warm and cool hues should be achieved. Leonardo da Vinci observed that 'colours seen in shadow will reveal more or less of their natural beauty in proportion as they are in fainter or deeper shadow'.

Colours exert a strong psychological effect upon the observer, affecting both mood and attitude to environment. Care should be exercised with the use of strong colours in confined areas and spaces. In courtyard planting design, for example, only a minimum of strong colour should be used for direction and emphasis. Harsh colours in confined spaces exert an overpowering, depressive influence. Colour can be used in the landscape in much the same way as an architect or interior designer might use it, to define spaces and give them a special character.

A thorough knowledge of the colours and textures of building materials and landscape artefacts such as fences, gates, seats, etc. plays an important role in the choice of colour when selecting suitable plant material. A blue-black semi-engineering brick suggests the use of silvery white and yellow, including light green and lemon green, whereas a dark red brick suggests deep, dark evergreens or blue, blue-grey and grey which are able to offer a

PLATE 4.10
Bold contrasting form and texture of *Iris pallida* **'Dalmatica' and** *Sedum spathulifolium* **'Atropurpurea'. The use of colour is subtle; both plants have a blue-grey bloom on the foliage.** *(Preben Jakobsen)*

PLATE 4.11
Contrasting texture of foliage and colour. Species include *Ballota, Hebe* **and** *Senecio maritima. (Preben Jakobsen)*

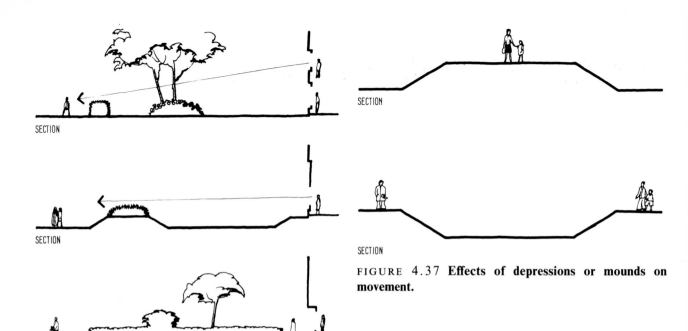

SECTION

SECTION

SECTION

SECTION

SECTION

FIGURE 4.36 **Defensible space. Psychological effect of landform, shrubs and groundcover discourages intruders in overlooked areas.**

FIGURE 4.37 **Effects of depressions or mounds on movement.**

FIGURE 4.38 **An artist's impression of a garden for blind people. Whitley Park, Ellesmere. The plants are aromatic and a handrail surrounds the planted areas.** (Landscape Architects: *Donaldson/Edwards Partnerships*)

sufficiently strong contrast. A fence stained dark blue or brown associates well with silver, white and yellow flowered and foliaged plants.

4.53 Special requirements

The sociological aspect of planting design is little understood, but there are definite effects upon the psychological well-being of individuals and the subsequent effect on their social behaviour. Some of the effects of colour have already been noted, and it has been shown that the landscape architect can influence the movements of an observer by the use of planting material. These facts can be used in a landscape design to discourage public access to semi-private areas overlooked from windows, as shown in Figures 4.36 and 4.37. People will normally tend to cross in a direct desire line between two points, but there is a distinct psychological objection to crossing dished or sunken grass areas. People will generally skirt the edge of a depression. The converse is true of a raised mound of grass, provided that the slopes are not too steep.

Planting can be specially selected for groups of people such as the blind or deaf. The blind appreciate rough and smooth textured bark, coarse and smooth foliage, aromatic shrubs and groundcovers, and the rustling of foliage in the wind, etc. The deaf, whose optical perception is sharpened, may particularly appreciate *contrajour* lighting which tends to highlight well sited multi-stemmed shrubs with distinct foliage.

4.6 GROUNDCOVERS

4.61 Grass, the universal groundcover

Throughout the world grass is the most commonly used groundcover, but perhaps nowhere more so than in Britain, where the climate is particularly well suited to turf culture. Its prime use is to cover the ground and provide a horizontal plane. The landscape architect in his role as landscaper, landshaper and land sculptor has in grass, when used in conjunction with contouring and earthworks, a tool well suited to the manipulation of spatial changes in level. The creation of grassed mounds and other features is also a useful way of disposing of surplus topsoil and subsoil.

The combined practical and ornamental values of a close-cropped sward of grass can be appreciated in a variety of ways, from the landscaping of historic ruins and monuments, to the grounds of stately homes, to the creation of modern grass amphitheatres. The list below is presented to indicate where grass cover has in the past been used to particular effect, in the hope that it will stimulate the imagination and perhaps suggest new ways of using grass effectively as groundcover.

Neolithic, religious	ornamental hill figures
Viking	fortresses and domestic hill settlements
Iron Age	fortresses and tumuli (e.g. Silbury Hill)
Roman villas	hill forts, dykes (e.g. Offa's Dyke)
Medieval castles	moats, dykes and seats
Renaissance	ideal towns in Italy, French engineers
Sixteenth century	Le Nôtre, *tapis vert*
Seventeeth and eighteenth century	Repton and Brown's great rolling landscapes
Puckler	pyramids of grass
Victorian and Edwardian	Jekyll, Lutyens; unmown grass, mown grasspaths, waterworks, bridge abutments.

PLATE 4.12 *Contrajour* **effect.** *Mahonia moserii* **Knaphill nurseries.** *(Preben Jakobsen)*

PLATE 4.13
Sculptural effects of large areas of grass. Grass steps of the restored jousting court, Dartington Hall. *(Preben Jakobsen)*

PLATE 4.14
Grass amphitheatre at Århus University, Denmark, designed by C. T. H. Sørenson. *(Preben Jakobsen)*

PLATE 4.15
Petasites fragrans **growing wild in Madron Churchyard near Penzance. Design despite neglect.** *(Preben Jakobsen)*

A modern movement in the use of grass and earth sculpture can be discerned from the end of the nineteenth century, gaining popularity in the twentieth. This includes grass amphitheatres in Scandinavia in the 1940s, the Aspen Memorial, Colorado in 1955, the Zurich Horticultural Exhibition in 1959, and the grass gardens of Burle Marx in the 1960s.

4.62 Mosses, lichens and ferns

Mosses and lichens are considered by some to be undesirable weeds. In Japanese gardens, however, moss has always been appreciated as a groundcover; some consist almost entirely of moss, with a few maples and bamboos juxtaposed against round boulders, formal or informal paving and buildings.

In Britain one of the most notable examples of the use of moss is in the Savill Garden at Windsor, under mature beech trees. Indeed, we may be about to see the revival of moss growing on a large scale. It has been fostered in the USA for some time. There are a number of Victorian gardening books on mosses, lichens and ferns which indicate the former popularity of these plants.

Whilst paving full of moss on a public path can be dangerous, in a less accessible space it can be used effectively in paving joints to create a feeling of age and mystery. Perhaps one of the most effective moss plantings of this type is at Dartington Hall, where moss on both the stone paving and walling is juxtaposed with large *Fatsia japonica*.

Good moss substitutes are *Sagina subulata*, *Arenaria* spp, *Saxifraga* spp, and *Cotula squalida*. In milder parts *Helxine solierolii* will rapidly spread to form close mats in semi-shaded areas, and in sunny sites *Bolax glebaria* can be used.

Lichen is not often considered as a groundcover but in a suitable climate, such as in Cornwall, where stony and rocky ground, roofs and walls often become invaded with lichen, the effectiveness of the plant as a cover can be seen.

Ferns are becoming more widely used amongst landscape architects. They have been used along the frontage of York University's Institute of Architectural Studies, and in courtyard design and exhibition areas.

Several ferns are low and ground-hugging, notably *Scolopendrium vulgare* and *Polypodium vulgare*. *Polystichum angulare* 'Proliferum' has a spreading habit and displays a neat rosette that when used *en masse* appears like a carpet of filigree snow crystals.

63

PLATE 4.16
South African Hottentot fig naturalized on rocky coast of Cornwall.

PLATE 4.17
Unusual effects of horizontal terraces, vertical grass and *Dipsacus sylvestris*, **in evening light. Herb garden at Odense Hospital.** *(Preben Jakobsen)*

4.63 Weeds as groundcover

The accepted definition of a weed is a plant in an unwanted place. To a landscape architect plants which are native to a locality or which adapt so well that they grow rapidly and with little maintenance can form useful and attractive groundcovers particularly where the need for economy is uppermost or where there is a concern to foster the use of native species and their associated wildlife (*see* Chapters 7 and 8). An example is shown in Plate 4.15 where *Petasites fragrans* grows naturally in a Cornish graveyard. It is a rampant groundcover which can sometimes be a nuisance, but if kept under control can in certain conditions be extremely effective and cheap.

Plate 4.16 shows how well the South African Hottentot fig *Carpobrotus edulis* has adapted to become a typical groundcover on the rocky coasts of Devon and Cornwall. Once more, it can become invasive and its spread should be controlled.

4.64 Climbers and ramblers

The early groundcover trials at the Arnold Arboretum in America did a great deal to indicate the possibilities of climbing and rambling plants as groundcovers.

They are useful in constricted urban situations to fuse the horizontal and vertical planes. *Hydrangea petiolaris* was used for this purpose in Arne Jacobsen's Harby School. Climbers and ramblers can also be used to good effect in permanent planting containers on overhanging parapets or balconies (*see* Chapter 9 and Figure 4.39).

On motorway banks in the USA various vines have been used extensively as an effective method of erosion control. The Road Research Laboratory in Britain has conducted tests to ascertain the shock absorption and impact resistance of shrubs, notably with a rambler *Rosa multiflora japonica*, with a view to using them as a buffer for central reserves.

4.65 Vegetables and herbs

A recent trend in Scandinavia has been to accept vegetables in their own right as part of landscape design. Perhaps the emphasis on economy and wholesome foods has helped this trend; no longer need it be considered socially and visually unacceptable to grow vegetables in the front garden. A well tended kitchen or herb garden is culturally and aesthetically as acceptable as ornamental groundcover and shrubs. Aromatic groundcovers include many culinary varieties and are of special value when designing for the blind.

4.66 Inert materials

The use of inert materials in conjunction with plant material stems from oriental landscape design, notably the stylized Japanese garden. Oriental designs featuring a

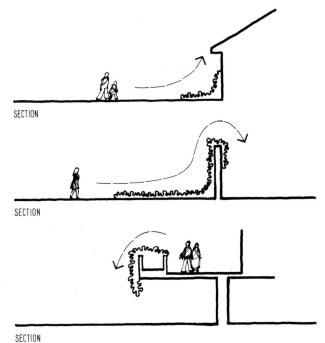

FIGURE 4.39 **Use of climbers and ramblers to fuse vertical and horizontal planes and on balconies.**

miniature river bed with carefully chosen and sited plant material, have been instrumental in the development of the typical American west coast garden. Although much larger in scale than those from which they derive inspiration, these gardens adhere to the basic stylistic principles of the oriental garden. During the last thirty years or so the idea of simulating beaches or dry river beds following the Californian example has won many ardent admirers in Europe, particularly amongst Swiss and German landscape architects.

The acceptable proportion of pebbles to planting can be critical, for example 1:1 is never very satisfactory; either plants or pebbles should appear to dominate. Russell Page in his *Education of a Gardener* declares that if he were given a white walled courtyard, a load of gravel as groundcover, and a golden elderberry bush, he could provide an effective landscape composition relying almost totally on the inert gravel.

Through close observation of nature one can arbitrarily create a particular landscape type within an enclosed and confined environment such as a courtyard. Sand, gravel, pebbles, cobbles and boulders are just as much groundcover as the plants themselves, their function being decorative and to act as a foil to the plant material.

The courtyard gardens of the Gulbenkian Museum in Lisbon by Professor Cabral are some of the more recent successful European examples of the use of inert materials and plants, relying mostly on tall grass species and pebbles.

65

PLATE 4.18
Space enclosure using clipped hedges. Villa Gamberaia, Florence. *(Preben Jakobsen)*

PLATE 4.19
Clipped hedge as a foil for varied groups of planting; note the contrast in texture and light and dark accents. Lutyens House. *(Preben Jakobsen)*

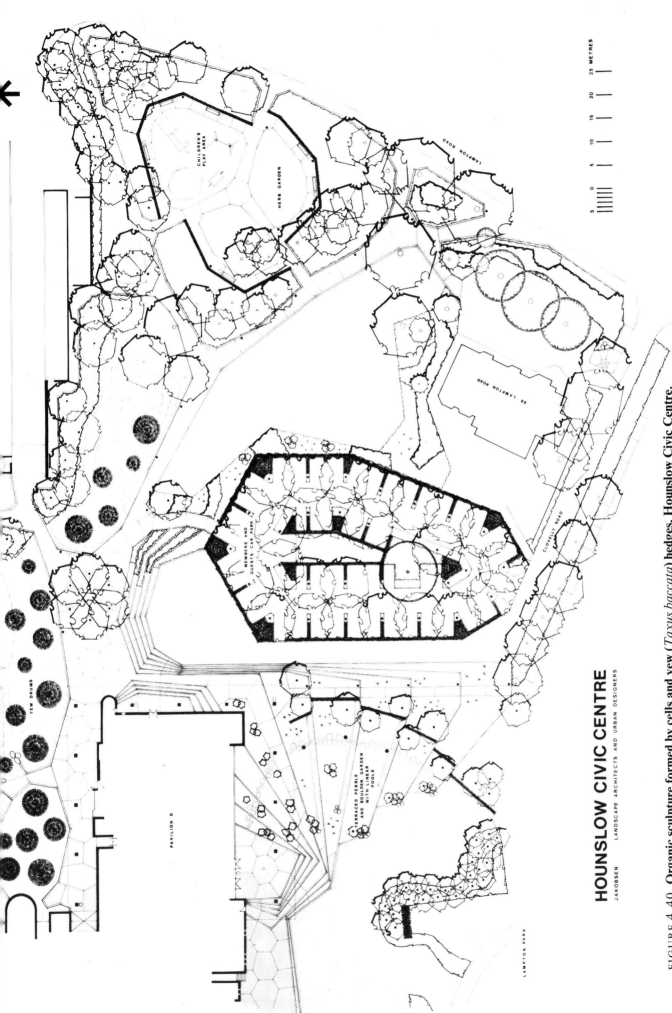

CHILDREN'S PLAY AREA

HERB GARDEN

LAMPTON ROAD

85 LAMPTON ROAD

CLIVELLY ROAD

MEMBERS AND GUESTS CAR PARK

TERRACED PEBBLE GARDEN AND BOULDER GARDEN WITH LINEAR POOLS

PAVILION D

YEW DRUMS

LAMPTON PARK

5 0   5   10   15   20   25 METRES

HOUNSLOW CIVIC CENTRE
JAKOBSEN LANDSCAPE ARCHITECTS AND URBAN DESIGNERS

FIGURE 4.40 **Organic sculpture formed by cells and yew (***Taxus baccata***) hedges. Hounslow Civic Centre.**
(Landscape Architects: *Jakobsen Landscape Architects and Urban Designers*)

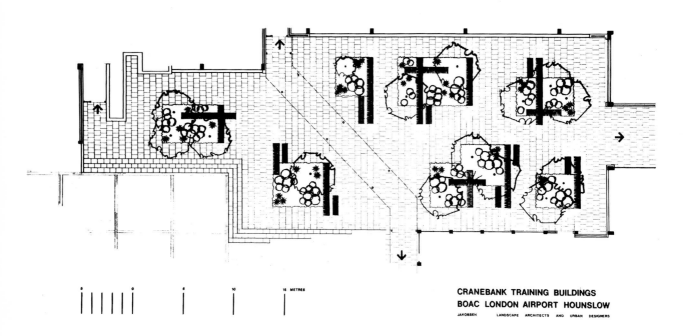

CRANEBANK TRAINING BUILDINGS
BOAC LONDON AIRPORT HOUNSLOW
JAKOBSEN   LANDSCAPE ARCHITECTS AND URBAN DESIGNERS

FIGURE 4.41 **Organic sculpture with constructivist influence. Tall dark green yew** (*Taxus baccata*) **hedges with penetrating lower, yellow-green** *Lonicera* **'Baggessen's Gold'. BOAC Training Centre.**
(Landscape Architects: *Jakobsen Landscape Architects and Urban Designers*)

Although bark mulches have been introduced primarily as a weed suppressor, their decorative aspects offer possibilities for wider use for offsetting plants, similar to the technique in interior planting where a terracotta 'leca' type aggregate is used for offsetting dark evergreen foliaged plants.

4.7 DESIGNING WITH HEDGES AND OTHER CLIPPED AND PRUNED ELEMENTS

Throughout the history of landscape gardening the hedge has in its many forms played an important role in aspects of planting design. Initially the function of the hedge was to define land ownership, create shelter and prevent stock from trespassing. Later, the hedge surrounding the main house, castle, or cottage became largely ornamental culminating in the elaborate *broderie parterres* associated with seventeenth-century French and Dutch gardens in particular.

Scandinavian landscape architects have relied heavily on inspirations from the past and still do with regard to low and tall hedges in clipped and semi-clipped form. A notable departure is the hedge in depth principle (giant groundcover) used in Denmark by both Arne Jacobsen in Klampenborg school, and Jørn Utzon at 'Kingo' Houses, Helsingor. They both planted common beech *Fagus sylvatica* to be clipped at a height of approximately 1·2 m. Such large-scale clipped groundcover, regrettably, requires intensive maintenance. These two schemes are distinctive and appear to work well. In the Jørn Utzon scheme particularly the idea 'less is more' has been taken to its ultimate—only two species, *Fagus sylvatica* and *Vitis quinquefolia*, appear to dominate the scene.

Another distinctive departure is the use of the simulated hedge, really 'fedge' which is an Old English term for a combined fence and hedge. Such a fedge was deliberately created in the sculpture garden of Louisiana Museum near Copenhagen and consists of a leaf mould container made of impregnated soft wood with open gaps between the boards. This has been planted with common ivy and the boards are now totally covered.

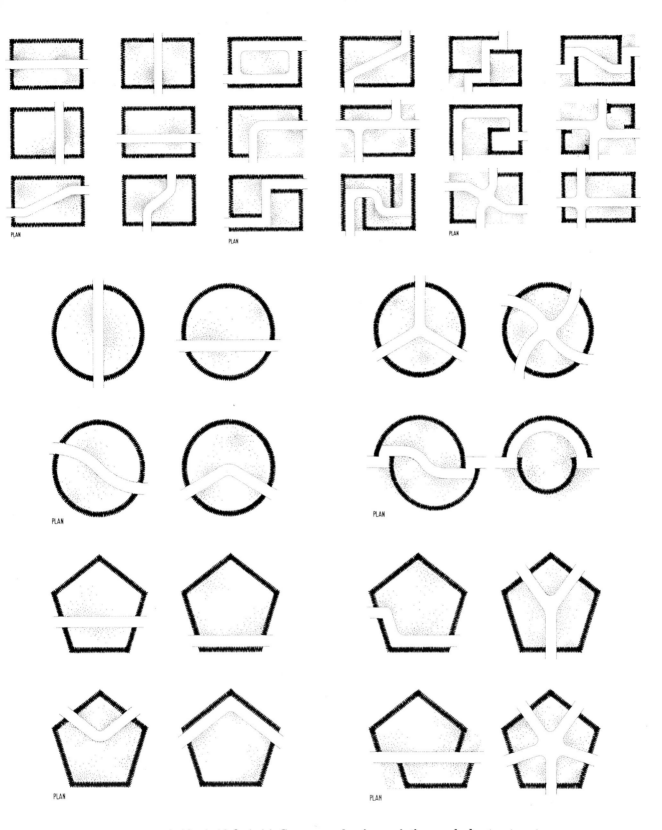

FIGURES 4.42. 4.43 & 4.44 **Sequences showing variations on hedge treatment.**

The cubistic clumps of box used by Gunnar Martinsson and S. I. Anderson in the Outdoor Room exhibition at Bastad in 1961 showed how this planting technique could be successfully used in the small private garden. C. Th. Sørensen made a notable contribution in front of Kalundborg Cathedral, with a design which changes with the height of the viewpoint. Due to its horizontal and simple layout the design avoids destroying the architectural unity of a distinctive townspace. The recent revival of labyrinths and mazes has a direct bearing for the landscape profession in the future, particularly in urban design. There is no doubt that hedges are a form of organic sculpture and their use is as varied as the designer's inventiveness.

Apart from being pure space-enclosing elements, shrubs used as hedges can serve a multiplicity of design purposes within an overall planting design. Hedges can be seen as sculptural volumes affording a neutral background against which to display a shrub or tree for emphasis, or to make carefully controlled design statements with other plants. They allow free use of herbaceous borders and colourful planting schemes which can be concealed within landscape cells formed by hedges so that they do not detract from the purity of the overall design. Lutyens' work with Gertrude Jekyll is an example. His sombre dark yew hedges provided the perfect background for her herbaceous borders and shrub planting.

ACKNOWLEDGEMENT

All drawings and sketches in Chapter 4 were produced by Jakobsen Landscape Architects and Urban Designers.

FURTHER READING

1. Design appreciation

Albarn, K. *et al. The Language of Pattern* (London: Thames and Hudson Ltd., 1974)

Arnheim, R. *Towards a Psychology of Art* (London: Faber and Faber, 1966)

Bagger, B. *Nature as Designer* (London: Frederick Warne and Co. Ltd., 1967)

Chermayeff, S. and Alexander, C. *Community and Privacy* (New York: Doubleday & Co. Inc., 1963; Harmondsworth: Penguin, 1966)

Clark, K. *Landscape into Art* (Harmondsworth: Penguin Books Ltd., 1949)

Critchlow, K. *Order in Space* (London: Thames and Hudson Ltd., 1970)

Edwards, E. B. *Pattern and Design with Dynamic Symmetry* (New York: Dover, 1967)

Ehrenzweig, A. *The Hidden Order of Art* (London: Weidenfeld and Nicolson, 1967)

Goodman, N. *Languages of Art* (London: Oxford University Press, 1969)

Gregory, E. L. and Gombrich, E. H. *Illusions in Nature and Art* (London: Gerald Duckworth and Co. Ltd., 1973)

Grillo, P. J. *Form, Function and Design* (New York: Dover, 1960)

Langer, S. K. *Philosophy in a New Key* (New York: Mentor Paperback 1954)

Matthews, W. H. *Mazes and Labyrinths, their history and development* (New York: Dover, 1970)

Norbergh-Schulz, C. *Intentions in Architecture* (London: George Allen and Unwin Ltd., 1963)

Papanek, V. *Design for the Real World. Making to Measure* (London: Thames and Hudson, 1972)

Vernon, M. D. *The Psychology of Perception* (Harmondsworth: Penguin Books Ltd., 1962)

White, L. L. *Aspects of Form* (London: Lund Humphries, 1968)

Wilson, F. A. *Art as Understanding* (London: Routledge and Kegan Paul, 1963)

2. Landscape design

Allen, G. *The Colours of Flowers* (London: Macmillan and Co. Ltd., 1882)

Brooklyn Botanic Garden *Creative Ideas in Garden Design* (Brooklyn Botanic Gardens, 1965)

Carpenter, P. L., Walker, T. D. and Lanphear, F. O. *Plants in the Landscape* (San Francisco: W. H. Freeman & Co., 1975)

Eaton, L. K. *Landscape Artist in America: The Life and Work of Jens Jensen* (University of Chicago Press, 1964)

Grant, J. A. and C. L. *Garden Design Illustrated* (University of Washington Press, 1954)

Hubbard, H. V., and Kimball, T. *Landscape Design* (New York: Macmillan, 1917)

Kramer, J. *Gardening with Stone and Sand* (New York: Scribners, 1972)

Newbigin, M. L. *Colour in Nature, a Study in Biology* (London: John Murray, 1898)

Robinette, G. O. *Off the Board, Into the Ground* (Dubuque, Iowa: Kendell Hunt Publishing Co., 1968)

3. Shrubs and Groundcover

Boddy, F. A. *Foliage Plants* (Newton Abbot: David and Charles, 1973)

Boddy, F. A. *Groundcover* (Newton Abbot: David and Charles, 1974)

Brooklyn Botanic Garden *Tree and Shrub Forms: Their Landscape Use* (Brooklyn Botanic Garden, 1972)

Fish, M. *Ground Cover Plants* (London: W. H. Collingridge Ltd., 1964)

Foley, D. J. *Groundcover for Easier Gardening* (New York: Dover, 1961)

Gorer, R. *Hardy Foliage Plants* (London: W. H. Collingridge Ltd., 1966)

Gorer, R. *Climbing Plants* (London: Studio Vista, 1968)

Gorer, R. *Multi-Season Shrubs and Trees* (Newton Abbot: David and Charles, 1971)

Haworth-Booth, M. *The Flowering Shrub and Garden* (London: Country Life, 1938)

Hillier, H. G. *Hilliers Manual of Trees and Shrubs* (Winchester: Hillier and Sons catalogue, published annually)

Lloyd, C. *Foliage Plants* (London: Collins, 1973)

Paturi, F. *Nature, Mother of Invention* (London: Thames and Hudson Ltd., 1976)

Philbrick, H. and Gregg, R. B. *Companion Plants* (London: Stuart and Watkins, 1967)

Robinette, G. *Design Characteristics of Plant Materials* (American Printing and Publishing Inc., 1967)

Robinson, W. *The Subtropical Garden* (London: John Murray, 1879)

Seabrook, P. *Shrubs for your Garden* (France: Editions Floraisse, 1973)

Sunset Books *Lawns and Groundcovers* (California: Lane Magazine and Book Co., 1964)

Thomas, G. S. *Plants for Ground Cover* (London: J. M. Dent and Sons Ltd., 1970)

Thomas, G. S. *Colour in the Winter Garden* (London: Phoenix House, 1957; Newton Centre, Mass.: Charles I. Blandford Co.)

Wyman, D. *The Saturday Morning Gardener* (London: Macmillan and Co. Ltd., 1962)

Lotus spp. *(Preben Jakobsen)*

CHAPTER 5

Herbaceous Plants and Bulbs

A. DU GARD PASLEY

5.1 INTRODUCTION

Within the time scale of the landscape, herbaceous planting has a place as fleeting as the shadows of the clouds drifting across the face of some ancient rock formation. As fleeting, and as important, for it is just those chance shadows which give added richness to the texture of landform, revealing new depths until that moment unperceived. The transitory nature of such planting has both dangers and rewards. Forgotten for a year or two, some cherished effect may vanish into bindweed and desolation. But how easily it can be replaced or altered, unlike the wrongly shaped oak wood or misplaced cedar standing for centuries in mute reproach to their planter.

The possibility of change and experiment is an essential element in designing with herbaceous plants—a constant process of evolution, impelled not so much by a desire for novelty as by a wish to express a little better some cherished vision or idea. To have the vision is one thing, to try to capture it in materials which not only change constantly, but are at the mercy of pests and diseases, sudden storms and late frosts, is another. As Gertrude Jekyll wrote: 'Those who do not know are apt to think that hardy flower gardening of the best kind is easy. It is not easy at all. It has taken half a lifetime merely to find out what is best worth doing, and a good slice out of another half to puzzle out the ways of doing it.'[1]

As with any other medium, it is first essential to understand its limitation, which in this case is an inability to provide permanent structural form. However solid the pattern at high summer, any scheme relying entirely on herbaceous planting will inevitably lack height and firm structure in winter. Whether it is the box patterns of a parterre, the informal groupings of rhododendrons and trees at a woodland edge or the subtle arrangements of dwarf evergreens and bold foliage shrubs in the border, all herbaceous planting needs a frame and a background. Although the details of such planting are considered

elsewhere, its presence remains implicit throughout this chapter.

Within the short span of a lifetime, changing social and economic conditions, to say nothing of the strange tides of fashion and ideas, can overturn accepted attitudes and just as easily reinstate them later. In the garden, scientific or mechanical advance may simplify an apparently complex process, making the practical and labour-saving ideas of the previous decade appear merely boring and sterile. While the long-term plans of the tree and shrub planter may not be much affected by these considerations, the question of maintenance vitally affects the use and extent of herbaceous planting. Not long ago it seemed that the day of the herbaceous plant—apart from those rampant enough to become groundcover or stolid enough to require little attention when once established—was over. Now new techniques and changed conditions have altered the situation and it is worth while considering those areas in which such planting is most appropriate today.

5.2 THE USE OF HERBACEOUS PLANTS AND BULBS

The term 'herbaceous border' has long been a household phrase—indeed a music hall joke in some circles—so it is perhaps justifiable to consider this feature first. At their best, in the hands of such sensitive artists as William Robinson, Gertrude Jekyll and Vita Sackville-West, these borders were beautifully controlled compositions in which trees, large shrubs, both deciduous and evergreen, shrub roses and drifts of small shrubs formed a constant framework to broad groups of plants, many of which were grown as much for their foliage colour and form as for their flowers. To such borders were admitted anything which could help the picture. Bulbs, lilies, annuals, tender bedding plants, and even vegetables had their place. The possibilities for experiment were almost limitless and despite those prophets of doom whose boring com-

PLATE 5.1 **The continuous background of** Clematis montana **provides an excellent foil to the bold sculptured foliage of** Paeony lutea **'Ludlowii'. Unfortunately the trivial treatment of the planting at the front of the border reduces the impact. Borde Hill.**
(*Preben Jakobsen*)

PLATE 5.2 **A clear cut rectangular pattern often proves a better setting for low herbaceous plants than the vaguely amoebic forms of 'island beds'.** (*Susan Jellicoe*)

PLATE 5.3 **In the wild garden herbaceous plants take on a new dimension.** *(Susan Jellicoe)*
PLATE 5.4 **Strong, well arranged contrasts of form and texture are quite as important as colour in the border. Here the interplay between rounded and spiky forms is particularly effective. Brodick.** *(Preben Jakobsen)*

positions of mown and roughcut grass covered so many post-war gardens, there is nothing to invalidate this style of gardening today. Indeed, there has probably never been a better vehicle for English garden genius. Our love of flowers, colour and endless variety of material can have full rein, while a strong basic composition holds the whole together.

The mixed border, then, has an important place in our gardens, although different emphasis may change its basic character. It is impossible to keep such a border in full bloom for more than two months, so that before any consideration is given to detailed planning a preliminary decision must be made about the purpose which it is to fulfil. In general terms, a border which relies largely on a good structure and where sculptural forms, foliage contrasts, and tone values predominate, will be the most satisfactory because they remain constant, while flower colour can create special effects and be used to highlight particular times of year.

Where space is available or other considerations allow, borders created for particular seasons of the year can be very effective. In this case, plant material need be considered only in relation to the chosen period and excellent effects can be obtained by using plants which have only a short season of beauty and are otherwise gross or unattractive—it is surprising how many of these there are. Such seasonal planting needs to be placed so that it does not appear obtrusive in its off periods, a problem particularly acute in the case of monocultures such as the iris garden, which is a dream of beauty for two weeks and either boring or hideous for the remaining fifty.

A later development of the old herbaceous border has been the island bed. The theory of fairly low-growing plants set out in the open away from down-draughts and problems of light caused by adjacent walls and hedges, and easily accessible on all sides, is an excellent one. As practised, the result—a selection of ill-assorted kidneys and amoebic shapes uneasily afloat on a sea of grass—has been deplorable. A simple dignified pattern of square or rectangular beds planted with these same low-growing perennials, perhaps with an asymmetric counterpoint of evergreen shrubs and foliage plants, would be exceedingly effective. If the beds could be edged with bands of brick or stone, at once emphasizing the pattern and reducing grass cutting problems, they would also be very easy to keep. Such an arrangement on a large scale was created by Norah Lindsay in the 1930s to replace the old Victorian parterre at Blickling Hall in Norfolk, and to this day it remains the most spectacular feature of that garden. There are also many old paved rose gardens, where the soil has become rose sick, to which such a solution could be applied with advantage.

How often, since the last war, have Victorian and other parterres been swept away under the plea of saving labour, and many stretches of tedious grass have remained to bore the eye thereafter? Sometimes, of course, such parterres were added to landscape gardens in which they had no place, and consequently they are better gone, but where parterre and setting were designed together, the loss is all too obvious. Now that mechanical and chemical aids have reduced the problem of maintenance, there is a good case to be made for restoring the balance of these gardens by re-creating, perhaps in a simplified form, the old parterres and filling them with

PLATE 5.5 **The natural method of one major effect at a time always looks well if there is sufficient space available, but it must be comprehensive. Mixed daffodils sold 'for naturalising' would have created a visual disaster instead of an harmonious unity. Hampton Court.** *(Preben Jakobsen)*

carefully chosen perennials rather than with time-consuming and gaudy bedding plants. A careful choice of good foliage plants, interspersed with suitable bulbs, would provide interesting contrasts of texture and colour, while the usual problem of too much bare earth in winter would not arise, since at that season the exact pattern of the cut box-work would be seen to its greatest advantage.

The old knot garden, too, might well be revived, since in its earliest form the 'open knot' was planted with herbaceous perennials, bulbs and lilies rather than concentrated bedding schemes. Such knots are well adapted to present conditions as they often formed the major part of gardens even smaller than many of those current today, and their firm simple patterns have a calming effect on the magpie collections of plants to which the average British gardener is so addicted.

Outside the confines of the formal garden, herbaceous plants take on a new dimension. In the woodland and wild garden they are, or can seem to be, in their native habitat, grouped naturally in long drifts under the trees, running out under shrubs and through the thin grass at the woodland edge. Apparently self-sown, certainly self-perpetuating and requiring a minimum of maintenance, many of the plants which are too rampant for the garden proper can find an ideal home there. As one eighteenth-century writer explains: 'Art should never be allowed to set foot in the province of Nature otherwise than clandestinely and by night', so however much nature is improved by art, the results must still appear natural, and this is one of the most difficult effects to achieve artificially. However carefully arranged, our groups tend to look stiff and lumpish, lacking the spontaneous flow of plants in the wild. Observation, aided by notebook or camera, and a careful study of plant groupings which please us, are essential if we are to achieve really satisfactory effects. Once again the most worth-while advice comes from Gertrude Jekyll, whose trained eye and meticulous power of observation produced some of the most penetrating examinations of the use of plant material. She it was who noted the proportions of dominant and sub-dominant plants in their natural setting and the way in which plant associations ebb and flow in the wild, the dominant's reversing roles, meeting, mingling and dividing again as soil, exposure or mere chance have affected them. She shows, too, how plants will grow in layers, their roots being at different levels, an important fact which we can use not only in the wild garden but also within the confines of our cultivated borders.[1]

Where the woodland opens to areas of rough or seldom mown grass, in the orchard or where the garden merges into paddock or parkland, there is an opportunity to practise that form of flowery meadow gardening beloved of William Robinson and described in his book *The Wild Garden*.[2] He was perhaps the first—although by no means the last, as it has become a very popular form of modern gardening—to point out the infinite charms of the flower-filled alpine meadow. This concept of the garden as an idealized meadow had a much earlier application in the 'flowery mead' of medieval romances and paintings, where so often the Virgin sits upon a carpet of grass scattered with flowers, each placed singly like the fleurettes of the tapestries. 'The orchard was fair beyond content. Herbs grew there of every fashion, more than I am able to name . . .'[3] In fact, massed planting was as alien to the vision of Botticelli as it was to Berthe Morisot, whose women rest in softly flowering meadows, enshrined in a sunny nineteenth century world before the hay was cut. Into a silvery carpet of grass are woven pointilliste spots of colour which form a complementary effect to balance the solid wood of bluebells or the bank of primroses.

However carefully we analyse, however objective our approach, our vision is influenced inevitably by subjective things—the half-remembered lines of Wordsworth (and I for one will always reject those great armies of brazen trumpets which march across our grass in springtime, simply because they spoil a cherished childhood vision; my heart could never dance with such rigid flowers and I am unable to see them for what they are, only for what they are not), the painting in some forgotten exhibition, the memory of a distant conversation. These echoes, just as much as our horticultural knowledge and our power to appreciate light, form and colour, will influence both our planting and that ideal of perfection which we try to achieve. For this reason there can be no absolute, merely a search for an ideal which may perhaps illuminate the lives of others beside ourselves, and in this respect the herbaceous planter has an advantage. The imagination can perceive the oak, but its planter will never live to see its perfection, whereas in a year or two the results of *Iris pallida* 'Dalmatica' spearing up beside a drift of *Ruta graveolens* can be seen, assessed and accepted or altered as our taste dictates.

5.3 WHAT TO PLANT

The possibilities are infinite, but are conditioned by various limiting factors which affect all forms of planting design. Soil, climate and exposure will force rejection of many plants which might otherwise be suitable, or at least they should do so. It is probably possible to grow anything anywhere, after a fashion, but to what purpose? Those who practise such gardening are no more than Commandants of concentration camps full of ailing and unwilling prisoners, and the visual results of such methods are little more agreeable. Then there is the human element which may reject otherwise desirable plants for purely personal reasons, but even so an almost daunting choice remains.

5.31 Colour, shape and texture

Every plant has form, texture and colour and of these elements it is the first two which are more important because if they are not fully considered any planting scheme will become a formless jumble. Only careful observation at every season—for effects change so markedly with the passage of the months that each plant can appear in half a dozen different guises—will make us fully aware of the quality and of the possibilities of each plant. Some are sculptural, holding shadows even deeper than those within carved stonework, others are pure form or pure texture, or some balance between these things. Each needs to be placed to make full use of its potential, whether it be striking or recessive, either by direct contrast or the juxtaposition of like and like. One can contrast form and texture, texture and colour, colour and form, but seldom all three elements at once or the planting will become like a Victorian letter, so full of underlinings and exclamation marks as to be incapable of any emphasis at all.

The ease and popularity of colour photography has brought many problems in its wake, not least an inclination to play down the importance of composition. Pleasing colours agreeably grouped may seem to make a picture, whereas if the scene is reduced to black and white a satisfying composition of forms and proper balance of light and shadow will be found to be lacking, with a resultant loss of effect. At the outset it is useful therefore to think of any new planting in terms of black and white, infilling the major structure of trees and shrubs with abstract compositions whose form, texture and tonal values are fully developed. When the abstractions are considered satisfactory, it is not difficult to turn these formal elements into plant material, remembering that any group of plants takes on the basic outline and quality of a single plant of the same species. Even at a distance too great to observe any detail of leaf or branch structure, a clump of oak could not be mistaken for a clump of beech because the shape of the two trees, individually or grouped, is different.

For some strange reason, colour seems to be regarded

PLATE 5.6 **The close, matt texture of clipped yew is a perfect background to detailed planting placed in front of it, particularly if this is of a pale and light reflecting nature. Great Dixter, Lutyens House.** *(Preben Jakobsen)*

by many people as a pure end in itself, without regard to what effect is being achieved. The results too often remind one of Elvira's exasperated remark in Noel Coward's *Blithe Spirit*: 'The border by the sundial looks like a fruit salad . . .' But green is also a colour, or more strictly an almost infinite variety of colours, and remains the most important because, as far as this country is concerned at least, it is predominant. 'No white nor red was ever seen as amorous as that lovely green' wrote Andrew Marvell and although our colour planting may not be dictated by its amorous quality, green has other advantages.[4] 'Annihilating all that's made to a green thought in a green shade' . . . what could be more restful in our frenetic age than that? The relief to the eye provided by a single stand of cool green aquatic plants in the big marquee at Chelsea Flower Show was very great, after the concentrated blast of multicolours everywhere else.

What then is colour to do, and how is it to be achieved? Colour can be soothing or stimulating, can create warmth or coolness, introduce light or shadow, create or emphasize a mood, underline the good or play down the bad points of a site, but it can do none of these things unless it is used with sensitivity and care. In general we will want our effects to be as long lasting as possible, and for this reason will make the greatest use of foliage which lasts for most of the season rather than flowers which have a fairly short life. This brings us back to green—or silver, grey, blue, yellow, white, purple, crimson, pink, apricot, and more besides—which leaves can provide. Indeed, one can make very satisfactory compositions from foliage plants alone, full of colour and interest without the rather ephemeral help of flowers at all.

There are two basic ways of using colour: by direct contrast (which produces a very restless picture if over-indulged) or by building up a series of related tones and shades, with occasional contrast for dramatic effect. The easiest and safest way to handle it is to decide on one theme colour and then use it in a series of variations against some neutral background. This can be most effective in a small garden or as part of a large one: the results will seem clever and original while in fact it is difficult to go wrong.

A yellow garden, with flowers and leaves in every available shade from cream to near orange against either a dark green or silver background, is always satisfying, especially if the strong colours are kept to the centre of the beds, working out to paler tones at the edges. A red garden, in a setting of dark green or purple leaves, is very stimulating, as the great red borders at Hidcote prove, while a purple garden can seem a little sombre, although the magnificent purple border at Sissinghurst Castle proves that it can be carried through with success. Blue or white gardens are cool and fresh, the first for a sunny, the second for a partly shaded position because while blue seems to absorb sunlight and looks drab without it, white flowers look best in partial shade or at least against a background of shadow.

When using a number of different colours it is best to keep to those which incline towards yellow or those which are based on blue. Although flower colours appear to be almost limitless in their variety, when one comes to examine them carefully it becomes obvious that very few of them are so pure that they do not have a touch of either blue or yellow in their make-up. Taking an absolutely pure white base and adding yellow to it produces first a warm white in which there is a hint of cream, then cream of deepening intensity, then yellow. Progressively adding red will produce all the oranges, salmons, apricots and orange pinks (which do contain a little blue also, but the yellow is dominant) until in the end there is pure scarlet. In the other range there are cold bluish whites working up to pure blue which, with a varying addition of red, will produce all the pinks varying from apple blossom to deep rose and through crimson to violet and purple. Even if there is no direct blue or yellow in the scheme, the flowers based on one or the other have a natural affinity and always look well together.

Working within one range of colour in a setting of complementary or carefully contrasted foliage, the results can be very harmonious, but it must be remembered that the eye needs a space of rest and refreshment before another colour group can be appreciated. It is here particularly that the cool grey, silver and bluish foliage plants come into their own, helping to clear from the eye the impressions from one set of colours before the next, which may not necessarily be in violent contrast, is introduced. The light in this country is always blue—visibly so on some days—and the blue atmosphere has a dramatic effect on flower colour, intensifying pale colours, particularly if they are blue based, and giving them a vibrant depth which they would never have under a harder, yellower sun. That is why all those sweet pea colours, swooning mauves and greyish pinks, blues and silvers, look so wonderful in our borders and so frightfully limp and washed out when similar effects are attempted in some less misty climate. Likewise, many of the dashing colour contrasts which look so stimulating under a southern sun appear tawdry and vulgar if copied here. Bright colour should always be seen in full sunlight, pale colours (other than certain blues) gain from a measure of shade or from being seen against a shadowy background. In fact certain plants (mostly those with white or pale yellow flowers) actually seem to glow in the dark and this ability can be used to create special effects where the garden is going to be used at night.

Sometimes it is possible to rely on a single sweep of unadulterated colour, an effect to which bulbs lend themselves particularly well. The bluebell wood, the orchard of daffodils, the churchyard carpeted with snowdrops, have a pure impact which any additional element would destroy. Except on a limited scale within a firm framework, the mixtures which are so often all that can be obtained are most unsatisfactory. The mixed daffodils, too much alike yet too different, and the mixed bedding plants which are guaranteed to destroy any carefully composed scheme of planting. The flowery mead works because the flowers are various, and set in a common matrix, but in the case of these mixed bags and boxes the flowers are all alike and the colours appear merely muddled.

5.4 PLANTING AND MAINTENANCE

The purely formal garden is the easiest of all types to make and to maintain. Single species planted at regular intervals and kept in a consistent way require a degree of labour but very little thought, an important factor today when it is easier to get help from an unskilled labourer than a professional gardener. With this in mind, the placing of blocks of plants, either symmetrically or asymmetrically, has much to commend it. Variations can still be obtained from the contrast of height, colour and texture, but the importance of a neat habit of growth, regular flowering pattern and interesting foliage, preferably evergreen but at least long lasting, is obvious. Obvious too is the desirability of plants which remain growing happily in one place without a constant need to lift and divide. In some cases it is perfectly possible to use plants with invasive tendencies, such as *Stachys lanata* for instance, by cutting round them every year to maintain the shape of the group, though of course in time the centre will become woody and the clumps will need division and replanting.

In association with static plant groups, which need little attention apart from the removal of weeds and the application of a yearly mulch, bulbs of various kinds come into their own in a way which is impossible in most areas of cultivated ground. The dying foliage of many bulbs is rather disagreeable, and it is a great help if it can be hidden by the new growth of associated plants. Early crocus and most small bulbs come well through thymes, dwarf campanulas, ajuga and similar things, while larger bulbs like narcissus, tulips and hyacinths tend to do better if the host plant is scarcely visible at their time of flowering but comes up later to engulf their fading leaves. Hostas, small geraniums, pulmonaria and many others are good in this way. Not only spring bulbs but alliums, autumn crocus and similar subjects can be used, often in the same group but planted in layers (although of course not directly on top of one another) to maintain a constant succession of interest through the season.

In the border the ability to plant in layers is important as it helps to prolong the season of full beauty or to create incidents of interest outside the major period of display. For instance, a group of Chinese paeonies could make the basis for three quite separate effects needing the minimum amount of labour and maintenance. In spring, the richly coloured young shoots might form an ideal setting for those white or white and salmon-pink daffodils which tend to look so artificial in the wild garden, together perhaps with tulips of an associated colouring which would extend the flowering period until the expanding paeony leaves concealed the unsightly dying foliage of the bulbs. In June, of course, the paeony flowers would be in full beauty, while later in the season the leaves, by now beginning to assume their fine autumn colouring, could make a base for a bold group of late orange lilies and later still a foreground to a drift of chrysanthemum or richly coloured asters. In this way the same area of ground might make an almost continuous contribution to the general effectiveness of the border while providing ideal growing conditions for a number of subjects all of which resent root disturbance.

With care, and understanding of the basic needs of various plants, any number of similar associations may be built up. Nor is it necessary to deal solely with purely hardy subjects, since in the warmer parts of the country at least, gladioli, dahlias, ixias and other half-hardy things can be overwintered outside with a little protection, and in colder parts they can always be lifted and replanted each year in the conventional way. When planting the border it is essential not to be dominated by preconceived ideas, and the use of dahlias and gladioli is a case in point. They are regarded as being stiff and ugly simply because they are associated with rows of bamboo canes, or with green-painted stakes crowned with straw-filled flower pots, while the flowers themselves are thought of in relation to the show bench or the market stall. Such thinking is very limited and lacks perception since there is scarcely any plant which is truly ugly or which cannot be grown to great advantage somewhere providing the setting and the method of cultivation are right. Smoky violet and rich purple gladioli rising through and supported by a strong drift of common lavender, the weight of the heads making them bend forward and sideways in graceful sheaves above the grey foliage, must surely banish all memories of bamboo canes and green twine, while crimson dahlias similarly supported by the lower branches of *Cotinus coggygria* 'Atropurpureus' are equally stunning.

Similarly, spaces can be left for the inclusion of bedding plants and annuals, spaces which in themselves need not be noticeable since thin drifts rather than large clumps are required. Geraniums of the right colouring can be very effective used in this way, and often old straggly plants, perhaps drawn up by being kept too long in the house and therefore of no use for bedding schemes, are ideal for the purpose. Other house plants can also be used, either plunged in their pots or set out and repotted again before the onset of winter. The tender plumbago, easily increased from cuttings, will introduce a note of clear pale blue which could be picked up and repeated in other parts by drifts of Cambridge blue lobelia. In the same way, many of the tender silver and grey leafed sub-shrubs can be propagated and planted out where time allows. Even a small greenhouse, or a house with sufficient broad window ledges, can provide a good variety of less hardy plants to increase the border's range in summer. Naturally hardy annuals, preferably grown in a patch of reserve ground and later planted out, or boxed bedding plants from the florist, can be used in the same way. In the latter case, however, it is essential that the exact variety of plant is known, since all too often the plants available commercially are only in colourings or mixtures which are difficult to use.

In an established garden nature itself takes a hand, often producing self-sown groupings which, if thinned out and reshaped, can become an agreeable feature of border or wild garden. To take advantage of such chance effects, it is essential that all weeding should be done by hand and with the greatest care, only known weeds being removed and all other seedlings being allowed to remain until they prove their worth. Even when misplaced such seedlings can be lifted and used elsewhere or passed on to others who are in need. This principle of self-seeding can be encouraged by removing plants which have reached the seeding stage, or cutting off the seed heads as the case may be, and throwing them down in a spare corner or between other plants where they will remain out of sight. Many chance seedlings can be obtained in this way without trouble although of course the seed can be allowed to ripen and then sown in a more conventional way where time and space allow.

Both in the border and in the wild garden the removal of fading flowers, foliage and excessive growth is important since even a few groups obviously past their prime can destroy the good effect of others still in bloom or yet to come. This is a task which is best undertaken daily and just ten minutes after breakfast or before dinner can make all the difference even to a large area of planting. No plant should ever look as though it has been cut back severely, but many can be cut back to half their size after flowering by careful reshaping, the complete removal of some growths and the shortening of others to points concealed by leaves either on the plant itself or on its neighbours. In this way natural outlines can be maintained and yet more space provided for the expansion of those plants which will produce their effects later in the season. Although these techniques are most necessary in the border, they can be extended to the wild garden, since even in an informal setting it is often necessary to remove excess leaves or shoots, or get rid of withered flowers in order to maintain the characteristic appearance of certain plan groupings.

Continuous adjustment and shaping do not only apply to the removal of fading material but also to the adaptation of plants to their positions as they grow. It is not always realized how many herbaceous plants can change their appearance, depending on the way they are treated. With some tall growing perennials, such as many of the asters, the height of flowering can be controlled by pinching out the shoots as they develop, and a sweep of a particular colour rising at different levels through the border can be achieved in this way. Other plants like helianthus and rudbeckia can be pulled forward and held down with long wire loops to cover bare spaces where oriental poppies, or even bulbs, flowered earlier in the season. These normally tall plants when grown almost horizontally form sheets of bloom from freely produced short side shoots. This habit allows groups of early flowering plants like lupins (which subsequently leave untidy gaps) to be grown quite far back in the border as the spaces can be covered from behind. Once again, even the wild garden can benefit from the possibility of creating sheets of colour rather late in

PLATE 5.7 **An occasional tall plant of strong character, used near the front of the border, creates a three dimensional effect which is helped considerably by carrying low planting back behind it.** *(Preben Jakobsen)*

the season when they might not be obtainable by more conventional means. In this, as in so many other realms of life, it is illusion rather than reality which is all-important.

Nothing is so boring as the old concept of the herbaceous border as a kind of highly coloured railway embankment, the plants all evenly graded from back to front in ever diminishing size, each group being neatly held in place with a ring of canes and string. The use of shrubs, trees, climbers and roses in the border helps to prevent this dreary effect, since low plants used as groundcover can sometimes sweep almost through to the back of the border, underplanting some shrub which is at once tall and bare below, while in other places tall plants can surge towards the front of the border like a wave, giving a three-dimensional effect. Staking and support will still be necessary, although the development of many varieties which are self-supporting has helped to reduce the extent of the problem. In some cases plants can help to support each other, bands of low shrubs helping to restrain the plants behind them, while the stout stems of delphiniums cut back to the right height could hold up weaker growths of asters or helianthus leaning forward over them. Otherwise there is really nothing to compare with brushwood inserted as the plants begin to grow in spring, any surplus pieces being cut out when full growth has been achieved, the whole aim being to ensure that the plant shows itself off to the best advantage without any appearance of artificiality.

The flowering orchard or meadow is perhaps the least affected by considerations of detailed maintenance, since this is largely a question of knowing exactly when to cut the grass to preserve order but to do the least damage to the various plants involved. However, flowering meadows do not spring up of their own accord and it is generally best to strip the grass from the required areas and resow them with a finer mixture to which the seeds of wild and suitable garden flowers, either bought from the seedsman or self-collected, have been added. Before sowing, bulbs can be planted and groups of plants put in to establish colonies which will then spread themselves gradually outwards by rooting and seeding. For the first few years undesirable weeds will have to be removed by hand but thereafter probably no more than a twice yearly cut will be necessary. Where it is not possible to treat the whole area in this way, it is best to prepare strategically placed patches to be planted and sown, so that plants and young seedlings do not have to contend with tough meadow grass until they are established. If the right species have been chosen, the plants will spread slowly to the untreated areas.

5.5 CONCLUSION

The effects to be achieved with herbaceous plants and bulbs are almost limitless in their variety, the only limiting factors being the extent to which we study their needs and habits of growth, and our perception of their visual qualities. Although plenty of information exists in the form of books and articles, there is no substitute for personal experience, observation and experiment, for all too often the writers merely follow one another and there is little advance in understanding. Never choose a plant or bulb solely from a catalogue description or the evidence of a specimen at a flower show, unless it is bought purely for experimental purposes to study its year-round effects and habits of growth, for otherwise time, money and effort may be wasted on something entirely unsuitable for its purpose.

The use of plants is not a purely practical matter, for scent, colour and form have an emotive power which can touch the springs of memory and emotion, giving an added dimension to our work and linking it firmly to the world of ideas. Plants are just as much the raw materials of art as are paint, bronze and marble. With these materials, the practical hands of the gardener and the trained eye of the artist achieve results as satisfying to the human spirit as anything to be found in the museums and art galleries of the world.

FURTHER READING

Fairbrother, N. *Men and Gardens* (London: Hogarth Press, 1956)

Jekyll, G. *Wood and Garden* (London: Longmans, Green and Co., 1914)

Robinson, W. *The English Flower Garden* (London: John Murray, 1883)

Sieveking, Albert Forbes *In Praise of Gardens* (London: J. M. Dent & Co., 1899)

REFERENCES

1. Jekyll, G. *Colour in the Flower Garden* (London: Country Life, 1908)
2. Robinson, W. *The Wild Garden* (London: John Murray, 1903)
3. Anon. *Arcassin of Nicolette* (Thirteenth century)
4. Marvell, A. *The Garden* (Seventeenth century)

CHAPTER 6

Water Plants

ALLAN HART

6.1 HISTORICAL BACKGROUND

The water lily is unique in having been an object of veneration for almost four thousand years. There is evidence that members of Egyptian royal families and priests of the nineteenth and twenty-first dynasties were buried with petals of the water lily covering their bodies. The religious significance of this plant was attributed to its ability, after the rainy season, to arise anew in all its purity from a resting place of dank, evil-smelling mud.

This lily was called the Nile Lotus, and the name was attributed to both *Nymphaea coerulea* and *Nymphaea lotus*—a white scented species. Authorities suggest that the true lotus, *Nelumbo nucifera*, was included within the all-embracing name of Nile Lotus. Nelumbo has many associations with Buddhism and was taken from India to China, and from there to Japan in the sixth century A.D. The flower has been formalized in many different ways; basins derived from the shape of both the closed bud and the open flower are to be found in the Court of the Lions at the gardens of the Alhambra in Spain.

There is little evidence to show that other water plants were held in such high esteem, and it is unlikely that there was any deliberate planting of aquatics until the mid-nineteenth century, when the discovery of the giant water lily (*Victoria amazonica*) aroused great interest. Its first flowering in 1849 started a craze amongst wealthy garden enthusiasts for the cultivation of tropical water plants, all trying to find and flower other rarities. In most cases any artificially constructed lakes, pools and canals would have been colonized naturally where the conditions were suitable, particularly around the margins, if the sides were not too steep or the bottom too deep. The great stimulus for water gardening and planting came about as a result of four separate influences arriving on the scene at about the same time.

i) The first influence was that of William Robinson, who passionately advocated the natural approach to planting using materials hardy to soil and climate. The publication of his book *The Wild Garden* in 1894 brought attention to the striking character of many indigenous foliage plants, in particular those associated with water.[1]

ii) This new awareness of native species was also felt by Gertrude Jekyll, who by writing *Wall and Water Gardens* and by her example was able to influence a wider sphere of appreciation.[2] The majority of her observations on the siting and dispositions of hardy plants are still valid today.

iii) Meanwhile, botanical and biological research was bringing to public attention the close inter-relationships between aquatic flora and fauna, and particularly the effect of the delicate balance between a host of organisms on the health of a pool or pond.

iv) Perhaps the greatest influence resulted from the pioneer hybridizing by Joseph Latour-Marliac of Temple-Sur-Lot in France. His name is now synonymous with water lilies, as a result of his carefully guarded methods of crossing North American species such as *Nymphaea odorata* and *Nymphaea tuberosa* with *Nymphaea alba-rubra* from Sweden and others, to introduce pink, red and yellow pigments. (It is interesting to note that Marliac's methods died with him, and Frances Perry records that the hybridizing of water lilies is generally so much fruitless labour; the efforts of her father-in-law, Amos Perry, a renowned horticulturalist, were to all intents and purposes a total failure.) The advent of striking shades and colours fostered a wave of interest in water lilies and their associated allies, and many gardens were designed to exhibit the rarities.

6.2 THE USE OF WATER PLANTS IN GARDEN DESIGN

In addition to aquatics (plants growing freely on or within the water) the subject of water plants includes those plants which inhabit the margins of streams, ponds or lakes, which are of a herbaceous and semi-woody nature. It

PLATE 6.1 **Water lilies on a pool near Copenhagen, Denmark.** *(K. Stansfield)*

PLATE 6.2 **A narrow stream is given a greater impression of apparent width by low profile contouring. Ayington Park near Winchester.** *(Allan Hart)*

excludes trees and shrubs, several of which will grow at the water's edge—for example, swamp cypress (*Taxodium distichum*), the wing nut (*Pterocarya × rehderana*), swamp birch (*Betula nigra*), although the planting of any such trees or shrubs should always be in sympathy with the water area and its margins, both aesthetically and ecologically. The design principles and the method of handling water plants are very similar to those used for other plant materials, with the exception that the great majority of aquatics die down in winter, and therefore a particular effect may be lost temporarily, until the following spring.

The art of the use of shadowed water was outlined by Sir George Sitwell in his book *On the Making of Gardens* in which he illustrated how dark evergreens were invaluable as a background to water; by the simple expedient of truncating the sun's lateral rays, they help to concentrate the deep blue of the water when the sun is directly overhead.[3] It is also possible to increase the apparent size of an area of water by designing grass banks which slope gradually down to the water's edge—this gives less shadow than planted banks.

The climate of the British Isles means that water for reflection has limited uses and must be carefully sited to take maximum advantage of a small amount of sunshine to realize its sparkling quality, otherwise it may appear dark and sombre. Water in Britain generally gives the impression of fading away into mist and trees, and a careful selection of plant materials can enhance this effect.

It is the quintessence of all design that the desired visual effect is determined as early as possible. In certain types of water features, particularly those in full sunshine, and where the reflective qualities of the surface are sought, aquatic planting must play a subordinate part, carefully located to add to rather than detract from the composition.

It is essential that the proportions of surface plant cover to open water are carefully determined, and that the aquatic plants are in scale with the surface area. Unless this balance is maintained, the surface of a sheet of water will be little different from that of an area of dry land covered with vegetation. The final effect of free growing plants can appear to reduce the apparent size.

Dramatic effects evoking a variety of moods can often be achieved by the simplest of detailing. The strong, arrow-like foliage of the giant rush (*Typha latifolia*) or common phragmite (*Phragmites communis*) standing in water, either reflected in sunshine or rising from a mist-covered lake, is an inspiring sight. A simple arrangement of the leaves of a solitary water lily or a total covering of duckweed (*Lemna minor*) on the surface of a still pool or basin in a shadowy glade can create a situation charged with mystery.

The tropical lushness of the huge leaves of *Gunnera manicata*, suddenly revealed, excite the imagination with thoughts of its Chilean jungle home. The same sense of wonder can be created by the first sight of the native great water dock (*Rumex hydrolapathum*) which usually

PLATE 6.3 **Water, clear of vegetation, reflects the sky overhead.** *(Allan Hart)*

PLATE 6.4 **The qualities of both planting and open water are negated when vegetation covers the whole surface.** *(Robert Adams)*

PLATE 6.5 **Balanced proportions of planting to surface area.** *(Allan Hart)*

PLATE 6.6 **Romantic water associations. Scotney Castle, Kent.** *(Allen Hart)*

reaches 15 m in height, particularly when the exotic size and shape of its leaves are transformed with its breathtaking autumn colour.

The composition of planting in and around the moat at Scotney Castle in Kent is a superb example of an idealized romantic setting for the ruins of the old castle, which would do credit to any of the artists of the pre-Raphaelite Brotherhood.

Britain has its own richly unique collection of indigenous water plants many of which possess particularly handsome foliage. This is a fact which may surprise many who think that lush foliage is usually associated with hot jungle climes. Many of our finest herbaceous plants grow by the waterside, and may be thought of as escapees from some distant country. Such a plant is the flowering rush (*Butomus umbellatus*), which has been favourably compared with the sacred lotus of ancient Egypt.

The grouping of *Butomus* with *Equisetum telmateia* by Robinson has almost become a classic. *Equisetum telmateia* may reach 1 m in height in deep shaded soil, and has long, closely grouped, slender branches, set in whorls. Similar to the flowering rush is the buckbean or bogbean (*Menyanthes trifoliata*), which has long stalked leaves topped with three leaflets, like a giant clover.

The yellow iris (*Iris pseudacorus*) and sweet sedge (*Acorus calamus*) exhibit strap-shaped leaves, the former

displaying bright red seed capsules in the autumn, and the latter producing a sweet scent when the foliage is bruised. It also has a curious horizontal ribbing on the stems which is an aid to identification. The branched bur-reed (*Sparganium erectum*) has sword-like leaves, with its flowers grouped in globular bur-like masses on the branches at the top of the stalk. The arrowhead plant (*Sagittaria sagittifolia*) has lanceolate leaves above the water, its submerged leaves being linear. This is a most handsome plant at the water's edge. Two plants which are often found growing naturally together and which complement each other perfectly are the yellow loosestrife (*Lysimachia vulgaris*), a member of the primrose family, and purple loosestrife (*Lythrum salicaria*).

Greater emphasis is now being placed on ecologically based planting, the principles of which must be thoroughly understood if the designer is to achieve the desired effect. Submerged and floating aquatics play an essential role in the maintenance of a correct ecological balance, without which the water would become cloudy and foul. The correct 'mix' of plants, animals, fish, micro fauna and flora gives a self-maintaining environment. Submerged plants release oxygen into the water for use of fish and insects—they also deprive algae (unicellular plants) of light and mineral salts. Aquatic plants provide food for insects, which in turn provide food for fish which find nesting places in the leaves and stems. The young fish are able to hide and shelter from predators. The protective aspect of underwater planting is therefore important.

6.3 AQUATIC COMMUNITIES

Perhaps with aquatic plants more than any other group, the designer must realize that the relationships between various groups of plants are rarely fixed or permanent but continually changing. The natural succession is a 'hydrasere', in which there is a progression from deep open water, through to marsh and finally to dry land. This is brought about by silt and dead organic material accumulating in depth on the bottom, so gradually reducing its suitability for deep-water plants, but making it more habitable for shallow-water species.

Eventually, if the process continues, only dry land species will find a home there. It is possible to see zones of vegetation around ponds and lakes, and these usually indicate the various stages of succession.

PLATE 6.7
Riverside marginal plants including *Butomus umbellatus. (Robert Adams)*

The main varieties of water plants described below are listed in Table 6.1. Most of the limited selection of plants are native British species, rather than exotic varieties.

a) *Plants growing adjacent to water*

Mixed herbaceous plants. The plants adapted to this situation include many which are renowned for their bold foliage and architectural form and are used for mixed herbaceous plantings. For example, goat's beard (*Aruncus sylvester*) has very distinctive plumes of creamy-white flowers, tall and arching, over multi-pinnate foliage, a more aristocratic version of the native meadowsweet (*Filipendula ulmaria*). Spiraeas or false goat's beard (*Astilbe × arendsii* and *Astilbe japonica* hybrids) in shades of white, through pink to red, and in heights ranging from 600–900 mm, make very effective groundcover. In complete contrast is that most delicate looking but persistent plant, lady's smock (*Cardamine pratensis*), surely one of our most beautiful native plants and best seen in association with grasses.

There are several bulbs adapted to these conditions, including snowflake (*Leucojum aestivum*), found along the banks of the Thames, and quamash (*Camassia quamash*), a native of North America, which can seed and colonize in water meadows if undisturbed. The various

Table 6.1
Plants associated with water

Location	Latin Name	Popular Name
1. Adjacent to water		
Mixed herbaceous	*Aruncus sylvester*	goat's beard
	Astilbe × arendsii	spireas or false
	Astilboides tabularis japonica hybrids	goat's beard
	Cardamine pratensis	lady's smock
	Hosta spp (various)	plantain lily
	Ligularia clivorum	giant groundsel
Bulbs	*Camassia quamash*	quamash
	Hemerocallis var.	day lily
	Leucojum aestivum	snowflake
Trees and Shrubs	*Alnus* spp	alder
	Betula nigra	water birch
	Clethra alnifolia	sweet pepper
	Corylus spp	hazel
	Nyssa sylvatica	tupelo
	Populus spp	poplar
	Pterocarya fraxinifolia	wing nut
	Salix spp	willow & dwarf spp
	Taxodium distichum	swamp cypress
2. Marsh Plants	*Carex* spp	sedges
	Eupatorium cannabinum	hemp agrimony
	Filipendula ulmaria	meadow sweet
	Gunnera manicata	Chilean rhubarb
	Iris kaempferi & var.	Japanese water iris
	I. sibirica	
	Juncus spp	rushes
	Lysichitum americanum	skunk lily
	Lysimachia nummularia	creeping jenny
	Peltiphyllum peltatum	umbrella plant
	Rheum palmatum	
	Rodgersia aesculifolia	
	R. podophylla	

Location	Latin Name	Popular Name
3. Marginal Plants	*Acorus calamus*	sweet flag
	A. calamus var.	
	Alisma lanceolatum	water plantain
	A. plantago-aquatica	
	Butomus umbellatus	flowering rush
	Caltha palustris	marsh marigold
	Carex pendula	sedge
	C. pseudo-cyperus	
	C. riparia	
	Cotula coronopifolia	brass buttons
	Cyperus longus	galingale
	Epilobium hirsutum	hairy willow herb
	Galium spp	water bedstraw
	Mentha spp	water mint
	Menyanthes trifoliata	
	Myosotis palustris	water forget-me-not
	Oenanthe crocata	hemlock dropwort
	Orchis spp	marsh orchids
	Parnassia palustris	grass of Parnassus
	Ranunculus lingua	great spearwort
	Scutellaria galericulata	skull cap
	Senecio aquatilis	water ragwort
	Trollius spp	globe flower
4. Reed Swamp	*Phragmites communis*	common reed
	Scirpus lacustris	bulrush
	Typha augustifolia	
	T. latifolia	great reed mace
Sword-like foliage	*Acorus calamus*	sweet flag
	Iris pseudacorus	yellow flag
Arrow-shaped foliage	*Sagittaria sagittifolia*	
Submerged species	*Ceratophyllum demersum*	hornwort
	C. submersum	
	Elodea canadensis	Canadian pond weed
	Myriophyllum verticillatum	water milfoil
Attractive foliage & flowers	*Hottonia palustris*	water violet
	Nasturtium officinale	watercress
	Ranunculus aquatilis	water crowfoot
	Utricularia vulgaris	bladderwort
5. Floating plants	*Aponogeton distachyos*	water hawthorn
	Callitriche spp	starworts
	Glyceria fluitans	flote grass
	Hippuris vulgaris	mare's tail
	Hydrocharis morsus-ranae	frogbit
	Nuphar lutea	yellow water lily
Native to Britain	*Nymphaea alba*	white water lily
	Nymphoides peltatum	fringed water lily
	Polygonum amphibium	floating persicaria
	Potamogeton natans	floating pondweed
	Stratiotes aloides	water soldier

PLATE 6.8 **Early development of a typical hydrasere. Canal at Bath.** *(Robert Adams)*

PLATE 6.9 **Canal abandoned less than a decade ago, and already in the final stages of colonization.** *(Robert Adams)*

forms of plantain lily (*Hosta* spp) associate well with the day lily (*Hemerocallis* varieties), though it is better to avoid the harsher tones of many modern varieties.

Foliage trees and shrubs. Hazel, willow and poplar, water birch (*Betula nigra*) together with dwarf species of willow, sweet pepper (*Clethra alnifolia*), a vastly underrated shrub, and tupelo (*Nyassa sylvatica*) are some of the trees and shrubs which would be found adjacent to water.

b) *Marsh plants*

These require moist soil conditions at all times. The sides of a pool can be stepped to provide pockets of soil at water level, or the banks of a river, stream or lake can be graded or excavated to provide similar conditions. It will be found that the stems and foliage will be more lush and exotic, none more so than the Chilean rhubarb (*Gunnera manicata*) and its visual allies, *Rheum palmatum* which has large toothed, red leaves; the umbrella plant from California (*Peltiphyllum peltatum*) with parasol shaped leaves; *Rodgersia aesculifolia* with its dark green chestnut-like foliage; *Astilboides tabularis* with plate shaped leaves and *R. podophylla* with palmate leaves. The Japanese water iris (*Iris kaempferi* and its varieties) must surely be the star of this particular galaxy, with its clematis-like flowers in delicate shades of white, blue, pink and red. However, it does need a certain amount of cosseting and it is better to use *Iris sibirica*, a more hardy and easily grown species.

Hemp agrimony (*Eupatorium cannabinum*) is a very handsome foliage plant with large heads of composite flowers. One of the most showy marsh plants rejoices in the name of skunk lily (*Lysichitum americanum*) with a typical aroid-like bright yellow flower which appears before the very large and dark green foliage. Creeping jenny (*Lysimachia nummularia*, and the variety *aurea*) is found covering the ground between individual plants, hiding a soil which otherwise appears dank and unappealing.

c) *Marginal plants*

Marginal plants, or those requiring a water depth of up to 500 mm, include many striking foliage plants, mainly reed-like or arrow shaped.

Water musk, or monkey flower (*Mimulus luteus*) is a native of Chile, now naturalized in several English rivers. There have been fewer more beautiful acquisitions by the British countryside than this plant, which usually establishes itself on the banks of streams as they emerge from the hills. Bogbean (*Menyanthes trifoliata*), marsh marigold (*Caltha palustris*) and globe flower (*Trollius* spp) are all worthy companions. Examples may also include hairy willow-herb (*Epilobium hirsutum*), marsh orchids, water mints (*Mentha* spp), hemlock dropwort (*Oenanthe crocata*) (extremely poisonous and similar to water cress in spring), water bedstraws (*Galium* spp),

water ragwort (*Senecio aquatilis*), water forget-me-not (*Myosotis* spp), grass of Parnassus (*Parnassia palustris*), great spearwort (*Ranunculus lingua*) and skull cap (*Scutellaria galericulata*).

d) *Reed swamp*

This zone of vegetation is generally a dense mass of plants with tall erect stems, the intermediate stage between marsh and water vegetation. As with most zones, it has no clear boundary, and one may find marsh plants on the land side and water plants on the other margin. For example the loose outer edge of reed swamp furthest from the pool or lake edge may have water lilies whose floating leaves occupy the spaces between the sparsely occurring shoots of the reeds. The floating leaves are thus protected from wave action. Generally, the plants are very vigorous and one species tends to become dominant, with others occurring locally and erratically.

Its associated plants include the common reed (*Phragmites communis*), which is readily recognized with its tall slender stem, 1·5–2 m high, with a grass-like leaf at each joint and flowers grouped into a plume-like paniche on top of the stem. The flowers are purple-brown at first, becoming silver as the seed ripens.

The great reed mace (*Typha latifolia*) is more commonly called bulrush (properly *Scirpus lacustris*) and requires plenty of room to develop as the rootstocks are very invasive. The reeds can reach a height of 5 m and are very handsome. It is possible, by creating an artifically restricted root run, to grow these majestic plants in fairly small pools. They may need replacing at intervals if the size of canes noticeably decreases.

Sweet flag (*Acorus calamus*) and its variety 'Variegatus', together with the yellow flag provide the sword-like foliage, *Sagittaria sagittifolia* the arrow shapes. This plant clearly exhibits the tendency of several of those plants growing partly submerged, to have more than one shape of leaf on the same plant. The aerial leaves are shaped like an arrow head, the floating leaves are lanceolate and those submerged are linear. The flowering rush is also an inhabitant of this area.

Submerged plants are of vital importance to the health and well-being of water. They generally have finely divided foliage below the surface: those species which grow above the water as well have a combination of dissected and entire leaves. Milfoil (*Myriophyllum verticillatum*) and hornwort (*Ceratophyllum demersum* and *submersum*) together with Canadian pond weed (*Elodea canadensis*) rarely appear above water, and consequently have little to contribute visually. The water violet (*Hottonia palustris*), water crowfoot (*Ranunculus aquatilis*), watercress (*Nasturtium officinale*) and bladderwort (*Utricularia vulgaris*) all possess very attractive foliage and flowers, and are all perfectly hardy plants native to Britain.

PLATE 6.10 **Marginal planting at a lakeside swimming lido, Zurich.** *(Ian Laurie)*

e) *Floating plants*

Floating plants obtain all their food by photosynthesis and have roots in the bottom of the pool or lake. They may be said to be the aristocrats of water plants, with their combination of handsome foliage and flowers. Native to Britain are the white water lily (*Nymphaea alba*) the fringed water lily (*Nymphoides peltatum*)—distinguished from the true Nymphaea by the frilled edges to its leaves and five fringed yellow petalled flowers—and the yellow water lily or brandy bottle (*Nuphar lutea*), the flowers of which have a strong alcoholic smell. There are many hybrids suitable for different depths or areas of water, ranging in colour from white to yellow, pink, red and blue, and many are scented. Discretion should be exercised concerning the setting and location of plants with the more strident colours.

There are other beautiful deep water aquatics. Floating pondweed (*Potamogeton natans*) has elliptic, leathery leaves 75 mm long, and differs from other aquatics in that the veins are parallel and not netted. Frogbit (*Hydrocharis morsus-ranae*) produces strawberry-like runners with heart-shaped leaves in tufts at the ends of them. The flowers are three petalled, white and very attractive. Water hawthorn (*Aponogeton distachyus*) is one of the most sweetly scented of plants and is thought to smell like vanilla; the common name refers to the shape of the flowers. Floating persicaria (*Polygonum amphibium*), flote grass (*Glyceria fluitans*), starworts (*Callitriche* spp) and mare's tail (*Hippuris vulgaris*) may also be present.

6.31 Controlling the cycle

If the designer wishes to maintain a certain effect, he must somehow contrive to halt the natural progression otherwise the next stage of the hydrasere will eventually be reached. This may be achieved by re-starting the cycle, or maintaining the *status quo* by sympathetic after management. A positive policy will be needed, with allowance made for adequate funds to implement the after care. It is important to realize how quickly one group of plants may develop at the expense of others.

92

This is particularly the case with newly created water areas. During early stages of ecological succession there may be great invasions of colonizing species. The balance between species may fluctuate wildly, especially if there is a source of aquatic plants nearby. The chosen planting may be overrun, and then the permanent planting may have to be re-established at a later date when the ecosystem has achieved some kind of balance.

The degree and rapidity of change and succession will be dependent on a number of factors:
i) the presence or absence of running water;
ii) the depth of water;
iii) the quality of water;
iv) the lack of toxicity;
v) the degree of alkalinity or acidity;
vi) the presence or absence of silt or decayed vegetation on the bottom;
vii) light penetration and variations in temperature.
All factors must be carefully analysed, and planting proposals based on the result of that analysis. Too often plant types alien to the location are chosen in preference to those particularly suitable, on the grounds that they do not meet the designer's aesthetic or visual requirements.

The introduction of alien species can upset the delicate ecological balance between naturally associating plants. The dividing line between survival and extinction is a fine one. Recent examples of such introductions are Canadian pond weed, planted in British waterways in 1847 and rapidly reaching pest status. Subsequent research has shown that after a period of several years' intense activity, it declines. But this is of little solace to the owner of a new pond or lake which is becoming rapidly choked. The most up-to-date introduction is that of tape grass (*Vallisneria spiralis*), normally a plant for the tropical aquarist. It can be found in canals, particularly near warm water outfalls from factories, but it is thought unlikely that it will ever become thoroughly naturalized. Both of these examples pale to insignificance when compared to the notorious water hyacinth (*Eichhornia crassipes*) from tropical America. When ten plants were introduced to the St. Johns River in Florida they increased to half a million in eight months and seriously hampered navigation: similarly, plants introduced into gardens have escaped their confines and found the new habitat very much to their liking. The Indian balsam (*Impatiens glandulifera*), a native of the Western Himalayas, is a fairly recent

PLATE 6.11 **A modern example of water planting at York University.** *(Allan Hart)*

PLATE 6.12 **Typical example of a lake bed requiring dredging. Note swollen underwater trunk of** *Pterocarya*. **Kew Lake.** *(Robert Adams)*

PLATE 6.13 **Dredging almost complete; clay base of lake exposed.** *(Robert Adams)*

addition to the British flora and has made rapid progress, spreading along water courses throughout the country. It is a very beautiful aromatic plant which extends its territory by the simple expedient of exploding its seed capsules and projecting the seeds a distance of several metres. The touch-me-not plant (*Impatiens noli-tangere*), a yellow flowered, smaller version, does not appear to be quite so invasive.

6.32 Planting and maintenance

The supply of many garden and exotic species poses few problems as water gardening is at present showing an upsurge in popularity to which the trade is responding. But for those concerned with the establishment of indigenous species for large-scale planting of lakes and rivers, the situation is quite different. As with the production of hardy nursery stock, the range of plants being grown is becoming smaller with each passing year, and many native aquatics are no longer commercially available. Alternative sources of supply could be explored—local authorities and water undertakings may be sympathetic to a competent person taking samples of plants for re-establishment elsewhere; similarly, local field centres and the Nature Conservancy may be able to help, particularly if the new schemes and planting have a sound ecological and educational basis. (These two organizations are useful contacts, as they may be able to help with suggestions of plants in which they have a special interest and which they would like to see given a wider distribution. In certain cases they may suggest that a research student be appointed to collect and plant the vegetation and if possible to monitor the project over a period of time. Where such arrangements are made, they would have to be included within any contract specification for new works.)

Planting times are fairly critical for many of the heavily rooted species such as nuphars and pontaderias, and planting is usually carried out as they are emerging from their dormant period from mid-April to mid-May, with temperatures around 20–25°C. From May to June is the period of most active growth which is necessary for new planting to become established before winter. The lesser aquatics, submerged oxygenators and marginal plants can be planted at almost any time during the growing season.

The new growth of established water lilies is such that the new leaves do not unfold until they reach the surface. Plants may be purchased pot-grown, with young leaves just above the surface of the container. It would be a tremendous shock to the plant's system if it were to be placed at its ultimate depth. It is therefore necessary either to lower it gradually into the water as the stems develop, or to raise the level of the water in stages to correspond with the stem growth until the correct depth is reached. If the tubers are dormant it is usually sufficient to tie them to a heavy weight and drop them into position in the mud.

This is the normal method of planting submerged aquatics. Cultural requirements are simple—heavy loam (free from organic matter to avoid decomposition and therefore pollution of the water) in open mesh containers of basketwork or plastic. For ease of operations, marginal planting may be carried out in prepared dry soil which is then allowed to become saturated.

The maintenance of water plants is relatively simple—smaller ponds may need emptying annually, while larger pools may need the removal of competing vegetation. It may be necessary to resort to dredging if the water area becomes badly silted. This can be a complicated and expensive operation.

There is a purely natural occurrence which causes concern, and that is the discoloration of the water. This is caused by algae, tiny unicellular plants which thrive on the soluble salts found in new water, or soil and mud disturbed during construction or dredging operations. In severe cases this can result in low dissolved oxygen concentrations which increases the danger of fish mortality. The introduction of daphnia (water fleas) quickly brings about a reduction in their numbers. The growth of oxygenating and floating plants helps to exclude light from the water and in turn this prevents further growth. Similarly, blanket or flannel weed, which is a filamentous plant, is best removed periodically by hand until the main planting covers the water's surface.

Certain plants may grow at the expense of others, and may be removed by hand cutting in late June or early July, or by chemical means. The Toxic Chemicals and Wildlife Division of the Nature Conservancy are currently investigating new methods of controlling aquatic vegetation. The following is a list of chemicals with low toxicity:

Chemical	Quantity	Controls
Simazine	3–6 parts per million	Duckweed
Monuron	4–12 parts per million	Underwater vegetation
Sodium arsenate	10 parts per million	Underwater vegetation
Dalapon	1 kg/litre of water sprayed onto foliage	Rushes, reed-mace, bur-weeds etc.

In newly established areas the more vigorous species such as reed sweet mace (*Glyceria maxima*) may invade cleared waters, and to reduce this an attempt should be made to diversify the glyceria swamps by using selective systemic insecticides. The resulting dead foliage is formed into mounds on which nettles, willow herb and other colonizers may establish. This technique was originated by RSPB at the Rye House Marsh Reserve in Hertfordshire. The floral diversification attracts birds and provides nesting sites.

The extent of winter maintenance will depend on the situation and use. Water plants can look very depressing after the first frosts have blackened and destroyed their lush features, and consequently they are better cut down in an urban setting. This will also remove the overwintering habitat of water-lily beetles and other pests. The natural breakdown of plants under water releases toxic gases which can prove fatal to fish or at best lower their resistance to disease. This normally applies to small ponds and is not usually a problem with larger areas. It may not be visually desirable to remove vegetation, for reed stems piercing the water can give an extra dimension to a water surface in winter. Plants such as water plantains (*Alisma*), irises and reed maces (*Typha*) which seed readily should have the seeds removed. Certain of the semi-hardy marginal plants, such as Brazilean rhubarb, need protecting with straw or bracken against frost.

6.4 CONCLUSION

The use of water plants in landscape design can be most rewarding. They establish themselves quickly and can produce a mature effect within the first year of planting. A practical contribution to the conservation of native species can be made and justified, as many of these are aristocrats of the plant world and worthy of a place in any planting scheme.

It can be an intellectual exercise in management techniques in determining the best means of maintaining the desired effect. It may be that the natural expression of succession should be allowed, to achieve a balance between the different plant types; or perhaps the development should be arrested at a particular stage, to freeze the composition. It will only be possible to achieve the right effects by a full understanding of the plants' physical characteristics and cultural requirements. There is good documentation on the needs of most ornamental species, but for many of the native water plants, personal observation and research will be needed, which is the best way to know and understand any group of plants.

FURTHER READING

Chaplin, M. *Riverside Gardening* (Feltham: W. H. and L. Collingridge Ltd., 1964)

Cook, C. D. K. *Water Plants of the World* (The Hague: Junk, 1974)

Crowe, S. *Garden Design* (London: Country Life Ltd., 3rd impression 1965)

Machin, T. T. and Worthington, E. B. *Life in Lakes and Rivers* (London: Collins, 1951)

Peters and Roemer, *Garden Pools for Pleasure* (London: Abelard Schuman, 1972)

Turrill, W. B. *British Plant Life* (London: Collins, 3rd edition 1962)

REFERENCES

1. Robinson, W. *The Wild Garden* (London: John Murray, 1894)
2. Jekyll, G. *Wall and Water Garden* (London: Country Life Ltd.)
3. Sitwell, Sir George *On the Making of Gardens* (London: Gerald Duckworth Ltd., 1951)

CHAPTER 7

The Use of Native Plants in Urban Areas

DICK HOYLE AND ALLAN RUFF

This chapter is divided into two separate parts designed to provide both a general background to the subject and specific examples of the practical use of native plants. Part A deals with the use of native plants in general, and outlines the possible different approaches to their use in landscape design. Some aspects of maintenance and availability are discussed.

Part B assesses the much more advanced practical work in Holland, following an ecological approach to the use of native plants in landscape design. Examples of Dutch schemes are described, and followed by a general discussion of relevant ecological principles necessary for an understanding of methods used in Holland. Techniques of management and maintenance are discussed at the end of the chapter.

PART A

Native Plants in Landscape Design

DICK HOYLE

7.1 INTRODUCTION

Part A discusses the use of native plants in landscape work, *native* being defined as 'not known to have been introduced by human agency'. *Naturalized* species are those which have been introduced by man and have established themselves in the wild. These may include garden escapes or remnants of earlier cultivation. To avoid confusion only truly native species have been considered here.

Although actual examples of plants given are species native to Britain, the principles have a universal application. It is necessary to evaluate each country's native flora, not only in terms of the individual qualities of each plant, but also in the wider concept of their use in landscape work.

In all there are about 1,800 British native species, out of which at least 500 can be considered suitable for the various requirements of the landscape architect. A precise guide to whether a plant is indigenous to a locality can be

Morwell Quay Woods, Cornwall. *(John Chitty)*

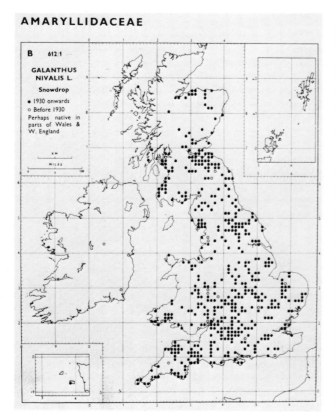

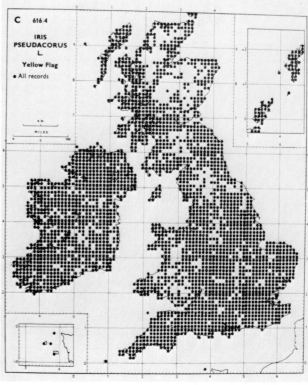

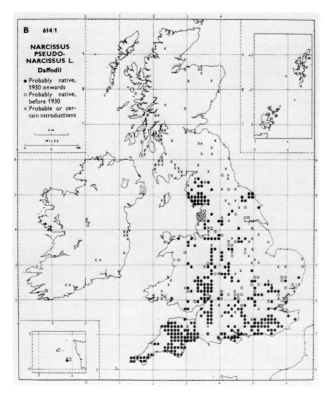

FIGURES 7.1, 7.2 & 7.3 **An example of the charts used in the** *Atlas of the British Flora.* *(Courtesy of the Botanical Society of the British Isles)*

found in the *Atlas of the British Flora.*[1] The charts, examples of which are given in Figures 7.1, 7.2 and 7.3 can be used by the landscape architect to assess the suitability of individual plants for a particular locality. Introduction of species not native to the locality can be unwise for a variety of reasons, but if this is attempted, prior consultation must be made with either the Botanical Society of the British Isles (c/o The Royal Botanic Gardens, Kew, Richmond, Surrey) or Biological Records Centre (Institute of Terrestrial Ecology, Monks Wood Experimental Station, Abbots Ripon, Huntingdon, Cambridgeshire).

7.2 HISTORICAL PERSPECTIVE

Traditionally wild plants were valued for their medicinal properties, and were closely linked with folklore. Nowadays, with increasing urbanization, the spread of towns and mechanized agriculture, native plants tend to be found in remote or inaccessible places, surviving in urban areas on wasteland, such as railway embankments, hedgerow verges and alongside canals.

The influx of exotic plants started by the early plant collectors fostered an interest in the science of plant breeding and non-native species became more popular amongst plantsmen and gardeners than our own native species. The balance was to some extent redressed by the English landscape traditions developed in the eighteenth century by 'Capability' Brown and Repton who discarded ornate formal designs in favour of simple, natural forms. Their ideas were further reinforced by the Victorian romantic movement when Gertrude Jekyll and William Robinson reacted against the ornate planting practised in their day:

PLATE 7.1 **The simple beauty of the tiny native daffodil,** *Narcissus pseudonarcissus.* *(Dick Hoyle)*

'... planting was made up of a few kinds of flowers which people were proud to put out in thousands and tens of thousands. It was not easy to get away from this false and hideous "art".... I began to get an idea (which should be taught to every boy at school) that there was (for gardens even) much beauty in our native flowers and trees ...'[2]

7.3 THE PRESENT USE OF NATIVE SPECIES

There have been significant examples of the successful use of native species in the Americas, Australia and in Europe, particularly in West Germany, Denmark and the Netherlands. The Dutch examples are further discussed in Part B.

The work of Burle Marx, the Brazilian landscape-garden artist, exemplifies a dynamic modern approach using natural materials employing the colours, textures and shapes of native tropical plants in very crisp, controlled designs closely related to man-made structures and features.

While many native plants, particularly trees and shrubs, are used with non-native plants in landscape design in Britain, little research has been carried out in this country concerning the more extensive use of a wider range of herbaceous native species. The remainder of Part A aims to show how these native plants can be used by landscape architects.

7.4 THE VALUE OF NATIVE PLANTS

Many native species are very much underrated as design material. As William Robinson wrote:

'... among them are included things of a high order of beauty that will flourish and keep their own ground without any watching or special preparation of the soil: and even for the sake of selecting plants wherewith to embellish the margins of lakes, rivers, ponds or beds of fountains in our parks, pleasure grounds or gardens, the subject is worthy attention.'[3]

The wide range of native species—from annuals, biennials and perennials to subshrubs, shrubs and trees, enables the landscape architect to find reliable plants for almost any urban situation or problem site. Many are

101

PLATE 7.2 **The Kennedylaan, Herrenveen, in Friesland, Holland: planting in the central reservation along a dual carriageway. Illustrated is recent planting with rubble and timber bark still visible.** (Landscape Architect: *LeRoy* Photograph: *Robert Holden*)

PLATE 7.3 **A butterfly attracted by** *Centaurea scabiosa* **or greater knapweed.** *(Dick Hoyle)*

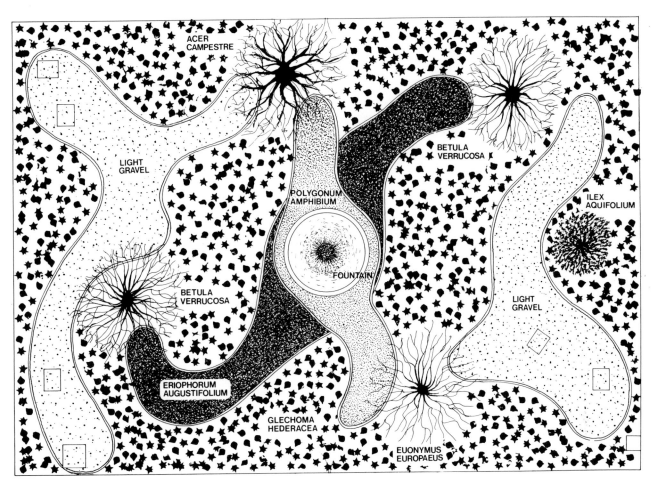

FIGURE 7.4 **A design for a small overlooked and partly shaded courtyard, requiring no topsoil and minimum maintenance, using a simple palette of aquatic native species in bold concrete pools around a fountain.** *(Dick Hoyle)*

suitable for landscape work, from small scale to large scale, from the single specimen to species suitable for hydroseeding and reclamation projects.

Native species can be relied upon for their hardiness and successful establishment if indigenous to the area, soil and conditions provided. They can be used in landscape schemes to provide local character, often lacking in urban developments.

In situations where no topsoil is available native species are at their most valuable. In fact topsoil is undesirable for many native species. Poor soil conditions prevent excessive growth and maintenance problems, and the plants tend to be longer lived in poor soil than in rich soil. A growing medium of crushed brick rubble, slag, shale or subsoil can provide optimum growing conditions for particular species. Some native plants are particularly tolerant of limestone soils with a high pH and can successfully be used as an alternative to grass in a mix specially prepared for low groundcover (*see* Table 7.1).

Conservation of our native flora and associated wildlife is becoming increasingly important. An ecologically

TABLE 7.1

Limestone species suitable for quarry waste, crushed brick rubble, slag, shale, or subsoil, all of high pH

Campanula rotundifolia	harebell
Centaurea scabiosa	greater knapweed
Dipsacus sylvestris	wild teasel
Leucanthemum vulgare	ox-eye daisy
Linaria vulgaris	common toadflax
Origanum vulgare	marjoram
Primula veris	cowslip

Suggested native species for inclusion in a low groundcover mix:

Achillea millefolium	yarrow
Bellis perennis	daisy
Lotus corniculatus	common birdsfoot trefoil
Plantago media	hoary plantain
Sedum acre	wall-pepper
Trifolium repens	white clover

103

PLATE 7.4 **The distinctive heads of** *Dipsacus sylvestris,* **the wild teasel, shown to effect against a dark background.** *(M. Nimmo)*

PLATE 7.5 **The juvenile form of** *Euphorbia lathyrus,* **or caper spurge, a very architecturally shaped biennial with fine pointed leaves.** *(Dick Hoyle)*

PLATE 7.6 **Large hairy leaves of** *Verbascum thapsus* **or mullein, before flowering. Note fifty pence piece to give an idea of scale.** *(Dick Hoyle)*

sound network of native planting infiltrating urban areas would link up rural habitats and encourage wildlife in our towns and cities (*see* Part B and Chapter 8).

Short-term demolition sites or land awaiting development can be usefully and attractively covered with annuals or biennials, including attractive corn weeds which are becoming increasingly rare and which thrive on disturbed ground. Associated populations of butterflies and other fauna may be boosted in this way. Examples of annuals or biennials suitable for such short-life sites are listed below:

Digitalis purpurea	foxglove (poisonous)
Dipsacus sylvestris	wild teasel (*see* Plate 7.4)
Echium vulgare	viper's bugloss
Euphorbia lathyrus	caper spurge (poisonous) (*see* Plate 7.5)
Papaver dubium	poppy (commonest in north)
Papaver rhoeas	corn poppy (commonest in south)
Verbascum thapsus	mullein (*see* Plate 7.6)

PLATE 7.7 **Educational aspects of native planting in urban areas. Herrenveen, Holland.** (Landscape Architect: *LeRoy*. Photograph: *Allan Ruff*)

PLATE 7.8 **The peat bog section of the** *bedreigde flora* **(flora under threat) garden at the Amsterdam Floriade, June 1972.** *(Robert Holden)*

PLATE 7.9 **The Kennedylaan, Herrenveen as in Plate 7.2, showing the state of planting after three or four seasons, as an example of LeRoy's work. One problem at the Kennedylaan has been that weeding by council gardeners has taken place which gives a 'tidier' effect than was intended, and self-sown plants have been removed.** *(Robert Holden)*

It is difficult to impute particular psychological advantages to the use of native plants in preference to other kinds of plants without the backing of actual examples to substantiate them, although work in Holland seems to be producing interesting results in this respect (*see* Part B).

The advantages to young children are often cited, in that native planting can provide an environment in urban residential areas similar to that found in natural woodlands and open fields, where there is considerable freedom to climb trees, pick flowers and so forth, often lacking in traditional landscape schemes.

Indigenous plants faithfully reflect the passing of the seasons, whereas exotic species may be introduced specifically for their non-seasonal characteristics. It may be that the familiar and enduring presence of native plants in a rapidly changing world can help to provide the reassurance that stems from a feeling of continuity with the past.

7.5 DESIGN APPROACHES

There appear to be three main design approaches:

i) *Ecological*—In this case the exact or simplified composition of a natural ecosystem is reconstructed, for example in the formation of woodland the introduction of native species of trees, shrubs and herbs is carefully carried out when conditions are right over a period of time. Pioneer, principal, filler

TABLE 7.2
Native plants for groundcover and foliage

1. Groundcover plants	
Allium ursinum	ramsons (Plate 7.10)
Anthemis nobilis	chamomile
Asarum europaeum	asarabacca
Athyrium filix-femina	lady-fern
Galeobdolon luteum	yellow archangel
Glechoma hederacea	ground ivy (Plate 7.11)
Hypericum androsaemum	tutsan
Lysimachia nummularia	creeping jenny
Petasites hybridus	butterbur
Polypodium vulgare	polypody
Polystichum aculeatum	hard shield-fern

2. Foliage plants	
Carex pendula	pendulous sedge
Crambe maritima	sea-kale
Cyperus longus	galingale
Dryopteris filix-mas	male fern (Plate 7.12)
Elymus arenarius	lyme-grass
Eryngium maritimum	sea holly
Foeniculum vulgare	fennel
Helleborus foetidus	stinking hellebore (evergreen) (Plate 7.13)
Iris foetidissima	gladdon, roast beef plant (Plate 7.14)
Osmunda regalis	royal fern
Salix lanata	woolly willow
Verbascum thapsus	mullein

PLATE 7.10 **Shiny leaves of** *Allium ursinum* **or ramsons for a close textured pattern in damp shady situations.** *(Dick Hoyle)*

PLATE 7.11 **Rounded leaves of** *Glechoma hederacea* **or ground ivy form a successful groundcover.** *(Dick Hoyle)*

PLATE 7.12 **Detail of** *Dryopteris filix-mas,* **the male fern.** *(Pam Hoyle)*

and edge species are used to establish the woodland and provide diversity (*see* Part B). Plants and habitats can be used to form 'wild' areas such as that in the *bedreigde flora* (flora under threat) garden at the 1972 Floriade in Amsterdam (*see* Plate 7.8). Polder planting begun in 1971 in the Lanwerszee by the Rijksdienst voor het Ijsselmeer uses native species for forestry, nature reserves, recreation and military practice areas, planted and maintained according to ecological principles.

ii) *Laissez-faire*—An example of this approach is to be found in the work of Le Roy, an artist gardener in Holland. He plants a mixture of native and exotic species, varied in relation to the growing medium which can be brick rubble or a soil and timber bark mix. The plants are allowed to develop with minimum maintenance.[4]

iii) *Selective*—In this case plants are selected from the palette of native material and are used in a more conventional way, together with non-native species. This has been the method generally adopted in

Britain. Some of the plants which can be used in this way are listed in Table 7.2.

7.6 MAINTENANCE AND MANAGEMENT

The consideration of maintenance is of paramount importance whatever method of design is adopted. The plants as design material have to be fully understood—their requirements, potentials, weak points, seasonal fluctuations and maintenance requirements.

Generally the use of native species in urban areas requires a change in attitude from normal horticultural practice and a sound ecological understanding of the site and locality (*see* Part B). Table 7.3 summarizes native species suitable for particular sites and maintenance considerations.

Most indigenous trees and shrubs are readily available in Britain. They are easily propagated and so may be grown by parks and landscape departments to meet their particular demands. Herbaceous plants for detail areas

107

TABLE 7.3
The use of native species in urban areas

Situation	Soil	Range of plants and suggested treatments	Maintenance considerations

Temporary derelict areas, sites after demolition	Crushed brick rubble usually high pH due to lime mortar	Leguminous species:
		  Trifolium arvense
		    hare's-foot clover
		  Trifolium repens
		    white clover
		Drought resistant species and pioneers:
		  Achillea millefolium
		    yarrow
		  Medicago lupulina
		    black medick
		  Papaver rhoeas
		    corn poppy
		  Plantago lanceolata
		    ribwort
		Limestone species:
		  Linaria vulgaris
		    common toadflax
		  Verbascum thapsus
		    mullein
		Direct sowing into crushed rubble, ensuring there is enough 'tilth' for establishment.
			Dependent on life of planting, from no maintenance to autumn clearing and if necessary disturbance of a percentage of the surface to ensure the germination of annuals and biennials the following year.

Derelict land	Various:
	Shale
	Rubble
	Slag
	Subsoil
		Thorough analysis of species already tolerating the conditions on site will indicate suitable species. Examples are given below.
		Limestone species:
		  Linaria vulgaris
		    common toadflax
		  Sedum acre
		    wall-pepper
		  Trifolium arvense
		    hare's-foot clover
		  Verbascum thapsus
		    mullein
		Drought resistant species:
		  Achillea millefolium
		    yarrow
		  Medicago lupulina
		    black medick
		  Plantago lanceolata
		    ribwort
		  Tussilago farfara
		    coltsfoot
		Leguminous species:
		  Cytisus scoparius
		    broom
		  Lotus corniculatus
		    birdsfoot-trefoil
			Various, depending on use and effect required, but grass cutting as such can be reduced with areas of low growing herbs.
			Forestry planting will also build up soil layer and at later stages underplanting or sowing with suitable woodland species can be introduced as the woodland develops.
			
			As a long term plan, leguminous species will help to increase the soil fertility. However, this is not always desirable and may lead to increased maintenance problems.

Situation	Soil	Range of plants and suggested treatments	Maintenance considerations

		Trifolium repens
		    white clover
		Ulex europaeus
		    gorse
		Vicia cracca
		    tufted vetch
		Many of the herbaceous and shrub species are suitable for hydroseeding.	

Embankments—railway, industrial, road and motorway	Subsoil	Low maintenance groundcovers:
		    Plantago lanceolata
		        ribwort
		    Trifolium repens
		        white clover
		or a low rate of fescues to provide initial cover but allowing local native species to colonize. In poor soil conditions the above plants may be used under trees and shrubs where root competition is not likely to be a problem. Vigorous agricultural strains should be avoided. Other stabilizing groundcovers are given below:
		    Achillea millefolium
		        yarrow
		    Calluna vulgaris
		        heather or ling
		    Cytisus scoparius
		        broom
		    Elymus arenarius
		        lyme-grass
		    Lotus corniculatus
		        birdsfoot-trefoil
		    Origanum vulgare
		        marjoram
		    Pteridium aquilinum
		        bracken
		    Ulex europaeus
		        gorse
			Can be minimum depending on effect required. Coarse weeds must be eradicated initially.
			
			Cutting of heather and gorse may be required to prevent them becoming leggy and control invading tree species

		Wildflower mixes for interest may contain the following:
		Perennials:
		    Centaurea scabiosa
		        great knapweed
		    Filipendula ulmaria
		        meadow-sweet
		Biennials:
		    Digitalis purpurea
		        foxglove
		    Verbascum thapsus
		        mullein
			Selected cuts 1, 2 or 3 times a year must be carefully worked out for the species used. Specialized cutting and removal of cuttings can be an expensive operation. Farmers may be encouraged to cut for hay if species suitable. Annuals and biennials should be encouraged to reseed themselves by disturbance of a percentage of the soil surface. Annuals and biennials are ideal over services that

Situation	Soil	Range of plants and suggested treatments	Maintenance considerations
		Annuals: *Centaurea cyanus* cornflower *Papaver rhoeas* corn poppy	are likely to be excavated and where tree and shrubs species would be a problem.
Housing areas Public open space Industrial areas Educational grounds Hospitals Parks	Subsoil and topsoil	The use of local species giving local character. Groundcovers: *Galeobdolon luteum* yellow archangel *Glechoma hederacea* ground ivy *Hypericum androsaemum* tutsan *Trifolium repens* white clover Foliage plants: *Foeniculum vulgare* fennel *Helleborus foetidus* stinking hellebore *Iris foetidissima* gladdon *Verbascum thapsus* mullein Ferns: *Dryopteris filix-mas* male fern *Phyllitis scolopendrium* harts'-tongue fern *Polypodium vulgare* common polypody *Polystichum aculeatum* hard shield-fern Shade plants for damper situations: *Allium ursinum* ramsons *Luzula sylvatica* greater woodrush *Lysimachia nummularia* creeping jenny *Trollius europaeus* globe flower Aromatic plants: *Anthemis nobilis* chamomile *Cyperus longus* galingale *Foeniculum vulgare* fennel *Origanum vulgare* marjoram	Maintenance requirements dependent on effect required and use. Generally maintenance increases with proximity to buildings. White clover works well on banks, e.g. as at Runcorn New Town provided coarse weeds are eliminated. Some areas may be left to establish naturally apart from clearing litter etc., but other areas will require careful maintenance to achieve the desired effect. Maintenance of areas designed for wildlife should be minimum to prevent unnecessary disturbance and at correct time of year, consistent with good wildlife management. Burning or the use of chemicals should be avoided if possible.

Situation	Soil	Range of plants and suggested treatment	Maintenance considerations
		Scented flowering plants: *Convallaria majalis* lily-of-the-valley *Filipendula ulmaria* meadow-sweet *Lonicera periclymenum* honeysuckle *Rosa pimpinellifolia* burnet rose The use of perennials, shrubs and trees together to form balanced woodlands. Hedgerow habitats on boundaries. Marsh habitats instead of land drainage. Stimulating 'natural' and designed features using native species. Aromatic areas: blind gardens. Wildflower pastures. Nature trails: planting for wildlife butterflies. Provision of biological material for schools and colleges.	

PLATE 7.13 *Helleborus foetidus* **or stinking hellebore with its distinctive winter flowers.** *(Dick Hoyle)*

on a relatively small scale, such as a garden or small park, are usually available from nurseries but larger quantities require contract growing. This often necessitates only one year's notice, in the case of herbaceous perennials or biennials, and can be easily arranged by the main contractor during earthmoving or building operations.

In a large scheme, it is often desirable to grow the plant material specially, possibly using as stocks plants or seed gathered from the site before earthmoving or building operations begin. Often phasing of the work in different parts of a site or locality will allow plants to be used from one area to plant up an area just completed. Voluntary conservation organizations may be able to carry out this work, or perhaps a trusted landscape contractor or direct works department.

It can be cheaper as well as more desirable and reliable to use plants dug up from nearby threatened or specially allocated 'reservoir' areas by the planting contractor. Other less well tried techniques for the establishment of native species include transferring pieces of turf to encourage the spread of the local flora and the use of a selected haycrop, seeded or hydroseeded on to the area. Care has to be taken to ensure that it is possible to provide the maintenance necessary for those species required and for the elimination of others that are not needed.

The vegetation layer scraped off an interesting area by machine and, if necessary, stored as topsoil for a year, should contain enough seed and roots to establish certain

PLATE 7.14 *Iris foetidissima* **or gladdon showing its graceful tapering foliage and orange-red seeds.** *(Dick Hoyle)*

PLATE 7.15 *Tussilago farfara*, **the coltsfoot, showing the form of the golden flowers.** *(M. Nimmo)*

PLATE 7.16 *Ammophila arenaria*, **marram grass. An important stabilizing plant for sand dunes.** *(Dick Hoyle)*

PLATE 7.17 *Veronica filiformis* **may be included in a grass mix to give a brilliant blue haze before the first cut at the end of April.** *(Dick Hoyle)*

PLATE 7.18 *Galanthus nivalis*, **the snowdrop; a close-up showing the delicate drooping flower heads.** *(Dick Hoyle)*

of the flora providing the created ground conditions are similar. Careful maintenance will be required initially as pioneer weeds will invade.

If attractive and suitable plants are locally abundant, new areas can be left to vegetate naturally if the results are predictable but this should only be done in poor growing media, eg, weathered steel slag will produce a flora where limestone species predominate, such as *Sedum acre* (wallpepper) and *Linaria vulgaris* (common toadflax).

The seed trade is working towards producing more commercial quantities of native species. Unfortunately, for reasons of economy, most of the material has to be imported, which may create problems. The 'foreign' stock may mix and spread and may include more vigorous cultivars which are undesirable from the maintenance point of view. Mixes should be specially prepared for each habitat from locally collected seed, containing only the

plants required. Commercial 'wildflower' mixes should be avoided. One firm in Britain is able to collect seed from their native habitats although for research purposes only. However a good landscape department should be able to collect their own supplies for their area. Direct works departments carry this out in Holland.

7.7 PLANT SELECTION

Table 7.4 lists a range of native plants for possible use in landscape work, their availability, habitats, use and particular features. It is not intended to replace a detailed knowledge of the plants but rather to indicate a few suitable for further study. Table 7.5 is a design checklist, from the survey stage through to the maintenance stage, summarizing for easy reference the main steps to be considered when using native species.

114

TABLE 7.4
A selected list of native plants

Latin name	English name	Availability		Habitats								Use				Interest				Comments
		Plants	Seed	Bare ground	Maritime habitats	Freshwater margins	Marsh	Grassland	Heath, moor, mountain	Scrub	Woodland	Groundcover	Shade	Derelict land	Wildlife	Aromatic/scented	Fruit	Flower	Foliage	
Achillea millefolium	yarrow	×	×	×				×				×		×		×		×	×	
Campanula latifolia	giant bellflower	×	×								×							×		
Crambe maritima	sea-kale	×	×		×							×		×				×	×	
Cyperus longus	galingale	×				×	×									×			×	
Digitalis purpurea	foxglove	×	×	×					×	×	×	×	×					×	×	Poisonous
Elymus arenarius	sea lyme-grass	×			×							×					×	×	×	
Eryngium maritimum	sea holly		×		×										×			×	×	
Filipendula ulmaria	meadow-sweet	×	×			×	×	×			×		×			×		×		
Foeniculum vulgare	fennel	×	×	×	×			×				×	×	×	×	×	×		×	
Galeobdolon luteum	yellow archangel	×									×	×	×					×	×	
Galium odoratum *(Asperula odorata)*	sweet woodruff	×	×								×	×	×					×	×	
Glaucium flavum	yellow horned-poppy	×	×	×	×							×		×			×	×	×	
Glechoma hederacea	ground ivy	×		×							×	×	×			×		×	×	
Helleborus foetidus	stinking hellebore	×	×							×	×	×				!		×	×	Poisonous
Hippuris vulgaris	mare's-tail	×				×									×				×	
Humulus lupulus	hop	×	×							×	×	×				×	×	×	×	Climber
Hypericum androsaemum	tutsan	×	×		×						×	×				×	×	×	×	
Iris foetidissima	gladdon, roast-beef plant	×			×					×	×	×	×			×	×	×	×	Poisonous
Lotus corniculatus	common birdsfoot-trefoil		×	×	×			×				×		×	×			×	×	
Luzula sylvatica	greater woodrush	×							×		×	×	×					×	×	
Lysimachia nummularia	creeping jenny	×				×	×	×			×	×	×					×	×	
Narcissus pseudonarcissus	wild daffodil	×						×			×	×						×		
Origanum vulgare	marjoram	×	×					×		×					×	×		×	×	
Osmunda regalis	royal fern	×				×	×				×	×							×	
Pteridium aquilinum	bracken	×							×	×	×	×	×	×					×	
Salix lanata	woolly willow	×							×			×			×			×	×	
Salix repens	creeping willow	×			×		×		×			×			×			×	×	
Trifolium repens	white clover		×					×				×		×	×			×	×	
Trollius europaeus	globe flower	×	×				×	×	×			×	×					×	×	
Verbascum thapsus	mullein	×	×					×				×						×	×	Biennial
Viola odorata	sweet violet	×	×					×			×	×	×		×	×		×	×	

TABLE 7.5
Design check list

Site Survey	Site Analysis	Design Stage	Contract Stage	Completion & Maintenance
Thorough analysis of native species present and their relationship with soil, slope, moisture and use.	Explore the possibility of retaining areas with established and interesting vegetation cover.	Consider the use of native species as part of the design concept for the site. Consider also the saving on topsoil, fertilizers, reduced maintenance and the avoidance of a sterile landscape. Consider supply & contract growing of species in phasing programme.	Protection of habitats and species including herb layers in woodland areas. Use of material for contract growing taken from site before operations begin. Salvage of plants for other jobs if not required, or turf pieces or hay cut techniques possibly from within site boundary.	Correct maintenance for the establishment and perpetuation of the design involving ecological principles, specially trained staff and new techniques.

PART B

Holland and the Development of an Alternative Landscape

ALLAN RUFF

In the post-1945 period there were sweeping changes in Holland, brought about largely by a change from a rural economy to a modern technological society; in the process many former values were lost and others threatened. Central to this was the extensive migration from the countryside into the urban centres, which paralleled events in Britain 150 years earlier. It made necessary the building of extensive suburbs around each of the towns and cities of the Randstad of Western Holland—Amsterdam, the Hague, Leiden, Utrecht, Delft, Haarlem, etc. This caused an increasing alienation of people from nature and further destruction of the countryside; in its place came the *ersatz* nature of the urban landscape, so familiar throughout Western Europe.

7.8 EARLY BEGINNINGS

By the middle 1960s public opinion, swayed by an open debate in press, radio and TV, was moving towards

accepting a semi-natural framework for urban living, and from this time onwards parks directors in the Randstad towns started to experiment with a radically new landscape form. Of these developments, two played perhaps the most significant part in what has followed: the biophysical approach by Amsterdam at the suburb of Bijlmermeer, and a sociological approach at Delft Zuid.

7.81 Amsterdam—Bijlmermeer

The Bijlmermeer is situated on the flat polders to the south-east of Amsterdam; the apartment buildings, eight-storey white concrete monolithic blocks, are used to create internal courts of some 1–2 hectares each (the development was inspired by the Park Hill Estate in Sheffield). The designers of the external space were faced with the enormous task of creating an hospitable environment from the uninspiring legacy of natural factors—sand dunes subjected to almost incessant and

PLATE 7.19 **A general view of Bijlmermeer and the surrounding polder landscape.** *(Allan Ruff)*

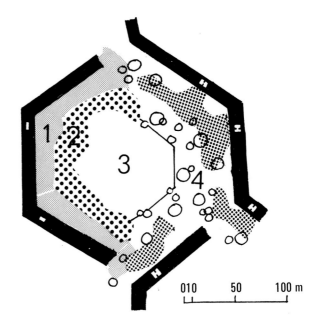

1. SERVICE ACCESS
2. WOODED TRANSITIONAL ZONE
3. PLAY MEADOW
4. CHILDREN'S PLAY, SITTING, etc.

FIGURE 7.5 **Internal courtyard zoning. Bijlmermeer, Amsterdam. Consideration of climate function and activities results in a clear framework for the residential court.** (Source: *Dienst der Publieke Werken, Amsterdam*)

often gale force winds—and the man-made factors of a turbulent micro-climate. Furthermore, the designers felt it unthinkable to house people in areas of new buildings given conventional landscape treatment which they considered to be totally alien to human needs. They endeavoured to create a new landscape by extending the principles of urban woodland, first developed at the Amsterdam Bos some thirty years earlier, into urban housing. From this had come two important management principles:

i) The selection of species must be on an ecological basis, which determined the maintenance towards a particular association over 60 years.
ii) No part of the woodland should serve merely an ornamental function, but should be strictly related to the needs of the people who were to use it.

The disposition of the woodland blocks in the internal courts was determined by climatological zoning (*see* Figure 7.5); the sunless Zone (1) next to the block is restricted to service and access; in Zone (2) the wind turbulence is ameliorated by block planting, which also serves to screen the individual from the Housing Block and vice versa. The centre of the court, Zone (3), varies between sun and shade depending on the time of day and

active games are located here. On the sunny side of the block, Zone (4), the passive activities of play, sitting, etc. are interlinked.

The Zoning of the courtyard works well (*see* Plates 7.20, 7.21, 7.22). The tree planting after eight years already has a woodland character. But early developments at the Bijlmermeer were, as recent stages have recognized, too architecturally designed, particularly such features as steps, paths, water edge, etc. One of the greatest difficulties of this new approach has been to achieve a non 'landscaped' appearance.

The Bijlmermeer project failed to achieve a real interaction between people and the land, which was to be the objective of the development at Delft.

7.82 Delft—Buitenhof

Translated, 'Buitenhof' means 'country garden', and this is precisely what the designers aimed to achieve in one area at Delft Zuid. During the 1960s there had been a gradual move away from the conventional architectural treatment of urban landscape to something more free and natural. In this, public opinion lent its support to an entirely new approach to urban landscape. This is best

117

PLATE 7.20 **A view through from the service access area (Zone 1) showing the concentration of planting in Zone 2.** *(Allan Ruff)*

PLATE 7.21 **The central activity area (Zone 3).** *(Allan Ruff)*

PLATE 7.22 **The play and sitting area (Zone 4).** *(Allan Ruff)*

expressed by the then Director of Parks, Mr Bos:

'... It is very difficult for children to play their own game, like their parents used to do, who lived in a less overpopulated country and could play in streets without lots of parked cars and dangerous traffic, as there is today.

'At the moment the only freedom of a child is that which adults allow him.

'When an architect is designing a playground for children, there are all kinds of standards to be taken into consideration ... but in spite of applying all the standards it is evident to every spectator that the playground is not a source of inspiration for the children, it gives them no possibility to play their own game. Children ignore architects' good intentions but are delighted to play in other areas such as water, ditches, buildings under construction. But also for adults it is difficult for them to go their own way. Likewise the green area between the housing is designed by standards and according to the ideas of the designer.

'Difference in thinking between the users and the designer!

'During the weekends many inhabitants of the cities migrate to the countryside, to the woods, the moors and the dunes, and everyone is delighted to walk on

118

PLATE 7.23 **Man-created wilderness at Delft-Buitenhof.** *(Allan Ruff)*

PLATE 7.24 **Children's play shelters at Delft-Buitenhof. The opportunities for informal play are virtually unlimited.** *(Allan Ruff)*

PLATE 7.25 **Native plants form 'landscape pictures' of great beauty. Part of the Jac. P. Thÿsse Park after 17 years.** *(Allan Ruff)*

small and winding paths, to sit on a bank among high growing weeds, to pick flowers in the field, to play with sand in the dunes and to run over hills.

'But at home everything is straight and tidy. Shouldn't we ask ourselves if it is possible to bring a piece of nature into the towns so that we can give the inhabitants some weekend fun during the week too?

'Of course it is impossible to copy a piece of nature reserve in a city, but for all that it is worth trying and with the co-operation among town planners, civil engineers, etc. it must be possible to break through the current trend of tidiness.'

To try out this experimental approach, the central area of one housing unit was given over to the creation of what to English eyes can only be described as a wilderness, having the appearance of scrub land reverting to woodland (Plate 7.23). Parking and vehicle access was removed to the periphery of the site. In the centre as many existing features were retained as possible, broken walls, ditches, low-lying wet areas, existing vegetation, as well as vegetation which had invaded during the course of construction. Then with minimal disturbance, limited earth mounding was used to create shelter and accent on an otherwise flat site. This work was executed without a conventional plan. Such features as secondary footpaths were to be trodden out by the residents before surfacing with an organic material. This has helped to create the non-landscaped character of the site today. A plan was used to place the small number of standard trees, whilst the positioning of the mass of whip planting was determined on site by the planters. Following planting, the seeding of a few species of native plants was augmented by natural invasion into the area; but because too rich a soil was used, the subsequent herb growth was vigorous and, as public attitudes prevented the use of herbicides, tree growth has been retarded. Cutting of the vegetation is necessary twice a year, by a hand-held rotary bank cutter as the nature of the ground and the rankness of the herbage prevents the use of more customary equipment. Following this, all herbage has to be removed from the site to minimize soil fertility and to obviate a fire risk. This special maintenance makes the cost of this approach no cheaper in the first ten years or so than conventional treatments. Socially however this experiment was an unqualified success.

The University of Leiden Department of Social Medicine was able to report after five years that it created an ideal environment for children, providing the opportunity for building shelters, hole digging, picking flowers, etc. (Plate 7.24). Adults also used the outdoors to create personal space.

Neither of the two developments overtly used native plant material in a planned way to create a semi-natural framework. At Bijlmermeer the first priority had been to create a physically comfortable environment by the use of forest planting techniques. At Delft the planting served a social function and the selection of species was not ecological but rather the customary horticultural one of using what is known to thrive. The quantity involved and the need for coppicing species determined that largely, though not exclusively, native species were used. It is impossible to say how far these approaches would have developed without techniques for using native herbs so painstakingly evolved by J. Landwehr, the Director of Parks at Amstelveen. It was the addition of these techniques in the early 1970s that made a radically new approach to the treatment of urban land possible, whether in housing, parks, road verges, or other urban areas.

7.83 Landwehr and the use of native plants

In 1940, faced with the task of planting a new public park, at a time when there was literally no money available, Landwehr took the simple but significant step of using native plant material. This initial planting was a public success. In the years after 1945 he went on to extend both the park and the knowledge of native plants which today extends to a use of over 500 species, with detailed information regarding their germination, establishment, rate of growth and stability. These are used in the park

aesthetically, to create what Landwehr calls landscape pictures, which are of great beauty. More recently, Landwehr's techniques have been used by others to create more strict ecological associations based largely on a *Salicetum* and a *Callunetum* by first manipulating the abiotic factors of soil and water. Since the mid '60s Landwehr has himself extended these techniques for more utilitarian uses on roadsides and in housing, for example, with the express purpose of reducing costs (Plate 7.25).

7.9 THE ECOLOGICAL PRINCIPLES

From what has been said, it should be evident that the use of native species marks a change from the horticultural traditions of the past 150 years of urban landscape. Native plants are used, as they are found, to recreate dynamic communities rather than unchanging garden compositions. This calls for a far greater understanding of ecological factors of both the plant and its relationship to natural conditions, which cannot come from text books alone. It must be supported by prolonged field observation. Further, as every site is going to be different there cannot be a manual for the use of native plants. This part of the chapter considers the main ecological principles and techniques involved in the use of native species of trees, shrubs and herbs. In order to explain the techniques being developed in the Netherlands and to dispel some of the myths that have already sprung up in England, some ecological background is necessary.

7.91 Plant communities

The use of native species to create artificially semi-natural communities is based upon the basic broad division between plant communities found in Europe; that is, the woodlands and the open grasslands, and the exploitation of the ecotone that exists between the two. An ecotone is defined as 'mixed communities formed by the overlapping or adjoining communities in the transition area' (Weaver & Clements, *Plant Ecology*, 1929).

The woodland community is the natural vegetation cover of western Europe and forms the climatic climax to most uninterrupted successional sequences; the main plant associations are those of the forest forming species of oak, beech, ash and pine. The maintenance of woodland communities is directed towards furthering the succession by operations like thinning and the introduction of tree and herb species at appropriate stages of development.

The open grassland community emerges when woodland is cleared and it forms a secondary climax dependent on biotic control; if this type of community is created, it follows that maintenance costs will be higher due to the need for such control, in the form of mowing or hand weeding.

The main difference between this and the traditional horticultural approach is the use of the ecotone. A great

TABLE 7.6

Examples illustrating the derivation of the competitive index

Species	Attributes i)	ii)	iii)	iv)	Competitive index (total/2)
Chamaenerion angustifolium	5	5	5	2	8·5
Arrhenatherum elatius	5	4	4	3	8·0
Brachypodium pinnatum	3	4	3	5	7·5
Ranunculus repens	3	5	3	1	6·0
Helictotrichon pratense	3	2	3	2	5·0
Taraxacum officinale	3	1	4	1	4·5
Festuca ovina	2	1	3	2	4·0
Campanula rotundifolia	2	2	3	0	3·5
Arenaria serpyllifolia	1	0	4	0	2·5

deal of the monotony of the urban landscape stems from the harsh line drawn between communities and functions; for example, between grass and pavement, shrubs and grass, water and water edge, trees and lawns. With native planting the broadest possible ecotone is formed to create the greatest possible diversity and perceptual interest. In design terms, this means, for instance, that if paths are laid horizontal to the ecotone the visual diversity will be limited and the variation will have to come from the walker's relationship to either of the two communities, an ideal arrangement for a meandering walk; if the path is put across the ecotone the visual diversity will be greater, an arrangement more suited to rapid movement, e.g. primary footpaths, roads, etc.

As the minimum width of an ecotone between woodland and open grassland is about 30 m, it is perfectly feasible to create such dynamic corridors in many otherwise sterile urban situations.

7.92 Plant types

One of the most difficult facts for anyone to grasp who has been weaned on horticulture and the notion that all native plants are weeds, is that native plants can be divided into two distinct groups—a fundamental distinction which has a very great influence on the establishment, appearance and management of native plant communities.

In order to appreciate this distinction one must turn to the work of J. P. Grimes of the former Nature Conservancy Grassland Research Unit at Sheffield University. Grimes has shown that herbaceous plants may be classified according to their competitive features, of which four can be recognized as being consistent:
i)   tall stature;
ii) a growth form that is usually tussocky or a large densely branched rhizome, which allows extensive and intensive exploitation of the environment both above and below ground;

iii) a high relative growth rate;
iv) a tendency to deposit a dense layer of litter on the ground surface.

From this it is possible to score plant species with respect to each of these features and so to provide a competitive index (C.I.) over a scale of 0–10. Leaving aside the derivation of the index, which can be seen in Grimes' original paper, an example of such grouping can be seen in Table 7.6.

The species of high C.I., that is, greater than 6·0, form communities that are low in the number of species (below 20 per m²). These are plants commonly regarded as weeds. The other species of low C.I. form communities where there is a considerable variety of species (above 20 per m²) in such areas as limestone screes and limestone meadows. Grimes suggests that there are two mechanisms that bring about the low incidence of species of high C.I. in vegetation of high species diversity:
i)   the result of environmental stress induced by such factors as drought and mineral nutrient deficiency
ii) the maintenance phenomena such as grazing, mowing, burning, trampling, which prevent potentially competitive species from attaining maximum size and vigour and reduce litter accumulation

In Grimes' model, reproduced as Figure 7.6, it can be seen that under conditions of low environmental stress,

FIGURE 7.6

Diagrams representing the impact upon species of:
a. **intensity of environment stress**
b. **intensity of grazing, mowing, etc.**
C. **species of high competitive index**
S. **species (or ecotones) of high resistance to the prevailing stresses imposed by environment or by grazing, mowing, burning or trampling respectively**
R. **remaining species.**

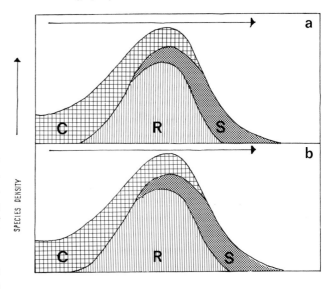

a) INCREASING ENVIRONMENTAL STRESS
b) INCREASING INTENSITY OF MANAGEMENT

productivity is high, species of high C.I. attain maximum vigour and species density is low owing to competitive exclusion. Under conditions of increased environmental stress, the competitive species decline in vigour and species of lower competitive ability are able to survive. With further reduction in productivity, species density falls as conditions of extreme stress are reached and species density is limited by the scarcity of species tolerant of the specific conditions limiting productivity. Such a gradient is found naturally, passing from lowland fertile arable land to unfertilized upland pasture and on to lead waste tips. A similar gradient is found with intensity of grazing, mowing, etc. These two groups of species can be referred to as Exploiters (sometimes known as Generalists) for the high C.I. species and Acceptors (Specialists) for the low C.I. species.

In the approaches described so far, the wilderness scheme at Delft encourages the exploiter species, with species-poor communities which are nevertheless able to take considerable wear and tear. Whilst Landwehr makes use of many more acceptor species in planned species-rich communities, these do not take active use but are perceptually more interesting. When both these techniques are combined with woodland communities which behave in the same way, it is possible to appreciate that the opportunities available to the user of native plant material are unlimited, especially as they range from high to exceedingly low cost.

Grimes' work also explains why native plant communities must be maintained—to keep the soil impoverished or to prevent the invasion of exploiter species. In addition, the chances of establishing a species-rich community in the short term, by a *laissez-faire* approach, are extremely slender.

7.93 Physical environment

From the preceding discussion, it should be evident that a great deal of attention has to be paid to soil and the soil/water relationship as this will determine the type of community, its maintenance and its cost.

For species-rich communities, the most satisfactory results are achieved with soils that are poor in nutrients, especially nitrogen, and yet, where trees are used, able to retain sufficient moisture. That trees and shrubs will grow adequately on poor soils, providing there is sufficient moisture, is evident from studying the colonization of waste heaps and development of afforestation on such sites. Many materials can provide the right growing conditions. Sub-soil following roadworks can be used, providing it is not clay, and the peat and brick rubble so freely available in urban redevelopment areas is an excellent growing medium for chalk and limestone flora without improvement, providing it is sufficiently finely ground and retains sufficient moisture. Good results can also be achieved with well weathered domestic refuse ash which is often freely available especially in industrial

towns. Much practical research is required in the UK to explore the different forms of growing media, but clearly there is no need always to import high cost topsoil into urban areas; neither is there any reason for improving all soils to a garden standard.

In preparation, the object is not to improve the soil, but to prepare it as a base; nutrient-rich topsoil should be replaced by low-nutrient materials and the surface metre must be freed of all unwanted vegetation likely to cause competition later. Also, advantage should be taken of existing site conditions, and every attempt should be made to retain not only existing vegetation but also wet and dry areas, gradients, acid and alkali places, areas of impenetrable and penetrable structure, etc., so as to give as much variety to the planting as possible. It is not usually possible, for economic reasons, to make great changes in the prevailing soil conditions, but localized variations can be created by introducing pockets of sand, brick rubble, and ash, all with different pH levels.

A greater variation in the habitat can be achieved by varying the height of the soil surface in relation to the underlying water table. By the use of gradual gradients, up to 1 m in height above water level, it is possible to create a broader ecotone with a range of wet and dry habitats (*see* Plate 7.25).

Added to the soil/water relationship is the light factor. In the early years of succession the maximum amount of light reaches the soil surface and conditions in general favour the growth of exploiter, ruderal species suited to disturbed arable ground. Later, the plant community creates physical conditions favourable to itself while the closed community, whether woodland or open herbs, discourages outside invasion.

In woodland planting, it is the light factor that makes it impossible to introduce woodland herbs at the early stage. Later, during the thicket stage, the amount of light reaching the forest floor is minimal and due to the impenetrable character, herbs are again prevented from successfully establishing themselves. As the woodland structure emerges, the light value at the forest floor does not increase but the structural organization (i.e. tree, shrub, herb and ground layer) makes it possible to introduce the woodland herbs associated with a closed canopy. However, the majority of woodland herbs are

TABLE 7.7
General effect of light at ground level in high forest

Illumination Level	Ground Flora
Below 16%	Forest floor bare
16–18%	Mosses
22–26%	Herbaceous material
30%	Regeneration of tree species

associated not with deep forest but with glades, whether as clearings, paths or even woodland edges which are, in effect, one-sided glades.

Where the glade is small in diameter, all the vegetation will be influenced by woodland conditions, but where it becomes larger it will be removed from this influence and take on the character of an open grassland community.

Thus, another important design consideration during later management is the creation of a sequence of woodland glades in which the path is the linking element; passing, for example, through the closed canopy, then through the centre of a glade and skirting the edge of another. The position of the path must always be carefully related to time and angle of sun penetration.

7.10 TECHNIQUES OF MANAGEMENT

7.101 Biotope planting

In order to distinguish this type of planting from forestry or amenity planting, the author uses the term biotope planting which can be defined as creating artificially semi-natural communities of trees, shrubs and herbs. Although woodlands and open grassland communities naturally form part of a sequence, the development of artificial techniques for creating the two communities has until now been separate in Holland.

The techniques for establishing woodlands stems from such sources as the work at the Amsterdam Bos where the State Forestry Service assisted in pioneering ecologically planned woodland. Incidentally, the combination of forester and landscape designer into a single management team appears to be the most successful formula for this work.

The development in the use of native herbs has already been mentioned in the work of J. Landwehr and later C. Sipkes. For the purpose of discussion and explanation in this chapter, it will be simpler to take the woodland and herb communities separately.

7.102 Woodlands

The plant associations are derived from the main forest-forming species already mentioned, viz. oak, beech, ash and occasionally pine. In special circumstances, determined largely by physical factors, the pioneer species of birch, willow and alder will form associations. The species composition will vary slightly from region to region, although suitability lists can be prepared from such sources as *British Islands and their Vegetation* by Sir A. G. Tansley.

On sites where there is an existing herb flora, a detailed floristic inventory will determine the plant association, as well as locating sites of interesting flora, both visually and ecologically, which can later be incorporated into the planting and serve as a useful seed source.

In newly formed areas, housing sites, road verges, etc. it is very important to control the type of soil and its profile and here the physical material will determine the plant association, in accord with the regional ecology.

An example of an association based on *Alnus glutinosa* is shown in Table 7.8. It should be noted that this was prepared for mainland European woodlands, although all the species listed will grow in Britain. It has further been modified for a specific location. The main tree species have been divided into both forest transplants and standard trees. This is partly to give a more natural appearance from the beginning by creating a mixed age woodland, but also it is important on exposed sites to gain as much shelter as possible in the early years. On more sheltered sites all the plant material could be 1–2 year old transplants. The species are divided into different functions within the woodland.

Principal species: these are the main woodland species and they occur as either dominants or co-dominants as in a natural woodland. The percentage of these species is determined by function, for example, shelter, filtering, screening, and the eventual ecological association desired. Their frequencies range from a pure stand of 100% to 25% but on average their presence is approximately 60–65%.

Filler species: these are the other species found in a woodland and give diversity. They are often colourful in leaf or flower, e.g. whitebeam, bird cherry, etc.

Pioneer species: these are used in the same way as in forestry, to screen and shelter other species. They are the faster growing birch, willow and alder, the particular species being determined by the prevailing physical factors. They are thinned out during the first fifteen years of the woodland except in specific areas, e.g. low-lying wet areas, dry mounds, etc.

Edge species: these are the marginal ecotone species and serve three functions:

i) ecological, in that for wildlife the most diverse and valuable part of the woodland is its edge;

ii) visual, in that it creates a more natural effect;

iii) cultural, because many of the edge species are thorny, e.g. rose, bramble, hawthorn and blackthorn (i.e. pioneer species of the thicket stage). These protect the planting on the inside and their untidy growth prevents the tidy-minded maintenance operator from mowing up to the woodland planting. The maximum length of edge should be created by making it irregular in outline.

The planting plan for woodland has traditionally been in the form of a grid. One advantage claimed for this was that the species were planted approximately as the designer intended. However, the disposition of trees and shrubs is not critical in the first fifteen years when all the planting is in the thicket stage. A grid also takes office time to prepare and cannot be accurately checked on site by the landscape architect or quantity surveyor. Where an experienced contractor or direct labour force is used, it is

TABLE 7.8
Tree Selection—Alnus woodland

	Species	Occurrence	Tree %	Forest Transplant %
Principal Tree Species	Alnus glutinosa	aa	23	10
	Fraxinus excelsior	aa	23	8
	Quercus robur	a	13	3
Filler Tree Species	Fagus sylvatica	z	8	3
	Populus nigra	a	13	5
	Alnus incana	zz	4	—
	Ulmus carpinifolia	zz	4	2
	Acer pseudoplatanus	z	8	3
	Salix caprea	zz	4	2
Edge (marginal) Species	Ribes sylvestre	zz		4
	Prunus padus	aa		8
	Viburnum opulus	z		3
	Sambucus nigra	a		6
	Salix viminalis	z		4
	Crataegus monogyna	a		5
	Rosa canina	z		4
	Prunus spinosa	zz		3
	Euonymus europaeus	z		3
	Cornus sanguinea	a		4
	Carpinus betulus	zz		2
	Sorbus aucuparia	a		4
	Frangula alnus	zz		2
	Salix cinerea	z		3

KEY
aaa	60%+	dominant
aa	30–59%	co-dominant
a	20–29%	abundant
z	10–19%	frequent
zz	5–9%	sparse
zzz	5%	rare

(Source: Dienst der Gemeenteplantsoenen, Den Haag)

sufficient to use a planting schedule which gives details of the number to be planted in each area according to the percentage occurrence. Details can also be included of specific requirements, for example, the location of edge species; waterside planting; where plants are to be single or in groups. The trees themselves are planted on a grid to facilitate maintenance and are spaced at 1 m intervals, although this can range between 0·80 m and 1·2 m depending on species. In instances where weed control is not practised, any wider spacing than this makes it difficult for the trees and shrubs to form a thicket and thus suppress the weeds, and stunting and other setbacks will occur.

It must be made clear that there are two different approaches to the maintenance of woodland communities depending on whether exploiter or acceptor species are used; these can be classified as being a coarse or a refined approach.

i) Coarse approach

A limited number of tree and shrub species are used and the herbs are of an 'exploiter' type, which may colonize naturally or may be sown during the second year of the plantation. The woodland receives little or no cultivation and it is left to the natural thicket forming process to suppress the coarse herbage. In the glades and other clearings, the herbage has to be cut and removed twice a year, after flowering in May/June and again after a second bloom in late August/September. Such an approach is used where a low-cost programme is intended in the initial works, but in areas of public access, where mowing is necessary, it can be up to ten years before a low cost is achieved in subsequent maintenance.

This approach can be used for forming the structure of forest areas, where there is to be some degree of wear and tear and in places where there is little control over physical conditions of soil and water, i.e. where the soil is too fertile and the removal of soil and the eradication of all ruderal species would be too expensive.

ii) Refined approach

A greater number of tree and shrub species are used and the physical conditions of soil and water are controlled, thus reducing the growth of unwanted herbs. In the woodland any unwanted herbs that do occur can be suppressed either by hand cultivations or the timely use of residual herbicides, like Simazine. Once the canopy has closed, such cultivations are kept to the outside of the plantation and herbs of an acceptor type can be introduced as and when conditions become favourable.

As much of the planting is done on pioneer sites, using a greater proportion of pioneer species like poplar, it is necessary to have a phased programme of planting spread over fifty years or more. As conditions move towards the middle range of the physical gradient, so additional species of climax and fillers can be added. Figure 7.7 shows how this is achieved.

Biotope woodland allows a range of thinning practices, each serving different functions; it is possible to range from the forming of individual trees in parkland, to coppice with or without standards which in turn can equally be diverted into a further alternative of high forest.

In this work the maintenance personnel, like the designer, must adopt a new approach and develop new techniques. There should be no attempt to 'garden', that is, to create a preconceived effect, whether ecological or aesthetic and a free dynamic interplay between species should be allowed. The aboriculturalist must learn to thin trees not according to silvicultural or forestry practice, but to select for ecological or aesthetic value, e.g. the retention of dead or malformed trees with twisted or double stems which will give visual effect, especially alongside paths.

Thinning commences when the trees and shrubs come into contact. During this initial thinning of pioneer species, the whole tree may be removed, or where this may allow too much light to reach the woodland floor and encourage weed growth, the first thinning can be a pollarding of the top two-thirds of the tree stem. This will allow sufficient light to reach other trees but cast sufficient shade to suppress unwanted herbs. Later, the remaining one-third can be removed.

FIGURE 7.7 **Phasing of woodland planting.** (Source: *Dienst der Publieke Werken Amsterdam*)

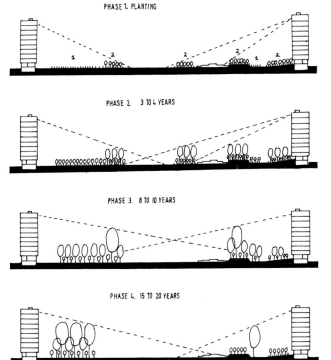

PHASE 1. PLANTING

PHASE 2.   3 TO 4 YEARS

PHASE 3.   8 TO 10 YEARS

PHASE 4.   15 TO 20 YEARS

7.103 Open herb communities

It is impossible to give specific instructions for the use of herb species, or to draw plans for their location. The initial effort goes into the creation of the physical environment required—soil, water and their relationship. Following preparation, the exact location for seeding or planting will depend on observation of the site conditions; this calls for intimate practical knowledge of species requirements. Thus, the designer uses the plant material as an artist, physically adding to the spatial composition. Unlike the artist, however, he can change the materials as the soil, water and vegetation factors alter.

Following establishment, the same principles of management apply, the objective being to eradicate high competitive species by hand weeding or mowing, but at the same time to allow a dynamic interplay within the community. Thus the appearance of the community is always changing as species wane or increase in importance, or disappear altogether and others are added.

The use of native species can be extended to the treatment of road verges; and the re-creation of man-made communities of a type that are fast disappearing from the countryside. For example:

i)   flower-rich grasslands, wet or dry
ii) perennial flower pastures without grasses
iii) railwayside flora
iv) annual flower pastures
v)   old road verges, ditches, etc.

In the treatment of roadsides and central reservations, native herbs can be used to create a more attractive appearance with lower maintenance costs than the customary rye-grass strip. The cost of maintenance depends on the number of species in the mixture. The more that are used, the greater the cost. There is no indication yet as to whether grass should be included or not, as success can be achieved with pure herb mixtures as well as a 50:50 ratio of herb to grass. If grass is used, it must be a slow growing, low biomass species, on poor dry soils. This means, for instance, *Agrostis canina* 'Montana', *Festuca ovina* 'Tenuifolia' and *Deschampsia flexuosa*.

In maintenance, cutting techniques have to be adopted which are more closely akin to traditional hay making, the time being governed by the species used rather than the calendar. If many species are used, the only cutting is in August/September. Cutting at other times will prevent other species from flowering.

Cutting should be with a finger-type mower, either tractor mounted or of Allan scythe type. All cuttings must be removed to prevent nutritional improvement of the soil, through the build-up of detritus material.

7.11 CONCLUSION

The techniques being developed in Holland stem from a social concern for people who are forced to spend their entire lives in the artificial urban environment. On the one hand, greater perceptual experience is brought to the individual by direct contact with the elements of the natural world. On the other, the semi-natural framework of the physical environment allows the individual greater opportunity for manipulation of his environment to suit his social needs. In this, the developments in Holland differ from the American-inspired 'Nature in Cities' movement of the late 1960s which was aesthetically and often sentimentally motivated.

A similar, radical new approach is necessary in England if the urban environment, especially in the inner city, is to be made relevant to people's needs. But the question has to be asked—are such developments possible in England? Technically the answer is 'yes', although much research is obviously needed in a country where there have been no similar advances to those in Holland in the use of native species.

The new techniques shift the emphasis away from the present fixed designs to the dynamic management of real landscape; once the crucial work of establishing the stage, with its raw materials of soil, water and vegetation has been done, the creative work of managing communities begins. The appearance of the landscape may pass through many unforeseen and exciting stages before maturity in fifty, sixty or even 100 years' time. In this, the landscape architect can be an initiator, catalyst, and orchestrator, but never master in the process of interaction between people and nature. This can only be achieved by the landscape architect, forester and parks personnel being part of a single urban land management team. In the Netherlands, the Parks Service has always included these people, and unless the same degree of co-operation takes place in England it is believed that the urban landscape and its people will continue to suffer from the application of outmoded and ineffective techniques.

FURTHER READING

Part A

Fitter, R. S. R. *Finding Wild Flowers* (London: Collins, 1973)

Grime, J. P. and Lloyd, P. S. *An Ecological Atlas of Grassland Plants* (London: Edward Arnold, 1973)

Mabey, R. *The Unofficial Countryside* (London: Collins, 1973)

Salisbury, Sir Edward. *Weeds and Aliens* (London: Collins, New Naturalist Series 1969)

Tansley, A. G. (Ed. Proctor, M. C. F.) *Britain's Green Mantle* (London: George Allen and Unwin Ltd., 2nd edition 1968)

Tansley, A. G. *British Islands and their Vegetation* (Cambridge: University Press, 1939) vols 1 and 2

Thomas, G. S. *Plants for Ground Cover* (London: J. M. Dent and Sons Ltd., 1970)

Part B

Grime, J. P. 'Competitive Exclusion in Herbaceous Vegetation', *Nature* vol 242, March 1973

Landwehr, J. and Sipkes, C. *Wilde plantentiunen* (Institute voor Natuurbeschemin educatie (Dutch only), 1974)

Tansley, A. G. *British Islands and their Vegetation* (Cambridge: University Press, 1939) vols 1 and 2

REFERENCES

1. Perring, F. H. and Walters, S. M. *Atlas of the British Flora* (Nelson, 1962; E. P. Publishing Ltd., 1976)
2. Robinson, W. *The English Flower Garden* (London: John Murray, 1898)
3. Robinson, W. *The Wild Garden* (London: John Murray, 1870)
4. Leroy, L. G. 'Natuur uitschakelen natuur inschakelen' 'nature chained: nature unchained' (Deventer, Ankh-Hermes B.V.: 1973) in Dutch

ACKNOWLEDGEMENTS

I wish to acknowledge the assistance given in preparing Part B of this chapter by:

Ir. R. van der Wal, Head of Parks Division, Public Works Department, Amsterdam

J. P. van Alf, Parks Director, Public Works Department, Utrecht

B. J. Galjaard, Director, Parks and Recreation Department, Amstelveen

H. J. Bos, Superintendent, Municipal Parks Department, The Hague

Mr. De Jong, Public Works Department, Delft

Dr. R. Benton and Ian C. Laurie, University of Manchester.

(This paper has been extracted from the author's thesis on *The Use of Native Species in Urban Areas*.)

CHAPTER 8

Planting Design and Management for Wildlife

ANNE YARROW

8.1 INTRODUCTION

Apart from nature reserves, which together account for only about 0·5 % of the land surface of Britain, no land is managed primarily for wildlife. Therefore the maintenance of our wildlife is dependent upon a whole range of semi-natural and cultivated areas used primarily for another purpose. These areas include farmland, woodland, hedgerows and road verges, transmission line wayleaves, commons, parks, reservoirs, and gravel pits. The wildlife value of these places can be maintained or improved by following certain design and management guidelines, the more important of which are outlined in this chapter.

Management for production (agriculture, forestry), amenity or recreation, and management for wildlife, are often incompatible. Where a conflict exists in the management of public access land precedence will normally be given to recreation interests unless the area is of special wildlife importance. In the latter case, the area probably is or should be designated a Site of Special Scientific Interest; details of these can be obtained from the County Planning Department, or Nature Conservancy Council Regional Office.

These guidelines refer to design and management measures that help towards the goal of *ecological diversity*, i.e. a range of habitats, with an associated diversity of species. This is an appropriate goal if there are no particular species or habitats in need of protection. This point should be checked with the appropriate regional office of the Nature Conservancy Council and local Naturalists' Trust. If there are such special habitats or species, they can then advise on appropriate management measures.

8.2 PLANTING DESIGN FOR WILDLIFE

A wide range of habitats should be retained or created. As well as different kinds of grassland or woodland there may be existing patches of scrub, pools or wet hollows, rock outcrops or walls that add to the richness of the area. These should be retained where they occur, or, where absent, they can be quite easily created.

Structural diversity should be retained or created wherever possible as this is correlated with species diversity; in other words, the different plant layers of canopy trees, shrubs and herbaceous plants, should all be present separately and/or one above the other. For example, woodland with field and shrub layers beneath the canopy will be biologically richer than a closed canopy wood with little or no understorey. Shrubs included in the planting design for the interior of a woodland must be shade tolerant, e.g. holly, yew.

The 'edges' between one habitat and another are often ecologically very rich and this is especially true of the gradual transition from woodland to non-woodland and the land/water boundary. Therefore the 'edge' between adjacent habitats should be as long as possible. Woodlands with an irregular boundary will be richer biologically than a block of woodland of the same area with a regular outline.

Links or corridors between several small areas of similar habitat will increase the effectiveness of that habitat in terms of wildlife conservation. Links of a diverse habitat in an ecologically barren area, such as arable farmland, can help species to spread and populations maintain themselves—hence the great ecological

PLATE 8.1 **Scrub being cleared to restore part of a site to grassland. The flail leaves a layer of chopped material which, unless removed, encourages worse 'waste ground' species.** *(F. L. Ryan)*

PLATE 8.2 **A site where part of the grassland is mown short, while other areas are left as long grass.** *(F. L. Ryan)*

importance of hedges, railway banks and road verges.

A variety of species should be planted, e.g. some hardwoods (ideally not less than 10%) in predominantly coniferous woodland or broad-leaved herbs in grass mixtures. 'Pure' grass-seed mixtures should be avoided. It is almost impossible to obtain wild-flower seeds commercially as listed 'wild' flower species are usually not from wild native stock. But the local Naturalists' Trust or universities may be able to help organize collection and sowing of wild herb seeds.

A breeding population of an animal species can only become established if a suitable habitat of adequate size is available. In general, the larger the animal, the larger the area required; for instance an insect population could develop in a single oak tree, whereas woodland birds such as blackbirds and warblers appear to need a minimum of half a hectare of scrub with a few canopy trees, and larger species such as deer obviously require far more extensive tracts.

The introduction of foreign plant species should be avoided since aliens may initially be so successful that they get out of control. Even the introduction of plant species not found in the area is undesirable unless specifically required, for instance, for colonizing a difficult site. The Society for the Promotion of Nature Reserves have produced a pamphlet on recommended policy for introductions and this should be consulted. Details of any proposed introductions from outside the area should be sent to the Biological Records Centre, Monks Wood Experimental Station, Abbots Ripon, Huntingdon. Animal introductions are even less desirable and should be avoided. Mammal introductions have often proved disastrous, e.g. coypu, muskrat, feral American mink and grey squirrel.

Disturbance to mammals and birds may be a problem in areas where the public have access. It may be possible to incorporate into the design refuge areas with restricted public access. Uses of an area may be zoned in time so that 'close seasons' allow animals to be undisturbed during particularly vulnerable periods. For instance, some areas are important breeding places for birds, while others are more important as refuelling points for migrating birds, or as overwintering areas. Designation of 'close seasons' would take these points into account. Birds, in particular, can tolerate moderate disturbance if it is constant; the unusual disturbance is most likely to cause breeding birds to desert the nest. Wherever possible, public access to important breeding areas should be limited to a single approach route.

Trees long-established in Britain generally carry the richest insect fauna, which in turn support insect-eating birds. Particularly rich are oak, birch, willow and

PLATE 8.3 **A fine old oak that provides a valuable habitat for insects, birds, and lichens (and will continue to do so even when dead).** *(D. Harvey)*

TABLE 8.1
The numbers of insect species associated with various deciduous and coniferous trees in Britain.

Species	Number of Insect Species
oak (*Quercus robur* & *Q. petraea*)	284
willow (*Salix* spp)	266
birch (*Betula* spp)	229
hawthorn (*Crataegus* spp)	149
sloe (*Prunus spinosa*)	109
poplars (*Populus* spp)	97
Scots pine (*Pinus sylvestris*)	91
alder (*Alnus glutinosa*)	90
elm (*Ulmus* spp)	82
hazel (*Corylus avellana*)	73
beech (*Fagus sylvatica*)	64
ash (*Fraxinus excelsior*)	41
spruce (*Picea abies*)	37
lime (*Tilia* spp)	31
mountain ash (*Sorbus aucuparia*)	28
hornbeam (*Carpinus betulus*)	28
field maple (*Acer campestre*)	26
larch (*Larix decidua*)	17
fir (*Abies* spp)	16
sycamore (*Acer pseudoplatanus*)	15
holly (*Ilex aquifolium*)	7
sweet chestnut (*Castanea sativa*)	5
holm oak (*Quercus ilex*)	2

(From Southwood 1961)

hawthorn. Table 8.1 shows the total number of insect species of five common orders which are associated with each of a number of tree species. The number of insect species associated with a plant is an indication of the plant's history and of its palatability. The interpretation of this table is not straightforward since the number of species feeding on a particular plant is not the only factor governing its importance for wildlife. Some plants are important not because of the variety of insect life that they support, but because they are the only food source of one or more species (e.g. the brimstone butterfly and alder buckthorn). Tables 8.2, 8.3 and 8.4 indicate shrubs and herbaceous plants that are good food-sources for butterflies and moths, seed- and berry-eating birds, and waterfowl. These tables must be used with caution since they can give the impression that animal species are specific to certain plants and that only those plants listed are worth planting. The truth is that most animal species are fairly catholic in their eating habits. The most important rule is to maintain a variety of habitats with as

130

wide as possible a range of native plant species of varied age-structure, consistent with the management aims of a particular area.

It must be borne in mind that, as well as needing food, animals also require suitable places for shelter, breeding and in some cases display. For instance, apart from a very few ground-nesting species such as larks and pipits, birds require trees, shrubs, holes, cliffs, or buildings in order to nest. With the same exceptions, virtually all species sing from posts, shrubs or trees.

8.3 MAINTENANCE AND MANAGEMENT

Management aims, objectives and operations should be explicitly set out in a management plan so that it is clear what has been done, what is to be done, and why.

8.31 Woodland

Structural diversity can be encouraged by heavy thinning so that the canopy is broken in places thus allowing rich field and shrub layers to develop. For this reason coppicing-with-standards is ecologically rich (as well as being an excellent visual screen, and resistant to vandalism) (*see* Figure 8.1). Although coppicing as a method of woodland management is now practised on a large scale only in S.E. England where chestnut coppice is managed for split fence stakes, much of the old-established woodland in lowland Britain was formerly coppice-with-standards. The wide-spaced standards were usually oak or occasionally ash, whereas the traditional understorey coppice was mainly hazel, ash, or hornbeam. These species support a richer fauna than the modern chestnut coppice.

Coppice-with-standards fulfils the following conditions necessary for wildlife diversity:
i) semi-natural associations of native trees and shrubs;
ii) a complex structure with a constantly changing mosaic of successional stages, allowing rich herb and shrub layers to develop and consequently a great variety of ecological niches for colonization by plant and animal species;
iii) a continuity of successional stages which allows many local or rare woodland species to survive;
iv) food plant variety in all seasons.

These conditions favour many species of insect, bird and mammal, and the characteristic spring displays of woodland flowers such as primroses, bluebells and wood anemones. The decline in coppicing and the resultant gradual dereliction of woodland is a serious threat to woodland wildlife. This is compounded by the drastic changes in management favouring the development of close-canopy, even-aged monocultures.

Scrub can be a valuable resting, feeding and nesting place for birds, but if left to itself will gradually become woodland. It can be managed, like coppice, on a

TABLE 8.2
Food plants—shrubs (native or naturalized species)

Latin name	English name	Birds		Butterflies		Rodents	Remarks on habitat, etc.
				Larvae	Adults		
Buddleia davidii	buddleia				×		Naturalized in S. England
Cornus sanguinea	hogwood	×					Especially on calcareous soils
Corylus avellana	hazel					×	Lowland woods and hedges
Cotoneaster simonsii		×					Naturalized
Crataegus monogyna	hawthorn	×	p	×	×	×	Hedging species
C. oxyacanthoides	hawthorn	×	p	×	×	×	Mostly in S. and E., on clay and loam. More shade-tolerant, therefore found in woodland.
Euonymus europaeus	spindle	×					Especially on calcareous soils
Ilex aquifolium	holly	×					
Ligustrum vulgare	privet	×		×			Calcareous soils
Lonicera periclymenum	honeysuckle	×			×		Woods and hedgerows
Malus sylvestris	crab apple	×					
Prunus avium, etc.	cherry	×		×			
P. domestica	plum			×			
P. spinosa	blackthorn		p	×			Chiefly calcareous soils in S. & E.
Rhamnus catharticus	buckthorn			×			
Rosa spp	wild rose	×					
Rubus caesius	dewberry	×	p	×	×		Less vigorous form. Mainly basic soils.
R. fruticosus agg.	blackberry, bramble	×	p	×	×		
Salix caprea	goat willow			×	×		
Sambucus nigra	elder	×	p		×		
Sorbus aucuparia	rowan	×	p				Mainly light soils
Symphoricarpos rivularis	snowberry	×	p				Naturalized
Taxus baccata	yew	×					Calcareous soils
Viburnum lantana	wayfaring tree	×					Not on acid soils
V. opulus	guelder rose	×			×	×	Neutral or calcareous soils

p—berries eaten by pheasants.
Butterfly larvae—generally three or more species found on each plant or group mentioned.

TABLE 8.3
Food plants—Herbaceous species (native or naturalized)

Latin name	English name	Birds		Butterflies		Bees	Remarks on habitat, etc.	Height
				Larvae	Adults			
Ajuga reptans	bugle				×		Damp woods and fields	L
Alliaria petiolata	garlic mustard			×			Hedgebanks, wood margins, damp places	M–H
Anthriscus sylvestris	cow parsley	×					Undisturbed ground	H
Armoracia rusticana	horseradish			×				M–H
Aster spp	michaelmas daisy				×		Locally naturalized	M–H
Cardamine pratensis	ladies smock			×	×		Moist places	M
Centaurea nigra, C. scabiosa	knapweed	×			×		*C. scabiosa* especially on calcareous soils and dry places	M–H

131

Latin name	English name	Birds	Butterflies Larvae	Butterflies Adults	Bees	Remarks on habitat, etc.	Height
Centranthus ruber	red valerian			×		Naturalized on old walls, cliffs	M
Cheiranthus cheiri	wallflower			×		Naturalized on cliffs and rocky places	M
Cirsium & Cardun spp	thistles	×		×		*Cirsium vulgare* and *C. arvense* are injurious weeds (statutory obligation to control spread)	M–H
Daucus carota	wild carrot	×	×			Grassy places, especially on calcareous soils and near sea	M
Dipsacus fullonum	teasel	×				Especially on clay soils	H
Erica & Calluna spp	heathers			×	×	Acid soils	M
Foeniculum vulgare	fennel		×			Locally naturalized in waste places especially near the sea	H
Heracleum sphondylium	hogweed	×				Rough grass	H
Knautia arvensis	scabious	×		×		Dry places, especially on calcareous soils	M
Leucanthemum vulgare	ox-eye daisy			×		Basic soils, pastures	M
Lotus corniculatus	birds-foot trefoil		×			Short grass	L
Lupinus arboreus	lupin				×	Locally naturalized, dry and gravelly places	H
Nepeta cataria	catmint			×		Calcareous soils	M
Oenothera biennis	evening primrose	×				Dry places	M
Origanum vulgare	marjoram			×		Usually calcareous soils	L–M
Papaver spp	poppy	×				Mainly in dry places, disturbed ground	M
Petasites fragrans	winter heliotrope			×		Naturalized in hedge-banks, etc.	L
Primula vulgaris	primrose			×		Woods, woodland margins	L
Reseda lutea	mignonette			×		Chalky and dry places	M
Rumex spp	docks	×	×			Waste places	M–H
Solidago virgaurea	golden rod			×		Dry places, cliffs	M
Taraxacum officinale	dandelion		×	×		Short grassland	L
Thymus spp	thyme			×	×	Calcareous and dry soils	L
Trifolium repens, T. pratense, etc.	clovers		×	×	×	Short grassland	L–M
Urtica dioica	nettle	×	×			Nitrogen-rich places	M–H
Valeriana officinalis	valerian			×		Rough grassy places	H

L — Low growing (normally below 30 mm)
M — Medium
H — High (commonly reaching 1 000 mm or more)
Butterfly larvae—generally three or more species found on each plant mentioned
Rough grass is the food plant of many kinds of butterfly larvae.

TABLE 8.4
Food plants—waterfowl

Latin name	English name	Habitat, etc.	Height
MARGINAL PLANTS			
Carex hirta	hairy sedge, hammer sedge	In damp grass and near ponds.	0·3–0·6 m
C. acutiformis	pond sedge	Fringes of still or slow moving water, swamps, especially in north.	0·6–1·5 m
*Eleocharis palustris	common spike-rush	Tufted. Wet meadows, marshes, by ditches and pools.	15–30 cm
Glyceria fluitans	flote-grass	Common in stagnant and slow-flowing water.	0·3–1·2 m
G. maxima	reedgrass	Usually deeper water than G. fluitans	1·2–1·8 m
Polygonum hydropiper	water pepper	Marshy fields, shallow water by ponds and ditches.	0·3–0·6 m
P. persicaria	redleg, redshank	Besides ponds and streams.	0·3–0·6 m
Ranunculus repens	creeping buttercup	Wet meadows by rivers and ditches.	
*Rumex hydrolapathum	great water dock	Wet places and shallow water. Rare in north.	1·2–1·8 m
Sagittaria sagittifolia	arrowhead	Best in silt or mud in approx. 15 cm of water. Rare in north.	0·3–0·9 m
*Scirpus lacustris	common bulrush	Margins of silted lakes, ponds, rivers.	1·8–2·4 m
S. maritimus	sea club-rush	Brackish water.	0·6–1·2 m
**Sparganium erectum	bur-reed	In water at edge of lakes, canals, rivers.	
Typha latifolia	reedmace, bulrush	Invasive, growing down to at least 90 cm. At edges of ponds, canals, etc.	1·2–2·4 m
TREES (SEEDS EATEN)			
Alnus glutinosa	alder		
Betula pubescens	birch		
Quercus spp	oak		
EMERGENT PLANTS			
*Hippuris vulgaris	marestail	Ponds, lakes, slow streams. Wide pH range.	
**Polygonum amphibium	amphibious bistort	Widespread and common. Pools, canals, etc.	
**Potamogeton natans	floating pondweed	Lakes, ponds, ditches. Prefers 0·3–1·5 m depths. More tolerant of acid conditions than other pondweeds. Likes highly organic substratum.	
Ranunculus aquatilis	water crowfoot	Swift streams or bog water. Will tolerate moderate acidity.	
R. baudotii	brackish-water crow-foot	Brackish water.	
FLOATING PLANTS			
Lemna spp	duckweeds	L. trisulca will grow in acid water.	
SUBMERGED PLANTS			
Chara spp	stonewort	Alkaline or brackish water. Still or stagnant. Very rapid growth.	
Potamogeton pectinatus	sago pondweed	Rich, fresh or brackish ponds, ditches, rivers.	
Ruppia maritima	tassel pondweed	Brackish ditches and ponds. In soil or sand from a few inches to several feet.	
PLANTS GIVING MARGINAL COVER			
Iris pseudacorus	flag iris, yellow flag	Marshes, shallow water.	0·3–1·2 m
Phragmites communis	common reed	Swamps and shallow water. Invasive.	1·8–3·6 m

*Species of value
**Species of particular value

Newly coppiced stools. Light demanding ground vegetation begins to develop.

After five years a thick and tangled vegetation develops.

Mature coppice, 15–20 years old and ready for cutting. Little ground vegetation.

FIGURE 8.1 **Managed coppice-with-standards woodland preserves a variety of habitats, changing in location through time.**

PLATE 8.4 **A fritillary on a bramble—a valuable plant for insects.** *(D. Harvey)*

rotational cutting system, over say fifteen years, so that there is a mosaic of different stages from stumps to tall leggy growths.

Ecological richness can be increased by making rides and clearings to encourage growth of the understorey layers. They should be wide enough to allow sunlight to penetrate and should be maintained by cutting. Rides should be designed so as to avoid creating wind tunnels.

In primarily coniferous woodland, edges should be created using a variety of native broad-leaved trees and shrubs, and islands of broad-leaved trees and shrubs should be maintained or created within the plantation.

Management should seek to maintain a diverse age-structure, ranging from saplings to dying trees. This will both maintain a variety of habitats, and also ensure the long-term continuity and stability of the woodland. Very old trees support a particular lichen flora and a fauna of

PLATE 8.5 **Coppiced woodland, especially with standards above, provides a rich variety of habitats, and could be a good way of managing a visual screen (although hazel would be of much more benefit to wildlife than the sweet chestnut in the photograph).** *(C. Yarrow)*

specialized insects, and when dead they are the home of rare insects not associated with younger trees.

Removal of dead and dying material should be kept to the minimum consistent with safety for the public and fire prevention. But elm logs should be removed, debarked and the bark burnt because of Dutch elm disease. Pest outbreaks are unlikely to occur as a result of retaining dead and dying timber in properly managed mixed woodland.

Dead and dying wood supports a very rich insect fauna and a wide variety of fungi, and in less polluted areas a rich lichen and moss flora. Many species of birds are dependent on tree holes for nesting sites. Where mature or overmature trees are absent, nest boxes should be provided.

If cleaning, trimming or scrub clearance operations are necessary, they should be carried out as seldom as

possible and in late autumn or winter to avoid disturbing nesting birds. Similarly, cutting and extraction of timber should be carried out in winter. Figure 8.2 shows a typical woodland/grassland sequence giving a wide variety of habitats.

8.32 Grassland

A consistent management method should be applied so that the vegetation can adapt to it.

Grassland which is correctly grazed or cut to keep the vegetation short will develop a fine-grained vegetation pattern and may contain species-rich communities. Sheep tend to graze favourite patches of sward very hard, while neglecting other parts, which therefore grow longer. Cattle graze less closely than sheep and are less selective. Cattle and horses pull at the grass leaving a rough surface,

135

Woodland canopy, plus understorey of saplings and shade tolerant shrubs and ground vegetation.

Woodland edge. Light demanding trees and shrubs.

Long grass

Short grass

FIGURE 8.2 **A woodland—grassland sequence giving a wide variety of habitats.**

PLATE 8.6 **A typical pond which would benefit from improvement.**

and horses in particular will not graze grass that has been contaminated with faeces, so that long patches develop. The likelihood of compaction and poaching increases with cattle and especially horses.

Frequent cutting, like grazing, favours short grassland species such as *Lotus corniculatus, Trifolium repens, Ranunculus repens*, etc.; but very frequent cutting or cutting at the wrong time of year removes all flower and seed heads. Cutting regimes must allow plants to ripen seed as well as flower.

Cutting in mid to late May with any of the conventional mowing machines will have a lasting effect on the height of the vegetation throughout the growing season. A cut in May followed by another in June will maintain an average height of about 30 cm in most seasons. If the vegetation is to be kept lower than 30 cm, then more frequent cutting will be required, because the natural vegetative growth of most herbaceous plants and grasses usually exceeds 15 cm, although seldom exceeding 30 cm.

A sudden stop in grazing or cutting produces a reduction in species diversity together with rapid growth of some potentially dominant grass species. Conversely, the introduction of mowing in tall grassland, or scrub, will finally lead to low grassland with a greater species diversity.

Grass is best cut at a season that allows maximum flowering for the sake of both plant propagation and insects. This will depend on the kind of vegetation. If ground-nesting birds are present, cutting should be avoided before July or August.

Grass cuttings left on the ground act as a fertilizer and mulch. Therefore it may be necessary to remove cuttings to prevent a build-up of minerals which favours growth of coarse grasses. Dense swathes of long grass cut by a hay mower in June or July will tend to favour coarse grasses. A flail mower chops the cuttings finely and distributes them evenly so that they can easily be broken down and re-assimilated, although these cuttings do add to the nutrient status of the soil.

Maleic hydrazide (a growth inhibitor) applied at high volume rates (at least 145 litres water per ha) at the beginning of the growing season will restrict the growth of herbaceous plants and grasses for ten to twelve weeks. If followed by a cut about six weeks after application, an average height of 30 cm can be maintained through the growing season. Maleic hydrazide tends to eliminate taller tufted species that spread by seed and favour rhizomatous species. Selective herbicides such as 2–4D eliminate most broad-leaved herbs and should be avoided.

There are advantages in maintaining different zones at different heights. An area of long grass, cut once late in the season to eliminate shrubs, will allow the flowering of umbellifers, knapweeds, etc., which are good food plants for birds and insects. The different zones must be treated consistently each year.

8.33 Water and marsh

Areas of open water and marsh should be retained. If possible, any artificial ponds or lakes should have a mud or gravel bottom rather than concrete. The water/land edge will be richest in wildlife where seasonal fluctuations in water level are small and gradual.

The wildlife interest of ponds and lakes can be increased by:

i) ensuring that there are broad-leaved trees near the margin; however, a continuous margin of trees should be avoided since it is important for sunlight to reach the water.

ii) increasing the edge by excavating the shoreline to form small irregular bays.

iii) artificially controlling water levels to prevent sudden irregular inundations of the margins.

iv) controlling silt deposition, if this becomes a problem, with silt traps or by planting woody species at inflow points of streams. All lakes and ponds silt up in time, and it may be necessary to clear silt out of existing ponds to increase the area and depth of open water.

v) providing artificial nest sites for waterfowl (e.g. rafts and duck baskets) and islands where birds can rest and nest undisturbed. Islands, whilst discouraging human interference, are of only limited value in protecting birds from predators since most predators are not deterred by a stretch of water. This is particularly true of feral mink.

vi) ensuring that there are shallow sloping margins, marshy banks and steep banks to give as varied a margin treatment as possible.

vii) providing an adjacent area of grass where waterfowl may graze.

viii) marshy areas should not be drained but should be managed so that the habitat is as varied as possible. This may involve cutting and clearing vegetation to open up pools and water courses, or excavating a number of interconnecting pools. This latter operation can be done quickly and inexpensively with carefully placed explosive charges.

ix) reducing disturbance by limiting access to one side of the expanse of water, by channelling the public by means of nature trails and hides and by providing extensive cover for nesting birds.

Figure 8.3 shows an 'ideal' pond providing a wide variety of habitats.

8.34 Hedges

Wherever possible hedges should be retained, and hedgerow trees should be retained and encouraged. A large proportion of the British fauna can be found in hedgerows, and the hedge system can be regarded as an

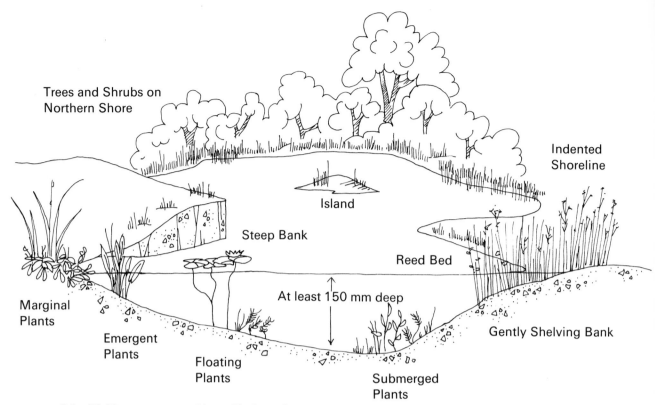

FIGURE 8.3 **Habitats represented in an ideal pond.**

FIGURE 8.4 **Habitats represented in an ideal roadside hedgerow.**

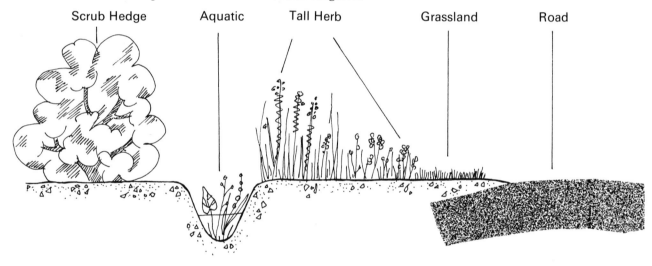

extension of rich woodland into agricultural land.

While tall, unkempt hedges are excellent for wildlife, this state usually presages their removal; as with other forms of habitat, regular management is essential for their survival.

Traditional hedge laying is an ideal form of management from the wildlife point of view, as it ensures a variety of hedge type from the newly laid to the tall hedge at the end of the cycle. However, it is rarely practicable these days. The alternative of mechanical trimming is best carried out every two or three years, rather than annually, to maintain some variety of form. Cutting should be carried out at the end of the winter, after the berries have been eaten by birds.

If the hedge is no longer required to enclose stock, because the land has been converted to arable, or perhaps to parkland, it could be maintained by coppice management, i.e. by cutting back to ground level every eight years or so rotationally. Figure 8.4 shows an 'ideal' hedgerow and roadside verge, providing a variety of habitats.

8.4 SUMMARY OF GENERAL GUIDELINES

i) Planting and management for wildlife conservation must be based upon sound ecological principles. Unless there is a particularly important species or habitat to be conserved, the aim should be to create and maintain a variety of habitats and of species. This is best achieved by encouraging structural diversity of plant form, a variety of plant species, and a varied age-structure. Wherever possible marginal habitats should be increased by producing an indented boundary.

ii) Management operations, and the reasons behind them, should be clearly set out in a management plan. This is particularly important in the case of woodland, where the management cycle may span decades or even centuries.

iii) Sudden, drastic changes in regime which are either natural (e.g. periodic inundation of lake margins; alternation between salt water and fresh water) or man-made (e.g. sudden cessation of a management regime or sudden enrichment by fertilizer application) will tend to decrease species diversity. If changes in management regime are necessary they should be as small and as gradual as possible.

iv) Planting schemes should use only native species unless an introduced species has a particular advantage for wildlife; they should be designed to increase plant and structural diversity.

v) Removal of dead plant material and general 'tidying-up' should be minimal and in any event only as much as is necessary to prevent accidents, fire or unsightly appearance.

vi) Application of pesticides, herbicides and fertilizers should be avoided except as a last resort.

vii) The landscape architect would be well advised to seek advice from the ecologist and the land manager at both planting design and management plan stages. The plant ecologist, in particular, should be consulted at an early stage about what is possible and advisable for the site and about plant selection.

FURTHER READING

*Barber, D. (ed.) *Farming and wildlife: a study in compromise* (RSPB, 1970)

*British Trust for Conservation Volunteers. *Hedging*. 1975

Campbell, B. 'Birds and Woodlands'. *Forestry Commission leaflet* 47 (London: HMSO, 1964)

*Devon Trust for Nature Conservation. 'Wildlife conservation and woodland management'. Supplement to *J. Devon Trust for Nat. Cons.* 1970

*Devon Trust for Nature Conservation. 'A plan to establish a Nature Reserve'. Bulletin No. 7, 1973

*Devon Trust for Nature Conservation. 'Wildlife Conservation and Lichens'. Supplement to *J. Devon Trust for Nat. Cons.* 1975

Duffey, E. (ed.) 'The biotic effects of public pressures on the environment'. Monk's Wood Experimental Station Symposium No. 3. (The Nature Conservancy, 1967)

*Eley Game Advisory Station. 'Forestry and pheasants'. Booklet 15, 1967

*Eley Game Advisory Station. 'Wildfowl management on inland waters'. Booklet 3, 1969

Fairbrother, N. *New Lives, New Landscapes* (London: Architectural Press, 1970)

*Fryer, J. and Makepeace, R. *Weed Control Handbook* (Oxford: Blackwell Scientific Publications, 1972) Vol II. Recommendations

Hamilton, F. 'Forestry and birds'. *The Forester*, Sept. 1968 pp. 14–16 (Forestry Division of Min. of Ag., N. Ireland)

Heal, H. G. 'The conservation of butterflies in N. Ireland forests'. *The Forester*, Sept. 1968 pp. 3–13 (Forestry Division of Min. of Ag., N. Ireland)

Heal, H. G. 'Conservation aspects of amenity planting' (Unpublished paper, 1969)

Helliwell, D. R. 'A methodology for the assessment of priorities and values in nature conservation.' Marlewood Research and Development Paper No. 28, (The Nature Conservancy, 1971)

Hooper, M. D., and Holdgate, M. W. (ed.) 'Hedges and hedgerow trees' (especially N. W. Moore, 'The Conservation of animals') Monk's Wood Experimental Station Symposium No. 4 (The Nature Conservancy, 1968)

*Nature Conservancy Council leaflets: 'Hedges and Shelterbelts', 'Wildlife on Farmland' and 'Ponds and Ditches', 1973; 'Tree planting and wildlife conservation', 1974

*Newman, L. H. *Create a butterfly garden* (Worlds Work, 1967)

Pollard, E., Hooper, M. D., and Moore, N. W. 'Hedges' New Naturalist (London: Collins, 1974)

*Royal Society for the Protection of Birds. 'The birds in your garden' and 'Feed the birds' (leaflet) 1972

*Society for the Promotion of Nature Reserves. 'Scrub clearance: a conservation code' (leaflets), and 'Recommended policy for introduced species'

*Soper, T. *The new bird table book* (Newton Abbot: David & Charles, 1974)

Southwood, T. R. E. 'The number of species of insect associated with various trees. *J. Animal Ecology* No. 30, 1961

*Steele, R. C. 'Wildlife conservation in woodlands.' Forestry Commission Booklet No. 29 (HMSO, 1972)

*Stubbs, A. E. 'Wildlife conservation and dead wood.' Supplement to *J. Devon Trust for Nat. Cons.* 1972

Way, J. M. (ed.) 'Road verges: their function and management' Symposium Proceedings. Monk's Wood Experimental Station (The Nature Conservancy, 1969)

Way, J. M. (ed.) 'Road verges in Scotland: their function and management' Symposium Proceedings (Edinburgh: The Nature Conservancy, 1970)

Way, J. M. 'Road verges on rural roads: management and other factors.' Monk's Wood Experimental Station Occasional Report, No. 1 (The Nature Conservancy, 1973)

* Publications giving practical advice.

ACKNOWLEDGEMENTS

Dr Way and Dr Wells of the Institute of Terrestrial Ecology, Monk's Wood Experimental Station, and various members of Land Use Consultants, have kindly suggested corrections and improvements, as have ecologists Roger Lee (Highlands and Islands Development Board) and Robert Edgar (East Sussex County Council).

Bodinnick Woods, Fowey, Cornwall. *(John Chitty)*

CHAPTER 9

Planting in Artificial Conditions

RICHARD BAKER, KATHY STANSFIELD AND RIK STURDY

The prevalence of paved or other hard surfaces in our towns and cities has meant that plants can only survive in these conditions where their needs are supplied artificially. As this chapter shows, plants can be successfully grown in pits in paved areas, plant containers, balconies, building courtyards, roof gardens, and in other artificial conditions.

The chapter is divided into three parts. Part A stresses the very considerable contribution which plants can make to the urban environment and considers the technical factors which determine the success or failure of plant growth in artificial conditions.

Part B discusses the methods, principles and techniques of planting in pits in paved areas, raised beds, plant containers and balconies. Special consideration is given to courtyards and roof gardens both of which present particular difficulties. These are illustrated by case studies since it is from practical experience that these problems and solutions can best be discussed. The Manchester Education precinct has been selected because the proposed design for this huge project incorporates most of the features of planting in artificial conditions described in Part A, in an admirable attempt to re-introduce landscape beauty into a degraded urban environment. Particular examples studied within the precinct are the courtyard of the Architecture and Town Planning Department and the roof garden of the Royal Northern College of Music.

Part C discusses plant selection, presents lists of plant material for particular urban areas and a discussion of maintenance aspects of planting in artificial conditions.

Reference should be made to Chapters 3 and 10 concerning tree planting and transplanting in urban areas, and to Chapter 13 for the effects of air pollution.

Part A

9.1 THE IMPORTANCE OF PLANTING IN ARTIFICIAL CONDITIONS

Extensive urbanization has meant that man has become increasingly divorced from nature: towns and cities have spread over what was once countryside and have become so densely built that buildings and hard ground surfaces have displaced soil and plants. This is the familiar working environment for most human beings in the western world. Contact with plants in such areas is dependent upon a conscious decision by man to provide conditions in which plants will grow, and to tend and foster them. By so doing a new dimension of natural beauty can be added to the built forms and spaces of urban areas. Other positive benefits are the reduction of air pollution, screening as a buffer against noise and wind, and generally increasing the well-being of the city dweller.

FIGURE 9.1 **Different forms of planting in artificial conditions.**

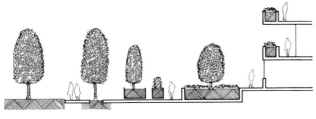

NATURAL GROUND   PAVED AREAS   PLANT CONTAINERS   RAISED PLANTING   HIGH LEVEL PLANTING

PLATE 9.1 **Varied planting at the entrance to a school in Zurich.** (Landscape Architect: *Walter Leder*. Photography: *Ian Laurie*)

PLATE 9.2 **Groundcover on the Central Station Roof Garden, Berne.** *(Ian Laurie)*

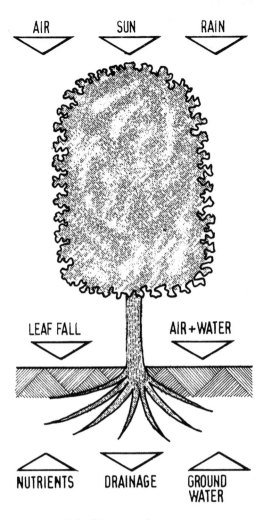

AIR   SUN   RAIN

LEAF FALL   AIR + WATER

NUTRIENTS   DRAINAGE   GROUND WATER

FIGURE 9.2 **Plant requirements.**

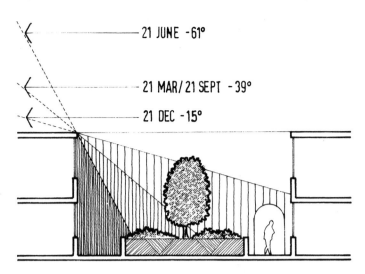

21 JUNE - 61°

21 MAR / 21 SEPT - 39°

21 DEC - 15°

FIGURE 9.3 **Effect of surrounding buildings on distribution of sunlight throughout the year.**

9.2 DETERMINING FACTORS

The success of planting schemes in artificial conditions will to a large extent be determined by the local microclimate, including the amount of shelter provided, the light and water available, and other factors such as drainage and soils (*see* Figure 9.2). All these factors must be analysed with reference to the site before the design is commenced and a selection of plants made.

9.21 Microclimate

Careful consideration should be given to the abnormal climatic effects arising from such factors as proximity and disposition of buildings, extensive hard surfaces, possible separation from natural terrain and other features of urban areas. The main effects are summarized below and are considered further where relevant in the sections following.

i)   Wind may be funnelled between buildings causing an increase in velocity. Other effects may be turbulence,

the venturi effect and eddying, particularly around high buildings.

ii) The amount of light is very much influenced by the height and proximity of buildings, degree of overhang, and texture and colour of cladding surfaces.

iii) The natural precipitation pattern is frequently altered, for instance plant material in areas of rain shadow or under overhanging structures will be deprived of water.

iv) Temperatures may be more extreme, for example frost pockets in winter, and heat reflection from pavings in summer. Where plant material is in containers separated from the natural terrain temperature extremes will be intensified.

9.22 Shelter

The adverse effects of microclimate discussed above stress the need for shelter and protection of plants from the damaging effects of wind, not only on exposed sites or on the roofs of buildings, but also at street level.

It is of the utmost importance that proper anchorage be provided for trees and shrubs to protect them from wind rocking which breaks the soil/root contact and may in extreme conditions sever the trunk. The normal development of the root system in plants growing in artificial conditions may be restricted by lack of space and shallowness of soil, particularly in the case of trees which develop tap roots.

Several methods of anchoring trees and shrubs are described below.

i)   *Staking.* This is the most conventional method where wooden stakes are pushed into the ground and the tree stems secured to them by means of a tree tie.

143

PLATE 9.3 **A sheltered sitting area in a neighbourhood park, Berne.** *(Ian Laurie)*

PLATE 9.4 **A sunken garden for changing rooms at an outdoor swimming lido in Zurich, Switzerland.** *(Ian Laurie)*

ii) *Above ground guying*. Three or four wire guys are passed between the main stem and a branch about half way up the tree, being encased in rubber tubing where the wire would otherwise come into contact with the trunk. They are secured to pegs, or deadmen below ground, and tensioned at an angle of 45° to the tree trunk. This method is commonly used for large or semi-mature trees, particularly in areas where there is little risk of vandalism.

iii) *Underground guying*. This is a technique used for large trees where an unobtrusive method of support is required. It has particular application in paved areas where aerial guys would be difficult to secure and prone to vandalism. A frame of timber is placed over the root ball for protection before wires are passed over it. These are attached to deadmen below ground, or to stakes driven in at an angle.

9.23 Light

Before the plant design stage a survey should be made of the heights of the surrounding buildings and the effects these will have on the distribution of sunlight throughout the year using sunpath diagrams for the appropriate latitude (*see* Figure 9.3). In new developments careful study will be necessary to determine the distribution and intensity of light from plans and detail drawings.

The surfaces of buildings and pavings will reflect varying amounts of light and heat. Light surfaces in particular can reflect sufficient heat on a summer day to cause plant scorch, especially on the bark of trees. This can be prevented by temporarily burlapping the trunk until the tree has adapted to the new conditions.

In countries with a low light intensity, such as Great Britain, areas in deep shade—overhangs or corners in particular—should be treated with caution as plants will be difficult to grow.

9.24 Water

One of the major problems of planting in urban areas is to ensure that plants have an adequate supply of water. In paved areas trees are often deprived of water because the drip line lies outside the spread of the tree roots. Figure 9.4 shows the different relationships between planting pit, tree size and paved areas.

a) The drip line falls outside the catchment of the planting pit and the paving levels shed the water away from it, thus depriving the tree of water.

b) The large planting pit ensures that the drip line falls within the soil area and the water falls onto open-jointed paving (or bare soil, tree grille or groundcover) thus reaching the roots. A constant fall across the pit enables the surface water to flow across the area but not to collect.

c) Paving falls are dished towards the tree, thus providing it with a source of water. However the water will be concentrated around the trunk area rather than the feeder roots where it would be absorbed, and rather than helping the tree to survive, it may cause collar rot.

Invariably the mains will be the source of water. Checks should be made with the Regional Water Authority as to their requirements and charges before embarking on the installation of a watering system. Care should be taken that the lime content of water from the mains will not have an adverse effect on the plants to be watered.

The importance of depths of soil with regard to water supply is considered in 9.26.

9.25 Drainage

Adequate drainage is essential to a plant's survival. Failure to provide it will lead to a lack of oxygen and deterioration in the quality of the soil resulting in reduced root growth and possibly death in severe cases.

FIGURE 9.4 **Tree drip line, pit size and paving falls in relation to water catchment.**

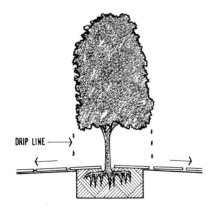

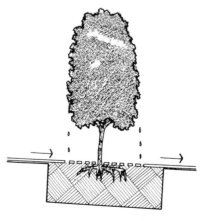

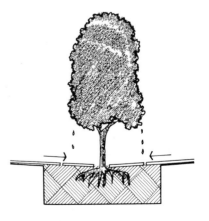

DRIP LINE ⟶

a) INSUFFICIENT WATER

b) ADEQUATE WATER

c) TOO MUCH WATER

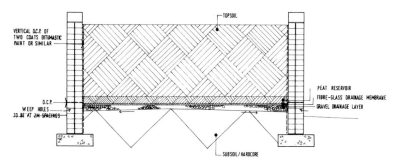

FIGURE 9.5 **Drainage system using topsoil, peat layer and hardcore.**

FIGURE 9.6 **Drainage system using peat, fibre glass and gravel.**

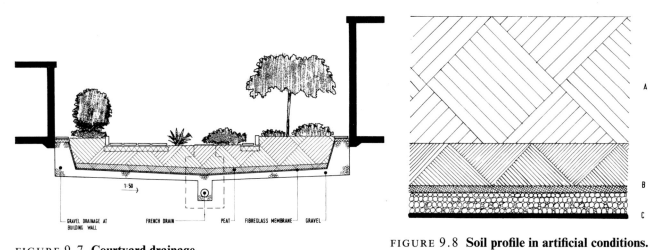

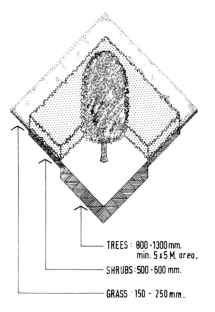

FIGURE 9.7 **Courtyard drainage.**

FIGURE 9.8 **Soil profile in artificial conditions.**

TREES : 800 - 1300 mm.
min. 5 x 5 M. area.

SHRUBS : 500 - 600 mm.

GRASS 150 - 250 mm.

FIGURE 9.9 **Recommended soil depths.**

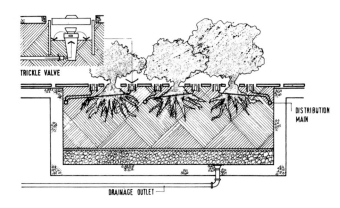

FIGURE 9.10 **Trickle valve irrigation system.**

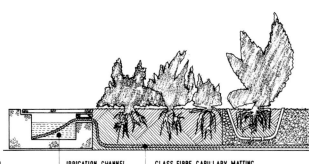

146   FIGURE 9.11 **Capillary irrigation system.**

If site analysis reveals poor drainage characteristics special measures should be taken. These may range from excavating deeper into the ground to break up any impermeable soil pan which may be present, to providing a drainage medium such as gravel or hardcore at the bottom of the planting pit, which can if necessary be linked to an outfall.

The simplest and most frequently used method of draining containers and raised beds involves laying topsoil directly onto a drainage medium such as gravel or hardcore, allowing the water to discharge through weepholes near the base of the container (*see* Figure 9.5). Over time the soil particles washed into the drainage layer will reduce the efficiency of this system.

If the container is made from brick tanking, with asphalt on the inside of the wall above the weepholes will prevent water seeping through the brickwork and reduce the risk of efflorescence on the outer brick surface.

A more sophisticated drainage system, costing more to install but more efficient and durable, combines the use of peat, fibre glass and gravel (*see* Figure 9.6). The base of the planting pit or bed should be laid to a fall of 1:50 to 1:80 to ensure that pockets of stagnant water do not form. The first layer is formed by a 100 mm (4 in.) layer of 20–50 mm rounded aggregate on top of which a 15 mm ($\frac{1}{2}$ in.) fibreglass blanket is laid. This filters out the fine soil and peat particles brought down by the water and prevents clogging up the drainage layer below. Above the filter a 100 mm (4 in.) layer of granulated peat which compresses by half when the growing medium is laid on top of it acts as a water reservoir. This is a refinement which can also be used in the topsoil-hardcore method.

The water is discharged through weepholes onto a paved area and subsequently directed to the surface water drainage system. Alternatively it can be piped direct into the drainage system or a soakaway or use may be made of a french drain (*see* Figure 9.7).

9.26 Soil

In urban areas, soils, if they exist at all, tend to be dry, shallow and of poor quality. Analysis should be carried out to determine the deficiencies of the soil and to suggest means by which it can be ameliorated. It may be necessary for soil to be imported from outside the site, in which case the soil type may be selected and specified to suit the specific plant requirements. In any event, it is advisable to ensure that a high quality topsoil is used and that it has an adequate supply of nutrients, a good structure and texture and an appropriate pH, that is, it is neither unduly acid or alkaline for the plant material concerned. Good moisture retaining properties, the ability to drain well and a rich nutrient status are essential qualities for planting in artificial conditions.

A natural soil profile is a section through the soil showing the different horizons or layers which extend downwards from the surface to the parent rock. These layers are usually designated by the letters *A, B* and *C. A* is the layer called the top or vegetable soil which contains the minerals, bacteria, moisture and organic materials so vital to plant growth. *B* is the subsoil, the nature of which has an important bearing on how the topsoil will drain, while *C* is the parent rock. In artificial conditions *A* can be regarded as the growing medium, *B* the drainage system, and *C* the container or hard surface base (*see* Figure 9.8).

Generally the greater the depth of soil provided, the larger can be the size of plants to be grown. Whilst trees will grow in shallow soils, the adverse microclimate in artificial conditions means that a generous depth should be provided. For trees a range of 800 to 1300 mm is recommended over an area of 5 m². Shrubs require between 500 and 600 mm, and grass 150–250 mm (*see* Figure 9.9).

The nutrient reserves of soils in containers, beds or pits quickly become impoverished owing to their isolation from natural replenishment processes. An annual application of a well balanced fertilizer will redress the deficiency and periodic mulching will be beneficial. In the case of small containers it may, after several years, be necessary to replace the exhausted soil with fresh material.

9.27 Irrigation

The decision whether to irrigate or not will be strongly influenced by climatic conditions, not simply in terms of arid or temperate climates, but by microclimatic variations within the countries. In England for instance, the dryer eastern part of the country is more likely to need irrigation than the wetter west. A careful assessment should be made of the likely soil water status by considering local rainfall figures, evapo-transpiration rates and, if applicable, water-table levels and ground conditions.

The type of system selected will depend on cost, labour available, and the characteristics of the area to be irrigated.

Watering may be carried out by hand using a watering can or hose, or water tanker, depending on the scale of operation. The use of sprinklers and permanently installed irrigation systems, of which there is a wide range, will save time and labour, but it must be remembered that there is no substitute for human judgement and constant supervision of a plant's water needs. Automatic watering systems that operate without regard for the needs of plants can be lethal by saturating the soil.

There are three main types of irrigation systems.
i) *Sprinkler irrigation*
    A wide variety of types is available, Sprinklers can be fitted to risers (as in the Edinburgh Botanic Garden rockery), but a pop-up sprinkler may be more suitable where a smooth surface without projections is required, e.g. a grassy area which has to be mown. The water can be sprayed either from a fixed jet or from a

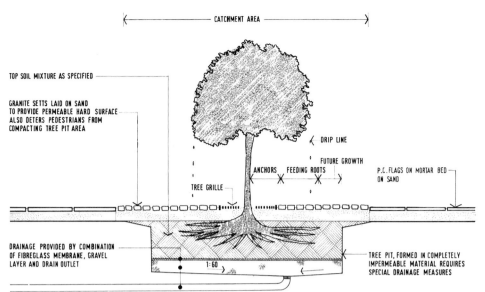

FIGURE 9.12
Planting pit in a paved area.

TOP SOIL MIXTURE AS SPECIFIED

GRANITE SETTS LAID ON SAND
TO PROVIDE PERMEABLE HARD SURFACE
ALSO DETERS PEDESTRIANS FROM
COMPACTING TREE PIT AREA

CATCHMENT AREA

DRIP LINE

FUTURE GROWTH

ANCHORS FEEDING ROOTS

P.C. FLAGS ON MORTAR BED
ON SAND

TREE GRILLE

DRAINAGE PROVIDED BY COMBINATION
OF FIBREGLASS MEMBRANE, GRAVEL
LAYER AND DRAIN OUTLET

1:60

TREE PIT, FORMED IN COMPLETELY
IMPERMEABLE MATERIAL REQUIRES
SPECIAL DRAINAGE MEASURES

rotary spray throwing water over a large area. The system is used mainly for lawns and large areas of groundcover, and may be manually or automatically controlled. Care should be taken in siting these appliances to prevent spraying passers-by.

ii) *Trickle-irrigation*

Plants are supplied with controlled amounts of water directly to the top of the root zone from trickle valves fitted with a control device which allows different flow rates. Figure 9.10 shows a detail of the trickle valve indicating the water flow. Most trickle irrigation systems are self-regulating, automatically compensating for water pressure variations within certain limits. Because these systems irrigate within the plant root area, an 80% water saving can be claimed as compared with flood irrigation and up to 50% by comparison with sprinkler systems. For this reason trickle systems have particular application in hot dry climates where water conservation is of prime importance.

iii) *Capillary irrigation*

The glass fibre capillary matting provides controlled amounts of water from the irrigation channel. This method is rarely used but has application in roof gardens, garden courts and indoors (*see* Figure 9.11).

Other methods of irrigation

A continuous water supply for planting above ground level can be provided by creating an artificial water table, that is, a permanently water-saturated layer over the entire roof area (e.g. the St. Martin roof garden, Lausanne, and Harvey's in Guildford where water from the pools on the roof is used).

A method of irrigating balcony planting is described in 9.34.

9.28 Waterproofing

This is of particular importance in roof gardens where a waterproof membrane is generally provided. The most commonly used method is a full asphalt specification, laid to a fall of about 1 in 60, directly over the entire roof area to provide an impermeable base (e.g. the Gross Schanze Park on the roof of Berne Railway Station). There are various bituminous products combined with milled glass fibres, yarns or asbestos felt which provide resilient water and rot-proof membranes. A protective screed over the waterproof membrane provides additional protection, particularly from invasive plant roots. The effectiveness of waterproofing may be increased by using two membranes separated by a screed. Sheet linings such as butyl or polythene can be used over small areas, such as a pool in a roof garden.

9.29 Anti-desiccants

Application of anti-desiccant sprays is rarely necessary at street level, but on roof gardens plants may lose more moisture as a result of the more extreme conditions. In such cases anti-desiccants can be sprayed on plants three times annually—once in late spring, once after leaf fall, and once around February.

Part B

9.3 PLANTING METHODS, PRINCIPLES AND TECHNIQUES

The way in which the plant requirements described above are met depends to a certain extent on whether the planting is to take place in paved areas, raised beds or containers. Careful thought needs to be given to the detailed planting technique to ensure satisfactory results. Some of the commonest methods are discussed below as a guide, but in practice the conditions in each individual case will determine the solution, which may be a combination of different methods.

9.31 Planting pits in paved areas

In practice a wide range of situations will be encountered where planting pits can be used, each requiring a different approach. Two main types can be distinguished which represent each extreme of the range. They are described briefly below.

i) *Planting pit set into the ground.* This is generally the most straightforward type. There should be no drainage problem provided that there is a permeable subsoil, and there will be little variation in ground temperature.

ii) *Planting pit isolated from ground terrain.* In this case water will have to be provided by irrigation if rainfall is insufficient, and a drainage system will have to be installed. Variations in soil temperature may be greater, and may result in frost damage to roots in winter or drying out of soil in summer.

Approach

Figure 9.12 is an example of a fairly typical situation and demonstrates the principles that should be considered. In this case the planting pit has been excavated in impermeable material, and the water table lies too deep to be of benefit.

i) The tree is almost mature, but note that the tree pit is sufficiently large to accommodate further root growth and that the drip line falls well within the generous catchment area of the pit. Granite setts are laid on sand to provide a permeable hard surface which at the

PLATE 9.5 **Civic square, Houston, USA, showing a variety of plants, including striking pattern formed by groundcover around tree boles.** *(Ian Laurie)*

PLATE 9.6 **Trees and shrubs in a strong architectural composition of containers, screening the City of London Girls School from the Barbican housing scheme.** *(Richard Baker)*

PLATE 9.7 **An assorted group of plant containers, Holborn, London.** *(Richard Baker)*

same time discourages pedestrians, thus preventing compaction of the rooting medium. Water and air are thus given the maximum opportunity to penetrate into the rooting zone.

ii) Owing to the completely impermeable sub-stratum, drainage is required to prevent the pit filling up like a sump in wet weather. A combination of fibreglass membrane, peat and gravel may be used, linked to a drain outlet.

9.32 Raised planting beds

Raised planting beds may be constructed from brick walls, *in situ* concrete, pre-cast units, concrete blocks, setts and other materials. They are more permanent, more robust and generally larger than plant containers and are often part of or associated with a nearby building.

Both raised planting beds and containers may be used to define space, provide enclosure and introduce planting into areas where it would otherwise be impossible.

As in the case of a planting pit isolated from the ground, drainage and possibly irrigation will be necessary. There will be additional problems because of the relatively small size of the bed. The small size of the catchment area and exposed walls will create a tendency for the soil to dry out more quickly. Root growth will be restricted to the size and depth of the container. There will be little or no natural replenishment of soil and over time nutrient reserves may become sufficiently depleted to make it necessary to add fertilizer or to replace the soil.

Approach

i) It is advisable to make planting beds as large as possible to contain the spread of mature roots.

ii) The peat layer, membrane and gravel drainage detail can be used, with weep holes in the walling or an alternative drainage outlet in the base (*see* Figure 9.6). Alternatively topsoil can be placed on either a gravel or hardcore drainage layer. A peat layer may be incorporated above the drainage layer to act as a water reservoir (*see* 9.25).

iii) Provide as generous a depth of topsoil as possible.

9.33 Plant containers

Plant containers provide a cheap, temporary and flexible means of growing plants. They can be obtained in a vast array of shapes and sizes and made out of many different materials. As far as public landscape schemes are concerned, the most widely used materials are pre-cast and *in situ* concrete, timber, brick, glass reinforced concrete and pvc. A number of manufacturers supply plant containers with seating as an integral part of the design or as separate matching units.

The plant container is generally constructed of relatively thin material and is completely separated from the ground terrain, thus the problems described in connection with planting pits and raised beds will be further exacerbated. The small size will restrict root growth and limit the choice of plants which can be successfully grown. Normally drainage holes are provided in the base of the container.

Approach

i) There will be more scope for planting if a large, deep container is used.

ii) A prepared mix of loam, peat and sand will aid the necessary balance of air, nutrients and water.

iii) A drainage layer will be needed at the bottom of the container, and consideration should be given to disposal of water from the drainage hole.

iv) Fertilizer and mulch can be added at periodic intervals to replenish nutrients, or the soil can be replaced, after a period of years.

9.34 Balconies

The hard surfaces and edges of high buildings can be relieved by planting on balconies which also allows users of high buildings to retain contact with nature by using a balcony as a miniature garden.

Balcony planting can be incorporated into existing individual balconies by using window boxes. Alternatively it may be designed as an integral part of the scheme with provision for drainage and irrigation where the balconies form part of higher level public open spaces or raised walkways giving access to flats.

The Byker housing development at Newcastle incorporates a variety of planting boxes on the upper level decks and balconies of the three- to eight-storey flats in the Byker Wall. Sometimes these are planted and carried up to the decks, or partially planted so that tenants can fill them up with plants of their choice. Other boxes are cantilevered onto the outside of the walls. Materials used include asbestos, fibreglass and brown plastic boxes, sometimes inserted into wooden containers. Drainage is by peat, gravel and weepholes. Much of the maintenance is left to tenants and the scheme is very popular.

In Westminster City Council's Lillington Street housing, planting on balconies is designed as an integral part of the scheme along upper level walkways. The planting is irrigated by a combination of natural and artificial methods.

On decks sheltered from the rain, water from the roof is piped into a catch-pit from which the water is conducted to the soil through perforated pipes. This drains through to the screed layer until sufficient water collects to spill into a collection silt catch-pit from which it passes into a drain.

There are many examples of the integrated design of balcony planting and housing developments in Switzerland. In some cases the balcony is located at the end of an upper level terrace, and planting is designed to give an immediate impression of contact with ground level, framing or underlining more distant views from the building. The advantages of integrated design are more

FIGURES 9.13 & 9.14
Before and after sketches of landscape proposals for the Manchester Education Precinct, showing a large open space replacing a road. (Landscape Architects: *Donaldson/Edwards Partnership*)

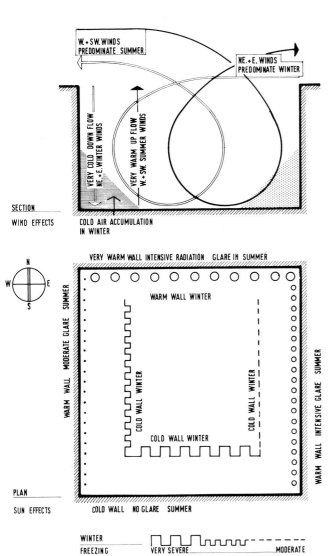

FIGURE 9.15
Typical microclimate conditions in a courtyard.

open space. The examples have been taken from the Architecture and Town Planning building and the Royal Northern College of Music, the former being a garden court, and the latter a roof garden.

9.35 Courtyards

Many modern buildings incorporate courtyards at ground level as part of their design, providing, as in the case of roof gardens, an area of open space for users of the building, with a varied range of uses. A courtyard is often the focal point of interest for views from the interior of the building, improving the quality of the work environment in rooms surrounding it, in addition to its use for outdoor activities.

Mention has already been made of microclimatic effects in artificial conditions, but there are specific points which have to be considered in courtyard design. A wide range of conditions such as sun pockets, frost corners and wind turbulence may be found, all of which must be anticipated at the design stage. Typical microclimatic conditions that can occur in a courtyard are shown in Figure 9.15.

The courtyard and the building should be designed together so that both are fully integrated. The distribution and design of hard and soft surfaces, seating areas, pools and so forth, and the height, shape and texture of plants should form a harmonious design in scale with the walls and windows of the enclosed building and relating to the activities within. Positioning of access points, for instance, may be a crucial factor in determining the extent to which the courtyard is used, particularly in areas of poor winter climate. There is considerable scope for features of special visual interest, including pieces of sculpture, natural rock groups and pools with fountains or small jets of water.

obvious in schemes incorporating larger elevated spaces than private balconies, where drainage, irrigation, night-lighting and maintenance can all be properly organized.

Having discussed the principles and techniques associated with planting in various conditions, it is proposed now to look at the more complex problems of planting in courtyards and roof gardens. The most effective method has been in each case to describe the general principles and then to make a case study of a specific example.

Both examples have been taken from the proposed Manchester Education Precinct which is planned as one of the largest education complexes in Europe. The Landscape Master Plan indicates planting in linear pedestrian spaces, courtyards, roof gardens, upper-level walkways, along roadside frontages, and in large areas of

Case Study: The Garden Court

The Architecture and Town Planning building, Manchester University, was in full occupation from October 1970. The garden court was planted during the autumn. It consists of a quadrangle surrounded by pre-cast concrete units with a surface of exposed Cornish granite aggregate designed to avoid staining in wet weather. The building was designed on a 2·7 m (9 ft) module, the standard two-storey units for the offices on the ground floor being 1·5 m (4 ft 6 in.) wide. All four walls are lined with windows overlooking the courtyard. The single entrance is from the main foyer of the building (*see* Figure 9.16).

Constraints
i) Although the building is largely symmetrical about the north–south axis, the thrust of the entrance from

153

PLATE 9.8 **One of a series of courtyards designed to give visual pleasure to public waiting areas, corridors and hallways. Textures of large, loose cobbles contrasted with smooth paving slabs. Contrasting plant textures of** *Viburnum rhytidophyllum, Cotoneaster salicifolius, Hypericum calycinum* **and** *Lonicera pileata.*
(Landscape Architects: *Derek Lovejoy and Partners.* Architects and photograph: *Building Design Partnership*)

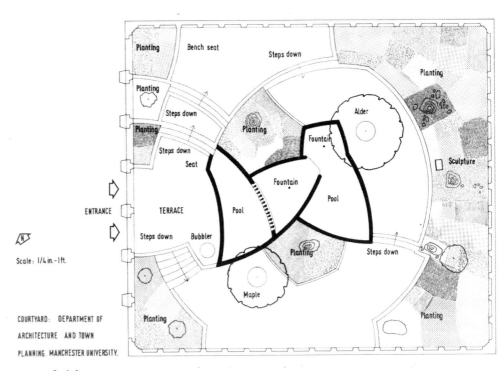

FIGURE 9.16
The plan for the courtyard, Department of Architecture and Town Planning, Manchester University. (Landscape Architect: *Ian Laurie.* Architects: *Hanson, Kantorowich and Partners*)

PLATE 9.9 **Natural rocks used with planting as a feature of the entrance court to a school in Zurich.** (Landscape Architect: *Walter Leder*. Photograph: *Ian Laurie*)

the east façade disturbs the symmetry in subtle but significant ways. The courtyard, eight grids deep and seven grids wide at ground floor level, leads off a two-storey exhibition area formed by the entrance foyer. The courtyard entrance is off centre, and this became the starting point of its design.

ii) The design was constrained by the single access point, and one of the aims was to draw the visitor to the farthest parts of the garden.

iii) It was the wish of the architects that the courtyard should be a foil to the severe geometric discipline of the building, at the same time being integrated with it. The court was expected to provide an outdoor extension to the large internal foyer space, designed to be a focus for views from several levels within the building, as well as a quiet area in which to sit or walk.

iv) Microclimatic conditions were important. Most of the court is in the shade for much of the day during the winter, but in the summer the northern end, particularly the north-eastern corner, receives sun. Light and warmth are reflected from the light-coloured concrete walls. The garden court is well sheltered but there is some down-draught eddying especially on windy days, which is reduced by the presence of two semi-mature trees.

Design

The design reflects symbolically the north-west regional landscape. The entrance platform at the upper level symbolizes the hill top, steps descending on either side to the valley floor. The higher tree is suggestive of uplands, the lower *Alnus* beside the bottom pool, the lowland plain. Water bubbles as if from a spring and gushes, spouts and falls, as in hilly country through descending pools, to the quiet pool, the lowland lake, at the lower level.

In plan the shape suggests a conch spiral, dislocated and fragmented because the curves are all of a constant radius of 16·5 m (54 ft), six times the building module. The coiled form is set along a slightly diagonal axis from north-west to south-east, following a line between the double entrance doors and main fountain, to the Hepworth bronze 'Head of Ra' in shade. The sculpture forms one of several 'incidents' to attract the eye in a walk around the garden.

The courtyard is designed as a working demonstration garden for study by students of landscape design, and thus contains a rich variety of plant material (*see below*).

Technical details

i)   The paving is of blue brick paviers of the same type as

155

PLATE 9.10 **The garden court, Architecture and Town Planning building Manchester University.** (Photograph: *Geoff Wheeler*)

used on the ground floor of the foyer. Because of the unusual and complicated shapes of the areas to be covered, it proved extremely difficult to lay the paving to a fall for drainage purposes. Except on the upper level the paviers were laid on sand, with sand joints to allow free drainage to open jointed land or tile drains of unglazed earthenware (230×75 m), connecting to the main sewers. A gradual clogging up of the pipes over time is characteristic of this system. Paving was laid to fall to a drain on the upper level, to direct water away from the building.

ii) The steps, curbs and copings are all formed in pre-cast concrete from a single mould, curved in plan, and cut to lengths as required. The width satisfied the requirements of the various wall sections devised for vertical tanking and retaining in the several parts of the construction.

iii) The interlocking pools were constructed of engineering brick. To avoid staining which may have resulted from rising damp into bricks above water level, a damp-proof course was provided in these areas. The original idea to form the pools from *in situ* concrete, which would have made the solution of problems easier, proved too expensive.

156

TABLE 9.1
Courtyard Planting—Architecture and Planning Building

Trees
  Acer negundo 'Elegans'
  Alnus incana
  Robinia pseudoacacia 'Frisia'

Large shrubs
  Arundinaria auricoma
  Cornus alba 'Elegantissima'
  Cornus stolonifera 'Flaviramea'
  Cotoneaster simonsii
  Hamamelis mollis
  Leycesteria formosa
  Phillyrea latifolia
  Pieris formosa forrestii
  Pyracantha atalantioides
  Rhus typhina 'Laciniata'
  Salix elaeagnos
  Stranvaesia davidiana
  Viburnum tinus

Small shrubs
  Camellia japonica 'Donckelarii'
  Chaenomeles × superba 'Knap Hill Scarlet'
  Cotoneaster conspicuus
  Cotoneaster 'Hybridus Pendulus'
  Skimmia fortunei
  Symphoricarpos × chenaultii
  Viburnum davidii

Climbers
  Actinidia chinensis
  Clematis montana rubens
  Hedera colchica
  Hedera helix 'Buttercup'
  Vitis henryana

Groundcovers
  Hedera helix 'Buttercup'
  Hypericum calycinum
  Pachysandra terminalis

Perennials, bulbs, ferns, etc.
  Acanthus mollis
  Allium karataviense
  Anemone 'Honorine'

Anemone hupehensis
Aruncus sylvester
Avena sempervirens
Camassia quamash
Campanula poscharskyana
Chionodoxa sardensis
Cimicifuga dahurica
Crocus 'Cream Beauty'
Crocus tomasinianus
Eranthis hyemalis
Euphorbia epithymoides
Euphorbia palustris
Helleborus foetidus
Heuchera 'Red Spangles'
Hosta fortunei hyacinthia
Hosta lancifolia
Hosta sieboldiana 'Elegans'
Hosta undulata
Iris foetidissima
Iris sibirica 'Snow Queen'
Lilium canadense
Lysimachia nummularia
Narcissus 'Pheasants Eye'
Osmunda regalis
Paeonia officinalis 'Rubra Plena'
Paeonia suffruticosa 'Duchesse de Nemours'
Phyllitis scolopendrium
Primula florindae
Primula japonica
Rodgersia pinnata 'Superba'
Schizostylis coccinea
Scilla sibirica
Senecio clivorum
Spartina michauxiana
Trollius europaeus
Tulipa fosterana
Tulipa praestans 'Fusilier'
Tulipa 'Princeps'
Tulipa 'Red Riding Hood'

iv) The fountains in the pools are operated by a system of re-circulating pumps.

v) Lighting is provided both in the form of general lighting from high floods on the wall of the building and from fluorescent tubes in waterproof fittings below the cascades to illuminate the waterfalls.

Planting

The main aim of the planting design was to provide interest during the academic year, particularly in May and June when the garden is mainly used by staff and students. The garden was designed to require little maintenance within two or three years from the initial planting. A light loamy soil was imported and laid to a depth of 1 m over tile drains. Shade-loving shrubs with all-year round interest, with groundcovers and bulbs in bays, provided the main framework of plants in the beds against the walls, while ivy and virginia creepers were planted to grow on the walls to soften their effect. In the central beds adjacent to the pools, waterside vegetation including primulas, lilies, ferns, woodrush and willows were planted. Additional textural contrast is provided, particularly in winter, from groups of rock within the plant beds.

The two semi-mature trees provide spatial punctuation when viewed from all four sides. The placing of the trees was carried out by a tower crane already on site, to save costs, before the opening of the building, and before construction work in the courtyard. The consequent building operations may have been responsible for the death of one of the trees. When it was replaced, water was found in the tree pit for which no explanation has been found. The replacement alder tree was raised above the paving on an ivy-clad mound.

Additionally the courtyard planting aimed to show that natural growth could be encouraged to return to a central city location formerly polluted to such a degree that nothing green could survive. In this it has been successful beyond expectations, with rapid plant growth of the varied species, selected to provide interest throughout the year and to require minimal maintenance (*see* Table 9.1). Aquatic plants and fish add interest to the pools, and in addition several birds including blackbirds, wagtails and tits have been attracted to the garden. A nesting box is to be fixed to one of the trees to encourage the tits to breed in the garden. There are also frogs in the pools.

9.36 Roof gardens

In our congested urban environment the roofs of buildings provide a valuable potential source of outdoor space readily accessible to users of the building. They may improve the quality of the view from surrounding higher buildings, and can be specifically designed to be viewed from above (e.g. The Water Gardens, Sussex Gardens in London). Alternatively roof gardens may be designed to mask the building (e.g. those in London above underground garages at Hyde Park, Cadogan Place and Lillington Street) or as landscape features in their own right (Kaiser Centre, Oakland, California).

The roof garden will influence the design of the whole building since any undue load on the roof is transmitted throughout the building. Heavy structures, containers, soil and trees can be sited above the load-bearing members. The floor below the roof deck will have to house the mechanical equipment, and incorporate the planting pockets, pools and so forth in the roof space. Heat from the building may be transmitted through the roof to the soil and plants where it may unnaturally stimulate growth during the dormant period. A soil temperature of 5–7°C (40–45°F) can be critical: evapo-transpiration may be increased and the plants may become dehydrated. This can be counteracted by a thermal insulation layer of vermiculite, fibreglass battens or an air layer between the weatherproof membrane and drainage layer. Plants should not be placed close to exhaust vents or hot surfaces.

The importance of determining at an early stage the access to the roof garden for bulky fragile plants and other materials, particularly heavy semi-mature trees and soil, cannot be over-stressed. There are numerous examples of enormous expense and difficulty encountered in trying to construct a roof garden after the completion of the building, when cranes may have to be used, or lifts and stairs, and plant material, particularly trees, may be damaged.

All the plant requirements discussed in Part A apply particularly to roof gardens where adverse effects of microclimate are intensified; for example, walls and pavings reflect heat and light and wind increases with the height of the building.

The paving should be selected bearing in mind restrictions due to weight, the need to protect the waterproof membrane, and to allow minimal thermal movement. Suitable pavings are asbestos tiles, lightweight slabs, brick tiles and hollow concrete tiles laid with an air space below. In addition timber decking or tarmacadam can be used.

A high parapet wall around the garden will help break the force of the wind as well as being a safety precaution and providing a background for planting. The space enclosed may need to be subdivided for further shelter by slatted fences or walls, which may give the designer scope to create different spaces and levels within the garden. Trees set flush with the ground in planted areas will be easier to guy for support against the wind.

Despite the doubts often voiced concerning the use of pools in roof garden design, there is no reason why such features cannot be used (e.g. at Harvey's in Guildford) and there is the additional advantage that water on the roof provides a natural insulation for the building. A pool can be designed simply for the reflective qualities of water in which case it can be very shallow (5–8 cm, 2–3 in.), but

PLATES 9.11 & 9.12 **Ground level view and view from above of an enclosed garden on top of an underground garage. Hyde Park redevelopment scheme, London. For use by residents. Plants range from shade-tolerant species under existing trees to sun-loving ones in the sunniest part of the garden.**
(Landscape Architects: *Derek Lovejoy and Partners, London*. Photograph: *Ben Johnson*)

PLATE 9.13 **Central Station Roof Garden Park, Berne, Switzerland.** *(Ian Laurie)*

there must be protection against frost by making allowance for expansion, unless the pool is drained in winter. The water should be circulated, even if there is no organic life, to keep it clean. If fish and plants are required the pool must be at least 45 cm (18 in.) deep.

Case Study: The Roof Garden

The roof garden of the Royal Northern College of Music in Manchester was opened in July 1974. The space is formed by an enclosed 'L' shaped courtyard at second floor level, surfaced with asphalt and containing two groups of skylights. It is constructed on two levels of 6·4 m (21 ft) and 10 m (33 ft) with the upper terrace and pedestrian link overlooking the lower level. There are entrances at both levels (*see* Figure 9.17).

Constraints

i)   The concrete roof slab was already constructed when the commission was given, and this meant that there were very severe loading restraints which determined areas of hard and soft landscape.

ii) There were problems of microclimate—glare, wind turbulence, and low humidity due to the enclosed nature of the garden, and heat dissipation from the building through the roof. This limited the choice of plants.

iii) The roof skylights situated almost in the middle of each wing of the courtyards, with a further, and higher, one along the whole length of the western wall were a tremendous limitation on the design.

FIGURE 9.17 **The plan for the roof garden, Royal Northern College of Music, Manchester.** (Landscape Architects: *Michael Brown Partnership.* Architects: *Bickerdike Allen and Rich*)

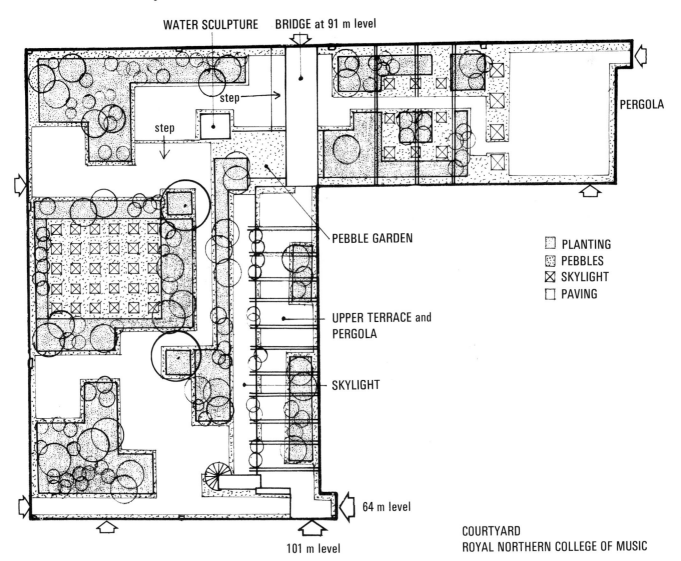

WATER SCULPTURE   BRIDGE at 91 m level

PERGOLA

step

step

PEBBLE GARDEN

PLANTING
PEBBLES
SKYLIGHT
PAVING

UPPER TERRACE and PERGOLA

SKYLIGHT

64 m level

101 m level

COURTYARD
ROYAL NORTHERN COLLEGE OF MUSIC

159

PLATE 9.14 **Central Station Roof Garden, Berne, showing access to the garden.** *(Ian Laurie)*
PLATE 9.15 **Royal Northern College of Music roof garden before landscaping.** *(Michael Brown)*

Design

The original design intention was for nothing more than grass, paving and plant boxes. The creation of a more exciting roof garden was made possible by Dame Kathleen Ollerenshaw who provided funds for the garden as a memorial to her daughter.

The courtyard was designed as a through way between the rooms facing onto it, providing a pleasant view from inside, and an outdoor sitting area. Use was made of both levels, access from one to the other being provided by a spiral staircase.

Paving was restricted to areas where the load-bearing capacity was sufficient, and related to access points. Non-paved areas were set aside for planting. Two column supports allowed two trees to be placed in the courtyard in large timber boxes. To provide a further canopy without using trees, timber pergolas were constructed at both levels to take climbers. Sitting spaces were provided, and a pottery water sculpture formed the focal point of the garden. Since the surrounding rooms are used in the evening, lighting was designed to illuminate trees, planting and water feature.

Technical Details

Hard and soft landscaping was constrained by loading problems and maintenance of the waterproof asphalt surface over the concrete slab. Pads underneath the paving keep an air layer free between it and the asphalt layer. Water drains through the paving slab joints.

A lightweight soil mix, mostly of peat, was used for planting with irrigation by pop-up sprinklers. After it was observed that the spray cast was obstructed by shrubbery, the sprinklers were raised 0·9 m (3 ft) and painted black to hide them amongst the planting. An auxiliary system of taps and hoses was provided, the narrow 25 mm (1 in.) pipes being concealed by a pebble border round the paved areas (which was used for other services including electricity cables).

Sailing turnbuckles were used to tension heavy gauge wire to support climbing plants (*see* Plate 9.16), more rustic supports being considered out of place.

Planting

The garden was designed to provide interest all the year round, shrubs and groundcovers being selected for their

PLATE 9.16 **Detail showing pebble border, concealing services, auxiliary irrigation system, and sailing turnbuckles used to tension wire for climbers.** (*Robert Trew*)

PLATE 9.17 **A view of the roof garden after landscaping, showing the pottery water sculpture.** (*Michael Brown*)

form and foliage, colour and texture throughout the year (*see* Table 9.2). The colour theme for flowering plants was deliberately limited mostly to whites and yellows, echoed by silver-grey foliage plants.

In the plant beds an understorey of groundcovers should eventually carpet the soil. Climbing plants will be an important feature up the walls and along the pergolas. A frame over the largest group of skylights was designed for climbing plants to reduce the visual impact of the skylights. Small plant boxes are recessed into the parapet wall of the upper terrace, containing *Cotoneaster* spp and *Lonicera* 'Halliana', planted to coat the edge and clematis to climb up the pergola.

Selection of trees was difficult: loading problems and restricted root space meant that species had to be selected which would not grow too large. Originally two *Cornus controversa* were used but these were damaged due to difficult access to the site (the lifts of the building) and were replaced with *Amelanchier laevis*.

TABLE 9.2
Roof Garden Planting—Royal Northern College of Music

Large Trees	Climbers
Eucalyptus gunnii	*Clematis armandii*
Pyrus salicifolia	*Clematis montana*
Small Trees/large shrubs	*Clematis tangutica*
Acer palmatum	*Lonicera japonica halliana*
Amelanchier laevis	
Magnolia × *soulangiana*	*Wisteria sinensis*
Rhus typhina	Groundcover
Shrubs	*Cotoneaster dammeri*
Camellia japonica	*Erica carnea* 'Springwood'
Cornus florida	
Cornus kousa	*Hedera helix* 'Glacier'
Cornus stolonifera 'Flaviramea'	*Hedera helix* 'Green Ripple'
Cotoneaster horizontalis	*Hebe pinguifolia*
Cotoneaster salicifolius floccosus	*Potentilla fruticosa* 'Longacre'
Cotoneaster × *watereri*	*Vinca minor*
Cytisus × *praecox*	*Vinca minor* 'Alba'
Leycesteria formosa	Ferns
Lonicera pileata	*Athyrium filix-femina*
Pernettya mucronata	*Polystichum setiferum*
Pinus mugo	Perennials
Potentilla fruticosa 'Vilmoriniana'	*Armeria maritima* 'Alba'
	Euphorbia epithymoides
Prunus laurocerasus 'Otto Luyken'	*Helictotrichon sempervirens*
Prunus laurocerasus 'Zabeliana'	*Iberis sempervirens* 'Snowflake'
Skimmia japonica	

Since the area of Manchester in which the roof garden is situated has become smokeless, a few other plants were tried experimentally, including *Magnolia* spp, *Acer palmatum* and *Eucalyptus* spp which exhibited good growth in the first season.

Part C

9.4 PLANT SELECTION

The selection of plant material for use in artificial conditions requires very careful thought. Attention has been focused in this chapter on the many adverse factors which militate against plant growth and the need for a thorough investigation of the site to assess microclimate, ground conditions such as soil quality and drainage characteristics, and user requirements. Other factors on which information should be sought include the possible risk of vandalism, pollution data (if applicable), the need and feasibility of providing irrigation and the likely maintenance input that may be expected.

Chapters 3 and 4 cover the general principles of plant selection and these need not be repeated here. However, particular selection criteria relevant to planting in artificial conditions may be summarized as follows:

i)   general hardiness and ability to tolerate climatic extremes;
ii) tolerance to high wind speeds;
iii) tolerance to dry and shallow soil conditions;
iv) robust and 'vandal proof';
v)   tolerance to pollution;
vi) low maintenance requirement;
vii) general reliability.

The tables that follow list species based largely on the above criteria. The tables are not intended to be comprehensive and are given as *aides-memoire*. They are based on what will satisfy a wide range of needs and limitations. There is more scope for imagination and experiment in roof gardens and courtyards with controlled access, as will be seen from reference to the comprehensive lists given in the case studies.

9.5 MAINTENANCE

Maintenance is particularly important in an artificial environment where plants are subject to extreme conditions and cannot exist without human aid. It is essential to consider from the outset of the design not only the maintenance operations required after implementation but the implications of carrying these operations out. Thus careful thought must be given to the layout and detailing of the scheme. The shape of planting beds, positioning of containers and paved areas should be such as to permit easy access for maintenance equipment such as a mower or water tanker (if required) and to facilitate such tasks as weeding, pruning and plant replacement.

TABLE 9.3
Trees for planting in artificial conditions

Large	Medium	Small
Acer platanoides	*Alnus cordata*	*Amelanchier laevis*
Acer pseudoplatanus	*Alnus glutinosa*	*Cornus florida*
Aesculus (several)	*Betula pendula*	*Cotoneaster* 'Cornubia'
Ailanthus altissima	*Fraxinus ornus*	*Cotoneaster frigidus*
Fraxinus excelsior	*Ilex aquifolium**	*Crataegus* (several)
Platanus hybrida (× acerifolia)	*Prunus avium*	*Laburnum × watereri* 'Vossii'
Populus (many)	*Prunus padus*	*Malus floribunda*
Robinia pseudoacacia	*Sorbus aria*	*Prunus amygdalus*
Tilia × euchlora	*Sorbus aucuparia*	*Prunus cerasifera*
Tilia platyphyllos 'Rubra'	*Taxus baccata**	*Prunus subhirtella*
		Pyrus salicifolia
		Salix purpurea 'Pendula'

Note: The trees listed in the 'Large' column are suitable for planting in street situations and within paved areas where space allows. The 'Medium' and 'Small' columns list species which are suitable for planting in paved areas and raised beds, and in the larger containers.
* Evergreen

TABLE 9.4
Shrubs and perennials for paved areas

Large	Medium to small	Groundcover
Aucuba japonica	*Berberis* (many)	*Ajuga reptans*
Berberis (many)	*Cotoneaster* (many)*	*Calluna vulgaris* & vars.
Buddleia (several)	*Cytisus* (several)*	*Cotoneaster congestus*
Chaenomeles (many)	*Euonymus japonicus*	*Cotoneaster dammeri*
Cornus alba 'Elegantissima'	*Genista* (several)	*Ericas* (many)
Cotinus coggygria	*Hebe brachysiphon**	*Galeobdolon luteum*
Cotoneaster (several)	*Hypericum patulum**	*Hedera* (many)
Elaeagnus (several)*	*Juniperus* (several)*	*Hypericum calycinum*
Forsythia (several)*	*Lavandula* (several)*	*Lonicera japonica* 'Aurea Reticulata'
Ligustrum (several)*	*Lonicera pileata**	*Polygonum affine*
*Olearia × haastii**	*Mahonia* (several)*	*Stachys byzantina (= S. lanata)*
*Pinus mugo**	*Potentilla fruticosa*	*Vinca major*
Prunus laurocerasus	*Prunus laurocerasus* 'Otto Luyken'*	*Vinca minor*
Pyracantha (many)*	*Rosa* (many)	
Ribes (several)	*Skimmia japonica**	
Sambucus nigra 'Aurea'	*Viburnum davidii**	
Viburnum (several)*		

* Evergreen

TABLE 9.5
Plants for containers

Small trees	Groundcover	Trailing plants/climbers
Alnus cordata	*Calluna vulgaris* & vars.	*Cotoneaster dammeri*
Alnus glutinosa	*Cotoneaster conspicuus*	*Cotoneaster* 'Skogholm'
Corylus avellana	*Erica* (many)	*Euonymus fortunei*
Cotoneaster (several)	*Hedera* (many)	*Hedera* (many)
Crataegus (several)	*Hypericum calycinum*	*Hydrangea petiolaris*
Malus (several)	*Lamium maculatum*	*Lonicera* (several)
*Pinus mugo**	*Pinus mugo pumilio**	*Parthenocissus* (several)
Prunus (many)	*Rosa* 'Max Graf'	*Rosa* (many)
Rhus typhina 'Laciniata'		*Rubus calycinoides*
Robinia pseudoacacia 'Frisia'		

Except in certain prestigious schemes a low maintenance regime is normally called for. Maintenance operations can be reduced by careful consideration at the design and specification stage. For example, topsoil can be specified as being completely weed free or a prepared, sterilized clean loam, sand, peat mix used. The use of a large proportion of evergreens will suppress weeds and minimize leaf litter. Weed problems can be further reduced by using plant material which establishes itself quickly forming a dense cover and underplanting deciduous shrubs with evergreen groundcover. Planting at close centres will help achieve quick groundcover, and use of plants which do not require a lot of pruning or staking will reduce maintenance at later stages.

Routine maintenance operations during the year will include regular weeding, pruning, firming after frost, fertilizer dressings, ensuring that trees are properly secured to stakes, mowing of grass areas, replacement of dead plant material and watering in dry periods, particularly during the initial establishment period. If automatic irrigation is used regular checks should be made to ensure that neither too much nor too little water is being supplied. Two or three years after planting the material should become sufficiently established to require only occasional maintenance.

FURTHER READING

General

Beazley, E. *Design and Detail of the Spaces between Buildings* (London: Architectural Press)

Edlin, H. L. *Guide to Tree Planting and Cultivation* (London: Collins, 1970)

D.O.E. Housing Development Notes II. *Landscape of New Housing* (London: HMSO, 1973–74)

MHLG *Trees in Town and City* (London: HMSO, 1958)
Design with Trees (Property Services Agency, 1974)
'Housing foundations on shrinkable clays' BRS Digest No. 3.

Tandy, C. R. V. (ed.) *Handbook of Urban Landscape* (London: Architectural Press, 1972)

Weddle, A. E. (ed.) *Techniques of Landscape Architecture* (London: Heinemann, 1967) Produced for the Institute of Landscape Architects.

Wood, A. D. B. *Terrace and Courtyard Gardens* (Newton Abbot: David & Charles, 1970) 2nd Edition

B.S. Standards Nursery Stock BS 3936
Large Trees BS 4043
Tree Work BS 3998
Glossaries BS 3975

Roof Gardens

Back, Jane, 'Swiss Roof Gardens' *Cement and Concrete Quarterly* 1973

Darbourne, J. 'Roof gardens for a local authority scheme' *Architects Journal* September 1968, pp. 587–9

Harris, Lynn M. F. 'Too good for tar and gravel' *Jnl. Amer. Inst. Arch.*

Howard, D. 'Living off the ground' *Arch. Jnl.* September 1968

Stansbury, J. 'Planting on rooftops and terraces' *Architecture* Canada, December 1967

Zion, R. 'Planting trees on rooftops' *Trees for Architecture and Landscape* (New York: Van Nostrand Rheinhold Company, 1968)

Microclimate

Bailey, J. 'Building Environment' section 1. Climate and Topography *Architects Journal* A. J. handbook series October 2–November 20 1968

Lacy, R. E. 'Survey of meteorological information for architecture and building' *Building Research Station* current paper CP 5/72, March 1972

London, A. G. and Petherbridge, P. 'Heating effect of sunshine' *Building Research Station* current paper, design series No. 40, 1966

Petherbridge, P. 'Sunpath diagrams and overlays for solar heat gain calculations' *Building Research Station* series 39 and supplement, March 1965

Sexton, D. E. 'A simple wind tunnel for studying air flow round buildings' *Building Research Station*

Wise, A. F. E. 'Wind effects due to groups of buildings'. *Building Research Station* current paper. C.P. 23/70, July 1970

ACKNOWLEDGEMENTS

We are indebted to Ian Laurie, Professor Kantorowich and Mr Schonegevel of the Department of Architecture and Town Planning at Manchester University for the information on the garden court and to Michael Brown and Ken Trew for the information on the Royal Northern College of Music roof garden.

Ralph Erskine and Partners kindly provided the information on balcony planting at Byker.

The figures were drawn by Richard Baker with the exception of Figures 9.5, 9.6, 9.13, 9.14, 9.15 and 9.16.

CHAPTER 10

Transplanting Semi-Mature Trees

R. L. HEBBLETHWAITE

10.1 INTRODUCTION

The British Standards Institution pamphlet *Transplanting Semi-Mature Trees* (BS 4043) gives the following definition: 'A semi-mature tree is a tree or shrub at an advanced stage of growth which is to be transplanted with a rootball, or in certain cases, bare roots, and is of such combined size and weight that special equipment is needed to carry out the operation. Such trees will generally be between 6–15 m in height and will weigh between 250 kg (5 cwt) and 10 tonnes (approx. 10 tons); they also include certain shorter trees and shrubs which weigh over 250 kg (5 cwt) and need special lifting equipment because of their spread and weight.'[1]

10.2 THE USE OF SEMI-MATURE TREES

There is a psychological requirement for new works of man—new buildings, recreational areas, industrial installations—to appear to have been set in well conserved landscape. If there were no large trees on site the scale of the semi-mature tree or a group of them gives an 'established' atmosphere. The scale in relation to the size of the new structure or space gives balance. Man relates the age and size of the tree to previous experience and is reassured in a newly created environment by the maturity and sense of security of the trees' visual impact.

No matter how attractive and aesthetically pleasing an architect's design for a building is, a new building gives a bare unameliorated impression unless it stands adjacent to conserved trees. It is most unlikely that a building is so badly designed and of such poor material that it has to be entirely screened. If partial screening is required to allow acceptance into the landscape, the scale of the semi-mature tree supported by younger trees and shrubs is of great benefit. Many buildings, attractive in their own right, are framed immediately by the use of these larger trees.

If it is necessary in the interests of the community to build a large construction, hundreds of feet in height, placing semi-mature trees adjacent to it is useless to the long-distance viewer. However, judiciously selected sites adjacent to sensitive viewpoints can be used to plant large trees and/or shrubs which can partially or completely screen the construction from the viewpoint. The exact height of the tree or trees required can be worked out by the Zone of Visual Influence Method taking into account the curvature of the earth and refraction of light.[2]

There are good reasons for choosing the majority of trees for planting in a new development of the same genus and species as those found locally to give a sense of continuity and integration. It is difficult for those not experienced in arboriculture, horticulture or silviculture to recognize the connection between young newly planted nursery stock of the same genus and species as those in the adjacent countryside. Semi-mature trees give an immediate visual continuity in size, form, scale and texture.

Vandalism of young newly planted stock is not unknown. It is probably true that the use of semi-mature trees or advanced nursery stock reduces the incidence of vandalism on newly planted stock. With very small stock the main stem may be broken and any penknife attack is almost fatal to the shape or existence of the tree. With semi-mature trees, providing that they are reasonably safeguarded by adequate fencing, a single penknife attack does little proportionate damage.

It has been estimated that a 25-year-old semi-mature beech in a deep loam has a leaf area of fourteen times the area over which the canopy extends on the ground. All the leaf area is capable, by transpiration and evaporation, of adding water vapour to the atmosphere thereby creating higher humidity. It has been estimated that a single 15 m (50 ft) silver maple may transpire as much as 268 litres (58 gallons) per hour.[3] The use of semi-mature trees may therefore be responsible for small localized increases in relative humidity which may be beneficial to the establishment of young stock in the area. This assumes that the

bark of the semi-mature *Arbutus unedo* (strawberry tree) is also attractive in the area from which it is seen.

The framework of branches is already formed in a semi-mature tree so that it can be chosen with a very good idea of its mature appearance. Smaller trees may need expert directional pruning to form them into a shape typical of the type. Semi-mature trees provide all the joys associated with well established trees—the movement of the shadow of leaves on the ground, the sound of wind among leaves, and drifts of leaves from the autumn fall from deciduous trees.

The importance of trees in a continental climate, where summer temperatures rise into the 30s Centigrade (90s Fahrenheit) and above, is enhanced by their shade value. In some of these countries trees which in maturity reach heights of over 21–27 m (70–90 ft) are known as 'shade trees'. The importance of shade for protection from the heat of the sun in Great Britain is perhaps not so great: however the cool shade of trees is appreciated on hot days.

Although semi-mature trees give an immediate effect, the planting of advanced nursery stock trees 3–5 m in height in advance of new building may be preferable to planting semi-mature trees after completion. Trees planted prior to or during construction must be protected from damage by post and rail fencing and their routine maintenance must not be neglected. There are also restraints on the site if an early planting of smaller trees is made; these are:

i) supervision of maintenance required throughout the contract;
ii) restriction of usable building space;
iii) possible interference with options of access;
iv) restriction of options for services.

Before deciding to incur the larger initial cost and involve site staff in maintenance responsibility the benefit of using semi-mature trees must be carefully analysed. All transplanted trees suffer a check in growth. The growth of well-prepared and carefully selected advanced nursery stock may overtake larger semi-mature trees after a period of seven to ten years unless selection, moving methods, conditions on site and after-care are particularly good for the semi-mature stock. Extensive plantings of semi-mature trees should always be supported with advanced nursery stock and possibly smaller trees.

10.3 RESTRAINTS ON USE

Before the decision is made to plant semi-mature trees, considerable thought must be given to the physiological

semi-mature tree has been moved properly and comes out into reasonable leaf.

The use of semi-mature trees with larger leaf area may help to control the air pollution of the environment in larger measure than if small nursery stock is used in the same positions. This is particularly true in the enclosed areas of towns. The advisability of starting with a large tree to help control pollution and 'sweeten' the air is recommended, for example lead, zinc and other heavy metals can be adsorbed and absorbed by leaves.

A semi-mature tree will already have started to show the characteristics of a mature specimen of the species in its bark texture: in many cases this can be aesthetically attractive to its immediate environment. For example, if a semi-mature *Acer rufinerve* (snakebark maple) is used the 'snakebark' effect is very pleasing: the reddish brown

PLATE 10.2 **Four Carolina Hemlocks** *(Tsuga caroliniana)* **transplanted at Furman University, USA. One lost its top in hurricane fringe winds.** *(R. L. Hebblethwaite)*

requirements, species, preparation, siting and moving and maintenance. Even though the requirements of the site demand a semi-mature tree, it may not be possible to move and plant such a tree on the site under consideration. A short check list is suggested which may help the decision.

A semi-mature tree and root ball may weigh on average between 5 and 10 tonnes; trees have been moved up to 20 tonnes:

i)   Can a truck and the tree and ball be brought over or under services into the site?

ii) Are there any services under the tree area that cannot stand the weight plus another ton or two of water?

A semi-mature tree often has a spread, even when being moved, of 5–7 m:

i)   Is there adequate head and spread room for tree and truck to be manoeuvred close to the planting area?

ii) Will it be necessary to remove telephone or electric overhead cable to bring the tree into the site and can this be done?

iii) Will there be room for the natural spread of branches when planted and when mature?

Or, will there be adequate skilled maintenance staff available to water, look after staking, spray against pest or disease and recognize deficiencies of mineral elements.

If some of these difficulties are insuperable it may be better to use lighter, advanced nursery stock, and if there is inadequacy in skilled maintenance staff one has less capital at stake.

10.4 PHYSIOLOGY: BASIC KNOWLEDGE FOR TREE MOVING

A good knowledge of physiology is necessary to move semi-mature trees successfully. The main problems are discussed below.

PLATE 10.3 **A Japanese Maple** *(Acer palmatum)* **during autumn after spring planting, New Jersey, USA.** *(R. L. Hebblethwaite)*

167

10.41 Desiccation

The most difficult problem is desiccation as a result of loss of water by the tree or shrub in excess of the amount entering the plant, causing wilting, and if continued, ultimately death. 90% of water taken in by the tree is lost by evaporation through the leaves (assuming transpiration to be a controlled water loss).

10.42 The root system

The root system is of prime importance in successful tree removal. Throughout the root system the newly formed young roots are the most important; root tips and root hairs absorb the major portion of the tree's moisture and solutes. Trees with a good fibrous root system can be moved successfully without preparation. Otherwise they should be prepared three or four years in advance of transplanting, to encourage fibrous roots to develop within the size of a movable rootball. (*See* 10.54.)

Trees absorb water most quickly through the growing roots just behind the meristematic region of the root cap, and through the root hairs produced from the cortex, a short distance back from the growing root tip. For successful moving, *it is essential to keep a mass of young roots intact, in contact with the soil, and without disturbance.*

10.43 Soil conditions

Protoplasm is less permeable and water more viscous at low temperatures; both factors reduce water absorption. Trees should therefore be moved when there is warmth in the ground in early autumn or spring; autumn is preferred. This point is most important with evergreens.

Intake of water by osmosis occurs when the soil solution concentration is less than the solution in the plant root cells. If the situation is reversed, water will be drawn out of the root cells (plasmolysis). It is therefore essential to use organic, slowly available fertilizers around the newly transplanted rootball according to the soil analysis requirement.

The fertilizer should be well mixed with backfill material before the operation, not thrown in with a bucket or spade as backfilling progresses. Very weak liquid feeds may be given every three or four weeks during spring and early summer growth periods for the first three years after transplanting.

Soil oxygen and carbon dioxide—relation to backfilling
i) Heavy tamping of backfill should be avoided, particularly of heavy and clay soils, to prevent exclusion of oxygen and build up of carbon dioxide.
ii) Insufficient oxygen restricts respiration of the root and slows metabolism and thereby absorption of salts, which lowers the Diffusion Pressure Deficit (DPD), slowing down the intake of water by osmosis.
iii) Accumulation of carbon dioxide increases pro-toplasm viscosity and decreases permeability slowing down the intake of water. [34]

A badly-drained planting pit will have the same results as above, with lowered oxygen and increased carbon dioxide. Field drains may be placed from the base of the pit to storm drainage or a sump, if water levels allow the latter. Cracking of a heavy soil can be accomplished before planting with a 'pop-shot' of 115 g (4 oz) gelignite charge, drilled in the hole from the base of a 'back hoe excavated pit' (*see Specification 1975*, 76th Edition, Architectural Press, pp. 1 and 51–2, which under 'Contractors Equipment' shows 'Backhoe' as recognized back-acting mechanical digger). Permission must be obtained and a licensed operator for explosives employed.

10.44 Water availability and requirements

Fine soils such as clays adsorb more water than sands. Each particle resists the pull on its adsorbed water by osmotic pressure with gravitation, adsorptive and hydrostatic forces. The adsorptive capacity of a fine clay has to be satisfied before water is freely available to a plant root. Clays above field capacity need watering less frequently than sandy soils.

A root-balled semi-mature tree has a very limited root area on transplanting; the surface area is usually within 25 m² for watering (approx. $\frac{1}{400}$ ha). The volume of water of 25 mm (1 in.) rainfall on a hectare is approximately 254 255 l (56 500 gal). The same amount of rainfall on 25 m² equals 636 l (140 gal). A reasonable amount of water per month during May to September for transplanted semi-mature trees would be 25 mm. If the rainfall is expected to be low, e.g. 8 mm, $\frac{2}{3} \times 636$ l will be necessary to make up the 25 mm required on the semi-mature tree's watershed area; i.e. 424 l (94 gal) to each tree, applied in two soakings of 212 l each, one week apart. (The two soakings are only for *this* application of 424 l, to avoid excess run off.)

10.45 Aids

Use of root-inducing hormones. A concentration of 10 ppm IAA (indole—3—acetic acid) will stimulate root growth. Higher concentrations inhibit root elongation and cause branching of roots. A very light dusting, so that the white coating can barely be seen (about 7 g ($\frac{1}{4}$ oz) per m²) on the outside of the rootball, is sufficient. [5]

Use of alginates to induce water intake. Water dispersed alginate concentrates form complex polyuronide hemicellulose substances. When roots are coated with these substances, the induction of water is enhanced. This is shown in practice in the following three examples.
i) After washing soil off the roots of *Aquilegia*, those soaked in alginates survived without wilting although in full flower and leaf. Roots of treated plants showed

tuberous swellings (*see* Plate 10.4).

ii) For the landscape plan of the new headquarters of the Central Electricity Generating Board's Generation Development and Construction Division, a semimature tree (*Arbutus unedo*) was moved. It was prewatered with alginate before digging, and granular alginate was used in the backfill. The tree, with a 5 ton ball, never flagged and has continued to grow, making 450 mm of new growth on some branches the following year. The total absence of wilting and the success of planting this subject, which is generally regarded as difficult to move, were significant.

iii) *Viburnum tinus* were field dug in June after prewatering with alginate. Roots were roughly balled, tops reduced, and the rest of the leaves sprayed with an anti-desiccant. Granular alginate was used in the backfill. The plants moved with negligible flagging, and in mid-June this is significant.

Although no confirmed theories are available on the action of alginates, they may act in the three following ways:

a) Polyuronide hemi-cellulose materials can absorb calcium, potassium and some other metals. In so doing they reduce the viscosity of the soil solution which would induce more water to flow into the root hairs by osmosis.

b) A polyuronide structure is capable of tremendous expansion by induction of water in and onto its structure. The expansion pressures may well overcome the viscosity of the liquid inside the root and force water into the plant.

c) Although it is not fully understood, the action of the alginate may overcome the balance of ions defined in the Donnen equilibrium and concentration pressure gradients.

10.46 Summary of steps to take to ensure necessary root action and prevent desiccation

i) Move the tree with an adequate sized ball which must not be broken after digging and balling to ensure conserving maximum fine roots.

ii) Always dig at right angles to the edge of the ball to prevent 'lever' breakage of the ball (*see* Figure 10.1).

iii) Trees with a normally poor root system must be prepared three years in advance of removal.

iv) Move when ground temperatures are warm, during early autumn or spring.

v) Use fertilizer sparingly; treat new roots like those of a seedling.

vi) Backfill with an 'open' mix of seven parts loam, three parts sphagnum peat, and two parts sharp sand. Do not over- or under-consolidate.

vii) Water well when planting and then as limited rainfall makes it necessary.

viii) Use root-inducing hormone on ball surface.

PLATE 10.4 **Tuberous roots on an alginate treated aquilegia.** *(R. L. Hebblethwaite)*

PLATE 10.5 **Field dug** *Viburnum tinus*, mid-June. **Alginate treated and turgid.** *(R. L. Hebblethwaite)*

169

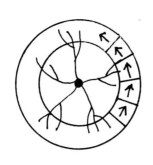

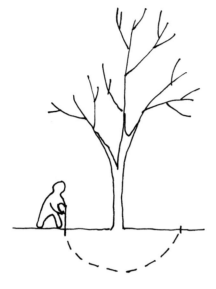

FIGURE 10.1 **Always dig at right-angles to the root ball to prevent 'lever' breakage of the ball. Arrows indicate direction of spade leverage.**

ix) Use alginates before moving and during backfill operations.

10.47 The stem, or trunk and branches

The aerial part of a semi-mature tree may be pruned to alleviate the imbalance of 'head' to root when transplanting. Judiciously retaining the form, it is better to reduce the head by removing two or three main branches, the cut ends of which can easily be painted with tree wound dressing. Many small cuts require far more cambium growth to cover them, causing a strain on the tree resources, and to paint all cut surfaces is wasteful of labour. Removal of large branches should be in accordance with BS 3998.

The bark of a semi-mature tree in a position exposed to full summer sun should be wrapped. The wrapping insulates the xylem tissue and may reduce the temperature of the leaf by one or two degrees, which will reduce transpiration loss (*see* 10.48).

Damage to the trunk or main stem should be avoided. Both parasitic and saprophytic fungi may enter through broken bark, the latter in some cases becoming parasitic.

Insects obtain easier access to soft tissue for egg laying and food supplying through broken bark, and may carry pathogens on their feet.

Deep damage to the xylem will prevent some water and solutes from reaching the leaves. Shallow damage through the cuticle and cortex into the phloem will limit the flow of elaborated materials to the root system.

If the tree suffers damage in the transplanting process, this will further strain the tree's ability to survive the move.

Damage to the stem inhibits the natural rhythm of diurnal expansion and its possible role in the movement of water to the top of a tree. According to the transpiration cohesion-tension theory, the sun evaporates water from the leaves and the xylem becomes a passive pipeline through which columns of solutes are pulled under tension. Measurements of the tensile strength of water have exceeded 300 atmospheres.[6]

To raise water to the top of a 120 m (400 ft) tree would require a difference of only 13 atmospheres. Although friction and adhesion forces and gravity oppose the movement of water upwards, it is thought that sufficient tensile strength is present to overcome them. Values of root pressure have been measured up to 6 atmospheres, but 2 atmospheres is nearer normal. The difference between the two pressures causes tension and narrowing of the diameter of the xylem cells, starting at the bottom of the tree and measurable on a dendograph. The minutely loosened perimeter gradually works its way up the tree having a squeezing effect on the solutes in xylem above it, thereby aiding the movement of xylem solutes and phloem materials along extended branches and to the top of the tree. At night with transpiration lessened and stomata enclosed, xylem tissues gradually fill out with a second wave of movement expanding the perimeter. If tissues are broken, both the continuous tube system and the xylem reduction effects are broken for the area of damage.

10.48 The leaves

Water may be taken into a tree through the leaves during rain or overhead spraying through channels of pectinaceous material in the upper epidermis. These form a continuous passage for water from the surface to vascular bundles. The channels are few in number, and normally the cutinous layer only absorbs water to a small extent, dependent on the DPD of the epidermal cells.

The main aid to a moved tree is to prevent moisture loss from any part of the plant until the root system can re-establish in the new root-environment. Only after new root hairs are made and water absorbed through them can a water balance be achieved between transpiration and evaporation and water induction.

Water from the root system moves into the leaf cells from the vascular bundles of veins, is transpired into the intercellular spaces between the mesophyll cells and moves through the stomates (when open) as water

PLATE 10.6 **Pin oak** *(Quercus palustris)* **transplanted two months previously. Note bark wrapping.** *(R. L. Hebblethwaite)*

vapour. The movement of water into the intercellular spaces depends on the difference in water vapour pressure between the atmosphere if the stomates are open and the vapour pressure inside the leaf. The atmosphere inside the leaf is generally assumed to be near saturation and of high water-vapour pressure; that of the atmosphere outside the leaf unsaturated and of less water vapour pressure. Water vapour will therefore move from high to low vapour pressure and diffuse through the stomata. This movement has to be restricted, which can be accomplished in several ways.

The stomata through which 90% of moisture vapour loss occurs, become closed during darkness, the intercellular spaces become saturated and water movement stops from the mesophyll cells as pressures inside the leaf equalize.

Digging and transportation between sites can be restricted to a period of dull days. The road transport period can be carried out, if the tree is evergreen or in leaf, during the evening. Medium sized trees or shrubs can have a canopy supported over them during transportation and for a week after transplanting. The canopy should not be such as to trap the heat of the sun e.g. not black or clear polythene—but rather tight hessian which can be wetted.

A leaf will heat up in the sun between 2° and 10°C higher than the surrounding atmosphere. Wrapping the bark reduces the temperature of solutes reaching the leaf by its insulating effect. An overhead spray will cool the leaf both on contact and during evaporation. Increased temperature in the leaf increases vapour pressure, increasing the DPD resulting in even greater transpiration and water loss on evaporation. Wrapping or overhead spraying help the tree to overcome the transplanting physiological condition.

A vaporizing nozzle fixed at the top of the tree to a 12 mm water hose can be turned on during dry or windy days. The air humidity caused will reduce the DPD, thus reducing transpiration, and the moisture will also cool.

Modified polyvinyl resins are used to form a membrane over the leaf almost impervious to water, but allowing the passage of gases. The membrane decreases transpiration and thereby evaporation. The leaves of evergreen trees should be sprayed before moving. Bare root trees benefit from a cover spray over their roots. Oedema of the leaves can be caused by anti-desiccants applied during periods of excessive transpiration.

Anti-desiccant is best put on in early morning or early evening or in dull humid weather.

171

10.49 Flowers and fruit

Flowers and fruit take energy and moisture from the tree or shrub. During the period of establishment, for two or three years, within reasonable labour cost, removal of flowers and fruit is beneficial to successful transplanting.

10.5 THE PRACTICE OF TREE MOVING RELATED TO PHYSIOLOGY

Trees should be chosen not only for their shape and size relative to the site, but also for their ability to tolerate the indigenous ground and air conditions (*see* Table 10.1). Appendix A of BS 4043 contains a list of trees suitable for transplanting when semi-mature.[7] The species listed below have been successfully transplanted and could usefully be added to the list:

Arbutus unedo	— strawberry tree
Magnolia grandiflora	— evergreen magnolia
Pinus strobus	— white pine
Quercus palustris	— pin oak
Tsuga caroliniana	— Carolina hemlock

10.51 Preparation

The tree pit should be dug before the tree is moved. Good drainage is essential. A 150 mm (6 in.) gravel layer at the bottom of the hole covered with turf upside down and linked to a sump or main drain is necessary in heavy clay soils. Providing the water table is at the bottom of the hole or below it, light soils do not usually need additional drainage.

In heavy clay or other compacted soil it is beneficial to crack the area around the pit and the sub-soil below the hole with a 115 g (4 oz) stick of 20% gelignite as follows:

i) Permission must be obtained in writing to carry out blasting from any authority with underground services within 20 m laterally from the tree pit site. Obviously one would not be blasting over the tops of services.

ii) Employ an operator with a licence to carry out gelignite blasting—e.g. operators who blast ditches for farm dams.

iii) Make a hole with a soil auger or steel pointed rod at the tree pit site, about 450–600 mm (18–24 in.) deep. The 115 g charge is fitted with an electric detonator and placed at the bottom of the hole. The hole is back tamped gently with sand or fine soil. A number of holes can be blown at once using a 12 volt car battery.

iv) After the pit has been excavated by hand or back hoe (workers should keep clear of smoke which may cause bad headaches if inhaled), a further charge can be placed 450–600 mm deeper than the bottom of the pit to crack the sub-layer, creating fissures for drainage and root expansion. Sharp sand can be beneficial if washed into the fissures to prevent them from closing up or being clogged with clay particles.

v) The sides of the pit should be roughened with a fork or pick to ensure a good bond with the backfill.

vi) The hole should be 450 mm wider all around than the width of the ball and 150 mm deeper to allow for 250 mm of good backfill mix, tamped firm to 150 mm.

TABLE 10.1

Deciduous tree species commonly used in landscape schemes suitable for semi-mature planting and easily available

Easily established	More difficult
Acer platanoides	*Betula alba*
Acer pseudoplatanus	*Carpinus betulus*
Aesculus hippocastanum	*Crataegus* spp
Alnus glutinosa	*Fagus sylvatica*
Platanus hybrida	*Fraxinus excelsior*
(× *acerifolia*)	*Prunus* spp
Tilia × *euchlora*	*Quercus* spp
Tilia platyphyllos	*Robinia pseudoacacia*
Ulmus spp (only use where trees isolated from diseased elms)	*Salix* spp
	Sorbus spp

10.52 Backfill mix

A satisfactory mix consists of seven parts friable loam, three parts sphagnum peat and two parts sharp sand. 10:10:10 N:P:K fertilizer should be added to the backfill and thoroughly mixed before use at the rate of $\frac{1}{2}$ kg (roughly 1 lb) per m³. The backfill mix should be ready at the hole before the tree is moved. Specifications for tamping vary according to the amount of clay particles in the loam: medium tamping for a heavy loam, heavier tamping for light loams. The heavy end of a pick-axe handle has a 'sheep's foot' effect as a tamper, in finding voids and pushing soil in and around the ball of the tree. Good results are generally obtained if a medium firm tamping is given to backfill every 150–200 mm, and when half full, the backfill is flooded for further settlement. After excess water has disappeared (which proves reasonable drainage), further soil is added, tamped, and a final watering given just before the final 75 mm of backfill is added.

10.53 Digging the tree

Preparation for moving non-fibrous rooted trees should start three years before moving.[8] This allows trenches to become tight with fibrous roots, and eventually makes it possible to move the tree. Less time is insufficient since much of the soil and new root will be too soft to obtain a hard ball periphery.

PLATE 10.7 **Ball of a strawberry tree** *(Arbutus unedo)* **dug and ready for hessian and rope binding.**
(R. L. Hebblethwaite)

Normally the rootball would be 300 mm (1 ft) diameter per 25 mm (1 in.) diameter of trunk of stem measured at 720 mm (2 ft 6 in.) above ground level. Below a stem diameter of 100 mm (4 in.) the diameter of the ball should be increased, and above a stem diameter of 200 mm (8 in.) it should be reduced. For example a 50 mm (2 in.) diameter tree would need a 700 mm (3 ft) diameter ball, and a 250 mm (10 in.) diameter tree would need only an 1800 mm (6 ft) diameter ball.

Sequence for digging a root ball

The sequence of operation is as follows (*see* Figure 10.2):

1. Three days before lifting, soak the ball in alginate solution.
2. One day before lifting, spray bark and leaves, if present, with an anti-desiccant.
3. Immediately before lifting judiciously remove some branches to balance the head and root, and paint cuts with an asphaltum or tree wound paint.
4. Tie up the lower branches to the centre of the tree, being careful to prevent chafing the bark. (Use an air hose with wire threaded through it, or strong hessian

or cloth loops with string attached.)
5. Measure off the radius from the bole of the tree for the ball.
6. Make a cut with a sharp spade all round the

FIGURE 10.2 **Sequence of digging a semi-mature tree.**

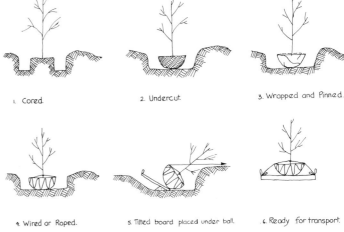

1. Cored.   2. Undercut.   3. Wrapped and Pinned.

4. Wired or Roped.   5. Tilted board placed under ball.   6. Ready for transport.

173

PLATE 10.8 **Balled semi-mature hornbeam** *(Carpinus betulus)* **moved in New York State. Note board and size of picks.** *(R. L. Hebblethwaite)*

PLATE 10.9 **Semi-mature yew** *(Taxus baccata)* **in USA moved on a steel sled. Note tyre chain.** *(R. L. Hebblethwaite)*

PLATE 10.10 **Semi-mature juniper** *(Juniperus virginia)* **moved on a wooden sled.** *(R. L. Hebblethwaite)*

circumference of the ball, a few inches wider than the final ball width.

7. Mark the outer circumference of the trench about 750 mm (2 ft 6 in.) wide, and cut this vertically with a spade.

8. Dig out the trench, facing ninety degrees away from the tree. Never dig towards the tree as this will break the edge of the ball.

9. Topsoil and subsoil should be kept separate.

10. When the tree has been 'cored' to a depth of about 900 mm (3 ft) undercutting can take place so as to leave the tree on a neck or pedestal of subsoil. The edge of the ball can now be combed with a hand fork to the correct width, heavy roots being cut back, and light ones retained.

11. Dust the ball with root-inducing hormone at 10 ppm strength.

12. Arrange strong hessian around the ball and use 'pinning nails' to secure it. These are specially long-pointed hardened nails, about 75 mm (3 in.) long.

13. Arrange a wire or rope concertina around the whole tree, a circle of wire or rope being fixed as far under the ball as possible, into the undercut. Make another circle of wire or rope on top of the ball and thread through the top loop of the 'concertina'. As the loops are pulled tight, the smaller loop of wire under the ball resists the pull of the upper circle. Cross ties across the circle make the ball even tighter. If wire is used a meat hook can be twisted through it to form a loop, the more twists, the tighter the ball. Experience teaches the breaking point of the wire.

14. Dig a ramp on the side from which the tree is to be removed. A very strong board, flat on top, is used for mounting the tree or shrub. A high hitch, well-padded, is attached two thirds of the way up the tree to lean it away from the ramp. Usually the ball breaks off the pedestal of soil and sometimes a tap root has to be sawn.

15. The board is placed under the ball, and the tree released back on the board. The ball is twisted with tyre chains or hessian until centrally placed on the board.

16. The ball is securely lashed to the board by means of a strong wire loop, or eye bolts at each corner. *From this time on, the ball is not touched.*

17. The board may be winched on planks and rollers, or lifted by slings and crane, onto a low loader trailer.

18. The process is reversed to get the ball into the tree pit on site. A further anti-desiccant may be sprayed. Backfilling and watering should be carried out as in section 10.52.

Bare-root moving

If a semi-mature tree is taken from a light sandy loam

175

and it is not possible to obtain a firm ball of soil and roots, it may be moved bare root with special precautions to prevent the roots drying out. A medium sized semi-mature tree can be lifted with a front-end-loader caterpillar tractor and a good operator. A trench is dug on three sides of the tree about 3·5 m away from the trunk. With the bucket on the fourth side about 750 mm deep the tree can be lifted and teased out of the soil by skilful manipulation. This type of operation is most successful with very fibrous, surface rooting trees such as maple and birch.

10.54 Transportation and planting

Transport should take place in the evening if possible, or in the case of a large shrub or small tree, under light sheeting. The vehicle should move slowly, at not more than 10 mph. Windy weather should be avoided. The hessian, leaves and bark should be soaked to create a humid atmosphere around the ball. The tree and board should be securely tied to the trailer to prevent movement during transit, always remembering to protect bark with expanded polystyrene cushions or wire rope covered with rubber hose.

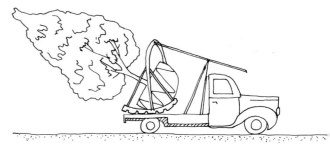

FIGURE 10.3 **Semi-mature tree in transport.**

Generally speaking it is best to place a tree in the same direction it faced before being moved. Planting mix and backfill procedure should be carried out as in 10.43. Staking should be secure and adequate for the size and weight of the tree when full of moisture and under heavy wind pressure.[9]

10.55 After care

The tree should never be short of 'available' water, particularly for the first two years after planting. This must take into account the adsorption, adhesion, and the

PLATE 10.11 **Semi-mature tree being lowered into position by crane at Manchester University, Department of Architecture and Town Planning Courtyard.** *(Ian Laurie)*

PLATE 10.12 **The same tree, showing detail of root ball and chains.** *(Ian Laurie)*

PLATE 10.13 **Transplanted tree prior to backfill.** *(R. L. Hebblethwaite)*

cohesive nature of very fine soil particles. With the 7:3:2 mix described in 10.52, water should be available to the roots under normal osmotic pressure.

BS 4043 shows turnbuckles in the staking wires.[10] These should be inspected every week and after heavy winds, and tightened as necessary in the first few months after planting when some stretching of the wire rope may occur. After four months, monthly inspections are enough.

A watch should be kept for disease. Most fungicides are preventative, not curative. If the species is known to be susceptible to disease, routine sprays should be applied.

Pests are usually noticed by the layman only after damage to the plant makes it obvious that the pest is present. A well trained arboriculturalist will look out for pests before they have had a chance to ruin the appearance and recuperative efficiency of the tree. Such pests as aphis, red spider, thrip, capsid and leaf hoppers can cause a great loss of liquids and leaf surface essential to the recovery of the tree, if left untreated.

A watch should be kept for mineral deficiencies particularly magnesium, nitrogen, potash, phosphate and

177

lime-induced iron deficiency. Expert advice should be sought with regard to the amount of corrective mineral to apply and its form.

10.6 CONCLUSION

The basic physiology regarding tree moving should be understood at least by the foreman of the moving crew, if not the crew themselves. Necessary specifications should include those based on physiology. The confidence of the general public and local authorities in planting semi-mature trees can only stem from a high success rate, and the latter is only achieved by giving due regard to relevant plant physiology in tree moving and after care.

FURTHER READING

Fox, D. G. 'Carbon Dioxide Narcosis' *J. Cell Comp Physiol* 1933. Vol. 3, p. 75.

Hartt, C. E. 'The Effect of Temperature upon Translocation of C14 in Sugarcane' *Plant Physiology* vol. 41, p. 309

Kramer, P. J. 'The Relation between Rate of Transpiration and Rate of Absorption of Water in Plants' *Am. Jnl. Botany*, 1937. Vol. 24, p. 10

Roberts, E. A., Southwick, M. D. and Palmer, D. H. 'A Microchemical Examination of McIntosh Apple Leaves showing Relationship of Cell Wall Constituents to Penetration Spray Solutions.' *Plant Physiology* 1948 Vol. 23, p. 557

REFERENCES

1. 'Transplanting Semi-Mature Trees' *British Standards Institution* 1966 B.S. 4043
2. Lovejoy, D. (ed.) *Land Use and Landscape Planning* (Aylesbury: Leonard Hill, International Textbook Co., 1973) Chapter 2 pp. 45–7
3. Cummings, W. H. A. 'A Method of Sampling the Foliage of a Silver Maple Tree' *J. Forestry* 1941 vol. 39 p. 382
4. Bonner and Galston. *Principles of Plant Physiology* (San Francisco U.S.A.: W. H. Freeman & Company, 1952)
5. Devlin, R. M. *Plant Physiology* (New York: Van Nostrand Reinhold Company; 1969) 2nd edition p. 316
6. Meyer, B. S. and Andersen, D. B. *Plant Physiology* (Princeton, New Jersey: D. van Nostrand Reinhold Company Inc., August 1952) Reprint: May 1959
7. Op. cit. B.S. 4043
8. Ibid.
9. Ibid. Appendix C. p. 111
10. Ibid. p. 25

University of York. *(Maurice Lee)*

CHAPTER 11

Reclamation and Planting of Spoiled Land

DR R. P. GEMMELL

11.1 INTRODUCTION

One of the greatest difficulties encountered in carrying out landscaping and planting schemes on spoiled land is the hostility of the ground materials towards plant growth. Consequently, such schemes often demand drastic treatments of the planting media in order to improve their growth potential. A further difficulty is that soil conditions are extremely variable, each site posing its own special problems. There is, therefore, no universally applicable treatment and it is necessary to carry out special investigations on every scheme where adverse growing conditions prevail. The information gained is then used to devise amelioration, cultivation and after-management treatments suitable for the planting and establishment of the type of vegetation required.

It is now recognized by experienced local authorities, contractors and consultants that the restoration of areas damaged by industrial and other activities requires a special kind of technical expertise in addition to the usual skills of planting and design. This is best achieved when landscape architects and ecologists work together, combining and complementing their particular skills. The role of the ecologist should be:
i) to advise on the feasibility and planning of schemes;
ii) to conduct investigations on the growth characteristics of the substrates concerned;
iii) to devise techniques for improving the ground conditions before planting;
iv) to advise on the choice of species and after-management.

In practice, the input of ecological expertise should be aimed at enabling the maximum design potential of schemes and subsequent improvement work to be realized.

11.2 FACTORS RESTRICTING GROWTH

A common feature of spoiled land is the absence of natural soil materials due to waste deposition, mineral extraction, pollution, and other kinds of disturbance. In the majority of cases humus is absent from the ground materials, the substrates are infertile due to a deficiency of the major plant nutrients, toxic chemical factors may be present, and physical conditions may be unfavourable for plant growth. Table 11.1 summarizes the problems likely to prevail on the different kinds of substrate found on spoiled land.

11.3 TECHNIQUES OF REVEGETATION

Six groups of waste material are discussed in detail:
1. Colliery spoil
2. Blast furnace slag
3. Power station ash
4. Metalliferous wastes
5. Chemical wastes
6. Infertile waste

In each case the main characteristics of the waste are discussed, details of establishment of grass and trees given, including suitable species, and analytical tests which can be carried out are described where appropriate.

11.31 Colliery spoil

See Table 11.2 for a simplified guide to planting on colliery spoil.

TABLE 11.1

General guide to planting problems on spoiled land

Substratum	Likely problems
Colliery spoil from deep mining and open-cast extraction	1. Acidity: initial and long-term 2. Deficiencies of nitrogen and phosphate 3. Fixation of phosphate 4. Salinity due to excess soluble salts 5. Compaction, consolidation and impermeability
Blast furnace slag from iron and steel making	1. Alkalinity: pH up to 10·8 2. Deficiencies of nitrogen and phosphate 3. Fixation of phosphate 4. Cultivations difficult due to fused slag 5. High porosity and low fertilizer retention
Metalliferous wastes including metal mine spoils, smelter wastes and fluorspar tailings	1. Zinc, copper and lead toxicities 2. Deficiencies of nitrogen, phosphate and potash 3. Acidity, particularly in copper wastes 4. Cultivations difficult due to fused slag 5. Low moisture holding capacity
Power station ash	1. Boron toxicity 2. Alkalinity: pH up to 12·0 3. Salinity due to excess soluble salts 4. Deficiencies of nitrogen and phosphate 5. Concretions
Chemical wastes	1. Acidity and alkalinity 2. Salinity due to excess soluble salts 3. Toxicities caused by chromates and other salts 4. Deficiencies of nitrogen and phosphate
China clay spoil	1. Mild acidity 2. Deficiencies of nitrogen and phosphate 3. High porosity and low fertilizer retention
Domestic refuse and municipal wastes	1. Toxic sulphides due to waterlogging 2. Boron toxicity from paper products 3. Poor aeration
Sand, gravel, brick rubble, ironstone spoil, foundry sand, furnace ash, cinders, exposed subsoil, clay and quarry sites	1. Deficiencies of nitrogen and phosphate 2. Mild acidity and alkalinity 3. Cultivations difficult due to stones and clay
Sewage sludge	1. Zinc, copper and chromium toxicities
Soils and vegetation affected by trampling and public access	1. Physical destruction of vegetation 2. Compaction and root shearing 3. Loss of soil structure and poor aeration
Soils affected by air and water pollution	1. Sulphur dioxide damage to plant foliage 2. Metal toxicity due to fallout from metal refining plants 3. Metal and pH toxicities from tip effluents
Unstable sand dunes	1. Wind erosion 2. Trampling effects

TABLE 11.2

Simplified guide to planting on colliery spoil

Operation or treatment	Specification
1. Deep ripping or subsoiling to relieve compaction	60 cm (2 ft) depth with rippers set at 45–60 cm (18–24 in.) centres. Use Caterpillar No. 4 ripper or Ransomes C. 1 subsoiler. Cross ripping may be useful.
2. Exposure to leaching (saline sites only)	Allow natural leaching for several months or throughout winter.
3. Ground limestone application	Apply ground limestone at 0–50 000 kg/ha (0–20 tons/acre) depending on lime-requirement tests and presence of potential acidity.
4. Incorporation of ground limestone	Rotovators, heavy duty fixed or spring tine cultivators, or disc harrows.

Operation or treatment	Specification
5. Soil spreading	Conserve topsoil prior to earthworks and spread over shale. Intensely acid and pyritic sites may require extra cover material.
6. Phosphate fertilization	Apply 250–500 kg/ha P_2O_5 (200–400 units/acre P_2O_5) depending on tests as either basic slag or triple super-phosphate.
7. Incorporation of phosphate	Rotovators or disc harrows.
8. Seed bed preparation	Choice of disc harrows, rotovators, tined harrows, chain harrows etc. depending on substrate conditions. Roll.
9. NPK fertilization	50–125 kg/ha (40–100 units/acre) nitrogen, 50–125 kg/ha (40–100 units/acre) phosphate, as P_2O_5. 50–100 kg/ha (40–80 units/acre) potash as K_2O depending on soil tests and after use
10. Grass seeding	Increase seed rates by up to 50 % if sowing direct on spoil. Use high proportion of clovers, particularly wild white varieties, for leys and low maintenance amenity areas
Carry out stonepicking cultivations.	at appropriate stages during

a)   Grassland establishment

Acidity. This is the most important factor restricting plant growth in many types of colliery spoil. Acid conditions down to pH 4·0 are not directly harmful to plants but they interfere with the uptake of phosphate and calcium, causing infertility problems. When the pH is below 4·0, as is commonly the case in colliery wastes, the acidity is directly harmful to plant roots and may result in aluminium and manganese toxicities. At the same time, deflocculation of the clay colloids occurs causing the waste to have an impermeable and particularly adverse physical structure. The development of acidity is caused principally by the action of oxygen and moisture on iron pyrites in the waste, the following reactions occurring:

$$2FeS_2 + 2H_2O + 7O_2 \rightarrow 2FeSO_4 + 2H_2SO_4$$
$$4FeSO_4 + 10H_2O + O_2 \rightarrow 4Fe(OH)_3 + 4H_2SO_4$$

The formation of sulphuric acid is of course responsible for the low pH of the waste. The oxidation of iron pyrites in the spoil is a very slow process and often proceeds over a period of many years. Because it commences only in the presence of both moisture and oxygen, freshly mined material or newly exposed spoil after the completion of earthworks is often of neutral pH. This means that acidity may develop after planting even though early tests indicate that the pH is satisfactory. Even when acidity is detected before planting, the pH then prevailing does not show how much acid will be generated by pyrite oxidation after planting. However, heavy clay-rich spoils with an initial pH below 3·0 or even 3·5 are quite likely to exhibit high potential acidity. On the other hand, potential acidity is absent from burnt spoil.

PLATE 11.1 **Experimental grass plots on colliery waste at Leigh. The trials were designed to investigate the effects of fertilizer and cutting treatments on the establishment and management of grass.**
(Courtesy of Joint Reclamation Team, Greater Manchester and Lancashire County Councils)

PLATE 11.2 **Dieback of grass on colliery waste caused by acidity released by pyrite oxidation. The pH of the spoil fell from 7·0 to 3·0.** *(Courtesy of Joint Reclamation Team, Greater Manchester and Lancashire County Councils)*

PLATE 11.3 **The effect of nitrogen deficiency on the growth of grass on colliery waste. Note the poor cover which could have been improved by the inclusion of clovers in the seed mixture or treatment with nitrogen fertilizer.** *(Courtesy of Joint Reclamation Team, Greater Manchester and Lancashire County Councils)*

Acidity in colliery spoil is usually neutralized by the addition and incorporation of ground limestone. Slaked or burnt lime are unsuitable because they make the spoil too alkaline if an excess is needed as is usually the case. Dolomitic or magnesian limestone should be avoided on highly acid sites because it may result in excessive levels of magnesium sulphate. The ground limestone must be thoroughly incorporated into the waste because its neutralizing effect in impermeable acid spoils is limited to its depth of incorporation. Deep incorporation also significantly increases the permeability of the spoil, thus improving the drainage. If acid spoil is covered with a layer of soil or other material, it is important to apply and incorporate the ground limestone before soil spreading.

On ordinary kinds of acid soil, the maximum rate of ground limestone which may be applied in one application is about 10 000 kg/ha (4 tons/acre). Highly acid types of colliery spoil often need much more than this and 30 000 kg/ha (12 tons/acre) is not unusual. When long-term or pyritic acidity is known to be present, it is essential to apply an excess or reserve of ground limestone so that the acidity produced after treatment is immediately neutralized. Highly pyritic spoils may require up to 50 000 kg/ha (20 tons/acre) or even 75 000 kg/ha (30 tons/acre) of ground limestone for long-term treatment of acidity. It is not feasible to apply the ground limestone at intervals as split-applications because top-dressings are ineffective. Ground limestone applied in this way remains at the surface and does not neutralize the acid spoil in the rooting zone beneath.

The method of incorporation of ground limestone into spoil is of crucial importance. First of all, the spoil must be deeply ripped in order to relieve compaction and permit subsequent cultivations and limestone integration. Ripping should be followed by ground limestone application (although some authorities recommend that the limestone should be spread before ripping). As soon as possible after liming, the spoil should be cultivated with either heavy duty fixed or spring tine cultivators, disc harrows or preferably rotovators depending on the ground conditions. When restoration is for agriculture, it is particularly important to incorporate the limestone deeply; if the spoil is intractable as far as surface cultivations are concerned then it is desirable to repeat the liming and cultivations after spreading a further layer of spoil.

Salinity. Salinity problems in colliery waste are less common than difficulties caused by acidity. The removal of excessive concentrations of soluble salts is generally achieved by exposing the shales to natural leaching, this process being facilitated by ripping operations which improve the drainage characteristics of the waste. It is usually necessary to delay planting for a few months in order to permit the removal of salts by rainwater percolation.

Deficiencies of nitrogen and phosphate. These are corrected by the application of fertilizers and/or manurial treatments. The phosphate status of colliery spoil is generally so low as to be immeasurable. Moreover, most spoils have the power to fix phosphate so that all or some of the fertilizer applied is not available for plant growth. Generally, about 250–500 kg/ha P_2O_5 (200–400 units/acre P_2O_5) should be applied as either basic slag or triple superphosphate depending on availability. The rate applied should, of course, be determined by chemical or growth tests on the shale. After spreading, the fertilizer should be incorporated into the waste by harrowing or rotovation.

The amount of nitrogen fertilizer required is influenced by land-use considerations but an initial surface-dressing of 50–125 kg/ha N (40–100 units/acre N) in a compound fertilizer is invariably needed. In the case of amenity grassland, the dose should be in the lower part of this range but higher for agriculture. It is generally advisable to apply a second dressing from one to four months after seeding. Of course, nitrogen may be applied in organic form as broiler manure or sewage sludge but care should be taken with the latter as some types of sludge contain high concentrations of toxic metals. The effects of toxic metals in sewage sludge on crops are discussed later in 11.34 and the levels of metals which cause toxicity are given in Table 11.6.

Grass seeding techniques are similar to those used on normal soils but higher seeding rates by up to 50% are advisable if seed bed conditions are unfavourable. The inclusion of clovers in agricultural and even some amenity grassland mixtures is of particular importance because of the necessity of building up nitrogen fertility rather than relying on expensive fertilizer applications. For amenity grassland, the persistent and dwarf wild white varieties are particularly valuable.

b) *Tree planting*

For the successful establishment of trees on acid colliery spoil, it is essential to carry out the same sequence of cultivation treatments as described for grass. In fact, it is strongly recommended that tree-planting areas be pre-planted to grass because a grass cover prevents erosion, restricts weathering reactions thus minimizing the release of soil acidity, initiates the early development of soil flora and fauna, and enriches the spoil in nitrogen if clovers are planted. Another important point is that the presence of a herbaceous groundcover brings about a rapid improvement in appearance and prevents weed infestation.

The mixtures of grass seed used for tree-planting areas must be chosen with care in order to avoid adverse competition effects on the developing trees. High yielding pasture species such as ryegrasses, timothy and cocksfoot must be avoided. The fine-leaved fescues and bents are preferable and may be sown with wild white clover so that nitrogen fertility is maintained. If possible, the time of seeding should be arranged so that the grass can be cut several times before tree-planting takes place.

Alder and birch are ideal as pioneer species,

particularly if the acid spoil conditions cannot be treated satisfactorily. Alder has the advantage in that it is a nitrogen fixer and is therefore ideal as a nurse species in mixed plantings. Conifers and other acid tolerant species are useful but if high rates of ground limestone are applied in order to neutralize intense initial and pyritic acidity, species tolerant of calcareous or high pH conditions must be selected.

c) *Analytical tests*

The Regional Laboratories of the Agricultural Development and Advisory Service (ADAS) are equipped to conduct analyses of soil and spoil materials. It must be emphasized that the interpretation of results will often differ considerably from that appropriate to normal soils. and ADAS do not conduct all analyses which might be required. Nevertheless, it is recommended that the ADAS facilities be utilized for analytical tests as they are convenient to arrange and the costs are reasonable. A further point in support of this recommendation is that it is desirable to standardize procedures for spoil analysis so that meaningful comparisons between results can be made leading to improved techniques of restoration.

It is essential that analyses be conducted on samples taken before earthmoving because the results may well influence the final placement of materials. Extremely hostile materials should be buried, the substrates with the greatest growth potential being best for placement as the surface growing media. It is recommended that sampling and analyses be conducted at the following stages of planting schemes:

i) before earthworks (as part of feasibility survey);
ii) after completion of earthworks but prior to planting;
iii) in the first year after planting (January–March);
iv) annually in the case of schemes where planting is direct on spoil (January–March).

TABLE 11.3
Chemical analysis of colliery spoil
(applicable to other types of waste material)*

Analysis	Procedure	Interpretation
pH (acidity/alkalinity)	Mix spoil and water in ratio of 1:2·5. Read pH.	Lime requirement test necessary if pH below 6·0.
Lime-requirement	Mix spoil with buffer solution (Shoemaker). Shake for 24 hours. Read pH. Repeat test with twice volume of buffer if final pH is below 5·5.	If initial pH of spoil is below 3·5 the result of the lime-requirement test should be doubled. This test assumes liming to 15 cm (6 in.) depth.
Phosphate	Mix spoil with 0·5N sodium bicarbonate solution. Shake for 1 hour and analyse solution for phosphate.	Results given in index form (0, 1, 2 etc.). Most colliery wastes give value of 0 indicating that 187·5 kg/ha P_2O_5 (150 units/acre P_2O_5) are required. However, test does not indicate fixation capacity so higher levels are needed (*see* text).
Potassium	Shake spoil with ammonium acetate or strong ammonium nitrate for ½ hour. Analyse solution for potassium.	Results given in index form (0, 1, 2 etc.). 0 indicates 125 kg/ha K_2O (100 units/acre K_2O) are required. 1–4 indicates 62·5 kg/ha K_2O (50 units/acre K_2O) are required.
Magnesium	Extract sample in ammonium nitrate solution. Analyse solution for magnesium.	Results given in index form (0, 1, 2 etc.). If low (0–1) apply lime as magnesian or dolomitic limestone.
Salinity	Make saturated extract in calcium sulphate. Measure electrical conductivity.	Results given as pH values (0, 1, 2 etc.). Values above 5 indicate salinity problems.

* For interpretation of ADAS analytical results consult 'The liming and fertilizing of arable crops and grassland'—*Booklet No. 1* from ADAS.

Ground materials should be sampled on a random basis.

At stage (i) the numbers of samples taken for analysis should be as follows:

Area (hectares)	Number of samples
0–4	6
4–12	12
12–24	15
24–40	20

Fewer samples are required at stages (ii)–(iv). Each sample should consist of ten or more sub-samples taken at random from within a 25 m radius of the sampling point, each sub-sample consisting of material extracted to a depth of 15 cm. It is important that the samples consist of equal amounts of material from the surface and at all levels to this depth.

Table 11.3 gives details of the types of analysis which ADAS are equipped to undertake. At the initial sampling and also before planting it will be found that phosphate status is often zero, but because of fixation of phosphate fertilizers added to shale, this value is meaningless. Analyses conducted after planting, however, will usually give a positive value and normal interpretation is then possible.

11.32 Blast furnace slag

See Table 11.4 for a guide to planting on blast furnace slag.

a) Grass establishment

Treatment of alkaline conditions. Like colliery spoil, blast furnace slag is devoid of nitrogen and phosphate but differs in respect of pH conditions for the waste is highly alkaline. Unweathered material may be as alkaline as pH 10·6 which causes immobilization of phosphates and possibly directly harmful effects on plant roots. This alkalinity is due to the presence of calcium hydroxide and the hydrolysis of calcium silicates in the slag.

Whereas acid conditions in soils and wastes are easily corrected by the addition of neutralizing agents such as ground limestone, alkaline conditions are difficult to treat. In the cases of some natural soils, acidifying agents such as sulphur and aluminium sulphate have been used but these cannot be employed for dealing with extremely alkaline materials because the action of sulphur is very slow, depending on the presence of oxidizing bacteria, and aluminium sulphate is prohibitively expensive when high application rates are needed. Further, chemical acidifiers are non-selective in their action on soil hydroxides and will react with calcium carbonate which is present in blast furnace slag. The only practicable method for reducing the high pH of the slag is by exposure to natural leaching after the completion of earthworks. Over a period of one year to eighteen months, the pH at the surface will fall to about 8·0 as a result of hydroxides

TABLE 11.4
Guide to planting on blast furnace slag

Operation or treatment	Specification
1. Exposure to natural leaching if pH is above 8·0	Allow natural leaching for 12–18 months or until the pH has fallen to about 8·0.
2. Phosphate fertilization	Apply 125–250 kg/ha P_2O_5 (100–200 units/acre P_2O_5) depending on pH of waste at planting time. Use superphosphate or triple superphosphate.
3. Seed bed preparation	Use minimal cultivations on account of stony nature of waste.
4. NPK fertilization	125 kg/ha (100 units/acre) nitrogen, 50 kg/ha (40 units/acre) phosphate as P_2O_5, 50 kg/ha (40 units/acre) potash as K_2O.
5. Grass seeding	Sow red fescue (*Festuca rubra*) and wild white clover (*Trifolium repens*). Increase normal seed rates by 50–100% on account of coarse and stony nature of substrate.
6. Repeat NPK fertilization	Apply compound fertilizer as above (4) but containing 50–100 kg/ha (40–80 units/acre) nitrogen.

being leached from the superficial material into the underlying waste.

Phosphate deficiency. Phosphate deficiency may be overcome by the application of superphosphate. Basic slag is inadvisable due to the high pH of the waste which will prevent the release of phosphate. The fertilizer should not be spread until the pH has dropped to about 8·0 otherwise insoluble calcium phosphates will be formed causing immobilization problems. The rate of phosphate application for grass seeding should be 125–250 kg/ha P_2O_5 (100–200 units/acre P_2O_5).

Due to the high porosity and poor fertilizer retention properties of blast furnace slag, the initial dressing of fertilizer should provide at least 125 kg/ha (100 units/acre) of nitrogen. This must be followed by a further application of about 50–100 kg/ha N (40–80 units/acre N) after planting, preferably after two to three months. Alternatively, organic sources of nitrogen such as

PLATE 11.4 **A landscape of waste from iron smelting: blast furnace slag. Vegetation is absent due to infertility and alkalinity.** *(R. P. Gemmell)*

PLATE 11.5 **Grass trials on blast furnace slag. The waste was allowed to weather, treated with nitrogen and phosphate fertilizers, and seeded to red fescue.** *(R. P. Gemmell)*

digested sewage sludge or broiler manure which have slow-release properties may be applied to give a longer lasting supply of nitrogen.

The most suitable grass species to sow on blast furnace slag is red fescue (*Festuca rubra*), this being highly tolerant of the dry and poor conditions as well as the prevailing high pH. Common bent (*Agrostis tenuis*) is intolerant of the waste and should never be planted. Because of the problems of maintaining nitrogen fertility, it is advisable to sow a mixture of grass and clover, preferably red fescue with wild white clover. The latter is persistent and grows well on the slag provided that ample phosphate is supplied and the pH is not above 8·0.

b) *Tree planting*

The range of species which may be established on blast furnace slag is rather limited because of the high pH and calcareous nature of the waste. Conifers and other species which prefer acid soils are intolerant of the conditions in the waste.

Alders are particularly useful as are other nitrogen-fixing species such as black locust (*Robinia pseudoacacia*), gorse (*Ulex europaeus*) and tree lupin (*Lupinus arboreus*) in mild areas. Sea buckthorn (*Hippophaë rhamnoides*), buddleia (*Buddleia davidii*), privet (*Ligustrum vulgare*) and many willows and sallows (*Salix* spp) are tolerant species.

11.33 Power station ash

a) *Grass establishment*

Early research on the grassing of power station ash, often known as pulverized fuel ash or fly ash, indicated that this waste contains toxic concentrations of aluminium and manganese. This was later disproved by further investigations which showed beyond doubt that the growth problems were due to boron. This element occurs in the ash as a soluble borate released by the hydrolysis of borosilicates.

Other chemical constituents which inhibit the growth of plants in the ash are soluble sodium and potassium salts. These are secondary in importance to boron toxicity but exert osmotic effects on plant roots, restricting the uptake of moisture and nutrients. An additional factor is high pH which usually falls between 7·5 and 10·5 but may approach 12·0. Like other wastes, power station ash is deficient in nitrogen and phosphate.

Toxicity. The chemical composition and toxicity of the ash are extremely variable, these properties being largely determined by the nature of the coal burnt in the power stations concerned. Although most ash types are extremely hostile to plant colonization, some are relatively innocuous on account of their low levels of boron, soluble salts, and near neutral pH. Many wastes from South Wales fall into this category and will support good plant growth if adequate levels of fertilizers are supplied. Applications of 125 kg/ha N (100 units/acre N) and at least 125 kg/ha P_2O_5 (100 units/acre P_2O_5) are needed in the first few years depending on land use and whether clovers are planted.

In the cases of toxic forms of ash, the layering or incorporation of bulky amendments is essential, particularly if agriculture is the desired land use. Agronomists have recommended the spreading of 30 cm (1 ft) soil layers on the most toxic ash types when arable crops are to be grown or if the land is to be heavily grazed. For amenity purposes, however, 10 cm of soil will suffice provided that high rates of phosphate and nitrogen are applied. Reasonable substitutes for soil are subsoil, peat, and neutral colliery spoil. Better still are sewage sludge (free of toxic metals and produced by the activated sludge process) and acid colliery spoil. All these materials, particularly the latter two wastes, should be incorporated into the ash rather than being spread as discrete surface coverings. Mixtures of acid colliery spoil and ash are particularly advantageous because the toxic properties of the two constituent wastes are alleviated and a reasonable soil structure intermediate to the extremes existing in the two wastes is achieved.

Cementation. Some types of power station ash undergo pozzolanic cementation with the effect that root penetration is impeded. If thin soil layers are applied or if soil substitutes are spread on the surface, it is essential to break up the ash concretions by subsoiling. This may be carried out either before or after the spreading of soil or other amendments.

Selection of grass species is often critical for successful plantings direct into ash or in media where ash is present in the rooting zone. A list of tolerant species of grasses and legumes is presented in Table 11.5. In establishing grass swards, the inclusion of clovers is advisable in order to enrich the soil in nitrogen and maintain fertility.

TABLE 11.5
Grasses and clovers tolerant of power station ash

Tolerance	Grasses	Clovers
High	—	*Medicago sativa*
Medium	*Cynosurus cristatus*	*Melilotus alba*
	Festuca pratensis	*Trifolium hybridum*
	Festuca rubra	*Trifolium pratense*
	Lolium multiflorum	*Trifolium repens*
	Lolium perenne	
	Phleum pratense	
	Poa annua	
	Poa pratensis	
	Poa trivialis	
Low	*Agrostis* spp	
	Dactylis glomerata	

187

PLATE 11.6 **Metalliferous waste tips in the Lower Swansea Valley. This waste is from a zinc smelter and is highly toxic to vegetation.** *(R. P. Gemmell)*

b) *Tree planting*

The breaking up of ash concretions, if they are present, must be tackled before tree planting. If analyses show that boron and salinity levels are high, trees must either be planted in pits filled with soil or on ash treated with a deep layer of cover material.

Included amongst the most tolerant woody plants are *Alnus* spp, *Salix* spp, *Robinia pseudoacacia, Betula, Acer, Crataegus, Hypericum* spp, *Tamarix* and *Ribes.* Conifers and other species preferring acid soil conditions are intolerant of the waste.

c) *Analytical tests*

Analytical tests should be carried out as described for colliery spoil with the inclusion of water-soluble boron

determinations. Lime requirement tests are unnecessary. If available boron levels are in excess of 10 ppm (parts per million) then a moderate degree of boron toxicity is likely. Even levels of 4–10 ppm may give rise to some toxicity.

11.34 Metalliferous wastes

Although non-ferrous metal mining has virtually ceased in this country, there are countless waste heaps from old workings of zinc, copper and lead mines scattered around parts of the country. Most of them are in the countryside, often in areas of high quality scenery, and many are in National Parks. Most are devoid of colonizing vegetation or support only a sparse flora due to metal toxicities and nutrient deficiency. They may also be sources of water pollution due to the heavy metal content of their drainage outflows.

The waste from the smelting of non-ferrous metal ores is generally more toxic than the corresponding mine spoil materials. The residue resulting from smelting is usually known as slag, referring to mineral concentrates which have been roasted with additives so that the metals are converted to a soluble form prior to separation. Consequently, the metals remaining in the smelter wastes are more soluble than those occurring in the tips of mine spoil which accounts for the greater difficulties encountered in establishing vegetation on metalliferous slags.

Certain other types of waste contain high concentrations of metals which may harm plants. The tailings resulting from fluorspar extraction exhibit metal toxicities of this kind. Sewage sludges, particularly those contaminated with industrial effluents, frequently contain toxic levels of metals such as zinc, copper and chromium. Natural soils may also become contaminated with copper and possibly other metals because of aerial fallout from nearby metal-refining plants.

a) *Establishment of grass and trees*

There are three methods available for planting vegetation on substrates contaminated with heavy metals.

i) The growth characteristics of the planting media can be improved by amelioration and cultivation treatments.

ii) The wastes can be completely blanketed with non-toxic material such as soil or subsoil.

iii) Species can be planted which exhibit tolerance to the toxic levels of metals prevailing in the wastes. Certain strains of the fescue and bent grasses derived from populations found colonizing old mine workings are known to possess a high degree of tolerance to certain metals. Seed of those strains, however, is not readily available and in any case the toxicity of some materials such as certain smelter wastes is too severe for plant tolerance to cope with.

Removal of toxicity. It is impossible to remove toxic metals from toxic planting media either by natural leaching or by artificial means. Natural leaching is ineffective because metal mine spoils and smelter wastes contain large reserves of metals in the form of sulphides. In some wastes the total concentrations of metal may reach 5% or more. These sulphides undergo weathering reactions and release metallic salts into solution over a long period and at toxic concentrations.

As soon as the metals in solution are leached from the surface by percolating rainwater, more metallic salts are brought into solution so that an equilibrium is attained which may prevail for hundreds or even thousands of years.

The only techniques which will permit plants to be grown in the presence of toxic metals involve the addition of organic materials and lime to the substrates.

Organic matter acts by 'complexing' the toxic metals,

rendering them unavailable to plant roots and removing them from solution. Good sources of organic matter for this purpose are peat, air-dried sewage sludge from the activated sludge process, and screened domestic refuse. The sewage sludge must, of course, be free from toxic concentrations of heavy metals. For metal mine spoils, levels of addition in the order of 5–10 cm (2–4 in.) depth will suffice but smelter wastes, because they are more toxic, require at least 10–15 cm (4–6 in.) of material. The organic matter should be incorporated into the surface layers of waste by disc cultivations.

Lime, as either ground limestone or hydrated lime, may be used to combat the toxicity of some metalliferous wastes. It is, however, rarely effective on its own and is best used in combination with organic matter treatments when the pH is on the acid side. Many copper mine spoils and copper smelter wastes are slightly to moderately acid and should be treated with ground limestone prior to the addition of organic matter. The raising of the pH causes copper salts to become insoluble, thereby reducing toxicity. The addition of calcium by lime addition also alleviates the toxic effects of copper and other metal salts in solution.

Blanketing metalliferous wastes with non-toxic growing media ensures that the plant roots are physically isolated from the underlying waste. Therefore, blanketing materials should be spread as discrete surface coverings rather than being incorporated into the underlying toxic substrates. The minimum thickness for grassland establishment should be at least 10 cm and preferably 20–30 cm (8–12 in.). For tree-planting schemes up to 2 m of cover material may be needed. Either soil or soil substitutes including subsoil, neutral colliery spoil, and similar non-toxic waste materials may be employed for this purpose but power station ash should never be used because it encourages the upward rise of moisture by capillarity bringing toxic metallic salts to the surface. Fine-grained, sandy or silty amendments may give rise to similar surface contamination problems.

Application of nitrogen and phosphates. Like colliery spoil and other materials, metalliferous spoils and smelter wastes require heavy rates of application of nitrogen and phosphate, both initially and during the after-management stages. Metal toxicities as well as nutrient deficiencies may reappear unless reclaimed sites are subjected to special after-management treatments. These must be directed towards building up the humus content of the soil by allowing grass to rot back on itself without cutting or by leaving the cuttings on site to rot back *in situ*. Further applications of organic matter and additional lime treatments may be needed if metal toxicities or acidity reappear. Vegetation established on metal-rich substrates should not be grazed by livestock unless it is certain that foliar absorption and accumulation of metals has not reached potentially toxic levels.

189

TABLE 11.6
Concentrations of metals causing toxicity in different wastes

Substratum	Extractant	Metal toxicity range
Zinc smelter waste and zinc mine spoil	Total (acid)	1–5 % zinc
	Acetic acid	10 000–20 000 ppm zinc
	Water	100–200 ppm zinc
Copper smelter waste and copper mine spoil	Total (acid)	0·1–1 % copper
	EDTA	1 000–3 000 ppm copper
	Water	20–100 ppm copper
Sewage sludge	Total	0·5–5 % zinc
	Total	0·2–1·2 % copper
	Total	0·03–0·4 % nickel
	Total	0·03–1·0 % chromium
	Acetic acid	1 700–3 500 ppm zinc
	Acetic acid	100–3 000 ppm copper
	Acetic acid	120–2 000 ppm nickel
	Acetic acid	20–100 ppm chromium

b) *Analytical tests*

In addition to the tests outlined in Table 11.3 for colliery spoil, the concentrations of heavy metals in suspected metalliferous materials should be determined. It is difficult to advise which of the alternative methods available should be adopted as this depends on the nature of the substrates under examination. Total metal levels may be meaningless as they do not indicate how much metal is actually dissolved in the soil solution although they may give some indication of potential toxicity. Extractions with ammonium acetate or acetic acid are commonly used to measure what are termed 'plant-available' metal levels. More recently, simple water extraction techniques have proved useful. In order to assist with the interpretations of results, Table 11.6 indicates the range of concentrations of metals which are known to cause toxicities in different wastes.

In recent years, ADAS has used the term 'zinc equivalent' in relation to the addition of metal-contaminated sewage sludges to soils. Many sludges are extremely toxic because of their high metal content and their addition to soils may give rise to toxic growing conditions. It has been found that about 250 ppm of total zinc is the maximum concentration of this metal that can be added to a soil over a long period without causing toxicity problems. This means that 560 kg (approx. 11 cwt) of zinc is the maximum amount that can be added to an area of 1 ha (2·5 acres) over, say, a 30-year period. On an annual basis, this is about 19 kg (42 lb) zinc.

Now, because sewage sludge may contain copper, nickel and chromium as well as zinc, allowances have to be made for these additional metals. Copper is about twice as toxic as zinc and nickel is about eight times as toxic. The term 'zinc equivalent' enables the levels of these other metals to be expressed in terms of zinc after making allowances for their different degrees of toxicity. Thus, the maximum amount of all metals that can be safely added to 1 ha is expressed as 560 kg zinc equivalent or, alternatively, 19 kg zinc equivalent per annum.

11.35 Chemical wastes

Chemical wastes are the most toxic of all materials likely to be encountered on landscaping and reclamation schemes. The presence in soil of only 0·1 % of some wastes may completely inhibit plant growth so that even trace contamination may cause difficulties in planting. A further problem is that chemical residues are frequently highly polluting materials due to the high solubility of their toxic constituents.

The conditions likely to affect growth in chemical wastes are extreme alkalinity, high acidity, toxic levels of various soluble salts such as chromates, sulphates and chlorides, and the presence of toxic metals such as zinc, copper, lead and chromium in solution. In many materials more than one of these conditions may prevail.

Wastes in which high pH conditions are found include alkali wastes from the manufacture of soda-ash, spent lime waste beds, chromate smelter waste and gas lime deposits; pH values of 12·0–12·7 are not uncommon in these materials.

At the other extreme, pyritic wastes from acid production processes have pH values of 2·0–3·0 and often lower. Due to pyrite oxidation, as occurs in acid colliery

PLATE 11.7 **A chemical waste tip. The dark areas are pyrite which is producing a highly acid run-off.**
(Courtesy of Joint Reclamation Team, Greater Manchester and Lancashire County Councils)

PLATE 11.8 **Acid run-off from a chemical waste tip containing pyrite. Note the toxic effect of the discharge on the natural vegetation. This could have been prevented by covering the pyrite with soil and stabilizing the tip by planting to grass and trees.** *(Courtesy of Joint Reclamation Team, Greater Manchester and Lancashire County Councils)*

spoil, such deposits release highly acid and polluting effluents. Freshwater flora and fauna are highly sensitive to even slightly acid conditions and are devastated by the heavy deposits of ferric salts on stream beds which occur in the presence of ferruginous effluents.

High salt levels are found in most chemical wastes. Chromates are responsible for the intense toxicity of chromate smelting deposits. Sulphates are high in alkali wastes from soda-ash production as well as in chromate smelter waste. Chemical sludges and residual sulphates consist almost entirely of soluble salts. In some cases, salts of toxic metals as described for metalliferous wastes are present.

a) *Establishment of grass and trees*

The only feasible method of establishing vegetation on the majority of chemical wastes is to spread a layer of suitable cover material so that the roots of plants can be isolated from the underlying toxic material. For grassland, about 20–30 cm (8–12 in.) is the minimum application rate of soil or similar ameliorant; for tree planting the depth should be increased to 2 m. The spreading of the surface covering must be carried out very carefully so that its thickness is even over the site and it does not become mixed with the underlying toxic waste. It should be realized that contamination of the soil cover by waste adhering to the tracks and wheels of earthmoving equipment may lead to toxicity problems. Also, deep cultivations may bring toxic waste to the surface; therefore only light harrowing can be performed during preparation of the seed bed.

Many of the soluble salts found in chemical wastes are extremely mobile in soil and may be transported upwards to the surface if moisture rises as in dry weather. For example, chromate salts are extremely mobile in loamy soils so that topsoil spread on chromate smelter waste may become contaminated and cause vegetation dieback. Therefore, cover materials which restrict mobility should be selected for chemical-waste planting schemes. Amendments like topsoil, power station ash and fine sandy media should be avoided; the best amendments for this purpose are granular, coarse subsoils. Alternatively, a layer of clay may be used to seal the waste. The subsoil or clay cover can then be covered with a layer of soil or further amended with sewage sludge.

Often, the ameliorating effects of soil spreading may have to be reinforced by chemical additives and/or organic matter, particularly if only a thin layer of cover material can be obtained or if contamination is unavoidable during spreading. Table 11.7 gives details of some chemical and organic amendments which may be used for this purpose.

There are many old alkali waste tips and lime waste beds in the north and west of England which have become colonized naturally over a period of up to a hundred years. Their flora is often rich in unusual and sometimes rare plants including wild orchids. Some of these sites are now recognized as important for scientific study, education and nature conservation. They should be preserved wherever possible.

TABLE 11.7
Some useful chemicals and organic amendments for revegetation of chemically contaminated sites

Amendment	Use	Application rates
Ground limestone ($CaCO_3$)	Neutralizes acidity. Counteracts some metal toxicities e.g. Zn, Cu, Mg, Cr, Ni and Mo. Reduces toxicities of some salts e.g. chromates.	2 500–30 000 kg/ha (1–12 tons/acre)
Gypsum ($CaSO_4$)	Counteracts certain metal toxicities e.g. Mg but does not alter pH.	1 250–5 000 kg/ha ($\frac{1}{2}$–2 tons/acre)
Ferrous sulphate ($FeSO_4\ 7H_2O$)	Reduces chromate toxicity. Neutralizes alkalinity.	2 500–20 000 kg/ha (1–8 tons/acre)
Organic matter e.g. peat, sewage sludge from activated sludge process, screened domestic refuse	Reduces metal toxicities by complex formation e.g. Zn, Cu, Ni, Pb etc. Reduces boron toxicity, Counteracts salt toxicities e.g. chromates and sulphates. Provides nutrients. Improves soil structure, moisture and nutrient retention.	Low levels: 50 000–250 000 kg/ha (20–100 tons/acre) High levels: 5–15 cm depth (2–6 in. depth)

b) *Analytical tests*

When obtaining specimens of chemical waste for analysis, the samples must be taken from deposits which have not been affected by natural leaching and weathering. This often involves extracting samples from up to a metre below the surface.

The analyses outlined in Table 11.3 should be supplemented by determinations of soluble hydroxides, carbonates and bicarbonates if the pH is high. If conductivity values indicate high soluble salt levels it is useful to measure the concentrations of sulphate, chloride, calcium, magnesium, potassium and sodium. Other worthwhile analyses include those for zinc, copper, lead, nickel, chromium, boron and sulphide. A wider range of analytical tests will be necessary if the presence of other contaminants is suspected.

11.36 Infertile wastes

Plant growth in many materials is restricted simply by nutrient deficiencies and adverse physical conditions. Deficiencies of nitrogen and phosphate are widespread; they prevail in sand and gravel deposits, china clay spoil, ironstone spoil, brick rubble, foundry sand, furnace ash, exposed subsoil and cinders. Some of these substrates may exhibit mild acidity as well.

These adverse growing conditions are readily corrected by fertilizer applications and the addition of nutrient-rich organic materials. Poor fertilizer retention is very common, particularly in relation to nitrogen, therefore wild white clovers should be included in grass seed mixtures and nitrogen-fixing trees should be included as pioneers.

11.37 Soils and vegetation damaged by trampling

In recent years, the increasing use of the countryside for recreation has caused damage to soils and vegetation in country parks, well known beauty spots such as Kynance Cove, Box Hill and Ilkley Moor, and parts of the Pennine Way. In some areas the vegetation has been completely destroyed leading to soil erosion and permanent scarring of the landscape. This damage is caused by physical injury to plants and the effects of soil compaction, both being the result of excessive trampling by walkers.

Certain vegetation and soil types are more sensitive than others to damage by trampling. Heathers (*Erica* spp), ling (*Calluna*) and bilberries (*Vaccinium* spp) are highly susceptible to trampling whereas most grasses, particularly annual meadow grass (*Poa annua*) and the ryegrasses (*Lolium* spp), are relatively tolerant. Poorly

PLATE 11.9 **An attractive landscape of grass and trees established on a former gravel pit entirely lacking in topsoil. Field-end Housing Scheme.** (Landscape Architects: *Eric Lyons Cunningham Partnership. Snoek Westward Photography*)

PLATE 11.10 **Destruction of vegetation by trampling in a country park. The effect of trampling is cumulative and maximum damage occurs when the soil is wet.** *(Courtesy of Joint Reclamation Team, Greater Manchester and Lancashire County Councils)*

PLATE 11.11 **Grass seeding and cultivation trials on a pathway denuded by trampling. Lime and fertilizers were needed in order to establish grass.** *(Courtesy of Joint Reclamation Team, Greater Manchester and Lancashire County Councils)*

drained and waterlogged soils are much more prone to damage than well drained and dry soils. Acid soils and their vegetation seem to be more sensitive to trampling than neutral or alkaline soil and vegetation types. It is also known that the ground flora of woodlands is vulnerable because of its relatively poor cover due to shading. Further, damage in general is particularly severe in the winter months on account of higher soil moisture content and the fact that regrowth of injured vegetation is very slow or nil due to the prevailing low temperatures.

The best way to minimize serious wear and deterioration of vegetation is by careful route planning. In selecting routes for paths, the following considerations should be made:

i) Avoid routes over waterlogged and impermeable soils; choose areas where drainage is good.
ii) If possible, direct walkers onto grassland rather than areas dominated by heathers, ling, and bilberry heath. Wet grassland dominated by purple moor grass (*Molinia*) should be avoided.
iii) Plan a flexible system or network of routes so that over-used paths are given time to recover. This will permit pathways over ground subjected to winter

TABLE 11.8
Techniques of renovation of turf damaged by trampling

Operation or treatment	Specification
1. Rotary cultivation to relieve compaction	Tractor drawn rotovator for large areas: tines may be needed for extreme compaction. Garden type rotovators for paths. Hand implements for small areas. Cultivate when soil is dry.
2. Liming	Apply ground limestone depending on pH values or lime-requirement tests.
3. Lime incorporation	Integrate lime by rotovation or hand cultivations.
4. Fertilization	Apply compound NPK fertilizers depending on results of nutrient tests. Use slow-release fertilizers rather than soluble types.
5. Grass seeding	Apply very high seed rates and use species tolerant of trampling e.g. *Lolium perenne, Poa annua, Phleum pratense, Festuca rubra* and *Agrostis* spp.

waterlogging or summer desiccation to be closed in the winter and summer months respectively.

iv) Allow for the provision of drainage ditches, cultivations, fertilization and seeding operations if recreation pressures are likely to increase.

If deterioration of trampled vegetation has not proceeded too far, regeneration will occur if trampling can be stopped for a period, provided that the soil structure has not been seriously impaired. If denudation has taken place, re-seeding will be necessary in order to achieve satisfactory recovery in a reasonable time. In most cases the damage to the soil is so serious that surface cultivations and growth amendments have to be applied. The adverse soil conditions induced by severe trampling are compaction, poor infiltration, and impeded drainage. These result in waterlogging in winter, desiccation in summer, de-oxygenation causing root growth inhibition and reduction in the activity of soil fauna and flora, and in many cases acidification.

Improvement can only be brought about by applying techniques similar to those used for turf renovation followed by seeding of appropriate grass seed mixtures. Details of the necessary procedures are given in Table 11.8. Before they are carried out it is advised that certain soil analysis tests be made: determination of pH followed by estimation of lime-requirement, nitrogen, phosphate and potash levels. After germination of the seed, the grass swards must be allowed to establish themselves for a reasonable period before they are subjected to public access and trampling.

11.4 AFTER-MANAGEMENT

Serious after-management problems have already been experienced on reclaimed land. The difficulties which have arisen are as follows:

i) development of acidity on colliery wastes;
ii) deficiency of phosphate on colliery wastes, blast furnace slag and power station ash;
iii) deficiency of nitrogen on most kinds of waste and subsoil;
iv) reappearance of metal toxicity on smelter wastes and mine spoils;
v) consolidation problems, particularly on colliery wastes.

Some of these difficulties have been the result of incorrect initial amendment and cultivation treatments but the commonest cause of regression is simply a lack of after-management. Restoration is rarely a 'once and for all treatment', it must involve follow-on treatments in order to be a permanent success. These maintenance operations must be considered and planned as part of the overall design strategy of schemes so that provision can be made from the outset for the costs involved and methods of implementation.

In order to detect adverse changes in soil properties at an early stage, a system of monitoring should be devised

PLATE 11.12 **Aerial view of reclamation site: Silksworth Colliery, Sunderland.** (Photographers: *Dennis Wompra Studios Middlesbrough*)

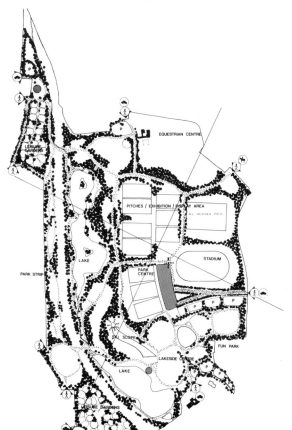

when plantings are made on wastes or difficult substrates. It is advisable for soil samples to be taken annually, preferably in late winter or early spring, and according to the procedure described in the section on colliery spoil. Appropriate modifications must be made in the cases of tests on wastes other than colliery spoil: these have been mentioned in the relevant sections.

The results of analytical tests, supported by information on the composition of species and growth levels, will enable the correct liming, fertilizing and manuring treatments to be worked out so that regression does not occur. Consolidation is a rather different matter and research on this and other likely long-term problems is now in progress.

FURTHER READING

Bradshaw, A. D. and Handley, J. 'Low cost grassing of sites awaiting redevelopment', *Landscape Design*, No. 99, 1972 pp. 17–19

FIGURE 11.1 **The plan for reclamation of Silksworth Colli** (Landscape Architects: *Brian Clouston and Partners*)

Chadwick, M. J. and Goodman, G. T. 'The ecology of resource degradation and renewal', *Brit. Ecol. Soc. Symp.* No. 14 (Oxford: Blackwell, 1975)

Duffey, E. and Watt, A. S. (Ed.) 'The Scientific Management of animal and plant communities for conservation', *Brit. Ecol. Soc. Symp.*, No. 11 (Oxford: Blackwell, 1971)

Gemmell, R. P. 'Colliery shale revegetation techniques', *Surveyor*, 6 July 1973, pp. 27–9

Gemmell, R. P. 'Planting trees on wasteland', *Surveyor*, 16 August 1974, pp. 30–2

Gemmell, R. P. 'Reclamation of chemically polluted sites', *Surveyor*, 2 November 1973, pp. 36–8

Gemmell, R. P. 'Revegetation of toxic sites', *Landscape Design*, No. 101, 1973 pp. 30–2

Goodman, G. T., Edwards, R. W. and Lambert, J. M. 'Ecology and the Individual Society' *Brit. Ecol. Soc. Symp.* No. 5, (Oxford: Blackwell, 1965)

Hilton, K. J. (Ed.) *Lower Swansea Valley Project* (London: Longmans Green, 1967)

Hutnik, R. J. and Davis, G. (Ed.) *Ecology and Reclamation of Devastated Land* (London: Gordon and Breach, 1973) vols. 1 and 2

Landscape Reclamation—a report on research into problems of reclaiming derelict land by a research team of the University of Newcastle upon Tyne. (Guildford: IPC Science and Technology Press Ltd., 1971 and 1972) vols. 1 and 2

Land reclaimed for golf course. (Landscape Architects: *Brian Clouston & Partners*. Photograph by *Judy Snaith*)

CHAPTER 12

The Landscaping of Reservoir Margins

C. J. GILL AND A. D. BRADSHAW

12.1 INTRODUCTION

In a country such as Great Britain with one of the densest populations in the world, the wholesale use of land for storage of water causes serious problems, not only because of the destruction of agricultural land, but also because of loss of public amenities. The loss to the public has been realized, and now, in contrast to past practice, the public are being allowed extensive access to every new reservoir being built.

In fact reservoirs are of great amenity value. The public, once allowed access, will be able to view the whole reservoir at close range and will hope to find not only sporting and recreational facilities, but also considerable aesthetic enjoyment. It is here that the problem lies, for reservoir levels fluctuate more than those in natural lakes (Figure 12.1). The low water levels which usually occur in the summer when recreational use is at its peak, expose bleak margins which are open to a great deal of criticism (*see* Plate 12.1). Landscape architects have long been concerned about the best treatment for reservoir margins but a satisfactory solution has yet to be found.[1]

Where trees have been used as a landscape feature in the past, the margins have been scrupulously avoided and other vegetation has not been consciously planted (e.g. Treweryn, Clywedog, Derwent).

A general aim of landscape design is to create a harmonious landscape in sympathy with its surroundings. In a rural area the landscaping should be as natural as possible and plants should be used which resemble closely in layout and species those that can be found locally. The main characteristic of natural water bodies is the lack of a bleak margin because adapted vegetation has colonized down to the average water level. If the margins of new reservoirs could be similarly covered with plants, they would resemble natural margins much more closely and be much more acceptable.

To provide a natural groundcover for the margin, the first step is to find suitable flood-tolerant plant species. Then the ecological difficulties set by the habitat must be overcome, and the quality of the water must not be endangered.

12.2 FLOOD-TOLERANT PLANTS

The different categories of plant material available are:
a) annuals replacing themselves by seed every year;
b) herbaceous perennials spreading vegetatively into the bare zone as it becomes exposed every year;
c) herbaceous perennials permanently rooted in the margin able to tolerate submergence and exposure;
d) floating vegetative mats which rise and fall with water level;
e) perennial trees able to grow at and just below top water level with their bases in the water.

Annuals and vegetatively spreading perennials, already grow in limited areas of the margins of most upland and lowland reservoirs.

Permanently rooted perennials are rarer, although there are good examples at Treweryn reservoir (Merionethshire), which was flooded in 1965. There small patches of pasture vegetation containing species such as *Ranunculus flammula* (spearwort) still become green and resume photosynthetic activity when unflooded. In the alluvial deltas of Lake Vyrnwy (Montgomeryshire) and Thirlmere (Cumberland), permanently rooted species such as *Phalaris arundinacea* (reedgrass), *Equisetum fluviatile* (water horsetail) and *Littorella uniflora* (shoreweed) thrive down to about 1, 1·5 and 2 m respectively below top water level.

The plant material of the first three groups is hardly of sufficient size to contribute much to the landscape. At best it will provide the reservoir with a green instead of a grey rim, which will not greatly alleviate the main aesthetic

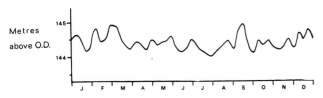

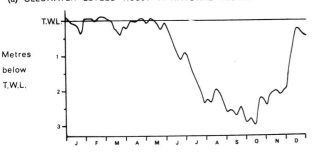

(a) ULLSWATER LEVELS (1966)—A NATURAL REGIME

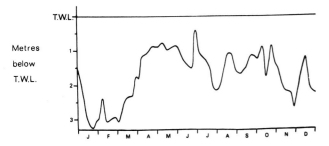

(b) VYRNWY LEVELS (1966)—A DIRECT SUPPLY REGIME

(c) TRYWERYN LEVELS (1966)—A REGULATORY REGIME

FIGURE 12.1 **Typical annual cycle in water level fluctuation in three water bodies.** *(C. J. Gill: Courtesy of a) North West Water Authority; b) c) Severn-Trent Water Authority)*

problem. In addition all three types of plant demand the presence of a hospitable soil surface relatively unexposed to erosion by waves. It may be possible to hasten what natural colonization will occur by introducing *Littorella, Ranunculus, Phalaris*, etc. on the appropriately sheltered margins of newly-filled reservoirs in which the species do not already exist.

Floating mats of vegetation are a common tropical phenomenon, but in existing natural and artificial areas of water in Britain they are almost completely absent because of the effects of wind, rather than total lack of appropriate species; this suggests that they are unlikely to succeed in Britain.

The common natural occurrence of trees on the margins of lakes and some reservoirs, and the success of tree planting for margin stabilization along Eastern European reservoirs, make the last category promising.[2] Trees are more likely to grow successfully and they provide a type of vegetation in scale with the landscape of

PLATE 12.1 **Summer drawdown in a quiet corner of the Elan Valley Reservoirs.** *(C. J. Gill. Courtesy of Welsh National Water Development Authority)*

FIGURE 12.2 **Reservoir planting and recreation. Artist's impression.** *(Andrew Donaldson)*

PLATE 12.2 **Montage demonstrating the visual effects of tree planting at and below TWL, at Treweryn (Llyn Celyn) Reservoir.** *(C. J. Gill. Courtesy of Welsh National Water Development Authority)*

a reservoir. Plate 12.2 shows by montage how groups of trees, judiciously planted, can break up the stark horizontal top water line and could greatly improve the appearance of the margin at times of drawdown. Trees have the added advantage that they are less likely to upset the quality of the water.

12.3 TREES

12.31 Tree growth in flooded conditions

It is no use planting trees on margins unless the ecological problem is understood. The subject has been discussed thoroughly elsewhere,[3] but the key points are:

i) Tree growth in waterlogged conditions is dependent on satisfactory root growth.

ii) Oxygen is necessary for root growth, for aerobic root respiration. In a soil at or below field capacity, sufficient oxygen can diffuse from the soil atmosphere to permit tree growth. Moisture levels above field capacity, as in a waterlogged or submerged soil, affect tree growth adversely by retarding oxygen diffusion.

iii) The amount of oxygen that can diffuse into a root in submerged soil is increased in soils of large particle size, and by well aerated water, i.e. where the water is shallow or moving.

iv) Because root growth is greater in spring and summer than in winter, respiration rates and therefore oxygen needs are also greater in spring and summer. Spring and summer flooding is thus more prohibitive to tree growth than winter flooding, not only because of

heavier oxygen demand, but also because of a relative oxygen shortage owing to high microbial respiration rates and to lack of wind-mixing.

v) Most tree species can survive short periods of flooding, especially in winter. Adapted species can withstand spring and summer flooding to a varying extent.

12.32 Tolerance of different species

Although there are general responses to flooding, tree species differ markedly in flooding tolerance. Evidence is emerging that flood-tolerant species owe their success to an ability to produce new roots very rapidly from the upper, older parts of the root system, in response to mortality of the deeper roots.[4] Flood-intolerant species lack this ability and cannot quickly replace drowned roots. The new roots are usually confined to the top soil horizons which are better aerated, although only relatively so. These roots may also possess anatomical and/ or metabolic adaptations enabling them to grow better in these conditions. (This behaviour has a bearing on the last part of this chapter.) To the landscape architect the important point is that certain species are much more tolerant of long periods of flooding than others. Table 12.1 has been compiled from various sources and indicates species which are likely to show considerable tolerance under British conditions. For further information more extensive lists are available.[5]

These tolerant species differ in the amount of flooding they will stand, and those particularly tolerant are singled out. In general adapted trees can probably survive prolonged periods of partial inundation, provided that on

TABLE 12.1
A list of some of the more tolerant species

Very tolerant	Tolerant
Alnus glutinosa (common alder)	*Betula pendula* (silver birch)
Alnus incana (grey alder)	*Cornus stolonifera* (red osier, dogwood)
Populus × euramericana— 'Robusta' 'Heidemij' 1–214, 'Serotina', 'Regenerata', 'Marilandica' (hybrid black poplars)	*Pinus contorta* (lodgepole pine)
	Populus nigra (black poplar)
	Populus trichocarpa (black cottonwood)
Salix alba (white willow)	*Salix caprea* (goat willow)
Salix cinerea (common sallow)	*Salix fragilis* (crack willow)
Salix hookerana (Hooker's willow)	*Salix phylicifolia* (tea-leaved willow)
Salix lasiandra (pacific willow)	*Salix purpurea* (purple osier)
Salix triandra (almond willow)	
Salix viminalis (common osier)	
Taxodium distichum (swamp cypress)	

* Recently introduced from Oregon and tested in the U.K. with some success.

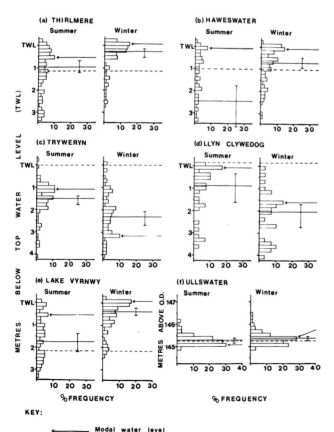

(a) THIRLMERE / (b) HAWESWATER / (c) TRYWERYN / (d) LLYN CLYWEDOG / (e) LAKE VYRNWY / (f) ULLSWATER — Summer / Winter. % FREQUENCY.

KEY:
— Modal water level
----- Present limit of natural colonization by woody species
—I— Median water level, and its 95% confidence limits

average they are unflooded for at least 50% of the growing season.

12.33 Natural tree growth on reservoir margins

Reservoirs and lakes differ in the amount of natural tree growth on their margins. In the Lake District and Wales some of the lakes and reservoirs which have been in existence for a long time have margins well colonized by trees (e.g. Ullswater, Windermere and Vyrnwy—*see* Plate 12.3). There are other reservoirs which are too young yet to have been colonized by trees. Some much older lakes and reservoirs still have no trees growing on their margins, which are often harsh and strongly eroded. The reasons could be either that the environment is too extreme, or that suitable trees do not grow nearby. It may be that natural colonization is rendered difficult by local conditions, but not growth, so that if trees were established by artificial means, they would flourish.

12.4 ENVIRONMENTAL VARIABLES DETERMINING PLANT GROWTH

There are four environmental variables operative in the drawdown zone environment obviously capable of determining the presence or absence of vegetation and its type:
1. Water manipulation patterns
2. Exposure to wave action
3. Soil type
4. Grazing

If these four variables are compared between a number of reservoirs (some colonized, others not), the possibility of tree growth under certain circumstances can be assessed, and the way prepared for a biotechnical solution to the aesthetic problems of new reservoirs.

12.41 Water manipulation patterns

These are important because they determine the frequency, duration and extent of flooding to which margin vegetation is subjected. Weekly water levels over certain years for several reservoirs are plotted as histograms showing percentage frequency of different levels for (*a*) the six months May–October and (*b*) the six months November–April (*see* Figure 12.3). From an ecological standpoint this diversion is more meaningful than that of second and third quarters versus first and last quarters because the period May–October approximates more closely to the growing season of woody species. On the histograms are marked:
i) top water level (TWL)—dam level;
ii) the point estimate of the median water level, the average during the years studied. The zone above this level would, on average, be unflooded for 50% of the period;

FIGURE 12.3 **Water level frequencies for five reservoirs and one natural lake.** (*C. J. Gill: Courtesy of a) b) f) North West Water Authority; c) d) e) Severn-Trent Water Authority*)

PLATE 12.3 **Natural colonization of drawdown zone at Lake Vyrnwy Reservoir.** *(C. J. Gill. Courtesy of Severn-Trent Water Authority)*

iii) the 95 % confidence limits of the median indicative of the range of fluctuation;

iv) the modal water level, the most commonly prevailing level and therefore that at which wave action ought to have been most severe;

v) the lowest limit of natural growth of semi-mature or mature trees at present.

When predictions are being made for the future, allowance for change in variables such as management must be made.

In the reservoirs shown the main points to notice are that Thirlmere, Haweswater and Lake Vyrnwy are all supply reservoirs and have a significantly lower median level in summer than in winter, whereas Tryweryn and Llyn Clywedog are both regulatory reservoirs operating with a system of retention levels which result in their winter median level being lower than the summer one. Lake Vyrnwy has the lowest and most widespread natural colonization. Only Thirlmere has a summer median level significantly higher than that of Lake

Vyrnwy, and this suggests that flooding itself is not prohibiting tree colonization in the other reservoirs (Haweswater, Tryweryn and Llyn Clywedog). It is interesting to compare the reservoir histograms with those for Ullswater (a natural lake at the time of analysis). The frequency distribution is approximately normal and tree colonization coincides with the median water level, which is the same in summer and winter.

Taken as a whole it is important to realize how far down the flooded margins trees can grow successfully. Observations on other lakes confirm this. The crucial point is that it is the summer median water level which is critical; in no case can tree growth be found much below this.[6]

12.42 Exposure and wave action

The effect of this on plant life is most difficult to assess or predict. But wave action particularly can be more important than flooding in prohibiting colonization

203

because it causes erosion and damage to plants.[7]

Changes in water level extend the zone subjected to erosion, the effects of which depend on the nature of the bank surface and its profile, the size of the waves, and the degree of exposure to them. These in turn are determined by the size and shape of the reservoir and its orientation and exposure in relation to the prevailing wind. In a natural lake where the level does not commonly fluctuate more than 2 m (6 ft), the effect of waves is to cut a terrace round the shore some 1–2 m below the mean water level. In terms of colonization this is extremely important because this terrace protects the shore above by causing waves to break, so that erosion is slowed down and something approaching equilibrium is gradually attained. Greater changes in levels disturb this quasi-equilibrium and cause renewed erosion in exposed areas.

Reservoirs differ in their exposure. Vyrnwy and Clywedog are certainly less exposed than Thirlmere, Haweswater and Tryweryn. At Haweswater the steady erosion of the afforested bank above TWL on the north shore (trees notwithstanding) bears witness to the potency of this factor, but at the south-western end there are a few sheltered areas, where tree growth should be possible.

At Tryweryn the strong erratic winds which prevented the establishment of a sailing club have a large reach over the lake surface, and incipient erosion can already be seen along most of the margin. Only time will show the extent and severity of wave action in this reservoir and in Clywedog, although it will certainly be less severe in the latter, whose narrow ramifying shape precludes any great reach of wind over water.

At Ullswater erosion has resulted in the formation of a very gently shelving terrace typical of natural lakes and the equilibrium described above has been attained; this equilibrium has allowed vegetation to colonize strongly down to median water level despite the erosion.

Species differ in their tolerance to erosion as well as in their tolerance to flooding. There is little critical evidence but species which have been recorded as particularly satisfactory, usually because of their ramifying root system and ability to regenerate from exposed roots, are listed in Table 12.2.

The effect of wind is not only to cause erosion by waves, but also to cause direct damage to plants themselves. In upland regions wind speeds are usually higher than in the lowlands, and may be further increased by the contours of the surrounding hills. It would be quite wrong to expect standard or half standard trees to survive even with staking. Even large bush trees will blow over or screw themselves off their roots. Planting material will usually have to be less than 60 cm tall.

At the same time such exposure may preclude the use of tall fast-growing material such as poplars or willows. In very exposed sites bush material such as the sallows (*Salix cinerea, S. caprea*), found naturally in very exposed habitats, may be the most satisfactory.

12.43 Soil type

The first attribute of soil type is its physical structure, whether composed of clay, silt, sand or rock. This depends mainly on the original parental material but it also depends on the amount of soil erosion which removes the finer particles. Margins made of clays and silts usually indicate lack of erosion and therefore sites suitable for tree planting. However, the fine particle size of these soils restricts air movements especially when they are water-logged, and drainage is slow, thus it is possible that trees will suffer from waterlogging more on these soils than on more freely draining coarser materials. The second attribute is pH (acidity) and nutrient status. Reservoir soils can be divided into those which are oligotrophic (lacking in nutrients and with a pH below 5), and those which are eutropic (with adequate nutrients and a pH above 5). Very few plants can grow in extremely oligotrophic conditions. Mostly upland reservoirs tend to be oligotrophic but it is unlikely that tree growth will be totally prevented by low soil nutrient status on any reservoir margin. But some species such as goat willow (*Salix caprea*), common sallow (*Salix cinerea*) and alder (*Alnus glutinosa*) are more tolerant of low nutrient conditions than others, such as willow (*Salix alba* and *S. fragilis*) and osier (*Salix viminalis*), and should be chosen for areas where soil analyses show poor conditions.

There is enormous variation in soil type from one part of any reservoir to another, due to geological accident and local drainage conditions. The consequences of this are particularly visible in lakes and old reservoirs in which there is good tree colonization, and a variety of species. In planting programmes on new margins different planting material may have to be chosen for different parts of the same reservoir. This necessity may have aesthetic virtues.

TABLE 12.2
Species noted for their relative resistance to wave action and undermining, grouped in order of decreasing resistance

Salix acutifolia	Most resistant
Populus deltoides	
Populus trichocarpa	
Populus × *euramericana*	
Salix alba	
Salix cinerea	
Salix triandra	
Taxodium distichum	
Alnus glutinosa	
Salix caprea	
Cornus sanguinea	
Ulmus pumila	
Acer negundo	least resistant

PLATE 12.4 **General view of Llyn Briane Reservoir, Dyfed, Wales showing tree planting close to the water's edge.** *(K. Stansfield)*

12.44 Grazing

This is a factor which can drastically modify colonization patterns on reservoir margins, because sheep frequently have extensive access to them especially in upland regions. Rabbit grazing may also be important locally. Tree seedlings on the Vyrnwy margin are grazed by hares and occasionally by trespassing sheep but of the five reservoirs considered here, Vyrnwy undoubtedly suffers the lightest grazing. The presence of sallow saplings on the islands of Thirlmere and Haweswater in contrast to the barren margins indicates that grazing by sheep may well be a critical factor in these two reservoirs. On the other hand the lack of tree regeneration within fenced field plots at Tryweryn suggests that grazing is possibly not so important there. Its significance at Llyn Clywedog is difficult to assess, there being no islands or sheep enclosures in this reservoir.

12.5 PLANTING PRINCIPLES

From both the landscape and ecological viewpoints, trees seem to be the most promising vegetation to use to combat the aesthetic problem of reservoirs. So far as flooding is concerned there are native species available which are sufficiently tolerant to be planted successfully down to about 2 m below TWL in many reservoirs, the exact limit of growth depending on the regime. This would allow plantings which would substantially break up the drawdown effect since plantings of woodland could be brought right down to the water instead of stopping at just that point where the rim is emphasized and made even more artificial.

One of the best examples of what can be achieved is provided by Lake Vyrnwy where natural colonization at the east end has completely transformed the bare margin. A great deal of planting has been done in reservoir drawdown zones in the USSR, Rumania and Czechoslovakia and although the aim was margin stabilization rather than aesthetic improvement, we could learn much from the sophisticated techniques used there.

Wave action, especially when it interacts with pedo-geological factors to produce highly-eroded substrates, must be recognized as the most powerful factor in limiting the sites on which planting would be practicable. Although some species are relatively resistant to wave action and undermining, very exposed shores would be best avoided in all planting schemes.

The wave action operating in a particular site can be easily assessed by an inspection of the soil structure. Sometimes the interaction produces a thin layer of stones or small rocks on the shore surface which are too large or too firmly embedded to be moved and hurled by the waves against any trees present. This layer acts as a wave shock-

205

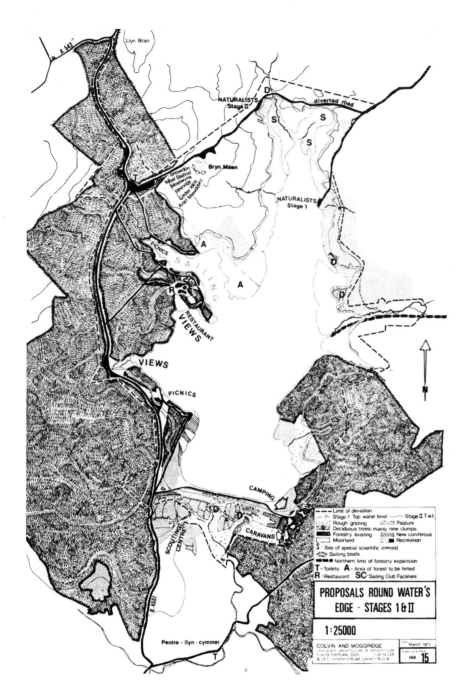

FIGURE 12.4 **Plan showing proposed margin development at Brenig Reservoir. Heavy afforestation of surrounding hills and broken contour forming the rim should help to alleviate problems of exposed shoreline. It is hoped that extensive exposed marshy, peaty land in the north of the lake will revegetate quickly as the water recedes, and prove attractive to birds.** *(Reproduced by permission of Colvin and Moggridge, Landscape Architects, and Welsh National Water Development Authority)*

absorber and often overlies an ideal planting medium consisting of a stable clayey soil (as at Vyrnwy) or even a truncated brown earth (as at Thirlmere).

In all but the most exposed reservoirs there are large parts of the margin in which planting could be attempted with a reasonable chance of successful establishment, given protection from grazing influences. There are a few other problems, but attention must be paid to ecological factors such as soil nutrient status, exposure, etc. Successful long-term growth will depend on finding trees whose ecological requirements are best suited or most adaptable to the environment in which they are to be planted.

12.6 PRE-PLANTING OF NEW RESERVOIRS

If the Water Authority gives careful consideration to planting the margins of new reservoirs at the design stage, rather than later in the process, the site can be pre-planted. There is every likelihood that the scheme will be more successful as a result since observation of mature trees under flood indicates that pre-planting of the future shore-lines as soon as the TWL can be predicted gives a better chance of survival than later planting. There are several reasons for this:

a) Flood damage increases with the proportion of the

shoot flooded.[8] A pre-planted tree, when eventually flooded, will be relatively tall and a smaller proportion of the aerial parts will be inundated.

b) The foliage will be well developed and better able to provide photosynthate for production of new surface roots when necessary.

c) The larger root system, although vulnerable to flooding, can provide firm anchorage against wave action.

d) From the landscape architect's viewpoint, pre-planting is also advantageous because the planting operation is unhindered by inundations, and because the trees will exert their visual and stabilizing effects immediately the reservoir is filled.

Selection of species suitable for pre-planting is not difficult. The natural distribution of tree species is largely determined by the seed and seedling ecology of the species concerned. It is well known that a given species can be artificially established in sites which could not be colonized naturally by that species. For example, *Alnus glutinosa* grows naturally on wet sites because its seed is dispersed by water and will germinate only under conditions of a high water-table.[9] Once established, although noted for its flood tolerance, it grows best in rather drier conditions and has been extensively used on well-drained motorway embankments in this country. Thus whilst it is unlikely that species noted for their flood tolerance will be found growing naturally on the upper slopes of a valley scheduled for reservoir construction, there is no reason why such trees should not be planted on the future shore-line long before the reservoir is filled.

12.61 Evaluation of margins before planting

When developing the landscape plan for a new reservoir, the architect and engineer between them usually have no difficulty in identifying those parts of the margin likely to present aesthetic or erosion difficulties which might benefit from planting. The ecologist can help to evaluate the suitability of these areas for planting.

a) *Horizontal limits*

Soil type and profile must be inspected carefully. Areas covered with deep peat should be avoided because although various species can grow successfully on drained peat, the same peat when flooded is often a poor substrate for tree growth owing to toxicity factors or to un-availability of mineral nutrients.

The profile of lighter mineral soils can become drastically changed under the influence of wave action. The smaller particles tend to be exported and the larger particles and pieces of parent material are left overlying the lower horizons of the truncated profile. When these soils occur in areas likely to be exposed to wave action, some erosion can be anticipated. But such soils are well-suited to planting and may gradually become stabilized against moderate wave action. It must be emphasized that erosion caused by large waves (more than 1 m observed on some reservoirs) cannot be combated by tree planting. The power of wave action will be determined by the prevailing winds and the reach of wind over water.

Heavy clay soils, common on many reservoir sites, are also well-suited to planting and are less susceptible to erosion after reservoir filling.

b) *Vertical limits*

How is one to determine the contour down to which planting is likely to be successful? The significance of flooding in the growing season has already been stressed. If one can characterize the average growing season at the reservoir site, and if one can predict the average annual pattern of drawdown, it is possible to determine the lowest contour which will, on average, be unflooded for at least 50% of the growing season. This contour is termed the 'summer median water level'.

This exercise has been carried out for the proposed Brenig Reservoir in Clwyd and for the Empingham pumped storage scheme in what was formerly Rutland, now Leicestershire. These are worth considering in detail.
Brenig reservoir

Vegetation in Britain generally begins to grow when the daily mean air temperature exceeds 4·4°C (40°F). The mean daily range between minimum and maximum air temperature is 8·8°C and cambial activity can therefore be assumed to begin when the daily minimum air temperature exceeds 0°C (32°F).[10] The cessation of growth is dependent on several factors but cambial activity is generally assumed to have ceased by 1 October.

The nearest meteorological recording station to Brenig is at the Alwen Reservoir, where a study of five years of temperature records, corrected for the difference in altitude, showed that at Brenig the start of the growing season varied between 18 March and 22 April. Draw-down patterns that would have occurred during the years 1959–69, had Brenig then been operating in accordance with the 'optimum' working rules, were analysed. These analyses were combined to show the proportion of the growing season for which the roots of trees, growing at a range of levels below TWL, would have been inundated on average over the 1959–69 period (Table 12.3). Two lengths of growing season have been considered, a 'long' one from 18 March to 1 October, and a 'short' one from 22 April to 1 October. From Table 12.3, it would appear that the vertical limit for pre-planting lies between 0·7 m and 1·0 m (2 ft 4 in.–3 ft 4 in.) below TWL depending on the date adopted as the start of the growing season. In the case of Brenig, this rather shallow limit is not surprising because proposed summer retention level is coincident with TWL and because the role of the reservoir in the regulation of the Dee is to provide water for substantial use only in reinforcing the releases from storage elsewhere in the system during severe droughts.

TABLE 12.3

Amounts of inundation experienced by different contours below TWL at Brenig 1959–69

Level (m below TWL)	Long growing season (2 167 days)		Short growing season (1 782 days)	
	No. of days of inundation	% inundation	No. of days of inundation	% inundation
0	0	0	0	0
0·2	503	23·2	294	16·5
0·4	608	28·1	358	20·1
0·6	860	39·7	558	31·3
0·8	1 122	51·8	753	42·3
1·0	1 322	61·0	937	52·6
1·2	1 488	68·7	1 103	61·9
1·4	1 680	77·8	1 301	73·0
1·6	1 820	84·0	1 435	80·5
1·8	1 942	89·6	1 557	87·4
2·0	2 005	92·5	1 620	90·9

Empingham pumped storage scheme

The success of the method is dependent on reasonably accurate prediction of the drawdown patterns of the future reservoir. This may be particularly complicated for pumped storage schemes, when rates of filling and of emptying are governed by a complicated and interacting set of factors. Even if the patterns can be predicted, levels in the first few years after filling may tend to be very high, with obvious complications for trees pre-planted to levels based on the expected drawdowns of subsequent years.

The future margins of the Empingham pumped storage scheme are currently being pre-planted with appropriate tree species, but the limit of 1·2 m below TWL represents a compromise between the drawdowns eventually anticipated and the sustained high water levels initially expected. In this case, the trees will have four years to establish before being flooded and some of them are being mound-planted to aid survival in the first years of flooding. Another treatment being tested, albeit only on a field-plot scale, is the use of a mulch designed to encourage the development of a strong lateral root system despite the initial free drainage.

12.7 CONCLUSION

Landscape architects have always been pioneers coping with novel situations. The richness of tree growth in city parks and country estates is witness to their tenacity and success in testing new species. Reservoirs are a very real problem which can benefit from their skills and energy, and this chapter has set out some guidelines for tackling one aspect of design that has traditionally caused difficulties.

REFERENCES

1. Gibberd, F. 'Landscape of Reservoirs', *J. Inst. W. Eng.*, 1961, 15, 88
2. Gill, C. J. 'The Flooding Tolerance of Woody Species—a review', *Forestry Abstracts*, 1970, 31 (4), 671
3. Op. cit. Gill, C. J. 1970
4. Braun, H. J. 'The growth of poplars under conditions of an alternating or constant high water table'. *Allg. Forst-u Jagdztg.*, 1973, 114, 89
5. Op. cit. Gill, C. J. 1970
6. Hall, T. F. and Smith, G. E. 'Effects of flooding on woody plants', West Sandy dewatering project, Kentucky reservoir, *J. For.*, 1955, 53 (4), 281
7. Gill, C. J. 'Studies of radial stem growth in *Salix cinerea* L., on a reservoir margin'. *J. Appl. Ecol.*, 1974, 11 (1), 215
8. Op. cit. Gill, C. J. 1970
9. McVean, D. N. 'Ecology of *Alnus glutinosa*: II, Seed distribution and germination', *J. Ecol.*, 1955, 43, 61. and McVean, D. N. 'Ecology of *Alnus glutinosa*: III Seedling establishment', *J. Ecol.*, 1956, 44, 195
10. Manley, C. *Climate and the British Scene*, (London: Collins, 1952)

A paper on the same subject by the authors of this article appeared in the *Journal of the Institute of Water Engineers*, 1971, Vol. 25, No. 3, p. 165 entitled 'Some aspects of the colonization of upland reservoir margins'.

ACKNOWLEDGEMENTS

This work was supported by grants from the Natural Environment Research Council and the Water Resources Board. Water level data and photographs are used by kind permission of the City of Birmingham Water Department, Liverpool Corporation Waterworks, Manchester Corporation Waterworks, the Clywedog Reservoir Joint Authority, the Cumberland River Authority, the Dee and Clwyd River Authority and the Welland and Nene River Authority. The authors are grateful to Mr. A. Tollitt for the plates.

CHAPTER 13

Plants and Air Pollution

DR P. J. W. SAUNDERS AND C. M. WOOD

13.1 INTRODUCTION

Air pollution may be defined as the disposal by man of any waste matter or energy into the atmosphere which produces adverse effects upon the environment. This chapter describes its adverse effects upon plants, and the ways in which plants can themselves be used to control air pollution.

13.11 Significance of air pollution in planting success

It is important to remember that air pollution is only one of several determinants of planting success. For instance, some plants require shelter from high winds and frosts. Compacted and contaminated soils can cause problems especially when planting derelict industrial sites and spoil tips. In severe cases, it may be necessary to recontour the land and to install land drains to improve the site and to import clean topsoil to overcome toxicity problems. Most schemes involve applications of organic material (e.g. peat, sewage sludge and manure) and fertilizer by broadcast (e.g. spraying) or specific techniques (e.g. bedding for tree roots). Ameliorants may be added to counter specific problems (e.g. extra lime to neutralize high acidity).

All these factors interact to produce growing conditions unique to each site; careful site preparation and species selection are therefore essential to mitigate establishment difficulties. Generally, air pollution is not a major problem in rural, suburban and outer urban areas. It is most important on sites close to busy roadways, older high density housing, urban commercial centres and various heavy industries, and generally in areas where the local topography promotes the concentration of atmospheric pollutants.

13.12 Trends in pollution and planting

Monitoring of air pollution is essential to discover local levels and trends in various pollutants. Most monitoring in Britain is conducted by the Warren Spring Laboratory (Department of Industry). The co-ordination and planning of routine monitoring programmes is the responsibility of the Air Pollution Monitoring Management Group (Department of the Environment). This group will collate, interpret and publish the results of air pollution monitoring in the UK.

Despite the popular belief that pollution is getting worse, the available information indicates that trends vary greatly between individual pollutants, and sometimes markedly between levels of the same pollutant in different parts of the country. It seems likely that although acute local pollution of many kinds may decline in the future, there will be more widespread low-level pollution.

In Britain, concentrations of smoke and sulphur dioxide in the atmosphere are expected to continue to decrease, with local exceptions in the latter case. By contrast, the quantities of sulphur deposited as sulphate and acid in rainfall have both increased over the last 10–20 years; the acidity of rain has steadily risen to between pH 4·2 and 4·6. Emissions from motor vehicles are increasing, thus raising local concentrations of ozone, oxides of nitrogen, peroxyacetyl nitrate, etc. (a pattern which will continue in the absence of automobile exhaust control measures). Trends in dust, grit and industrial pollutants (e.g. fluorides and metals) are generally uncertain.

There is a widespread impression that local planting conditions are improving with the decline in smoke and sulphur dioxide pollution, and better control of most industrial pollutants. (In the case of smoke, the decline in

PLATE 13.1 *Tulipa gesnerana.* **Tulips are in general susceptible to damage by air pollutants, particularly fluorides. The photograph shows necrosis (tip burn) at the leaf tips and margins. This is a characteristic symptom of acute fluoride damage.** *(Courtesy of Rothamsted Experimental Station, Harpenden, Herts)*

pollution has improved light intensity in urban areas with possible benefits to plant growth.)

In Greater Manchester, 72% of urban/industrial local authorities (prior to the 1974 reorganization) reported great improvements in growing conditions compared with 28% (rural/semi-urban) which observed no change. Generally sensitive plants such as apple, rhododendrons and many conifers can be grown in most urban and industrial areas, except where pollution is still severe and soil and weather conditions are unfavourable.

On a wider front, there is growing concern about the long-term effects of sulphur pollution. Investigations are under way to determine the dispersion of sulphur pollutants emitted in this country and their subsequent effects on the UK and Scandinavian environments.

Much forest in the orographic rainfall area associated with the mountains of southern Norway is composed of coniferous trees growing on acid podsols. Here atmospheric concentrations of sulphur dioxide are low but the deposition of sulphate as acid rainfall is greater than in the UK. Nevertheless, the overall exposure of forests to all forms of sulphur pollution is broadly similar in both countries. It is claimed that some Norwegian soils cannot buffer the acid which has adverse effects upon tree growth. The acid may also be leached from the soil into

streams with adverse effects on freshwater fauna, including salmon and trout. Similar effects have not been observed yet in the rural UK. Of more interest to landscape designers, however, are the indications that acid rain may have serious long-term effects on nutrients available for plant growth on thin sandy soils in urban areas.

13.2 EFFECTS OF POLLUTION ON PLANTS

13.21 Symptoms of pollution damage

These vary greatly according to:
i)   the species or cultivar exposed;
ii) the pollutant and the conditions of exposure;
iii) the health and maturity of the plant;
iv) other environmental stresses, e.g. temperature, windspeed.

It must also be remembered that plants may be exposed to more than one type of air pollution and that air pollution often coincides with and contributes to other forms of pollution (e.g. contamination of land) especially in industrial areas, thus exposing plants to multiple stresses. It is very difficult to discriminate between the direct and indirect effects of pollution and the diverse effects of disease, nutrient deficiency and 'mechanical' damage (e.g. due to frost and wind).

For convenience, the visible effects of air pollution may be described in relation to three general types of exposure:

i) *Acute exposure* to high levels of pollution over relatively short periods of time (e.g. approximately 750 μg of sulphur dioxide per m³ of air for 6 to 24 hours) results in marginal and tip necrosis of leaves and causes new shoots to die back. The affected leaves will change colour according to the pollutant involved but often they will be bleached white and may also be blackened with soot and grime. The particular effects of pollutants are described below:

Pollutant	Typical Effect on Plants
Sulphur dioxide and sulphuric acid	Initially leaves are bleached white becoming brown and water-soaked.
Hydrogen fluoride	Thin red line of red cells close to leaf margin which may be bleached white.
Peroxyacetyl nitrate	Bronzed leaves.
Ozone	Black stippled leaves.
Nitrogen dioxide	Intensification of green colour of leaves: leaf margins curl.
Ethylene	Distortion of leaves; very early fall of leaves, flowers and buds.
Corrosive dusts and aerosols	Black, water soaked spots or larger areas on leaves.

Eventually leaves affected in the above ways will become brown and die. Conifers which are sensitive to most pollutants suffer discoloration (general yellowing and blackening of tips) and early loss of needles.

ii) *Chronic exposure* to lower levels of pollution over relatively longer periods of time (e.g. approximately 300–600 μg SO$_2$/m³ for several days) results in vague marginal and interveinal chlorosis (yellowing) of leaves which may be associated with early leaf fall and advanced senescence.

Growth losses in plants suffering from acute and chronic exposure to air pollutants are generally in direct proportion to the area of leaf surface injured.

iii) *Cryptic injury.* Exposure to even lower concentrations of pollutants over very long periods of time (e.g. 50–150 μg SO$_2$/m³ for many weeks or months) is probably more typical of general UK conditions. Its effect is more insidious because it causes no visible leaf injury, hence the name 'cryptic injury'. Advanced senescence and leaf fall may occur together with considerable loss of growth. Inert dusts can produce similar results by blocking stomata and reducing the amount of light available to the leaf for photosynthesis. Modifications of soil conditions by pollutants (e.g. by acid rainfall) can also reduce growth rates. Cryptic injury is not usually of immediate concern to the landscape architect attempting to revegetate severely polluted areas. However, its long-term consequences should be considered because they can be ameliorated by proper selection of species and good soil conditions.

The total effect of pollution is rarely confined to one of the above categories. In practice plants are exposed to fluctuating levels of pollution thus suffering two or more types of exposure over the growing season or year. Wide variations in exposure conditions can occur over much shorter periods of time (i.e. hours or days). The total effect of pollution is thus rarely discrete but more a matter of degree and type of exposure. This is especially true of perennial herbs, shrubs and trees which, when exposed to chronic long-term pollution, develop slowly with poor flowering and fruiting characteristics, and early senescence. The continual sapping of a plant's strength may have fatal results.

PLATE 13.2 *Gladiolus* **'Snow Princess'. Like the tulip in Plate 13.1, necrosis has occurred initially at the tip of the leaves, but presumably as a result of prolonged exposure to air pollutants, probably sulphur dioxide and/or fluorides.**

PLATE 13.3 Tall trees adjacent to an industrial site in North Lancashire appear to have been affected by air pollutants (mainly sulphur dioxide, nitrogen dioxide and ammonia). Close to the points of emission shorter trees and hedgerows are less affected, probably because the concentrations of pollutants are lower near ground level. *(K. Oates; University of Lancaster. Reproduced courtesy of Department of Biological Sciences)*

PLATE 13.4 *Hypericum calycinum*. The damage illustrated in the photograph, probably from sulphur dioxide and/or flourides, is relatively slight, occurring on only a few leaves. This may be a reflection of the age of the leaves, as they are generally more susceptible at certain stages of development than others. In addition exposure may have been restricted by shading from other leaves. The leaves in the foreground show the characteristic necrosis at the tips and on the edges of the leaves. *(Courtesy of Rothamstead Experimental Station, Harpenden, Herts)*

Trees exhibit a range of responses including the 'stag-head'. This may be a result of the crown being exposed to plumes of concentrated pollutants which kill the leaves or cause severe die-back of apical shoots. Stunted top growth is often compensated by the development of adventitious shoots from the stem base. Some responses to pollution may be determined partly by the structure of the plant community. Thus, poor top growth may occur in the upper, more exposed region of the canopy which screens out some pollution permitting smaller and more sensitive plants to survive below. However, contaminants caught in the upper foliage are transported to the soil in droplets falling from leaves and in water flowing downwards over the stem during periods of rain and mist. The species of tree also affects the quality of this water. Many species increase its sulphate content but most reduce its acidity (e.g. maple, birch, beech). Norwegian spruce is apparently unique in its ability to increase markedly the sulphate and acid contents of rainfall passing through the canopy. In any case the contaminated water may influence plant growth indirectly as a result of its effects on soil chemistry and microbial activity.

13.22 Sensitivity of plants

Most precise information on the sensitivity of different plants to air pollution has been obtained by experimental fumigations and controlled observations in the USA, Germany and Eastern Europe. Furthermore, most data relate to acute and chronic conditions of exposure of plants, usually to sulphur dioxide pollution. Indigenous and ornamental plants used in this country are not well represented although some new UK research may partly remedy this deficiency in relation to pollution by sulphur dioxide, ozone, fluorine, oxides of nitrogen and vehicle emissions. Table 13.1 summarizes the results of fumigation trials conducted mainly overseas by grouping plants into three arbitrary categories of sensitivity. Many of the plants listed are of limited interest to the landscape designers but are included for illustrative purposes; some (e.g. tobacco) are being used as indicators of specific atmospheric pollutants in the UK. It is emphasized that this and succeeding lists are by no means comprehensive and that other trees and shrubs not included may well be sensitive to some degree.

There are differences in the recorded sensitivities of some individual species and cultivars which are associated with the following factors:
i) variations in the levels and durations of exposure to pollution;
ii) variations in environmental conditions during exposure to pollution.

For instance, the average concentration of sulphur dioxide required to injure the leaves of a plant after a 24 hour exposure can be halved under warm, moist conditions but more than doubled under dry, cold conditions. Windspeed is another crucial factor; plants exposed to high winds suffer far more damage in polluted areas than do those growing in sheltered sites.

Although conifers and other evergreens are *generally* more sensitive to most air pollutants than are deciduous plants, the relative order of sensitivity of plants to sulphur dioxide is almost the reciprocal of that for fluorine and fluorides. More information about the relative sensitivities of indigenous species and cultivars to individual pollutants would be most useful to landscape designers. In particular it would extend the range of options for planting around specific industrial sites. However, it must be used in conjunction with practical experience of planting in polluted environments.

Table 13.2 summarizes some recent observations of planting success in this country, mainly in Greater Manchester, Sheffield and Teesside. Considerable emphasis is placed upon the identification of the more tolerant plants. The categories of pollutants (i.e. urban, industrial, roadside) are much broader than those used in Table 13.1. Nevertheless, there is considerable agreement between the results for sulphur dioxide pollution in Table 13.1, and urban pollution in Table 13.2, although the latter also includes smoke pollution and traces of vehicular and industrial pollutants to which some plants may be particularly sensitive.

In Greater Manchester, most plant damage occurred where summer average concentrations of sulphur dioxide and smoke exceeded 100 $\mu g/m^3$ with peak values greater than 750 μg smoke and 500 μg SO_2/m^3 24 hours respectively. Reduced growth was reported at lower average and peak concentrations. The effects of concentrations below 150 μg SO_2/m^3 over periods of many weeks or months are uncertain. Recent research with perennial ryegrass and conifers has produced conflicting results; in some cases yield has been reduced and in others it has been increased. These responses seem to be closely connected with the sulphur nutrition of plants. It has been implied that atmospheric sulphur dioxide may compensate for soil sulphur deficiency in some marginal grasslands.

It has been shown that air pollution can affect plant pathogens including fungi and arthropod pests. In some cases this can be turned to advantage where the pathogen or pest (e.g. blackspot of roses, maple leaf tar spot, certain aphids) is inhibited by pollution. In others, however, pollution may assist the establishment of pathogenic organisms by predisposing the plant to infection (e.g. mould fungi on damaged wood, certain mites), or by inhibiting competitive species which previously limited the activities of the pathogen.

These subtle effects of pollution are not of immediate interest to landscape designers but the results of current research into such problems may eventually provide better techniques and guidelines for successful planting in

TABLE 13.1

Ranking of plants according to their sensitivity to gaseous pollutants in fumigation trials

Very Sensitive		Sensitive (intermediate)		Less sensitive (tolerant)	
Herbaceous etc.	Trees and shrubs	Herbaceous	Trees and shrubs	Herbaceous	Trees and shrubs

1. Sulphur dioxide

Very Sensitive		Sensitive (intermediate)		Less sensitive (tolerant)	
Herbaceous etc.	Trees and shrubs	Herbaceous	Trees and shrubs	Herbaceous	Trees and shrubs
Abutilon spp	Conifers** (e.g. Picea)	Begonia spp	Aesculus hippocastanum	Aster spp	Acer campestre
Arabis spp	Hebe spp	Cheiranthus (wallflower)	Calluna spp	Convallaria (lily of the valley)	Carpinus betulus
Heliotropium spp	Juglans regia	Fuchsia spp	Cedrus spp	Crocus spp	Conifers*
Lolium perenne* (ryegrass)	Malus spp (apple)	Grasses (incl. ryegrass)	Corylus avellana	Gladiolus spp	Erica spp
Lupinus spp	Quercus spp*	Lavandula spp	Fraxinus excelsior	Lolium perenne	Hebe spp
Medicago sativa (lucerne)	Rhododendron spp	Lolium perenne**	Ilex spp	Rumex acetosa (sorrel)	Laburnum spp
Primula spp	Ribes nigrum	Nicotiana spp	Prunus spp (peach, plum, sour cherry)	Trifolium spp**	Ligustrum spp
Trifolium spp* (clover)	Ulmus spp	Petunia spp	Quercus spp**	Tulipa spp	Platanus spp
		Salvia spp*	Taxus baccata		Populus spp
					Prunus spp (damson)
					Pyrus spp (pear)
					Sambucus spp
					Sorbus aucuparia
					Syringa (lilac)
					Tilia spp
					Ulmus spp

2. Fluorine and Hydrogen fluoride

Very Sensitive		Sensitive (intermediate)		Less sensitive (tolerant)	
Herbaceous etc.	Trees and shrubs	Herbaceous	Trees and shrubs	Herbaceous	Trees and shrubs
Begonia spp	Acer pseudoplatanus**	Aster spp	Betula spp*	Antirrhinum spp	Acacia spp
Crocus spp	Amygdalus persica (peach)	Dianthus spp	Conifers**	Chrysanthemum spp	Acer pseudoplatanus*
Gladiolus spp	Bougainvillea spp	Grasses**	Fagus spp	Medicago sativa	Alnus spp
Grasses*	Conifers*	Lupinus spp	Fraxinus excelsior	Nicotiana spp	Betula spp**
Hyacinthus spp	Jasminium spp	Viola spp	Larix decidua*	Petunia spp	Cotoneaster spp
Narcissus spp	Platanus spp		Populus spp*	Plantago spp (plantain)	Croton spp
Scilla non-scripta (bluebell)	Populus tremula		Quercus spp	Solanum spp (nightshade)	Juniperus spp
Trifolium spp**	Prunus spp (plum and cherry)		Ribes spp (blackcurrant)	Trifolium spp*	Larix spp**
Tulipa spp			Rosa spp*		Mahonia spp
			Sorbus aucuparia		Populus spp**
			Syringa spp		Quercus spp*
					Taxus baccata

214

Very Sensitive		Sensitive (intermediate)		Less sensitive (tolerant)	
Herbaceous etc.	Trees and shrubs	Herbaceous	Trees and shrubs	Herbaceous	Trees and shrubs
3. Ozone					
Begonia spp *Nicotiana* spp** *Solanum* spp (tomato) *Syringa vulgaris* (lilac)	Conifers	*Chrysanthemum* spp *Cistus* spp (rock rose) *Nicotiana* spp* *Petunia* spp	*Cornus sanguinea* (common dogwood)	*Geranium* spp *Gladiolus* spp *Mentha* spp *Nicotiana* spp* *Zinnia* spp	*Acer campestre* *Juglans nigra*
4. Nitrogen dioxide					
Hibiscus spp *Nicotiana* spp**	*Azalea* spp *Bougainvillea* spp	*Gardenia* spp *Nicotiana* spp	*Citrus* spp** Conifers** *Jasminum* spp		*Citrus* spp* Conifers* *Croton* spp
5. Peroxyacetyl nitrate					
Bluegrasses* *Petunia* spp**	Conifers (esp. *Pinus* spp)**	Bluegrasses** *Viola tricolor* (pansy)	Conifers*	*Petunia* spp*	*Citrus* spp Deciduous trees
6. Ethylene					
Orchis spp *Solanum* spp (e.g. tomato, potato, nightshade) *Urtica* spp (nettle)	Cotton	Grasses* Legumes *Mentha* spp	Conifers (esp. pines)* Deciduous trees**	Grasses**	Conifers Deciduous trees* *Malus* spp (apple)

Note: Plants may vary greatly between strains, cultivars and species in their sensitivity to an air pollutant. This may be seen in the use of leaf injury to strains of tobacco as an indicator of different levels of ozone pollution. Usually the majority of types of a plant fall within one category (**) but a small minority (*) can be much more or less sensitive.

TABLE 13.2

Ranking of plants according to their sensitivity to pollutants as observed in the field

1. URBAN AREAS (Primary pollutants are smoke and sulphur dioxide)

Very sensitive		Sensitive (intermediate)		Less sensitive (tolerant)	
Herbaceous etc.	Trees and shrubs	Herbaceous etc.	Trees and shrubs	Herbaceous etc.	Trees and shrubs
Aubrieta spp	Bush fruits (generally)	Ageratum spp	Acer platanoides*	Alyssum spp	Acer campestre**
Begonia spp	Evergreens* (incl. Abies, Cedrus, Ilex, Picea and Pinus† spp)	Bellis perennis (daisy)	Aesculus hippocastanum	Antirrhinum spp (roadside)	Acer pseudoplatanus
Hebe spp*	Fagus spp	Cheiranthus (wallflower)	Ailanthus altissima	Aster spp	Alnus spp
Heliotropium spp	Hebe spp	Festuca spp (& other grasses)	Berberis spp	Campanula spp	Amorpha spp
Lolium perenne* (ryegrass)	Magnolia spp	Fuchsia spp**	Betula pendula*†	Fuchsia spp*	Aucuba spp (roadsides: A. japonica)
Lupinus spp	Malus spp* (apple)	Gladiolus spp*	Calluna spp	Geranium spp	Berberis spp
Medicago sativa (lucerne)	Pernettya spp	Hebe spp**	Castanea sativa	Gladiolus spp**	Buddleia spp
Myosotis palustris (forget-me-not; dust, roadsides)	Philodendron spp	Nemesia spp	Cornus spp*	Grasses** (most ryes and Poa spp)	Buxus spp
Nicotiana spp** (tobacco)	Prunus spp* (incl. plum and sour cherry)	Nicotiana spp* (roadsides)	Erica spp (roadside)	Tagetes spp (roadside)	Catalpa spp (incl. C. bignonioides)
Petunia spp (roadsides)	Quercus spp†	Pelargonium spp	Evergreens* (incl. Chamaecyparis spp, Ilex aquifolium, Pinus nigra 'Austriaca', Taxus baccata)	Trifolium spp**	Calluna spp (roadsides)
Potentilla spp (roadsides)	Rhododendron spp	Petunia spp	Fatsia spp	Tulipa spp	Cercis siliquastrum
Primula spp (roadsides)	Rosa spp*	Primula spp	Juglans regia**		Chaenomeles spp
Trifolium spp* (clovers)	Viburnum spp*	Zinnia spp	Larix decidua		Cornus spp** (C. alba)
			Liriodendron tulipifera		Cotoneaster spp
			Mahonia spp**		Crataegus spp
			Malus spp** (apple, incl. ornamental crab)		Cytisus spp
			Prunus spp (incl. flowering cherries and P. laurocerasus)		Deutzia spp
			Pyrus spp** (pear)		Euonymus spp (E. japonicus; E. radicans)
			Ribes spp		Fraxinus excelsior
			Robinia pseudoacacia		Genista spp
			Rosa spp**		Ginkgo biloba
			Spiraea spp		Juglans regia*
			Ulex spp*		Laburnum spp
			Viburnum spp**		Lavandula spp
			Weigela spp		Ligustrum spp
					Mahonia spp**
					Philadelphus spp
					Platanus spp (incl. P. hybrida)

			Populus spp† (P. nigra)
			Pyracantha spp
			Pyrus salicifolia
			Rhus spp
			Rosa spp
			Salix spp
			Sambucus spp
			Sorbus aucuparia
			Sorbus intermedia
			Spartium spp
			Syringa spp
			Tilia europaea
			Ulex spp and cultivars**
			Ulmus spp

2. INDUSTRIAL AREAS (Species generally tolerant and markedly tolerant of specific pollutants except SO_2 and smoke (incl. above))

Most other plants regarded as generally sensitive to severe industrial pollution; Evergreens** especially so. N.B. *Acer pseudoplatanus* (sycamore; sensitive to fluorine) *Platanus hybrida* (plane: fluorine)	*Acer platanoides* *Alnus incana* *Cytisus* spp* *Elaeagnus* spp* *Ilex* spp* *Larix* spp *Picea omorika* *Pinus mugo* *Populus* spp (also fluorine) *Prunus laurocerasus* & cultivars *Ribes* spp* *Rosa* spp* *Salix* spp *Sorbus aucuparia* *Taxus* spp*	Grasses (esp. *Poa annua* and *Agrostis* spp)	*Acer campestre* *Alnus cordata*** *Alnus glutinosa*** *Acer pseudoplatanus* *Berberis* spp *Cotoneaster* spp *Cornus alba* & cultivars *Crataegus* spp *Cytisus* spp** *Elaeagnus* spp** *Fraxinus excelsior* *Hippophae rhamnoides* *Ligustrum* spp *Philadelphus* spp *Platanus hybrida* (×*acerifolia*) *Populus* spp** (incl. P. nigra) *Ribes* spp** (incl. blackcurrant) *Rosa* spp** *Salix* spp *Sambucus* spp *Ulex* spp & cultivars *Ulmus* spp (fluorine)

Note: (**) Majority of cultivars, etc. of a species falls into this category but a minority (*) may be much more or much less sensitive.　(†) Many species and cultivars exhibit a high degree of variability in sensitivity to air pollution. Variation within clones has been observed in the species indicated.

PLATE 13.5 *Mahonia aquifolium.* **As in the other photographs the damaged areas are the tips and margins of the leaves, probably from sulphur dioxide and/or fluorides.** *(Courtesy of Rothamsted Experimental Station, Harpenden, Herts)*

polluted areas. Generally there is insufficient data to specify the precise pollution limits or even relative sensitivities of many indigenous and ornamental plants used in the UK. Nevertheless, research and practical experience have shown that certain plants grow better than others in polluted urban and industrial areas (Table 13.2). Local, specific problems still arise with less common pollutants (e.g. cement dust, and ethylene) around industrial sites. Busy roads appear to be creating new problems as the impact of sulphur dioxide and smoke declines. For instance, some plants are adversely affected by dust and fumes (e.g. *Potentilla* spp) and even by road salt sprays (e.g. heathers of the *Calluna* type). Since photochemical pollution has been reported in this country, some attention is now being paid to the sensitivity of indigenous plants to ozone, peroxyacetyl nitrate, oxides of nitrogen, ethylene and dusts when landscaping roadways.

218

13.3 POLLUTION CONTROL BY PLANTING

It is not widely appreciated that local planning authorities can exercise considerable control over air pollution by determining the location and design of polluting activities. They can also reduce the effects of air pollution by ensuring that sensitive receptors—including plants—are not located in areas where air pollutant concentrations are high. There are, in fact, a large number of techniques for controlling pollution available to planning authorities, which possess a wide range of powers to implement them. For example, conditions may be attached to planning permissions relating to the development of both emitters and receptors to further mitigate pollution damage.

Some authorities are recognizing the contribution of planning to pollution control in the preparation of their structure plans and there are signs that better use of planning powers in controlling development is being made. (This trend would probably be accelerated if some form of environmental impact analysis was introduced into the planning procedure.) Furthermore, suitable planting and design (e.g. contouring) techniques can help to reduce the impact of pollution on the area surrounding each source. The landscape architect can thus assist local planning authorities, and industry, by stipulating suitable landscaping schemes around industrial and residential sites to ameliorate the level of air pollutants.

Open spaces planted with trees, shrubs and herbaceous species, especially grass, alter the local climate, thus increasing the dispersion of pollutants. Simple grass swards absorb twice as much pollution as does bare soil. This scavenging effect increases with the inclusion of shrubs and trees. Thus the average concentration of a pollutant in the atmosphere declines with increasing proportions of well planted open space in industrial and urban areas.

The air beneath a tree canopy contains only a fraction of the pollution found above and around the wooded area. The vegetation acts as a filter, the rate of pollutant removal being controlled by its physico-chemical nature, the species and the height of the vegetation, and the prevailing weather conditions (especially wind velocity and air humidity). Dusts and aerosols are filtered out most rapidly with sulphur dioxide, hydrogen fluoride and nitrogen dioxide being removed less efficiently but more quickly than nitric oxide and carbon monoxide.

Tree barriers between industrial and residential areas can reduce air pollution considerably; a plantation of 30 m depth gives almost complete dust interception and significant reductions in gaseous pollutant concentrations. Even one row of trees can reduce air pollution levels markedly if planted on green verges with or without an underlaying of shrubs (e.g. 25% reduction in dust concentrations observed in tree-lined streets). Free circulation of air within the canopy of a tree barrier helps promote the filtering of pollutants.

Successful planting of trees in shelter belts etc. in polluted areas demands consideration of several important factors:

i) The location of the planting site in relation to the source of pollution affects the degree of exposure of plants to the pollutants. Expert advice should be sought on the likely dispersion of pollutants from a particular source. As a rule of thumb, the maximum ground level concentration of pollution will usually occur approximately fourteen chimney lengths downwind of the source. In valleys subject to frequent temperature inversions, however, abnormally high and prolonged exposure may occur.

ii) Recontouring of land may be carried out to improve the appearance of the site, to promote drainage and to minimize erosion. It may also provide some shelter for plants during the early stages of establishment.

Adequate topsoil should be provided to a depth of about 15 cm (6 in.). Greater depths may be required for planting of larger trees and shrubs. If the original soil is contaminated (e.g. with metals) it will be necessary to import sufficient quantities of clean topsoil. Soil compaction should be avoided at all costs because good drainage is essential for early growth.

iii) Organic material (e.g. manure, sewage sludge, peat) and compound fertilizers are usually applied to the soil by broadcast techniques followed by ploughing into the topsoil layer. This will help early growth of shrubs and herbs. Spraying techniques may be used to apply grass and clover seed in a slurry with organic material and fertilizers. Trees and larger shrubs are usually planted in deep furrows or individual pits packed with organic material, etc. and with ample room for early root growth. The organic material helps conserve water in dry, rocky soils. On some sites it may be necessary to apply special ameliorants to alleviate specific problems of nutrient deficiency (e.g. additional nitrogen) and toxicity (e.g. lime to counteract acidity).

iv) Careful selection of plants is essential to ensure establishment in severely polluted areas. Obviously, insensitive plants must be used close to sources of pollution. For instance, poplar, lime, and elm are more effective than beech, false acacia and especially spruce on sites exposed to dust, smoke and sulphur dioxide pollution. In the initial phases of establishment, dense tree barriers may be planted. Density can be increased by the pruning of young trees, etc. to promote adventitious growth from the stem base. Later, however, a more open plantation may be created to give a better appearance; this also promotes air circulation within a canopy. Mixed plantations may be established provided the outer and upper limits of the community are composed of insensitive species which will shelter more sensitive plants.

Most of these considerations are familiar to the landscape designer who is concerned to give young plants the best possible chance of establishment on polluted sites. However, if the conditions are particularly adverse it may be necessary to consult a specialist.

Noise is not significantly reduced by tree barriers of less than 30 m depth but the cosmetic and psychological benefits of planting are considerable. Soft areas do not, in any event, reflect sound to the same extent as hard surfaces and are thus to be preferred on noise abatement grounds.

Some local projects to reduce air and noise pollution by planting have been conducted, especially around schools, hospitals and offices, although their benefits are probably more psychological than real. On a larger scale, Warrington New Town Development Corporation proposes to employ shelter belts to reduce urban air pollution, and other local authorities are believed to have prepared similar plans.

To summarize: risks of planting failure in polluted areas can be minimized by obtaining all the available information and by testing site conditions. Similarly, the control of air pollution can be maximized by employing the most suitable plants and planting techniques in an effective manner.

A wealth of unpublished but practical information on the problems of planting in polluted areas has been accumulated by individual members of the landscape design profession. Similarly, there is a small but growing U.K. research effort in this field but there is a need to codify this body of knowledge and to make it generally available. As a sound first step it should not be difficult to exchange experiences of planting problems and techniques in polluted areas both within the profession and with workers in other relevant disciplines. This might be associated with the formation of a central information service, perhaps under the aegis of the ILA. In the longer term there is a need for a vigorous examination of existing facts and opinions; consideration might then be given to the establishment of a collective programme to select and to breed plants tolerant to different forms of air and land pollution.

FURTHER READING

Department of the Environment *The Monitoring of the Environment in the United Kingdom* (London: HMSO, 1974)

Derwent, R. G. and Stewart, H. N. M. 'Elevated ozone levels in the air of Central London'. *Nature.* 1973, pp. 241, 342–343

Van Haut, H. and Stratmann, H. *Farbtafeldatlas uber schwefeldioxid-wirkungen an pflanzen* (Berlin: Giradet Bro. 1971)

Heagle, S. 'Interactions between air pollutants and plant parasites'. *Ann. Rev. Phytopath.* 1973, 11, 365–88

Hindawi, I. J. *Air pollution injury to vegetation* (US Dept of Health, Education and Welfare; National Air Pollution Control Administration, N. Carolina, 1970)

Inter-Research Council Committee on Pollution Research *Report of a Seminar on 'Gaseous Pollutants'* Royal Society, 1976

Jones, L. H. P. and Cowling, D. W. *Effects of air pollution on plants* 39th Conference National Society for Clean Air, Brighton, pre-print 1972

Lee, N. and Wood, C. M. 'Planning and pollution' *JTPI* 1972, 58, 153–8

Malmer, N. *On the effects on water, soil and vegetation of an increasing atmospheric supply of sulphur.* Nat. Swedish Environment Protect. Board, SNV PM 402 E, Somna. 1974

Ødelian, M. *Preliminary field experiments with sulphur fertilisation* Agricultural College of Norway, Institute of Fertilisation and Soil Management Rept. 62, 79–115, 1966 (In Swedish)

Raad, A. 'Green spaces and air pollution' *Arbor. Ass. Jnl.* 1969, 1, 234–45

Roberts, B. R. 'Foliar sorption of atmospheric sulphur dioxide by woody plants' *Environ. Pollut.* 1974, 7., 133–40

Saunders, P. J. W. 'Effects of atmospheric pollution on leaf surface microflora' *Pestic. Sci.* 1973, 4, 589–95

Saunders, P. J. W. and Wood, C. M. 'Sulphur dioxide in the environment, its production, dispersal and fate'. *Air Pollution and Lichens* (London University: Hawksworth, D., Baddeley, S. and Ferry, B. Athlone Press, 1973)

Scurfield, G. 'Air pollution and tree growth: Part I' *For. Abstr.* 1960, 21, 339–47; 'Part II' *For. Abstr.* 1960, 21, 517–28

Smith, W. H. 'Air pollution—effects on the structure and function of the temperate forest ecosystem' *Environ. Pollut.* 1974, 6, 111–30

Webster, C. C. *The effects of air pollution on plants and soil* (London: Agricultural Research Council, 1967)

Winning, A. L. *Recommended planting materials for seasonal and permanent landscaping in Sheffield after application of clean air legislation.* City of Sheffield Recreation Department, 1972

Wood, C. M., Lee, N., Luker, J. A. and Saunders, P. J. W. *The Geography of Pollution: a study of Greater Manchester* (Manchester University Press, 1974)

Wright, T. 'Planting for ecological success' *Landscape Design,* 94, 12–13

ACKNOWLEDGEMENTS

We wish to acknowledge the technical assistance given in preparing this chapter by: R. A. Bee (Manchester CB), K. Furnell (ILA Research Committee), O. L. Gilbert (Sheffield University), I. C. Laurie and A. Ruff (Manchester University), R. Sturdy (Brian Clouston and Partners), C. R. V. Tandy (Land Use Consultants), A. L. Winning (Sheffield CB), and numerous local authority officers.

CHAPTER 14

Planting to Stabilize Steep Slopes

JILL FOISTER

14.1 EROSION PROBLEMS OF STEEP SLOPES

14.11 Types of instability

Steep slopes present an obvious problem of potential instability and two major types may be defined:

i) *inherent instability*—This is a condition of slopes whose gradients are greater than the natural angle of repose of the slope material. Overloading of existing slopes (as in the case of tipped waste heaps), and problems of saturation can also lead to deep-seated instability, when major land slips may occur.[1] Planting alone cannot overcome this type of instability and in order to achieve stable conditions the degree of slope must relate to its specific soil structure and drainage conditions (although a continuous vegetation cover may help to lessen water percolation through porous soils). Grades should be achieved which ensure stability even under conditions of extreme saturation. Alternatively extensive sub-surface drainage, together with constructional methods of erosion control, may need to be employed.

ii) *surface instability*—This covers two main types; soil creep and sheet erosion. Both of these occur naturally and form part of the overall cycle of denudation of the earth's surface in which mountains are 'worn down' and the sediments are carried by rivers to be laid down in the sea.[2]

14.12 Soil creep

This is a natural process on steep slopes where the surface soil moves over an impervious layer. In colder areas, for instance, the topsoil is subject to alternate freezing and

thawing and tends to work its way downhill. Such soil creep or solifluction is a very slow process wherever the soil is bound by vegetation and examples may be seen in most of our upland districts (*see* Plate 14.1).

More extensive slumping of the surface soil may occur on steep man-made embankments as shown in Plate 14.2. Even after grass establishment the topsoil has slipped over a very compacted subsoil; the problem being accentuated by a steep-sided toe drain.

Suitable cultivation techniques are necessary to ensure that topsoil is sufficiently 'keyed' in to the slope material or subsoil. A close growing groundcover with vigorous root systems which penetrate into the subsoil can then be established to stabilize the surface.

14.13 Sheet erosion

This occurs on steep, unvegetated slopes where the velocity of surface water run-off will tend, even on slopes as shallow as 1:10, to wash away the top particles of the soil or other surface material.[3] Loss of topsoil and organic matter due to this process may render the slope sterile, making it difficult to establish a vegetation cover. Sheet erosion can easily lead to gulley erosion and water courses may be formed which result in even faster denudation of the slope.

The very rapid development of road communications and subsequent landscaping has meant that steep slopes are being artificially created which have their natural equivalent in sea cliff and mountain landscapes. Other examples are slopes of industrial waste heaps, degraded river banks, road and railway cuttings, all of which require visual integration into the landscape and physical protection from erosion.

Adequate drainage provision is essential in these situations to ensure that surface water run-off is con-

PLATE 14.1 **'Soil creep' on a Lake District hillside.** *(Jill Foister)*

PLATE 14.2 **Slumping occurring on a highway embankment where the topsoil has not been 'keyed in' to the subsoil beneath.** *(Pam Hoyle)*

trolled before it reaches the slope and whilst it is on the slope. However, drainage alone cannot prevent some surface sheet wash and further steps may need to be taken to hold the soil.

Tandy describes the various measures which can be taken to prevent surface erosion of steep slopes greater than 1:3 as follows:[4]
i)   the maintenance of a natural rock face;
ii)   the introduction of constructional methods such as retaining walls;
iii) the use of vegetative material.

In this chapter the specific use of different types of plant material on slopes will be discussed, looking at those characteristics which make them particularly suitable for stabilizing slope surfaces and at the various techniques required to enable them to become established.

14.2 THE EFFECT OF PLANT MATERIAL IN STABILIZING SLOPES

An established vegetation cover reduces the surface soil wash in the following ways:[5]
i)   surface vegetation and shallow, vigorous root systems 'bind' the soil and physically impede the movement of soil (or other surface material) down the slope;
ii)   rainfall is intercepted so that water passes directly into the soil rather than being washed over it;
iii) water evaporates directly from the leaves and stem and thus less actually reaches the slope;
iv)   water is absorbed by the plant roots and is transpired through the leaves, thus decreasing surface water and soil movement down the slope.
Other major effects of a vegetation cover are a reduction in soil temperature extremes and protection from wind erosion.

After consideration of determining site factors, a main criterion in the choice of plant species for use on steep slopes is the need for the establishment of a continuous groundcover. The plant material should help to bind the soil and intercept rainfall so that it does not run off the slope too rapidly, washing away the surface material, or in certain soil conditions, percolate down through the slope to contribute to any deep-seated instability.[6] (See 14.11.)

Secondly, as steep slopes are rarely easily accessible by machine, maintenance requirements should be as low as possible.

Thirdly, any vegetation cover must be established quickly and the period during which the slope remains vulnerable to surface sheet erosion kept to a minimum.

Finally, the choice of species must be aimed at integrating the slope into the landscape, and the use of trees and shrubs in association with an attractive grass sward or low shrub ground cover should be considered. Different types of vegetation cover will be discussed as follows:

i)   Seeding of grasses and herbaceous plants to produce a stabilizing groundcover. Various methods of binding the slope surface during the establishment of a grass cover will be considered.
ii)   Low shrub planting to form a continuous groundcover on steep slopes.
iii) Establishment of trees and large shrubs to provide a more permanent cover on suitable slopes.

14.3 SEEDING OF GRASSES AND HERBACEOUS PLANTS ON SLOPES TO ESTABLISH A STABILIZING GROUNDCOVER

Often the seeding of low growing grasses and herbaceous species is the most economic method of binding steep slopes and the following list gives some of the main characteristics necessary for a successful seed mix for this purpose.
i)   *Ability to bind the soil.* Species which spread by producing creeping rootstocks or rhizomes are particularly useful. They include *Festuca rubra rubra* (creeping fescue), *Agrostis* spp such as *A. canina* (brown bent grass) and *A. tenius* (brown top), as well as some of the *Poa* (meadow grasses) and *Bromus* (brome) varieties.

   Certain of these grasses and others such as *Agrostis stolonifera* also spread by overground runners or stolons and these help to hold the soil round the plant and prevent excessive soil movement. Various native grasses and plants have developed creeping stolons and rhizomes in order to hold a growing medium in naturally unstable situations such as sand dunes, salt marshes and river banks. A list of plants for use in these situations is given in Table 14.2.
ii)   *Development of a continuous groundcover.* Fescues and bents have the added advantage of good tillering capacity and when they are cut, or cropped by animals, new growth is encouraged and a dense close sward results. The 'closeness' of grass cover is important on porous soil or very heavy clays which are subject to cracking in periods of drought. If the vegetation cover is not complete, rain may percolate through the slope and cause instability at lower levels.
iii) *Low maintenance.* Species which grow slowly such as the fescues, and those of a low or prostrate habit such as the clovers and other legumes and many herbaceous plants, can all be considered for low maintenance. These species are being increasingly used to replace standard rye grass mixes, especially on very steep slopes and in planting areas where grass cutting becomes extremely difficult. Low growing groundcover is required in these situations for reasons of safety (for clear sight lines and

223

TABLE 14.1
**Grass and herbaceous species for use in low maintenance
seed mixes for slope stabilization**

Species	Comments	Species	Comments
Achillea millefolium yarrow	80–450 mm (3–18 in.) Rhizomatous perennial herb with strong horizontal root stock. Occurs naturally on soil of pH 4·0–6·5 on slopes up to 1:2.[12]	*Lotus corniculatus* bird's foot trefoil	100–400 mm (4–16 in.) Perennial herb with prostrate or ascending shoots. Grows well in poor soil, pH 5·2 to 8·4. Drought and heat resistant. Occurs naturally on slopes 1:4 to 1:1, especially south facing.[16] Leguminous.
Agrostis canina subsp. *montana* brown bent grass	100–600 mm (4–24 in.) Densely tufted rhizomatous perennial. Wide tolerance of soils. Drought resistant. Occurs naturally on very steep slopes (up to 1:1) although above 1:5 it is rarely found on south facing slopes. Attractive flower head.[13]	*Plantago lanceolata* ribwort plantain	100–150 mm (4–6 in.) Perennial rosette herb common in pasture. Occurs naturally on slopes 1:4 to 1:1.[17]
Agrostis stolonifera creeping bent	80–400 mm (3–16 in.) Spreads by leafy stolons to form a close turf.[14] Wide tolerance of soils.	*Poa pratensis* meadow grass	100–900 mm (4–36 in.) Slender rhizomes. Mainly occurs on well drained sand, gravel and loam soils.
Agrostis tenuis common bent or brown top	100–200 mm (4–8 in.) Tufted perennial spreading by short rhizomes and stolons. Wide soil tolerance, more prevalent on dry acid soils on gentle slopes. Lower frequency on south facing slopes. Attractive flower head.	*Poa trivialis* smooth stalked meadow grass	200–1000 mm (8–39 in.) Loosely tufted perennial with creeping leafy stolons.
Anthemis nobilis sweet chamomile	Particularly useful on sandy soil.	*Stachys officinalis* betony	150–600 mm (6–22 in.) Rhizomatous perennial herb. Commonly found in association with *Agrostis tenuis* and *Lathyrus montanus* on mildly acidic soils.
Bromus inermis awnless or Hungarian brome	Extensively creeping rhizomes. Drought resistant.	*Trifolium repens* white or Dutch clover	Up to 500 mm (20 in.) Creeping perennial herb with wide soil tolerance. Occurs naturally on all slopes and aspects, but most frequently on gradients up to 1:2.
Festuca rubra rubra creeping fescue	Rhizomatous perennial. Occurs naturally on moist soils from sea level to nearly 1 200 m (4 000 ft). Higher density recorded on slopes of northerly aspect although high frequency on all slopes and aspects.[15]	*Calcareous soils*	
		Arrhenatherum elatius oat grass	600–1 200 mm (2–4 ft) Creeping root stock. Found naturally on all slopes of all aspects, and on mountain screes.
Lathyrus montanus bitter vetch	Erect perennial herb with creeping tuberous rhizome. Mainly on slopes of 1:5 to 1:2, of north-western aspect.	*Origanum vulgare* marjoram	300–800 mm (9–32 in.) Rhizomatous perennial herb. Occurs naturally on slopes with southern aspect.

Examples of seed mixes are given by Tandy.[18]

reduction of fire risk), aesthetics and to reduce the problem of competition to newly planted trees. Being low growing, or 'bottom' grasses, these species are themselves subject to competition from taller, more aggressive grasses and weeds in better soils, unless the latter are kept under control by mowing or weeding. To establish grasses such as fescues and bents on steep slopes where there is to be no maintenance, the surface material should preferably be a poorer subsoil rather than topsoil, and fertilizer avoided.

iv) *Short period of establishment.* The period after seeding and before germination should be as short as possible to minimize the danger of erosion of both soil and seed and of invasion by other species. Slow growing species included for low maintenance such as the fescues and bents are slow in establishing themselves and it is during this time that they are particularly vulnerable to invasion and erosion. Seed rates should be higher than usual to encourage more rapid vegetative reproduction after germination.

Experiments have been carried out using rapidly establishing, non-persistent annuals in mixes for stabilization. In America, for instance, brome is used to shorten the establishment period.[8] This annual shows particularly vigorous root growth in the early part of the season, the heavy fibrous root system holding the soil initially and giving the other permanent species chance to develop.

In this country various strains of ryegrass are being experimented with by at least one major seed firm. It has been found, however, that the ryegrass, which would normally be killed off during a reasonably hard winter, has persisted during the last few years of very mild winter weather and in many cases has taken over from the slower and lower growing species in the mix. One seed firm offers a mix for steep slope stabilization and this includes 20% of a new low growing strain of perennial ryegrass for quick establishment. This is claimed to produce a turf of dense, low habit even in areas where mowing is impossible. The ryegrass, as well as being extremely prostrate, has the advantage of being green throughout the winter period and is recommended together with 40% *Festuca rubra rubra* (creeping red fescue), 30% *Poa trivialis* (smooth stalked meadow grass) and 10% *Agrostis tenuis* (brown top). All of the grasses are OECD certified strains.

v) *Ability to withstand drought.* Individual site factors may often considerably influence the choice of species for use on a steep slope. The problem of drought is very common, especially on slopes of porous material and those with a southerly aspect. Both fescues and bents are thus particularly useful, as they both occur naturally on poorer soils and the fine leaves of the fescues are xerophytic or drought resistant.

vi) *Winter hardiness.* Research is being carried out into this aspect of experimental seed mixes for slope stabilization by a leading seed firm. Unfortunately recent winters have been too mild to give any positive results.

vii) *Disease resistance.*

viii) *Attractive appearance.*

The inclusion of wild flowers and herbaceous species into seed mixes for steep slopes is becoming increasingly popular as a method of reducing maintenance and integrating steep slopes into the landscape. Whilst there is considerable scope for research into suitable species, seeding rates and maintenance techniques necessary, there are certain species which may be particularly suitable for slope stabilization and could usefully be included in mixes for that purpose.[9] Examples are given below.

> *Achillea millefolium* (yarrow)
> *Anthemis nobilis* (sweet chamomile)
> *Lathyrus montanus* (bitter vetch)
> *Stachys officinalis* (betony)

On calcareous soils:

> *Arrhenatherum elatius* (oat grass)
> *Origanum vulgare* (marjoram)

Various legumes have been used to aid stabilization of steep slopes as they possess the added advantage of fixing nitrogen and increasing the nutrient status of the soil. These include:

> *Lotus corniculatus* (bird's-foot trefoil)
> *Medicago lupulina* (black medick)
> *Trifolium pratense* (red clover) and cultivars
> *Trifolium repens* (white clover) and cultivars

In the United States, leguminous species have been sown on highway embankments with considerable success.[10] The rhizomatous crown vetch (*Coronilla varia*) in particular, though slow in establishment, provides excellent cover by a third season, tolerating dry conditions but faster growing with adequate moisture. Trials in this country, however, have been disappointing as the plant does not appear to be particularly hardy.

Bird's-foot trefoil on the other hand has been tried quite successfully in this country and should be included in a low maintenance grass mix as it grows well in poor soil and is both drought and heat resistant. In the United States a special bacterial inoculum is usually added with the seed.

Lupins are being increasingly used especially on areas of poor, sandy soil where they will last longer than on clay soil. They can be used as groundcover between tree seedlings, although they have to be cut back in autumn, unless they can be controlled by trampling during weeding operations.

In Switzerland, roadside banks and verges are stabilized by seeding immediately with two leguminous species, white clover and black medick, included in a seed mix sown at 15 g/m² ($\frac{1}{2}$ oz/yd²), before planting with trees and shrubs in soil pits.[11]

Vigorous agricultural strains of clover should be avoided where it is to form a groundcover beneath newly planted transplants as it may be too competitive.

14.31 Grasses and herbaceous species for use in low maintenance seed mixes for slope stabilization

New strains of grasses are being experimented with at present in situations such as the Wash Barrage. It is hoped that the results may mean a wider range of low maintenance grasses are available for slope stabilization, tolerant of various sites and attractive throughout the year. Table 14.2 lists some of the species suitable for direct planting on special sites.

14.4 TECHNIQUES TO ESTABLISH GRASS COVER

Direct planting methods will be covered in 14.5. Seeding to establish a grass cover on steep slopes presents particular problems. One of the main difficulties is the delay before germination during which the ground surface, together with the grass seeds, remains vulnerable to surface sheet erosion, and various techniques may be employed to minimize this danger.

14.41 Cultivations

In areas of heavy clay soils, slopes less than 1:2 should be harrowed or ripped before seeding to produce an uneven surface. Rain falling onto the slope will percolate through the surface more readily and seed and mulch material will not be washed away so easily. As the seed bed will not be rolled or compacted in any way, some of the seed will not be in sufficient contact with the soil to utilize the soil moisture. The seeding rate should therefore be slightly increased to compensate for this and mulching is advisable to protect the seed. All cultivation work should be carried out along the slope, moving gradually upwards to prevent soil moving down the slope to the lower levels.

14.42 Hydroseeding techniques

Hydroseeding involves the application of seed and fertilizer, together with mulch and anchoring material in a variety of combinations on areas where difficult site conditions make conventional seeding impractical. It is usually necessary on slopes with gradients greater than 1:2 or where slope material is particularly soft (e.g. PFA).

Equipment for hydroseeding most commonly used in this country consists of a tank in which the seed together with mulch and fertilizers are evenly distributed by mechanical stirring in solution with water. A British machine developed for this purpose has a capacity of 4 500 litres (1 000 gallons) which is sufficient quantity to cover approximately 2 000 m² (0·5 acre). A spray gun

attached to the tank is able to direct the seed solution over a horizontal distance of 6 m (20 ft) and vertical height of 2 m (6·5 ft). With an extension fitted to the hose, these distances can be increased and a horizontal distance of up to 14 m (46 ft) can be reached. One machine can cover 2 hectares (5 acres) per day. The particular components of a

TABLE 14.2
Grass species etc. suitable for special sites

Species	Comments
1. For stabilizing sand dunes and sandy soils	
Agropyron junceiforme sand twitch	
Ammophila arenaria marram grass	Long, spreading rhizomes.
Elymus arenarius lyme grass	Stout rhizomes, light green foliage.
Poa subcaerulea spreading meadow grass	Long rhizomes. Found naturally in wet meadows and sands.
2. For stabilizing river banks	
Catabrosa aquatica water whorl grass	Stoloniferous. Grows naturally on banks of ponds and streams.
Glyceria maxima reed sweet grass	Stems 900–1 800 mm (3–6 ft).
Phragmites communis common reed[19]	Stout stems 1 800–2 700 mm (6–9 ft).
Scirpus lacustris common bulrush or club rush	Stems 1 200–1 800 mm (4–6 ft).
3. For stabilizing shingle banks (salt marshes)	
Agropyron pungens sea twitch	Long creeping rhizomes.
Glyceria maxima common salt marsh or grass	Stoloniferous, stems spreading.
Glyceria procumbens	Stems spreading or prostrate.

hydroseeding solution will obviously depend on a number of factors relating to site conditions and costs. Several firms offer free advice on suitable mulch and binding materials, seeding specification and rates and fertilizers.

14.43 Mulches

The application of a mulch alongside or after seeding has considerable advantages:
i) it reduces the force of the rain on the slope and increases percolation of water thus minimizing seed and soil wash;
ii) it insulates the seed against temperature extremes;
iii) the mulch preserves the soil moisture. This is particularly important on south-facing slopes with porous subsoil, where extreme drought conditions may result;
iv) certain mulches encourage the build-up of humus content and micro-organic activity within the soil;
v) the need for expensive topsoil is eliminated;
vi) weed competition is reduced.

Straw and hay mulches. These should be applied at a rate just sufficient to cover the soil from view, at about 0·4–0·5 kg/m² (1½–2 tons/acre). Any deeper mulch may smother young seedlings.[20] Although straw mulch may be applied by hand and folded into the soil with tractor-mounted discs, it is normally applied in this country as a mulch for use with hydro-seeding methods.

Wood cellulose fibre. This has been a popular form of mulch in America for some years. It disperses in water to form an aqueous slurry of separate fibres which can be sprayed on to slopes together with seed and fertilizer to produce a continuous adsorbent 'coating' which allows water penetration and reduces erosion. Recommended application rate is 1 120 kg dry weight per hectare (1 000 lb/acre), but this should be higher on very steep slopes with a clay-silt fraction less than 30%.[21]

Ideally the seed should be under the mulch, but if the two operations are carried out together for economic reasons, the normal seeding rate should be increased by at least 10%. A green dye can be included in the spray to indicate complete coverage.

Organic manure. Application of animal manure or sewage sludge encourages rapid build-up of humus content and micro-organic activity within the soil. On slopes accessible by tractor, they may be applied dry by normal agricultural methods. Application rates vary from 2·5–5·0 kg/m² (10–20 tons/acre), and should take into account levels of concentration of trace elements and metals particularly in the sewage sludge. On the steepest slopes, organic manure may be blown dry on to the seedbed, together with a binding material, or else sprayed in solution with a more fibrous mulch. Application of 250 kg (5 cwt) of dried animal manure or air dried sewage sludge and 500 kg (10 cwt) of wood pulp fibre is recommended by a hydroseeding firm for use on a mineral subsoil of between 1:1 and 1:6 gradient.

Various other materials may be employed to hold mulch on to the slope surface, which provide protection against erosion and encourage seed germination. These include jute and polypropylene nettings, paper mesh and glass fibre. (A summary of their relative effectiveness is given in *Landscape Development of Steep Slopes*.) Two methods may be mentioned here:
i) Glass fibre is reported to be a successful but expensive technique. The fibre is applied through a compressed air gun and forms a dense web of fibres which germinating seeds have no difficulty in penetrating.[22]
ii) Experiments with jute nettings have also been successful. It is recommended by an American Research Board that the nettings are pegged tightly to the soil with wooden pegs or 150–200 mm (6–8 in.) wire staples made from no. 8 gauge wire.[23]

A polypropylene netting has been developed which can similarly be pegged to the slope to aid germination in particularly vulnerable situations.[24] A further development is the combination of netting and mulch in a single product for stabilization now on the market in America. It consists of a knitted construction of paper strips, interwoven with a plastic yarn. The paper acts as a degradable mulch, temporarily protecting the slope from soil wash, whilst the net remains to hold the grass cover as it develops.

14.44 Binding materials

Bitumen and asphalt emulsions may be used as mulches on their own to stabilize seed, but they have been applied more commonly in conjunction with dry organic mulches. Many different types are available and they are normally applied by bitumen sprays of 10–28 tonne/m² (15–40 lbs/in.²), although knapsack sprayers may be used on inaccessible but firm slopes.[25]

Various types of plastic and resin emulsions have now been developed which are easier to apply and which have many of the benefits of ordinary mulches in stabilizing the vulnerable slope surface and controlling moisture loss. They may be divided into those emulsions which provide a continuous impervious film and so prevent water escaping from the soil, and those materials which penetrate the surface and harden to form an absorbent stable layer in which seeds can germinate and plant minerals may be retained for long periods. In general they are applied after seeding and mulching although they may also be contained in the hydroseeding slurry.

Film emulsions

These include plastic binders which are used for dust control and also on steep slopes to counteract limited surface and water erosion, and latex rubber emulsions.

Rubber emulsions are diluted with water and applied with fertilizer and seed at a rate recommended by the manufacturers of between 120 and 240 g/m² (3·5–7·0 oz/yd²) made up to 11 400 litres/ha (1 000

TABLE 14.3
Low shrub groundcover species for steep slopes

Species	Comments	Species	Comments
1. Species with surface runners[28]		*Parthenocissus tricuspidata* virginia creeper	Used in Swiss roadside planting.[31]
Climbers which spread, without support, by means of tendrils and adventitious roots can be included in this category.[29]		*Rosa* 'Max Graf'	A prostrate shrub which grows quickly to form a dense cover.
Arctostaphylos uva-ursi nevadensis bearberry	100–150 mm (4–6 in.) high, 1 200 mm (4 ft) spread. Prostrate evergreen shrub of rapid spreading habit. Suitable for acid sandy soils.	*Rosa* × *paulii*	
		Rosa wichuraiana	A prostrate rose, spreading to 3 000 mm (10 ft) and forming a dense carpet.
Clematis vitalba[30]	For use on dry banks.	*Rubus tricolor*	
Cotoneaster dammeri	80–100 mm (3–4 in.) high, 1 500–2 100 mm (5–7 ft) spread. Vigorous prostrate evergreen shrub.	*Vinca* spp	Particularly useful for shade conditions.
Hedera helix	One of the hardiest and most useful species for groundcover, as well as a climber. *Hedera helix hibernica* especially suitable as it grows rapidly but will not so readily climb over adjacent shrubs (*see* Plate 14.3).	**2. Species with underground runners[32]**	
Lathyrus latifolius everlasting pea	A vigorous plant, useful for covering banks.	*Cornus canadensis*	100–150 mm (4–6 in) high. Low growing perennial with extensively creeping root stock. Suitable for sandy soil in broken shade.
Lonicera periclymenum woodbine, honeysuckle	Again useful for covering banks.	*Hypericum calycinum* rose of Sharon	300–460 mm (12–18 in.) high. Vigorous shrub forming dense carpet (*see* Plate 14.4).

gals/acre) with water. The spray penetrates to a depth of between 3 to 6 cm (1–2½ in.).

Care must be taken to avoid coagulation of the rubber constituents and breakdown of the stabilizing system by mechanical stirring or the use of hard water. The main disadvantage of such emulsions is that if the surface is broken, water may penetrate and cause erosion underneath it.

Surface penetrating sprays and emulsions
These vary considerably in ease of application. Generally they are sprayed on to slopes using knapsack or crop sprayers, bitumen sprayers or pumping equipment.

i) Emulsions of liquid plastic are easier to apply than latex as there is no danger of coagulation. Penetration is up to 10 cm (½ in.) and it is within this absorbent, adhesive layer that seeds can germinate.

Application rates vary enormously according to the particular situation. One manufacturer recommends 20 g/m² (0·6 oz/yd²) of concentrate for use with mulch in a general hydro-seeding slurry. It is important to ensure that the rate is kept below a certain limit if plant growth is required for permanent stabilization. Liquid plastic emulsions of this sort have proved to be particularly useful for stabilizing slopes to be seeded or planted as they present few obvious problems of

PLATE 14.3 *Hedera helix hibernica,* **three months after planting on a 1:2 slope at six plants m².** *(Jill Foister)*

phytotoxicity or growth retardation when applied at the correct rate.

ii) Starch powder.

iii) Calcium sulphate or gypsum also forms a water retentive surface layer, improving the soil structure of materials with a high silt-clay fraction and stabilizing mulch and seeds. It should be applied to the surface and worked into the top few inches.

iv) In the manufacture of seaweed extract polyuronides, seaweed is dried and broken down by chemical means to release polyuronides. These can be applied in the form of a spray and act both as a binder and conditioner, increasing the availability of nutrients and reducing leaching.

Such seaweed extracts also provide valuable trace elements and encourage rapid build-up of micro-organisms in the soil.

14.45 Fertilizer application

The particular fertilizer to be used in a given situation obviously relates to a number of factors including the physical and chemical status of the surface material and these should be carefully assessed before treatment is specified. Certain points which have particular relevance to steep slopes are considered below.

Lateral movement of water down slopes may be exaggerated by the presence of an impermeable layer immediately below the surface.[26] The soil becomes rapidly impoverished, especially towards the top of the slope. The required fertilizer treatments should therefore be applied at a higher rate than normal along the top of steep embankments. Rates of fertilizer application must also relate to the anticipated maintenance of the slope and to the species of grasses and other groundcover used. Heavy applications of nitrogen, for instance, will tend to stimulate top growth as opposed to root growth and subsequently increase the need for cutting. It will also tend to discourage the growth of clovers and other nitrogen-fixing legumes which may be desired for long-term stabilization.

Phosphates, on the other hand, will tend to stimulate root growth and encourage tillering. On lighter soils, high phosphate applications are not advisable.[27]

Hackett recommends the use of hand cranking machinery for distribution of fertilizer (and seed) on steep

229

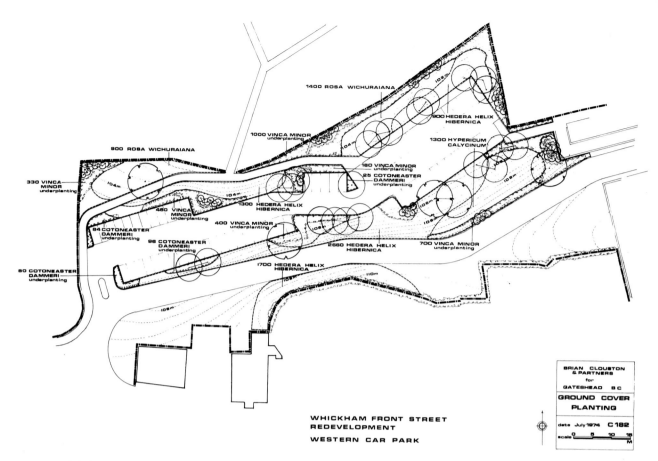

FIGURE 14.1 Plan showing planting areas surrounding a car park extension to a new shopping centre at Whickham, Gateshead M.B.C. (Landscape Architects: *Brian Clouston and Partners*)

slopes. The spread, which can be adjusted, should be kept fairly narrow as distribution will tend to be greater downhill and uneven coverage would otherwise result. Pelleted fertilizer applied by hydroseeding methods is also recommended.

14.46 Turfing

Turfing as a technique to stabilize slopes is usually used in a limited way as it is comparatively expensive. It does have one very important advantage over other methods of establishing grass cover in that it has an immediate effectiveness in stopping surface erosion.

A disadvantage of ordinary turf is that choice of species is difficult and consequently maintenance is high. There are now, however, several products on the market which can be grown to include specified mixes. These are sown in various ways to produce turf mats which are easily transportable and can be laid down in large sections 1 m (3 ft 4 in.) wide and from 2–12 (6·5–39·5 ft) in length. On steep slopes turf needs to be pegged in place and various techniques can be employed using ordinary turf over brushwood and wire netting secured by pins.

14.5 LOW SHRUB PLANTING FOR CONTINUOUS GROUNDCOVER ON STEEP SLOPES

Direct planting of steep slopes with plants which quickly spread by vegetative means to provide complete cover, is an effective method of protection against sheet erosion. It is more costly than grass seeding and is usually employed in limited situations. The eventual low maintenance requirements of such areas should, however, be taken into consideration when deciding on the relative advantages of both methods.

Species which are most useful for stabilizing steep embankments in this way may be divided into those that spread rapidly by means of surface runners or tendrils (e.g. climbers) and those that propagate by means of underground runners (*see* Table 14.3).

The planting distances suitable for groundcover plants can vary according to the site conditions, the degree of slope, the visual effect required and the nature of any associated planting.

Figure 14.1 shows planting areas surrounding a car park extension to a new shopping precinct at Whickham,

230

Gateshead M.B.C., Tyne and Wear. Here 1:2 slopes presented a problem of potential erosion and before cultivations the top soil was already beginning to break away from the top of the slope, over a compacted subsoil.

Groundcover planting was specified as shown, spaced on the slopes at 6 plants/m². Wherever low growing planting was specified as underplanting to the shrub areas, the spacing was reduced to 4 plants/m².

14.51 Cultivations

Planting should not be carried out on slopes which are still inherently unstable and which are steeper than their natural angle of repose.[33] With further movement the plants may be buried or their roots exposed.

With consolidation of the subsoil before topsoil is replaced, an impervious layer is very often formed below the surface. Lateral water movement may exaggerate the problem and result in the topsoil slumping down the slope (*see* Plate 14.2). Initially plant material has little effect in holding the soil and care must be taken to ensure that the subsoil is well broken up before placing the topsoil. If topsoil has already been spread, cultivations should include forking over, deep enough just to break up the surface of the subsoil.

At Whickham all cultivations of the soil were specified as hand work and especial care was taken to avoid increasing the danger of erosion. Work was carried out methodically along the slope so that a series of small terraces were formed by treading and digging. Work continued uphill rather than down so that disturbed soil was not continually pushed down the slope.

The terraces helped to conserve moisture and were planted after the application of a mulch. Formation of a small hollow adjacent to each plant would also encourage the percolation of moisture towards the roots.

14.52 Mulching

Retention of moisture and nutrients within the soil by mulching is very important. Mulching also helps to keep weeds down from what would otherwise be bare earth during the initial establishment period. Dry materials such as those which are liable to be blown away should be well forked into the top 150 mm (6 in.) of soil and on heavy clays it is an advantage if the soil is in a reasonably workable condition. Surface mulches should be relatively heavy and at Whickham well rotted farmyard manure applied to a depth of 50 to 77 mm (2–3 in.) provided a good insulation layer (*see* Plate 14.5)

PLATE 14.4 *Hypericum calycinum,* **three months after planting.** *(Jill Foister)*

and readily intercepted rainfall falling on to the slope. It has also been shown to be an effective deterrent to children. Peat blocks have been used in a similar way between groundcover plants on slopes, within the grounds of the University of Reading. On particularly steep gradients these may require pegging down as otherwise when they are saturated, their weight may lead to slipping.

14.53 Maintenance

Species of groundcover planting suitable for slope stabilization are those which not only spread rapidly to cover the ground but which also require very little maintenance apart from the initial weeding.

Some of the trailing plants such as ivy may need to be encouraged to branch by trimming back the longer stems. They may also require pegging towards the end of the summer in order to encourage rooting, especially in windswept areas and where the soil is loose.

Climbing plants such as *Lonicera* (honeysuckle) and most of the ivies should not be grown in close association with other shrubs and trees as they will very soon ascend their stems and foliage. *Hedera hibernica* (Irish ivy) is one of the few exceptions to this.

14.6 TREES AND SHRUBS FOR TEMPORARY AND PERMANENT STABILIZATION

Although low growing groundcover provides the most effective initial protection against surface erosion, the establishment of trees and shrubs produces a more permanent cover, less subject to disturbance and which can help to integrate the slope visually within the landscape.

Trees and shrubs can be of value in helping to stabilize steep slopes in two main respects:
i) when used as part of constructional methods to stop initial surface run-off on a regraded slope, or to halt degradation that has already occurred:
ii) as mature plants, when spreading vigorous root systems hold the soil, and when both foliage and natural mulch help to intercept rain falling on to the slope.

A summary of constructional methods of stabilization involving a combination of the use of live and woody material is given by Tandy.[34]

They include:
i) 1 m (3 ft 4 in.) sections of willow stake can be set $\frac{1}{3}$ to $\frac{1}{4}$ of their length into the slope, 0·5 m (1 ft 8 in.) apart. It

PLATE 14.5 **Manure mulch round** *Rosa rugosa.* *(Jill Foister)*

has been found that planting parallel to the slope, with diagonal planting in between, is the most effective method.

ii) Wood fascines can be formed from bundles of live wood (willow) and set into the slope to give both temporary and permanent stabilization.

iii) Live material such as willow, poplar or privet may be used to form wattle hurdles, leaving $\frac{1}{4}$ of the growth protruding.

These hurdles may be used simply to retain the slope, or else to form horizontal or sloping platforms which can be filled with topsoil and planted with shrub willow.

As trees and shrubs develop they have a significant effect in intercepting heavy rainfall which then finds its way more slowly into the ground and is taken up by the root system.

The rates of interception for different woodlands are given below.[35]

Mature spruce	
forest	40% of annual rainfall intercepted
Oak woodland	20% of annual rainfall intercepted
Mixed hardwood	
(in leaf)	25% of annual rainfall intercepted
(leafless)	16% of annual rainfall intercepted

In periods of heavy storm, the intensity of rainfall is very much reduced in all cases. On the steepest slopes, however, it is important that a continuous groundcover is present and Tandy suggests that an 'open' cover of small-leaved trees and shrubs would allow a grass sward (or groundcover planting) to flourish, whilst providing some interception of the rainfall.[36]

The roots of established trees and large shrubs can be effective in helping to stabilize permanently the soil on steep slopes. The type of root system that any tree or shrub produces depends very much on the site conditions and it is difficult to generalize about particular species which are more suitable than others in this respect. Spreading root systems, especially vigorous ones such as those of ash, poplar and willow, are obviously effective in holding the slope material. These species have a high water consumption; the root systems often spread to 15–25 m (50–100 ft) and well beyond the extent of the tree crown thus helping to support it even in exposed situations.[37]

Trees with an open canopy, such as beech, allow rain to travel down through the branches and the trunk and consequently the root systems tend to be shallow and limited in extent around the trunk. They offer no resistance in windy situations and can be particularly vulnerable on slopes. Other species with shallow circular roots, which may be easily uprooted, are spruce, Douglas fir, birch and hornbeam.

Trees with deep tap roots and few branch roots are more resistant to wind blow and include Scots pine, juniper, larch, oak, walnut and ash.

Trees and shrubs for slope planting must obviously be suited to the particular conditions of soil and climate. Ideally they should be of compact habit, with vigorous roots and preferably a deep tap root for anchorage.[38] Unfortunately trees best suited to dry sites—sycamore, birch and elm—are not ideal for slope situations and the black locust, mountain ash, oak and willow are recommended. Tandy also lists a number of tree and shrub species used on dry banks in Germany, America and Switzerland. The need for maintenance should be kept to a minimum and large-leaved trees and shrubs should be avoided, together with those species that require pruning.

Trees are best planted as whips or young transplants, but if larger plants are used, care must be taken to ensure that the correct planting depth is obtained. The slope material should be such that the roots of the tree are encouraged to grow deeply in order to anchor the tree. A method adopted by Dr John Sheldon of Liverpool University encourages deeper rooting in infertile material which could well be applied to a slope situation. The transplant is planted in a bag of fertilizer above a drainpipe buried in the soil and filled with a porous drainage material to encourage the growth of a tap root.[39]

One of the main disadvantages in seeding trees and shrubs is the length of time required before firm establishment takes place. Where cheap mass planting is required and speed of establishment is not essential, such a method may be quite acceptable, as in the reclamation of strip mining waste in North America, where enormous areas are being afforested by aeroseeding.

Treatment of the seed prior to seeding is not normally required. Gorse and broom seeds, however, should be soaked in a tank of water for a few hours. Mature seed should be specified which can be expected to germinate immediately it is planted. Otherwise it should be stratified by storing in peat for several months.

In choosing species for including in a grass mixture, the site conditions must be taken very much into account. Gorse and broom, for instance, have been shown to be most successful on lighter soils (PFA) when they should be seeded together with an organic mulch.

Tree and shrub species which can be grown from seed are given below. (The success rate is described by a hydroseeding firm as only fair at 50%. Very often tree species may take up to two years to germinate.)

Alnus glutinosa	*Rosa multiflora*
Betula alba	*Rosa wichuraiana*
Cornus alba	*Spartium junceum*
Cornus sanguinea	*Symphoricarpos albus*
Crataegus monogyna	*Ulex* spp
Robinia pseudoacacia	*Viburnum* spp

FURTHER READING

Hackett, B. *Landscape Development of Steep Slopes* (Newcastle: Oriel Press, University of Newcastle upon Tyne, 1972)

Hudson, N. *Soil Conservation* (London: B. T. Batsford Ltd., 1971)

Tandy, C. *Landscape of Industry* (London: Leonard Hill, 1975)

Proceedings of the Institution of Civil Engineers Conference: Biology and Civil Engineering, September 1948, I.C.E., 1949

Proceedings of the International Symposium on Ecology and Revegetation of Drastically Disturbed Areas, Penn. State University, August 1969 (New York: Gordon and Breach, 1973)

REFERENCES

1. Tandy, C. *Landscape of Industry* (London: Leonard Hill, 1975) p. 203
2. Strahler, A. N. 'The Nature of Induced Erosion and Aggradation' *Man's Role in Changing the Face of the Earth* (Chicago: The University of Chicago Press, USA, 1956) p. 622
3. Tandy, C. Op. cit., p. 223
4. Ibid.
5. Hackett, B. *Landscape Development of Steep Slopes* (Newcastle: University of Newcastle upon Tyne, Oriel Press, 1972) p. 19
6. Tandy, C. Op. cit., p. 223
7. Ibid. p. 231
8. Button, E. F. 'Establishment of Slope Vegetation'. Reprint from *Public Works Magazine,* Ridgewood NJ, USA, 1964
9. Hoyle, R. M. R. *A Guide to the Use of British Native Plants in Landscape Work, with Particular Reference to Urban Areas.* Unpublished thesis. Department of Landscape Architecture, Gloucestershire College of Art and Design, Cheltenham, 1973
10. Johnson, A. G., White, D. B. and Smithberg, M. H. *Development of Ground Covers for Highway Slopes,* University of Minnesota, Department of Horticultural Science, Interim Report, 1965, p. 57
11. Tandy C. Op. cit., p. 231
12. Grime, J. P. and Lloyd, P. S. *An Ecological Atlas of Grassland Plants,* N.E.R.C. Unit of Grassland Research, Botany Dept., Sheffield University (London: Edward Arnold, 1973) p. 18
13. Ibid. p. 20
14. Hubbard, C. E. *Grasses* (London: Penguin Books, 1954) p. 305
15. Grime, J. P. and Lloyd, P. S. Op. cit., p. 78
16. Ibid. p. 108
17. Ibid. p. 124
18. Tandy, C. Op. cit., p. 234
19. Tandy, C. Op. cit., p. 255
20. Button, E. F. Op. cit.
21. Ibid.
22. Hackett, B. Op. cit., p. 106
23. Ibid. p. 39
24. Ibid. p. 42
25. Tandy, C. Op. cit., pp. 221–2
26. Hackett, B. Op. cit., p. 106
27. Ibid. p. 109
28. Stuart Thomas, G., *Plants for Ground Cover* (London: Dent and Sons, 1970) pp. 42–6
29. Ibid. pp. 96–100
30. Tandy, C. Op. cit., p. 231
31. Ibid. p. 231
32. Stuart Thomas, G., Op. cit. pp. 46–8
33. Hackett, B. Op. cit., p. 44
34. Tandy, C. Op. cit., pp. 223–5
35. Robertson, F. C. F. 'The Influence of Vegetation on Floods', *Proceedings of the Institution of Civil Engineers Conference: Biology and Civil Engineering,* September 1948, I.C.E., 1949, p. 65
36. Tandy, C. Op. cit., p. 231
37. Pokorný, J. *Trees* (London: Octopus Books, 1974) pp. 22–5
38. Tandy, C. Op. cit., p. 231
39. Ibid. p. 230

CHAPTER 15

Planting in Tropical Lowland Areas

W. BOWEN, B. T. SIEDLECKI
AND DR T. G. WALKER

15.1 INTRODUCTION

Tropical countries experience very varied climatic conditions, ranging from a completely arid regime, through pronounced wet and dry seasons to the perpetually hot, humid, wet conditions found in many equatorial regions. At one end of the scale the sun may burn out of a cloudless sky without remission for most or all of the year, whilst at the other, although its heat may be felt, the sun may be more or less permanently obscured by overcast skies. As a result, using plants for amenity in tropical climates requires the acceptance of different and possibly unfamiliar values by persons trained in the horticultural and landscape traditions of the temperate regions, and the conscious rejection of some strongly held precepts.

There are great differences between the arid and non-arid tropics, therefore it has been necessary to devote a separate chapter to each field. (Chapter 16 is devoted specifically to arid areas.) This chapter is limited to the tropical lowlands, as a consideration of mountainous areas with their attendant lowering of temperature and its effect upon plant life is a further subject in itself. Nevertheless, many of the general principles will be applicable, although different plants may have to be used. Some of the problems most likely to be encountered in tropical lowland planting are discussed here, and suggestions outlined for their solution, together with a consideration of some of the planting materials available and the functions they can fulfil. Where a number of plants are mentioned in a particular section, they are listed at the end of that section for quick reference. Lists of trees, shrubs and climbers appear at the end of the chapter. Inevitably there are factors which are common to all tropical areas, thus where a topic is pertinent to both

chapters or is more fully discussed elsewhere, this is indicated in the text. The term 'tropical' generally refers both to non-arid and arid areas.

Plant Information Sheets for Tropical Humid Climates appear in Part III and reference should be made to these for plant descriptions and photographs in addition to those in the text. They cover foliage plants, climbers, groundcover, and ferns. An asterisk indicates that a photograph of the plant mentioned appears in the sheets.

15.2 CLIMATE

The sun plays a far greater part in the pattern of life in tropical regions than it does in temperate or even warm temperate areas. Under prolonged and intense sunlight, colour qualities change, and many of the very bright, vividly coloured trees and shrubs which may be considered too flamboyant or overwhelming in other conditions may be planted with advantage. In contrast, many of the softer tones tend to have a washed out appearance in full sunlight, and are more effective in shady areas.

It should be remembered that the glare of sunlight on white painted buildings or large areas of whitish concrete can be painful to the eyes. Pastel shades will frequently serve the purpose of creating an impression of lightness and coolness without reflecting the sun to the same degree.

Soil temperatures at the surface may vary by as much as 28°C (50°F) between seven o'clock in the morning and three in the afternoon as a result of the fierce sun. At a depth of 5 cm this variation drops by 17°C (30°F), while at 1·2 m it is only 1°C (2°F). Such temperature variations can play havoc with shallow rooted plants which are not given adequate protection against the sun.

Temperature statistics can be somewhat misleading if humidity is not considered. This can vary tremendously within a few hours. In the hot dry season it will be negligible, and the air may be laden with microscopic dust particles which penetrate and clog the leaves and other parts of the vegetation, as well as machinery and instruments. In places where the air is often still and humid, the creation of stifling enclosed areas should be avoided, and designs should take advantage of any local breezes to funnel and direct air movements to desired points.

Rainfall varies in amount from virtually zero to many hundreds of centimetres a year and the plants chosen must obviously be suited to the local conditions. Of equal importance to the total amount of rainfall is the seasonal distribution—some regions may be very dry for part of the year and wet for the remainder, whilst in others the rain may be more or less uniformly distributed throughout the year.

Where rainfall is permanently or seasonally low, thought may have to be given to supplementation, depending on the availability and legality of using water for such purposes. It should be borne in mind, however, that giving some plants a uniform and adequate supply of water may not in fact achieve the desired end, especially if the plants are adapted to a different regime. Oleander (*Nerium oleander*) will do exceedingly well vegetatively under such conditions but will fail to flower satisfactorily—this it will only do if given a dry period stimulus. Many of our spectacular tropical trees are ones which flower in the dry season in their natural habitats and positively require this stimulus to flower. Thus it may be that some parts of the landscaped area will need regular irrigation whilst others will need it only at intervals or not at all. (Irrigation is considered in detail in Chapter 16.)

Tropical rain is frequently of great intensity; 5 cm (2 in.) or more may fall in an hour and often more than 30 cm will fall during the course of a day. Consequently the ground is unable to absorb these large amounts of water and severe erosion can occur in which the topsoil is stripped off. In regions where this pattern of rainfall occurs special care should be taken when planting on sloping sites to counter these effects. Good practice may involve leaving the original site as little disturbed as possible during planting operations, clearing just enough ground to plant the new trees and shrubs individually, and gradually altering conditions as they establish successfully. Such a procedure, however, is very time-

PLATE 15.1 **A magnificent specimen of** *Pithecellobium saman (Samanea, saman)*, **the rain tree, in the gardens of the British Embassy, Bangkok.** *(Maurice Lee)*

consuming and can rarely be followed by the landscape designer who is working to a time limit. Nevertheless, other effective precautions can be taken, such as not exposing large areas of bare earth at any one time whilst planting is taking place and protecting the soil by providing it with a temporary cover such as brushwood, coconut husks, stones or netting, or by planting grasses or suitable herbaceous plants to hold the soil with their roots.

The siting of paths along contours may provide barriers to erosion and in areas of heavy rainfall it is often customary to have drainage channels running alongside them. Such drains should be open to enable easy cleaning, as much soil and litter is liable to accumulate. They can be incorporated as a part of the design forming part of lawns or road verges; maintenance problems can be reduced by giving them gently sloping mowable sides.

The paths themselves when on a slope should be bitumen emulsion or of concrete slabs *in situ* etc. to prevent their surfaces being washed away. In public areas it may be necessary to provide paths wide enough to allow heavy equipment and lorries to be used without damaging the grass. In many regions it has proved a positive tourist attraction to allow cars to be driven slowly along the main avenues of botanical gardens and parks, with adequate stopping and parking places where passengers can alight and proceed on foot along the narrower paths.

Many buildings have no rain gutters and water either cascades over the whole length of the roof or is discharged through protruding gargoyles. The area where the water hits the ground must be suitably treated by grass planting combined with loose cobbles etc. to prevent erosion and splash stains.

In parks or other public open spaces, the provision of shelters against the torrential tropical downpours should not be overlooked.

Wind is often a problem in the tropics, bringing both discomfort to the individual and damage to the plants, especially if it is salt- or sand-laden. The provision of windbreaks on a larger scale than that provided by conventional hedges may be desirable and suitable trees are *Casuarina* spp and *Andira inermis*. The former is very adaptable, and because of its very flexible branches and twigs is more likely to break the force of the wind and diffuse it rather than create an impenetrable barrier which can lead to wind turbulence damage. *Casuarina* is equally effective by the sea and here windbreaks of the screw pine (*Pandanus*), the sea-grape (*Coccoloba uvifera*) and the seaside mahoe (*Thespesia populnea*) make useful variants.

In some areas hurricanes, cyclones or typhoons may be encountered. There is little or nothing that one can do to mitigate their effect except to bear them in mind when carrying out design work and avoid the use of materials which can be easily whipped away and become lethal objects, e.g. galvanized sheeting, and the planting of especially fragile trees in exposed situations.

15.3 SOILS

Tropical soils are usually poor, except in special conditions, e.g. where rich volcanic ash or alluvium is present. (For further details, *see* Chapter 16.) Generally, the rapid decomposition of vegetable matter, unless replenished constantly by fresh leaf fall, is soon exhausted and either leached into deeper layers of the soil, or washed away by rains. This rapid exhaustion has led to the 'swidden' type of agriculture of 'slash and burn'. Shallow rooted agricultural crops exhaust the upper strata of the soil within a few years, and farming has to move into a new area leaving the old area to be colonized by trees. With their deep roots, they will not only reach the nutrients but also the moisture, often as deep as 15 m or more below the ground.

When a landscape scheme is planned, a soil analysis should be made to find out whether or not nutrient supplementation is required and what artificial fertilizers to add. Maximum use should be made at all times of natural manures and compost, as they have the properties not only of providing some nutrients but also of improving the soil texture and its water retentive properties.

When planting trees and shrubs, adequate planting holes should be prepared in advance and the soil to be replaced in them enriched with humus and fertilizer if necessary. Under more extreme conditions fresh soil may have to be imported for the purpose. It is advisable to stake trees (stakes to be treated against termite attack) and also to provide protection from the depredation of grazing animals if the whole area is not enclosed.

15.4 WATER

Before any initial proposals are drafted, it is essential to establish the source of local water supplies. In hot climates some watering of plants will almost certainly be necessary. The designer must ascertain whether the public water supply is subject to periodic restrictions (normally at times when the plants need water), and if suitable water for plants is available from reliable independent sources. Most young plants will require initial watering before they become established and this can be helped by judicious positioning of soakaways that will take water from roofs, car parks, roads, etc. Even silt chambers and manholes can be modified to act as soakaways. If they are constructed of honeycomb brickwork without a solid base and filled with gravel or crushed stone up to the outlet level, they will supplement soil moisture. Only during storms or torrential rains will they conduct water to the main soakaway or drainage channel. Citrus fruit and bananas are commonly grown with irrigation from a domestic bathroom, and several paw-paw plants (*Carica papaya*) are a usual feature of the soakaway from kitchen sinks.

PLATE 15.2 **A pool surrounded by clumps of plants featuring** *Pterocarpus indicum* **and** *Hymenocallis* **A.I.T. Bangkok.** *(Maurice Lee)*

The presence of water as a feature of the design has been traditionally a vital ingredient in the tropical or arid region garden, from the Moorish courtyard well to the immaculate mirror pools of India or the modern fountain in city squares. But water also brings its problems of mosquito breeding, algae, snakes, scorpions, noise from frogs, etc., all of which must be appreciated and countered.

15.5 THE HUMAN FACTOR

There are three main human factors that have a considerable bearing on landscape design in tropical areas—the client, the general attitude of the population and the labour force.

It is up to the landscape architect to temper some of the more enthusiastic and ambitious demands which a client may make. Sometimes even before completion of the design the initial enthusiasm and interest wanes and switches to new schemes. With landscape projects once the attention and money are withdrawn, it is almost impossible either to finalize them, or even to keep the plants alive when the scheme has been completed.

Local custom is an important consideration which can only be ascertained by first-hand experience on the part of the designer, but it is dangerous to assume that the behaviour regarded as standard throughout temperate regions has any parallel in some of the areas under discussion. Two examples will serve: it is difficult to persuade a man who has spent his life cutting and burning back a tropical forest in order to win a meagre living, that he should not break a branch from a tree to serve his immediate need; it is also not surprising that if an ornamental pool is made in an area which has never known piped water, the local people will drink it and wash themselves and their clothes in it. These are not points made to condemn their actions, but to guide the designer in his.

Local customs may influence various aspects of the design, for example the attitude to grazing rights, real or imaginary, may influence the type of fencing necessary. Where there are strong local traditions these may often profitably be used as the basis for designs, such as the tradition of walled gardens in the Middle East, the extensive use of potted plants in parts of the West Indies, or fish ponds in Indonesia.

238

In the tropics, as elsewhere, the long-term success of any landscape design is in the hands of the maintenance staff. Even in areas where landscape design is reasonably well established, the labour available for maintenance may be poorly trained by western standards or even totally untrained and lacking in appreciation of the objectives of cultivating plants for aesthetic reasons. Tools may be of local origin or made by the maintenance staff themselves; machinery, if installed, may last only a short time and once broken may not be repaired. Existing trees on the site may be used by workmen for fuel, or shelter for cooking fires, and thus must be protected. It is often difficult for straight, curved or parallel lines to be maintained by local people. After a few trims these designs may become so distorted as to be unmanageable. (Some form of edging with brick, stone or concrete would ensure the survival of the design, although at a greater initial cost.)

This attitude towards maintenance affects most aspects of the design, including drainage and irrigation, and allowance should be made for it. For instance small gullies with silt traps that need regular inspection are liable to become ineffective within a short time. Thus most drains, silt chambers, etc., should be capable of functioning reasonably in spite of neglect. The capacity for plant survival if operations such as watering are irregular must be taken into consideration.

Often the best labour force is to be found in local agricultural undertakings where a 'feel' for plants has been developed. These undertakings are also worth examining, for horticultural practices which have been tried and tested locally may be valid for amenity plants in the area.

The above points are not made out of a spirit of pessimism and do not apply in all areas, but they are emphasized to instill into the designer that his efforts will only survive if he gives high priority to simplicity of maintenance. Many schemes fail even in countries where skilled staff are available for such work because the maintenance is too complex, too expensive or too time-consuming.

Many countries impose severe import restrictions on plants, some excluding certain species and genera only, while others have a more or less blanket embargo. Most require import licences and health inspection procedures to be followed. Certain types of propagules, e.g. seeds, may be exempt from such orders. The practitioner has a clear moral duty to be careful what new plant he introduces, since even if few legal restrictions exist in a particular country, there are a number of cautionary examples of uncontrolled invasion on a spectacular scale following an alien introduction, e.g. prickly pear and *Lantana* in Australia and privet (*Ligustrum*) in Mauritius. This is probably especially true of floating aquatic plants

PLATE 15.3 **A slatted plant house at a nursery in Heliopolis, Cairo.** *(Maurice Lee)*

which have caused considerable difficulties on rivers and lakes in the past such as *Eichhornea, Salvinia*, etc. Their introduction into a number of countries carries severe penalties. Care should also be taken that a request for plants does not result in orchids etc. being stripped from the nearby forest rather than being raised in local nurseries.

Importation of plants may also be prohibited or restricted not only to avoid the introduction of pests and disease but also in the interests of conservation of rare species. Implementation of the terms of the Washington Convention on Trade in Endangered Species of Wild Fauna and Flora, held in March, 1973, introduces new restrictions of which landscape architects should be aware.

15.6 OTHER FACTORS INFLUENCING DESIGN

The provision of shade to escape the sunlight and heat has been the mainspring of planting in tropical and arid regions for many centuries. It is often difficult for temperate region dwellers without experience of hot climates to appreciate this blessing. Shade provided by plants can be as important in the tropics as a sound roof is in more temperate regions, reducing the glare and heat reflection from hard surfaces, cooling the surroundings, and providing the psychological benefit of greenness and seclusion.

Shade is essential at certain stages of horticultural practice. If permanent shady conditions are required, a shade house may be used. This is a light structure with a slatted roof and walls which allow dappled sunlight to fall on the plants—such as collections of orchids or ferns. Protection of this sort is usually essential for raising seedlings etc., and some temporary shade will normally be necessary for newly transplanted specimens.

The types of plant used to provide shade are to some extent determined by the purpose for which it is required: shade for car parking, for instance, will be different from that for walking areas. However, as a generalization the shade plants should be evergreen or be without leaves for only a very short period in the year. They should not produce heavy or pulpy fruits which may be a hazard when they fall.

The use of isolated trees or small groups under which cars may be parked is very important as the metal work and car seats can become blisteringly hot when parked in the open, even on an overcast day. Although carports will almost certainly be an integral part of house design it is advisable to provide additional shade trees bordering the driveway to cope with visitors' cars. Naturally, scale must be taken into account and care must be taken not to plant trees which grow to a large size in restricted areas. One of the most impressive shade trees on a grand scale is the rain tree, *Pithecellobium saman*. This has a short trunk and produces a flattened canopy; furthermore the grass under

its shade usually remains green, even though it may be brown and parched a few yards away. Some specimens may reach a diameter of almost 60 m (200 ft) under good conditions, thus it needs careful siting where there is plenty of space. (An excellent specimen may be seen in the grounds of the St. Augustine site of the University of the West Indies in Trinidad.) *Cordia sebestena* is a small evergreen which may be used in drives and has the added advantage that it produces clusters of conspicuous attractive orange flowers and can tolerate dry conditions.

For the shading of roads and wide avenues it is desirable to achieve a quick cover and it may be advisable to plant trees at about half the final planting distance and then remove alternate trees when their canopies meet. Again, trees which produce large or pulpy fruit should be avoided as they constitute a hazard to safety and for this reason also some palms are not to be particularly recommended as they might shed their very heavy leaves thus causing damage or accidents. *Pithecellobium saman* has a more restricted growth under lower rainfall regimes and makes a very useful shade tree, as does the tamarind (*Tamarindus indica*), a very handsome tree with attractive feathery foliage.

When designing large schemes involving golf courses, riding paddocks etc., shade must never be overlooked. It is always welcomed if not by the users, then by the maintenance staff and animals.

In contrast to temperate regions, the tropics experience twelve hours ($\pm$ *c*. 1 hour) daylight all the year round, and there is a sharp transition from day to night. This affects social and family life very considerably and entertaining frequently takes place out of doors after sundown. Consequently there is a need for cool, level spaces on which to sit out, barbecue areas etc., and for screening for privacy and quietness. The use of exterior lighting at night can play a much more significant part in tropical landscape design than it does in temperate regions. The effect of majestic plant material such as *Monstera, Musa*, and many night-flowering species can be greatly increased by lighting. The illuminated trunks of palms can have an almost architectural effect in suggesting colonnades.

The need for protection and shelter from the hot sun and wind together with the pleasure to be gained from outdoor activities in tropical climates have influenced landscape design. Enclosed outdoor spaces offer privacy and security as well as physical and psychological benefits. Many tropical plants can be used to deter undesirable intrusion of humans or animals. *Bougainvillea* with its bayonet-like spines is an effective barrier when trained on wires, where the coloured bracts which occur on young shoots should be tied back rather than trimmed off. *Euphorbia milili* (christ-thorn) and other spined specimens including agaves and cacti are useful in this respect. Sisal plants should be sited a safe distance from paths, otherwise the sharp, shiny, steel-like ends of the leaves will cause a nuisance to passers-by and the plants may be disfigured if trimmed.

PLATE 15.4 **A broad spreading** *Albizia lebbeck* **providing shade in Jeddah.** *(Maurice Lee)*

PLATE 15.5 **A well-planted enclosed space in the Petromin Compound, Jeddah.** *Phoenix canariensis* **in the foreground with** *Nerium oleander* **and** *Duranta plumieri* **in mid-picture. The overhanging foliage is** *Ficus benghalensis.* *(Maurice Lee)*

In tropical regions plant pests are many and varied; some are catholic in their tastes, others are highly specific and it is beyond the scope of this chapter to list them all and their respective treatments. There is a large armoury of insecticides, fungicides, etc. now available to deal with such problems. It should be noted that in many countries certain treatments are banned, thus one should make local enquiries before using certain chemicals.

Termites and ants, however, are almost universal pests and a sharp lookout should be kept for their attacks and steps taken to deal with them. Termites are particularly troublesome in that they burrow under the bark of trees and into the woodwork of buildings and can do considerable damage if they are not noted in time. Tree stakes, fencing and timberwork of all kinds need to be treated to combat termite damage. In the Americas, leaf-cutting ants can be a nuisance in stripping shrubs of their leaves and carrying the fragments back to their nests. Special care needs to be taken in the nurseries where seeds and seedlings are particularly vulnerable and are liable to be eaten or carried away.

15.7 PLANT MATERIAL AND ITS USE

15.71 Diversity of plants

The range and scope of the tropical flora is far in excess of that found in temperate regions, which gives the land-scape architect faced with the ubiquity of modern architecture the opportunity to use indigenous species to help maintain the local character. There are widely grown pantropic species such as *Delonix* (*Poinciana*), *Bougain-villea* and *Hibiscus* which will nearly always be available to the designer, but his work will retain a greater degree of individuality if he makes as much use as possible of indigenous plants. Not only are the results aesthetically pleasing, they may in addition be well received locally. For instance, the oil palm (*Elaeis guineensis*) is looked upon with affection by the Ghanaians, thus the planting of an avenue of oil palms would receive the approbation (and protection) of the local populace, similarly with many plants which are sacred or of religious significance.

Liaison with local botanists or horticulturalists will prove of great value in identifying indigenous plants, which can then be tracked down in a regional flora.

Because of the wide range of climates, the radically different floristic regions, and the still fragmentary development of landscape design, or even gardening for pleasure in the regions under discussion, the plants available in Mexico, Brazil, West Africa, India, and the Far East are still, except for the ubiquitous few, quite distinct and used only within their regions. The landscape architect should familiarize himself with the local flora and use it to the maximum. This, however, is not meant to deprecate the use of many of the species which, while possibly not being strictly pantropic, may be common to

PLATE 15.6 *Plumeria acutifolia* **displaying flowers, leaves and bare branches all at the same time.** (*Maurice Lee*)

two or more continents. These, after all, are usually the adaptable species and it is from many of these that numerous very valuable cultivars have been bred in much the same way as roses in temperate regions.

15.72 Plant behaviour

While there are many very clear examples of evergreen and deciduous trees in the tropics, in numerous species the distinction is blurred in that leaf fall may not occur simultaneously over the whole tree but in waves that may affect a branch or portion of a tree at a time, new leaves being produced on some parts whilst old ones are shed elsewhere. Some trees may be showing all growth stages at the same time. Thus, it is not unusual to see a mango tree which has old leaves on some branches, is dropping them on other parts, has new leaves on yet other branches and is also producing flowers and maturing fruits.

In some species not all individuals act in concert, some being at a different stage from others, perhaps producing new leaves, whilst others are fruiting. This is often seen in the silk cotton tree (*Ceiba pentandra*), one specimen of which has even been observed showing different behaviour in the two vertical halves of the tree—one half in full leaf, the other bare and fruiting.

Other trees have well marked phases such as a leafy period, followed by leaf fall and bare branches, then flowering occurring on the bare branches and fruiting, followed by a flush of new leaves. Such trees can be made a feature as they show a new and interesting aspect at different times of the year. By careful selection of trees and plants one can give an impression of stability in some areas or exciting change in others.

A number of plants are monocarpic and will die after flowering, such as agaves, some palms and bamboos. In a sense, therefore, such plants are temporary even though it may be a decade or much longer before flowering and death; and some thought must be given to their replacement, or initial planting to give a range of ages where this is possible. Particular care should be taken with some of the bamboos, especially those from the Indian region, as many have a fixed life cycle. All the plants will flower in the same year and die, so that having a group of plants of different ages in this case does not solve the problem as it does with most other monocarpic plants (*see* 15.88).

15.73 Growth rates

The designer used to making various allowances for the time taken for his plantings to mature, such as dense planting or use of fast-growing infill species to be removed early in the maturity of the scheme, will need to re-adjust to tropical growth rates, matching these to the design purpose. In trees a growth rate of up to 6 m (20 ft) a year is commonplace, and in some bamboos, 12–18 m (40–60 ft) a year is not uncommon in areas of good soil and rainfall.

If this adjustment is not made, the designer may overplant, or plant species will attain a size too great to be acceptable for their designed purpose. For example, *Ricinus communis*, the castor oil plant, is commonly used in temperate regions as an ornamental foliage plant for summer bedding and attains a height of about 1 m (3 ft). When used in the tropics it fulfils the original purpose for a few months only and if overlooked will rapidly form a small tree, the original foliage bed being transformed into a miniature forest. A further example of this growth rate is *Solanum macranthum* in which a height and spread of 10 m (30 ft) was recorded in Trinidad two years after planting the seed.

15.74 Establishment techniques

Most tropical plants, shrubs and trees are planted out at an early stage in their growth. It is possible, because of the rapid growth rates, even to plant tree seeds in the final desired position, thinning three seeds to one after germination.

Transplanting risks are high in tropical areas because of risks of desiccation, termite attack, broken root ends, lack of subsequent watering, irreparable damage to tap roots etc. These factors can be avoided by container culture if it is established in the area, or by good nursery practice and the use of anti-desiccants and good aftercare, and temporary shading or windbreaks of hessian, brushwood, etc.

The use of heavy nursery stock or semi-mature trees is less valid in tropical than in temperate regions because growth rates of normal size planting material are so rapid.

Generally tree pits should be 1 m³ (35 ft³) and average shrub pits $\frac{1}{8}$ m³ with infilled topsoil. These should be finished to a slightly lower level than the surrounding area to facilitate watering and retention of rain. Where the soil is wet and heavy it is advisable to dig deeper holes and put drainage stones in the bottom before infilling with compost etc. Stakes should be termite-proof, and of treated eucalyptus or borassus or similar, and tree ties of a durable synthetic material, light-coloured to avoid overheating.

In many tropical areas establishing grass by seed is not practicable because of lack of rainfall and insect problems. Grass is customarily planted by establishing nursery beds of a stoloniferous species like *Cynodon dactylon* and subsequently planting small clumps of stolons at 25 cm (10 in.) distance at the commencement of the rainy season. These clumps soon proliferate and a sward is rapidly formed, checking run-off and erosion during the rains, and being well established by the following dry season.

The normal back-up services of good nurseries and skilled contractors are available in relatively few tropical or arid regions thus it is of vital importance to discover any plant-growing undertakings in the area. Local sources may include government nurseries, local

PLATE 15.7
Flowers of *Plumeria rubra* **(frangipani).**
(Dr T. G. Walker)

authorities, existing private gardens, botanic gardens and educational establishments. As propagation from seed or by vegetative means is rapid, a project of any size or duration would be justified in setting up a small nursery at an early stage, especially if plant material has to be brought from a distance. It is recommended that seed and plant material be purchased as much as possible from sources within the climatic region concerned, as a greater chance of success is likely using acclimatized material. The seed of many tropical species loses its viability in a very short time (a matter of weeks in some cases) and storage in reduced temperatures and humidities is necessary.

15.75 Siting of trees

When planting trees near buildings their ultimate size and properties should be considered from several aspects. The obvious difficulties arise from placing too large a tree near a house, resulting in damage to the roof and blocking of the gutters. Other features, however, may be overlooked because of differences in the structure of houses and their services in the tropics as compared with those in temperate climates. Thus it is common practice to bring

not only telephone wires into a house by overhead cables but also power supplies, and care must be taken that trees do not encroach on them and have to be mutilated at frequent intervals. The generally light construction of houses also brings its problems: plants slapping against the walls or roof in a wind can make an exceedingly irritating din in the tropics which would go unnoticed in a brick- or stone-built house.

The provision of septic tanks is widespread and trees which have invasive roots, such as *Spathodea* should be treated with the same caution in their siting as are poplars in temperate regions, and planted well away from any underground services. *Spathodea* has the further disadvantage that if allowed to grow too large it is susceptible to wind damage.

15.76 Planting for visual effect

By its very nature a landscape is a dynamic, not a static thing. Imaginative planting can reinforce the feeling of change which becomes even more important in a climate which is non-seasonal. While some of the landscape plants are used deliberately as features because of their form and therefore need to be more or less constant to fulfil their function, counterbalances to this effect of permanency can be provided by the use of annual bedding plants. These, however, need a tremendous amount of upkeep. Judicious selection of trees which show marked differences at different times of the year can have a similar, although less formal effect, and help to give the impression of change in the environment. Thus a particular tree may produce brightly coloured leaves (whether young or old), attractive foliage, conspicuous flowers and leaf fall. The use of tall climbers which have their own pattern of flowering may introduce yet another dimension of change.

Changes in appearance may occur not only from month to month but also between one part of the day and another when flowers such as those of the morning glory (*Ipomoea*) may open in the early morning and be finished by dusk, by which time a number of other plants such as the night-blooming cacti, *Selenicereus grandiflorus* and *Hylocereus triangularis*, may be opening their flowers. This diurnal effect is subtly underlined by scented plants which tend to be more prominent in the evening and night-time.

Further reference should be made to 15.8 for descriptions of visual effects obtained from particular plants.

15.77 Planting for audible effect

The fact that sound can have a psychological role in helping to give the illusion of coolness has tended to be somewhat neglected in design plans. Casuarina trees produce this effect *par excellence*. The slightest air movement makes the feathery branches and twigs move and make a soughing sound which gives the illusion of a refreshing strong breeze. This is particularly marked at night if a casuarina is planted near a bedroom. Another tree that similarly gives an enhanced impression of air movement is *Albizia lebbeck*. In this case the seeds are rattled in the pod by a light breeze giving rise to the rather sardonic West Indian name of Woman's Tongue. Not all sound, however, has the same evocative quality—for example the rattling dry sound of dead palm leaves can be both irritating and an unwelcome reminder of great heat.

15.78 Planting for scent

No garden, no matter how beautiful and colourful it may be, is complete without scent and this is especially true in the tropics where scented plants help to mitigate the effects of the heat and dust. Careful thought should be given to the siting of the plants, especially where scent is required at night, so as not to get incompatible combinations in the same area. Whilst scent is mainly produced by flowers it should be remembered that leaves and fruits are other common sources.

One of the most beautifully scented trees and one which is used extensively in the perfume industry is the ylang-ylang, *Cananga odorata*. It is in bloom for much of the year and the yellow flowers are particularly fragrant in the cool of the evening. In time it may grow into a large tree. Another highly scented tree with creamy yellow flowers is *Michelia champaca*, a fast-growing evergreen.

Of the night-scented shrubs the lady of the night (*Nyctanthes arbor-tristis*) and queen of the night (*Cestrum nocturnum*) are especially valuable, whilst the large white flowers of *Gardenia jasminoides* provide a useful daytime supplement. The delicately perfumed frangipani, *Plumeria rubra,* has many virtues, bearing beautiful waxy cream, yellow or red flowers and still being striking when almost bare of them. In addition it is very tolerant and thrives in dry positions and by the sea. The shedding of leaves is less marked where adequate water is available throughout the year.

The huge pendant white flowers of angel's trumpet (*Datura suaveolens*) make this shrub or small tree a feature plant. The sweet scent is particularly strong in the evening and is believed by some people in the Pacific area to ward off mosquitoes.

Scent may be provided in a space-saving form by the use of climbers which may also be used to provide a fragrant screen. Suitable examples are the climbing ylang-ylang (*Artabotrys odoratissimus*), various species of *Jasminum*, the apricot flowered *Odontadenia grandiflora* and the white waxy-petalled *Stephanotis floribunda*. Honeysuckles are represented by the yellow flowered *Lonicera hildebrandiana*.

Amongst the herbs the ginger lily, *Hedychium*, is outstanding, *H. coronarium* with white flowers being suitable for planting by a stream or pond and *H. gardneranum* with yellow and red flowers for higher elevations. These are exceptionally heavily scented plants and should be used with discretion, for whilst the scent is delightful when wafted from a distance, it can prove to be overpowering and sickly at too close quarters.

Effective use may also be made of plants which require more conscious action in releasing the scent, e.g. by brushing against the foliage or by rubbing the leaves between the fingers. *Eucalyptus* species are especially refreshing and many can also be pollarded or be kept as bushes.

The bay rum tree (*Pimenta racemosa*) and the related pimento or allspice (*P. officinalis*) have aromatic leaves when crushed. The latter tree has, in addition, a curious habit of producing a twisted bark which is attractive.

Lippia citriodora is a small shrub which will give off its scent when the leaves and stems are brushed in passing. Thought should be given to the strategic placing of plants near paths where they may be brushed against accidentally.

The nutmeg tree (*Myristica fragrans*) bears the highly scented fruit used in commerce but suffers from the disadvantage that the sexes are borne on separate trees and are indistinguishable until flowering occurs, hence two is the absolute minimum required.

PLATE 15.8 **An atmosphere of mystery created by the imaginative use of plants and water in Pemsai Amranaud's garden, Bangkok.** *(Maurice Lee)*

Citrus trees, especially limes and lemons, should not be ignored when planting for fragrance, the leaves and fruits having a refreshing aroma when rubbed or carried in the hand and the flowers being sweetly scented.

Reference list of plants for fragrance

Artabortrys odoratissimus	*Lippia citriodora*
Cananga odorata	*Lonicera hildebrandiana*
Cestrum nocturnum	*Michelia champaca*
Citrus spp	*Myristica fragrans*
Datura suaveolens	*Nyctanthes arbor-tristis*
Eucalyptus spp	*Odontadenia grandiflora*
Gardenia jasminoides	*Pimenta officinalis*
Hedychium coronarium	*P. racemosa*
H. gardneranum	*Plumeria rubra*
Jasminum spp	*Stephanotis floribunda*

15.8 DOMINANT PLANT FEATURES

15.81 Habit

The tropical environment allows the landscape architect to employ a whole range of forms in plants that are not available in temperate regions and these shapes can be used individually or in combination to give exciting and interesting effects. A few examples are given below, with sketches to give an indication of the range of shapes available (not to scale).

Small-leaved *Araucaria* species provide very majestic examples of evergreen columnar trees which may reach heights of between 30–60 m (100–200 ft) and make superb specimen plants. The Norfolk Island pine, *A. heterophylla*, is a broadly-tapering very symmetrical species whilst *A. columnaris* (*A. cookii*) as its name implies is very erect and columnar. By contrast broad flattened headed crowns are seen in well-grown plants of *Pithecellobium saman*. Whorled branches may give quite a dramatic effect, especially when leaf fall has occurred and the tropical almond, *Terminalia catappa* and various members of the Bombacaeae such as *Ceiba*, *Bombax* and *Ochroma* are outstanding in this respect. Horizontal branches grow in wide spreading circles at different levels on the trunk.

The travellers' tree (travellers' palm—*Ravenala madagascariensis*) has one of the more spectacular shapes, its

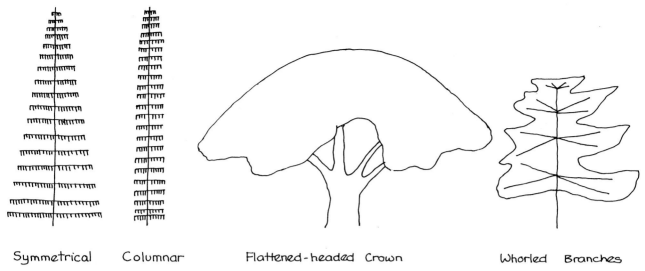

Symmetrical   Columnar   Flattened-headed Crown   Whorled Branches

FIGURE 15.1 **Examples of tree forms. (Not to scale).**

FIGURE 15.2 **Large leaved plants such as** *Musa* **spp,** *Heliconia* **spp and** *Strelitzia* **spp form pleasing groups. (Not to scale.)**

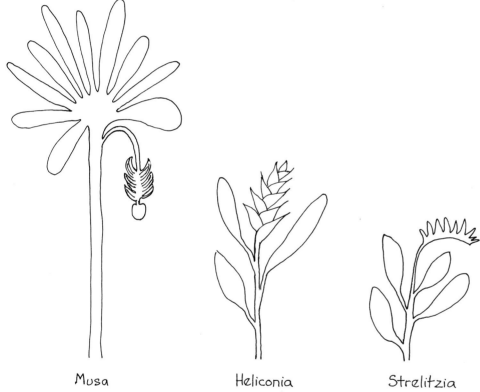

Musa   Heliconia   Strelitzia

enormous leaves being arranged in the form of a fan. It thrives best in a humid atmosphere. There is a strong belief that the fans orientate themselves along a constant axis, but this is not the case.

Large herbaceous plants related to the travellers' tree include the bananas (*Musa* spp, *see* Plate 16.27), *Heliconia* spp and the Bird of Paradise flower (*Strelitzia*)*. All these have colourful inflorescences. Grouped together in various combinations they can make pleasing clumps. Some members of the ginger family have

somewhat similar foliage and the large brightly coloured bracts of the flowering heads provide prominent splashes of colour. The red ginger (*Alpinia purpurata*)* is a very vigorous plant, producing erect, scarlet inflorescences in contrast to the more delicate-looking pink, hanging ones of *A. nutans*. *Phaeomeria magnifica* is somewhat taller, reaching 4·5 m (15 ft) in height and ending in a spectacular large broad head which has given rise to the common name of torch ginger.

The crowns of very large stiff leaves of *Agave* and

*Photographs of all plants asterisked appear in Part III.

247

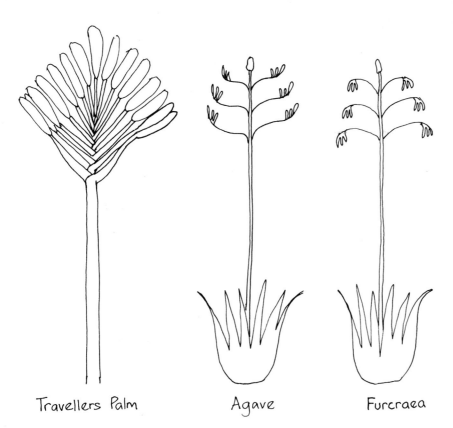

FIGURE 15.3
**Plants with distinctive appearance.
(Not to scale.)**

Travellers Palm   Agave   Furcraea

Furcraea make useful spot plants or provide high points in a bed. There are a number of colour forms, ranging from glaucous to dark green and yellow. Flowering occurs after a number of years (usually about ten) after which the plant dies. However, whilst in flower it is a spectacular sight with the central spike rapidly shooting up to 4·5 or 6 m (15 or 20 ft) and producing the clusters of erect bright yellow flowers (*Agave*) or pendulous white ones (*Furcraea*).

Palms occupy a unique position in design and are treated separately (*see* 15.88) as are also some herbaceous plants which are grown primarily for their foliage (*see* 15.82).

Reference list of plants in 15.81

Agave spp	Crowns of large stiff leaves, sometimes variegated. Monocarpic, with huge 'maypole' bearing clusters of erect yellow flowers. Dry conditions. Good specimens or as barriers (Figure 15.3).
Alpinia zerumbet (=*A. speciosa*) (shell ginger)	Large leaves; pendulous inflorescence of pink-flushed white flowers.
A. purpurata	Large leaves; erect inflorescence with prominent large red bracts. Good cut flowers.

PLATE 15.9 **Distinctive leaves of the aroid** *Scindapsus aureus* **in an attractive setting of varied planting.** *(Maurice Lee)*

Furcraea spp	Crowns of large stiff leaves. Monocarpic, with huge 'maypole' bearing large numbers of pendulous creamy-white flowers. Dry conditions. Good specimens or as barriers (Figure 15.3).
Heliconia spp	Large banana-like leaves; very conspicuous red bracts.
Musa spp (bananas, etc)	Large leaves and stems; useful foliage effect e.g. as a backdrop; some species used as windbreaks.
Nicolaia elatior (= *Phaeomeria magnifica*) (torch ginger)	Large leaves; spectacular round inflorescence, bright red borne on long stalk. Excellent indoor decoration.
Ochroma pyrimidale (balsa)	(= *O. lagopus*) Large tree; fast; the lightest wood known.
Ravenala madagascariensis (travellers' tree)	Very large leaves in fan. Valuable specimen plants.
Strelitzia reginae (bird of paradise)	Large leaves; handsome and unusual inflorescence.

also:
Araucaria columnaris
Bombax   *Pithecellobium saman*
Ceiba   *Terminalia catappa*

15.82 Foliage

Form and colour of leaves greatly enhance the value of certain trees and shrubs. Fresh greens such as are found in *Delonix* help to give an impression of coolness. A number of leaves have attractive undersides, as in the star apple, *Chrysophyllum*, where the contrast between the green upper surface and the brown velvety lower one is best appreciated when stirred by a breeze. Autumn-type colours tend to be rare in the tropics but the large leaves of the tropical almond, *Terminalia catappa*, turn red before dropping. In contrast the leaves of trees are often highly coloured when young and tend to hang down in limp bunches, ranging in colour from bright reds to blue or purple; more rarely whites are also to be found. The total effect may be very spectacular and from a distance the tree may seem to be in full flower. *Amherstia nobilis*, considered by many people to be the most beautiful tropical tree, has leaves which behave in this way, the bunches being a brown-pink. *Eugenia* spp, *Cinnamomum* spp and the iron wood tree (*Mesua ferrea*) also have brightly coloured leaves.

Species of *Eucalyptus* are very valuable in providing a large mass of blue-grey foliage which makes a sharp contrast with the dark greens of other trees. Pinnate or feathery leaves are found in abundance in *Cassia*, *Delonix, Amherstia, Jacaranda* etc., whilst the oval, glossy, thick leaves of *Ficus elastica* provide a sharp contrast. The palms present the ultimate in sheer size and have a great variety of shapes.

Variegation and richly coloured leaves and stems are present in many of the more slender plants and these are considered in a little more detail under the sections dealing with hedges and herbaceous leafy plants.

Many flowering trees and shrubs such as *Jacaranda, Delonix*, etc. have beautiful foliage and in some such as *Hibiscus* and *Bougainvillea* variegated-leafed cultivars have been developed. Over and above this, however, there is available in the tropics a wide range of plants, many of which are herbaceous, with large showy leaves—some green, some highly coloured. Suitable groupings of them can be used to create either a colour palette or a cool, green, restful area as required.

A number of coloured-leaf forms have already been considered and this section is mainly devoted to a consideration of the herbaceous foliage plants. Many of the genera in this category contain a large number of species and cultivars of ornamental value. A fuller consideration of these is outside the scope of the present chapter but it is hoped that enough general information is given of the possibilities presented by such plants and that more specialized works will be studied and local suppliers consulted as to what is available before a final detailed choice is made.

The aroids are among the most conspicuous of this group including *Alocasia, Anthurium, Colocasia* and *Dieffenbachia**. *Alocasia* and *Anthurium* are somewhat similar in having large leaves with a wide range of forms being available in various colourings and markings of the veins. A number of *Anthurium* species, such as *A. andreanum*, have the additional merit that they produce inflorescences with brightly coloured spathes which are useful in the house for flower arrangements because of their long-lasting quality. Possibly the widest range of leaves may be seen in *Caladium** which are not only variegated or with coloured veins but also have spots or dabs of colour scattered over their surface. This genus has a higher moisture requirement than the anthuriums and alocasias and does best in a damp, shady situation, although it also makes a useful pot plant. *Calathea** spp, with their green leaves bearing coloured stripes, have similar requirements to those of *Caladium*.

A variation in height can be given to a planting of these aroids by the use of dumb cane (*Dieffenbachia*) which has both plain green and white variegated forms.

Cannas are very valuable plants in that they not only produce leaves in many shades of green, bronze, dark red and purple but also give a handsome display of flowers ranging in colour from white, through yellows and oranges to deep reds, either singly or in combination. Many named cultivars are available and these may be used equally effectively in borders or in massed plantings in island beds. To give of their best cannas should be

249

Alocasia macrorhiza

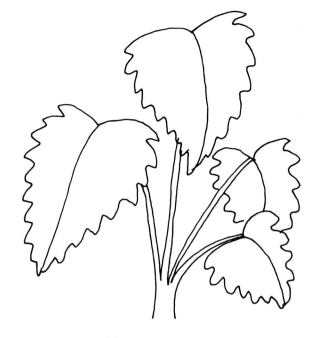

Alocasia sanderiana

FIGURE 15.4 **Examples of plants with conspicuous large leaves varying in shape, colourings and markings. (Not to scale.)**

grown in generously manured, deeply-dug, well-watered soil. The clumps should be kept vigorous by breaking up and planting once or twice each year, at which time more manure should be incorporated.

Large dissected foliage is characteristic of the tall shrubs *Panax, Jatropha* and castor oil (*Ricinus communis*). (It should be noted that many people are allergic to the latter plant and even minute traces of seed material can cause acute distress.) Other useful shrubs include *Graptophyllum* and *Strobilanthes dyeranus** with their coloured leaves.

The massive sword-shaped leaves of *Agave* have already been mentioned but the much smaller ones of *Rhoeo discolor** which are borne stiffly erect exposing their purple undersurface make a useful variant in both size and colour. These leaves are much shorter than those of the aroids and *Rhoeo* can be used as an edging to large plantings. It is easily propagated and very undemanding in its requirements. A much smaller plant which can also be used effectively in front of a foliage arrangement in moist shady situations is *Fittonia argyroneura* with its white-veined small leaves and creeping habit.

Reference list of foliage plants

Alocasia spp	Aroid; large leaves, some vars. with markings.
Caladium spp	Aroid; large foliage; innumerable forms, some with variegation, coloured veins or coloured spots.
Calathea spp	Large leaves, sometimes with coloured stripes.
Colocasia spp	Aroid: large foliage.
Dieffenbachia spp	Aroid; large leaves, sometimes with spots of white or very dark green.
Fittonia argyroneura	Small, herbaceous; very attractive white-veined leaves.
Rhoeo discolor	Short, erect, sword-shaped leaves with purple underside. Very adaptable and decorative *en masse* or as edging. Var. *vittata* also with yellow stripes on upper surface.

also:

Amherstia nobilis
Anthurium
Bougainvillea
Chrysophyllum
Cinnamomum
Eugenia
Ficus elastica
Graptophyllum

Hibiscus
Jacaranda
Jatropha
Mesua ferrea
Panax
Ricinus communis
Strobilanthes dyeranus
Terminalia catappa

15.83 Flowers

The great joy of many tropical trees and shrubs lies in the spectacular profusion of flowers that they bear and in the vast range of colour shown, from the most flamboyant

PLATE 15.10 **A gigantic baobab at Mana Pools, Rhodesia.** *(B. T. Siedlecki)*

PLATE 15.11 **A close-up of the bark of the same tree.** *(B. T. Siedlecki)*

reds and yellows to subdued blues and violets. Many bear flowers whilst the trees are in full leaf such as *Delonix, Jacaranda, Spathodea*, etc. whilst others such as the yellow poui (*Tabebuia serratifolia*) become a mass of colour when the branches are bare. There is an enormous range of form, and selection can be made to suit the mood of the surroundings, varying from the magnificent orchid-like sprays of *Amherstia* to the small clusters of say *Melia* or *Guiacum*. *See* Tables 15.1–15.3 for further information.

15.84 Curiosities

These are special feature plants having a limited use in planting designs to display their unique attributes; a few examples are described out of the large number of such plants available. The cannon-ball tree (*Couroupita guianensis*) is widely planted for this purpose and exerts endless fascination with its bizarre large red flowers, which are borne on rope-like stems hanging down the trunk and followed by the large round fruit from which the tree takes its name. The sausage tree (*Kigelia pinnata*) produces large sausage-like fruits hanging down from the branches. Discretion should be used in positioning these trees as the flowers of *Kigelia* have a rather unpleasant odour at night and the fruits of *Couroupita* stink if allowed to rot.

PLATE 15.13 **Unusual clipped, decorative** *Casuarina* **hedge.** *(Maurice Lee)*

The calabash (*Crescentia cujete*) is a small tree bearing the rounded fruits which when dried are used as water receptacles or as ornaments. The shape of the calabashes may be altered at whim by tying the fruits in the young stages. An additional feature of this tree is its rather stiff form and its habit of holding its leaves upwards at an angle which gives it an interesting appearance. Furthermore it is fairly tolerant of salty winds.

A somewhat similar fruiting habit is shown by the small, very branched candle tree (*Parmentiera cereifera*). The large greenish white flowers are borne on the trunks and branches and are followed by candle-like fruits from 30–90 cm (1–3 ft) in length, suspended on long stalks.

A tree which never fails to arouse interest is the Indian banyan (*Ficus benghalensis*) whose huge canopy is supported by aerial roots which grow down from the branches, take root and develop into supporting trunks. One specimen is recorded as having a diameter of 620 m (2000 ft) and with 320 root trunks. Historically, the most famous one sheltered the entire army of Alexander the Great beneath its shade. The African baobab (*Adansonia digitata*) is one of the longest lived trees in the world. It is of enormous girth, and venerated by Africans who use it for a wide variety of purposes including food, medicine, fibre, rubber, glue, soap and ornaments.

Another interesting African tree is *Euphorbia ingens* or the candelabra tree. Spiny 'cabbage heads' branch into many upright brittle branches borne atop the trunk. The scale-like leaves on younger trees (*see* Plate 15.12) are absent from older specimens adapted to dry conditions.

Finally, the small herbaceous *Tacca* is well worth a mention with its chocolate coloured flowers, from which long whip-lash projections hang down which stir in the slightest breeze.

15.85 Hedges

Hedges may have to fulfil one or several of a variety of functions. They can help to ensure privacy, give protection against larger animals such as cattle or deer, or against intrusion by humans; provide windscreens and screening for sheds, refuse bins etc.; or they can be planted simply for decoration.

In the establishment of a new garden or landscape design it is often desirable to have a quick-growing decorative hedge but this may not give adequate protection against human intrusion. In some areas of the tropics this situation is dealt with by planting an inner barrier of moderately low-growing prickly plants such as various species of *Euphorbia*, *Aloë pinguin*, *Opuntia*, etc.

Fast growing species which may be combined with this inner protective layer if necessary include several with decorative leaves. *Cordyline terminalis** has erect stems bearing long narrow leaves which differ widely in colour according to the variety, being red, white, green or striped in various ways. Individual plants are often used as boundary markers in Trinidad, where this use is widely

recognized. Very similar to *Cordyline* (and often confused with it) is the tall growing *Dracaena fragrans** which grows 6–9 m (20–30 ft) and makes a useful windbreak. This plant has the advantage that it can be propagated from stem cuttings 2 m (6 ft) long. Others with decorative foliage include *Acalypha* (with long crimson catkins), croton (*Codiaeum*) and *Panax fruticosum*. The latter has large pinnate leaves and like *Dracaena* forms a tall hedge, establishing quickly from long cuttings.

Decorative shrubs which are widely used to form flowering hedges include *Stenolobium stans* with yellow trumpet flowers, *Hibiscus* in a wide range of colours, the red *Malvaviscus*, *Plumbago capensis* with characteristically blue flowers but with a white form also, *Lagerstroemia indica* (white, pink or red) and oleander (*Nerium oleander—see* Plate 15.5). The latter, which will grow in arid regions, forms a very attractive flowering hedge in a variety of shades of red, pink and white but it should be remembered that it is very poisonous.

Plants which are prickly to a greater or lesser extent and make effective protective hedges include various species of *Euphorbia* (also suitable for dry regions), *Pereskia grandifolia* (often called *P. bleo*), *Pithecellobium unguis-cati*, *Bougainvillea* and Barbados pride (*Caesalpinia pulcherrima*). The last shrub has handsome feathery leaves and bears very attractive red or yellow flowers which are in evidence for much of the year if kept well pruned. Where hedges are required to grow in the difficult situation of deep shade the palm *Rhapis* may be used.

Reference list of plants suitable for hedges

Aloë pinguin	Long, stiff sharp leaves—good barrier plant. Dry areas.
Euphorbia spp	Many are spinous and make good barrier plants. Dry areas.
Opuntia spp (prickly pear)	Cactus; long spines, good barrier plant. Dry areas. May become invasive.
Rhapis spp	Small palm; useful for deep shade and for hedging.

also:

Acalypha	*Lagerstroemia indica*
Bougainvillea	*Nerium oleander*
Caesalpinia pulcherrima	*Panax fruticosum*
Codiaeum	*Pereskia grandifolia* (*P. bleo*)
Cordyline terminalis	*Pithecellobium unguis-cati*
Dracaena fragrans	*Plumbago capensis*
Hibiscus	*Stenolobium* (*Tecoma*) *stans*

15.86 Climbers

Climbers can perform a variety of functions such as clothing bare fences or walls, screening and shading. They are especially useful in rapidly creating cool arbors and shady walks, on pergolas and for screening off verandah

PLATE 15.14 **Sharp pointed leaves of** *Sansevieria trifasciata* **form a low hedge underneath** *Ficus retusa* **trees, Jeddah.** *(Maurice Lee)*

areas. Most of the climbers used for these purposes are brightly flowered and in addition a number are also heavily scented. A smaller category are cultivated for their foliage to give an impression of coolness and their flowers are relatively unimportant in a landscape context.

Care should be taken in the selection of climbers that they are not too vigorous when planted against a building otherwise damage to the roof may result, or they may become a nuisance by invading the interior via jalousies (slatted shutters) etc. Similarly, vigorous climbers should not be trained up small trees otherwise their weight (which may be considerable when wet) may smash off branches or even pull down the tree.

A number of species are widely used to clothe pergolas and to make arbors. Among these the most popular are the following: *Allamanda cathartica,** which has bright yellow trumpet flowers in evidence for most of the year and is a fast grower; the pink Corallita, *Antigonon leptopus,* which can be very spectacular as a curtain draping over a tree or as a large screen, and *Congea tomentosa,* with mauve-pink flowers which retain their colour long after the petals have fallen by virtue of their persistent coloured sepals. The potato creepers, *Solanum*

wendlandii and *S. seaforthianum* are among the most popular of plants used to form large arbors or to screen off verandah areas, as they are very fast growers and will flower only a few months from planting as cuttings.

Other climbers can be used on trellis, in hedges or fences or on trees to give particular splashes of colour. Several species of the Bignoniaceae such as *Doxantha unguis-cati, Pyrostegia venusta* and *Saritaea magnifica* produce very attractive yellow or orange flowers and like so many members of this family usually depend on a dry spell to induce good flowering. The very appropriately named *Gloriosa superba* and *G. rothschildiana* are herbaceous and produce their magnificent flowers before dying back in the dry season. *Ipomoea learii* is a perennial morning glory and its short-lived but brilliant blue flowers are one of the sights to be experienced in an early morning in the tropics. *Petrea volubilis** has violet flowers and, like *Congea**, has a prolonged colourful period by virtue of its persistent sepals. Many regard this as one of the most beautiful climbers and if staked it may be grown as a very attractive standard. Bougainvilleas are woody climbers and a considerable effort in breeding has resulted in a vast range of cultivars which may be used to

254

supply splashes of a particular colour in appropriate areas or to relieve a plain expanse of wall. The two commonly grown species of *Thunbergia* occupy very different places in the garden; black-eyed Susan (*T. alata*) is a small plant with orange flowers having blackish throats which may be grown on a trellis, whilst *T. grandiflora** is rapid growing and vigorous with bluish mauve or white flowers, much in demand for screening large areas of wall etc.

The chalice vines, especially *Solandra maxima* and *S. grandiflora* are popular in the Western tropics with their large cup-like flowers. They may be used in trees and to cover wall surfaces but are sometimes so vigorous that they can become a nuisance as the young shoots are apt to penetrate through windows, louvres, etc. and invade the house.

Finally, there are the delightfully scented climbers such as *Jasminum, Odontadenia** and *Stephanotis*.

Foliage climbers

The number of climbers which are grown primarily for their foliage tends to be very limited. *Ficus repens* and *F. pumila* are employed in much the same way as ivy or virginia creeper is used in temperate zones to adhere to the walls of buildings and soften the effect of large areas of concrete or stone. However, when they have reached the top of the support the plants will develop large branches bearing coarse leaves and fruit. These branches should be cut off as they are formed.

Both *Pothos* and various species of *Philodendron* may be planted with advantage at the bases of large green trees which they can climb up. Their large dark green glossy leaves help to break up the stark outline of the tree trunks and give the impression of coolness. This is particularly marked if a small group of trees is treated in this way.

The elephant climber (*Argyreia speciosa*) to some extent occupies an intermediate position between these two categories of flowering and foliage climbers. Although it produces big purple bell-shaped flowers the large heart-shaped leaves with silvery undersurface are most conspicuous. It is a rapid grower and requires plenty of space.

Reference list of climbers

Philodendron spp	Aroids; large leaves, Some are handsome foliage creeping plants for tree trunks, others are pot plants.
Pothos spp	Aroids; large-leaved creeper. Useful for clothing tree trunks.

also:

Allamanda cathartica	*Jasminum*
Antigonon leptopus	*Odontadenia*
Argyreia speciosa	*Petraea volubilis*
Bougainvillea	*Pyrostegia* (*Bignonia*) *venusta*
Congea tomentosa	*Saritaea* (*Bignonia*) *magnifica*

Doxantha (*Bignonia*) *unguis-cati*	*Solandra grandiflora*
Ficus pumila	*S. maxima*
F. repens	*Solanum seaforthianum*
Gloriosa rothschildiana	*Stephanotis*
G. superba	
Ipomoea learii	

15.87 Epiphytes

The prevalence of a wide variety of plants growing epiphytically on trees is a striking feature of tropical vegetation. In the landscape scheme added interest and a sense of luxuriance may be created by the establishment of epiphytes, particularly as many of these plants are extremely attractive in their own right. A wide variety of subjects are available such as orchids, ferns, gesneriads, bromeliads and aroids. Care should be taken to get the scale right and not to use on small trees some of the large anthuriums, for example, which produce huge baskets of leaves some 1·5 m (5 ft) or so in length. Similarly, overloading with large epiphytes should be avoided as

PLATE 15.15 *Cordyline australis,* **similar to** *C. terminalis.* *(Maurice Lee)*

PLATE 15.16 *Ficus pumila* **as both a climber and groundcover with distinctive leaves of** *Heliconia metallica* **in the foreground. Suan Pakkad, Bangkok.** *(Maurice Lee)*

PLATE 15.17 **The birds nest fern** *(Asplenium nidus)* **in the fork of a tree.** *(Maurice Lee)*

breakage of branches can occur or even the collapse of trees.

Bird's nest ferns (*Asplenium nidus, see* Plate 15.17) and similar species are found virtually throughout the tropics and have their stiff simple leaves in a basket arrangement, whilst the various species of the stag's horn fern (*Platycerium*)* have additional interest in producing two types of leaf, one being dissected and giving rise to the common name of the plant because of its shape, the other being rounded and adhering close to the tree trunk (Plate 15.18).

The green of the ferns may be supplemented by the reds or oranges shown by the flowers of many epiphytic species of *Columnea* or *Aeschynanthus*.

Many orchids are easily grown on trees and a common practice is to hang them from trunks and branches growing on pieces of a suitable substrate such as potting medium held in coconut fibre. This has the advantage that plants in strategic positions can easily be changed as they come into flower and returned to the maintenance area when flowering is over. Orchid growing has become very popular in many tropical countries and supplies will normally be available commercially together with advice from local societies as to the most suitable species and hybrids for the area.

Bromeliads are a marked feature of neotropical forests and show a wide variety, some having decorative inflorescences and others with quite spectacular leaves, which are often banded with red or white. Many of them can also be grown on the ground, hence it is quite feasible to have some growing on the tree and others grouped around the base. These plants will tolerate a wide variety of conditions and will root in almost any light porous medium which is rich in humus, such as coconut fibre and compost. Various species of *Cryptanthus, Aechmea, Bilbergia, Guzmania* and *Nidularium*, have very attractive leaves, varying from rich green or grey to highly coloured or variegated. *Neoregelia carolinae* is particularly striking with its radiating green leaves which are brilliant red at the base, giving the effect, seen from above, of a red inner circle surrounded by a green outer one. Some decorative pineapple (*Ananas*) cultivars also available.

PLATE 15.18 **Stags horn fern on tree trunk. Note the different shapes of the leaves.** (*T. Walker*)

The leaves of many bromeliads are tightly pressed to one another at the edges, forming water-tight 'tanks'. Whilst this habit enables the plant to survive in dry periods, it can be troublesome if mosquitoes are allowed to breed in them.

Propagation of bromeliads is predominantly by offshoots or from seeds and in many countries interest in this group of plants has grown, ensuring reasonable commercial supplies of a wide variety of forms.

Reference list of epiphytes

Aechmea spp	Bromeliad; broad leaves often with coloured stripes.
Aeschynanthus spp	Gesneriad; several epiphytes, with orange or red tubular flowers.
Ananas spp (pineapples)	Bromeliad: stiff leaves, sometimes variegated, unusual fruits.
Anthurium spp	Aroid; attractive foliage, some with markings. Conspicuous spathes, often brightly coloured and long lasting.
Asplenium nidus (bird's nest fern)	Large basket-shaped fern; epiphytic.
Bilbergia spp	Bromeliad; leaves of some species variegated.
Columnea spp	Gesneriad; several epiphytes, usually with orange or red tubular flowers.
Cryptanthus spp	Bromeliad; attractive broad leaves, striped, mottled or variegated.
Guzmania spp	Bromeliad; attractive leaves.
Neoregelia carolinae	Bromeliad; vivid red bands at base of leaves, very spectacular.
Nidularium spp	Bromeliad; bright scarlet leaves in centre.
Platycerium spp (stag's horn fern)	Very decorative epiphytic fern, clasping tree trunks.

In addition the vast numbers of species and cultivars of orchids may be used in a variety of ways, including as epiphytes or hanging in temporary positions, etc.

15.88 Palms

Because of their anatomical structure and method of growth palms require careful tending for success. They should be well nourished from the start in order to develop the broad base which is essential for the production of strong stout trunks. They must also grow without check, as any impediment to growth results in a constriction of the trunk which will persist and be visible for the life of the palm, even if normal development is

FIGURE 15.5 **Characteristics of different palms. (Not to scale.)**

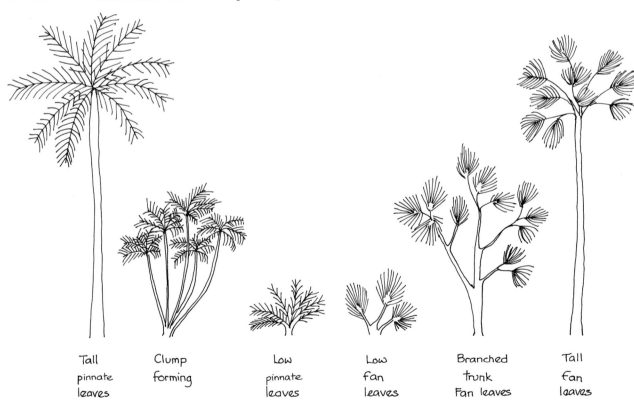

Tall pinnate leaves	Clump forming	Low pinnate leaves	Low fan leaves	Branched trunk Fan leaves	Tall fan leaves

PLATE 15.19 **The clump forming
Prostachys lakka or sealing-wax
used as a barrier.**
(Maurice Lee)

PLATE 15.20 **Delicate foliage of
Caryota or Fish tail palm.**
(Maurice Lee)

resumed afterwards. This becomes particularly obvious where the plants are grown as specimen trees or in avenues.

Amongst the palms there is a wide variety of habit, size and leaf-shape from which to choose and whilst traditionally palms have tended to be treated in books primarily on the basis of the form of their leaves, from the landscape point of view it is probably more useful to consider their growth habit first.

A number of palms produce single tall trunks which may ultimately reach from 20–30 m (60–100 ft) or more in height and bear crowns of immense leaves which may be either pinnate or fan-shaped according to the genus. It is this group which is so outstanding when used as specimen or avenue trees and includes species of *Caryota, Arenga, Elaeis, Roystonea* and *Oreodoxa*, which are all pinnate-leaved, and species of *Borassus, Sabal* and *Corypha*, which have fan-shaped leaves. *Areca catechu*

can be used to make less lofty avenues. Smaller single-stemmed species are to be found in the genus *Thrinax*, which may range from pot plants up to about 10 m (30 ft).

Several palms have fairly long stems which are, however, produced in clumps instead of singly and these can be used to great advantage. One of the most popular and effective of this group is the sealing-wax palm (*Cyrtostachys lakka*) which grows to about 10 m (30 ft) and has the outstanding feature of the bright red leaf stalks and sheaths which give this plant its popular name. Despite being a clump-former, *Cyrtostachys* makes a very effective small avenue palm in addition to being a good spot plant. *Chrysalidocarpus lutescens* is another member with this type of growth but with much shorter stems and may also be grown as a pot plant or near the margins of pools.

In yet other species the trunk is reduced in height until little or none is visible above ground and the crowns of

PLATE 15.21 **Distinctive fanshaped leaves of the Sabal palm.** *(Maurice Lee)*

leaves are produced at soil level. Clumps of long spiny pinnate leaves are borne in this way by *Salacca edulis* which also produces fruit with a very refreshing sub-acid taste. Fan leaves are produced by the popular *Licuala grandis*, which may eventually also form a short trunk. This plant has the further advantage that it can tolerate shade and can be grown under a large tree.

Finally, among the various growth forms the doum palms (*Hyphaene*) are most unusual in having branched trunks and could probably be more widely grown in the non-arid tropics than at present.

A number of palms are monocarpic and although it may be up to several decades before flowering and subsequent death takes place, thought should be given to replacement, especially where they form ceremonial avenues. *Caryota, Arenga* and *Corypha* all behave in this manner. The latter is particularly spectacular when in flower with its huge branching inflorescence surmounting the giant crown.

Reference list of palms

Areca catechu (betel nut)	Pinnate leaves; single trunk, medium height.
Borassus flabellifer (palmyra palm)	Fan leaves, single trunk, tall.
Chrysalidocarpus lutescens	Pinnate leaves; clump-forming, relatively short trunks.
Corypha umbraculifera (talipot palm)	Fan leaves; single trunk, tall, monocarpic.
Cyrtostachys lakka (sealing-wax palm)	Pinnate leaves with bright red bases and sheaths; clump-forming, medium trunks.
Hyphaene spp (doum palm)	Fan leaves; branched trunks.
Licuala grandis	Fan leaves; very short trunk.
Oreodoxa spp	Pinnate leaves; single trunk, tall.
Roystonea spp	Pinnate leaves; single trunk, tall.
Sabal spp	Fan leaves; single trunk, tall.
Salacca edulis	Pinnate leaves; single trunk, very short; sexes on different plants, fruit edible.
Thrinax spp	Fan leaves; single trunk, ranging from short to tall.

15.89 Bamboos

The great size of some palms is matched by the giant bamboos *Dendrocalamus giganteus* and *Gigantochloa asper*, forming huge graceful clumps up to 30 m (100 ft) or more in height, and the somewhat smaller *Bambusa vulgaris*. Like the palms these giant bamboos may be used as impressive specimen plants or in the creation of avenues. In the latter case the arching habit leads to the two rows meeting at the top, giving an enclosed cathedral-like quality to the avenue. Probably the most famous of these is Bamboo Walk in Jamaica where these features may be seen to perfection.

A large number of smaller bamboos are available for use. Among these may be mentioned *Arundinaria fortunei* and *A. hindsii* with dark green stems and foliage, whilst *Bambusa multiplex* may be green, yellow or striped and makes an excellent hedge. Another useful hedging bamboo is *Phyllostachys aurea* with thick yellow stems, growing to 4–6 m (13–20 ft) in height. The much smaller *Shibataea kumasaca* has very short stems and makes a useful plant for small gardens.

Bamboos originating in the Indian region are peculiar in being monocarpic and all individuals of the species will flower communally and die in the same year, the new generation being produced from seed. Unless this habit is taken into account very awkward gaps may appear in the planting layout. The time scale for several species is of the order of thirty years.

Reference list of bamboos

Arundinaria spp	Small to medium.
Bambusa spp	Small to tall, often with coloured stems or leaves.
Dendrocalamus giganteus	Massive.
Gigantochloa asper	Massive
Phyllostachys spp	Small to medium.

15.810 Aquatics

The use of water as a focal point or in creating the impression of coolness hardly needs emphasizing, especially if it is accompanied by the sound of cascades or fountains.

The building of ponds or water gardens has been much simplified in recent years with the advent of rot-resistant, flexible butyl (sub plastics) liners which may be used equally effectively in the construction of a tiny garden pool or a large lake. Construction can be carried out using unskilled labour and there are virtually no subsequent problems of leakage (apart from those caused by careless damage) such as frequently used to bedevil the more traditional concrete lined structures.

Equally, planting has also been simplified in that open-work plastic baskets are available for the purpose in a range of sizes. These should be lined with coarse woven sacking or coir (coconut fibre) and filled with a suitable compost. Such baskets can be lifted out when the plants need attention without disturbance to the other inhabitants of the pool and with less risk of damage to the fabric than when the plants are rooted directly on the bottom.

The pool should be sited in full sun to enable vigorous growth of the ornamentals to occur, which in their turn

261

PLATE 15.22 **Informal pool with heavily planted margins. Contrast with Plate 15.23.** *(Maurice Lee)*

PLATE 15.23 **Formal water feature—part of the canal system at A.I.T. Bangkok. A large bushy papyrus clump in the foreground.** *(Maurice Lee)*

will help to suppress undue algal growth by shading at a lower level. Dead leaves can cause a considerable amount of pollution when they rot and should be removed from the water surface before they can accumulate. Mosquito larvae can be kept under control by the use of suitable fish which also add further interest and pleasure and planting should not be so dense that there are areas of the pool that the fish cannot reach in their search for the larvae.

Most aquatic plants have an optimum depth of water in which they will flourish and for ornamental purposes the most useful range of depth is from about 0·5 m (18 in.) for the smaller water lilies and lotus to about 1 m (36 in.) for the larger lilies. Little is normally gained by working outside these limits. If the water is too shallow overheating is liable to occur, and if too deep the number of plants that will grow becomes limited and construction costs rise with no increase in benefit.

The shape is of great importance, a regular shape such as a square or a circle being suitable in a formal garden setting but very dull and jarring where the background is of an informal nature. Here irregularity of outline is desirable.

In order to avoid complications in the construction and to give greater flexibility in the planting it may be more convenient to make the pool of a uniform depth and to raise the baskets on bricks or stones where shallow water is called for. Drainage outlets in two positions should be provided, although they may empty into the same conduit. A bottom outlet, which is plugged, allows the pool to be drained when necessary in order to carry out cleaning or repairs, whilst a permanently open outlet just above the required water level ensures that heavy storms do not lead to the pond overflowing and possibly flooding the surrounding area.

Water lilies belonging to the genus *Nymphaea* exist in a large number of species and cultivars, with a wide range of colours. Attention should also be paid to the behaviour of the flowers; some open from late afternoon to early morning, whilst others open for most of the day and close towards night. A careful selection can ensure a different aspect to the pool at various times of the day. Most water lilies will grow satisfactorily in small pools, although with a larger water mass more variety of forms is possible. Where space is available, the giant water lily (*Victoria amazonica*) is a superb feature plant with its enormous round leaves up to almost 2 m (6 ft) in diameter. The scented flowers open towards dusk, remaining open for part of the following day and this is repeated once more before the flower withers. *Victoria* is propagated from seed and will last for many years when grown outside in the tropics, unlike its behaviour in heated houses in temperate regions which leads to it being treated as an annual.

The lotus, *Nelumbo nucifera,* favours shallow water and carries its attractive rounded blue-green leaves on long stalks well above water level as it does also its scented flowers and decorative fruiting head. (Where baboons are found these may be troublesome, as they pull up and eat the rhizomes.)

The moist margins of the pond support a variety of plants but discretion should be used as it is very easy to overplant, thereby not only producing a crowded effect but also hiding much of the water from sight. Groups of shrubs and low herbs interspersed with grassy areas provide additional interest without destroying the original purpose of the pond. Amongst such plants the small palm, *Chrysalidocarpus lutescens*, makes effective clumps on the damp banks and *Cyperus* species can be grown in the wetter areas. The dark-green leaves of *Spathiphyllum cannifolium* may be up to 1 m (3 ft) in length and are well set off by the large white spathes of the inflorescences. The arrowroot, *Maranta arundinacea*, thrives in the damp soil if it is enriched and this species also has variegated cultivars. Job's tears (*Coix lacryma-jobi*) is a moisture-loving grass and has decorative fruits, whilst an abundance of scent may be obtained by planting the white-flowered *Hedychium coronarium*.

Reference list of aquatics

Coix lacrymi-jobi (Job's tears)	Grass; with large ornamental fruits.
Cyperus spp	Sedge; pond marginal; various sizes.
Maranta arundinacea (arrowroot)	Pond marginal; large leaves, sometimes variegated.
Nelumbo nucifera (lotus)	Aquatic; free-standing leaves and flowers, attractive coloration and interesting fruits.
Nymphaea spp (water lily)	Aquatic; floating leaves and flowers; great range of flower colour.
Spathiphyllum cannifolium	Aroid; large leaves; conspicuous white spathe.
Victoria amazonica (giant water lily)	Aquatic; enormous floating leaves, requiring much space; large flowers; of great appeal.

plus: *Chrysalidocarpus lutescens* (*see* 15.88), *Hedychium coronarium* (*see* 15.78).

15.9 LISTS OF USEFUL PLANTS

A selection is given here of plants, some of which have proved to be of great merit, having been widely planted in the tropics, and others which deserve to be better known and more commonly used than at present. The species are grouped into trees, shrubs and climbers for convenience but the accompanying comments should enable the reader to abstract names of subjects for a particular purpose e.g. scented plants, those with red flowers, etc. If mention has been made of the plant in the text the section number is given in parenthesis.

PLATE 15.24 **Plate-like leaves of** *Victoria amazonica*, **the giant water lily, with Crinums in the background.** *(Maurice Lee)*

The lists refer particularly to the lowland non-arid tropics, although a large number of the plants will succeed at low to medium elevations. (Chapter 16 contains a list of plants suitable for hot arid climates.)

In a number of cases whether the plant develops into a small tree or shrub will depend upon local conditions and treatment, hence a few items listed as trees could equally well be listed as shrubs. The size grouping normally reached when mature is given and where the growth rate tends to be exceptional this is noted as rapid or slow as appropriate. Common names have been included only when they are widely used and may be of use in locating supplies from nurseries, etc.

TABLE 15.1
Trees

Species	*Flowers*	*Comments*
Acacia auriculiformis	small, yellow, scented	medium
Adenanthera pavonina (jumbie bead)	small, white	medium; seeds red, used as beads; rapid; for shade
Albizia lebbeck	small, yellow	large; feathery leaves; rattling seed-pods (15.77)
Aleurites moluccana (candlenut tree)	small, white, in clusters	large, spreading; greyish handsome leaves
Amherstia nobilis	large red and yellow sprays—outstanding	medium; handsome leaves, drooping and pinkish when young (15.82)
Andira inermis	red-pink	medium; almost evergreen; rapid, good windbreak (15.2)

Species	Flowers	Comments
Araucaria columnaris (= *A. cookii*)	produces cones	very tall, narrow; magnificent specimen tree (15.81)
A. heterophylla (= *A. excelsa*) (Norfolk Island pine)	produces cones	very tall, broadly tapering; magnificent specimen tree (15.81)
Bauhinia blakeana	large red-purple; produced when tree is very young	small; can be pruned to shape and size
B. purpurea	large, red-purple	small; rapid
B. variegata	large, variegated pink/white	small
Bixa orellana (anatto)	pink, in clusters; fruit scarlet	small; fruit used as dye
Bombax malabaricum	large, crimson, borne when leafless	very large; symmetrical branching; rapid (15.81)
Brassaia actinophylla (= *Schefflera actinophylla*)	red, in spikes	medium; handsome large leaves
Brownea capitella	orange-red, in large heads	small-medium
B. grandiceps	red, in large heads	small-medium
Calliandra surinamensis	pink in heads	small, almost trunkless
Calophyllum inophyllum	white, heavily scented	medium; rapid; salt tolerant
Cananga odorata (ylang-ylang)	yellow, fleshy, very heavily scented	medium (15.78)
Cassia fistula	yellow sprays, like laburnum	small-medium
C. grandis	pink	medium
C. nodosa	pink, scented	medium
C. siamea	yellow; in flower most of the year	large; very rapid
C. spectabilis	bright yellow	large
Casuarina equisetifolia	small, red; produces cones	medium-large; rapid, very elegant (15.2; 15.77)
Chrysophyllum cainito (star apple)	edible fruit	large; leaves velvet brown beneath (15.82)
Citrus spp (orange, lemon, lime etc.)	white, very fragrant	small-medium; aromatic fruit and foliage (15.78)
Coccoloba uvifera	white, small; fruit in clusters like grapes	varies from low shrub to large tree; attractive leaves (15.2)
Cochlospermum vitifolium	large yellow, borne when leafless	small; stands heavy pruning, good for dry situations
Cordia sebestena	orange, large	small; good in dry regions; rapid; good shade tree (15.6)
Couroupita guianensis (cannon ball tree)	large, red, white and yellow	large; big cannon ball-like fruit hanging down the trunk (15.84)
Crescentia cujete (calabash)	greenish	small; leaves stiffly erect; ornamental fruit (15.84)
Delonix regia (poinciana, flamboyant)	large, bright red varying to yellow, in clusters	medium; large light green feathery leaves; large pods; rapid; very decorative; rich soil (15.82)
Dillenia indica	large, white	medium; evergreen; large attractive leaves
Erythrina crista-galli	red, profuse	small; needs dry season for good flowering
E. indica (immortelle)	scarlet, profuse	medium; needs dry season for good flowering
Eucalyptus deglupta	red	tall; attractive bark; blue-grey aromatic leaves (15.78)
Fagraea fragrans	white, very heavily scented	tall, upright; useful for avenues

Species	Flowers	Comments
Ficus benghalensis (banyan)		large, spreading; for shade enormous spread (15.84)
F. elastica (India-rubber tree)		ultimately large, spreading; large shiny decorative leaves (15.82)
Gliricidia sepium	pink, abundant	small; rapid
Guaiacum officinale (*Lignum vitae*)	blue	small; evergreen; very attractive; slow
Hibiscus tiliaceus (seaside mahoe)	yellow, large	small to medium; withstanding salt
Jacaranda filicifolia	blue-mauve	medium; very decorative feathery leaves; flowers best with dry season (15.82)
J. mimosifolia	blue-mauve	as above (15.82)
Kigelia pinnata (sausage tree)	purplish, unpleasant smell	medium; large sausage shaped fruit on long stalks (15.84)
Lagerstroemia speciosa (pride of India)	mauve to pink, showy	variable in size; slow, but flowers when young
Melia azedarach (Indian lilac)	lilac, in large clusters	medium; rapid
Mesua ferrea (iron wood)	large, white, scented	medium; slow; young leaves bright red (15.82)
Michelia champaca	large, yellow, very fragrant	medium; rapid
Parmentiera cerifera (candle tree)	white, borne on branches and trunk	small; branches low down; long, candle-shaped fruits (15.84)
Peltophorum pterocarpum (= *P. inerme*)	yellow, erect spikes, scented	large; feathery leaves; rapid; spreading—good for shade
Pimenta dioica	insignificant	small; attractive bark; aromatic leaves and berries
Pithecellobium saman (rain tree)	pink	very large; spreading; excellent shade tree (15.6; 15.81)
Posoqueria trinitatis	very long, white, tubular; stamens 'explode' on touch	small–medium; rapid; flowers when very young
Pterocarpus indicum	yellow, scented	large; rapid; spreading, good shade
Punica granatum (pomegranate)	bright scarlet; pomegranate fruit	small; very decorative
Saraca taipingensis	yellow orange clusters	small; very decorative; needs shade
Solanum macranthum (potato tree)	blue, fading to white	medium; exceedingly rapid; sometimes deteriorates after a few years; useful for quick feature (15.73)
Spathodea campanulata	large, scarlet, very showy	large; rapid; but *see* 15.75; can be heavily pruned
Tabebuia pentaphylla (pink poui)	pink trumpets, when leafless	large; very rapid; flowers when very young, good in dry season
T. serratifolia (yellow poui)	bright yellow trumpets, when leafless	as above (15.83)
T. spectabilis	bright yellow trumpets, when leafless	small; very rapid; flowers when very young; good for dry season
Tamarindus indica (tamarind)	white and red	large; spreading; good for avenues and shade (15.6)
Terminalia catappa	almond-shaped fruits	medium to large; rapid; large leaves turn yellow and red before falling (15.81)
Thespesia populnea	large yellow to purple	small; spreading; good for coast (15.2)

Species	Flowers	Comments
Thevetia peruviana	yellow, funnel-shaped, scented	small; evergreen; very rapid; good for quick shade
Warszewiczia coccinea (chaconia)	large, brilliant red sepals in clusters	small; very decorative; a double form exists

TABLE 15.2
Shrubs

Species	Flowers	Comments
Acacia farnesiana	yellow, in small heads	fragrant
Acalypha spp	red catkins	wide variety of good foliage forms; also for hedges (15.85)
Allamanda schottii	large, yellow trumpets	
Aralia spp		several foliage forms
Ardisia crispa (= *A. crenata*)	white	persistent showy red berries
Barleria cristata	mauve, white or purple	spiny; good hedge plant; useful in dry conditions
B. lupulina	yellow, large	as above
Bauhinia galpinii	red, large	attractive cleft leaf
Beloperone (Drejerella) guttata (shrimp plant)	white, with red bracts	
Brunfelsia americana	white or yellow	strongly scented at night
Caesalpinia pulcherrima (Barbados pride)	red, orange or yellow, large and showy	prickly; good hedge plant; amenable to pruning, attractive leaves (15.85)
Calliandra brevipes	pink, in heads	
C. haematocephala	red, in heads	
Carludovica palmata		large, fan, palm-like leaves
Cassia alata	yellow-orange, in erect spikes	
Cestrum aurantiacum	yellow	
C. nocturnum (queen of the night)	greenish white	straggly; very powerful scent at night (15.78)
Clerodendrum fragrans	white-pink	small; scented
C. nutans	white, drooping clusters	leaves shed several times a year
Codiaeum vars. (croton)	small	numerous cultivars with leaves in many colours; hedges (15.85)
Cordyline terminalis	pink	many cultivars with coloured leaves (15.85)
Crossandra undulifolia	orange-red spikes	small; useful in dry areas
Datura suaveolens (angel's trumpet)	huge pendulous white trumpets	heavily scented (15.78)
Dracaena vars.		several cultivars for foliage (15.85)
Duranta repens	white and purple, persistent yellow berries	good hedge plant if untrimmed
Euphorbia pulcherrima (poinsettia)	bright red (or white) bracts	rich soil, in sun
Gardenia jasminoides	large white	heavily scented flowers; shiny leaves (15.78)
Graptophyllum pictum	red, in spikes	variegated leaves (15.82)
Hibiscus mutabilis	white, changing to red during course of the day	rapid; hedge (15.85)

267

Species	Flowers	Comments
H. rosa-sinensis	vast range of colours	many named cultivars
H. schizopetalus	red, with incised petals	
Holmskioldia sanguinea	orange	
Ixora coccinea	red, in large heads	rather slow; in sun; hedge
I. javanica	orange in large heads	tolerates light shade; hedge
Jatropha spp	small scarlet flowers in heads	some species with handsome, divided leaves; in sun (15.82)
Kopsia fruticosa	pink and white	
Lagerstroemia indica (crêpe flower)	red, pink or white	good hedge plant; very adaptable (15.85)
Lantana hybrids	white, yellow, pink, orange, in heads	in sun; aromatic flowers and leaves can be invasive (see 15.5)
Malvaviscus arboreus (sleeping hibiscus)	red, pendant; petals do not open out fully	good hedge plant (15.85)
Mussaenda erythrophylla	enlarged scarlet sepals	very showy
M. luteola	enlarged pale yellow sepals	
Nerium oleander* (oleander)	shades of white to red	excellent as hedge or specimen; good also in dry areas; poisonous in all parts (15.2; 15.85)
Nyctanthes arbor-tristis	large, white with orange	heavily fragrant at night (15.78)
Ochna mossambicensis	yellow petals soon falling but persistent red sepals	attractive small fruit; evergreen
Panax fruticosum	inconspicuous	Rapid; feathery leaves (15.82; 15.85)
Pandanus sanderi		very long, strap-shaped leaves, striped yellow and green
Pereskia grandifolia (= P. bleo)	pink	spiny; useful large hedges (15.85)
Pithecellobium unguis-cati	greenish-yellow, scented; prominent seeds	short spine at base of leaves; good hedge, spiny, not eaten by cattle (15.85)
Plumbago capensis	light blue	hedges (15.85)
Plumeria rubra (frangipani)	large, waxy, white to red in heads	very beautiful; heavily scented; also for dry conditions and near sea (15.78)
Quassia amara	scarlet	
Randia maculata	long, whitish	
Ricinus communis (castor oil plant)	in spikes	Herbaceous, becoming woody and tall; drought and salt-resistant; temporary ornamentals, also as windbreaks (15.73; 15.82)
Rondeletia backhousei	reddish, in trusses	
R. odorata	orange-red	suitable for small gardens
Russelia equisetiformis	scarlet	drooping stems; also for dry conditions
Solanum mammosum	curiously shaped yellow fruit	prickly; small
Stenolobium stans (= Tecoma stans)	large, yellow, tubular, prolific flowering	also for dry conditions; very rapid; hedge, prune to keep in shape after flowering (15.85)
Strobilanthes dyeranus		leaves green and purple above, purple beneath; grow in shade (15.82)
Thunbergia erecta	large violet or white	
Yucca spp (Adam's needle)	white in long spikes; often takes several years to flower	good spot plant with stiff linear leaves

TABLE 15.3

Climbers

Species	Flowers	Comments
*Allamanda cathartica	large yellow, continuous flowering	very adaptable; can be shrub, climber, canopy, or hedge. Var. *hendersoni* is climber only (15.86)
Antigonon leptopus (coralita)	pink or white	very prolific flowerer for most of the year (15.86)
Aristolochia elegans (Dutchman's pipe)	brownish purple and white	many species, but this has less offensive smell than most
Argyreia speciosa	large purple bells	large heart-shaped leaves, silvery beneath; rapid (15.86)
*Bougainvillea glabra	mainly purple bracts	rich soil for profuse flowering; also hedge (15.85; 15.86)
*B. hybrids	vast range of colour	very many named cultivars; performance sometimes variable (check locally)
*B. spectabilis	purple to red bracts	more vigorous than *B. glabra*; best in seasonal climate (15.85, 15.86)
Clerodendrum thomsonae	red and white in trusses	slender
Clitoria ternata	deep blue, to white	rapid; slender
Combretum grandiflorum	bright red in spikes	young leaves near tips bright red; on walls
*Congea tomentosa	pink or mauve bracts	(15.86)
Doxantha unguis-cati (= Bignonia unguis-cati)	yellow with orange; needs dry period to flower	tendrils like cat's claws cling to bark, etc.; rapid (15.86)
Ficus pumila		small foliage; self-clinging good for wall cover (15.86)
Gloriosa rothschildiana	large, deep red and yellow	in rich soil and sun (roots shaded): dies back seasonally; poisonous (15.86)
G. superba	large, red and yellow	as above (15.86)
Hoya spp	waxy flowers in heads	many local species in Malesian region
Ipomoea bona-nox (moonflower)	large, white	strong grower; night scented
I. horsfalliae	red, very prolific	rich soil, sunny position; on houses, verandahs, etc.
I. learii (=Pharbitis) (morning glory)	large, bright blue	rapid; short-lived, propagate annually (15.76; 15.86)
I. quamoclit	red	slender, annual
*Jasminum multiflorum	white; somewhat variable in scent	(15.86)
J. officinale	white; fragrant	(15.86)
*J. sambac	white; very fragrant	(15.86)
Lonicera hildebrandiana (honeysuckle)	yellow, large flowers	(15.78)
Mucuna nova-guineensis	bright red, in hanging trusses	excellent on avenue trees or strong support
Odontadenia grandiflora	yellow-orange; fragrant	strong climber, can cover tree, good for arbors (15.78; 15.86)
Passiflora vitifolia	large, bright red	rapid
Pereskia aculeata	white flowers; edible yellow berries	spiny
*Petrea volubilis	violet; persistent coloured calyx	evergreen; flowers several times a year (15.86)
Pyrostegia venusta (= Bignonia venusta)	bright orange	magnificent but needs dry period for flowering (15.86)

Species	Flowers	Comments
Quisqualis indica	white, turning to pink and red; scented	suckers vigorously
*Saritaea magnifica (= *Bignonia magnifica*)	pale purple	very vigorous; full sun (15.86)
Solandra grandiflora (silver chalice)	large white with purple lines	vigorous (15.86)
S. maxima	large yellow with purple lines; scented	vigorous; often called *S. guttata* by horticulturalists (15.86)
Solanum seaforthianum (potato creeper)	blue with prominent yellow stamens	rapid; in rich soil and sun (15.86)
S. wendlandii	blue	very vigorous (15.86)
Stephanotis floribunda	white, waxy; very fragrant	needs supporting (15.78; 15.86)
Strongylodon macrobotrys	pendulous racemes of jade-green	very unusual flower colour
Thunbergia alata (black-eyed Susan)	yellow with black throat	in sun; slender (15.86)
T. grandiflora	blue or white	very vigorous; sun and rich soil; very good screen or on pergola (15.86)
T. mysorensis	yellow or red-brown	vigorous; good on pergola

* Will climb up a support but without support develop as a shrub.

FURTHER READING

This book list makes no pretence to be exhaustive. Apart from the few books dealing with gardening in the tropics the titles have been selected on the basis of useful comments about widespread tropical plants or contain good illustrations of mature specimens.

Adams, C. D. *Flowering plants of Jamaica* (Glasgow: University Press 1972) for University of the West Indies

Adams, C. D. *The Blue Mahoe and other bush* (Singapore: McGraw Hill Far Eastern Publishers (S) Ltd., 1971)

Bardi, P. M. *The tropical gardens of Burle Marx* (London: Architectural Press, 1964)

Bor, N. L. and Razada, M. B. *Some beautiful Indian trees* (Bombay: Bombay Natural History Society, 1954) 2nd Edition, revised W. T. Stern

Bruggeman, *Tropical plants and their cultivation* (London: Thames and Hudson, 1962)

Corner, E. J. H. *Wayside trees of Malaya* (Singapore: Government Printing Office, 1940) Vols. 1 and 2

Dale, I. V. and Greenway, P. T. *Kenyan trees and shrubs* (Nairobi: Buchanans Kenya Estates Ltd., 1961)

Gibberd, A. V. and Gibberd, V. L. *A gardening notebook for the tropics* (London: Longmans, Green & Co., 1953)

Graf, A. B. *Exotica* (N.J.: Roehrs, Rutherford, 1963) 3rd Edition

Hargreaves, D. and Hargreaves, B., *Tropical blossoms of the Caribbean* (Portland: Hargreaves Industrial, 1960)

Hargreaves, D. and Hargreaves B., *Tropical trees* (Portland: Hargreaves Industrial, 1965)

Holttum, R. E. *Gardening in the lowlands of Malaya* (Singapore: Straits Times Press, 1953)

Hutchinson, J. and Dalziel, J. M. *Flora of West Tropical Africa* (London: HMSO, 1954–1972) 3 Vols., 2nd Edition, revised by F. N. Hepper

Kunkel, G. *Arboles exoticos, Los arboles cultivados en Gran Canaria* (Edicias del Exemo Cabildo Insular de Gran Canaria; 1969)

McCurrach, J. C. *Palms of the world.* (New York: Harper & Bros., 1960)

Macmillan, H. F. *Tropical planting and gardening* (London: Macmillan, 1956) 5th Edition

Menninger, E. A. *What flowering tree is that?* (Menninger, Stuart, Fla. 1958)

Menninger, E. A. *Flowering trees of the world. For tropics and warm climates* (New York: Hearthside Press, 1962)

Menninger, E. A. *Seaside plants of the world* (New York: Hearthside Press, 1964)

Menninger, E. A. *Flowering vines of the world* (New York: Hearthside Press, 1970)

Millar, A. *Gardening with Andrée Millar* (Port Moresby: South Pacific Post Pty. Ltd., 1971)

Pertchik, B. and Pertchik, A., *Flowering trees of the*

Caribbean (New York: Rinehart & Co. Inc., 1951)

Whitmore, T. C. *Palms of Malaya* (London: Oxford University Press, 1973)

Williams, R. O. and Williams, R. O. *The useful and decorative plants in Trinidad and Tobago* (Port-of-Spain: Guardian Commercial Printing, 1951) 4th Edition

ACKNOWLEDGEMENTS

Special acknowledgement is given to Dr Trevor Walker for Sections 7, 8 and 9 of this chapter and for the bibliography. Figures 15.1–15.5 have been redrawn from his original suggestions.

Asian Institute of Technology, Bangkok. *(Maurice Lee)*

CHAPTER 16

Planting in Hot Arid Climates

ANN WILLENS

16.1 INTRODUCTION

Over a third of the earth's surface can be classified as arid to some degree, including countries of widely differing character. This chapter cannot attempt, therefore, to do more than provide useful information for landscape designers gained from the author's own experience, and does not include all arid areas within its scope. Nevertheless, knowledge of the characteristics of particular arid climates, the nature of the soils, salinity problems, and plant physiology can act as a guide to the likely conditions, problems and solutions in other areas, provided that time and trouble is taken to become familiar with local conditions. This is particularly necessary when considering which decorative plant species may be introduced from areas of similar eco-climates, and how conditions may be modified to ensure their successful propagation and establishment.

Intensive landscaping is a relatively new development in most of the arid areas. Much of the information required for successful implementation is still in the experimental stage and new techniques are continually being developed.

The arid areas of the world in North and South America, North and South Africa, Egypt and the Sudan, the Arabian Peninsula, Iran, India and Australia, share a common distinction in being some of the least known regions on earth. The inhabitants, despite great differences in their history, religion and culture, are united in the reality of the life which they live, dominated by the ever-present scorching sun, long periods of drought, and sudden torrential rains. An awareness of the characteristics of arid areas will enable the landscape designer to produce sympathetic designs, in keeping with a background of traditions possibly alien to his own.

Aridity is due chiefly to the interaction of temperature, rainfall and evaporation, where 'the amount of water available through rain, soil moisture and groundwater is not sufficient to balance the loss caused by run-off, evaporation and transpiration by plants'.[1]

The resulting general desiccation is normally associated with a virtual absence of plant cover and frequently with soil erosion due to wind. The participation of man in creating arid areas cannot be ignored although it is in most cases controversial. Many deserts of today were once fertile and extensively cultivated. However, the relative importance of overcultivation, overgrazing and the felling of forests as compared to climatic changes has not been satisfactorily established.

16.2 CLIMATE

The desert effects of climate on plants in arid areas are essentially twofold. Physiological heat stress may result from high temperature and solar radiation levels, and water stress may result from high evapo-transpiration levels.

Characteristic lack of cloud cover results in arid areas receiving very high levels of solar radiation. The total amount of sunshine received can often be over 85% of the theoretical maximum and can easily be double that received in humid zones of comparable latitude.

High radiation can directly affect plant growth, particularly the size and shape of leaf canopies, but its more important effect is to increase the temperature of intercepting objects.

Maximum air temperatures often exceed 40°C (104°F) with ground temperatures reaching even higher levels. Surface temperatures can exceed 80°C (175°F) in mid-afternoon. Such conditions, apart from causing considerable dessication, can result in severe physiological stress and in some cases death in non-adapted species.

Minimum temperatures rarely drop to freezing point although in non-coastal areas frost and snow may occur,

PLATE 16.1 **Desert scrubland.** *Acacia nilotica.* **Seeb, Oman** *(Gordon Bell)*

PLATE 16.2 *Prosopis spicigera* **giving shelter to local inhabitants. Mesquit, Seeb, Muscat.** *(Gordon Bell)*

FIGURE 16.1 **Artist's impression of a water garden overlooked by a restaurant. Park Master Plan, Mecca.**
(Andrew Donaldson. Landscape Architects: *Brian Clouston and Partners.* Architects: *John S. Bonnington Partnership)*

particularly with increasing altitude. Coastal temperatures are generally less extreme than those of the interior.

Rainfall in arid areas is not only extremely low but is commonly unreliable. Quoted figures for average rainfall (typically 20–200 mm ($\frac{3}{4}$–8 in.) and rarely exceeding 500 mm (20 in.) are often misleading since the frequency of occurrence can be very erratic. The total annual rainfall may fall during a very few days of the year and in many areas 3–5 years with no rain at all is not uncommon. Even where the quantity of rain is fairly reliable it may occur in April one year and in December the next.

Indigenous plants are highly adapted to such precarious conditions. Most landscape planting must however be irrigated throughout the year as the contribution of rainfall to the water requirements of non-adapted plants is negligible.

Rainfall when it does occur in arid areas often causes problems. Light rains may wash surface accumulated salts into plant root zones causing root injury, scorch, defoliation and terminal dieback. Heavy rain, falling as intense short-lived showers, typically causes extensive surface erosion as dry valleys are turned into raging torrents and flat land is widely flooded. Afforestation and chemical and biological methods of soil stabilization can help to reduce erosion but landscape projects in apparently dry wadi beds should always be designed with the possibility of flash floods in mind.

In less arid areas such as North Africa, rainfall is sufficiently predictable and of adequate quantity to allow some species to be grown without irrigation. Adapted species of *Acacia, Prosopis, Casuarina* and *Eucalyptus* can survive when mature without irrigation, following an initial irrigated establishment period of 1–3 years. Less adapted shrubs and annuals generally still require irrigation although in some cases they can be established successfully on 'winter' rainfall. Anti-transpirants, moisture retentive mulches, soil stabilization and root dips usefully assist establishment in such cases.

Humidity varies widely in arid areas, ranging from 30% in low rainfall areas in the interior of land masses with water tables at considerable depth, to 100% usually near coasts, e.g. along the west coast of Saudi Arabia, and the Gulf coasts. Heavily cuticled *Ficus* spp can survive low humidities, whereas other plants such as *Terminalia catappa* thrive in humid conditions.

Winds can frequently reach gale force proportions and damaging sandstorms can develop. Wind increases evapo-transpiration and causes sand abrasion, defoliation, plant burial or blow out, dune movement, and carries salt spray from the sea. It sieves out and transports fine soil particles creating soils of poor texture and structure.

Shelter belts can be planted and tree guards used for protection against wind. Anti-transpirants and soil mulches will decrease evapo-transpiration. Chemicals, dead vegetation and indigenous stabilizing species will help to stabilize the soils.

Evaporation and evapo-transpiration rates are extremely high in arid regions, particularly where high winds and low humidities combine with high temperatures. Analysis of these rates necessitates detailed study of local conditions, using Penman equations, evaporation pans etc.[2]

High temperatures increase evapo-transpiration to such rates that if insufficient moisture is available, plants suffer both aerial and subterranean stress. Irrigation

274

PLATE 16.3 *Terminalia catappa* **in Jeddah.** *(Maurice Lee)*

schedules have to be designed to minimize this stress and frequent light irrigations are usually preferable to long irrigation intervals.

Overhead irrigation must be carried out with care since water on leaf surfaces in direct sunlight can cause scorch. In addition to being unsightly this can increase the fire hazard in dense tree plantings. Shelter belt and shade plantings should therefore be designed not only for human benefit but also to afford some protection to the more sensitive plant species.

16.3 SOILS

The soils associated with arid areas vary considerably in depth, texture and composition, and in the degree to which water will percolate through them. A particular characteristic is the upward movement of soluble salts in the soil profile when evapo-transpiration exceeds rainfall. This is a difficulty which must be overcome before successful planting can take place of species not adapted to saline soils.

PLATE 16.4 **Shade planting in the American Embassy compound, Jeddah, including** *Sansevieria trifasciata* **and** *Scindapsus aureus*. *(Maurice Lee)*

TABLE 16.1
Examples of soils in arid areas
(derived from the American system of soil classification)

ARIDISOLS	Form where potential evaporation greatly exceeds precipitation and water rarely percolates through the soil except in extreme years. Lack of moisture inhibits chemical erosion and soil morphology is therefore related to the parent material.
Properties:	i) High base status (minerals) but low organic matter due to rapid oxidation; ii) a surface pavement of gravel; iii) a 'desert varnish' of manganese and iron oxide staining upper stone surfaces black; iv) 'caliche' layers of carbonate accumulation or gypsum banding.
Examples:	Grey and brown steppe soils; soils with calcareous and gypsum crusts; saline soils; hard calcium cemented silty sands.
Cultivation:	Limited chiefly by water availability; lack of internal permeability and percolation may cause problems of salinization and alkalinization (*see* halomorphic soils, 16.31). Nitrogen levels are usually low, phosphorus adequate, potassium high, trace elements adequate although often made unavailable by high alkalinity. Foliar applications of iron and trace elements may be necessary.
ENTISOLS	Soils of slight and recent development; little or no horizon development.
Examples:	Dunefields exposed to bedrock areas, Hammadas, alluvial soils associated with wadi and sea-flooding loess.
Cultivation:	Fertility ranges from extremely low to very high depending on origin. The main problem is stability and most are susceptible to erosion by wind, water, or mass wasting. Can be salt affected.
MOLLISOLS	Soils with deep, dark, relatively fertile topsoil formed under grassland vegetation; found where arid areas grade into steppe or prairie.
Properties:	Light coloured, salt affected patches often found in depressions.
Examples:	Brown soils of steppe, prairie and savannah; often alluvial and sometimes hydromorphic (e.g. high water table).
Cultivation:	Extensively used for food production although water availability is limited.

16.31 Soil types

It is a common misconception that soils in arid areas are dominated by shifting dunes and rocks. There is in fact a variety of arid soils, and a simplified indication of their characteristics is listed in Table 16.1.

Under the American system of soil classification most soils of arid areas are classified as aridisols. Entisols, only recently and slightly developed (e.g. dunes) are also common and mollisols, the typical grassland soils of prairie and steppe, are often associated with the cooler, moister fringes of arid areas. Thirty-five per cent of the earth's surface is classified as 'arid' (*see* Table 16.1).

All of these soils can be affected by high contents of salts or highly alkaline conditions. These may be called halomorphic soils and can be developed by
i) low humidity and a high mineral content of the parent material;
ii) evaporation from saline ground water and capillary rise;
iii) sea-water flooding.
It can therefore be seen that irrigation of such soils, or irrigation of non-saline soils with saline water can itself result in salinization.

In simplified terms, saline soils form where total salts are high; alkali soils result where the sodium percentage is high and the resultant sodium carbonate raises the pH.

Salt-tolerant species survive in saline soils; alkali soils display the additional disadvantage of sodium causing deflocculation of clay and humic particles resulting in a solid, airless, dusty soil when dry, and amorphous when wet. Where periodic flooding from above or irrigation leaches salts and clay particles downwards, salt and impervious clay 'pans' can result.

These soils present a number of complicated cultural problems specific to each site, but these can be solved by careful water management and specific methods of irrigation, salt interception, aeration and drainage.

16.32 Soil analysis

Although many plants can be used to indicate the type and quality of the soil (e.g. *Suaeda* spp and *Tamarix passerinoides* in saline areas, *Arthrocnemum* and *Atriplex* spp in high water table areas) it is absolutely essential that an accurate analysis of all soil components is obtained for the whole area of each individual site, and at different depths prior to planting. The analysis should include:
i) soil structure and texture;
ii) pH value;
iii) total content of soluble salts—usually measured by electrical conductivity techniques (EC values) with particular emphasis on:
    a) Any macro- or micro-nutrients that are lacking (e.g. nitrogen) or in excess and toxic (e.g. boron).
    b) The sodium hazard (relative level of sodium to other cations in the exchange complex). If this is

PLATE 16.5 **A magnificent avenue of date palms,** *Phoenix dactylifera*, **with** *Pithecellobium dulce* **in the foreground. Jeddah.** *(Maurice Lee)*

high it will cause root injury, aerial scorch and dieback to all but the most adapted species (e.g. *Atriplex* spp and *Phoenix dactylifera*).

c) The soil percolation rates, and any changes in soil structure with depth (e.g. a silt layer 2 m down) which can impede drainage and the leaching away of harmful salts.

This information will aid the identification of possible plant cultural problems.

The problem of salinity can be overcome by leaching in irrigated areas with adequate drainage. Other main problems include lack of soil stability, poor water retention or poor drainage, lack of nutrients and low quantities of organic matter and soil organisms.

16.33 Soil fertility

Fertility can be improved by the addition of nitrogen, decayed animal and organic plant manures and clay (for fast draining soils) or sand (in silty or waterlogged soils). Nitrogen, potassium and micro-nutrients together with sequestered iron, can be applied in sweet water foliar sprays or through the irrigation system.

Phosphates are usually insoluble and must be applied as solids. (A new soluble glycerophosphate is efficient but expensive.)

Leguminous plants, e.g. *Acacia* and *Prosopis* spp, can add nitrogen to the soil by acting as host to nitrogen fixing bacteria in their root nodules. Mixing local soils to obtain a better texture often produces better results than searching for topsoil which may not exist close to the site. For productive plants a regular monitoring of plant nutrients and soil fertility is essential.

16.34 Soil moisture

The total moisture tension against which the plant takes up water increases with both moisture depletion and increase in salinity (due to increased osmotic pressure of the soil solution). The critical level for healthy plant growth varies widely with species and is little documented.

In order to minimize stress on the plant, irrigation systems should be designed to maintain soil moisture close to field capacity. Water application rates should be calculated for the worst foreseeable conditions, to

277

determine the peak capacity required of the irrigation system.

Ideally soil moisture levels should be continually monitored by a series of tensiometers. If required these can be directly linked to the irrigation system to provide a fully automatic system. Where salinity build-up is of greater importance than moisture depletion, sensors can be used in place of tensiometers.

16.4 WATER

16.41 Quality and sources

The quality of water available is as important as the quantity, and both these factors need to be carefully assessed prior to planting.

Surface water in arid areas tends to be relatively saline

PLATE 16.6 **Courtyard garden of Government Hostel at Islamabad New Capital City, Pakistan, showing water channels used as an ornamental feature and part of irrigations system. Plants include** *Cupressus sempervirens, Salix tetrasperma* **and** *Jasminium* **spp.** (Landscape Architects: *Derek Lovejoy and Partners*)

due to the high evaporation rates. When soil water rises from the water table by capillary action to the soil surface, dissolved salts are deposited after evaporation of the water. If recharge of the water table is slow due to low precipitation, slow flowing underground aquifers, or over-use of the water, the salts may become further concentrated in soil solution. In addition, surface water tends to contain more silt and suspended matter, and is often fouled by plant and animal organic matter.[3] Underground water supplies therefore assume vital importance in arid areas particularly for drinking purposes, and are generally more reliable water sources.

16.42 Water analysis

It is essential in arid areas to obtain a complete water analysis and to calculate the rate at which water can be used without severe depletion of the water table 'reservoir'. For example, perched water tables in sand dunes, formed from rainfall accumulating above an impermeable soil layer, can be quickly exhausted if used to irrigate large areas with little or no water recharge. The water analysis should include:

i) quantity (and therefore number of wells to be dug);
ii) pH value;
iii) total salinity (expressed in ppm, Me/litre or EC values);
iv) sodium content and SAR values;
v) concentrations of specific ions noting those that might be low or excessive.

Measurement of the depth to the water table will indicate the types of wells to dig and whether a tree planted during heavy seasonal rainfall or with initial irrigation will survive eventually without irrigation. Seasonal fluctuations of the water table should also be recorded to avoid plant death due to waterlogging.

16.43 Irrigation systems

The choice of irrigation systems depends on the water quality and quantity, the site topography, the duration and season of rainfall, evaporation rates, wind and costs. There are four principal types:

i) *Surface*—simple to operate, costs mainly depending on labour wages. Uses large quantities of water with high evaporation and drainage losses.
ii) *Sprinkler*—uses approximately $\frac{1}{3}$ of the water used in (i); costs of equipment higher, but cheaper to operate. Large areas can be covered by automated travelling systems. The output is not specific for plants with different water requirements and causes scorch with saline water.
iii) *Trickle*—uses $\frac{1}{10}$ water of the surface system. High capital cost but can be fully automated to maintain soil near field capacity, and leaches salts out of the root zones continuously. It can give specific amounts of water to each plant and apply pesticides and

fertilizers etc. if soluble.
iv) *Managed water tables and hydroponics*—these have been successfully used but require better quality water than is generally available. Such water can be provided by desalination plants, solar stills, and occasionally effluent treatment plants.

Waterproof membranes creating artificial water table conditions assist in water retention and prevent the rise of salts from the water table. Saline irrigation water, however, can cause salts to accumulate within the soil above the membrane. Another method involves raising plant beds, and interrupting the capillary rise (and therefore the salt rise) from the water table by placing graded rocks and rubble above the water table, and backfilling with sweet soil. Leaching can also be accomplished efficiently.

16.5 THE PLANTS

The warm climatic conditions of arid areas and prolonged sunlight ensure rapid growth of plants when water is available. Desert plants are characterized by the ways in which they adapt to drought conditions and can be categorized into three main groups showing morphological and physiological adaptations:

i) *Xerophytes* are protected from drought in a variety of ways. Some, like *Ficus* spp have heavy leaf cuticles; others like *Acacia* spp have small leaves; cacti and succulents store water in their tissues, and plants like *Acacia cavenia* and *A. nilotica* have thorns which store water. Yet others lose their leaves or die back in hot periods, e.g. *Haloxylon* spp, *Lantana* and *Bauhinia* spp and most ornamental species when subjected to insufficiently modified aridity.

ii) *Halophytes* are protected from salt damage by the high osmotic values of their cell sap and low transpiration rates, e.g. *Suaeda*, *Arthrocnemum* and *Nitraria* spp.

iii) *Hydrophytes* are protected from possible flooding in high water table areas by comparatively low osmotic values and high transpiration rates, e.g. *Atriplex*, *Tamarix* and *Prosopis* spp.

Table 16.2 indicates plant species which are naturally tolerant of extreme conditions.

It is essential to understand the local ecology and to assess the viability of introducing plants from equivalent environments elsewhere. For example although *Eucalyptus* spp transplant successfully, their transpiration rates are so high that their use is precluded in areas of low water availability.

Once the site characteristics are known, the balance between hard and soft landscaping can be assessed. Particular thought should be given to the potential visual quality of planting carried out under conditions of exposure, salinity and low water availability. Comparisons of the cost of irrigation equipment with that of hard materials should be made. The heating and light reflecting problems of hard materials should also be assessed. Where irrigation is too expensive, it is possible to establish main plantings of succulents, cacti and indigenous trees and shrubs, highlighted with a few drought tolerant specimen trees. It may be necessary to limit grass and groundcover plants and to concentrate on interesting and sheltered hard surfaces with spaces for attractive plant groups.

16.6 SOME PROBLEMS OF PLANTING

Grazing of camels, goats, rabbits, Australian mammals etc. can prevent the establishment of new plants and prohibit recovery of indigenous plants. Over-cultivation by man without replacement of plant nutrients and his collection of wood for fuel also degrades the soils and vegetation. Fencing, tree guards, education in crop rotation and public awareness of the reasons for planting

TABLE 16.2
Some naturally tolerant species indigenous to arid areas

Extremely tolerant of:	*Species*	*Extremely tolerant of:*	*Species*
1. Poor soil structure		5. High water table	*Arthrocnemum; Atriplex nummularia; Avicennia mariina; Casuarina* spp; *Prosopis juliflora; Tamarix*
Gravel	*Anabasis articulata*		
Sandy	*Haloxylon; Parkinsonia aculeata; Zizyphus spina-christi*		
Waterlogged, silty	*Acacia arabica; Eucalyptus* spp; *Tamarix* spp	6. High soil moisture tension due to drought	
2. Wind damage		Trees	*Acacia* spp; *Balanites aegyptica; Prosopis* spp; *Zizyphus* spp
Trees	*Acacia mellifera; A. pendula; A. seyal; A. tortilis; Casuarina* spp; *Eucalyptus* spp; *Prosopis juliflora; Tamarix aphylla; Zizyphus* spp	Shrubs	*Calligonum; Capparis* spp; *Fagonia* spp; *Haloxylon; Parkinsonia aculeata; Salvadora persica;* cacti and succulents, and all included in the following salinity tolerant category.
Shrubs	*Calligonum* spp; *Dodonea viscosa; Haloxylon salicornicum; Nerium oleander; Parkinsonia aculeata; Pithecellobium dulce*		
3. Grazing and over-use	*Acacia; Haloxylon; Kochia indica; Prosopis; Salsola* spp; *Tamarix*	Trees	*Casuarina equisetifolia; Phoenix dactylifera; Prosopis juliflora; Tamarix aphylla; T. passerinoides*
4. Dune movement	*Acacia cyanophylla; Atriplex* spp; *Calligonum comosum; Citrullus* spp; grasses (e.g. *Cyperus glomeratus, Panicum turgidum*)	Shrubs	*Atriplex nummularia; Kochia indica; Nitraria* spp; *Suaeda* spp; *Zygophyllum coccineum*

These trees and shrubs show the greatest tolerance to highly saline conditions, even where soil and water table have been contaminated by sea water. The salinity of water or the soil solution may be measured directly as parts per million (ppm) of dissolved solids. It is more conveniently measured by the electrical conductivity (EC). The standard unit of electrical conductivity (mho/cm) is a large unit. It is therefore customary to choose a smaller subunit which gives a more convenient location of the decimal point. The units most commonly used are $EC \times 10^3$ (millimho/cm), $EC \times 10^6$ (micromho/cm). For example 3 000 ppm is equivalent to an EC of 0·0047 mhos/cm or $EC \times 10^3$ 4·7 mmhos/cm or $EC \times 10^6$ 4 700 mmho/km.

Salinity tolerances of the more decorative species will be given, together with plant descriptions, in the next table. These salinity figures are appropriate to plant survival under optimum conditions of shelter, water, drainage and humidity. Survival at salinities higher than stated can be possible under trickle irrigation with its continual leaching properties. Survival on a windy, arid site can be substantially lower, reducing salinity tolerance by as much as 1–2 mmhos/cm (600–1 400 ppm TDS).

These guideline figures should never replace on-site plant trials previous to final species selection.

PLATES 16.7 & 16.8 **Interesting groupings of plants for shape, texture and colour, including** *Yucca aloifolia, Aloë arborescens* **and** *Centaurea candidissima* **(Plate 16.7) and** *Ailanthus* **(Plate 16.8).** *(K. Stansfield)*

FIGURE 16.2 **Artist's impression of landscaping for a housing scheme in Iran incorporating umbrella pines and eucalyptus.** *(Andrew Donaldson)*

all help to overcome this problem.

Most implementation problems can be overcome by proper management. Tree guards can protect new planting; sand must be cleared and stabilized, silts and clays must be hoed; mulching and use of fertilizers will improve soil quality. It must be remembered that planting can only be carried out in the cooler months, and that some form of pest control which does not break down in the heat will be necessary in the early growth stages. An efficient system of irrigation is essential, as one week's loss of irrigation can be fatal to young plants. Sand and salt can wear out or block any working parts of machinery; regular pipe flushing and salt leaching must be carried out.

Motionless water surfaces exposed to the light will encourage algae which can block irrigation systems and make water features unsightly. Water should be continually moving and aerated to keep it clear. Polythene sheets and pvc pipes can be degraded in hot climates. They should be of heavy quality and sunk, covered or painted.

It will be easier to manage and maintain the planting scheme if workshops, stores etc. are erected near to the site and are easily accessible.

16.7 ADVANTAGES

i) There is little need for expensive propagation units due to high temperatures and frost-free areas.

ii) The growth rate per annum is very fast. Many plants grow 2–3 m (6–10 ft) per year, and fast eucalyptus will grow 4 m per year.

iii) There is a low level of pests and diseases in hot, dry climates.

iv) There is a definite improvement of micro-climate accompanied by increases in all types of wildlife, together with social and psychological benefits of the people living close to the planting.

v) Shelter belts assist in desert reclamation, growth of crops, and reduction of winds around housing.

vi) Technological advances and research are stimulated by the urge to overcome climatic problems, e.g. desalination, plastic mulches, water table control, and breeding of salt tolerant species.

Adverse effects will also occur and must be constantly monitored and corrected, e.g. rapid depletion of sweet water for domestic use due to plant over-watering, salt accumulation in the soil, and salt-pan developments due to irrigation wetting patterns.

16.8 SUMMARY OF INFORMATION REQUIRED FOR DESIGN PROCESS AND PLANTING

Aerial survey and interpretation for large area surveys. Investigation and analysis of surface and sub-surface geology.

FIGURE 16.3 **Artist's impression of a picnic area shaded by trees and tents. Park Master Plan, Mecca.**
(Andrew Donaldson. Landscape Architects: *Brian Clouston and Partners.* Architects: *John S. Bonnington Partnership)*

Collection and analysis of soil samples.

Collection and analysis of meteorological data.

Determination and analysis of topography, drainage and soil conservation requirements.

Analysis of hydrology to determine water availability and quality.

Ecological analysis and selection of suitable planting material.

Analysis of present and proposed land use.

Recruitment and training of operating and maintenance personnel.

Choice of species, establishment of design criteria, preliminary and final design.

Design and establishment of tree and shrub nurseries and production of planting material.

Design and installation of irrigation systems for tree and shrub planting.

Establishment of shelter belts, dune stabilization, soil amelioration and preplanting irrigation.

Establishment and management of planting.

Irrigation and plant maintenance.

16.9 PLANT LISTS

The monotony of the buffs and beiges of arid sandy surroundings has always stimulated the inhabitants to create the tranquil, relaxing coolness of greenery, water and fragrances, punctuated by vivid colour displays and patterns of grass, gravel, hedges, climbers and annuals.

The following plant lists are confined to those species most tolerant of irrigated conditions. Many other species can be included if adverse site conditions can be reliably ameliorated (*see* Chapter 15). The plants have been grouped into several sections for easy reference for design use, and cover shade trees, shelter belt plants, shrubs, hedges, climbers, groundcover, plants for colour displays, fruit and fragrance. A list of palms appears in Chapter 15.

To avoid repetition, capital letters have been used to indicate whether the plant is deciduous or evergreen.

  D deciduous

  E evergreen

283

PLATE 16.9 **Residential section G.7 of Islamabad New Capital City, Pakistan. Public paths in 2 × 2 pre-cast slabs and each private garden planted with one** *Jacaranda mimosifolia* **to give tree structure to the area.** (Landscape Architects: *Derek Lovejoy and Partners*)

PLATE 16.10 **Plane trees in the courtyard of the Theological College, Isfahan, Iran. This design epitomizes the tranquil, shady refuge from the desert.** *(Gordon Bell)*

PLATE 16.11 **Vivid contrast between the arid, untended desert and greenery, concealed by high walls around the garden, Haft-tan, Shiraz, Iran.** *(Michael Timmons)*

TABLE 16.3
Shade trees

a) Spreading canopies casting dense or intermittent shade

Albizia lebbeck sirus (Leguminosae) D	Fast growing but relatively short-lived, brittle stems; pinnate compound leaves; intermittent shade; yellow ball-shaped flowers have protruding stamens; large flat seed pods rattle; poor survival of decorative underplanting and untidy leaf fall; 8–10 m. (*See* Plate 15.00) Survives salinity up to 9·5 mmhos/cm (6 000 ppm)
Azadirachta indica neem (Meliaceae) E	Large evergreen compound leaves with serrated leaflets; heavy shade; vigorous roots; white inconspicuous flowers; poor survival of underplanting; 8–10 m. 9·5 mmhos/cm (6 000 ppm)
Ficus bengalensis Indian banyan (Moraceae) E	Large, oval leathery leaves with red brown underfelt; needs humidity; Spreading tree. 12 m. 7 mmhos/cm (4 500 ppm)
Ficus religiosa bo or peepul tree (Moraceae) Semi-E	Glossy, pointed heart-shaped leaves giving attractive light and shade effects in sunshine. Large, spreading tree. 12 m. 9·5 mmhos/cm (6 000 ppm)
Ficus retusa (Moraceae) E	Medium-sized single ovate leaves; dense shade, some aerial roots. Moderate growth, needs humid, sheltered conditions. 7 mmhos/cm (4 500 ppm)
Tamarindus indica tamarind (Leguminosae) Semi-E	Large, spreading tree; dense feathery pinnate foliage; 3 petalled pale yellow flowers and pulpy red pods; needs some shelter and humidity. 12–24 m, depending on conditions. 4·7 mmhos/cm (3 000 ppm)

285

b) Lighter textured more decorative species casting less shade and generally (with the exception of indigenous acacias) less tolerant of wind, drought, heat and salinity

Acacia spp (Leguminosae) E	Trees and large shrubs, many indigenous, e.g. *A. pendula* in Australia, *A. tortilis* in the Gulf; light textured compound bi-pinnate leaves; yellow ball-shaped flowers. *A. tortilis, raddiana, gerrardii, mellifera* are least tolerant to salts. Good desert species. *A. nilotica* can induce hayfever. Least tolerant survive 2·5 mmhos/cm (1 600 ppm) Most tolerant survive 14 mmhos/cm (9 000 ppm)
Bauhinia spp camel's foot or butterfly tree (Leguminosae) E or D	Small trees, sometimes scandent; twin-lobed leaves like camel's footprints may brown in very arid summers; butterfly-shaped white and purple blossom. 4–6 m. 2·4 mmhos/cm (1 500 ppm)
Cassia spp e.g. Indian laburnum (Leguminosae) E and D	Small trees and large shrubs; bi-pinnate leaves; pendulous racemes of yellow or pink flowers e.g. *Cassia fistula* (yellow) and *C. javanica* (pink). Need a dry period to stimulate flowering. 3–4 m. 2·4 mmhos/cm (1 500 ppm)
Delonix regia poinciana, flame or flamboyant (Leguminosae) D	Bi-pinnate, bright green leaflets; strikingly beautiful dense clusters of scarlet blooms; tolerates sandy soils, sea coast; wood brittle and roots invasive. Needs a dry period to stimulate flowering. 15 m. 2·4 mmhos/cm (1 500 ppm)
Erythrina crista-galli cockspur coral tree (Leguminosae) D	Shrub or small tree, branches with pink to dark red blossom—cluster at tip. Requires sheltered, humid conditions. 0·96 mmhos/cm (600 ppm)
Jacaranda spp fern tree (Bignoniaceae) D or Semi-E	Open irregular head; fern-like leaves; clusters of lavender blue white or pink bell-shaped blossoms. 2·4 mmhos/cm (1 500 ppm) with leaching
Melia azedarach Indian lilac (Meliaceae) D	Serrated pinnate leaflets; giant clusters of fragrant, pale pink or lilac blossoms; round yellow poisonous berries. 12 m. 11 mmhos/cm (7 000 ppm)
Schinus molle pepper tree also *S. terebinthifolius* (Anacardiaceae) E	Heavy limbs, light branches droop gracefully; bright green divided leaves; tiny white flowers in drooping clusters; rose coloured berries. Not good near buildings or paving because of litter and surface roots. 7 m. 7 mmhos/cm (4 500 ppm)

c) Species to accentuate axes and avenues

Eucalyptus spp (Myrtaceae) E	Fast growing trees and shrubs of great beauty and variety; attractive functional forms; sometimes grey-blue and pendulous; greedy roots. *E. rostrata* and *E. sargentii* are salt tolerant. 20 m.
Phoenix × *dactylifera* date palm (Palmaceae) E SS	Slow growing; bears fruit at five years; long-lived; variety of uses. 10 000 flowers to each cluster; 141 kilos dates to each tree. Can survive with little water, but less fruit; more shrub-like in arid conditions. EC 35 (25 000 ppm). Other successful palms include *P. canariensis* and *Oreodoxia regia* but these are much less salt tolerant.

c) *Species to accentuate axes and avenues*

Terminalia catappa
   tropical almond
   (Combretaceae)
   D
	Large leathery leaves turn red before fall; horizontal branches spread in circles; edible plum-like fruit; withstands salt spray and sandy soil but needs adequate moisture and humidity. 10–15 m.
	7 mmhos/cm (4 500 ppm)

Washingtonia filifera
   fan palm
   (Palmaceae)
	Fast growth; long stalked leaves open crown; mature leaves bend down forming layers tapering to trunk. 10 m.
	38 mmhos/cm (25 000 ppm)

TABLE 16.4
Shelter belts

a) *Wind tolerant species which allow underplanting with indigenous shrubs*

Acacia spp (Leguminosae)	*See* Table 16.1

Casuarina equisetifolia
   ironwood or she oak
   (Casuarinaceae)
   E
	Long thin drooping stems with tiny leaves tufted like bird's feathers; tiny red flowers; bears cones; fastigiate, superficially similar to a pine; greedy roots will grow waterlogged even in saline water. Good desert tree. 15 m.
	32 mmhos/cm (20 000 ppm)

C. glauca	An attractive blue-grey relative of *C. equisetifolia*. 15 m. 14 mmhos/cm (9 000 ppm)
Eucalyptus spp	*See* Table 16.3.

Parkinsonia aculeata
   (Leguminosae)
   Jerusalem thorn
   D
	Small tree with slender 'fronds'; bright yellow blossoms; useful for re-afforestation in dry soils and as a hedge. 5–7 m.
	14 mmhos/cm (9 000 ppm)

Prosopis spicigera
   (Leguminosae)
   E
	Large tree with long tap root; small bi-pinnate blue-green leaves; slow growing initially. Good desert tree. 10 m.
	7 mmhos/cm (4 500 ppm)

P. juliflora
   mesquite
   (Leguminosae)
   D
	Tree or large shrub; wide spreading diffuse shade; tiny pinnate bright green leaflets; spines; white 'bottlebrush' flowers. Produces much pollen and sometimes induces hay fever. Good for sand binding, high water tables and saline water.
	47 mmhos/cm (30 000 ppm) if propagated from salt tolerant specimens.

Tamarix aphylla
   athel tree
   (Tamaricaceae)
   E
	Fast growth; evergreen appearance from green branchlets; minute leaves; small white-pinkish flowers at ends of branches. Adapted to sea coast and salt spray.
	32 mmhos/cm (20 000 ppm)

Ziziphus spp
   jujube or crown of thorns
   (Rhamnaceae)
   E
	Spatulate bright green leaves, spines; small yellow flowers in clusters; round cherry-like edible fruits; deep rooted. Adapts well to desert conditions. *Z. jujube* has larger fruit, leaves and form than *Z. spina christi*. 8–10 m.
	14 mmhos/cm (9 000 ppm) only in sheltered conditions.

b) Less extreme climates where Mediterranean maquis vegetation is established in the wild. These species can withstand temperatures near to 0°C but are rarely tolerant of salinities more than 1 mmhos/cm

Arbutus unedo strawberry tree (Ericaceae) E	Slow to moderate growth. Rich red-brown bark and branches; dark green, red stemmed leaves; clusters of white flowers; red or yellow fruit. Susceptible to aphids. Tolerates wide variety of soils, especially calcareous.
Ceratonia siliqua carob (*Leguminosae*) E	Small spreading tree; domed crown; wavy, leathery leaves; nutritious pods; invasive roots. 8 m.
Cupressus arizonica Arizona cypress (*Cupressacae*) E	Pyramidal form, glaucous foliage. 8–10 m.
Olea europa olive (*Oleacae*) E	Small tree; grey green lanceolate leaves; non-productive in very hot areas; very long lived. 6 m.
Pistacia lentiscus lentisk (Anacardiaceae) D or Semi-E	4·7 mmhos/cm (3 000 ppm) only if temperatures do not rise above 30°C for long periods. Divided leaves; good tree for autumn colour; females bear fruit if males nearby. Best for poor sandy, stony lime soils. *P. vera* produces edible pistachio nut; *P. chinensis* colours scarlet in desert. 4·7 mmhos/cm (3 000 ppm)
Pittosporum spp (Pittyosporaceae) E	Shrubs and trees. Mainly attractive for foliage and form; some have fragrant flowers and interesting fruits; susceptible to aphids.
Populus alba (Salicaceae) D	Resistant to salt spray, but high water demand. 10 m. *P. bolleana* is more salt tolerant.
Quercus spp (Fagaceae) D or E	Many varieties; lobed leaves generally typical; acorns, e.g. *Q. calliprinos* (E) *Q. ithaburensis* (D). Slow growing.

TABLE 16.5
Shrubs

a) Will tolerate up to 2 mmhos/cm (1 500 ppm) with leaching techniques

Caesalpinia pulcherrima small poinciana or peacock flower (Leguminosae) Semi-E	Bushy shrub; clear green bi-pinnate leaves; red, orange or yellow showy flowers with protruding stamens. EC 2 (1 500 ppm)
Ficus spp (Moraceae)	Evergreen or deciduous. Interesting large leaves, generally leathery. *F. mysorensis* withstands coastal winds and heat. *F. laurifolia* and *F. nitida* withstand low humidities with some shade.
Hibiscus rosa-sinensis tropical hibiscus (Malvaceae)	Showy trumpet flowers, white, pink to red, or yellow to orange; glossy foliage. 3–4 m. EC 1 (600 ppm) with no leaching.

b) Will survive higher salinities than (a)

Callistemon lanceolata
  bottlebrush
  (Myrtaceae)
	Pendulous, narrow radially arranged leaves; colourful flowers form dense spikes or round clusters, followed by persistent woody capsules. Fast growing; easy to train. 4 m.
	14 mmhos/cm (9 000 ppm)

Nerium oleander
  (Apocynaceae)
  E
	Slender, pointed, dull green leaves. Branches tipped with clusters single or double flowers in varied colours. Poisonous latex affects the eyes. Good roadside shrub. 3–4 m.
	14 mmhos/cm (9 000 ppm)

Punica granatum
  pomegranate
  (Lythraceae)
  Semi-E
	Small tree or large shrub, young shoots red, orange-red tubular flowers and large edible fruits. Needs shelter but tolerant of full sun. In arid conditions are decorative rather than productive.
	11 mmhos/cm (7 000 ppm)

Tecoma stans
  yellow trumpet
  (Bignoniaceae)
	Large tree-like shrub; bright yellow trumpet-shaped clusters of flowers. Tolerates well-drained dry soils in full sun. 3–4 m.
	4·7 mmhos/cm (3 000 ppm)

Thevetia peruviana
  yellow oleander
  (Apocynaceae)
  E
	Small open tree or large shrub; narrow leaves appear wrinkled; fragrant yellow funnel-shaped flowers; short lived, smaller than hibiscus flowers, but continuous. 4–5 m.
	11 mmhos/cm (7 000 ppm)

Vitex agnus-castus
  chaste tree
  (Verbenaceae)
  D
	Broad, spreading habit, multiple trunks; divided fan-shaped grey-green leaves; conspicuous spikes, lavender blue flowers. 4–5 m.
	9·5 mmhos/cm (6 000 ppm)

TABLE 16.6
Hedges

Low hedges can be infilled with annuals to give a parterre effect

Clerpdendrum inerme
  (Verbenaceae)
  E
	Rounded, fresh bright green leaves. Can be clipped. Fragrant white flowers. 2 m.
	12·5 mmhos/cm (8 000 ppm)

Dodonea viscosa
  hop bush
  (Sapindaceae)
  E
	Fast growing. Many upright stems; willow-like bright green leaves. Can be clipped or pruned hard back. Salt tolerant. 3 m.
	11 mmhos/cm (7 000 ppm)

Duranta plumieri
  (Verbenaceae)
  E
	Arching multiple stems; green or variegated oval leaves; tubular violet-blue flowers; orange fruit clusters. Needs pruning after flowering. 1–3 m.
	2·4 mmhos/cm (1 500 ppm)

Ipomoea carnea
  (Convolvulaceae)
  D
	Lobed, heart-shaped leaves; showy funnel or bell-shaped flowers, varied colours, open in morning only.
	2·4 mmhos/cm (1 500 ppm) with leaching.

Lantana camara
  (Verbenaceae)
  D or Semi-E
	Rough dark green leaves; clusters yellow-orange or red flowers, or mixed on same bush; pungent odour especially when in flower. 1–1·5 m.
	Up to 6·2 mmhos/cm (4 000 ppm) with leaching.

Lawsonia alba or *inermis*
  (Henna)
  (Lythraceae)
  D or Semi-E
	Fragrant white flowers, small privet-like leaves. 1–1·5 m.
	Up to 6·2 mmhos/cm (4 000 ppm) with leaching.

TABLE 16.7
Climbers

a) *Easiest species if given protection and high humidity*

Bougainvillea spp (Nyctaginaceae) E	Shrubby climber; vibrant colour from bracts round flowers; dense cover medium sized leaves. *B. glabra* with purple bracts more vigorous and tolerant of sea air than *B. spectabilis*.
Clerodendrum splendens (Verbenaceae) E and D	Dark green leaves, various shapes and sizes; attractive flowers with scarlet calyces. *C. inerme* can be trained as a climber. *C. thomsonae* can be used only in very sheltered conditions.
Jasminum spp (Oleaceae)	Shrubs or climbers. Not always fragrant. Needs frequent attention to control growth. e.g. *J. sambac* is a scandent shrub 2 m high. *J. officinale* is a twining climber, semi-evergreen and fragrant.

b) *Tolerate less extreme conditions and salinities, i.e. less than 2·4 mmhos/cm (1 500 ppm)*

Antigonon leptopus coral creeper (Polygonaceae) Semi-E	Fast growing; requires shade. Open airy foliage; sprays of dark green heart-shaped leaves; trailing trusses of elegant pink flowers, some fragrant. In adverse conditions may need annual re-sowing.
Clitoria ternata butterfly pea (Leguminosae)	Twining climber; pinnate oval leaves; pea-shaped blue flowers.
Luffa cylindrica (= *aegyptiaca*) loofah (Cucurbitaceae)	Rambling climber with large cut leaves, yellow single flowers and cucumber-shaped rattling 'gourd'. Usually annual.
Quisqualis indica Rangoon creeper (Combretaceae) E	Large woody climber; tubular flowers open white and turn light pink to deep red; scented at night; oval fruits. Needs shade.
Tecomaria capensis Cape honeysuckle (Bignoniaceae) E	Climber or shrub. Divided dark green shiny leaves; fine textured; brilliant orange-red tubular clusters blossom.

TABLE 16.8
Groundcover
This is not so widely used as in less harsh climates because of water shortage.

a) *Tough low water-demanding, creeping species*

Euphorbia spp (Euphorbiaceae) E	Shrubs, sub-shrubs, perennials, biennials, annuals and succulents. Inconspicuous flowers in coloured bracts. Milky sap can be poisonous or an irritant.
Ipomoea pes-caprae (Convolvulaceae) E	Large glossy, dark green leaves shaped like camel's foot. Tubular flowers in white and pink. Fast growing. Can be trained as a climber. Very tough but needs humidity.
Mesembryanthemum and *Lampranthus* spp ice plant (Aizoaceae) E	Succulent perennials, sub-shrubs or annuals. Many varieties. Good for soil erosion control and vivid colour effects. Thrive in wide variety of soils; sun-loving. *L. roseus* good groundcover with fleshy green leaves and white flowers.
Sempervivum spp (Crassulaceae) E	Perennial succulents; tight rosettes of leaves; small white to pink star-shaped flowers.

b) Plants with strong character for punctuation and silhouettes

Aloë spp (Liliaceae)	Succulents; clumps fleshy pointed leaves and branched or unbranched clusters orange-red or yellow flowers. Miniature to tree size.
Yucca spp (Agavaceae) E	Evergreen perennial shrubs. Clusters tough sword-shaped leaves and clusters white flowers. Miniature to tree size.

c) Plants useful where irrigation water more plentiful

Cynodon dactylon hybrids (Gramineae) Bermuda grass	Grow from seeds or stolons. Most tolerant species for arid saline conditions and coastal areas. Salt tolerant hybrids available.
Portulaca spp (Portulacaceae)	Spreading plant; multicoloured flowers appear continuously. Annuals and perennials. Wild species are suitable for problem areas but require irrigation.

d) Plants for cooler arid climates, requiring some shade

Jacquemontia pentantha (Convolvulaceae)	Small dense foliage; delicate lilac blue flowers.
Lippia nodiflora (Verbenaceae)	Herb used as grass substitute. Roots at nodes; minute pink flowers. No mowing required.

TABLE 16.9
Plants for colour

Begonia spp	Perennials. Hundreds of species and varieties. Tend to scorch in very dry conditions.
Canna spp	Tuberous root stock. Large green-brown-red leaves similar to banana. Flowers bloom on stalks; various colours, sizes and shapes. Group same colours against plain background; border, pool and pots. Some fragrant. Better in higher humidities but attract mosquitoes.
Coleus	Perennial; brilliantly multi-coloured leaves.
Gazania	Perennial; very bright coloured daisy-like flowers. Evergreen leaves. Form clumps; trailing species with silver grey leaves and yellow flowers.
Helianthus	Annuals and perennials. Coarse, tough and sturdy; bold flowers.
Kochia	Foliage plants, like fine textured coniferous shrubs; feather-like bright green leaves. Can be shaped.
Petunia	Perennial grown as annual. Autumn planting in desert areas; fragrant funnel-shaped flowers, many colours.
Tagetes marigold	Annuals; easily grown; yellow-gold-orange flowers; some varieties have odour.
Tropaeolum nasturtium	Perennial grown as annual. Dwarf species or trailers; round bright green leaves; red-orange-yellow flowers.
Verbena	Perennial herb; scented flowers and leaves; usually pink or blue flowers.
Vinca or *Lochinera rosea* Madagascar periwinkle	Perennial grown as annual. Summer-autumn colour in hot climates; bushing erect plant; glossy leaves; white-pink flowers. For massing in beds; persistent flowering.
Zinnia	Round flower heads; many bright colours.

Colour displays

The red 'flame' *Delonix* and showy *Cassia* flowers will strongly highlight duller background plants, whilst blue *Jacaranda* flowers offer more subtle tones, particularly if underplanted with glossy greens and white flowers e.g. *Clerodendrum* or silvery *Cineraria maritima* in milder areas. The clear fresh green of *Clerodendrum* and *Dodonea* hedges contrast strongly with the white-washed walls so often seen in arid countries. Walls and archways are often covered in *Bougainvillea* and fragrant climbers with bright green plants and annuals at their bases. Annuals are used to make patterns and breathtaking colour displays and are at their best in the cooler periods.

Caesalpinia, yellow *Tecoma stans*, and all shades of *Hibiscus* and *Nerium oleander* highlight the middle layers, contrasting in leaf colour and texture. Annuals may be grown in pots and containers for rapid colour changes.

Table 16.9 lists some of the most common annuals for colour displays. Water should be less than 1 000 ppm.

Fruit

Plants commonly grown for their fruit include dates (*Phoenix dactylifera*), citrus species; figs (*Ficus carica*); pawpaws (*Carica papaya*); mangoes (*Mangifera indica*); banana (*Musa* spp); pomegranates (*Punica granatum*); mulberries (*Morus alba*); guavas (*Psidium guajava*). All require regular irrigation with low salinity water. The coconut palm (*Cocos nucifera*) thrives best in monsoon areas. Pistachio nuts (*Pistacia vera*); olives (*Olea europaea*) and carobs (*Ceratonia siliqua*) can be grown in less extreme conditions.

Fragrance

In addition to fragrant plants already mentioned in the plant lists clerodendrum have fragrant summer flowers as do *Nicotiana* some of which open at night. In easier conditions, *Agapanthus*, *Stephanotis*, lavender (*Lavandula*) and rosemary (*Rosmarinus officinalis*) may be grown. *Millingtonia hortensis*, the jasmine tree, is also highly scented but somewhat stunted in arid conditions (e.g. 6 m–20 ft) and not salt tolerant.

FURTHER READING

Adams, R. 'Technical Considerations of Salinity in Hot Territories' *ILA Journal*, May 1976

Blatter, E. and Millard, W. S. *Some beautiful Indian trees* (London: John Bale and Curnow 1937, 2nd ed. 1954 Bombay)

Bor, N. L. and Raizada. *Some beautiful Indian climbers and shrubs* (Bombay: Natural History Soc., 1954)

Broun, A. F. and Massey, R. E. *Flora of the Sudan* (Sudan Govt. Office, London: 1929)

Cowen, D. V. (Mrs. Gardiner-Lewis) *Flowering trees and shrubs in India* (Bombay: 1950, 4th ed. Bombay 1965)

Gubb, Alfred S. *La flore Saharienne* and *La flore Algerienne* (Alger: 1913)

Palmer, E. and Pitman, N. *The trees of South Africa* (Cape Town: AA. Balkema, 1961)

Palmer, E. and Pitman, N. *The trees of Southern Africa* 3 vols. (Balkema: 1972)

Post, G. E. *Flora of Syria, Palestine and Sinai* (Beirut: American Press 1932) American University of Beirut National Science Series No. 1. 2nd ed. 2 vols.

Rechinger, K. H. *Flora Iranica* (Akademische Druck und Verlagsanstalt, P.O. Box 598, A8010 Graz. 1963 onwards)

Russell, E. W. *Soil Conditions and Plant Growth* 9th ed. (London: Longmans, Green 1961)

Stamp, L. Dudley. *Asia* (London: Methuen, 1967)
Flora of Iraq. Iraq Min. of Agric. Several Volumes:
Guest, E. and Ali Al-Rawi, 1966, Vol. 1
Townsend, C. C. and Guest, E. 1966, Vol 2
Bor, N. L. with Ali-Rawi (ed. Townsend, C. C. and Guest, E.) Baghdad, 1968, Vol. 9
Townsend, C. C. and Guest, E., Baghdad, 1974, Vol. 3

USDA. *Soil Survey Manual*. Soil Classification and supplement. (Washington: 1957)

REFERENCES

1. Hills, E. S. *Arid Lands: A Geographical Appraisal* (London: Methuen & Co. Ltd. 1966. Reprint 1969)
2. Ibid. pp. 41–6
3. Ibid.

PLATE 16.16 **Detail of the same tree showing fine texture of tiny leaves and spiny branches.** *(Maurice Lee)*

PLATE 16.17 *Tecoma stans* **in flower. Cairo.**
(Maurice Lee)

PLATE 16.18 *Nerium oleander* **bush in flower. AlAin Hilton, Abu Dhabi** *(Gordon Bell)*

PLATE 16.19 **Detail of same bush showing flower.** *(Gordon Bell)*

PLATE 16.20 *Duranta plumieri* **(variegata) hedge in Cairo.** *(Maurice Lee)*

PLATE 16.21 *Lawsonia inermis* **hedge. Jeddah.** *(Maurice Lee)*

PLATE 16.22 *Quisqualis indica* **in flower. Jeddah.** *(Maurice Lee)*

PLATE 16.23 *Ipomoea pes-caprae* **in flower, as a groundcover. Jeddah.** *(Maurice Lee)*

PLATE 16.24 **The same plant makes a good climber or trailer. Jeddah.** *(Maurice Lee)*

PLATE 16.25 *Lochinera (Vinca) rosea.* **Al Ain Hilton, Abu Dhabi.** *(Gordon Bell)*

PLATE 16.27 **Banana plant, Salalah, Oman. Other species of** *Musa* **can add interest to a design with their distinctive large leaves.** *(Gordon Bell)*

PLATE 16.26 **Detail of** *Carica papaya* **showing paw-paw fruits and silhouetted leaves.** *(Gordon Bell)*

CHAPTER 17

Landscape Management and the Fourth Design Dimension

RALPH COBHAM

17.1 INTRODUCTION

Plants, when grown both as individual specimens and particularly in communities, require time in which to display their many virtues—like all living things which we value. Happily maturity cannot be designed or commanded at an instant. It comes with time and only then if the plants have received the right type of treatment, which can range from intensive care even to conscious neglect.

Of all the dimensions with which the landscape designer has to contend, time—the fourth dimension—invariably poses the greatest problems. Achievement of the visual effects ultimately desired is dependent upon so many factors which are beyond the designer's complete control at either the drawing board or initial contract stages of a landscape scheme.

It is significant that the preceding chapters all make reference, if not specifically at least by implication, to the importance of considering management and maintenance when designing and implementing landscape schemes. This is just as it should be. Without the involvement and sensitive support of these two activities, the efforts and money expended in the initial design and implementation works may not come to fruition. It is with the help of management and maintenance skills that the evolution of the physical and aesthetic effects intended by designer and desired by the client can be achieved. These skills need to be applied as much in the broad rural landscape as in the intimate scale of a new town or refurbished housing estate.

The landscape management and maintenance examples mentioned in this chapter are almost exclusively from British scenes. However, the principles described are thought to be relevant for readers in other regions of the world, America and Europe particularly.

In financial terms, management and maintenance usually involve relatively small annual outlays when compared with the capital expended at the outset, this annual figure amounting to between 5% and 15% of the initial total. Such a seemingly insignificant figure may explain why in the past the two activities have either been overlooked or received inadequate attention. Yet when reviewed over the lifetime of a changed landscape, the annual management and maintenance costs will probably far exceed those of the initial works.

The broad components of a landscape design or plan vary widely in terms of capital and annual costs. Water bodies, whilst being expensive to install, normally require relatively little annual maintenance (£25–£100 ($43–$173)) in comparison with amenity woodland/meadowland (£50–£400 ($ 86–$692)) and highly manicured urban scenery (£1000–£4000 ($1730–$6920) (Figures correct at time of going to press.) In the case of some of the more prestigious schemes, the cumulative annual costs may soon outweigh the capital outlay.

Thus the design process calls not only for artistry in balancing physical and aesthetic considerations, but also in matching financial requirements and resources over the lifetime of the landscape scheme.

17.2 PROFESSIONAL ROLES

The report of the Landscape Management Discussion Group[1] set up to advise the ILA on the possible future role of the landscape manager in relation to the whole landscape profession included the following definition:

'*Landscape Management* is a task undertaken by professionals to ensure that the objectives of the landscape designer are achieved on the ground in such a way that the landscape evolves and matures over time to the satisfaction of both designer and user. Management concerns the establishment and development of physically and visually acceptable relationships between the land and its living communities.'

Landscape maintenance, which differs from management in both extent and degree, was defined thus:

'*Landscape Maintenance* concerns the routine care of land, vegetation and hard surfaces in the manner prescribed for their satisfactory establishment and continued future performance.'

For landscape design to succeed it is essential that a number of professions should work together as a team. The activities of the landscape designer, the earth and social scientists, the landscape manager and the maintenance officer need to be closely related until landscape schemes are well on the way to maturity. With the decision of the Institute of Landscape Architects to expands its role, and thereby encourage more professional co-operation, there is greater scope for achieving better solutions to the landscaping problems of our changing society.

The remainder of the chapter is devoted to
i) describing the different skills which are required for the landscape management profession to be effective;
ii) outlining some of the ways in which this profession can help the designer;
iii) mentioning a few of the many unresolved problems faced by members of the landscape profession collectively.

TABLE 17.1

Structure of the professional team during different phases of a large landscape scheme*

	Site Appraisal & Resource Surveys	Initial Feasibility Study	Planning & Design Sketch Detailed	Preparation of Specification and B.o.Q.	Tendering	Contract	Establishment Maintenance Maturity ←Monitoring→
Land Scientist							
Landscape Planner							
Landscape Architect							
Engineer							
Quantity Surveyor							
Landscape Manager							
Landscape Maintenance Officer							
Landscape Clerk of Works							

Approximate Relative Time Scale ←——————— x years ———————→ At least (10–20)x yrs.

* In practice the structure is usually not so clear cut as the Table indicates.

Key:
——————— period of close and regular involvement
– – – – – – period of observation and possibly occasional involvement

PLATE 17.1 **At New Ash Green the village is being constructed in an area of classic Kent countryside.** *(Ralph Cobham)*

17.3 PROFESSIONAL SKILLS AND STRUCTURE

In the report of the Landscape Management Discussion Group, landscape management was described as a many-faceted profession, founded on various disciplines including

'Horticulture, Agriculture, Ecology, Estate Management, Design, Surveying, Planning, Economics, Sociology, Administration . . .'

in short, a 'vascular bundle' of skills. It was stressed that to be successful, those practising the profession should have considerable knowledge in at least one of the above disciplines together with a sound appreciation of many more—particularly ecology.

This profession is the concern of *three* groups of experienced people: the landscape clerk of works, maintenance officer and manager.

The main responsibility of the *landscape clerk of works* is for the correct short-term implementation of landscape designs and management plans. This calls for careful supervision to ensure that the landscape is treated and changed in strict accordance with the standards specified. Success depends on many practical skills, in particular horticulture and construction.

The chief concern of the *maintenance officer* centres on the development of landscapes according to the plans and standards agreed for one or more years. The key activity involves assisting with the preparation of annual landscape maintenance plans, followed by taking responsibility for their execution. One of the most important skills in the execution of these plans is the ability to deploy scarce manpower, materials, machinery and financial resources between the needs of several types of landscape in such a way as best achieves the desired objectives. The relative economics of different maintenance methods and landscape treatments call for detailed attention by the landscape maintenance officer.

The *landscape manager* has a wide ranging responsibility for helping designers, planners and the members of several other professions and their clients to achieve the objectives which are agreed to be in the best *long-term* interests of the landscape and its users. 'Thus it is to be expected that the concern of professional landscape managers for the landscape will be wider than that of most farmers, estate managers, foresters, recreation managers . . .'

Table 17.1 attempts, in a simplified form, to indicate the types and sequence of involvement which are required from these three skills in the creation and evolution of new landscapes.

PLATE 17.2 **Woodland fringes are vulnerable to pressures from the new residents, many of whom have come from urban areas.** *(Ralph Cobham)*

17.4 MANAGEMENT PROBLEMS

The most important situations which call for the services of the landscape manager and maintenance officer are those where existing or potential conflicts are greatest, namely:

i) between the land users and the landscape;
ii) between the plants to be established and their immediate environment.

Whilst there are usually no easy answers to these problems, at least a number of options frequently exist for their solution. The first type of conflict occurs in at least three forms, brief descriptions of which follow with examples.

17.41 Changed land uses in the existing landscape

The major conflicts tend to occur where a radical change of use is proposed for a traditional and relatively undisturbed landscape. This is the case where new settlements are being built in the countryside.[2] Milton Keynes New Town[3,4,5] and New Ash Green 'Village'[6,7] are two such examples. The first, designated in 1967, is, despite the most carefully laid plans, making a considerable impact on the surrounding farmland. At New Ash

Green the village is being constructed in an area of classic Kent countryside, consisting of chalk predominantly overlain by clay-with-flints and thin layers of sand or brickearth. Its vegetation is a mixture of semi-mature deciduous woodland including neglected hazel coppice, herb-rich permanent pasture and arable land. All of this, despite the best intentions and plans of the parties involved, is vulnerable to an influx of primarily urban residents. Local participation in the upkeep of both the internal village areas and the surrounding landscapes is often the key to integration in such situations. At New Ash Green this is being fostered by a far-sighted group of residents, with the support of the progressive developer, the local authority, and the help of a number of management plans which have identified the objectives, resources and operations required. The action taken to date is most encouraging.

17.42 Conflicts through increases in existing land uses

There are many areas of the countryside where recreational pressures, aggravated by weathering, have increased to such an extent that they threaten the very resources to which the visitors are attracted. Amongst the best known examples are the sites chosen by the Countryside Commission for conducting Experimental Restoration Projects, namely: Tarn Hows,[8] Kynance Cove, Box Hill, Snowdonia,[9] and Ilkley Moor.[10] The landscape manager has much to contribute in such places where the pressures of cars and feet, together with the accumulation of litter, combine to cause physical and visual deterioration on an unprecedented scale. The type of help which he can provide includes:

i)   identifying the areas which are most vulnerable to use by visitors, and conversely those which are resilient;

ii) advising on the alternative strategies for solving the problems, ranging from the dispersal of visitors and their cars over a wider area, to their concentration in carefully selected sites equipped with litter collection and toilet facilities. By establishing a well-marked network of footpaths, and alternative transport systems, such as guided mini-bus and cycle services radiating from these chosen sites, the visitor pressures on the surrounding countryside can be contained;

iii) specifying the restoration techniques which are likely to be most successful along footpaths, in car parks and picnic areas;

iv) setting up the most effective system for managing and monitoring the areas both during and after restoration. Such systems may involve at least one or more of the following: the establishment of a Management Committee, the appointment of Countryside Wardens, the use of local volunteers such as the County Durham Countryside Rangers, and the preparation of management and access agreements.

PLATES 17.3 & 17.4 **The landscape manager has much to contribute to Ilkley Moor where the pressures of cars and feet combine to cause physical and visual deterioration.** *(Ken Curry)*

FIGURE 17.1 'Hey, where's the ref . . . the Landscape Manager, don't you mean?' *(Brian Iley)*

17.43 Conflicts arising through the numbers of users and incompatible activities

Increasingly situations are reported where there is competition between different interest groups for the same piece of land or the same resource. Conflicts are commonplace between:

i) the ardent conservationists and those seeking re-creation, particularly the flower pickers (including the amateur botanist!);

ii) casual walkers and horse riders;

iii) anglers and birdwatchers, on all but large water areas;

iv) water skiers and other water-based sportsmen.

Methods of management such as the spatial zoning, rationing or rotation of uses can help in some situations. Similarly charging a fee for the use of facilities can be a moderating influence. Nevertheless, it has to be recognized that there are some uses which are totally incompatible as far as the respective parties are concerned.

17.44 Plant-environment conflicts

These conflicts are amongst those most commonly faced by landscape managers and maintenance officers. Climate and site conditions, particularly in exposed coastal situations (as at Teesmouth), often militate against the establishment and development of a successful vegetation cover. Experience, both in N.E. England and on the Dutch coast, has shown that the effects of an adverse climate—particularly prolonged drought in spring, due to a combination of low rainfall and persistently strong winds—can to a large extent be mitigated. The pursuit of carefully conceived management and after-care operations ranks high in achieving success, along with important and closely related design features, such as:

i) the wise choice of locally indigenous nurse and quick cover plant species;

ii) the use of small stock, densely planted in large areas, which following selective thinning can be inter-planted with long-lived species;

iii) the use of protective ground contouring;

305

Development of new industrial landscapes; Europort, Holland. The results of co-operation between industrial developers, landscape designers, contractors and managers in coming to terms with alien conditions.

PLATE 17.5 **Land just reclaimed from the sea.** *(Richard Cass)*

PLATE 17.6 **Planting and subsequent establishment treatments commence within eighteen months.** *(Richard Cass)*

PLATE 17.7 **With proper maintenance an effective and attractive screen is created within eight years.** *(Richard Cass)*

iv) the execution of planting operations earlier rather than later in the planting season.

Whilst the techniques of establishing and maintaining vegetation on reclamation sites are well documented, success is by no means automatic. New problems continually arise. One example is that being encountered on the site designated for the creation of a beach park on the coast of Irvine New Town in Scotland.[11,12] There, a diverse and interesting but vulnerable flora (including vipers bugloss (*Echium vulgare*), dwarf willow (*Salix repens*), sheeps bit (*Jasione montana*), wild thyme (*Thymus serpyllum*), white flax (*Linum cartharticum*)) has colonized the site, the greater part of which was until recently used for the tipping of chemical factory waste. Whilst the vegetation is undoubtedly of educational value and a recreational asset in the area, it is not robust enough to withstand the public pressures normally associated with a beach park. The problem is to reconcile the desire to retain as much floristic interest as possible, both during and following the reclamation process, with the required function of the area. It is recognized that ultimately the vegetation may become increasingly difficult to maintain on account of public pressure and a gradual build-up of soil nutrients.

17.45 The re-establishment of semi-natural habitats

In recent years all categories of the country's rich and highly valued semi-natural wildlife habitats have come under increasing development pressure from a number of activities, such as reclamation for industrial use and drainage for more productive agriculture. Those categories subjected to greatest attack are the estuarine (e.g. Teesmouth[13] and Merseyside), coastal and inland freshwater habitats. In the circumstances it is natural that landscape managers should be involved in assisting other professions, notably ecologists and naturalists, to devise conservation and management measures which are most appropriate for the residual habitat areas. Their contribution is even more important when opportunities arise for creating conditions in new locations suitable for re-establishing as closely as possible the habitats which are under threat or have been lost. For many complex reasons, complete simulation is usually not possible. It is often for these very same reasons that the establishment and subsequent management of such areas undoubtedly presents the greatest challenge to the professional skills of all the parties involved.

A challenge of this type also exists at Irvine, which although in certain respects not unprecedented, is probably unique in degree. A substantial area of sand dunes has been lost due to over-greedy sand-winning operations, further aggravated by strong on-shore winds. Now there exists the problem of trying to re-establish a dune system within a time-scale which may preclude sole reliance on probably the cheapest and in the long term most effective method—namely, the man-aided process of sand accumulation using chestnut paling fences followed by the planting of sea lyme and marram grass setts. It may unfortunately prove necessary to by-pass the semi-natural and inevitably slow processes by fixing appropriately graded and uncontaminated sand, transported from inland areas of the site. As with an increasing number of problems, it becomes necessary to undertake on-site trials to evaluate which of the possible overall solutions and detailed establishment prescriptions are likely to be most successful, before proceeding with full scale operations. The trials at Irvine are proving helpful in directing attention to the type of compromise solution which is most likely to succeed. This is a typical example of a situation where the land scientist, landscape architect and manager can benefit from close co-operation.

17.5 SOME OF THE MANAGEMENT AIDS

The range of 'tools' at the disposal of the landscape manager and maintenance officer for coming to terms with these and other problems is continually being increased. They fall broadly into four categories.

17.51 Technical aids

There are growing numbers of agricultural, forestry and horticultural aids, such as slow release fertilizers, selective herbicides and precision machinery, which make many maintenance operations much simpler than hitherto. As the number of landscaped areas grows and the shortages of skilled men persist, such aids have an increasingly important role to play, just so long as they are used judiciously.

17.52 Recreation management aids

The provision of facilities such as interpretive centres, nature trails and long distance walks enable large numbers of people to be attracted into areas specially designed and managed for their enjoyment. As a result other places less able to withstand public pressure come to be both better respected and protected. Carefully designed waymarks and explanatory notice boards, appropriately located, are essential in helping people to enjoy popular parts of the countryside in ways which are in the long-term interests of all parties. With such aids, worn footpaths and grassy areas can be rested, often using nothing more elaborate than a single strand of nylon string. Excellent examples include the National Trust's work at Tarn Hows in the Lake District and that of Hampshire County Council at Danebury Hill Fort.

Use of these and other aids is particularly helpful to the landscape manager where an area of land is required to accommodate multi-purpose activities, such as farming, forestry, recreation, sporting and conservation. Grizedale Forest, the Beaulieu and Goodwood estates, and the

PLATE 17.8 **A woodland character and some feeling of maturity has developed after twenty years.** *(Richard Cass)*

PLATE 17.9 **Dune re-establishment trials being undertaken at Irvine. (***See also*** Plates 17.10 and 17.11.)** *(Ralph Cobham)*

PLATE 17.10 **The use of brushwood and chestnut paling fences to trap wind-borne sand.** *(Ralph Cobham)*

PLATE 17.11 **The planting of sea lyme and marram grass setts to stabilize accumulated sand.** *(Ralph Cobham)*

PLATE 17.12 **Yarner Wood National Nature Reserve.** *(Ralph Cobham)*

PLATE 17.13 **At the approach to Danebury Hill fort.** *(Ralph Cobham)*

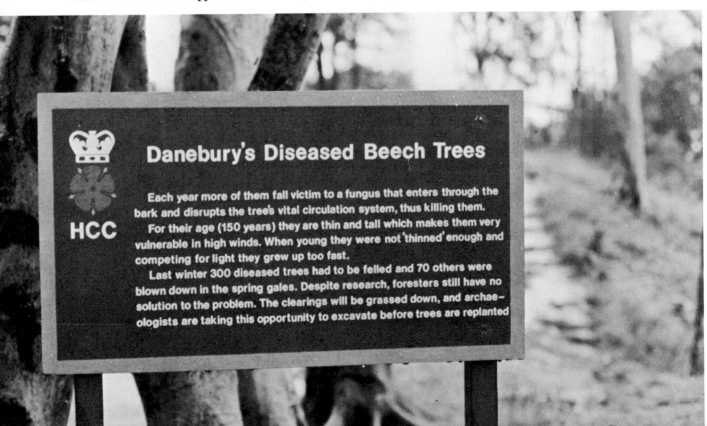

Danebury's Diseased Beech Trees

Each year more of them fall victim to a fungus that enters through the bark and disrupts the tree's vital circulation system, thus killing them.
For their age (150 years) they are thin and tall which makes them very vulnerable in high winds. When young they were not 'thinned' enough and competing for light they grew up too fast.
Last winter 300 diseased trees had to be felled and 70 others were blown down in the spring gales. Despite research, foresters still have no solution to the problem. The clearings will be grassed down, and archae-ologists are taking this opportunity to excavate before trees are replanted

HCC

PLATE 17.14 **Experimental work undertaken by the National Trust at Tarn Hows to restore worn footpaths with the aid of a single strand of nylon string.** *(Ralph Cobham)*

Kennermerduinen[14] and Veluwe National Parks in Holland are amongst the places where they can be seen to good advantage.

17.53 Plant selection and other design aids

The way in which a landscape scheme is designed at the outset can do much to influence the subsequent management task. Plants themselves provide some of the most effective aids to management. Such is the wealth of plant material available that the landscape designer and manager are often faced with the difficult task of selecting those species which it is most appropriate to plant for meeting such needs as the provision of either low cost groundcover or an effective prickly barrier against people and livestock (*see* Table 17.2). Both the species chosen and the variation in the height to which grass is allowed to grow are further well established techniques by which managers can save costs and persuade people to walk along certain routes.

The use of the ha-ha was and still is a classic example of the way in which design of simple differences in ground level can aid the management task.

17.54 Financial aids

Finally there are many financial aids upon which management can call. The assessment of external sources of finance available for assisting the establishment and after-care of multi-purpose use and landscaping schemes is a main responsibility of the landscape manager. These sources include:

i) the sizeable D.o.E. grants for reclamation sites covering the establishment phase of both grass areas (3 years, normally only in situations where less than

TABLE 17.2
Plants as management aids

Some of the main species best suited for either individual or mixed use as barriers which are difficult to penetrate

	Deciduous (D) or Evergreen (E)	Appropriate for Rural (R) &/or Urban (U) Sites	Best Time for Trimming	General Comments
Berberis darwinii	E	U	May/June	Prickly. Normally used in semi-formal situations.
Berberis stenophylla	E	U		
Carpinus betulus	D	R & U	July/Sept	Does well on heavier soils and withstands shade.
Corylus avellana	D	R & U	Sept/Oct	Good for chalk and dry situations.
Crataegus monogyna	D	R & U	Late summer	Prickly. Grows well in most soils and situations. Suitable for windy conditions.
Crataegus oxyacantha	D	R & U		
Fagus sylvatica	D	R & U	Mid-summer	Does best on soils with pH higher than neutral. Suitable for windy conditions.
Hippophae rhamnoides	D	R & U	After flowering	Prickly. Salt tolerant. Think twice before planting because of its very vigorous growth.
Ilex aquifolium	E	R & U	Late summer	Prickly. Can be slow to establish, but succeeds better than many species in shade.
Ligustrum ovalifolium	E	U primarily	Sept	Quick growing and withstands pollution.
Lonicera nitida	E	U primarily	Sept	Quick growing. Normally used in formal situations.
Mahonia aquifolium	E	U primarily	After flowering	Prickly points to the leaves. Normally used in informal situations.
Prunus cerasifera	D	R & U	July	Slightly thorny. Grows quickly.
Prunus spinosa	D	R & U	Late summer	Prickly. Particularly suitable for coastal and windy conditions.
Pseudosasa japonica	E	U	Early spring if required	Prone to damage by firing.
Pyracantha angustifolia	E	U primarily	May/July	Prickly and very hardy.
Rosa canina	D	R	After fruiting	Prickly.
Rosa rugosa	D	R & U		Prickly. In urban areas used informally.
Rubus fruticosa	D	R	After fruiting	Prickly and vigorous.
Sambucus nigra	D	R & U	Early spring	Grows very quickly. Suitable for windy conditions.
Taxus baccata	E	R & U	Aug/Sept	Tolerates shade.
Ulex europaeus	E	R	After flowering	Prickly. Suitable for coastal and windy conditions, also for dry sandy soils. Prone to damage by firing.

10 cm (4 in.) of top soil have been used) and tree planted areas (5 years, amounting to a total equal to the value of the original contract sum);

ii) the Forestry Planting grants which are now weighted significantly towards amenity considerations;

iii) the Countryside Commission grants available to assist local authorities with tree planting and landowners entering into access or management agreements;

iv) the grants available from charitable organizations, such as the Carnegie Trust, for the establishment and management of educational and interpretative facilities;

v) the aid given by such organizations as the Tourist Board and Sports Council.

17.6 PLANS AND SCHEDULES

It may seem that the responsibilities and contributions of the landscape manager are varied and diffuse. Yet there is usually a unifying or co-ordinating element. As with the solicitor and his deeds, or the accountant and his balance sheet, the landscape manager and maintenance officer are required to prepare formal documents involving disciplined thought and calculation. For any major landscaping

TABLE 17.3
Features of a management plan
A summary of the management task for a London borough new housing development area

The Main Landscape Maintenance Areas	Levels of Council Financed Maintenance Recommended/Required	Assumed/ Estimated Components (hectares)	Dimensions Total (hectares)
1. GRASS			
Very High Maintenance Areas	3–7 cuts per week during the season of use	0·15	
High Maintenance Areas	18 cuts per season	2·87	
Intermediate Maintenance Areas	7–11 cuts per season	8·30	
Low Maintenance Areas	4–6 cuts per season	4·56	
Very Low Maintenance Areas	1–2 cuts per season	10·47	
TOTAL: GRASS			26·35
2. TOTAL: HARD SURFACES	Daily/frequent attention	1·03	1·03
3. FORMAL PLANTING			
Shrub Areas	Low—intermediate levels of maintenance,	2·13	
Tree Areas	but high standards	1·89	
TOTAL: FORMAL PLANTING			4·02
4. TOTAL: INFORMAL TREE AND SHRUB PLANTING	Initially high levels of maintenance, but low thereafter	9·14	9·14
5. TOTAL: LAKE	Intermediate level	0·42	0·42
6. OTHER			
Maintenance Area: Depot & Nursery	High level	0·18	
Allotments	High level	0·40	
Hedges	Low level	0·24	
School Garden: Cultivation Area	High level during the holidays	0·07	
TOTAL: OTHER			0·89
GRAND TOTAL			41·85

project these documents consist of the overall management plan and its essential companion, the short-term establishment or maintenance schedule. Tables 17.3, 17.4, 17.5 and 17.6 indicate some of the main features typical of these documents, though naturally the format and contents will differ according to the particular management problems concerned.

Such documents provide a basic reference for regular use by the managers, maintenance officers and designers concerned with the continuing evolution of new landscapes. Preparation of these documents often means enlisting the help of an amalgam of skills including those of the ecologist, agricultural and horticultural specialists, ornithologists etc.

The management plan usually commences with a statement of general aims and objectives, followed by a description of the levels and standards of maintenance which are desired for each of the main landscape areas. It is normal for there to be a review of the possible strategies whereby the objectives can be achieved. This involves an evaluation of:
i) which maintenance operations should best be undertaken by direct, contract or voluntary labour;
ii) whether machinery is best purchased, hired or

313

TABLE 17.4
Features of a management plan
Broad use and management recommendations for some main areas at New Ash Green

Main Land Areas	Use	Level of Maintenance/Action to be taken (H = High; M = Medium; L = Low)
Existing Woodland Nine Horse Wood	Walking; riding; visual amenity; adventure areas for children; (pillaging and dumping ground for residents as development proceeds and children grow up, unless careful).	H in accessible areas, M in protected areas where coppice being converted to standards. Woodland fringes allowed to grow wild and form impenetrable barrier. During development, high level of care for trees to be retained.
Redhill and Bowes Woods	Buffer framework/visual screen for housing developments; walking; tree-house style play areas; picnicking by adjacent residents; (motorized litter dump for residents, unless careful).	H wherever access is free. In all woods consideration should be given to the scope for zoning and rotating active and non-use areas. Protection of newly planted areas and fringes. Access points and routes to be well defined.
Bazes Shaw Wood	Nature reserve and nature trail/study area for use by local naturalist society and by children attending nearby school as an outdoor laboratory.	Management based on *conservation* practices and geared to the demonstration of ecological principles of vegetational succession, etc. Work by naturalist society and school volunteers. Protection from residents moving to and from meadow essential: access points to the wood should be counter to popular demand.
New Woodland Redhill and Bowes Woods	As above	Protection until established. H in any areas which are subsequently accessible.
Western and Northern Belts	Wind break; visual screen/framework for future neighbourhoods.	L, after initial three years 'beating up' and weed control.
Tree, Shrubs and Grass Buffer Zones between Housing Areas	Increasing demand for informal 'let-off steam' play areas. The 'thread of Kent countryside . . .'	L, apart from twice annual tree survey and occasional grass cutting. Once trees established, grass within the drifts might be mown 2–3 times annually. Alternatively it can be left unmown.
Grassland Cricket Square	Progressively increased match use as good sward and surface becomes established.	Relatively H to provide for enjoyable village class matches.
Outfield/soccer playing field	Increasing use for sports as population grows and good sward is established. (Planting of tree groups and gentle earth contouring will give sense of enclosures.)	M, apart from *high* level of care in the case of worn areas, e.g. goal mouths; rotational siting of pitches and goal areas.

Main Land Areas	Use	Level of Maintenance/Action to be taken (H = High; M = Medium; L = Low)
Outer sports ground area	Area for tree screen planting and scout camping. Fair/gymkhana/bonfire ground.	L.
The Minnis	Increasing use as the village green once reasonable sward and a more inviting character are established.	M.
Nine Horse Meadow	Parkland for picnicking and walking.	L, involving removal of grass mowings to increase botanical variety and interest of the sward.
Apple Orchard	Apple trees retained but thinned to provide an attractive picnicking/playing area for local residents.	L.
Woodland grass fringes and rides	Walking, riding and nature study.	L, involving a twice yearly mowing of *narrow* strip alongside paths.
Hedges	Increasing importance as visual screens and physical barriers.	H where gapping up or replanting required; H where sight lines involved and adjacent to houses. Other hedges require L or M according to whether or not they are in wilderness areas.
Neighbourhood units—communal space	An increasing range of active and passive uses as the population grows and its structure diversifies.	Generally H throughout.
Prestige areas such as the Manor House, car parks and shopping centre		Generally H throughout.

Source: *New Ash Green Master Plan*, Brian Clouston and Partners and Clouston Cobham and Partners, 1973

TABLE 17.5
Features of a management plan: resource requirement appraisals

(i) *Estimated machinery requirements*

	The Village Association £	The Residents' Societies £	Total £
A Joint Village Associations/Residents' Societies requirements			
Tractor, MF 20	520	780	1 300
Trailer	140	210	350
Flymo	24	36	60
2 Knapsack sprayers	16	24	40
Hand tools	80	120	200
Sub-Total:	780	1 170	1 950

(i) *Estimated machinery requirements*

B Village Association requirements

3 unit Gang mower for playing field and Village Green	600		
Tractor mounted, Triple Hayter for cutting meadowland and large rough fringe areas	300		
Rotary Hayter Condor 76 cm cut for pedestrian use in cutting woodland fringes and smaller rough fringe areas	350		
Set of harrows } Roller }	200		
Foreloader and bucket attachment	250		
1 'Atco' mower, 61 cm cut for the cricket square	180		
2 Hedge trimmers and generator	120		
1 Chain saw	80		
Agricultural rake for meadowland	150		
Auger/post hole digger	120		
Sub-Total:	2 350	—	2 350

C Residents' Societies requirements

1 Triple Ransome mower for neighbourhoods		1 000	
3 'Atco' mowers, 61 cm cut } 1 Antelope mower, 51 cm cut } for smaller lawn areas		540 90	
1 Tractor mounted sprayer with hand lances		200	
Sub-Total:	—	1 830	1 830
TOTAL	3 130	3 000	6 130

(ii) *Estimated total annual resource requirements*

	The Village Association	The Residents' Societies	Total
Total hectares involved	63·2	19·8	83·0
	£	£	£
Manpower:			
Estates Manager	800	1 200	2 000
Foreman	1 000	1 500	2 500
3 permanent staff	2 160	3 240	5 400
6 temporary staff	1 800	3 600	5 400
Sub-Total:	5 760	9 540	15 300
Machinery:			
Depreciation (20% p.a.)	600	600	1 200
Maintenance/repairs	600	600	1 200
Sub-Total:	1 200	1 200	2 400
Materials:			
Fuel, fertilizers, sprays, fencing, gravel, replacements, stakes etc.	1 500	2 500	4 000
Administration/overheads	1 000	1 000	2 000
TOTALS	9 460	14 240	23 700
COST PER HECTARE	150	719	286

Source: *New Ash Green Master Plan*, Brian Clouston and Partners and Clouston Cobham and Partners, 1973

TABLE 17.6
Features of a management plan: total estimated annual costs for a London Borough

The Main Landscape Maintenance Areas	Ha.	Machinery £	Materials £	Manpower £	Total £
1.Grass Areas					
Very High Maintenance					
Bowling Green	0·07	292	279	1 945	2 516
Cricket Table	0·08	267	142	1 626	2 035
High Maintenance					
Central Precincts	0·017	60	2	7	69
Sports Fields	2·85	286	394	260	940
Intermediate Maintenance					
Housing Open Space/Occasional Sports Areas	8·30	996	175	625	1 796
Low Maintenance					
Open Areas and Verges	4·56	344	—	519	863
Very Low Maintenance					
Wildlife Conservation and Verges	10·47	—	—	374	374
Sub-Total: Grass Areas	26·35	2 245	992	5 356	8 593
2. *Hard Surface Sports Facilities*					
Hard Porous Pitches	0·90	1 439		5 214	
Tennis Courts	0·13	25		218	
Sub-Total: Hard Surface Sports	1·03	1 464	1 176	5 432	8 072
3. *Formal Planted Areas*					
Shrub Areas	2·13	12	831	4 204	5 047
Tree Areas	1·89	12	1 603	484	2 099
Sub-Total: Trees and Shrubs	4·02	24	2 434	4 688	7 146
4. *Informal Trees and Shrubs*	9·14	10	1 426	5 514	6 950
5. *Lake*	0·42	38	20	201	259
6. *Other Areas*					
Maintenance Area					
Depot		900		3 598	
Nursery	0·18			720	
Allotments	0·40	60		692	
Hedges	0·24	117		938	
School Garden	0·07	250		208	
Sub-Total: Other Areas	0·89	1 327	313	6 516	7 796
7. *General Site Use**		1 100	2 000		3 100
Total 1–7 inclusive		6 208	8 361	27 347	41 916
plus overall contingency 2·5%	155	209	684	1 048	
GRAND TOTAL	41·85	6 363	8 570	28 031	42 964

*Includes: Transport: 3-ton wagon, Tractor—David Brown, Fuel

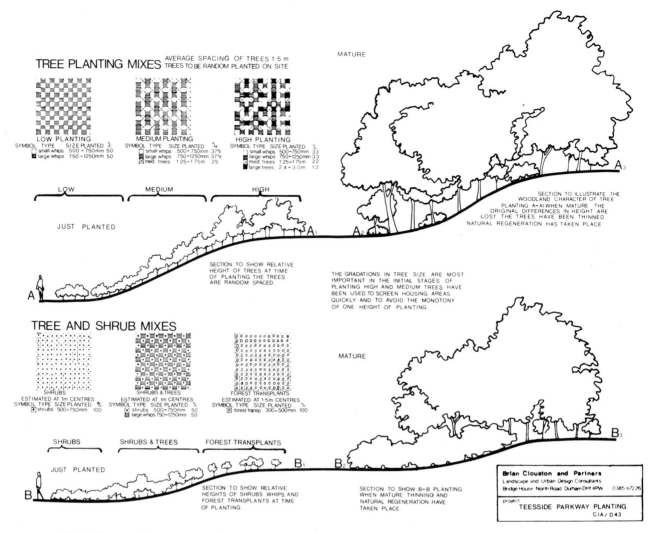

FIGURE 17.2 **Short and long-term design and management guidelines for Teesside parkway planting.** *(Pam Hoyle)*

obtained by engaging a contractor. A description of the reasons for the choice of the preferred strategy is normally given, coupled with a summary (as indicated in Table 17.5) of the resources which it is estimated will be required.

Both the management plan and the maintenance schedule require the close involvement of the landscape designer concerned, since it is essential that these documents should relate specifically to the visual effects which the designer wishes to evolve over a particular time period. Figure 17.2 displays two examples of the types of illustration which are essential companions to the two documents. They should be the product of discussions between designer, manager and maintenance officer.

17.7 BASIC DATA: AVAILABILITY AND SOURCES

The general advances in both the landscaping of many derelict and neglected sites and in the planning of large land areas for multiple use will inevitably require the supporting services of an efficient landscape management and maintenance profession.

To fulfil the essential management and maintenance functions there must be access to adequate technical performance data and costing information, the sources of which are at present unfortunately diffuse. The landscape manager is currently not as well served as either his professional design or agricultural counterparts by a central pool of information. He has no equivalent to the design handbooks (e.g. *Spons*) or the Annual Report of the Provincial Agricultural Economics Centres upon which to draw. Some of the main information sources are listed in the bibliography, including the helpful D.o.E. Schedule.[15]

In addition there is a substantial amount of unpublished technical and financial data which exists within central and local government and other organizations, which if and when published would undoubtedly be of benefit to the profession. There would be much to

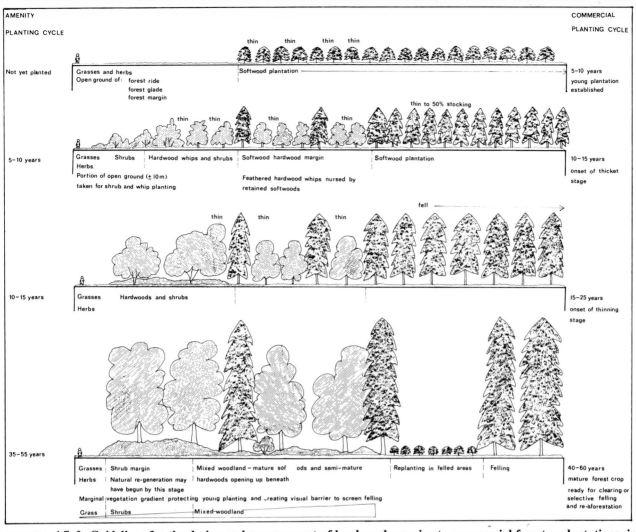

Not yet planted | Grasses and herbs
Open ground of: forest ride
forest glade
forest margin | Softwood plantation | 5-10 years
young plantation
established

thin thin thin thin

5-10 years | Grasses   Shrubs   Hardwood whips and shrubs   Softwood hardwood margin   Softwood plantation
Herbs.
Portion of open ground (±10m)
taken for shrub and whip planting | Feathered hardwood whips nursed by
retained softwoods | 10-15 years
onset of thicket
stage

thin to 50% stocking

thin   thin   thin

10-15 years | Grasses   Hardwoods and shrubs
Herbs | 15-25 years
onset of thinning
stage

thin   thin   thin

fell

35-55 years | Grasses   Shrub margin   Mixed woodland – mature sof ods and semi–mature   Replanting in felled areas   Felling
Herbs   Natural re-generation may   hardwoods opening up beneath
have begun by this stage
Marginal vegetation gradient protecting young planting and creating visual barrier to screen felling

Grass   Shrubs   Mixed woodland | 40-60 years
mature forest crop
ready for clearing or
selective felling
and re-aforestation

FIGURE 17.3 **Guidelines for the design and management of hardwood margins to commercial forestry plantations, in situations where visual, wildlife conservation, sporting and informal recreation considerations are important.**

FIGURE 17.4 **Conserving a sensitive landscape and maintaining a balance between multiple uses demands special management measures.**

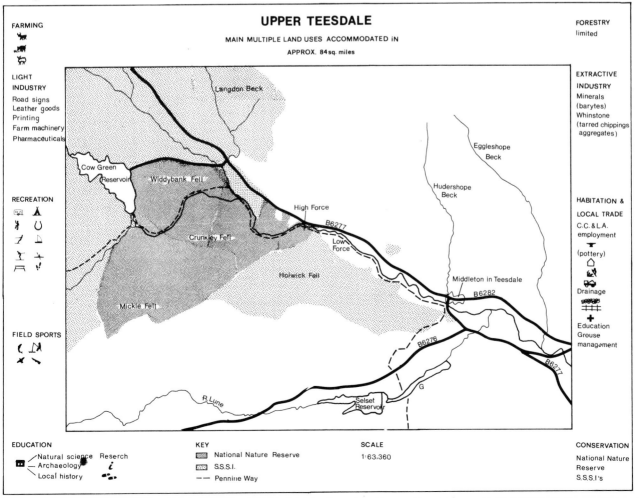

FARMING

FORESTRY
limited

UPPER TEESDALE

MAIN MULTIPLE LAND USES ACCOMMODATED iN

APPROX. 84 sq. miles

LIGHT
INDUSTRY

Road signs
Leather goods
Printing
Farm machinery
Pharmaceuticals

EXTRACTIVE
INDUSTRY

Minerals
(barytes)
Whinstone
(tarred chippings
aggregates)

RECREATION

HABITATION &
LOCAL TRADE

C.C. & L.A.
employment

(pottery)

Drainage

Education
Grouse
management

FIELD SPORTS

EDUCATION

Natural science   Reserch
Archaeology
Local history

KEY

National Nature Reserve
S.S.S.I.
Pennine Way

SCALE

1:63,360

CONSERVATION

National Nature
Reserve
S.S.S.I's

commend the co-ordination of all the known landscape management data in the form of an annual reference manual or information digest.

17.8 FUTURE DEVELOPMENTS

Provided that the landscape management profession organizes its information and other resources efficiently, it faces a challenging future from at least two points of view:

17.81 Management plans

There is the need for management plans to be prepared, executed and monitored for a large number of areas, particularly those where the land is, or will be, used for multiple purposes. It is a difficult enough task to manage land where single uses are involved, but the difficulty is compounded considerably where competing activities such as commercial farming, forestry, mining, recreation, education, field sports, conservation and human habitation require to be carried out in juxtaposition. The complexity and challenge of this type of management exercise can be observed in practice in the National Parks[16] and other significantly large land areas, such as Upper Teesdale[17] (*see* Figure 17.4) and 'corridor landscapes' like Hadrian's Wall and the coastline. Many of these areas, including even some important Nature Reserves which are accessible to the public, and coastal strips, despite the excellent intentions expressed in *The Coastal Heritage*,[18] are managed without recourse to any documented plan. This is not to imply that they are consequently not well managed. Instead it suggests that there is scope both for improvement and for benefit to be derived from involving many disciplines in what should be a comprehensive planning exercise. By its very nature, multiple land use is only likely to succeed where a balance is maintained between the interests concerned. As with semi-natural habitats, it is necessary to manage multiple land use areas in such a way as to maintain their wildlife and visual diversity. The richness of such areas, in both human and natural resource terms, lies in ensuring that no single interest or ownership becomes totally dominant.

17.82 Research

Planning and management on their own are not enough; they need to be backed by a vigorous research programme. This is essential if multiple land use ventures are to be successfully established and managed. Much work has already been undertaken in a number of fields such as the management of reclamation sites, road verges, hedgerows, recreation areas etc. However, many other fields are relatively untouched and what research results there are tend to be uncoordinated. The following are amongst the topics meriting greater investigation:

i) *The physical and financial implications of a range of different types of landscape schemes, using a variety of maintenance methods.* It is important that the capital and maintenance cost interactions, covering the lifetimes of all major types of landscape schemes, should become known. Assuming that there is only a certain proportion of GNP available for landscape works and maintenance it is important to know what types of capital and annual maintenance investments are likely to represent the best 'value'.

ii) *The manner in which certain areas at present devoted primarily to recreation use, might in future be simultaneously farmed or fished,* if so dictated by national food requirements. Possibly the resources of the relatively untrained recreators might be harnessed. A form of farming combined with recreational involvement may, in an age of public participation, come to have a greater place in the landscape of the future. Already visitors help to pick their own produce on some commercial farms and this may possibly extend to activities associated with supervised farm holidays involving such tasks as planting up gappy hedgerows and otherwise idle areas of land. Research could help to provide management guidance for these and other important land areas such as the vast rural-urban fringes surrounding most conurbations,[19] including the ineptly named Green Belts. In terms of land use, appearance and management these areas call for considerable improvement.

iii) *The most effective forms of groundcover from a maintenance point of view,* in both open and tree-shrub planted areas, bearing in mind the now high costs of grass cutting due to rising fuel and labour charges. The many different shrub and groundcover communities which are being used in the landscaping of New Towns merit investigation in relation to several factors, such as:
—their relative longevities under different environmental conditions,
—the total expenditure required for the initial planting and subsequent maintenance over their lifetimes,
—their relative growth performances and resource requirements.

When it comes to grass, the research work undertaken by Sayers and Gaman[20] into the responses of certain low maintenance mixtures to different treatments needs to be carried further, especially in view of the somewhat unexpected results. Their work would merit extension to include research into the types of grass mixtures and treatments, which will both provide an adequate cover for soil stabilization and visual purposes, and encourage colonization by indigenous herb species. The means of achieving botanically diverse, low maintenance and inexpensive swards has so far eluded professional and commercial interests alike. Research could show the extent to which it is possible to establish a vegetation

Positive management measures are required to deal with the problems of land uses and visual degradation in the rural-urban fringe landscapes.

PLATE 17.15 **The raw interface between residential and farming areas at Ashford.** *(Ralph Cobham)*

PLATE 17.16 **Motorized litter on British Rail land at Ashford.** *(Ralph Cobham)*

cover reliably and cheaply on sites without providing top-soil, thereby saving considerable capital outlay and a valuable resource.

17.9 CONCLUSION

This chapter has contained a simple message: to 'design with plants' successfully requires careful attention to the fourth design dimension and thereby to management and maintenance considerations. It is a fitting conclusion to the book, since it stresses the need for the development of closer working relationships between like-minded professions and—just as important—with the nurserymen who produce the required plants and the contractors who carry out much of the work. In short, the subject concerns a family of skills.

For many people the modern world is the scene of much dissension: consequently it is all-important to develop those human bonds whereby a better place can be provided for plants and people alike.

FURTHER READING

Agricultural Development and Advisory Service, with the Countryside Commission. *Cowbyers Conference Report* July 1974

Aldridge, D., *Guide to Countryside Interpretation:* Part 1 'Principles of Countryside Interpretation and Interpretative Planning' Countryside Commission (HMSO, 1975)

Arboricultural Association *Advisory Leaflets* No. 2 'A Guide to Tree Pruning', 1972 No. 3 'The Care of Trees on Development Sites', 1972

Barber, D. (Ed), 'Farming and Wildlife, a Study in Compromise' *Silsoe Conference* 1970 RSPB in association with FWAG

Carter, R. W. G., 'A Discussion of the Problems Associated with the Restoration and Management of Sand Dunes and Beaches' Unpublished paper, *The New University of Ulster*, 1975

CEGB, 'Economy in Landscape Maintenance' *Symposium Summary* 1967

CEGB, *Landscape Code of Practice* 1972. Vol. 1

Cobham, R. O. and Gill, C. J. 'Management and Maintenance' *Gardener's Chronicle* 1976 Vol. 179 No. 26 pp. 39–43; Vol. 180 No. 2 pp. 16–19, Vol. 180 No. 3 pp. 16–18

Conover, H. S., *Grounds Maintenance Handbook* (McGraw Hill, 1958)

Countryside Commission, Landscape Agreements, CCP 61, 1973

Countryside Commission, *Upland Management Experiment* (HMSO, 1974)

Colvin, B., 'Landscape Maintenance of Large Industrial Sites' ILA Journal No. 84 November 1968

DOE and SDD, *Housing Development Notes* II. 'Landscape of New Housing', February 1973 and 1974

Duffey, E., Morris, M. G., Sheail, J., Ward, L. K., Wells, D. A. Wells T. C. E. (Editors), *Grassland Ecology and Wildlife Management* (London: Chapman and Hall, 1974)

Duffey, E., and Watt, A. S. (Editors), *The Scientific Management of Animal and Plant Communities for Conservation* (Oxford: Blackwell Scientific Publications, 1971)

East Lothian County Council Planning Department, *Dune Conservation—a twenty year record of work in East Lothian*, 1970

East Lothian County Council Planning Department, *Dune Conservation 1970* (North Berwick Study Group Report, 1970)

Fairbrother, N., *New Lives New Landscapes* (London: Architectural Press, 1970)

Fairbrother, N., *The Nature of Landscape Design* (London: Architectural Press, 1974) Chapter 7

Farming and Wildlife Advisory Group, Essex Exercise: *Farming, Wildlife and Landscape* 1975

Hebblethwaite, R. L. *Landscape Maintenance* (CEGB, 1967)

Hewett, D. G. 'Human Pressures on Soils in Coastal Areas' *Welsh Soils Discussion Group Report* No. 14, 1973

Hookway, R. J. S., *The Management of Britain's Rural Land* (Countryside Commission, 1967)

Hooper, M. D., and Holdgate, M. W. (Editors) *Hedges and Hedgerow Trees:* Symposium Proceedings Monks Wood Experimental Station, 1968

Huxley, T., *Footpaths in the Countryside* (The Countryside Commission for Scotland, 1968)

ILA *Landscape Maintenance* Report of Symposium, June 1963

Institute of Recreation Management (Editors), *The Recreation Management Yearbook* (London E. & F. N. Spon Ltd, 1975)

Keenleyside, C. B., *Farming, Landscape and Recreation* (Countryside Commission, 1971)

Laurie, I. C. (Editor), *Nature in Cities* University of Manchester, Landscape Research Group Symposium 1974

Lovejoy, D. (Editor), *Land Use and Landscape Planning* (London: Leonard Hill Books, 1973)

Lovejoy, D. & Partners (Editors), *Spon's Landscape Handbook* (London: E. F. & N. Spon Ltd) revised annually

McHarg, I. C. 'Can We Afford Open Space? A Survey of Landscaping Costs' *Architects' Journal* March 8 and 15 1956 pp. 261–74

Marren, P. R. Ecology and Recreation, *A Review of European Literature* University College, London 1975

Nottinghamshire County Council, *Sherwood Forest Study*. The Sherwood Forest Study Group, 1974

Pennyfather, K., *Guide to Countryside Interpretation,*

Part II 'Interpretive Media and Facilities', Countryside Commission (HMSO, 1975)

Pollard, E., Hooper, M. D. and Moore, N. W., *The New Naturalist* (London: Collins, 1974) Chapter 16

Speight, M. C. D., 'Outdoor Recreation and its Ecological Effects' *Discussion Papers in Conservation* (London: University College, 1973)

Steale, R. C., 'Wildlife Conservation in Woodlands', Forestry Commission Booklet 29, (HMSO, 1972)

Tandy, C. (Editor), *Handbook of Urban Landscape* (London: Architectural Press, 1972)

Tandy, C., *Landscape of Industry* (London: Leonard Hill Books, 1975) pp. 256–61

University of Newcastle upon Tyne *Landscape Reclamation* (Guildford: IPC Business Press, 1972) Vols I & II

Warnock, T., 'A Surveyor Looks at Landscape Maintenance' *The Surveyor* September 1967

Warren, A. and Goldsmith, F. B., *Conservation in Practice* (Chichester: John Wiley & Sons, 1974)

Way, J. M., *Road Verges: The Function and Management.* Symposium Proceedings, Monks Wood Experimental Station 1969

Weddle, A. E., *Techniques of Landscape Architecture* (London: William Heinemann Ltd, 1967)

Weddle, A. E. and Pickard, J., 'Landscape Management: Site Conservation at Heriot-Watt University' *ILA Journal* No. 94 May 1971

Westmacott, R. and Worthington, T., *New Agricultural Landscapes* (Countryside Commission, 1974)

Woodhouse, A. R. 'Further Assessment of the Effectiveness of a Slow Release Nitrogen Fertilizer on Sports Turf' *Journal of the Sports Turf Research Institute* 1974 No. 30

Wright, T., 'Landscapes: The State of Welfare' *Gardeners' Chronicle* 1975 Vol. 178 No. 24 pp. 26–8

Wye College, Kent, *Aspects of Landscape Ecology and Maintenance* 1972

Wye College, Kent, *Tree Growth in the Landscape* 1974

REFERENCES

1. 'Expansion of the Profession' Report prepared by the Ad Hoc Committee, ILA 1974
2. Boddington, M. A. B. 'Urban Pressure—coming to terms with the towns'. *Farm Business* 1971 pp. 6–12
3. *The Plan for Milton Keynes*. Milton Keynes Development Corporation, 1971
4. Boddington, M. A. B. 'Agriculture in Milton Keynes'. *The Plan for Milton Keynes*. Technical Supplement No. 9, 1971
5. 'Milton Keynes Revisited: 1971', University of Reading—Department of Agricultural Economics and Management. *Miscellaneous Study No. 51*, 1972
6. Best, R. H. and Rogers, A. W. *The Urban Countryside* (London: Faber, 1973)
7. Brian Clouston and Partners *New Ash Green Landscape Master Plan*, 1973
8. Barrow, G., Brotherton, D. I. and Maurice, O. C., 'Tarn Hows Experimental Restoration Project'. The Countryside Commission, 1973. *Recreation News Supplement No. 9.*
9. Leonard Manasseh and Partners. *Snowdon Summit.* The Countryside Commission, 1975
10. Brian Clouston and Partners. *Ilkley Moor Experimental Restoration Project.* Summary Report for The Countryside Commission and Ilkley UDC, 1974
11. Irvine Development Corporation, *Irvine New Town Plan.* 1971
12. Brian Clouston and Partners and Irvine Development Corporation. *Irvine Beach Park, Proposals for an Urban Park for Leisure and Recreation on the Clyde Coast*, 1974
13. Brian Clouston and Partners in Association with Teesside County Borough. *Tees Riverside Plan* 'Part I Landscape and Recreation', 1973
14. Roderkerk, Dr E. C. M., 'Kennermerduinen National Park'. *Nature in Focus.* No. 18 (Council for Europe, 1974)
15. *Schedule of Rates for the Preparation and Maintenance of Land* D.o.E. (HMSO: 1973)
16. *Report of the National Park Policies Review Committee* D.o.E. (HMSO 1974)
17. Bradshaw, Dr M. E. (Ed.) *The Natural History of Upper Teesdale* (Durham County Conservation Trust, 1976)
18. *The Coastal Heritage.* The Countryside Commission (HMSO 1970)
19. Rawling, J. T., Ratcliffe, J. E., and Shelton, A. J., *A Planning Study of Rural Leeds.* (Civic Hall: Leeds 1972) Vols. 1 and 2
20. Gaman, J. H. and Sayers, C. D., 'The Amenity Potential of Low-Maintenance Grasses.' *Journal of Environmental Planning and Pollution Control* No. 4, 1973, Vol 1

ACKNOWLEDGEMENTS

In the preparation and presentation of this chapter, the author gratefully acknowledges the assistance received from the following colleagues and friends: Brian Iley (Figure 17.1); Mrs Pam Hoyle (Figure 17.2); Michael Thompson, Roger Lee and Tony Smith (Figure 17.3); Dr Tim Bines (Figure 17.4); George Cobham (Table 17.2); John Parker and Norman Leddy (Tables 17.5 and 17.6); Judy Snaith for assistance with selection of photographs.

Part III

PLANT AND TREE INFORMATION SHEETS

Plant Information Sheets

KEY

The plant information sheets are based on the plant list prepared by the Landscape Institute which consists of over 600 items ranging from trees to groundcover plants. This number does not include herbaceous perennials grown for floral display (e.g. delphiniums, phlox, lupins) or cultivars of *rosa syringa*, etc. All plants included are readily available commercially.

Most of the plants are divided according to height, with subheadings in each category where appropriate and there are some special groups (Sections 6 to 8).

1   *Groundcover under 300 mm high*
          Herbaceous perennials
          Evergreens and semi-evergreen
          Carpeting plants
          Bulbs, corms and tubers
2   *Low plants and shrubs 300 to 1 000 mm high*
          Herbaceous perennials
          Evergreen and semi-evergreen
          Deciduous
3   *Plants and Shrubs 1 000 to 1 500 mm high*
          Herbaceous perennials
          Evergreens and semi-evergreen
          Deciduous
4   *Plants, shrubs and small trees 1 500 to 3 000 mm high*
          Evergreen
          Deciduous
5   *Large shrubs and small trees 3 000 to 7 500 mm high*
          Evergreen
          Deciduous
6   *Climbing plants*
7   *Marginal aquatic plants*
8   *Grasses and rushes*
9   *Plants for tropical humid climates*
          Groundcover
          Foliage plants
          Ferns
          Climbers

The list of plants cannot claim to be exhaustive, but aims to include the most important plants in each group.

Information about each plant is divided into two parts:

a) a brief description of the plant, together with country of origin;

b) its requirements and uses.

No recommendations are made for associating plants. Natural associations can be obtained from ecological text books; other groupings will depend on the effect the designer wishes to obtain.

No recommendations are made for planting distances (except for hedging) as these will depend on the initial size of the plants, the money available, the effect required etc. The ultimate spread of the plant will give some indication of the space needed.

All measurements are in millimetres, unless otherwise indicated.

327

Robinia Hispida, **Hidcote Manor, Gloucestershire.** *(John Chitty)*

a) Plant description

Name. Latin name and source (synonyms), common name, plant family. The Latin name follows the nomenclature used in Hillier and Sons catalogues.

Height and spread at maturity. This can only be very approximate as growth depends on soil and climatic conditions, planting density etc. Rate of growth is only given when it is relatively fast, slow or invasive.

Form and habit. Any change in habit which occurs with age is noted and form described when not apparent from the photograph.

Density. When the combined effect of stems and leaves differs from the average it is described as dense, light or irregular. Thorns or other deterrents are noted.

Stems or bark. These are described only where of special interest.

Foliage. Winter effect—evergreen, deciduous, semi-evergreen, persistent. Form—compound, palmate, lobed, rounded, lanceolate, linear, scale. Colour will be described when it differs from mid-green or where autumn colour is important.

Flowers. Colour and season, scent, type of inflorescence.

Fruit. Colour and season, when important.

Special remarks. As and when necessary.

b) Uses and requirements

Soil. Special requirements or tolerances e.g. alkaline, acid, wet, dry, saline. 'Any soil' denotes that a plant will grow on a wide range of soil types excepting excessively acid, excessively alkaline etc.

Conditions. Light requirements (e.g. full sun, half sun, shade). Ability to withstand drips. Ability to withstand exposure (inland, coast). Ability to tolerate air pollution.

Size of plant. Size recommended is that suggested in the British Standard Specification for Nursery Stock N.S. 3936. Part I. Larger sizes of many items may be obtainable but would cost more and might require more care after transplantation. Smaller sizes are not suitable for landscape work.

Cost. Actual prices are not quoted but an indication is given of the relative cost of plants within each group i.e. cheap, expensive.

Maintenance. Most plants have been chosen for their ability to grow with the minimum of regular care once established. 'High maintenance' denotes plants needing skilled attention. 'Low maintenance' denotes plants needing no regular care once established.

Use. Any special use or value a plant may have in the landscape is noted. No attempt is made to list all possible uses.

Special remarks. As and when necessary.

ACKNOWLEDGMENTS

Patricia Booth, BSc Hort (Lond), FILA
supplied most of the photographs for the plant information sheets.

William Bessler, DipLD (Newcastle), AILA
supplied the following photographs in addition to those for Section 7:

Fabiana imbricata	*Rosa* 'Nevada'	*Daboecia cantabrica*
Cistus purpureus	*Rosa* 'Penelope'	*Erica vagans*
Cotoneaster amoenus	*Rubus cockburnianus*	*Liriope muscari*
Deutzia × *elegantissima*	*Viburnum opulus* 'Sterile'	*Sasa veitchii*
Myrtus communis		

Clifford Tandy, PPILA, RIBA
Gaultheria procumbens

G. S. Thomas
Tellima grandiflora

Maurice Lee, FRIBA, FSIA, LILA
supplied both text and photographs for Section 9.

328

1. Groundcover under 300 mm high

HERBACEOUS PERENNIALS

Ajuga reptans 'Atropurpurea'—Bugle—Labiatae
150 high spreading quickly by runners to form a dense leafy cover.
Semi-evergreen purplish leaves 50–75 long.
230 to 300 high loose spikes of blue flowers May to July.
A.r. 'Variegata' has grey-green leaves marked with cream.
Europe incl. Britain.

Any soil. Best in moist.
Sun or shade. Not very hot, dry sites.
Plant from small pots.
Excellent groundcover under shrubs or trees and for waterside planting.

Alchemilla mollis—Lady's Mantle—Rosaceae
230 to 300 high clumps which spread by seeding to form a dense cover.
Large soft greyish-green hairy leaves die down in winter but do not disappear completely.
455 high feathery sprays very tiny greenish yellow flowers in early summer.
Carpathians to Asia Minor.

Any soil.
Sun or half shade.
Plant strong clumps.
Groundcover or border plant.

Asperula odorata (Galium odoratum)—Sweet woodruff—Rubiaceae
150 to 230 high upright stems spreading rapidly by creeping roots to form a dense cover.
Narrow bright green leaves about 25 long are borne in whorls.
Small white flowers in May–June.
Drying plants smell of new-mown hay.
Europe incl. Britain, Siberia.

Any soil.
Sun or shade, but prefers shade.
Plant well rooted clumps or from small pots.
Low maintenance.
Excellent groundcover; will grow round plants without smothering them.

329

Cerastium tomentosum—Snow in Summer—
Caryophyllaceae

150 high creeping rapidly to form a close mat.
Tiny silvery woolly leaves persist through the winter.
White flowers in June–July.
S. and E. Europe.

Any soil.
Sun or shade.
Plant well rooted clumps or from small pots.
Good groundcover on poor dry soils.

Convallaria majalis—Lily of the Valley—Liliaceae

150 to 230 high leaves spreading by creeping rootstock to form a dense summer groundcover.
Pale green leaves 50–150 long.
Loose racemes of white bell-shaped flowers May–June. Scented.
Round red berries are not persistent or showy.
Europe incl. Britain, Asia, North America.

Any soil.
Sun or shade. Prefers partial shade.
Town.
Cheap.
Low maintenance.
Plant strong rhizomes with good terminal buds.
Very good ground-cover where it grows well, but does not always thrive where expected.

Geranium macrorrhizum—Geraniaceae

300 to 380 high spreading by brittle woody stems to form a dense ground-cover.
Semi-evergreen divided round leaves are light green, sticky and very fragrant.
Some leaves develop bright autumn tints.
Soft pink flowers in loose heads from May to July.
G.m. album has white flowers, is slightly more compact and colours better than the type.
G.m. 'Ingwersen' is slightly taller and has larger rose-pink flowers.
A good border plant.
S.E. Alps, Balkans.

Any soil.
Sun or shade.
Plant strong clumps.
Very good decorative groundcover in light shade especially *G.m. album.*
Best autumn colour on poor soil in sun.

Geranium sanguineum—Bloody Cranesbill—Geraniaceae

230 to 300 high wide-spreading hummock with many stems.
Deeply cut dark green leaves colouring in autumn.
Numerous magenta-pink flowers over a long period in summer.
G.s. lancastriense is a dwarf form with pale pink flowers.
Europe incl. Britain.

Any soil.
Sun or partial shade.
Plant well rooted clumps or from small pots.
Groundcover, border.

Lamium galeobdolon 'Variegatum' (Galeobdolon luteum 'Variegatum')—Labiatae

300 to 380 high spreading very rapidly by long stolons to form a dense groundcover.
Invasive.
Silvery variegated leaves are evergreen and attractive throughout the year.
Loose spikes of soft yellow flowers in spring.
Europe incl. Britain.

Any soil.
Sun or shade.
Plant strong clumps.
Low maintenance.
Excellent groundcover under trees and large shrubs.
Very rampant on moist soils when it will smother small shrubs.

Lamium maculatum—Spotted Dead Nettle—Labiatae

150 to 300 high spreading by creeping rootstocks to form a thick evergreen groundcover.
Dull sage-green leaves with a central white stripe.
Heads of rosy-purple flowers throughout the summer.
Europe incl. Britain.

Any soil.
Sun or shade.
Plant well rooted clumps or from small pots.
Good groundcover.

Omphalodes cappadocica—Boraginaceae

230 high thick mats of evergreen foliage.
Deep green leaves with greyish undersides.
Deep blue forget-me-not flowers 13 across in May–June and again in autumn.
Asia minor, S. Turkey.

Any soil.
Partial or full shade.
Expensive.
Plant well rooted clumps or from small pots.
Groundcover, border in shade.

Origanum vulgare 'Aureum'—Golden Marjoram—Labiatae

230 to 300 high mats of annual stems from perennial creeping rootstocks.
Small fragrant leaves, bright yellow in spring turning green towards autumn.
Inconspicuous heads of flowers.
Europe incl. Britain.

Any soil. Best in well-drained.
Sun.
Plant well rooted clumps or from small pots.
Groundcover, border.

331

Polygonum affine—Knotweed—Polygonaceae

100 to 150 high dense mat of narrow leaves turning bronzy-crimson in autumn and persisting through the winter as a rich brown mat.

Stiff spikes of pink flowers 300 high in August, changing to reddish-pink.

P.a. 'Donald Lowndes' has a more compact growth and shorter thicker flower spikes deepening to garnet-red in autumn.

Nepal.

Any soil. Best in moist.
Sun or shade.
Plant strong clumps.
Groundcover or border.
Not reliably hardy on poor soils in very cold areas.

Pulmonaria saccharata (P. picta)—Bethlehem Sage—Boraginaceae

230 to 300 high gradually spreading clumps of tongue-shaped leaves.

Evergreen leaves are deep green with conspicuous grey-white markings.

Clusters of small pink flowers, turning blue, from April to May.

France, Italy.

Any soil except very dry.
Sun or shade.
Plant strong clumps.
Groundcover.

Saxifraga umbrosa (S. × urbium)—London Pride—Saxifragaceae

150 high dense mat of evergreen foliage spreading by underground stems.

Small green leaves in rosettes sometimes colouring towards autumn.

300 to 380 high sprays of tiny pink flowers in May–June.

Europe.

Any soil.
Sun or shade.
Town.
Plant well rooted clumps or from small pots.
Groundcover, border.

Stachys byzantina (S. lanata)—Lamb's Tongue, Sow's Ear—labiatae

150 to 230 high dense mats of woolly, grey leaves.

Evergreen.

455 high spikes of tiny pink-purple flowers in July.

S.l. 'Silver Carpet' is a non-flowering form suitable for groundcover.

Caucasus to Iran.

Any soil.
Sun or light shade.
Plant strong clumps.
Good groundcover—particularly for poor dry soils. Border plant.

Viola cornuta—Violaceae

150 to 230 high foliage forming a dense mat.
Bright green leaves, some persisting through the winter.
Large violet flowers borne for a long period in spring and summer.
Cut back after summer flowering to produce autumn flowers.
V.c. 'Alba' has white flowers and is usually a stronger grower.
Pyrenees.

Any soil.
Sun or shade.
High maintenance.
Plant well rooted clumps or from small pots.
Groundcover, border.

EVERGREENS AND SEMI EVERGREENS

Cotoneaster dammeri (C. humifusus)—Rosaceae

50 to 150 high evergreen shrub spreading quickly by trailing shoots which shape themselves to the ground and root to form a dense cover.
Glossy oval leaves 20 to 30 long turning reddish in autumn.
White flowers in May.
Bright red berries in autumn.
China.

Any soil.
Sun or shade.
Town, seaside.
Plant from pots.
Groundcover, banks, particularly on poor soils.
Groundcover: plant about 600 apart.

Cotoneaster salicifolius 'Autumn Fire' (Herbstfeuer)—Rosaceae

150 to 300 high quick growing shrub with spreading stems forming a thick cover.
Evergreen willow like leaves 40 to 75 long.
Small white flowers in May.
Clusters of red berries in autumn.
W. China.

Any soil.
Sun or half-shade.
Town, seaside.
Plant from pots.
Expensive.
Groundcover, banks, particularly on poor soils.
Groundcover: plant about 1 200 apart.

333

Erica carnea—Heath—Ericaceae

255 to 300 × 300 to 600 forming a low rounded bush becoming more prostrate with age.
Evergreen dark green linear leaves 5–10 long.
Racemes of deep rosy-red flowers January to April.
E.c. 'Springwood' with white flowers is a vigorous form 125 to 205 high and more spreading than the type, rapidly making a very dense groundcover.
Many other named cultivars available.
Alps of C. Europe.

Any soil, including soil containing lime.
Sun or half shade.
Plant at 100–150 spread or pot plants with a minimum spread of 75.
Cheap. Low maintenance.
Groundcover: plant about 300 to 380 apart.

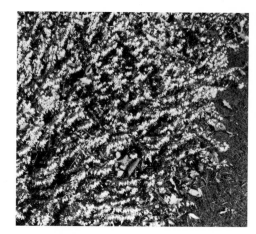

Gaultheria procumbens—Creeping Wintergreen, Partridge Berry—Ericaceae

75 to 150 high evergreen shrub creeping vigorously to form a dense mat.
Thick leathery shiny oval leaves 20 to 40 long are dark green turning reddish in autumn.
Tiny pink-tinged white flowers in July–August.
Bright red berries in autumn.
Oregon, California.

Lime free soil. Best in peaty soil.
Half or full shade.
Drip tolerant.
Low maintenance.
Excellent groundcover on soils with humus under trees.
Groundcover: plant about 300 apart.

Hebe pinguifolia 'Pagei'—Scrophulariaceae

230 to 380 × 750 to 900 low spreading bushy shrub, forming a thick groundcover.
Small evergreen glaucous blue leaves.
Short spikes of tiny white flowers May–June.
Not reliably hardy in very cold areas.
New Zealand.

Any soil. Best in well drained soils.
Sun or half-shade.
Town, seaside.
Plant at 75 to 230 high from pots.
Groundcover, banks particularly near sea.
Groundcover: plant about 380 to 450 apart.

Hedera helix—Common Ivy—Araliaceae

230 to 300 high dense evergreen groundcover or vigorous self-clinging climber up to 30 m high.
Thick leathery dark glossy green leaves.
Clusters of yellowish-green flowers in October produced only on special bushy branches, not on creeping or climbing shoots.
Many cultivars available, usually slower growing than the type.
H.h. hibernica—Irish Ivy—has large bright green leaves and quickly forms an excellent ground cover.
Europe incl. Britain.

Any soil.
Sun or shade.
Drip tolerant.
Town, seaside.
Plant at 600 to 1 200 high from pots.
Low maintenance.
Screen or hedge if supported, excellent groundcover in deep shade under trees.
Groundcover: plant about 900 apart.

334

Juniperus horizontalis (J. sabina 'Prostrata')—Creeping Juniper—Cupressaceae

255 to 380 high prostrate-branched shrub spreading widely by rooting of branches.

Coniferous evergreen with tiny glaucous green leaves forming a dense carpet with a rough, ruffled appearance.

Several cultivars available, usually more glaucous blue in colour.

J. conferta is a similar prostrate mat-forming species giving a bright green groundcover.

N.E. America.

Any soil. Best in well-drained soil. Sun or half-shade. Seaside. Plant at 230 to 450 diameter. Expensive. Groundcover: plant about 600 apart.

Pachysandra terminalis—Buxaceae

150 to 230 high semi-woody evergreen carpeting plant spreading by creeping rootstocks to form a dense cover.

Bright green leaves 25 to 50 long in whorl-like clusters.

Spikes of greenish-white flowers February–March.

P.t. variegata has leaves edged with creamy-white and spreads more slowly than the type.

Japan.

Any soil. Best in moist lime-free soil. Sun or shade. Town. Plant well-rooted clumps. Cheap. Good groundcover under trees and shrubs where the soil suits it. Groundcover: plant about 230 to 300 apart.

Vinca minor—Lesser Periwinkle—Apocynaceae

230 to 380 high prostrate evergreen spreading by trailing shoots which root as they go.

Growth slow at first but spreads rapidly once established.

Small shining dark green leaves forming a dense groundcover.

Soft blue flowers 25 across in March–May.

Large flowered, and white and purple cultivars available.

V.m. 'Aureo-Variegata' with leaves splashed with yellow is less vigorous than *V. minor*.

Europe.

Any soil. Sun or shade. Seaside, town. Drip tolerant. Plant well-rooted clumps or from pots. Cheap. Groundcover: plant about 300 apart.

335

CARPETING PLANTS

Acaena microphylla—Rosaceae

25 to 50 high spreading rapidly by creeping shoots to form a dense mat.
Evergreen.
Bronzy pinnate leaves 20 to 50 long.
Close heads of tiny flowers followed by showy and persistent spiny crimson burrs.
Withstands light foot traffic but burrs may stick to clothing.
New Zealand.

Any soil.
Sun or shade.
Drip tolerant.
Town.
Plant from small pots.
Low maintenance.
Paving, groundcover under trees.

Armeria maritima—Thrift, Sea Pink—Plumbaginaceae

100 to 150 high spreading to form a dense compact turf.
Dark green linear leaves.
Evergreen.
Rounded heads of lavender-pink flowers in July–August.
Persistent papery seed heads.
Withstands light foot traffic.
Named cultivars have flowers in white, pink and red shades.
Europe incl. Britain.

Any well drained soil.
Full sun.
Seaside.
Plant from small pots.
Low maintenance.
Paving, dry walls, groundcover in sun.

Cotula squalida—Compositae

20 to 50 high spreading by long creeping slender branched stems to form a dense mat.
Evergreen.
Tiny fern-like dark green leaves 25 to 50 long.
Insignificant flowers.
Withstands light foot traffic.
New Zealand.

Any soil.
Sun or half shade.
Town.
Plant from small pots.
Paving joints, groundcover for bulbs.

Helxine soleirolii—Urticaceae
10 to 30 high creeping rapidly to form a dense mat.
Herbaceous perennial.
Tiny bright glossy green rounded leaves.
Very small inconspicuous flowers.
Blackened by frost but grows away quickly in spring.
Corsica.

Any moist soil.
Full or half shade.
Town.
Plant from small pots.
Invasive groundcover in cool moist places.

Lysimachia nummularia—Creeping Jenny—Primulaceae
20 to 80 high spreading rapidly by long creeping shoots to form a prostrate groundcover.
Persistent leaves.
Bright green rounded leaves.
Showy bright yellow flowers June–September.
L.n. 'Aurea' has golden yellow leaves.
Europe incl. Britain.

Any soil. Best on moist.
Sun or shade.
Town. Drip tolerant.
Plant from small pots.
Low maintenance.
Groundcover under shrubs, moist banks.

Sagina subulata—Caryophyllaceae
20 to 80 high with very branched stems forming a dense mat.
Evergreen.
Tiny linear leaves.
Tiny white flowers in summer.
Corsica, Sardinia.

Any soil.
Sun or partial shade.
Town.
Plant from small pots.
Paving joints.

Saxifraga moschata—Saxifragaceae
75 to 150 high rapidly spreading to form a dense tufted mat.
Evergreen.
Tiny bright green leaves in rosettes.
Numerous showy pink flowers borne above the leaves April to May.
The many named cultivars vary in colour from white to pink and red shades.
Pyrenees to Caucasus.

Any soil.
Sun or shade. Best in partial shade.
Plant from small pots.
Groundcover.

337

Sedum spurium—Crassulaceae

150 high dense mat of leaves borne in rosettes.
Evergreen.
Fleshy oval leaves 25 long and 18 wide.
Pink flowers in dense flat cymes 50 across in July and August.
S.s album splendens (Green Mantle) is a non-flowering cultivar which makes a very good groundcover.
Caucasus, N. Iran, naturalized in Britain.

Any soil.
Sun or partial shade.
Plant from small pots.
Dry walls, ground-cover on banks.

Thymus serpyllum (T. drucei)—Thyme—Labiatae

50 to 75 high spreading by creeping stems to form a dense mat.
Evergreen.
Very small dark green oval leaves.
Aromatic.
Short loose spikes of purplish flowers on upright stems June to July.
Withstands light foot traffic.
Named cultivars vary in colour from white to pale pink and deep purplish-red.
Europe incl. Britain.

Any well drained soil.
Sun or partial shade.
Seaside.
Plant from small pots.
Paving, dry walls.

BULBS, CORMS AND TUBERS

Anemone blanda—Mountain Windflower—Ranunculaceae

Small brown tubers producing foliage up to 75 high, sometimes spreading freely by seeding—especially on warm chalky soils.
Deeply divided mid-green leaves produced in winter and die down by midsummer.
Flowers 25 to 50 across with many strap-shaped petals in early spring—pale or deep blue, mauve, pink or white with yellow centres.
Many named varieties.
A. appenina grows to 150 tall and will naturalize in shade or in thin grass.
Greece.

Any well-drained soil.
Chalk.
Full sun.
Use tubers, not less than 40 circumference, and plant 50 to 75 deep in September.
Low maintenance.
Borders.

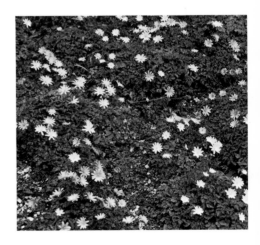

338

Anemone nemorosa—Wood Anemone—Ranunculaceae

Small black thickened rhizomes producing 2 or 3 leaves and a single flower stalk 100 to 150 high. Spreads freely in open woodland.
Deeply divided mid-green leaves on long leafstalks, producing in late winter and die down by midsummer.
White flowers, pale mauve or pink outside, up to 50 across.
Named varieties are suitable for gardens.
Europe incl. Britain.

Any soil that is not too dry.
Good on loam or clay.
Partial or full shade.
Plant strong clumps after flowering.
Cheap.
Low maintenance.
Woodland, under deciduous shrubs, thin grass.

Chionodoxa luciliae—Glory of the Snow—Liliaceae

Small bulbs producing leaves and flower stalks up to 150 high. Increases freely by offsets and seed. Glossy green strap-shaped leaves grow in late winter and die down by late spring.
Star-like blue flowers 20 to 25 across borne 8 to 10 on a stem in early spring.
White and pink flowered varieties have only 2 to 3 flowers per stem and are not so vigorous.
Crete, Asia Minor.

Any soil. Best in light.
Semi shade or full sun.
Use bulbs not less than 40 circumference and plant 75 deep in September.
Cheap.
Low maintenance.
Borders, under deciduous trees or shrubs.

Crocus tomasinianus—Iridaceae

Small bulbs rapidly increasing by offsets to form strong clumps and also spreading by seed.
Narrow linear leaves up to 150 long enclosed at the base in a sheath growing from the bulb.
Die down by early summer.
Slender buds, pale mauvish-blue outside, open to bright lilac-mauve flowers in early spring.
Several named forms have stronger colours but do not spread as rapidly.
E. coast of Adriatic.

Any well-drained soil.
Drought resistant.
Sun or partial shade.
Use bulbs not less than 40 circumference and plant 50 to 75 deep in September.
Cheap.
Low maintenance.
Woodland, grass, borders.

Cyclamen neapolitanum—Primulaceae

Brown corms slowly increasing in size to produce dense clumps of foliage 100 high.
Also spreads by seeding on suitable sites.
Ivy-shaped leaves, dark green with variable silver marking, appear in winter and die down by end of June.
Rose-pink flowers are borne singly on slender stems 100 to 150 high and start in September to November before the leaves appear.
Plants are very variable and the flowers are sometimes scented.
C.n. 'Album' is a pure white form.
S. Italy, Greece.

Any well-drained soil that is not too acid—preferably limy.
Sun or partial shade.
Plant small pot-grown plants or plant dormant tubers 50 deep in July to August.
Expensive.
Low maintenance.
Will grow under deciduous trees and shrubs including beech.

339

Eranthis hyemalis—Winter Aconite—Ranunculaceae

Small tubers spreading freely and naturalizing in suitable sites.
Ruff of much divided green leaves just below flower.
Bright golden-yellow buttercup-like flowers on 50 to 75 tall stems from January to February.
Other species and hybrids are attractive but do not naturalize well.
Europe, naturalized in parts of Britain.

Any soil. Best in fairly moist.
Sun or partial shade.
Use tubers of not less than 20 circumference and plant 50 to 75 deep in September or October.
Cheap.
Low maintenance.
Naturalize in thin grass under deciduous trees or among shrubs.

Galanthus nivalis—Common Snowdrop—
Amaryllidaceae

Small bulbs increasing by offsets to form clumps of foliage up to 150 high. Also spreads by seeding.
2 or 3 narrow linear greyish-green leaves grow from each bulb, shorter than flower stem at flowering time but growing to 300 after. Leaves die down by early summer.
Drooping white flowers borne single on stems 150 to 200 high in February to March.
Many other Galanthus species and cultivars of *G. nivalis* may be grown in borders but are not generally suitable for naturalizing.
Europe, incl. parts of Britain.

Any soil. Best in cool, slightly moist places.
Sun or shade.
Plant pot-grown clumps or divide and replant immediately after flowering in March.
Bulbs with a minimum circumference of 40 may be planted 75 deep in September.
Cheap.
Low maintenance.
Naturalize in thin grass under deciduous trees or among shrubs.
Borders.

Muscari armeniacum—Grape Hyacinth—Liliaceae

Small bulb spreading very rapidly to form dense clumps of foliage. Also increase by seeding.
Deep green grass-like leaves appear in autumn and die down in late spring.
Small bright blue flowers grow in dense heads on stems 100 to 150 high in April.
Other Muscari species can be grown in borders but do not spread as rapidly.
Europe, W. Asia.

Any soil.
Sun.
Use bulbs with a minimum circumference of 60 and plant 75 deep in early autumn.
Cheap.
Low maintenance.
Borders, thin grass.

Scilla sibirica—Squill—Liliaceae

Small bulb spreading slowly.
Strap-shaped bright green leaves die down by midsummer.
Very bright blue drooping flowers borne 3 or 4 on flower stems 100 to 150 high in March. Each bulb produces several flower stems.
C. and S. Russia.

Any soil.
Sun or partial shade.
Use bulbs with a minimum circumference of 60 and plant 75 deep in September.
Low maintenance.
Borders. Will grow in thin grass but does not spread much.

2. Low Plants and Shrubs 300–1 000 mm high

HERBACEOUS PERENNIALS

Acanthus mollis—Bear's Breeches—Acanthaceae

600 to 900 high foliage from slowly increasing deep rooted clumps.
Deeply divided heart-shaped leaves 600 long, 300 wide, almost evergreen in mild areas.
Spikes of purple and white flowers 900 to 1 200 high in July.
Has better foliage but is not so free flowering as *A. spinosus*.
A. mollis latifolius has larger leaves and is more robust.
A. spinosus is less vigorous with dark green deeply cut leaves and more persistent flower spikes.
Italy.

Any soil.
Sun or partial shade.
Drought resistant.
Plant well rooted clumps with a strong terminal bud.
Specimen, group, border.
In cold areas, may need winter protection until established.

341

Agapanthus campanulatus—African Lily—Liliaceae

300 to 450 high clumps of radical leaves growing from a short creeping rootstock with thick fleshy roots.
Strap-shaped green leaves.
Bell-shaped sky-blue flowers in umbels on erect stems 600 to 800 high in July to September.
A.c. 'Albus' has white flowers.
Headbourne Hybrids are a strain of seedlings varying in colour from pale to deep blue.
Natal.

Light well-drained soil. Chalk.
Sun or light shade.
Plant strong clumps in spring.
Expensive.
Border, specimen, containers.
Hardy in S. England but may need protection in cold areas.

Anemone × elegans (A. japonica)—Japanese Anemone—Ranunculaceae

600 to 1 000 high with thick basal foliage spreading by woody roots to form a dense clump.
Dark green three-lobed leaves, sometimes elegantly divided.
Saucer-shaped flowers 50 to 75 across in August to September.
Garden hybrid.
Many named cultivars varying in height and in colour from deep pink to white.
A. 'September Charm' is free flowering soft pink.
A. 'Luise Uhink' has semi-double white flowers.
Garden hybrid derived from S.E. Asia.

Any soil. Prefer heavy soil with some lime.
Sun or partial shade.
Town.
Plant pot-grown plants.
Border. Good ground-cover on heavy soil.
Slow to establish and do not grow strongly until second year.

Astilbe × arendsii— Saxifragaceae

600 to 1 000 × 450 to 600 slowly increasing clump of weed-proof groundcover.
Feathery leaves on thin, much branched upright stems. Leaves usually green but some are purplish in spring.
Conspicuous feathery plumes of tiny flowers in July to August on upright or arching stems.
Many named cultivars varying in colour from deep red to pink and white.
Garden hybrid derived from S.E. Asia.

Any moist soil.
Sun or partial shade.
Plant strong clumps.
Moist border, water-side.

Brunnera macrophylla (Anchusa myosotidiflora)—Boraginaceae

300 to 450 slowly spreading clumps.
Heart-shaped hairy leaves, small at first becoming large and coarse after flowering.
Forget-me-not like blue flowers on 450 stems during April–May.
W. Caucasus.

Any soil including chalky.
Best in moist well drained.
Half or full shade.
Cheap.
Plant well rooted clumps.
Good groundcover under trees.

342

Bupthalmum speciosum (Telekia speciosa)—Compositae

600 to 1 000 high dense foliage forming a good groundcover.
Herbaceous perennial.
Lower leaves very large and coarse.
Deep orange-yellow daisy flowers on thick upright branching stems 1 500 high June–August.
Showy seed heads.
C. Europe east to the Caucasus.

Best in moist soil.
Sun or shade.
Plant well-rooted clumps.
Border, wild garden, waterside.

Campanula glomerata 'Dahurica'—Campanulaceae

300 to 700 high spreading quickly by underground stems to form leafy clumps.
Narrow hairy leaves 40 to 80 long.
Rich violet funnel-shaped flowers in clusters on erect stems. June to August.
Europe incl. Britain.

Any soil, good on dry. Chalk.
Sun or half shade.
Plant strong clumps
Border.

Centranthus ruber (kentranthus)—Red Valerian—Valerianaceae

600 to 900 stout stems growing from a much branched perennial stock.
Greyish-green ovate-lanceolate leaves.
Dense cymes of tiny pinkish-red flowers at ends of stems from May to August.
C.r. 'Albus' is a white form.
Europe.

Any soil. Good on chalk.
Full sun or partial shade.
Plant strong plants or sow seed *in situ*.
Low maintenance.
Border, banks.
Spreads by self-sown seedlings.

Crambe cordifolia—Sea kale—Cruciferae

600 to 900 high foliage from spreading clumps with thick fleshy roots.
Dark green deeply-lobed cabbagey leaves 300 to 900 long.
Clouds of tiny white flowers in loose panicles up to 1 500 high in June.
Caucasus.

Any soil, best not acid.
Sun or partial shade.
Plant well rooted clumps with a strong terminal bud.
Specimen, group, border.

343

Dierama pulcherrimum (Sparaxis)—Wand Flower—Iridaceae

600 high foliage from slowly increasing clumps.
Stiff grassy leaves about 15 wide.
Wiry arching stems 1 000 to 1 500 high with pink or purple bell-shaped flowers July–August.
Named cultivars include low growing and selected colour forms.
S. Africa.

Best in deep well drained soil.
Sun or light shade.
Plant well rooted clumps in spring.
Specimen, border.
Not hardy in cold areas.

Echinops ritro—Globe Thistle—Compositae

900 to 1 200 high slowly increasing clumps with deep fleshy roots.
Divided greyish, prickly leaves.
Steely-blue flowers in globular heads on stiff erect stems in July to September. Border.
S. Europe, Balkans.

Any soil.
Sun or half shade.
Seaside.
Plant strong clumps.
Border.

Eryngium variifolium—Umbelliferae

100 high dense clumps of foliage from thick fleshy roots.
Basal leaves heart-shaped. Upper leaves and bracts deeply cut and veined with silver.
Blue teasle-like flowers on stiff branching stems 600 high in July persisting until autumn.
E. alpinum has large pale green leaves and metallic-blue flowers and upper stems.
N. Africa.

Any well-drained soil.
Sun.
Seaside.
Plant strong clumps.
Border.
Short-lived on heavy soil.

Euphorbia wulfenii (E. venata)—Euphorbiaceae

900 high evergreen bush with thick fleshy stems which die back after flowering.
Narrow bluish-green hairy leaves—evergreen in mild winters.
Broad terminal heads of greenish-yellow flowers in April to July up to 1 250 high.
E. characias has greyer-green leaves and green flowers with a maroon eye.
Turkey, Caucasus.

Any soil. Chalk.
Sun or partial shade.
Seaside.
Plant young pot-grown plants.
Expensive.
Border, specimen.

344

Geranium ibericum 'Johnson's Blue'—Geraniaceae
500 to 600 high spreading clumps of loose foliage.
Finely cut five-lobed light green leaves.
Profuse bright blue flowers June to August.
Cultivar.

Any soil.
Sun or half shade.
Plant strong clumps.
Border, groundcover.

Geranium psilostemon (G. armenum)—Geraniaceae
750 to 1 000 × 750 to 1 000 dense, slowly increasing clump.
Bright green deeply cut five-lobed leaves turning colour in autumn.
Brilliant magenta-crimson, black eyed flowers about 40 across. May to June.
Armenia.

Any deep soil.
Full sun or partial shade.
Plant strong clumps.
Border.

Hemerocallis cultivars—Day Lilies—Liliaceae
600 high fairly fast increasing clumps.
Broad grassy leaves are bright yellowish green in early spring becoming bright green and arching in summer.
Stout flower stems with clusters of lily-like flowers, each usually lasting only one day.
Many named cultivars available with flowers in the red, pink, orange, yellow colour range.
Hybrid.

Any soil including chalk or clay.
Sun or shade.
Wind tolerant, drought resisting.
Town.
Plant well rooted clumps.
Groundcover, border.
Will grow in grass on moist soils.

Hosta crispula (Funkia)—Plantain Lily—Liliaceae
450 × 450 slowly increasing clumps.
Dark green undulating leaves with a conspicuous white border, die down in autumn.
Loose racemes of pale mauve flowers on stems 600 high in June.
H. 'Thomas Hogg' is slightly smaller but very similar to, and more widely available than *H. crispula*.
Japan.

Any soil.
Sun or shade.
Town.
Plant well rooted clumps.
Expensive.
Waterside, group border, summer groundcover.

Hosta sieboldiana (H. glauca)—Plantain Lily—
Liliaceae

450 × 450 slowly increasing clumps.
Large blue-green glaucous leaves turn yellow in autumn before dying down.
Short dense racemes of pale lilac flowers on stems 600 high in June.
Decorative seed heads last through winter.
H.s. elegans has more rounded and bluer-grey leaves.
Japan.

Any soil.
Sun or shade.
Town.
Plant well rooted clumps.
Waterside, group, border.
Summer ground-cover.

Hosta undulata erromena (H. lancifolia fortis)—
Liliaceae

450 × 450 slowly increasing clumps.
Large rich green leaves dying back early in autumn.
Loose racemes of dark lavender flowers on stems 900 high in August.
H. undulata is only 380 high and has wavy green leaves with white central variegation and pale lilac flowers.
Japan.

Any soil.
Sun or shade.
Town.
Plant well rooted clumps.
Waterside, group, border.
Good groundcover in summer.

Iris, bearded or German cultivars—Iridaceae

450 to 600 high clumps of foliage from thick rhizomes at ground level.
Fans of stiff sword-like grey-green leaves.
Clusters of showy flowers on stout stems for a brief period in June.
Cultivars.
Named cultivars cover a very wide colour range.
I. pallida dalmatica has light lavender-blue fragrant flowers and grey foliage which remains in good condition through the summer.

Well drained soil containing lime.
Full sun.
Town.
Plant strong well rooted rhizomes.
Border.
Need replanting every 2–3 years to encourage flowering

Iris ochroleuca—Iridaceae

900 high clumps of stiff sword-like foliage.
Tough dark green leaves about 30 wide.
Clusters of large white flowers with a broad yellow mark on the falls, June–July.
Attractive seed heads.
Asia Minor.

Any soil.
Sun or partial shade.
Plant well rooted clumps.
Border, wild garden.

Iris pseudacorus—Yellow Flag—Iridaceae

600 to 1 000 high clumps of foliage from a thick horizontal rootstock.
Stiff erect leaves 25 to 50 wide, pale glaucous green.
Clusters of bright yellow flowers in May–June.
Good seed heads.
I.p. 'Variegata' has yellow stripes on the leaves in spring turning green later.
Europe incl. Britain, Asia.

Any soil that is not too dry.
Sun or partial shade.
Plant well rooted clumps.
Cheap.
Low maintenance.
Border, banks of streams, marshes and shallow water.

Iris sibirica—Iridaceae

600 to 1 000 high strong growing clumps from tufted roots.
Brown leaves persist. Stiff grassy leaves about 10 to 15 wide. Purple-blue flowers on strong stems above the leaves in June.
Decorative seed heads persist through the winter.
Named cultivars vary in colour from white to purple, blue and pink.
C. Europe, Russia.

Any soil. Best in moist.
Sun or partial shade.
Plant well rooted clumps.
Border, waterside.

Kniphofia uvaria (Tritoma)—Red Hot Poker—Liliaceae

600 to 1 000 high strong growing clumps.
Herbaceous.
Arching grey-green leaves up to 300 wide.
Flowers in spikes on stout stems above the leaves, in August–September.
Coral red, becoming orange and greenish yellow.
K. galpinii has grassy leaves and deep orange flowers on 600 high stems; only suitable for well drained soil and mild areas.
S. Africa.

Any well drained soil.
Sun or partial shade.
Wind tolerant.
Plant well rooted clumps in spring.
Border.
Not suitable for cold wet sites.

Limonium latifolium (Statice)—Sea Lavender—Plumbaginaceae

600 to 900 high flower branches above a clump of basal leaves. May take several years to establish but is long lived.
Broad leathery dull dark green leaves.
Large panicles of tiny lavender-blue flowers on wiry, much branched stems, July to August.
Dried flower stems remain attractive on plant over a long period.
Bulgaria, S. Russia.

Any well-drained soil.
Sun.
Seaside.
Plant strong clumps.
Border.

347

Lysimachia punctata—Primulaceae

600 to 1 000 spreading by fleshy roots to form a clump of upright stems.
Invasive on moist soils.
Bright green ovate leaves.
Whorls of bright yellow star-shaped flowers on erect leafy stems, July to August.
S.E. Europe.

Any soil. Best in moist.
Sun or partial shade.
Plant strong clumps.
Low maintenance.
Border, waterside.

Peltiphyllum peltatum (Saxifraga peltata)—Umbrella Plant—Saxifragaceae

600 high foliage from thick creeping rhizomes spreading to form wide clumps.
Large rounded leaves on single stems develop after flowering.
Wide heads of pale pink flowers in April.
California.

Any moist soil.
Sun or shade.
Plant well rooted rhizomes with a strong terminal bud.
Group, waterside.
Good for binding water-margins to prevent erosion.

Polygonatum multiflorum—Solomon's Seal—Liliaceae

600 to 1 000 spreading by slowly creeping fleshy rootstock to form a thicket of arching stems.
Light green ovate leaves 75 to 100 long along one side of upright or arching stem.
Greenish-white flowers like hanging bells in June.
Europe incl. Britain, N. Asia.

Any damp soil.
Part or full shade.
Drip tolerant. Town.
Plant strong roots with several buds.
Low maintenance.
Woodland, shady border, groundcover under trees.

Polygonum bistorta 'Superbum'—Polygonaceae

250 to 300 high dense clumps of foliage from thick, spreading rootstock.
Lanceolate leaves 75 to 150 long.
Pink flowers in poker-like spikes on stems up to 600 high in June to August.
P. bistorta grows naturally in moist meadows.
Europe incl. Britain.

Any soil, best in moist.
Sun or partial shade.
Seaside.
Plant strong clumps.
Border.

Rheum palmatum—Sorrel Rhubarb—Polygonaceae

600 to 900 high foliage from slowly increasing clumps.
Large rounded five-lobed rhubarb leaves.
Panicles of creamy flowers on stout stems 1 500 to 1 800 high June–July.
R.p. 'Bowles Crimson' has crimson flowers and the leaves have red undersides.
Tibet, China.

Any deep soil, best in moist.
Sun or partial shade.
Plant well rooted clumps with a strong terminal bud.
Expensive.
Specimen, group, waterside.

Rodgersia aesculifolia—Saxifragaceae

600 to 900 high foliage from slowly spreading underground shoots.
Large bronzy chestnut-like leaves.
Pinkish-white flowers in spikes 900 to 1 200 high in July.
R. pinnata has pinnate leaves and pink or white flowers.
China.

Any moist soil. Best if peaty.
Sun or partial shade.
Needs wind shelter.
Plant well rooted clumps with a strong terminal bud.
Expensive.
Specimen, group, waterside.

Rudbeckia fulgida—Compositae

750 to 900 high erect bushy growth spreading to form a wide clump.
Coarsely-toothed greyish-green leaves.
Deep yellow daisy flowers with a dark centre July to October.
S.E. USA.
R.f. 'Goldsturm' has larger flowers.

Any soil.
Sun or damp shade.
Plant strong clumps.
Border.

Salvia × superba (S. nemorosa 'superba')—Labiatae

900 to 1 000 spreading to form a dense clump with numerous upright branching stems.
Sage-green leaves up to 75 long.
Massed spikes of tiny violet-purple flowers, July to August.
Garden origin.
S. 'Lubecca' is a dwarf form growing 450 to 600 high.

Any soil.
Sun or partial shade.
Plant strong clumps.
Border.

349

Sedum spectabile—Crassulaceae

450 high clumps of straight stems from a woody rootstock.
Glaucous green fleshy oval leaves.
Flat heads of bright pink flowers in August to September.
S.s. 'Brilliant' has large heads of deeper pink flowers.
S.s. 'Autumn Joy' is taller and more vigorous with flowers fading to deep coppery-rose in October.
China.

Any well-drained soil.
Good in dry soil.
Sun or partial shade.
Seaside.
Plant strong clumps.
Border, groundcover.

Smilacina racemosa—Liliaceae

600 to 1 000 slowly spreading clump of upright stems. Slow to establish.
Soft green lanceolate leaves.
Panicles of fragrant creamy-white flowers at end of stems in May.
N. America.

Any soil. Best in cool moist lime-free soil.
Part or full shade.
Drip tolerant.
Plant strong clumps.
Expensive.
Low maintenance.
Woodland, shady border.

Verbascum chaixii (V. vernale)—Mullein—Scrophulariaceae

300 to 500 dense rosette of basal leaves producing stout flower stems up to 2 000.
Short lived perennial.
Very large greyish-green basal leaves.
Bright yellow flowers on branching spikes remain showy from early summer onwards.
Will seed itself and become naturalized under suitable conditions.
S. and C. Europe.

Any soil. Best on chalky soil.
Sun.
Plant strong clumps or sow seed *in situ*.
Border, wild garden.

EVERGREEN AND SEMI-EVERGREEN

Arundinaria fortunei (Pleioblastus variegatus)—
Gramineae

300 to 900 high tufted bamboo spreading rapidly to form a very dense groundcover of slender leafy stems. Evergreen.
Dark green leaves, striped white, 50 to 180 long. Leaves are persistent but are freshest from July to September.
A. vagans has bright green leaves and creeps to form a very dense cover about 300 high.

Any soil. Best in moist.
Sun or partial shade.
Seaside.
Plant strong clumps in late spring.
Expensive.
Low maintenance.
Groundcover, waterside.

Berberis candidula—Berberidaceae

600 to 900 × 1 200 to 1 800 slow growing, dense dome-shaped bush with rigidly arched branches.
Small spiny evergreen leaves 15–25 long, dark green above, silvery white beneath.
Bright yellow flowers 15 across in May. Oval fruits with a purple bloom.
W. Hupeh, China.

Any soil.
Sun or shade.
Good in towns.
Plant at 230 to 300 diameter.
Grouping, massing.
A very good groundcover but slow growing.

Bergenia cordifolia (Saxifraga Megasea)—Saxifragaceae

300 high foliage from slowly creeping roots.
Evergreen.
Large leathery, glossy green leaves roundly heart-shaped with undulate margins.
Pink flowers in large drooping sprays on stems 300 to 450 high.
March–April.
B.c. 'Purpurea' has purple-pink flowers and the leaves turn purplish-crimson in winter.
Siberia.

Any soil including chalky.
Sun or shade.
Plant well rooted clumps.
Groundcover, border.

351

Calluna vulgaris (Erica vulgaris)—Heather, Ling—Ericaceae

300 to 600 × 600 to 700 straggling much branched shrub forming a dense groundcover.
Evergreen.
Tiny deep green scale-like leaves.
Long racemes of purplish-pink flowers from July to October.
C.v. 'Alportii' is a vigorous erect form with spikes of crimson flowers 600 to 1 000 high.
C.v. 'H.E. Beale' has very long spikes of pale pink double flowers.
Many other named cultivars available.
N.W. Europe incl. Britain, naturalized in E. USA.

Any lime-free soil.
Best in well-drained peat.
Full sun.
Very hardy, wind tolerant.
Plant at 150 to 225 spread or pot grown plants with a minimum spread of 75.
Cheap.
Low maintenance.
Dry banks, groundcover, border.
Groundcover: plant 400 to 450 apart.

Cistus × corbariensis—Cistaceae

600 to 900 × 1 200 to 1 500 low spreading bush.
Small pointed leaves 20 to 50 long, dark dull green above, paler below. Evergreen.
Profuse crimson-tinted buds opening to white flowers 40 across in June.
Quick growing but somewhat short-lived.
Hybrid of *C. populifolius* × *C. salviifolius.*

Any soil. Best in light well-drained soil.
Sun or light shade.
Plant 230 to 300 high from pots.
Cheap.
Grouping, groundcover.
Good on dry banks as it is drought resistant.
Not reliably hardy in cold areas.

Cotoneaster conspicuus 'Decorus'—Rosaceae

600 to 900 × 1 200 to 1 800 wide vigorous spreading bush with long arching branches.
Tiny oval leaves, shining dark green above, grey beneath. Evergreen in mild winters.
Masses of solitary white flowers in June.
Showy long lasting round scarlet berries late September–February.
C. conspicuus is similar in appearance but the branches reach 1 500 to 1 800 high.
S.E. Tibet.

Any soil, including clay or chalk.
Sun or half shade.
Good in towns.
Plant root-balled or pot-grown plants 300 to 600.
Grouping, massing, groundcover.

Daboecia cantabrica—St Daboec's Heath—
Ericaceae
Low spreading shrub 300 to 600 high of dense growth.
Evergreen.
Narrow leaves, 5 to 10 long which are dark glossy green above and silvery beneath.
Flowers pitcher-shaped, rose-purple in erect racemes 75 to 100 long in June to November.
D.c. 'Alba' a good variety with white flowers.
D.c. 'Porter's Variety' a dwarf plant up to 300 high with rose-purple flowers.
D.c. 'Praegerae' is of dwarf spreading habit with deep pink, narrow flowers.
Ireland, France, Iberian peninsula.

Peaty or light sandy loam.
Intolerant to lime.
Full sun or partial shade.
Town.
Plant container-grown plants 100 to 150 high.
Useful for complete groundcover over large areas.

Epimedium pinnatum—Berberidaceae
300 to 450 high strong growing herbaceous perennial spreading by solid interlocking rhizomes to form a dense cover.
Persistent foliage.
Leaves have 5–11 ovate leaflets, green in spring, turning colour in autumn.
Tiny yellow spurred flowers on wiry stems in spring.
E.p. colchicum has larger flowers and is often evergreen.
Iran, Caucasus.

Any soil.
Sun or shade. Prefer light shade.
Drip tolerant.
Town.
Plant pot-grown plants.
Cheap.
Groundcover, border.

Erica × darleyensis—Ericaceae
450 to 600 × 450 to 800 vigorous shrub spreading rapidly to form a dense rounded bush.
Evergreen.
Tiny dark green linear leaves.
Numerous spikes of soft purple flowers from November to May.
Named cultivars have darker purple or white flowers.
Hybrid of *E. carnea* × *E. mediterranea*.

Any soil. Lime tolerant if humus is present.
Sun or partial shade.
Plant at 150 to 225 spread or pot-grown plants with a minimum spread of 75.
Cheap.
Low maintenance.
Groundcover, group, border.

353

Erica vagans 'Mrs. D. F. Maxwell'—Cornish Heath—Ericaceae

Low spreading shrub 300 to 600 high of compact habit.
Evergreen. ·
Mid-green leaves arranged in whorls 4 to 8 long.
Deep rose-pink flowers borne in racemes 150 to 200 long from July to November.
E.v. 'Grandiflora' tall loose-growing habit with long tapering sprays of pink flowers.
E.v. 'Lyonesse' has pure white flowers with distinctive brown anthers.
Europe incl. Britain, naturalized in E. USA.

Any light soil but intolerant to chalk conditions.
Best in full sun.
Town.
Plant root-balled or container-grown plants 100 to 150 high.
Good for sunny slopes or planting in large drifts.
To encourage more profuse flowering, plants should be clipped back in spring before growth commences.

Euonymus fortunei 'Variegatus'—Celastraceae

A trailing or climbing plant which can reach a height of more than 2 000 if grown against a wall, otherwise 300 to 500 when growing prostrate, spreading by rooting stems.
Evergreen.
Leathery ovate leaves up to 30 long, greyish-green, margined white and often tinged pink.
Insignificant small greenish-white flowers are borne in cymes in May and June on adult plants. Does not set seed. The type has glossy green leaves and sets orange seeds encased in a pink capsule.
Japan.

Any fertile soil.
Sun or shade.
Town.
Plant container-grown plants 150 to 200 high in autumn or spring.
Will tolerate considerable amounts of shade but less hardy than the type and should be grown with the protection of a wall or under trees.

Euphorbia amygdaloides robbiae—Euphorbiaceae

450 to 600 high herbaceous perennial Spreading to form a dense groundcover.
Evergreen.
Dull dark green leaves up to 100 long, forming neat rosettes.
Pale green-yellow flowers with showy green bracts opening in January and persisting until autumn.
Excellent groundcover for shade and under trees.
N.W. Asia Minor.

Any soil.
Sun or shade.
Drip tolerant.
Plant strong clumps.
Low maintenance.
Groundcover, group, waterside.

× **Fatshedera lizei**—Araliaceae

A vigorous and sprawling shrub with stout shoots which tend to grow erect and then flop over and growing in a scandant fashion.
Evergreen.
Leaves leathery, dark glossy green, 100 to 250 across.
Numerous pale creamy-green flowers are borne in October in terminal panicles 200 long and composed of numerous umbels each 25 in diameter.
Bigeneric hybrid between *Fatsia japonica* 'moseri' and *Hedera hibernica*.

Any well-drained soil.
Sun or shade.
Town or industrial areas.
Plant container-grown plants 150 high in autumn or spring.
Specimen in border if staked, otherwise as a groundcover on banks and in shady conditions.

Galax aphylla—Diapensiaceae

300 to 450 high herbaceous perennial spreading to form a thick groundcover.
Evergreen.
Shining green rounded leaves 75 across, becoming bronzy in winter.
Slender racemes of tiny white flowers in June–July.
N. and E. America.

Any lime-free soil.
Best in peat.
Full or partial shade.
Drip tolerant.
Plant strong clumps.
Groundcover, group.

Genista hispanica—Spanish Gorse—Leguminosae

450 to 900 × 1 200 to 1 800 dense mass of spiny branches forming a cushion-like bush.
The tiny leaves are deciduous but the crowded green twigs give an evergreen effect.
Covered with clusters of bright golden yellow pea-like flowers in May and June.
Small flat seed pods are insignificant.
Makes a good dense prickly barrier.
Spain, S.W. Europe.

Any soil. Best in well-drained soil of moderate quality.
Sun.
Plant pot-grown plants 150 to 300 high.
Cheap.
Grouping, ground-cover.
Not reliably hardy on rich soils or in shade.

Hebe cupressoides—Scrophulariaceae

600 to 1 000 × 600 to 1 000 much branched shrub forming a dense rounded bush.
Evergreen.
Grey-blue scale-like leaves giving the effect of a dwarf cypress.
Heads of tiny pale blue flowers in June to July, profuse in some seasons.
New Zealand.

Any soil, including chalk.
Full sun.
Seaside.
Plant at 200 to 400 high.
Group, border, low hedges.
Hedges: plant 450 apart.

Hebe rakaiensis (subalpina)—Scrophulariaceae

450 to 900 × 900 to 1 200 low spreading shrub forming a neat dense rounded bush.
Evergreen.
Small bright grass-green leaves, oval, arranged in four vertical rows on the stems.
Short spikes of tiny white flowers June–July.
Changes very little through the seasons and gives a very good winter effect.
New Zealand.

Any soil.
Sun or light shade.
Good in towns, seaside.
Plant pot-grown or root-balled plants 150 to 300 high.
Cheap.
Grouping, ground-cover.

Helleborus corsicus—Ranunculaceae

300 to 450 × 600 slowly increasing sub-shrubby clumps.
Evergreen.
Large leathery glaucous leaves with 3 spiny leaflets.
600 high panicles of pale green flowers February–March.
Corsica, Sardinia.

Any soil including chalky.
Best in partial shade.
Needs wind shelter.
Plant well rooted clumps.
Specimen, group.

Helleborus orientalis

300 to 450 × 450 slowly spreading clumps.
Evergreen.
Deep green leathery leaves with 5 to 11 elliptic leaflets.
Panicles of flowers varying from white to crimson November–April.
Greece, Asia Minor.

Any soil including chalky.
Best in partial or full shade.
Plant well rooted clumps.
Good groundcover under deciduous trees and shrubs.

Hyssopus officinalis—Hyssop—Labiatae

300 to 600 × 600 to 900 bushy shrub with dense upright stems.
Partially evergreen.
Densely packed dark greyish-green linear leaves.
Terminal spikes of deep blue flowers June–August
H.o. 'Roseus' has pinkish flowers.
H. aristatus is a dwarf species with purple-blue flowers and rich green foliage.
Leaves and young growth have a mint-like smell.
Mediterranean regions to C. Asia.

Light dryish soil.
Sun.
Plant pot-grown plants.
Group, groundcover, low hedging.
Hedges: plant 300 apart.

356

Iris foetidissima—Iridaceae

600 high fairly fast spreading clumps of foliage from a thick rootstock.
Evergreen.
Stiff deep green leaves about 30 wide.
Dull purplish-green flowers in June.
Seed pods open to show bright orange-scarlet berry like seeds.
I.f. 'Variegata' has green and cream striped leaves.
Europe incl. Britain.

Any soil including chalk and clay.
Sun or shade.
Drought resistant.
Drip tolerant.
Town.
Plant well rooted clumps with well developed foliage.
Low maintenance.
Good groundcover in almost any situation.
Best in moist shade.

Juniperus sabina tamariscifolia—Cupressaceae

450 to 600 × 1 200 to 1 800 dense spreading prostrate conifer with a tabular habit.
Rich green aromatic evergreen foliage, grey-green when young.
Good groundcover but rather slow.
S. Europe and Asia.

Any soil. Good on chalk.
Sun or light shade.
Plant root-balled or pot-grown plants 230 to 450 spread.
Expensive.
Specimen, grouping, groundcover.

Lavandula spica 'Hidcote'—Lavender—Labiatae

300 to 450 × 300 to 450 compact bush.
Evergreen.
Silvery-grey downy linear leaves 300 to 450 long.
Deep violet flowers freely born in compact spikes about 205 above the foliage.
Leaves and flowers are very fragrant.
Cut back in early spring to keep bushy.
Cultivar of Mediterranean origin.

Any well drained soil.
Full sun or partial shade.
Seaside.
Plant at 150–230 high.
Cheap.
Group, low hedging.
Hedges: plant 300 apart.

Liriope muscari (L. platyphylla)—Liliaceae

A hardy perennial growing in compact clumps 300 to 450 high.
Evergreen.
Leaves broad linear and glossy deep green.
Mauve bell-shaped flowers similar to grape hyacinth are borne on long wiry brownish-purple stems 150 to 300 long in August and November.
L. spicata has more erect and narrower leaves.
Japan, China.

Best in neutral or slightly acid sandy soil.
Full sun or partial shade.
Town.
Plant root-balled or container-grown plants 400 apart in March and April.
Large groups at the front of border or under trees. It is drought resistant and useful for dry banks once it is established.
Flower spikes should be removed after flowering.

357

Lonicera pileata—Caprifoliaceae

600 to 900 × 1 200 to 1 500 horizontally branched shrub with a neat spreading habit.

Evergreen elliptical leaves 15 to 40 long, bright green when young turning dark lustrous green.

Inconspicuous yellowish-white flowers in May.

Clusters of attractive violet berries.

Young plants tend to be more evergreen than older ones which may shed their leaves in cold winters.

China.

Any soil.
Sun or shade.
Seaside.
Plant at 300 to 450 high.
Cheap.
Grouping, massing, underplanting, groundcover.

Pernettya mucronata—Ericaceae

600 to 1 500 high spreading by suckers to form a dense thicket of thick stems.

Small dark green ovate leaves.

Numerous small white flowers near the ends of each shoot in late May and June.

Round berries coloured pink, white or purple produced freely and persist for several months.

May be cut by frost in very severe winters but will shoot again from the base.

S. America.

Lime-free soil. Best in sandy peat.
Full sun or half shade.
Plant at 230 to 380 high.
Grouping or massing.
Plant in groups to ensure cross-pollination.

Phlomis fruticosa—Jerusalem sage—Labiatae

750 to 900 × 1 200 to 1 500 fairly fast growing bushy shrub.

Evergreen.

Soft ovate leaves wrinkled and green above, white and hairy beneath.

Whorls of bright yellow flowers in late May and intermittently until August.

Mediterranean and S. Europe.

Any well-drained soil. Best on light sandy soil.
Full sun or partial shade.
Seaside.
Plant at 230 to 300 high.
Expensive.
Group.
Not hardy in very cold areas.

Phyllitis scolopendrium (Scolopendrium vulgare)—Hart's Tongue Fern—Aspleniaceae

300 to 450 high fern spreading by stout rhizomes to form a dense cover of fronds growing in tufts. Fronds persist until new growth appears in spring.

Long rich green strap-shaped fronds with undulate edges and a thick mid-rib.

May grow up to 1 000 high in mild, moist conditions.

Circumpolar N. Hemisphere incl. Britain.

Any soil including chalk.
Grows on poor soil but best in shade or moisture.
Sun or shade.
Drip tolerant.
Plant strong clumps or pot-grown plants.
Cheap.
Low maintenance.
Groundcover, group, specimen.

Polystichum aculeatum—Hard Shield Fern—Aspidiaceae

450 to 600 × 600 to 750 fern growing in circular clumps of fronds.
Evergreen.
Pale green scrolls of young fronds unroll in April–May and are fully developed by late June.
Mature fronds have a hard, leathery texture and are glossy, dark green with many lance shaped pinnae forming the frond 100 to 300 wide and 600 to 900 long.
Cosmopolitan.

Any well-drained soil.
Best in partial shade.
Town.
Plant strong clumps or pot-grown plants.
Groundcover, group, specimen.

Rubus tricolor—Rosaceae

A vigorous plant 300 to 700 high with long trailing stems densely covered with ginger bristles, spreads by rooting stems.
Evergreen.
Leaves cordate, 75 to 100 long, dark glossy green above and white felted beneath.
White flowers 25 diameter are borne singly in leaf axils in July, occasionally followed by bright edible fruits.
China.

Any moist soil.
Sun or shade.
Town.
Plant root-balled or container-grown plants 300 high.
Ideal for low ground-cover planting and used in contrast with other foliage plants.

Ruscus aculeatus—Butcher's Broom—Liliaceae

450 to 900 high dense low shrubby growth spreading by suckers from the base.
Dark dull evergreen rigid stems and spine-tipped 'leaves'.
Tiny dull white flowers in spring.
Small red berries on female plants September onwards.
Plant male and female plants or hermaphrodite form to produce berries.
Europe incl. Britain.

Any soil.
Light or dense shade.
Drip tolerant.
Low maintenance.
Grouping, massing, groundcover.
Good in dense shade under trees or shrubs.

Santolina chamaecyparissus (S. incana)—Cotton Lavender—Compositae

450 to 600 × 600 to 900 bushy sub-shrub spreading to form a low mound.
Evergreen.
Silver-grey leaves 25 to 38 long, densely crowded onto grey stems.
Bright yellow button-like flowers in July.
Flowers may be sheared off to improve appearance of shrub.
May be pruned back to near base of previous year's growth in April to keep bushy.
S. France.

Any soil. Best in poor soil.
Full sun.
Seaside. Very wind hardy.
Plant pot-grown plants.
Cheap.
Group, groundcover, low hedging.
Hedges: plant 300 apart.

Sarcococca humilis—Buxaceae

300 to 450 × 450 to 600 slow growing shrub spreading by new stems from the ground to form a dense leafy, neat bush.
Evergreen.
Narrowly oval glossy green leaves 25 to 75 long.
Small fragrant white flowers in early spring.
Shiny black berries in autumn.
China.

Any soil.
Full or partial shade.
Plant pot-grown or root-balled plants.
Groundcover, group.

Sasa veitchii—**(Arundinaria veitchii)**—Gramineae

A low growing, dense, thicket-forming bamboo with thin purplish-green stems 600 to 1 000 high, spreading by underground rhizomes.
Evergreen.
Leaves 100 to 250 long by 25 to 50 wide, deep green in summer withering to a straw colour along the margins in autumn giving the effect of variegation which lasts throughout the winter.
Not known to flower in this country.
Japan.

Any moist soil.
Sun or shade.
Town.
Plant container-grown plants 300 to 400 high.
Specimen where space permits, otherwise ideal for large areas to be completely covered also for ornamental use near water.

Tellima grandiflora—False Arum Root—Saxifragaceae

300 high clumps spreading to form a thick cover.
Evergreen.
Rounded hairy leaves are pinkish in spring, green in summer and turn crimson in autumn.
Spikes of fringed bell-like flowers on stems 600 high in May to June.
Flowers greenish at first becoming pink later.
T.g. purpurea has purplish leaves turning coppery-purple in autumn and winter.
Alaska to California.

Any soil.
Sun or shade.
Plant well-rooted clumps.
Cheap.
Group, border.
Groundcover under trees and shrubs.

Viburnum davidii—Caprifoliaceae

600 to 900 × 1 200 to 1 500 neat, compact, wide spreading bush.
Oval evergreen leaves 50 to 150 long, dark green above, paler below with deep longitudinal veins.
Tiny dull white flowers crowded in flat heads.
Bright turquoise-blue berries on female plants.
China.

Any soil, including chalky.
Sun or light shade.
Plant root-balled or pot-grown plants 300 to 380 high.
Expensive.
Specimen, grouping, groundcover.

Vinca major—Apocynaceae

450 to 600 high sub-shrub spreading rapidly by long shoots which root where they touch the ground. Invasive. Dense groundcover once established. Evergreen.
Glossy deep green leaves up to 75 long. Large bright blue flowers from May to September borne on erect shoots.
May be trimmed over in spring.
V.m. 'Variegata' grows 450 high and has leaves blotched and margined in creamy white.
C. and S. Europe incl. Britain.

Any soil that is not waterlogged.
Sun or shade. Best in shade.
Drip tolerant.
Town.
Plant well-rooted clumps.
Cheap.
Groundcover under trees.

Yucca filamentosa—Liliaceae

450 high rosette of leaves slowly spreading by short side growths.
Evergreen shrub.
Stiff slightly glaucous grey-green leaves.
1 000 to 1 500 high spikes of lily-like flowers in July–August.
Usually flowers when rosettes are about 3 years old.
S.E. USA.

Any soil—best in well drained.
Sun.
Wind tolerant.
Seaside.
Plant well-rooted clumps with strong foliage.
Expensive.
Specimen, border.

DECIDUOUS PLANTS AND SHRUBS

Caryopteris × clandonensis—Verbenaceae

600 to 1 000 × 1 000 to 1 250 slender branching twigs forming a dense rounded bush.
Lanceolate leaves 25 to 50 long dull green above and silver-grey beneath; dormant until late April.
Showy clusters of tiny violet-blue flowers at the ends of the current years shoots from August to October.
Best pruned to base of young growth each spring.
Hybrid of *C. incana* × *C. mongolica*.

Any well-drained soil including chalk, sand and gravel.
Full sun.
Plant pot-grown plants 300 to 450 high.
Group, border.

361

Ceratostigma willmottianum—Plumbaginaceae

600 to 1 000 high spreading freely by shooting from the base to form a low rounded bush.
The semi-woody stems usually die to the ground in cold winters.
Lanceolate leaves 25 to 50 long turning purplish-red in autumn.
Terminal clusters of very bright blue flowers from July to September.
W. China.

Any soil.
Sun.
Seaside.
Plant pot-grown plants.
Group, border.

Cotoneaster horizontalis—Rosaceae

Low spreading shrub rarely more than 300 to 400 high unless grown on a wall where it may reach 2 000.
Branches are arranged in characteristic herringbone fashion.
Leaves broadly ovate, glossy dark green which colour in the autumn.
Flowers are pale pink, 7 to 10 diameter and appear in May and June, followed by glossy red berries.
China.

Any well-drained soil.
Full sun or partial shade.
Town, industrial areas.
Plant container-grown or root-balled plants 200 to 300 high.
Group, groundcover or specimen.
Good on banks, open areas or against north and east facing walls.

Genista lydia (Spathulata)—Leguminosae

450 to 600 × 1 000 to 1 200 slender wiry grey-green arching shoots forming a pendulous wide spreading bush.
Tiny grey-green linear leaves.
Masses of deep yellow pea-like flowers in May to June.
E. and S.E. Europe, Syria.

Any soil.
Full sun.
Seaside.
Plant pot-grown plants.
Expensive.
Rock garden, dry wall.

Petasites fragrans—Winter Heliotrope—Compositae

Herbaceous perennial 300 high spreading by thick underground rhizomes.
Leaves dark green, cordate at base and rounded with toothed margins.
Small purplish-pink or white, vanilla scented heads of flowers, 5 to 10 diameter in short racemes 250 high in February just before the leaves.
Europe.

Any moist soil.
Best in shade.
Town and industrial areas.
Plant container-grown plants or roots in autumn and February or March.
Large groups to colonize banks or under trees, useful for coastal cliffs.
A rampageous spreader in moist soil.

Potentilla 'Elizabeth'—Rosaceae

600 to 1 000 × 1 000 to 1 250 bright brown twiggy growths forming a dense spreading bush.
Dainty light green pinnate leaves.
Large deep yellow buttercup-like flowers from May to September.
N. Hemisphere incl. Britain.
Hybrid of *P. arbuscula* × *P. fruticosa mandshurica*.

Any well-drained soil, including chalk.
Full sun or half shade.
Seaside.
Plant at 300 to 450 high.
Group, border.

Rosa pimpinelli folia—Scotch or Burnet Rose—Rosaceae

300 to 600 high forming a dense thicket of erect much branched shoots spreading by creeping roots.
Armed with prickles.
Deep green leaves 25 to 60 long consisting of 5–9 oval leaflets.
White or pale pink flowers 40 to 50 across in May to June.
Europe incl. Britain, W. Asia.
Many named cultivars usually much taller than the species.

Any soil. Best in dry sandy soil.
Sun.
Seaside. Hardy and wind tolerant.
Plant strong plants with well ripened shoots.
Low maintenance.
Group, groundcover.
Good on dry soils on hills or near sea.

Spiraea × bumalda 'Anthony Waterer'—Rosaceae

600 to 1 000 × 1 000 to 1 250 erect branches forming a bushy rounded shrub.
Coarsely toothed lanceolate leaves up to 100 long.
Flat heads of tiny bright crimson flowers July to August.
Best pruned back hard in March.
Hybrid *S. japonica* × *S. albiflora*.

Any soil
Sun or partial shade.
Plant at 250 to 450 high.
Group, border, low hedges.

3. Plants and Shrubs 1 000–1 500 mm high

HERBACEOUS PERENNIALS

Aruncus sylvester (Spiraea aruncus)—Rosaceae

1 000 to 1 200 high clumps of upright stems with dense foliage increasing slowly.

Deep green pinnate leaves with serrated leaflets 30 to 70 long.

Large plumes of tiny creamy-white flowers in June rising above leaves to 1 250 to 1 800 high.

Flowers rather short-lived but foliage remains attractive until autumn.

N. Hemisphere.

Any moist soil.
Full sun or partial shade.
Plant well-rooted clumps.
Border, specimen, wild garden.
Will grown in thin grass.

Cynara cardunculus—Cardoon—Compositae

1 200 to 1 500 high foliage from slowly increasing clumps with thick fleshy roots.

Very large, deeply cut silvery-grey spiny leaves.

Large spine-tipped blue thistle-like flowers August–September.

C. scolymus 'Glauca'—Globe Artichoke—has a similar habit but is less spiny.

Any deep soil.
Full sun.
Plant well-rooted clumps.
Specimen, group, border.
Plant in spring.

Digitalis purpurea—Foxglove—Scrophulariaceae

200 to 300 high dense rosette of leaves in first year.

Hardy biennial or short lived perennial.

Greyish-green oblong or lanceolate leaves 200 to 300 long.

Spikes of purple, mauve or white flowers.

900 to 1 500 high in early summer of second year.

Plants usually die after flowering but produce large quantities of seed and will naturalize under suitable conditions.

W. Europe incl. Britain, Asia.

Any soil.
Sun or shade.
Cheap.
Plant young seedlings or sow seed *in situ*.
Woodland, wild garden.

364

Filipendula purpurea (Spiraea palmata)—Rosaceae

900 to 1 200 high dense clumps of foliage.
Large deep green leaves 5 to 7-lobed.
Flat heads of tiny crimson flowers on leafy stems rising above basal foliage.
Japan.

Best in moist soil.
Sun or partial shade.
Plant well-rooted clumps.
Border, wild garden, waterside.

Foeniculum vulgare—Fennel—Umbelliferae

1 200 to 1 500 dense clump of stout erect branching stems.
Short lived herbaceous perennial.
Greyish-green feathery pinnate leaves with very narrow linear segments.
Yellow flowers in large umbels in August–September.
Showy seed heads.
All parts of the plant are aromatic.
F.v. 'Smoky' has blackish-red young leaves.
Europe incl. Britain.

Any soil. Good on chalk.
Sun.
Seaside.
Plant well-rooted clumps.
Border, wild garden.
Self-sown seedlings may become invasive.

Ligularia dentata (Senecio clivorum)—Compositae

1 000 high dense clumps of foliage increasing slowly to form a good groundcover.
Very large deep green leathery lower leaves.
Orange-yellow daisy flowers in large loose heads up to 1 500 high in July–August.
Named cultivars available.
China, Japan.

Any soil moist in summer.
Sun or partial shade.
Plant well-rooted clumps.
Border, waterside.

Macleaya cordata (Bocconia)—Plume Poppy—Papaveraceae

1 200 to 1 500 high close set leafy stems quickly spreading by running roots.
Large roundish glaucous leaves white beneath.
Plumes of tiny creamy-white flowers up to 2 000 high at ends of shoots.
M. microcarpa is a taller species with buff-coloured flowers.
China, Japan.

Any well-drained soil.
Sun or partial shade.
Town.
Plant well-rooted clumps.
Border, specimen.
May become invasive in good soil.

365

Osmunda regalis—Royal Fern—Osmundaceae

1 200 to 1 800 high deciduous fronds from a woody rootstock.
Feathery fronds are light green in spring becoming darker with age.
Upper portion of fertile fronds densely covered with spore capsules in summer and resemble brown flower spikes.
Fronds quickly cut by frost in autumn.
Cosmopolitan except Australia.

Any moist soil.
Sun or partial shade.
Plant strong clumps.
Expensive.
Low maintenance.
Specimen, group, waterside.

Reynoutria japonica (Polygonum cuspidatum)—Polygonaceae

1 500 to 2 300 high quickly spreading to form a dense thicket of outward curving unbranched stems.
Red-brown stems are attractive in winter.
Large oval-oblong deep green leaves.
Tiny creamy-white flowers in showy feathery panicles July to October.
Japan.

Any soil.
Sun or partial shade.
Plant well-rooted clumps.
Wild garden, waterside.
Very rampant and can become invasive.

EVERGREEN AND SEMI-EVERGREEN

Artemisia abrotanum—Southernwood—Compositae

900 to 1 200 × 900 to 1 200 shrub with erect stems densely furnished with leaves to form a rounded bush.
Evergreen.
Soft greyish-green finely cut aromatic leaves.
Insignificant flowers in terminal spikes in late summer.
May be kept bushy by pruning previous year's growth to base in early spring.
S. Europe.

Any well-drained soil.
Full sun or partial shade.
Plant at 230 to 455 high.
Group.

Berberis gagnepainii—Berberidaceae
1 200 to 1 800 × 900 to 1 500 strong growing erect bush forming a dense thicket of spiny branches and prickly leaves.
Narrowly tapering dark green leaves 40 to 100 long with undulating toothed margins.
Clusters of small bright yellow flowers late May to June.
Inconspicuous black berries.
W. China.

Any soil. Good on chalk.
Sun or half shade.
Plant at 300 to 600 high.
Hedge specimen or group.
Hedges: plant 300 apart.
Makes a good dense barrier.

Berberis verruculosa—Berberidaceae
900 to 1 500 × 1 500 to 2 100 slow growing arching branches forming a compact dome-shaped bush.
Dense with prickly stems and leaves.
Small shiny dark green leaves, whitish underneath, with wavy prickly margins.
Small primrose yellow flowers in May.
Inconspicuous black berries.
W. China.

Any soil.
Sun or half shade.
Tolerant of air pollution.
Plant at 300 to 450 high.
Specimen or group.

Cistus × purpureus—Cistaceae
1 000 to 1 500 high shrub or rounded habit.
Young branches downy and resinous.
Evergreen.
Leaves oblong, dull greyish-green, scented, 25 to 50 long.
Flowers appearing in June and July, 60 to 75 across, reddish-purple with a conspicuous dark red blotch at the base of each petal.
Hybrid.

Any well-drained soil.
Full sun.
Town.
Plant container-grown plants 300 high.
Specimen or group.
Not reliably hardy in the coldest districts.

Cotoneaster amoenus—Rosaceae
1 000 to 1 500 high shrub of a graceful spreading habit.
Semi-evergreen.
Oval leaves 25 long, glossy green on surface, thick grey wool beneath.
Flowers white, numerous, borne in corymbs, followed by bright red berries in late summer.
Yunnan, China.

Any soil.
Sun or partial shade.
Town, industrial areas.
Plant root-balled plants 300 to 600 high.
Specimen or group.

Erica mediterranea (E. erigena, hibernica)—
Ericaceae

1 200 to 1 800 × 1 200 to 1 800 dense bushy shrub.
Tiny dark green linear leaves.
Numerous small rosy-red fragrant flowers from March to May.
E.m. 'Superba' is a free-flowering form with a neat upright habit.
E.m. 'W. T. Rackliff' has white flowers and dense compact growth.
S. France, Spain, N. Ireland.

Any soil. Will grow on chalk.
Sun or half shade.
Plant at 150 to 230 spread.
Cheap.
Grouping and massing.

Escallonia 'Apple Blossom'—Escalloniaceae

1 200 to 1 800 × 1 200 to 1 800 forming a rounded compact bush.
Evergreen.
Glossy dark green oval leaves 10 to 25 long.
Showy heads of small pink and white flowers in June–July.
Hardy in warm sheltered places inland or in coastal areas.
Cultivar originating from S. America, Chile.

Any soil, including chalky.
Best in sandy soil.
Sun.
Seaside.
Plant root-balled or pot grown plants 450 to 900 high.
Informal hedging, group, border.
Hedges: plant 750 apart.

Fabiana imbricata—Solanaceae

1 000 to 1 500 high heath-like shrub.
Evergreen.
Leaves heath-like, narrow, pale green.
Small white tubular flowers festoon the branches in May and June.
F.i. violacea is similar but with lavender-mauve flowers.
Chile.

Moist, well-drained neutral or acid soil.
Full sun.
Town.
Plant container-grown plants 300 high.
Specimen or group.
Requires some shelter.

Gaultheria shallon—Ericaceae

900 to 1 500 high spreading indefinitely by underground suckers to form a dense thicket of stems.
Broadly ovate leathery leaves 40 to 100 long.
Racemes of small pinkish-white flowers in May and June.
Dark purple edible berries.
W. and N. America.

Any soil. Best in moist peat.
Sun or shade.
Good under trees.
Plant strong clumps.
Cheap. Low maintenance.
Massing. Good covert plant under trees.

Hebe brachysiphon (traversii)—
Veronica—Scrophulariaceae
1 500 to 1 800 × 1 800 to 2 400 wide spreading neat rounded bush.
Small dark, dull green leaves densely arranged on the shoots.
Racemes of tiny white flowers in July.
New Zealand.

Any soil.
Half shade or sun.
Good in towns. Salt resistant.
Plant at 300 to 750 high.
Hedge specimen or group.
Hedges: plant 380 apart.

Hypericum patulum 'Hidcote'—Guttiferae
1 200 to 1 800 × 1 200 to 1 800 forming a rounded bush of dense twiggy branches.
Semi-evergreen.
Deep green oval leaves 25 to 60 long.
Showy golden saucer-shaped flowers 50 across July–October.
Himalayas, S.W. China, Japan.

Any soil, including chalky.
Sun or half shade.
Plant at 300 or 600 high.
Group, border.

Juniperus × media 'Pfitzeriana'—Pinaceae
1 200 to 1 800 × 3 000 or more, wide spreading conifer with drooping tips to the branchlets.
Greyish-green foliage, juvenile leaves awl-shaped, adult leaves scale-like.
Foliage gives off a strong aromatic odour when bruised.
Hybrid of *J. sabina* × *J. sphaerica*.

Any soil. Good on chalk.
Full sun or light shade.
Plant at 300 to 750 spread.
Expensive.
Specimen or group.

Pieris floribunda (Andromeda)—Ericaceae
1 200 to 1 800 × 1 500 to 2 400 slow growing rounded bush.
Leaves ovate, 40 to 75 long. Dark glossy green above, paler below.
Numerous erect panicles of tiny white flowers in March and April.
S.E. USA.

Lime-free soil. Best in moist peat.
Half shade. Best in open woodland.
Plant at 300–900 high.
Expensive.
Specimen or group.

Rosmarinus officinalis—Rosemary—Labiatae

900 to 1 500 × 1 500 to 1 800 loose spreading shrub.
Evergreen.
Linear leaves 20 to 50 long dark shining green above, white downy below.
Tiny pale violet-blue flowers in April to May.
Best pruned after flowering to keep bushy.
R.o. 'Pyramidalis' (Miss Jessop's Upright) is a more erect form with paler flowers.
S. Europe, Asia Minor.

Any well-drained soil. Sun or partial shade.
Seaside. Wind tolerant.
Plant at 230 to 450 high.
Group, low hedging.
Hedges: plant 300 apart.
Not hardy in very cold areas.

Ruta graveolens 'Jackman's Blue'—Rue—Rutaceae

900 to 1 200 × 900 to 1 200 sub-shrub forming a dense rounded bush.
Evergreen.
Finely cut glaucous-blue foliage.
Small bright yellow un-showy flowers June to September.
Leaves have a pungent smell when crushed.
Trim in April to keep bushy.
S. Europe.

Any soil.
Full sun or partial shade.
Seaside.
Plant pot-grown plants.
Groundcover, group, low hedging border.
Hedges: plant 300 to 380 apart.

Salvia officinalis 'Purpurascens'—Purple Sage—Labiatae

750 to 900 × 1 200 to 1 500 shrub spreading to form a rounded bush.
Evergreen.
Soft greyish-purple leaves 25 to 40 long.
Purplish flowers in June.
Leaves have characteristic sage smell when crushed.
S. Europe.

Any well-drained soil.
Full sun or partial shade.
Seaside.
Plant at 230 to 380 high.
Group, border.

Senecio greyi (S. laxifolius)—Compositae

750 to 1 500 × 1 200 to 1 800 spreading bush, becoming straggly if not trimmed.
Evergreen.
White felted oval leaves 50 to 80 long.
Clusters of golden yellow daisy-like flowers June to July.
The plant in cultivation is probably a hybrid but is usually known as *S. greyi*.
New Zealand, N. Island.

Any soil, including chalky.
Best in sandy soil.
Sun or half shade.
Seaside.
Plant root-balled or pot-grown plants 200 to 400 high.
Border, dry banks.

Skimmia japonica—Rutaceae

900 to 1 500 × 75 to 100 slow growing broadly dome-shaped bush.
Yellowish-green oval leaves 75 to 100 long.
Small fragrant white flowers in terminal panicles during April and May. Male and female flowers on different plants.
Bright red berries on female plants persist through the winter.
S.j. 'Foremanii' is a female form with larger dark green leaves and large scarlet berries.
Japan, Sakhalin, Kuriles.

Any soil. Chalk or acid.
Best in moderate shade.
Good in towns.
Plant at 230 to 455 high.
Group to ensure berrying.

Ulex europaeus—Common Gorse, Furze or Whin—Leguminosae

900 to 1 500 × 1 500 to 2 100 forming a broadly spreading bush of tightly packed branches.
Very dense and spiny.
Dark green linear leaves 5 to 15 long or reduced to spines.
Small bright golden yellow pea flowers through most of the year but make a blaze of colour in May.
Dead twigs are retained within the bush and burn very readily during dry spells.
U.e. plenus—Double Gorse is a more compact form suitable for gardens.
W. Europe incl. Britain and E. to Italy. Extensively naturalized in C. Europe.

Best in poor dry soil.
Not shallow chalk soil.
Full sun.
Wind and salt resistant.
Plant at 230 to 455 high.
Cheap. Low maintenance.
Grouping and massing.
Not recommended for rich soils when it gets leggy and does not flower freely.

DECIDUOUS SHRUBS

Berberis thunbergii—Berberidaceae

1 200 to 2 000 × 1 500 to 2 200 dense bushy shrub with stiff reddish-brown thorny branches.
Fairly quick growing.
Light green leaves 10 to 40 long turning bright scarlet in autumn.
Small pale yellow flowers in April–May.
Showy scarlet berries in autumn.
B.t. 'Atropurpurea' has reddish-purple foliage turning red in autumn; taller than the type.
Japan.

Any soil, including clay.
Sun or half shade.
Town. Seaside.
Plant root-balled or pot-grown plants 300 to 600 high.
Group, border.
Hedges: plant 600 apart.

Cytisus × praecox—Leguminosae

1 200 to 1 500 × 1 500 to 2 000 arching and spraying green branches forming a dense bush. Rapid growth.
Grey green leaves about 10 long.
Masses of pale yellow flowers in April–May. Heavy scent which may be unpleasant in a confined space.
Garden origin *C. multiflorus × C. purgans*.

Any soil.
Full sun.
Seaside.
Plant pot-grown plants 300 to 600 high.
Group, border.

Deutzia × elegantissima—Philadelphaceae

Upright bushy shrub 1 200 to 1 500 high.
Leaves lanceolate, slender pointed and matt green.
Fragrant, star-shaped, pink to rose-purple flowers in paniculate corymbs 50 to 75 dia. in May and June.
D. × e. 'Fasciculata' is a clone with bright rose-pink flowers.
Hybrid of *D. purpurascens × D. sieboldiana*.

Any fertile soil.
Full sun or partial shade.
Town.
Plant root-balled or container-grown plants 300 to 500 high.
Specimen or group.

Kerria japonica—Rosaceae

1 200 to 1 800 × 1 500 to 2 000 arching and spraying branches forming a wide bush. Bright green twigs.
Lanceolate leaves 40 to 100 long.
Yellow buttercup-like flowers April–May.
K.j. 'Pleniflora' has orange-yellow double flowers and a taller, more upright habit.
China, Japan.

Any soil, including clay.
Sun or half shade.
Plant at 600 to 1 200 high.
Group, border.

Perowskia atriplicifolia—Labiatae

900 to 1 500 × 900 to 1 500 sub-shrub with upright silvery stems.
Silvery white coarsely toothed leaves 300 to 750 long, 150 to 300 wide.
Attractive spikes of lavender blue flowers in late summer.
Leaves have a sage-like aroma.
Prune to base of previous year's growth in April.
Afghanistan, W. Himalaya to Tibet.

Any well drained soil. Chalk.
Full sun.
Plant pot-grown plants 230 to 380 high.
Expensive.
Border, group.

Potentilla fruticosa 'Katherine Dykes'—Rosaceae

1 200 to 1 500 × 1 200 to 1 500 bright brown twigs forming a dense bush. Dainty pinnate leaves 25 to 40 long. Yellow buttercup-like flowers 25 to 40 across May–October.

P.f. 'Vilmoriniana' makes a neat rounded bush with silvery green foliage on upright branches and creamy-white flowers.

Europe incl. Britain, Asia, America.

Any soil, including chalky.
Best in sandy soil.
Sun or half shade.
Seaside.
Informal hedges, group, border.
Hedges: plant 600 apart.
Best if old growth is thinned out each March.

Rosa rugosa—Rosaceae

1 200 to 1 800 × 1 500 to 2 000 thicket of stout thorny stems forming a dense rounded bush.
Leaves 75 to 125 long consisting of 5–9 leaflets, turning yellow in autumn.
Pink saucer-shaped flowers about 90 across in June and after. Very fragrant.
Showy large red shiny hips.
Many named hybrids with flowers of white, pink and deep red, and of varying habit.
Japan, N.E. Asia.

Any soil, including clay.
Sun.
Seaside.
Plant at 450 to 900 high.
Hedges, border.
Hedges: plant 900 apart.

Weigela florida (amabilis) (rosea)—Caprifoliaceae

1 400 to 1 800 × 1 800 to 2 500 spreading and arching branches forming a wide shrub.
Oval leaves 50 to 100 long.
Showy flowers in clusters along previous year's shoots in May and June, pink, white or red.
'Bristol Ruby' has deep red flowers.
'Eva Rathke' has dark foliage, crimson flowers, and slow compact growth.
Japan, Korea, N. China, Manchuria.

Any soil, including chalky.
Sun or half shade.
Seaside. Town.
Plant at 450 to 900 high.
Informal hedging, border, group.
Hedges: plant 600 apart.

4. Plants Shrubs and Small Trees 1 500–3 000 mm high

EVERGREEN

Berberis × Stenophylla—Berberidaceae
2 400 to 3 000 × 3 000 to 3 600 wide spreading bush with slender arching branches forming a dense thicket.
Narrow dark green, spine tipped leaves.
Masses of tiny golden-yellow flowers in April and May.
Blue-black berries in August fall quickly.
Hybrid of *B. darwinii* × *B. empetrifolia*.

Any soil.
Best in sun.
Seaside, town.
Plant root-balled or pot-grown plants 395 to 750.
Formal and informal hedges, grouping.
Hedges: plant 395 apart.

Buxus sempervirens—Common Box—Buxaceae
3 700 to 5 500 × 3 700 to 5 500 rounded bush or small tree according to its early treatment.
Oval leaves 15 to 25 long, shiny dark green above, paler below.
Insignificant pale green flowers in April.
Many cultivars including pendulous, erect, large leaved and variegated forms.
S. Europe, N. Africa, W. Asia.

Any soil. Good on chalk.
Sun or dense shade.
Fairly resistant to air pollution.
Plant at 300 to 900 high.
Low maintenance.
Formal hedges, topiary, screen or windbreak.
Hedges: plant 300 to 600 apart.

Choisya ternata—Mexican Orange Blossom—Rutaceae
1 800 to 3 000 × 2 400 to 3 000 rounded bush.
Bright green shiny leaves usually consisting of three leaflets.
Clusters of sweetly scented white flowers from April to June.
Best planted in spring on heavy soils or in colder areas. Not quite hardy until established.
Mexico.

Any soil.
Half shade.
Good near sea but needs shelter from cold winds.
Plant root-balled or pot-grown plants 300 to 600 high.
Specimen, group.
Not suitable for cold, exposed sites.

Cotoneaster franchetii—Rosaceae
2 400 to 3 000 × 2 400 to 3 600 shrub
with graceful arching branches.
Small greyish-green leaves.
Inconspicuous whitish flowers May to
June.
Orange-red berries.
C.f. sternianus is a better form with
sage-green leaves that are silvery
underneath and large bright berries.
China.

Any soil.
Sun or shade.
Seaside.
Plant 450 to 1 050
high.
Specimen, group,
formal and informal
hedges.
Hedges: plant 600
apart.

Elaeagnus × ebbingei—Elaeagnaceae
3 000 to 4 600 × 3 000 to 4 600 fast-
growing forming a roundish bush of
thin twiggy shoots.
Thin silvery green oval leaves 40 to 100
long.
Small fragrant white flowers in
October–November.
Has a lighter effect than most evergreens.
Hybrid of *E. macrophylla* × *E. pungens*.

Any soil.
Sun or light shade.
Salt and wind re-
sistant.
Plant at 450 to 750
high.
Low maintenance.
Screen, hedge,
windbreak.
Hedges: plant 450 to
600 apart.

Elaeagnus pungens—Elaeagnaceae
2 400 to 3 600 × 3 000 to 4 500 vigorous
spreading shrub.
Sometimes spiny.
Leathery oval leaves 40 to 100 long,
dark glossy green above, dull white
below.
Small fragrant white flowers in
October–November.
E.p. 'Variegata' has pale yellow mar-
gins to the leaves.
There are many other less attractive
forms.
Japan.

Any soil. Chalk,
sand.
Sun or shade.
Resistant to salt
winds and air
pollution.
Plant at 300 to 600
high.
Low maintenance.
Screen, hedge.
Hedges: plant 380 to
455 apart.

Euonymus japonicus—Celastraceae
3 000 to 4 500 × 3 000 to 4 500 fast-
growing shrub or small tree.
Narrowly oval leaves 25 to 75 long,
leathery dark shiny green.
Insignificant greenish-white flowers
May–June.
Many forms available including silver
and golden variegated varieties.
Japan.

Any soil. Chalk.
Sun or dense shade.
Very resistant to
salt spray and air
pollution.
Plant at 300 to 750
high.
Cheap. Low
maintenance.
Screen, hedge,
windbreak.
Hedges: plant 380 to
455 apart.

375

Fatsia japonica (Aralia sieboldii)—
Araliaceae
1 800 to 4 500 high wide-spreading shrub or small tree. Thick stems, sparsely branched.
Large shiny dark green palmate leaves 300 to 400 across.
White globular flower heads in October.
Japan.

Well-drained soil.
Semi-shade.
Town, seaside.
Needs wind shelter.
Plant pot-grown plants 300 to 600 high.
Cheap.
Specimen, border, group.

Kalmia latifolia—Mountain Laurel—Calico Bush—
Ericaceae
1 800 to 3 000 × 1 800 to 3 000 dense bush, slow growing at first.
Rich glossy green leaves 50 to 125 long, 20 to 40 wide.
Clusters of flowers in May and June varying in colour from pale pink to deep rose.
Eastern N. America.

Lime-free soil. Best in moist.
peaty soil.
Half shade.
Plant root-balled or pot-grown plants 300 to 600 high.
Expensive.
Specimen, group.

Ligustrum vulgare—Common Privet—Oleaceae
1 800 to 3 000 × 2 400 to 3 600 wide spreading bush with arching branches. Semi-evergreen.
Narrowly oval leaves 25 to 65 long.
Dull white heavily scented flowers in erect panicles, June to July.
Showy black berries are eaten by birds.
N.E. Europe, Britain.

Any soil. Best on calcareous.
Town, seaside.
Wind tolerant.
Plant 450 to 900 high.
Cheap.
Low maintenance.
Shelter belts, covert planting, specimen, group.

Mahonia japonica—Berberidaceae
1 800 to 3 000 high stiff, bushy spreading shrub.
Large deep green pinnate leaves.
Fragrant lemon-yellow flowers in long pendulous clusters in March and April.
Purple berries.
China.

Any well-drained soil, including chalky.
Sun or half shade.
Seaside.
Plant root-balled or pot-grown plants 300 to 600 high.
Specimen, border.

376

Myrtus communis—Common Myrtle—Myrtaceae
1 500 to 2 500 high densely leafy shrub, wide spreading.
Leaves glossy, mid to deep green, ovate, 25 long, aromatic.
Flowers white, 25 wide with a brush of fluffy stamens from the centre, slightly fragrant, produced in July and August and sometimes followed by purple-black ovoid fruits.
Mediterranean, S.W. Europe, W. Asia.

Any well-drained soil, chalk.
Full sun.
Town, seaside.
Plant container-grown plants 300 to 450 high.
Requires shelter in exposed cold districts.

Olearia haastii—Daisy Bush—Compositae
1 500 to 2 400 × 1 800 to 3 000 dense rounded bush.
Thick leathery oval leaves 12 to 25 long dark shiny green above, white felted below.
Flattish clusters of fragrant white flowers in July and August.
Seed heads covered with brownish down persist through winter.
New Zealand.

Lime-free soil.
Sun or shade.
Town, seaside.
Plant at 300 to 600 high.
Specimen, group, informal hedging.
Hedges: plant 300 apart.

Phillyrea decora (P. vilmoriniana) (medwediewii)—Oleaceae
1 500 to 3 000 × 2 400 to 3 600 rigidly branched shrub.
Narrowly oval pointed leathery leaves 50 to 125 long, very dark glossy green above, paler below.
Clusters of small fragrant white flowers in April.
Oval, reddish fruits in September turning purplish-black.
W. Asia.

Any soil.
Sun or shade.
Fairly resistant to air pollution.
Plant at 300 to 600 high.
Low maintenance.
Screen, informal hedge, specimen.
Hedges: plant 300 to 750 apart.

Phormium tenax—New Zealand Flax—Agavaceae
1 500 to 3 000 high dense clumps of foliage with semi-woody rootstocks spreading by thick fleshy roots.
Rigid leathery sword-like grey-green leaves.
Bronzy-red flowers in panicles up to 4 500 high in summer.
P.t. 'Purpureum' has bronze-purple leaves.
P.t. 'Variegatum' has a creamy-white margin to the leaves.
New Zealand.

Any soil, likes moisture.
Sun or half shade.
Seaside, town.
Plant strong clumps.
Group, specimen, border, waterside.
Hardy except in very cold areas.

Prunus laurocerasus—Common or Cherry laurel—Rosaceae

4 500 to 6 000 × 6 000 to 9 000 quick growing wide spreading bush with hungry roots.
Dark shiny green oblong leaves 100 to 150 long.
Racemes of insignificant white flowers in April.
Black-purple fruits in autumn.
Many forms available varying in hardiness, leaf size, and habit.
E. Europe, Asia Minor.

Any soil. Chalk, peat.
Sun or shade.
Moderate resistant to salt winds.
Not draughty or exposed.
Plant at 450 to 1 200 high.
Cheap. Low maintenance.
Hedge, screen, windbreak.
Hedges: plant 300 to 900 apart.

Prunus lusitanica—Portugal Laurel—Rosaceae

3 000 to 7 500 × 4 600 to 9 000 wide bush or round-headed small tree according to its early treatment.
Pointed oval leaves 60 to 125 long, very dark glossy green above, paler below.
Showy racemes of small scented white flowers in June–July. Spikes of dark purple fruits.
Spain, Portugal.

Any soil. Chalk, peat.
Sun or shade.
Fairly resistant to air pollution.
Plant at 450 to 900 high.
Low maintenance.
Specimen, screen, windbreak.
Hedges: plant 450 to 900 apart.

Rhododendron ponticum—Ericaceae

2 400 to 4 500 × 3 600 to 6 000 rounded shrub or may form a small tree.
Becomes leggy and sparse in dense shade.
Narrow oblong leaves 100 to 205 long, very dark glossy green above, paler below.
Showy heads of mauve flowers in May–June.
Poisonous to cattle, but usually avoided.
Spain, Portugal, Asia Minor.

Any soil. Not good on chalk. Likes moist peat.
Sun or dense shade.
Resistant to air pollution.
Plant at 450 to 900 high.
Low maintenance.
Screen, hedge, woodland, windbreak.
Hedges: plant 900 to 1 200 apart.

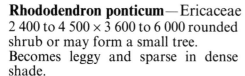

Spartium junceum—Spanish Broom—Leguminosae

2 400 to 3 000 × 2 400 to 3 000 forming a leggy bush of rush like green stems.
Very few tiny deciduous leaves.
Large rich yellow scented pea-like flowers in terminal racemes from June to September.
Becomes leggy at base unless pruned back each spring.
Mediterranean, Canary Isles.

Any soil, including chalky.
Best in dry sandy soil.
Sun.
Seaside.
Plant pot-grown plants 450 to 750 high.
Group, mass.
Good for hot, dry banks.
May be sown *in situ*.

Viburnum tinus—Laurustinus—Caprifoliaceae

1 800 to 3 000 × 2 400 to 3 600 much branched bush, furnished to the ground.
Narrowly oval dark glossy green leaves 40 to 100 long.
Pink buds opening to form flat cymes of tiny white flowers any time between November–April.
Several forms available, usually less hardy than the type.
S.E. Europe.

Any soil. Best in moist loam.
Sun or shade.
Fairly resistant to air pollution.
Plant at 300 to 450 high.
Low maintenance.
Screen, hedge, grouping.
Hedges: plant 450 apart.

DECIDUOUS

Aesculus parviflora (Pavia macrostachya)—Hippocastanaceae

2 500 to 3 000 high shrub spreading by sucker growths at the base. May be grown as a small tree if trained to a single stem.
Leaves consist of 5 or 7 leaflets radiating from the end of a long stalk.
Turn yellow in autumn.
White flowers with red anthers, in erect spikes during July and August.
S.E. USA.

Any soil.
Sun.
Town.
Plant at 450 to 900 high.
Expensive.
Specimen, group.

Aronia arbutifolia—Red Chokeberry—Rosaceae

2 000 to 3 000 high vigorous bushy shrub spreading slowly by suckers.
Narrow oval leaves 40 to 80 long, dark green above, grey and felty beneath.
Bright red autumn colour.
Corymbs of small white flowers in May.
Bright red berries.
A.a. 'Erecta' has a narrow upright habit and brilliant crimson autumn tints.
E. North America.

Any soil except shallow soil over chalk.
Damp sites.
Sun or half shade.
Plant at 450 to 750 high.
Specimen, group.

Buddleia 'Lochinch'—Loganaceae

2 000 to 3 000 high shrub with bushy, compact habit.

Lanceolate leaves, grey and downy at first becoming green above with age.

Fragrant violet blue flowers in dense conical panicles at end of current year's shoots. May be hard pruned in March.

Buddleia davidii cultivars, in many colours, may be hardier but are usually leggier in habit.

All are very attractive to butterflies.

Hybrid of *B. davidii* × *B. fallowiana*.

Any soil.
Sun.
Seaside, town.
Plant root-balled or pot grown plants 450 to 900 high.
Specimen, group.

Ceanothus 'Gloire de Versailles' (Delinianus group) Rhamnaceae

1 500 to 2 500 high bushy, strong growing, branching shrub.

Deciduous.

Soft green oval leaves.

Large panicles of tiny powder-blue flowers July to October.

Prune in April, if required.

May be cut by severe frost but usually shoots again from the base.

Any soil.
Sun.
Town.
Plant pot-grown plants 450 to 900 high.
Group, wall plant, border.

Cytisus scoparius (Sarothamnus scoparius)— Common Broom—Leguminosae

1 500 to 2 000 high quick growing, bushy shrub with dense green stems giving an evergreen effect.

The dark green leaves 6 to 15 long.

Rich yellow pea flowers in May, followed by seed pods 35 to 50 long.

Will naturalize by seeding.

Short-lived and may be used as a temporary filler.

Many named cultivars available.

Europe including Britain.

Any soil, except shallow soil over chalk or very acid soil.
Sun.
Town, seaside.
Plant pot-grown plants 300 to 600 high or seed *in situ*.
Cheap.
Group, dry banks.

Ficus carica—Common Fig—Moraceae

2 000 to 3 000 high small spreading tree or shrub spreading rapidly by suckers.

Large deep green lobed leaves 100 to 200 long.

Flowers produced inside fleshy receptacle which afterwards develops into edible fruit.

Needs warm sheltered position and restriction of roots for fruit production.

W. Asia.

Any soil, including chalky.
Sun.
Town, seaside.
Needs wind shelter.
Plant well-rooted suckers or pot-grown plants 450 to 1 200 high.
Wall plant, specimen.

380

Heracleum mantegazzianum—Giant Hogweed—
Umbelliferae

1 500 to 1 800 high foliage from deep rooted clumps.
Very large deeply divided leaves.
Immense heads of tiny white flowers on stout stems 2 400 to 3 000 high.
May die after flowering but spreads rapidly from seed.
Hairs on leaf and stem may produce blisters on people allergic to them.
Caucasus.

Any soil.
Sun or shade.
Plant strong clumps or sow seed.
Low maintenance.
Specimen, group.
Not suitable for confined areas.
Will naturalize under suitable conditions.

Rosa × cantabrigiensis—Rosaceae

2 000 to 3 000 high shrub with arching branches. Dense bristly stems.
Fragrant fern-like leaves with 7 to 11 leaflets.
Fragrant creamy-yellow rose flowers 50 across in May–June.
Small round orange hips in late summer.
R. hugonis is similar but less vigorous.
Hybrid of *R. hugonis* × *R. sericea*.

Any soil.
Sun.
Town.
Plant well-rooted plants with at least 2 well-ripened shoots.
Specimen, group, border.

Rosa 'Nevada'—Rosaceae

1 500 to 2 000 high dense shrub rose with almost thornless arching branches.
Rich green pinnate leaves varying in size with 5 to 9 leaflets.
Single ivory-white flowers. 100 across, often flushed pink in hot weather are borne profusely in May and June and intermittently onwards.
Hybrid *R. moyesii fargesii* × Hybrid tea.
R. 'Marguerite Hilling' is a sport from *R.* 'Nevada' with semi-double flowers, deep flesh pink and more fragrant.

Any soil.
Sun.
Town, industrial areas.
Plant bare-rooted plants 450 to 750 high with strong root systems and well-ripened shoots.
Group, screen, specimen.

Rosa 'Penelope'—Rosaceae

1 500 to 2 000 high sturdy and vigorous hybrid musk rose with strong branching shoots.
Broad glossy pinnate leaves with 5 to 7 leaflets.
Free flowering, semi-double, scented, rich creamy-pink on opening, fading paler.
Coral pink hips covered with grey bloom.
Hybrid Musk Shrub Rose.

Any soil.
Sun.
Town.
Plant bare-rooted plants 400 to 700 high with a strong root system.
Specimen, group.
Hedge or screen.

381

Rubus cockburnianus (giraldianus)—Rosaceae

2 000 to 2 500 × 1 500 to 1 800 strong growing shrub with purple arching thorny stems, covered with a white bloom.
Leaves pinnate, fern-like and composed of 7 to 9 leaflets, pale green above and white or grey beneath.
Flowers rose-purple, 10 to 15 wide, appearing in June are of little merit and are often followed by inconspicuous bloomy black fruits.
N. and C. China.

Any soil, best in moist conditions.
Sun or partial shade.
Plant container-grown or root-balled plants 450 to 700 high.
Group planting for effect of white stems.
Old stems should be pruned out after flowering.

Rubus × tridel—Rosaceae

2 500 to 3 000 high vigorous shrub with erect, peeling thornless shoots, arching with age.
Three to five-lobed leaves 40 to 75 long.
Rose-like white flowers 50 across borne singly along arching branches in May.
'Benenden' is a selected clone.
Hybrid of *R. deliciosus* × *R. trilobus*.

Any soil.
Sun or light shade.
Plant pot-grown 450 to 750 high.
Specimen, group, border.

Spirea × arguta—Rosaceae

1 500 to 2 100 × 1 500 to 2 100 slender branches forming a bushy shrub.
Narrow bright green leaves 20 to 40 long.
Clusters of pure white flowers along upper side of previous year's shoots in April and May.
Hybrid of *S. multiflora* × *S. thunbergii*.

Any soil.
Sun.
Plant at 600 to 1 200 high.
Group, informal hedging.
Hedges: plant 450 to 600 apart.

Symphoricarpos × chenaultii—Caprifoliaceae

1 800 to 2 400 × 2 700 to 3 600 broad spreading twiggy bush.
Small fresh green oval leaves.
Small pink bell-shaped flowers June to July.
Pale pink to bright purple-red rounded fruits.
Hybrid of *S. microphyllus* × *S. orbiculatus*.

Any soil.
Half or full shade.
Towns.
Drip resistant.
Plant at 450 to 900 high.
Group, mass, underplanting.

382

Viburnum × bodnantense—Caprifoliaceae

2 500 to 3 000 high vigorous shrub with a strong upright habit.
Dull green leaves 50 to 100 long.
Tiny fragrant tubular flowers, pinkish in bud, opening to white, in dense clusters December–February.
V. farreri (fragrans) is upright at first becoming rounded with age. It has smaller flower clusters but is very hardy.
Hybrid of *V. farreri* × *V. grandiflorum.*

Any soil.
Sun or half shade.
Town.
Plant at 450 to 900 high.
Expensive.
Specimen, group, border.

Viburnum opulus 'Sterile' ('Roseum')—Snowball—Caprifoliaceae

2 000 to 2 500 high shrub of upright bushy habit.
Maple-like dark green leaves with 3 to 5 lobes, 75 to 100 long, colouring richly in the autumn.
Flowers are totally sterile and are gathered into conspicuous globular creamy-white heads which become white with age.
V. opulus is more vigorous and open, with flat corymbs of flowers followed by copious bunches of glistening red fruits.
Europe, incl. Britain, N. Africa.

Any moist soil.
Sun.
Town, industrial areas.
Plant root-balled plants 400 to 600 high.
Specimen, group.

Viburnum plicatum 'Mariesii' (V. tomentosum)—Caprifoliaceae

2 500 to 3 000 high, wide-spreading shrub with tiered horizontal branches.
Green pleated oval leaves up to 100 long, turning dark red in autumn.
White flowers in umbels in May and June. Small fertile flowers in centre surrounded by conspicuous sterile florets.
V.p. 'Lanarth' is stronger growing and less horizontal in habit. *V. plicatum tomentosum* is the wild form with slightly smaller ray florets and less horizontal habit.
China, Japan, Taiwan.

Any soil.
Sun or light shade.
Plant at 450 to 900 high.
Expensive.
Specimen or group.

383

5. Large shrubs and small trees 3 000–7 500 mm high

EVERGREEN

Arundinaria japonica (Pseudosasa)—Gramineae

3 000 to 4 500 or sometimes higher dense thickets of olive-green canes arching at the top. Spreads slowly by underground suckers.
Dark glossy green leaves 180 to 300 long and 20 to 50 wide.
Very hardy.
Japan.

Any soil. Best in moist.
Sun or half shade.
Seaside.
Plant strong clumps in spring and cut to half height after planting.
Cheap.
Low maintenance.
Specimen, group, screen.

Arundinaria murieliae (Sinoarundinaria)—
Gramineae

2 500 to 3 500 clumps of graceful arching canes, at first bright green changing to dull yellow. Spreads by underground suckers.
Bright green leaves 60 to 100 long and 10 to 20 wide.
A. nitida is usually taller than
A. murieliae and has narrower leaves and purplish stems.
China.

Any soil. Best in moist.
Sun or half shade.
Needs shelter from cold winds.
Plant strong clumps in spring and cut to half height after planting.
Specimen, group, waterside.

Cotoneaster lacteus—Rosaceae

3 000 to 4 000 × 3 500 to 4 500 wide bush with graceful spraying growth.
Large leathery oval leaves dark green above, grey beneath. 30 to 55 long and 20 to 30 wide.
Small creamy-white flowers in corymbs 50 to 75 wide in July.
Long lasting berries become red in late autumn.
China.

Any soil including chalky.
Full sun or partial shade.
Seaside. Town.
Plant pot grown plants 450 to 750 high.
Hedges, screen, group, specimen.
Hedges: plant 600 apart.

Cotoneaster salicifolius floccosus—Rosaceae

3 500 to 5 000 × 3 500 to 5 000 with slender spraying branches forming an arching bush.
Evergreen in mild winters. Leathery lanceolate leaves 20 to 60 long and 5 to 20 wide, the upper surface wrinkled dark green, grey white beneath.
Tiny white flowers in corymbs 25 across in June.
C.s. rugosus has broader leaves, larger flowers and coral red berries.
China.

Any soil including chalky.
Full sun or partial shade.
Seaside. Town.
Plant pot grown plants 450 to 750 high.
Specimen, group.
Hedges: plant 500 apart.

Cotoneaster × watereri—Rosaceae

4 500 to 6 000 × 5 000 to 7 000 fast growing open bush or small tree, depending on early training, with wide spraying arching branches.
Evergreen in mild winters.
Dark dull green leaves 40 to 75 long.
Tiny flowers in corymbs June–July.
Profuse clusters of showy scarlet berries in autumn persisting for a long time.
Hybrid of *C. frigidus* × *C. henryanus* × *C. salicifolius*
C. 'John Waterer' is a named clone of *C.* × *watereri*.

Any soil including chalky.
Sun.
Seaside. Town.
Plant pot grown or root-balled plants 600 to 1 250 high.
Specimen, group, screen.

Griselinia littoralis—Cornaceae

5 000 to 8 000 high dense shrub or growing to a tree 1 200 high in mild areas.
Leathery, glossy yellowish-green oval leaves 25 to 120 long.
Inconspicuous yellowish-green flowers in May.
Liable to frost damage in cold inland areas.
New Zealand.

Any soil. Chalk.
Sun.
Seaside.
Plant at 300 to 750 high.
Hedging, coastal shelterbelts.
Hedges: plant 450 apart.

Magnolia grandiflora—Magnoliaceae

6 000 to 9 000 slow growing, round-headed shrub or tree.
Glossy green leathery leaves, reddish-brown beneath, 150 to 250 long.
Very large fragrant, creamy-white flowers during summer and early autumn.
Flowers more freely with wall protection in Britain.
Named clones include 'Exmouth' which flowers at an early age.
S.E. USA.

Any soil, including deep soil over chalk.
Full sun or half shade.
Needs wind shelter.
Plant root-balled or pot-grown plants 300 to 600 high.
Expensive.
Wall plant, specimen.

385

Pyracantha coccinea 'Lalandei' — Rosaceae

3 500 to 4 500 × 3 500 to 4 500 bush, taller if wall trained. Vigorous and upright when young becoming arching at maturity.

The very dense branches are often spine-tipped.

Oval leaves 25 to 60 long, dark glossy green above, paler beneath.

Masses of small pinkish-white flowers in corymbs in June.

Large bright orange berries usually eaten by birds.

S. Europe, Asia Minor.

Any soil.
Sun or shade.
Seaside. Town.
Plant pot-grown plants 450 to 750 high.
Hedge, screen, group, north wall.
Hedges: plant 600 to 1 000 apart.

Stranvaesia davidiana — Rosaceae

4 000 to 6 000 × 4 000 to 6 000 very vigorous shrub or small tree with upright branches and spreading side shoots.

Dark green leathery lanceolate leaves 70 to 1 000 long. Oldest leaves turn bright red in winter.

Clusters of small white flowers in June.

Clusters of bright red globular fruits last until January.

W. China.

Any soil.
Sun or partial shade.
Industrial areas.
Plant at 450 to 900 high.
Informal hedges, specimen, group.
Hedges: plant 600 to 900 apart.

Viburnum rhytidiphyllum — Caprifoliaceae

3 000 to 6 000 high wide spreading, fast growing shrub. Stout branches covered with brownish down.

Large corrugated oval leaves 80 to 200 long, dark green above, grey beneath.

Flat heads of creamy-white flowers in May or June.

Oval fruits, red at first, turning black.

Plant in groups for free fruiting.

C. and N. China.

Any soil. Chalk.
Sun or half shade.
Needs wind shelter.
Plant pot-grown or root-balled plants 450 to 1 000 high.
Specimen, group, border.

DECIDUOUS

Acer ginnala—Aceraceae

5 000 to 7 500 × 6 000 to 8 000 wide-spreading tree or bush.
Bright green three-lobed leaves 60 to 90 long.
Brilliant orange and red autumn tints but leaves usually fall soon after colouring.
Small clusters of yellowish-white fragrant flowers in May.
China, Manchuria, Japan.

Any soil. Clay.
Sun or partial shade.
Plant at 450 to 750 high.
Specimen, group.

Acer palmatum—Aceraceae

4 500 to 7 500 rounded tree often wider than its height. Bushy when young becoming more open with age.
Palmate leaves with 5 or 7 lobes, 50 to 90 long and wide, green at first becoming bronzed or purplish and turning orange in autumn.
Small purple flowers in erect clusters.
Small winged fruits.
Many different forms obtainable including 'Atropurpurea' with reddish purple leaves and 'Osakazuki' with deeply toothed green leaves turning brilliant scarlet and orange in autumn.
Japan, C. China, Korea.

Any good soil. Best on lime-free.
Sun or half shade.
Need protection from cold winds for young leaves.
Not hardy in cold areas.
Plant root-balled or pot-grown plants 450 to 900 high.
Specimen.

Amelanchier laevis (A. canadensis)—Rosaceae

6 000 to 9 000 high wide-topped round tree or bush.
Slow-growing.
Oval leaves 40 to 75 long, 25 to 40 wide, bronzy-purple when young becoming green later and changing to a soft red before falling.
Fleeting white flowers at end of April when leaves are unfolding.
Showy when in full bloom.
N. America.

Any soil.
Sun or half shade.
Smoke tolerant.
Plant at 600 to 1 200 high bush or standard.
Cheap.
Specimen, group.

Buddleia alternifolia—Loganiaceae

3 000 to 6 000 × 3 000 to 6 000 very vigorous shrub or small tree with graceful long arching branches.
Greyish lanceolate leaves 40 to 100 long.
Bright mauve fragrant flowers densely crowded in clusters along pendulous shoots in June.
Best trained to tree form when it looks like a small weeping willow.
China.

Any soil. Best in sandy loam.
Full sun.
Seaside.
Plant root-balled or pot-grown plants 450 to 1 000 high.
Specimen, group.

Cercis siliquastrum—Judas Tree—Leguminosae

4 500 to 7 500 spreading low-forking bush or sometimes a taller tree on a distinct trunk. Slow growing until established.
Roundish, glaucous green leaves 60 to 100 across.
Bright rose-purple pea flowers produced in May to June before the leaves.
Seed pods 75 to 125 long remain on plants throughout the winter.
E. Mediterranean.

Any soil. Tolerant of dry soils and chalk.
Sun.
Sheltered position.
Smoke tolerant.
Plant at 450 to 1 000 high in May.
Cheap.
Specimen.

Colutea arborescens—Bladder Senna—Leguminosae

3 000 to 4 000 × 3 500 to 5 000 wide spreading much branched bush.
Bright green pinnate leaves 75 to 150 long.
Numerous small pea-shaped yellow flowers from June until the frosts.
Showy inflated bladder-like seed pods.
S. Europe, Mediterranean.

Any soil that is not waterlogged.
Sun or shade.
Town.
Plant at 600 to 1 000 high.
Low maintenance.
Specimen, group, dry banks.
Will naturalize by seeding itself.

Cornus mas—Cornelian Cherry—Cornaceae

4 500 to 7 500 high slow-growing bushy shrub or spreading small tree.
Dark dull green ovate leaves 40 to 100 long, 20 to 40 wide.
Good autumn colour on poor soils.
Showy clusters of tiny yellow flowers during February and March on leafless stems.
Bright red fruits not often seen in Britain.
C.m. 'Variegata' has a creamy white border to the leaves and is less vigorous.
C. and S. Europe.

Any soil. Chalk.
Sun or half shade.
Plant at 450 to 1 000 high.
Cheap.
Specimen, group, hedging.

388

Corylus avellana—Hazel, Cobnut—Corylaceae

4 500 to 5 500 × 4 500 to 5 500 bushy shrub usually forming a dense thicket of erect much branched stems suckering from the base.
Rounded leaves 50 to 100 long, 40 to 75 wide.
Showy soft yellow male catkins 40 to 60 long in February.
Edible nuts ripen in autumn and leaves turn soft yellow before falling.
C.a. 'Aurea' is a form with soft yellow leaves.
Europe incl. Britain, W. Asia, N. Africa.

Any soil including chalky.
Sun or shade.
Plant root-balled plants 450 to 1 000 high.
Low maintenance.
Screen, woodland.
Hedges: plant 300 to 600 apart.

Corylus maxima 'Purpurea' ('Atropurpurea')—Purple-leaf Filbert—Corylaceae

4 000 to 5 000 × 5 000 to 6 000 wide-spreading shrub or small tree.
Roundish dark purple leaves 50 to 125 long.
Purple catkins in February.
Cultivars of *Corylus maxima* are grown for their edible nuts.
S. Europe, W. Asia.

Any soil. Clay.
Chalk.
Sun or partial shade.
Plant at 450 to 900 high.
Specimen, group, hedging.
Hedges: plant 300 to 600 apart.

Cotinus coggygria (Rhus cotinus)—Venetian Sumach—Anacardiaceae

3 000 to 4 500 × 3 500 to 5 000 much branched dense rounded bush.
Ovate green leaves 40 to 75 long.
Fawn plume-like inflorescences cover the bush in June–July, turn pinkish and then smokey-grey by late summer.
Leaves turn orange and red in autumn.
C.c. 'Royal Purple' has dark purple leaves and purplish-pink inflorescences.
C. and S. Europe.

Any soil. Best not too rich.
Sun.
Town.
Plant at 300 to 750 high.
Specimen, group.

Cytisus battandieri—Leguminosae

3 500 to 4 500 × 3 000 to 4 500 forming an open bush of rather upright branches growing from the base.
Trifoliate leaves 40 to 70 long covered with silky white hairs giving a silvery appearance.
Erect racemes of fragrant golden yellow flowers in June.
In very cold areas is only hardy when trained against a wall.
Morocco.

Well drained soil, including chalky.
Sun.
Town.
Plant pot-grown plants 300 to 600 high.
Expensive.
Specimen, group, wall plant.

389

Elaeagnus angustifolia—Elaeagnaceae

4 500 to 6 000 × 4 500 to 6 000 loose growing large shrub or small tree, the young shoots covered with silvery scales.
Silvery willow-like leaves 25 to 100 long.
Tiny fragrant white flowers in June.
Yellowish oval fruits 12 long.
Whitest foliage produced in full sun.
Temperate Asia; naturalized in S. Europe.

Any soil. Best in sandy loam.
Full sun.
Wind resistant.
Plant root-balled or pot-grown plants 450 to 750 high.
Expensive.
Specimen, group.

Genista aetnensis—Mount Etna Broom—Leguminosae

4 500 to 6 000 × 3 000 to 4 500 with erect shoots forming a leggy bush when young, becoming a small tree with numerous pendant green shoots.
Very sparse foliage consisting of tiny linear leaves.
Numerous golden yellow pea-like flowers scattered singly on current year's shoots in July and August.
Sardinia and Sicily.

Any soil. Best in sandy.
Sun.
Seaside.
Plant pot-grown plants 500 to 1 000 high.
Specimen, group.

Gunnera manicata—Gunneraceae

3 000 to 3 600 high slowly spreading clumps.
Enormous rhubarb-like leaves 1 200 to 1 800 across coarsely toothed.
Flowers in long stout spikes, dull green turning reddish.
Leaves cut early by frost in autumn.
Herbaceous.
Brazil.

Deep moist soil.
Full sun.
Needs wind shelter.
Plant strong clumps.
Expensive.
Specimen, waterside.
Best planted in spring.
Cover crowns in winter in cold areas.

Hamamelis mollis—Chinese Witch Hazel—Hamamelidaceae

4 000 to 5 500 × 4 000 to 5 000 shrub or small tree with upspreading branches.
Roundish soft hairy leaves 75 to 125 long turning yellow in autumn.
Rich golden-yellow fragrant flowers with strap-shaped petals, from December to March.
H.m. 'Pallida' has large soft sulphur yellow flowers.
China.

Any lime-free soil.
Clay.
Sun or partial shade.
Plant pot grown or root-balled plants 450 to 900 high.
Expensive.
Specimen, group.

Hippophae rhamnoides—Sea Buckthorn—Elaeagnaceae

3 500 to 4 500 × 3 000 to 3 500 shrub with open branching habit when young becoming dense and rounded with age. The stiff twigs are often spine tipped. Narrow silvery leaves 25 to 75 long, 3 to 6 wide. Very small flowers in April in clusters along twigs. Showy orange-yellow berries from September–February on female plants. Plant both sexes to ensure berrying. Europe, temperate Asia.

Any soil. Good in sandy. Damp sites. Sun. Very wind resistant and salt tolerant. Plant at 450 to 1 250 high. Cheap. Low maintenance. Group, rough hedges, windbreak. Hedges: plant 600 to 1 000 apart.

Magnolia × soulangiana—Magnoliaceae

4 500 to 7 000 high × 7 500 to 10 000 wide spreading slow-growing tree or shrub. Oval green leaves 75 to 150 long. Large goblet-shaped flowers start in April on bare shoots and continue until early June. Flowers are white inside and purplish outside. Many named forms including 'Alba' with pure white flowers and erect growth and 'Rustica Rubra' with deep rosy-purple flowers and more vigorous growth. Hybrid of *M. denudata* × *M. liliiflora* 'Nigra'.

Any soil that is not too dry. Clay. Sun. Town. Plant pot-grown or root-balled plants 450 to 900 high in April or May. Specimen.

Morus nigra—Common Mulberry—Urticaceae

6 000 to 9 000 high tree with a dense spreading head and short rough trunk. Fairly fast growing at first becoming rugged with age. Deep glossy green ovate leaves 60 to 120 long start to unfold at end of May—usually turn yellow in autumn. Dark red edible fruits 20 to 25 long ripen and drop from end of July to mid-October. *M. alba* is a taller tree without the rugged charm of nigra—the leaves are fed to silkworms. W. Asia.

Any well-drained soil, chalk. Sun. Town, seaside. Not for cold areas. Plant young plants with strong single stems. Expensive. Specimen. Falling fruits may be a nuisance near paths or seats.

Parrotia persica—Hamamelidaceae

5 000 to 8 000 × 7 000 to 10 000 large shrub or small tree with vigorous outward spreading branches. Patchwork grey bark on older stems. Ovate leaves 70 to 125 long. Flowers consist mostly of clusters of red stamens in March. Very showy autumn tints of gold and crimson. N. Iran to Caucasus.

Any soil. Lime-tolerant. Sun. Plant at 900 to 1 800 high. Expensive. Specimen, group.

391

Prunus spinosa—Blackthorn—Rosaceae

3 000 to 5 500 high dense suckering shrub or small bushy tree.
Dark spiny branches.
Small oval leaves 20 to 45 long.
Small white flowers in March and early April on naked branches.
Blue-black round plum-like fruits 12 diameter.
P.s. 'Purpurea' is a compact form with rich purple leaves.
Europe incl. Britain, N. Africa, W. Asia.

Any soil. Dry or damp. Chalk.
Sun or partial shade.
Cold exposed areas.
Seaside.
Plant at 450 to 1 000 high.
Cheap.
Hedges, shelterbelts.
Hedges: plant 300 apart in double row.

Prunus × yedoensis—Yoshino Cherry—Rosaceae

6 000 to 9 000 quick-growing bush or tree with semi-arching branches spreading upwards and out.
Dark green oval leaves 60 to 110 long, narrowing to a point.
Very pale pink buds opening to single pure white flowers at end of March and April—usually before leaves.
Hybrid of *P. speciosa × P. subhirtella* introduced from Japan.

Any soil, clay, deep soil over chalk.
Sun.
Plant bare-rooted bushes or standard trees.
Specimen, group.

Pyrus salicifolia 'Pendula'—Willow-leaved Pear—Rosaceae

5 000 to 7 500 small tree with weeping branches. May become dense and bushy unless pruned and trained to tree shape.
Narrow silvery grey leaves 40 to 90 long becoming greyish-green later.
White flowers in April.
Cultivar originating from Caucasus.

Any well-drained soil. Chalk.
Town.
Plant feathered trees 1 800 to 2 500 high or standards.
Expensive.
Specimen, group.

Rhus typhina—Stag's Horn Sumach—Anacardiaceae

3 000 to 6 000 high wide spreading, sparsely branched small tree or large shrub spreading by suckers to form a thicket in light soils. Thick branches covered with reddish-brown hairs.
Large pinnate leaves 300 to 600 long turning orange and red in autumn.
Showy conicle crimson fruit clusters persisting through winter on female plants.
R.t. 'Laciniata' has deeply cut leaflets and is less vigorous.

Any soil.
Sun.
Town.
Plant bare root plants 600 to 1 200 high.
Cheap.
Specimen, group.
May be pruned to ground in February to provide luxuriant foliage.

392

Salix caprea—Goat Willow—Salicaceae

4 500 to 5 500 × 5 500 to 6 000 shrub or low tree with a bushy habit.
Oval leaves 60 to 100 long and 25 to 55 wide, grey-green wrinkled above, downy beneath.
Catkins produced on bare shoots in March and April. Showy male catkins about 25 long with bright yellow stamens; female catkins are silvery, about 50 long.
Europe, W. Asia.

Any soil.
Damp sites.
Seaside.
Plant at 600 to 1 250 high.
Cheap.
Low maintenance.
Group, screen.

Salix purpurea—Purple Osier—Salicaceae

3 000 to 5 500 × 4 000 to 6 000 shrub or small tree with thin graceful branches forming a loose spreading plant. The shoots are yellowish, or purple where exposed to the sun.
Narrow leaves 40 to 100 long, dark glossy green above, glaucous beneath.
Catkins appear before the leaves in April.
Europe, C. Asia.

Any soil. Will grow on dryish soils.
Sun or shade.
Plant at 600 to 1 200 high.
Low maintenance.
Group, waterside.

Salix viminalis—Common Osier—Salicaceae

5 000 to 6 000 × 3 500 to 4 500 erect growing vigorous bush or small tree with long straight shoots.
Shoots greyish at first becoming yellowish.
Narrow leaves 1 250 to 3 000 long, dull green above and glistening silver-grey beneath.
Roundish catkins produced in March and April on naked branches.
Very common native species cultivated for basket making.
Europe incl. Britain to N.E. Asia and Himalaya.

Any soil. Clay.
Plant at 600 to 1 250 high.
Waterside, shelterbelts.

Sambucus nigra—Common Elder—Caprifoliaceae

3 500 to 5 500 × 3 500 to 5 500 shrub or may grow into a taller tree with a rough, crooked trunk.
Pinnate leaves 100 to 300 long usually of five sharply toothed ovate leaflets 40 to 125 long.
Tiny yellowish white flowers in large flat umbels in June. Heavy scent.
Shiny black berries in September.
S.n. 'Aurea' has bright gold foliage.
Europe, N. Africa, W. Asia.

Any soil including chalky.
Sun or shade.
Very tolerant of atmospheric pollution.
Seaside. Wind tolerant.
Plant at 600 to 1 000 high.
Cheap.
Low maintenance.
Specimen, group, screen, windbreak.

393

Sorbaria arborea—Rosaceae

3 500 to 4 500 × 3 500 to 4 500 loose growing branches forming a large shrub.
Elegant deep green pinnate leaves 300 to 700 long.
Very large plumes of cream coloured flowers in August–September.
S. aitchisonii grows to 3 000 high, has similar foliage and reddish stems.
It flowers in July.
C. and W. China.

Any soil.
Sun, or light shade.
Plant at 600 to 1 200 high.
Specimen, group.

Tamarix pentandra—Tamarisk—Tamaricaceae

3 500 to 5 000 × 3 000 to 4 000 shrub or small tree with long slender drooping plumose branches.
Very small pointed leaves.
Numerous tiny pink flowers in dense slender racemes in August and September.
May be cut back hard each April to keep bushy.
W. and C. Asia.

Any soil except shallow chalk.
Full sun.
Seaside, wind-resistant.
Plant at 450 to 1 000 high.
Specimen, group, hedging.

Viburnum lantana—Wayfaring Tree—Caprifoliaceae

3 500 to 4 500 × 4 500 to 5 500 dense vigorous rounded bush.
Downy ovate leaves 50 to 125 long, 40 to 100 wide.
Cymes of tiny white flowers in May–June.
Clusters of red fruit turning black.
May have red autumn tints.
C. and S. Europe, N. Asia Minor, N. Africa.

Any soil including chalky.
Sun or partial shade.
Plant at 450 to 1 000 high.
Cheap.
Low maintenance.
Group, screen.

6. Climbing Plants over 6 000 mm high

Clematis montana—Ranunculaceae

6 000 to 9 000 high vigorous climber clinging by means of twining leaf stalks.
Deciduous.
Mid-green leaves consisting of 3 leaflets.
Masses of fragrant white flowers 50 to 60 across borne lightly on slender stalks in May.
C.m. 'Grandiflora' has larger white flowers, no scent.
C.m. rubens has rose-pink flowers in June and the young leaves are purplish. Hardier than the type.
Himalaya.

Any soil. Best in heavy moist loam. Roots like shade. Shoots like full sun or shade. Seaside, town, wind tolerant. Plant pot-grown plants 600 to 900 high. Low maintenance. Will cover old trees, north walls.

Hydrangea petiolaris—Hydrangeaceae

7 000 to 18 000 high very vigorous climber clinging by aerial roots.
Deciduous.
Dark, bright green roundish leaves 40 to 90 long.
Numerous flat corymbs in June, large white sterile flowers on edges, small fertile flowers in centre.
Japan, Kuriles, Sakhalin, S. Korea.

Any soil. Partial or full shade. Plant root-balled or pot-grown plants 300 to 600 high. Low maintenance. Will cover old trees, north walls, forms a spreading bush over stumps. Groundcover in shade.

Lonicera japonica halliana—Caprifoliaceae

6 000 to 9 000 high rampant climber clinging by twining stems.
Semi-evergreen.
Mid-green ovate leaves 40 to 90 long.
Very fragrant white flowers, changing to yellow, borne in pairs from June onwards.
Tiny round black fruits not eaten by birds.
L.j. 'Aureo Reticulata' has leaves with netted golden yellow variegation, insignificant flowers. May be killed back in cold winters.
Japan, Korea, Manchuria, China.

Any soil. Sun or shade. Plant pot-grown plants 600 to 1 200 high. Wall plant, groundcover on banks and in shade.

Parthenocissus henryana (Vitis henryana)—Vitaceae

6 000 to 8 000 high vigorous climber clinging by pads on the end of tendrils. Deciduous.
The pinnate leaves consist of 3 to 5 oval leaflets, dark purplish-green with silvery veins. The leaves develop the best colour in shade.
Insignificant flowers.
C. China.

Any soil.
Sun or shade.
Plant pot-grown plants 600 to 900 high.
Wall plant. Best on north or north-west.

Parthenocissus tricuspidata (Vitis inconstans)—Vitaceae

10 000 to 18 000 high very vigorous climber clinging by pads on the end of tendrils.
Deciduous.
Leaves of old plants are deep green glossy and three lobed, up to 200 across. Brilliant crimson-red autumn colour.
Small yellow-green cymes of flowers on older plants.
P. quinquefolia has bright green five-fingered leaves and brilliant orange and scarlet autumn tints.
Japan, Korea, China.

Any soil.
Sun or shade.
Town. Seaside.
Plant pot-grown plants 600 to 900 high.
Low maintenance.
Wall, tall trees.

Polygonum baldschuanicum—Russian Vine—Polygonaceae

10 000 to 12 000 rampant climber clinging by slender twining stems.
Deciduous.
Pale green oval leaves 40 to 100 long.
Feathery sprays of tiny pinkish-white flowers cover the plant July to October.
S.E. Russia (Tadzhikistan)

Any soil.
Sun or shade.
Town. Seaside.
Plant pot-grown plants 900 to 1 200 high.
Low maintenance.
Will cover old trees, fences.

Rosa filipes 'Kiftsgate'—Rosaceae

10 000 to 15 000 bushy rambler with very vigorous arching shoots armed with hooked spines. Slow to establish.
Light green pinnate leaves with 5 to 7 leaflets.
Corymbs of blossom up to 450 across consisting of many small creamy-white single flowers with yellow stamens in July. Very fragrant.
R. longicuspis is similar to the above but with dark green leaves, less vigorous but more easily established.
R. 'Wedding Day' is another vigorous rose with large trusses of yellow buds opening to creamy-white with orange-yellow stamens.
W. China.

Any soil.
Full sun or partial shade.
Plant bare root plants with a strong root system and at least 2 shoots not less than 750 long.
Cheap.
Will cover old bushes or trees or grow in the open in a sheltered site.

396

Vitis coignetiae—Vitaceae

12 000 to 18 000 high very vigorous climber clinging by tendrils.
Deciduous.
Dark green, toothed, roundish leaves 100 to 250 across. Brilliant scarlet autumn colour.
Insignificant flowers followed by small black berries.
Japan, Korea, Sakhalin.

Any soil.
Sun or partial shade.
Needs wind shelter.
Plant pot-grown plants 600 to 1 200 high.
Expensive.
South or west walls, tall trees.

Wisteria sinensis (W. chinensis)—Leguminosae

1 000 to 30 000 high very vigorous woody climber supporting itself by twining stems. Old plants will make a thick trunk and can be pruned to tree form.
Pinnate leaves 250 to 300 long made up of 11 ovate leaflets.
Fragrant mauve pea-like flowers in dense racemes 200 to 300 long in May and June.
W.s. 'Alba' has white flowers.
China.

Any soil.
Full sun.
Plant root-balled or pot-grown plants 1 000 to 1 500 high.
Expensive.
South or west walls, old trees.

7. Marginal aquatic plants

Butomus umbellatus—Flowering Rush—Butomaceae

Hardy herbaceous perennial up to 700 high of tufted habit, spreading by creeping rhizomes.

Leaves up to 700 long, narrow and fleshy, sometimes twisted, bronze-purple when young becoming deep green.

Rose-pink flowers 25 across, borne on umbels on smooth round stems from June to August.

N. Asia, Europe incl. Britain.

Any loamy soil.
Water depth up to 200 or any bog or marshy bank.
Full sun.
Plant moist bare-rooted plants in spring.
Grows best in sheltered still water.

Caltha palustris—Marsh Marigold—Ranunculaceae

200 to 400 high hardy herbaceous perennial of compact rounded habit, spreading by creeping stems.

Shiny dark green rounded leaves 50 to 75 across with lightly toothed edges. Summer leaves often larger and more sharply toothed.

Flowers 25 across, light to golden yellow, many stamens and 5 or more prominent sepals, borne in profusion in April and May.

C.p. 'Alba' does less well in water.

C.p. 'Plena' is very free flowering.

Europe incl. Britain, N. America, Arctic.

Any neutral or slightly acid loamy soil.
Water depth up to 150.
Plants in ground above water level must always be kept moist.
Sun or partial shade.
Plant moist bare-rooted plants from March to September.

Cyperus longus—Galingale—Cyperaceae

Hardy strong-growing perennial with erect three-angled stems 600 to 1 200 high and 350 spread, with a tough creeping rootstock.

Narrow grass-like leaves, grooved, bright shiny green above and paler beneath.

Chestnut brown plumes with 3 long pendulous shiny green bracts are borne in August and September.

Europe incl. Britain.

Any soil.
Water depth up to 400.
Full sun or partial shade.
Plant moist bare-rooted plants between April and June.
Suitable for grouping at a large pool or lake, or as a single specimen in a small pool if roots are restricted in a container.
Clear old foliage in autumn or spring.

398

Iris laevigata (beardless laevigatae group)—Iridaceae

Deciduous herbaceous perennial with slender rhizomes and stems up to 600 high.
Leaves pale green, smooth, 600 to 800 high.
Usually 3 flowers per stem, clear uniform blue with a white streak, 100 to 150 across borne in a terminal spathe in June.
I. kaempferi is related but differs with ribbed deep green leaves and there are many colourful varieties.
China, Manchuria, Korea, Japan.

Most soils preferably slightly acid.
Full sun.
Water depth up to 150.
Plant moist bare-rooted plants in early spring or autumn.

Mimulus luteus—Monkey Musk—Scrophulariaceae

Hardy herbaceous perennial 100 to 500 high with soft leafy rooting stems and without a definite rootstock.
Mid-green leaves 25 to 50 long, oblong-ovate.
Snapdragon-like, open mouthed flowers 25 to 40 long, yellow and variably marked with crimson-brown spots at the mouth, produced from May to August.
M.l. guttatus is lower growing but with larger flowers with prominent purple-brown blotches.
N. America, naturalized in Britain.

Any soil.
Full sun or light shade.
Best in wet waterside soil or in water up to 100 deep.
Plant container grown or moist bare-rooted plants in spring.
Most species will grow in any ordinary moist garden soil.

Myosotis scorpioides (M. palustris)—Water forget-me-not—Boraginaceae

Hardy evergreen perennial 200 high and creeping at base.
Leaves elongated spoon-shaped and covered with hairs.
Flowers variable, 6 to 8 across, pale blue with yellow eye, borne on stems 200 to 250 long from April to May.
M.s. 'Mermaid' has thicker stems, dark green leaves and deep blue flowers.
M.s. 'Semperflorens' is more compact than the type.
Europe incl. Britain.

Heavy loam.
Full sun or partial shade.
Water depth up to 75, but does best at water level.
Plant moist bare-rooted plants in spring or autumn.

Pontederia cordata—Pickerel Weed—Pontederiaceae

Hardy strong-growing herbaceous perennial of neat compact habit, 450 to 600 high, spreading by creeping rhizomes.
Thick heart-shaped leaves, bright glossy green and sometimes with maroon-brown patches, on rounded smooth stems.
Flowers purple-blue small and numerous on terminal spike 50 to 100 long. After flowering spikes submerge until seeds are ripe.
N. America.

Deep loam.
Full sun.
Water depth up to 300 above crowns for established plants.
Plant moist bare-rooted plants from April to June.
Best grown in sheltered position at margin of pond or lake or slow flowing stream.

Typha angustifolia—Small Reed Mace—Typhaceae

Up to 1 500 high hardy aquatic perennial with vigorous creeping rhizomes deep in the mud.
Dark green strap-shaped leaves 10 to 20 wide, tapering slightly.
Dark brown poker heads of inflorescence 10 to 20 wide produced in July on cylindrical stems.
Europe incl. Britain.

Rich deep loam.
Full sun.
Water depth up to 300.
Plant moist bare-rooted plants in April and May.
Not as invasive as other species but specimen in a small pool should be restricted in a container.

Zantedeschia aethiopica (Richardia)—Arum Lily—Araceae

Evergreen rhizomatous herbaceous perennial 450 to 900 high of bold appearance.
Large arrow-shaped leaves, twice as long as broad and varying in size, deep green with long stout stalks.
Flowers consist of a yellow spadix surrounded by a white spathe 120 to 225 long, narrowing to a recurved cuspidate point, March to June.
Z.a. 'Crowborough' is reputedly hardier.
S. Africa.

Rich loam.
Sun or partial shade.
Water depth up to 300.
Plant moist bare-rooted or container grown plants in spring.
Group or specimen at edge of pool or moist bank. Generally hardy anywhere if submerged at least 100 deep safe from frost damage.

8. Grasses and Rushes

Cortaderia argentea (C. selloana)—Pampas Grass—Graminae

900 to 1 500 high clump of slender, arching glaucous leaves.
Forms a dense barrier of sharp-edged leaves.
The dry leaves persist until fresh foliage is produced in spring.
Showy silvery-grey plumes of flowers on stiff stems 1 800 to 3 000 high from September to November.
C.a. pumila is a more compact form 1 200 to 1 500 high.
Argentine.

Any soil. Deep loam or sand preferred.
Sun or partial shade.
Sheltered position for best flower spikes.
Expensive.
Specimen, group.
Old foliage may be cut or burned off in April.

Elymus arenarius—Lyme Grass—Gramineae

600 to 1 200 high dense grass spreading rapidly by long stout rhizomes. Invasive on light soils.
Attractive blue-grey arching leaves about 510 long, 15 wide.
Stiff blue-grey flower spikes in May to July.

Any soil. Sand.
Sun or partial shade.
Very salt tolerant.
Cheap.
Low maintenance.
Excellent for binding loose sand to prevent erosion.

Festuca ovina glauca—Grey Sheep's Fescue—Gramineae

150 to 230 high densely tufted perennial grass.
Very narrow rigid blue-grey evergreen leaves.
Small, slightly one-sided panicles of purplish flowers from May to July.
Europe.

Any soil.
Sun or partial shade.
Cheap.
Specimen, group, mass.

Helictotrichon sempervirens—(Avena candida, A. sempervirens)—Gramineae

455 high dense slowly spreading clumps.

Narrow blue-grey arching persistent leaves.

Flower stems up to 900 high in June and July.

S. Russia, Turkestan.

Any soil.
Sun or partial shade.
Specimen or group.

Luzula maxima (L. sylvatica)—Wood Rush—Juncaceae

300 to 600 high tufted perennial spreading by short creeping rootstocks to form a dense cover. Tough evergreen leaves 152 to 300 long, 15 wide.

Pale brownish flowers in May and June.

Any soil.
Sun or shade.
Drip tolerant.
Cheap. Low maintenance.
Very good ground-cover under trees and shrubs and on dry soil.

Miscanthus sinensis gracillimus—(Eulalia japonica)—Gramineae

900 to 1 500 high clump-forming grass.
Narrow arching blue-green leaves with a whitish mid-stripe, turning amber in autumn.

Attractive pinkish-brown flower spikes may be produced from August to October but are infrequent in Gt. Britain.

M. sinensis has broader leaves, about 15 wide, *M.s. zebrinus* has transverse yellow bands on light green leaves.

China, Japan.

Any soil.
Sun or partial shade.
Specimen or group.

Molinia coerulea variegata—Variegated Moor Grass—Gramineae

230 to 300 high slowly increasing tufted grass.

Rather rigid upright white striped leaves 5 wide.

Panicles of purplish flowers on slender upright stems 600 high from July to September.

Soft orange autumn tints.

Any soil.
Sun or partial shade.
Specimen, group, waterside.

Phalaris arundinacea picta—Ribbon Grass, Gardener's Garters—Gramineae

900 to 1 200 high upright stems spreading freely by creeping rhizomes to form a dense clump.
Leaves 12 to 20 wide and 150 to 300 long striped with white. Turn pale straw colour in autumn and die down.
Whitish-green flower spikes from June to August.
N. Hemisphere.

Any soil.
Sun or half shade.
Cheap.
Group, mass, waterside.

Spartina pectinata aureo-marginata—Prairie Cord Grass—Gramineae

900 to 1 800 high compact clumps spreading freely by creeping rhizomes.
Leaves up to 600 long and 15 wide with pale gold stripes.
Flower spikes June to September.

Any soil.
Sun or partial shade.
Salt tolerant.
Low maintenance.
Group, mass, waterside.

403

9. Tropical humid climates

GROUNDCOVER

Alternanthera versicolor—Amaranthaceae—Joyweed

Texture: Fine.   Sun.
Leaves: Small oblong pointed.   Any soil.
Red and yellow-green varieties   Height 150.
Flowers: inconspicuous.
Perennial cover plant which needs clipping occasionally.

Axonopus compressus—Carpet or Malaysia Grass—Gramineae

Texture: Fine to medium.   Shade/semi-shade.
Leaves: Broad pointed 25–50.   Dry to moist soil.
Dark green.   Spreads rapidly.
Good transition plant between finer grass and foliage.   Low groundcover.
Fully shade tolerant.   Height 25.
S.E. Asia.

Episcia fulgida—Gesneriaceae

Texture: Medium, velvety.   Shade/semi-shade.
Leaves: Flat ovate serrated 50–75.   Good moist soil.
Russet green with silver veins above, purple below.   Good drainage.
Spreads by stolons.
Flowers: Small, bright scarlet.   Bright, colourful groundcover.
Height 75–100.

Ficus pumila—Climbing Fig—Moraceae

Texture: Small, matt.
Leaves: Ovate 20.
        Medium grey-green.
Flowers: Inconspicuous.
Also a useful climber.
Close and dense.
China.

Shade/semi-shade.
Any soil.
Spreads rapidly and widely by nodal roots.
Dense groundcover.
Height 50–75.

Hemigraphis colorata (also H. repanda)—Acanthaceae

Texture: Medium to small.
Leaves: Ovate serrated 25–30.
        Green, silvery above, purple below.
Flowers: Small white.

Shade/semi-shade.
Any soil.
Spreads widely by nodal rooting.
Height 100.

Melampodium spp—Compositae

Texture: Fine.
Leaves: Oblong seriated rich green.
Flowers: Yellow, daisy-like.
Trailing habit giving close cover.

Sun.
Any soil.
Height 800.
Spread indefinite.

Pilea nummulariifolia—Urticaceae

Texture: Fine.
Leaves: Oval, green with silver variegation.
Flowers: Inconspicuous.
Creeping, self-rooting.
S.E. Asia.

Shade/semi-shade.
Any soil.
Height 75.
Spread indefinite.

Rhoeo discolor—Commelinaceae

Texture: Medium spiky.
Leaves: Stiff narrow pointed in rosettes 300.
Dark green above, purple below.
Flowers: Small white in axils of leaves.
C. America.

Sun/semi-shade.
Good moist soil.
Spreads by basal shoots forming new rosettes.
Groundcover height 300.

Sansevieria hahnii—Liliaceae

Texture: Medium.
Leaves: Ovate pointed.
Mottled grey-green.
Excellent low cover plant.
Spreads by offsets from base.
W. Africa.

Sun/semi-shade.
Any soil.
Height 200.

Sansevieria trifasciata—Whipcord Hemp—Liliaceae

Texture: Bold.
Leaves: Stiff and upright.
Grey-green variegated 900.
Good deep texture groundcover massed.
W. Africa.

Sun/semi-shade.
Any soil.
Height 900.

Scindapsus aureus—Araceae

Texture: Medium to bold.
Leaves: Heart shaped 100.
Mid-green streaked yellow.
Flowers: Inconspicuous.
Alternatively a climber with much larger leaves.
S. America.

Shade/semi-shade.
Good moist soil.
Spreads rapidly and widely if pinched out.
Tumbling groundcover.
Height 200.

Selaginella spp Selaginellaceae
Texture: Fine matted.
Leaves: Lacy fronds about 150.
Good enveloping groundcover.
Malaysia.

Shade.
Rich moist soil.
Spread 300–400.

Setcreasea purpurea—Purple Heart—Commelinaceae
Texture: Medium lanceolate.
Leaves: Oblong leaves 150 in tufts
with stems 300 rich purple.
Flowers: Small rose pink.
Mexico.

Sun.
Any moist soil.
Spreads widely by
nodal rooting.
Height 200.

Strobilanthes dyeranus
Texture: Medium.
Leaves: Ovate 25–50.
Blue, purple-green above,
red-purple below.
Burma.

Shade.
Good moist soil.
Low bushy plant 450.
Height 450.

Syngonium podophyllum—Araceae
Texture: Bold.
Leaves: Five-lobed mid-green 200.
By habit a climber but very useful for
trailing groundcover,
S. America.

Shade.
Moist soil.
Spread indefinite.

Verbena spp—Verbenaceae
Texture: Fine.
Leaves: Oval seriated.
Flowers: Small clusters mauve.
Good trailing cover on dry banks.
S. America.

Sun.
Good well-drained soil.
Height 300.
Spreading.

Zephyranthes rosea—Wind Flower—Amaryllidaceae
Texture: Fine.
Leaves: Grassy clumps.
Flowers: Pink crocus-like bells.
Bulbous plant, multiplies by offsets.

Sun.
Good well-drained soil.
Height 200.

FOLIAGE PLANTS

Alpinia purpurata—Red Ginger—Zingiberaceae
Texture: Bold.
Leaves: Oval lanceolate fronds.
200–300—dark green.
Flowers: Vertical inflorescences of crimson bracts 150.
S.E. Asia.

Semi-shade.
Rich moist soil.
Height 1–2 m.

408

Arundo donax variegata—Gramineae

Texture: Large, grassy.
Leaves: Lanceolate 300–500.
Yellow/grey-green serrated.
Flowers: Stiff panicle sprays.
600–900.

Full sun.
Any moist soil.
Height 3 m.
Spread 3 m.

Caladium candidum—Araceae

Texture: Medium.
Leaves: Broad arrow-shaped.
75–100.
White with green veins.
Flowers: Whitish green.
S. America.

Shade/semi-shade.
Rich moist soil.
Rhizomatous.
Height 450.

Calathea ornata—Marantaceae

Texture: Bold.
Leaves: Lanceolate 300–500.
Dark green with rose-pink
lines, underside purple.
Columbia.

Shade.
Rich moist soil.
Height 1 m.

Calathea zebrina—Zebra Plant—Marantaceae

Texture: Medium, velvety.
Leaves: Oval 300–400.
Deep green on emerald.
Brazil.

Shade.
Very moist soil.
Height 450–600.
Spread 600.

Cordyline terminalis—Liliaceae
Texture: Bold.
Leaves: Oval lanceolate 300 bunched
         in terminal heads. Crimson
         and green.
S.E. Asia.

Shade/semi-shade.
Good moist soil.
Height 900–1 500.

Crinum amabile—Amaryllidaceae
Texture: Bold.
Leaves: Long, strappy 600–700.
         Yellow-green.
Flowers: Umbels 4–6 white with rose-
         pink reverse.
         150 diameter.
S.E. Asia.

Sun.
Moist rich soil.
Bulbous.
Height 750.
Spread 900.

Dieffenbachia picta exotica—Dumb Cane—Araceae
Texture: Large.
Leaves: Oblong-ovate 300–400.
         Pale yellow with green edges.
Brazil.

Shade/semi-shade.
Any moist soil.
Height 1·5 m.
Spread 1 m.

Dracaena fragrans—Liliaceae
Texture: Bold.
Leaves: Oblong lanceolate up to 750.
         Green with gold lateral
         stripes.
W. Africa.

Sun/semi-shade.
Good moist soil.
Height up to 2 m.

410

Dracaena sanderi—Liliaceae

Texture: Medium.
Leaves: Oblong-lanceolate.
200–250.
Dull green/pale yellow edge.
Zaire.

Semi-shade.
Any moist soil.
Height 1·5 m.
Spread 600.

Heliconia metallica—Musaceae

Texture: Bold.
Leaves: Oval 300. Green above, underside purple.
Flowers: Red and white.
Brazil.

Shade/semi-shade.
Rich moist soil.
Height 1 800.

Heliconia psittacorum—Japanese Canna—Musaceae

Texture: Bold, shiny.
Leaves: Ovate-pointed 300.
Yellow green.
Flowers: Bright orange 100.

Full sun.
Rich moist soil.
Rhixomatous.
Spread 1 m.

Hymenocallis speciosa—Spider Lily—Amaryllidaceae

Texture: Bold.
Leaves: Linear arching 450.
Yellow green.
Flowers: White with narcissus form centre.
S. America.

Sun/semi-shade.
Rich moist soil.
Height 900.

411

Nicolaia elatior (Phaeomeria magnifica)—Torch Ginger—Zingiberaceae

Texture: Very large.
Leaves: Oblong large 600. Dark green on long rigid stems.
Flowers: Brilliant red 100 on independent stems from ground about 1 m high.
S.E. Asia.

Semi-shade.
Rich moist soil.
Height 5–6 m.
Spread 2 m.

Pandanus sanderi—Variegated Screw Pine—Pandanaceae

Texture: Bold striped.
Leaves: Linear finely toothed 600–1 200. Green/yellow variegation.
Papua New Guinea.

Sun/semi-shade.
Good soil.
Height 3–5 m.

Philodendron elegans—Araceae

Texture: Very bold.
Leaves: Deeply lobed ovate 600 × 450. Rich green. Non-climbing.
Brazil.

Shade.
Rich moist soil.
Height 1–1·5 m.

Spathiphyllum cannaiefolium—Araceae

Texture: Bold.
Leaves: Oval 200. Rich green.
Flowers: White spathe 150. Yellow green spadix.

Shade/semi-shade.
Rich moist soil.
Height 600–900.

412

Strelitzia nicolae alba—Bird of Paradise—Musaceae

Texture: Very large.

Leaves: Paddle shaped 1 000.
Grey-green.

Flowers: Blue and white boat-shaped
bract 250–300.

(In background is the more common *S. reginae*, 1 m–1·5 m, with orange and blue flowers.)

S. Africa.

Full sun.
Rich moist soil/good drainage.
Height 2–3 m.
Spread: 2 m.

FERNS

Adiantum cuneatum—Maidenhair fern—Polypodiaceae

Texture: Fine, feathery.

Leaves: Small rhomboidal on black wiry stems.
Fronds 500–700.

Brazil.

Shade/semi-shade.
Moist well-drained soil.
Spread 1 m.

Asplenium nidus—Bird's Nest fern—Polypodiaceae

Texture: Bold, strappy.

Leaves: Feathery with shiny surface, up to 1 m in bold rosettes.

Epiphytic but adaptable as pot plant or on ground.

Tropical Africa.

Full shade.
Moist soil.
Spread up to 2 m.

413

Cyathea contaminans—Tree Fern—Cyatheaceae
Texture: Bold, feathery.
Leaves: Fronds up to 1 m.
Malaysia.

Full shade.
Moist soil.
Prefers lush
humidity.
Spread 2 m.

Nephrolepis biserrata—Polypodiaceae
Texture: Medium.
Leaves: Curly fronds about 300–400.
S.E. Africa.

Semi-shade.
Rich soil well
drained.
Spread 600.

Nephrolepis exaltata—Sword Fern—Polypodiaceae
Texture: Medium.
Leaves: Narrow sword-like up to
600.
S.E. Asia.

Semi-shade.
Rich soil well
drained.
Spread up to 900.

Phymatodes scolopendria—(**Polypodium
phymatodes**)—Polypodiaceae
Texture: Bold, angular.
Leaves: Simple fronds up to 500.
A good groundcover in shade and
semi-shade.
N. Hemisphere.

Semi-shade/shade.
Moist soil.
Spread up to 800.

414

Platycerium grande—Stags Horn Fern—Polypodiaceae

Texture:	Very bold.
Leaves:	Fleshy, antlered fronds fully 1 m.

Shade.
Humid conditions.
Spread 2 m.

Epiphytic tree parasite.
Most darmatic of all epiphytes.
Malaysia.

Selaginella spp—Selaginellaceae

Texture:	Fine.
Leaves:	Lacy fronds about 150.

Shade.
Rich moist soil.
Spread 300–400.

Malaysia.

Stenoloma chinensis—Lace Fern

Texture:	Fine, lacy.
Leaves:	Short fronds about 200.

Shade.
Rich moist soil.
Spread 500.

Spreads quickly in shade and forms a good groundcover.
China.

CLIMBERS

Allamanda cathartica (var. hendersonii)—Apocynaceae

Texture: Woody sprawling. Full sun.
Medium. Any soil.
Leaves: Oval, pointed 75–100. Height 4·5 m.
Rich green.
Flowers: Rich yellow, trumpets, five
lobes 75.
S. America.

Beaumontia multiflora—Apocynaceae

Texture: Woody, vigorous. Sun.
Bold. Any soil.
Leaves: Dark green, oblong, 150. Height 10 m.
Flowers: White, cup-shaped, 50, in
terminal clusters. Fragrant.
Thailand/Malaysia.

Camoensia maxima—Leguminosae

Texture: Woody. Large. Sun.
Leaves: Oblong, 200. Good soil.
Yellow green. Height 4·5 m.
Flowers: Large white flowers 200.
Heavily fragrant.
Zaire.

416

Congea velutina—Verbenaceae
Texture: Scandent. Small.   Sun.
Leaves: Oval 50. Medium.   Good soil.
Flowers: Panicles of soft pink violet   Height 2–3 m.
         bracts 30.
Thailand/Malaysia.

Jacquemontia pentantha—Convolvulaceae
Slender twining.   Semi-shade.
Texture: Fine.   Good soil.
Leaves: Cordate 50. Fresh green. Height 2 m.
Flowers: Cerulean blue clusters
         small bells 25–30.

Mucuna bennettii—New Guinea Creeper—Leguminosae
Rampant twining.   Sun to semi-shade.
Texture: Medium.   Rich loamy soil.
Leaves: Trifoliate 100.   Height 6 m.
         Mid-green.
Flowers: Brilliant red, like upturned
         beaks, about 80 in racemes
         4–500 long.
Papua New Guinea.

Odontadenia speciosa—Apocynaceae
Vigorous woody.   Sun.
Texture: Bold.   Rich soil.
Leaves: Oblong 100. Medium green. Height 2–3 m.
Flowers: Apricot yellow trumpets, 50
         in terminal clusters.
         Fragrant.
Guyana.

417

Petrea volubilis—Purple Wreath—Verbenaceae

Woody twining.

Texture: Medium, rough.

Leaves: Oval pointed 75. Grey green.

Flowers: Lilac to purple, five strap petals about 30 diameter in long racemes, up to 200.

S. America.

Semi-shade.
Good soil.
Height 6 m.

Thunbergia grandiflora—Acanthaceae

Woody twining.

Texture: Medium to bold.

Leaves: Oblong 100. Mid-green.

Flowers: Violet bluet trumpets, pendulous and best seen from below. Also white form.

N. India.

Semi-shade.
Good soil.
Height 3 m.

Tree Information Sheets

KEY

The information sheets are based on the plant list prepared by the Landscape Institute, which includes a range of evergreen and deciduous trees. All the trees included are readily available commercially and are reasonably hardy throughout the British Isles.

Each sheet describes one main tree but in some cases it has been possible to describe a second species which is illustrated with a smaller photograph.

The data is divided approximately into two parts:
a) general information and design use;
b) a description of the tree and its requirements.

a) General description and design use

Name. Latin name, source and common name.
General information. Including history where known, general form, distribution and limitations.
Design use. Special feature (e.g. autumn colour, flowers etc.) and any special value a tree may have. Suitable locations for planting.

b) Detail description and requirements

Height and spread at maturity. Approximate dimensions only as growth depends on many factors.
Bark. Where possible bark descriptions are given for both young and mature trees.
Foliage. Colour, size and shape. Autumn colour is described where it is exceptional.
Inflorescence. Colour, type and season.
Fruit. Colour, size and season.
Growth Rate. Relative rate e.g. fast slow or moderate.
Habit. Description of form and habit together with any change that occurs with age.
Tolerances. Degree of tolerance of soil and climatic factors that are specifically harmful to the tree.
Planting. Recommended sizes. Planting distances are not given because they vary according to initial size, effect required and available money.
Culture. Any special soil and light requirements and ability to tolerate pollution and wind exposure.
Other forms. Other interesting forms and varieties that are commercially available and reasonably easy to grow. Special features of habit or form are indicated.

ACKNOWLEDGMENTS

Peter Styles, Dip Hort, Dip LA, AILA
designed the tree information sheets, wrote the text, drew the details and supplied the photographs of *Ilex × altaclarensis*.

Maurice Nimmo
supplied all the remaining photographs.

Acer campestre

Field Maple

A native deciduous tree, common on calcareous soils in the South and East of Britain mainly along hedgerows. It can form an attractive low, domed tree with small leaves that turn golden yellow in autumn.

DESIGN USE

As a hardy medium sized tree it is useful for shelterbelt planting and exposed hill sites. It can also be clipped to form tall, rough hedges. A good tree for embankment planting because it seeds and colonizes quickly.

DETAIL INFORMATION

Height: 25 m.

Spread: 13 m.

Habit: Low spreading crown, often a mere bush.

Bark: Grey-brown with shallow fissures and pale ridges.

Foliage: Three to five-lobed greyish-green leaves 80 mm long. Autumn colour varies rich gold to red and purple.

Inflorescence: Open upright clusters of small greenish-yellow flowers in May opening with the leaves.

Fruit: Paired winged seeds 50 mm across, in mid-autumn.

Growth rate: Moderate. Fast as a hedge.

Tolerances: Waterlogged, acid soils.

Planting: Up to semi-mature tree size transplanting.

Culture: Lime-rich soil where it quickly spreads.

OTHER FORMS

Only one other obtainable form:

A.c. 'Postelense'—which has bright gold young leaves. Mature leaves are only slightly golden.

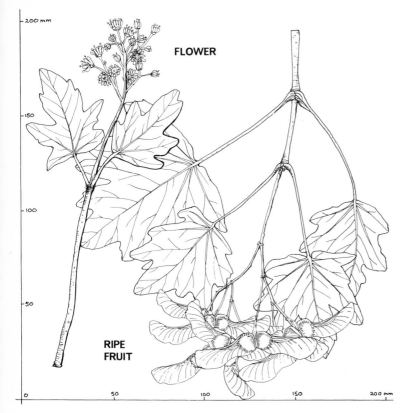

FLOWER

RIPE FRUIT

A. pseudoplatanus—Sycamore.

Free-seeding hardy dense tree. Very good for difficult, urban places and shelterbelts. Prefers lime soils.

420

Acer platanoides

Norway Maple

A deciduous tree first introduced from Scandinavia, it is now common in S. England. Free-growing and round-headed it is one of the most adaptable of trees, capable of thriving in a wide range of soil types and climatic conditions. It is self-seeding in some residential areas.

DESIGN USE

Its attractive habit and tolerance to polluted atmospheres makes it a good tree for urban use, particularly for street or park planting. As an ornamental tree it has a profusion of early flowers before the foliage is fully emerged and in autumn the leaves turn lovely shades of yellow and gold.

DETAIL INFORMATION

Height: 26 m.

Spread: 20 m.

Habit: Tall-domed form with open winter habit and dense summer foliage.

Bark: Brown becoming grey, smooth or shallowly ridged.

Foliage: Five-lobed, bright green leaves with broad incisions. 120 × 150 mm with petioles 80–180 mm long. Yellow autumn foliage.

Inflorescence: Bright yellowish-green flowers in erect panicles of 30–40 flowers in May.

Fruit: Yellow-green fruit and wing 30–50 mm across, falling in autumn.

Growth rate: Rapid in early stages, slowing down after 4–5 years.

Tolerances: Exposed, windy sites and dry poorer soils.

Planting: Easily moved up to semi-mature size.

Culture: Best planted on well drained sandy loam where it may self-seed.

OTHER FORMS

A.p. 'Crimson King'—dark red foliage.

A.p. 'Cucullatum'—fastigiate form with crinkled round leaves.

A.p. 'Goldsworth Purple'—large, dark purple leaves in summer.

A.p. 'Schwedleri'—purple-green summer foliage, pinkish in spring.

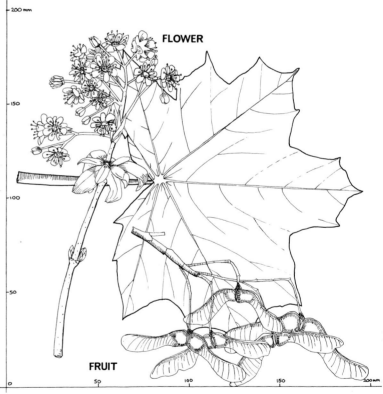

FLOWER

FRUIT

Acer saccharinum—Silver Maple.

A rapidly growing tree with pendulous branches. Requires space and a moist loamy soil to develop. Ideal for urban parks and open spaces. Good autumn colour.

421

Aesculus hippocastanum

Horse Chestnut

Common deciduous tree found all over England. First introduced from the Balkans in the 17th century. Usually a large tree with a domed crown, it does well in urban situations, forming magnificent specimens where space allows.

DESIGN USE

A strictly ornamental tree, it is ideal for open space, park and avenue planting, both in urban and rural situations. Spring flowering is an impressive sight with a profusion of white flowers. Autumn colour varies from scarlet to gold and is equally impressive.

DETAIL INFORMATION

Height: 40 m.

Spread: 28 m.

Habit: Large round crown. Branches on older tree curve upwards.

Bark: Grey-brown, smooth when young, flaking with age.

Foliage: Compound, palmate leaves up to 250 mm long with serrated edges. Dark green with yellowish-green undersides.

Inflorescence: Flowers in panicles up to 300 mm long in early May, white with large yellow blotch at base. Abundant.

Fruit: Green globular fruit ripens in September splitting to reveal 'conkers'.

Growth rate: Vigorous. Life expectancy is 150 years.

Tolerances: Very dry soils or cold exposed sites.

Planting: Best transplanted in sizes up to 6 m.

Culture: Deep loam soil in an open position.

OTHER FORMS

A.h. 'Baumannii'—white double flowers producing no fruit.

A.x. carnea 'Briottii'—a hybrid between *A. hippocastanum* and *A.pavia*. Bright red flowers and glossy leaves.

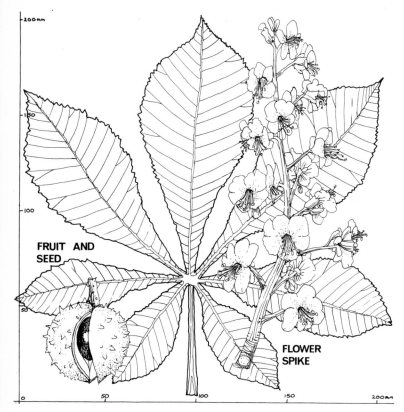

FRUIT AND SEED

FLOWER SPIKE

Aesculus hipposcastanum in winter.
The gradual unfolding of the bright green leaves in early May is a splendid sight.

422

Ailanthus altissima

Tree of Heaven

Introduced from N. China it is commonly found in urban places. A beautiful, hardy, deciduous tree it thrives in virtually any type of soil, producing root-suckers freely. Its bold foliage and open forked branches make it a very picturesque tree.

DESIGN USE

Because of its smoke resistance and its ability to survive in poor soils the Ailanthus is a useful urban tree, particularly good in squares and streets. It can be coppiced to produce a bold shrub type or planted close to buildings where its open pinnate foliage throws a dappled shade.

DETAIL INFORMATION

Height: 26 m.
Spread: 19 m.
Habit: Tall, irregular domed crown on a straight bole.
Bark: Grey-brown, smooth with dark streaks.
Foliage: Deep green, pinnate leaves 300–400 mm long, pale green underneath. Unpleasant odour when crushed.
Inflorescence: Dense clusters of cream male flowers in July. Male and female flowers usually on separate trees.
Fruit: Bunches of winged bright red seeds 40 mm long in autumn.
Growth rate: Fast when established. Slow in early stages.
Tolerances: Wet, cold soils in exposed positions.
Planting: Transplants well up to 6 m high.
Culture: Sunny position in well drained soil.

OTHER FORMS

A. vilmoriniana—an uncommon tree with dark green, drooping leaves 300 mm long. Leaves are pubescent underneath with red rachis.

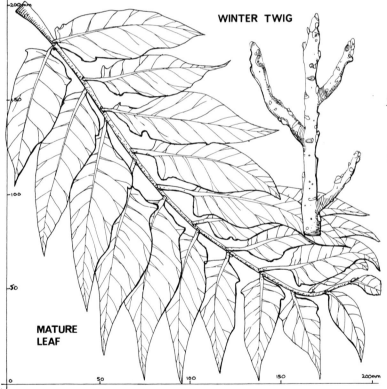

WINTER TWIG

MATURE LEAF

A. altissima in winter. Small ovoid reddish buds become scarlet as they swell in April. When the leaves appear in mid-June they are bright red.

423

Alnus glutinosa

Common Alder

A native deciduous tree found growing wild near open water either as a multi-stemmed bush form or with a pyramidal habit. Alder has a symbiotic relationship with a soil bacterium. This bacterium is only found on marshy ground and it develops on the roots in nodules which in turn fix free nitrogen from the air.

DESIGN USE

A useful tree for river and lakeside planting in rural and urban situations. It can be planted on slag heaps where it quickly establishes itself into natural groups. It has attractive spring catkins and the leaves remain green in autumn until they fall. The common form is not a good specimen tree and is more effective planted in groups or coppiced to produce bush forms. Useful also for screening clay pits where the roots help to stabilize soil erosion on the wet banks.

DETAIL INFORMATION

Height: 25 m.

Spread: 10 m.

Habit: Pyramidal, pointed crown, with open horizontal branches.

Bark: Smooth and greenish-brown when young, becoming dark grey and cracked with age.

Foliage: Serrated, oval leaves in May, 10 mm long. Dark green, lighter green underneath with tufts of hair on the vein axils.

Inflorescence: Long pendulous, dark yellow male catkins in March. Female catkins in erect clusters, dark red when open, ripening to green ovoids.

Fruit: Female catkin become dark brown and woody, dispersing the seeds during winter.

Growth rate: Fast in early stages, particularly on rich soil.

Tolerances: Will not grow on well-drained, poor soils.

Planting: Small trees up to 4 m transplant more successfully.

Culture: Any moist soil except acid peat. Sun or shade.

OTHER FORMS

A.g. 'Aurea'—yellow leaves until late summer.

A.g. 'Imperialis'—a slender tree with finely cut leaves.

A.g. 'Laciniata'—deeply cut leaves—makes a good specimen.

MALE CATKINS

RIPE FRUIT

Alnus glutinosa in winter. A beautiful winter tree with slender horizontal branches and black 'false cones'. The buds are brownish-violet and sticky.

424

Betula pubescens

Hairy Birch or Common White Birch

A common wild tree abundant in the North and West of Britain where it is found growing mainly on wet or moist sites. It is usually the first tree to establish itself on swampy ground and on commons when grazing has ceased. A rather picturesque tree with its spreading, twisting branches, it makes a good alternative for planting on badly drained sites.

DESIGN USE

For maximum effect plant in groups rather than singly. Good as a pioneer tree for wild rural sites where it quickly establishes itself and spreads naturally, particularly around water. This tree like all other birches has peeling white bark when established and in autumn the foliage turns a golden yellow. Multi-stemmed specimens can be easily produced by cutting back saplings to the base or planting two or three saplings together.

DETAIL INFORMATION

Height: 25 m.

Spread: 17 m.

Habit: A spreading irregular crown with open branches and shoots.

Bark: When mature it is greyish-white and peels away in horizontal strips.

Foliage: Dull green leaves broad at base, 60 mm long. Pubescent underside of leaves and petioles, shoots covered in white hairs.

Inflorescence: Purple-brown male catkins and green female flowers open in April. Male catkins turn pale yellow when ripe.

Fruit: Tiny, winged seeds, ripening in late autumn and dispersed during winter.

Growth rate: Fast. Reaches 10 m in 20 years.

Tolerances: Does not tolerate dry, well-drained soils.

Planting: Small trees up to 4 m transplant well.

Culture: Any moist, acid soil.

OTHER FORMS

No other forms available but other good *Betula* species include:

B. pendula—graceful common birch.

B.p. 'Dalecarlica'—narrow crown with cut foliage.

B.p. 'Youngii'—a dome-shaped weeping form.

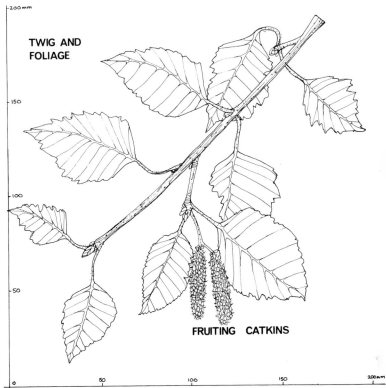

TWIG AND FOLIAGE

FRUITING CATKINS

Betula pendula in winter. A fast growing native tree with a narrow graceful habit. Prefers well-drained soils and is a good urban tree for planting around buildings.

425

Carpinus betulus

Hornbeam

A native, deciduous tree, confined in its wild state to S.E. England. It is basically a forest type tree and is similar in every respect to beech except that it grows well on heavy wet soils. It forms a magnificent specimen tree with rounded head, fluted grey trunk and gold autumn foliage.

DESIGN USE

This hardy tree withstands wind and shade thus making it a slow but very useful shelterbelt tree. Also good as a specimen in cold, exposed urban and rural sites or as a street tree. Hornbeam can be clipped to form hedges and it provides shelter and colour throughout the winter by retaining its brown, dead leaves. It is not usually damaged by grazing animals.

DETAIL INFORMATION

Height: 28 m.

Spread: 22 m.

Habit: High domed, conical crown with arching branches.

Bark: Smooth light-grey, striped pale-brown.

Foliage: Rough-toothed elliptical leaves, dark green above, yellow-green beneath, unfolding in May.

Inflorescence: Pendulous male catkins in late April produce large quantities of pollen. Smaller terminal female catkins.

Fruit: In pairs with nuts attached to lobed wings, ripening in autumn.

Growth rate: Fast when young but slows later.

Tolerances: Easily grown, chalk and clay tolerant.

Planting: Can be transplanted up to semi-mature tree size.

Culture: Any soil in sun or shade.

OTHER FORMS

C.b. 'Columnaris'—fastigiate form.

C.b. 'Incisa'—upright form with deeply toothed leaves.

C.b. 'Purpurea'—bright reddish young growths.

WINTER TWIG

FRUITING TWIG

C.b. 'Fastigiata'

A good street tree with upright habit spreading with age. Bright green leaves turning bright gold in autumn.

426

Castanea sativa

Sweet Chestnut

First introduced by the Romans, it is naturalized only in S. England because of climatic restrictions to ripening of fertile seeds in the north. It is vigorous and as a specimen tree it can grow to huge dimensions. It is the longest-lived of all deciduous trees, some specimens living for over 400 years.

DESIGN USE

For park and open space it is a spectacular sight with its bold foliage and creamy flower spikes. Plant singly for good specimens or in groups for screening purposes. Can also be planted to form avenues. The swirling deep fissures in the older specimens give the trunk a sculptural quality. Very attractive yellow and brown autumn foliage.

DETAIL INFORMATION

Height: 37 m.

Spread: 20 m.

Habit: Tall with heavy domed crown.

Bark: Smooth and grey when young, brown and deeply fissured with age.

Foliage: Glossy, dark green oval leaves up to 300 mm long and 80 mm wide. Distinct ribbed veins ending in a spined tooth.

Inflorescence: Creamy white male flowers in catkins 250–350 mm long, opening in June. Green female flowers at the base of catkins.

Fruit: Fruit ripens in October. Bunches of green spiny husks with two nuts in each.

Growth rate: Moderate. Reaches 12 m in 20 years.

Tolerances: Wet, exposed or very cold sites.

Planting: Can be transplanted up to semi-mature size.

Culture: Prefers well-drained soils. Easily raised from seed.

OTHER FORMS

C.s. 'Albomarginata'—a rare form with white margined leaves.

C.s. 'Laciniata'—attractive leaves, the teeth having long filamentous points.

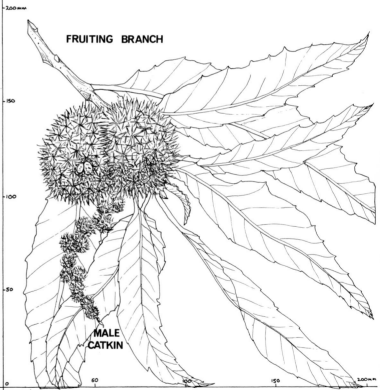

FRUITING BRANCH

MALE CATKIN

Castanea sativa in winter. Equally attractive in winter with dark brown, spiralled trunk and angular, ridged twigs. Pinkish-brown buds.

427

Catalpa bignonioides

Indian Bean Tree

A large, deciduous tree introduced from S.E. USA in the 18th century. Commonly found now in S. England where the warmer climatic conditions suit the tree's growth. Although a relatively fast grower it is short-lived and most specimens have a life expectancy of about 100 years.

DESIGN USE

Catalpa makes an impressive specimen tree with its broad habit, large bright leaves and beautiful white flowers. It tolerates polluted atmospheres so is a good urban tree for planting in parks, open-spaces and city squares. It requires a warm, sunny situation for good development and is not suitable for exposed, rural sites where the soft shoot tips can be easily killed by an early frost.

DETAIL INFORMATION

Height: 17 m.
Spread: 19 m.
Habit: Low, spreading crown with dense foliage.
Bark: Grey-brown with shallow fissures.
Foliage: Large cordate leaves, bright green above with pale green undersurfaces. Smooth pale green petioles.
Inflorescence: Panicles of white flowers spotted with yellow and purple, in July and August.
Fruit: Long, hanging pods, dark brown, persisting through winter.
Growth rate: Moderately fast, reaches 7 m in 20 years.
Tolerances: Cold, wet exposed sites.
Planting: Up to 4 m high standards transplant well.
Culture: Deep, moist loam with sunny aspect.

OTHER FORMS

C.b. 'Aurea'—bright yellow foliage, sparse flowering.
C.b. 'Purpurea'—dark purple young leaves and shoots turning dark green.

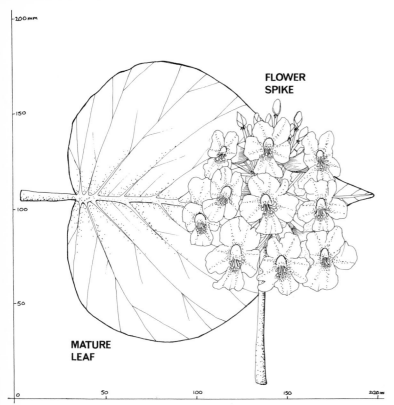

FLOWER SPIKE

MATURE LEAF

C. bignonioides in winter. A short stout bole which is often bent with age. Decay usually sets into the bole as the tree matures.

428

Cedrus libani

Cedar of Lebanon

First introduced in the 17th century, it is now common all over Southern England in parks and gardens. It makes a magnificent specimen tree but is not suitable for instant effect because of its slow growth.

DESIGN USE
Cedars will not tolerate extremely polluted atmospheres but can be grown in urban situations where space allows. As a large spreading tree it is only suitable as a specimen in parks, gardens and open spaces. Older specimens usually require bracing of the larger branches to avoid damage by snow. Mature cedars, like oaks, give a feeling of age and strength and therefore can be used to provide character in a site.

DETAIL INFORMATION
Height: 38 m.
Spread: 32 m.
Habit: Open, flat-topped crown with tiered branches.
Bark: Brown and deeply fissured in older trees.
Foliage: Bunches of 10–20 blue-green, stiff leaves, which are slightly curved.
Inflorescence: Pale green male and female flowers in October.
Fruit: Grey-green, barrel-shaped cones ripening to grey-brown the following year.
Growth rate: Slow, reaching 10 m in 20 years.
Tolerances: Waterlogged or very poor, dry soils.
Planting: Small trees 1 m high in early autumn. 7 m high specimens available.
Culture: Deep, neutral loams in full sun.

OTHER FORMS
C.l. 'Aurea'—rather a rare form with bright yellow foliage and dense habit.

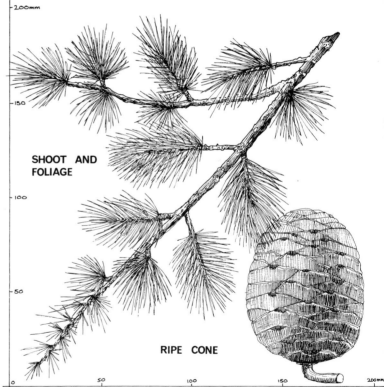

SHOOT AND FOLIAGE

RIPE CONE

C. deodara
Moderately fast growing, with dense foliage that varies from light to dark green.

429

Crataegus monogyna

Common Hawthorn

A native, small tree abundant all over Britain, it is one of the commonest hedge and windbreak plants. As a tree it is picturesque with its dense, round head and gnarled, twisted branches. Hawthorn is able to tolerate a wide range of soils and will grow densely in any exposed position.

DESIGN USE

This tree has something of interest all the year round, with attractive form and flowers and red fruit in autumn. Planted in groups it is a good small urban tree for street, park and development schemes. Also good for shelterbelt and hedge planting in cold exposed places such as coastal sites or motorway embankments. For small garden planting they make interesting specimens.

DETAIL INFORMATION

Height: 14 m.

Spread: 8 m.

Habit: Varies with degree of site exposure but usually has dense, low, shapeless crown.

Bark: Reddish-brown becoming grey and cracked with age.

Foliage: Deeply laciniate leaves 110 mm long, dark shiny green with dark pink veins underneath.

Inflorescence: Dense bunches of fragrant white flowers May–June. Profuse white globular buds.

Fruit: Dark red, globular with single stone.

Growth rate: Rapid in spread, slow in height.

Tolerances: Will not survive extreme acid or wet conditions.

Planting: Up to 4 m high standards.

Culture: Any well-drained soil.

OTHER FORMS

C.m. 'Biflora'—leaves produced earlier.

C.m. 'Stricta'—a vigorous columnar tree with erect branches and white flowers. Good for street planting.

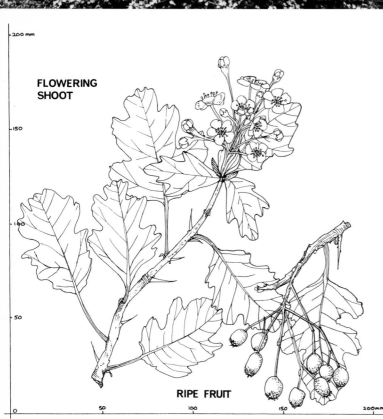

FLOWERING SHOOT

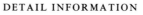

RIPE FRUIT

Crataegus monogyna in winter.
Thickly branched crown with 15 mm long reddish-brown thorns on the shoots.

430

Fagus sylvatica

Common Beech

One of our most beautiful native trees, it can be found growing wild in S.E. England and the Midlands, on chalk and well-drained soils. Used extensively in forestry planting it can also make a good specimen tree in urban situations. As a forest tree it develops a tall slender form, while specimen trees have huge, spreading crowns.

DESIGN USE
Beech is very hardy and wind-firm and tolerates a moderate degree of pollution thus making it both a useful shelterbelt tree and for planting in parks and open spaces. An excellent tree for group planting but requires space to develop. It has delicate green spring leaves and golden autumn foliage and there are several attractive varieties suitable for specimen planting. Suitable also for hedging.

DETAIL INFORMATION
Height: 41 m.
Spread: 36 m.
Habit: Mature specimens have huge, domed crowns with ascending or horizontal branches.
Bark: Smooth, metallic-grey with age.
Foliage: Oval, dark shiny-green leaves, pale green underneath, turn yellow to orange-brown in May.
Inflorescence: Inconspicuous greenish-yellow flowers in catkins that open just after leaves in May.
Fruit: Shiny-brown triangular nuts in pale-brown prickly husks in October.
Growth rate: Slow until established, then fairly fast.
Tolerances: Water-logged acid soils.
Planting: Can be obtained up to semi-mature size.
Culture: Prefers well-drained soils.

OTHER FORMS
F.s. heterophylla—the Fern-leaved Beech with deeply serrated leaves.
F.s. 'Pendula'—Weeping Beech.
F.s. purpurea—Copper Beech with dark purple foliage.

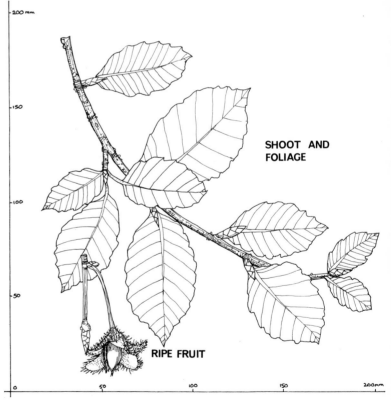

SHOOT AND FOLIAGE

RIPE FRUIT

Fagus sylvatica in winter. Beautiful smooth, straight trunk and arching branches that can root as layers.

431

Fraxinus excelsior

Common Ash

A native deciduous tree, abundant where the soil is rich and damp. It is basically a forest tree with wide spread open branches that produce leaves late in May. It is an extremely hardy and wind-firm tree with light foliage that casts little shade.

DESIGN USE

This tree withstands smoke and exposed positions well, making it a useful tree for cold, urban sites such as windy exposed terraces and courtyards between tall buildings. Its light crown means that shrubs can be grown successfully underneath with no problems of heavy shade. Not suitable for shelterbelts.

DETAIL INFORMATION

Height: 40 m.

Spread: 28 m.

Habit: Tall-domed form with open wide-spreading crown.

Bark: Pale-grey, smooth at first becoming thick and ridged.

Foliage: Opposite pinnate leaves 200–300 mm with 10 mm leaflets. Dark green above, pale green underneath with shallow toothing.

Inflorescence: Bright yellow, fragrant male and female flowers in dense bunches before leaves appear in April.

Fruit: Bunches of winged ash fruits 40 mm long in autumn.

Growth rate: Fast, quickly establishing itself.

Tolerances: Dry sandy soils and wet stagnant conditions.

Planting: Easily moved up to semi-mature size.

Culture: It likes a rich soil and grows best on deep loam.

OTHER FORMS

F.e. 'Aurea'—yellow wood and yellow leaves, in autumn and spring.

F.e. 'Diversifolia'—Single-leaved Ash with an open crown and smooth bark.

F.e. 'Pendula'—long, weeping shoots to the ground.

F.e. 'Transoni'—the golden-leafed Ash, less vigorous habit.

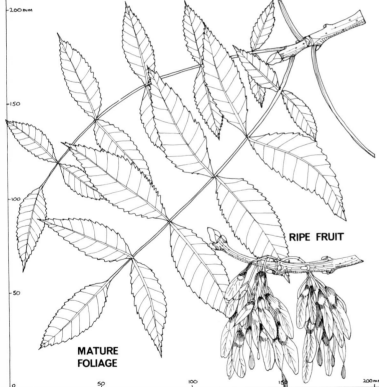

RIPE FRUIT

MATURE FOLIAGE

Fraxinus ornus — Manna Ash.
Grows well on light soils dense rounded head and spreading habit, with panicles of creamy-white fragrant flowers in May. A good urban tree for street and courtyard planting.

Ilex aquifolium

Holly

One of our few native, broadleaved evergreens, it can be found all over England, reaching a height of 20 m where conditions are favourable. In its wild form it is usually found growing in association with oak and beechwoods, as a spreading shrub. It is invaluable as a hardy, shelter tree on exposed sites.

DESIGN USE

Holly grows well in shade and in a variety of soils, and for this reason is excellent for understorey planting in shelterbelts, particularly in coastal situations. Also a good urban tree, able to withstand wind and smoky conditions. It has a habit of retaining dense foliage near the ground and can be trimmed as a hedge. As an ornamental tree or hedge there are many attractive cultivars available.

DETAIL INFORMATION

Height: 20 m.

Spread: 8 m.

Habit: Dense, conical crown, with rather pendulous branches.

Bark: Smooth, grey when young becoming warty.

Foliage: Great variation, but usually glossy, dark green, elliptical leaves with yellowish spines. Dull light green undersurfaces.

Inflorescence: Fragrant, white male and female flowers on separate trees. Short-lived they open in May.

Fruit: Scarlet, globose fruit remaining throughout winter.

Growth rate: Slow, but more vigorous in mild climates.

Tolerances: Dislikes extreme moisture or drought.

Planting: Up to 5 m high, but young 1 m plants are best.

Culture: Any well-drained soil, sun or shade.

OTHER FORMS

I.a. 'Argenteo marginata'—silver marginated leaves.

I.a. 'Golden Queen'—golden marginated leaves.

I.a. 'Pyramidalis'—self-fertile. Pyramidal growth.

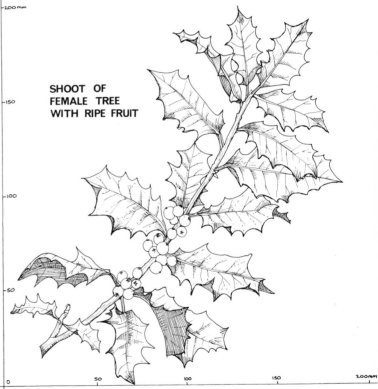

SHOOT OF FEMALE TREE WITH RIPE FRUIT

Ilex × *altaclarensis*—Highclere Holly.
A strong growing hybrid it is more vigorous than *I. aquifolium*, attaining 15 m or more. It has broad, flat leaves up to 75 mm across. Many cultivars available.

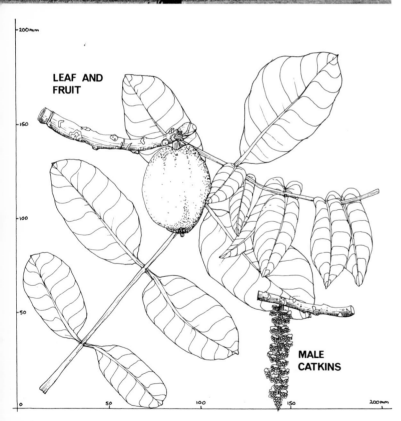

Juglans regia

Common Walnut

Introduced by the Romans as a cultivated nut tree from Asia Minor, it is now commonly found all over England except in the extreme North. A large, handsome, deciduous tree with a spreading crown and deep roots, its wood is very valuable as a veneer and for carving.

DESIGN USE

A tree for long-term planting because of its slow growth. Makes a wonderful specimen for park and open space planting. The foliage is very attractive and has a short summer life which provides excellent conditions for under-planting with shrubs that like partial shade. Suitable also for groups and avenues where space permits. It will not produce fruit for the first fifteen years.

DETAIL INFORMATION

Height: 24 m.
Spread: 18·5 m.
Habit: Spreading crown with big open branches.
Bark: Grey and smooth, fissured with age.
Foliage: Compound, dark yellow-green leaves with yellow veins, aromatic when crushed. The juice will stain brown.
Inflorescence: Greenish male catkins produced in mid-May with leaves. Sparse female flowers.
Fruit: Familiar walnuts in dark green fruits, 50 mm long.
Growth rate: Very slow when young.
Tolerances: Cold, exposed situations and wet soils.
Planting: Plant small standards 3 m high.
Culture: Well-drained, rich soils.

OTHER FORMS

J.r. 'Laciniata'—an unusual, small form, with deeply cut leaflets and purple veins. Not a common tree.

LEAF AND FRUIT

MALE CATKINS

Juglans regia in winter. An attractive appearance in winter with sinuous branches and trunk.

434

Larix decidua

European Larch

A deciduous conifer, introduced into Britain during the 17th century from Central Europe. Valuable as a timber producer, it has many uses in the building industry. It is also a good pioneer tree with very rapid early growth.

DESIGN USE

Larch has particularly good ornamental qualities in spring and autumn when the foliage is very attractive. Plant in groups to show the graceful foliage at its best. useful also as a shelterbelt tree where it makes a fast-growing 'nurse-tree' for slower broad-leaved trees. Not suitable for heavily polluted industrial sites and towns but attractive for parks and open-space planting in urban situations.

DETAIL INFORMATION

Height: 40 m.

Spread: 20 m.

Habit: Varies with age. Old specimens have broad, flat crowns.

Bark: Smooth, greenish when young, becoming brown and ridged.

Foliage: Needles emerge bright green in March, in clusters or singly. They darken through summer and turn yellow in autumn.

Inflorescence: Yellow male flowers and female flowers with dark rose bracts in April.

Fruit: Brown, ovoid cone which takes one year to ripen.

Growth rate: Fast. Reaches 16 m in 20 years.

Tolerances: Very dry or cold water-logged soils.

Planting: Can be transplanted up to 8 m high.

Culture: Tolerant of most soils. Sun or shade.

OTHER FORMS

L.d. polonica—the Polish Larch. A good form often used in forest plantations in Britain.

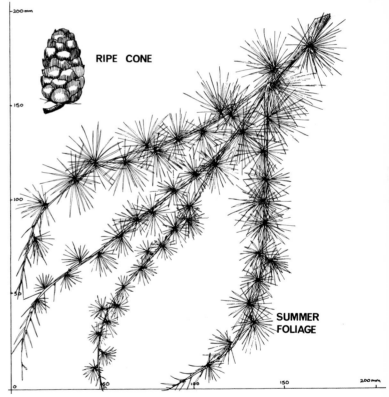

RIPE CONE

SUMMER FOLIAGE

L. decidua in winter. The dead cones are retained throughout winter on pendulous twigs.

435

Liriodendron tulipifera

Tulip Tree

A handsome deciduous tree first introduced from the USA it is commonly found in parks and gardens. It has very good ornamental value with its unique shaped leaves, tulip-like flowers and vigorous growth—a tree of great character in every respect. Liriodendron is closely related to magnolias and it has similar fleshy roots.

DESIGN USE

Particularly suitable for town planting where the young growth is not so easily affected by late frosts. Tolerates polluted conditions very well. Magnificent as a specimen or in groups in parks, squares and courtyards, or as an avenue tree. The foliage remains a rich green during summer, and in autumn turns a superb bright gold.

DETAIL INFORMATION

Height: 36 m.
Spread: 21 m.
Habit: Tall, narrow-domed, dense crown when young.
Bark: Grey, turning orange-brown with age.
Foliage: Four-lobed, ovate-triangular, shiny, bright green leaves. Autumn colours last until November.
Inflorescence: Tulip-like, pale green flowers with orange linings, opening in May–June. Prolific in a good summer.
Fruit: Brown papery fruit persisting through winter.
Growth rate: Very fast, reaching 12 m in 20 years.
Tolerances: Very dry soils and exposed cold sites.
Planting: Best planted as a small standard 3 m high.
Culture: Deep, rich loam in sunny position.

OTHER FORMS

L.t. 'Aureomarginatum'—uncommon form with yellow leaf margins.
L.t. 'Fastigiatum'—fastigiate form.

MATURE LEAF

OPEN FLOWER

Liriodendron tulipifera in winter.
Open winter crown, with low curving branches.

436

Picea omorika

Serbian Spruce

An attractive, tall conifer first introduced in the 19th century from Yugoslavia. It is a very hardy tree and is tolerant of a wide range of soils from limestone to acid peats. Useful also as a timber producer for the building industry.

DESIGN USE

Tolerant of polluted atmospheres, it is a good town tree. The architectural form and dark green foliage is of particular design merit in association with buildings. An excellent feature tree planted in groups or as a specimen in parks and open spaces. A tree of interest all the year round with its graceful flowering branches and egg-shaped cones. Can be planted in woodlands.

DETAIL INFORMATION

Height: 29 m.
Spread: 10 m.
Habit: Narrow, conical crown, with dense branches.
Bark: Orange-brown, flaking with age.
Foliage: Dark, bluish-green needles with white, striped undersides, radiating from shoot.
Inflorescence: Red male flowers in clusters and bright red female flowers, in May.
Fruit: Dark brown egg-shaped cones.
Growth rate: Fast when young, reaches 12 m in 20 years.
Tolerances: Extreme waterlogged soils.
Planting: Best planted when young, 1 m high.
Culture: Light, well-drained soils.

OTHER FORMS

No other forms available but *P. mariana* (the Black Spruce) and *P. rubens* (the Red Spruce) have similar crowns with different foliage.

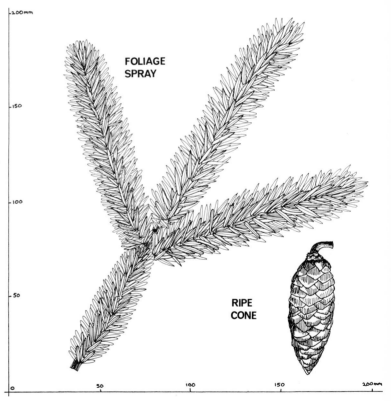

FOLIAGE SPRAY

RIPE CONE

P. brewerana
The Brewer Spruce, with unique crown of hanging branches and blackish-green foliage.

437

Pinus sylvestris

Scots Pine

The only native British Pine found wild in South, Central and Northern England. As a timber-producing conifer it is very important and is widely used in the building industry. Its mature form is very picturesque with rugged trunk and asymmetrical habit.

DESIGN USE

Scots Pine is not suitable for planting in central town or industrial sites because of its intolerance to polluted atmospheres. It will survive in less polluted urban situations and makes a good tree for parks and open spaces. A very good shelter tree in exposed places, particularly coastal sites. Because it is usually transplanted as a small specimen it is best interplanted with fast growing trees which will provide shelter and give visual impact. Very effective when planted with its natural partner, Silver Birch.

DETAIL INFORMATION

Height: 30 m.

Spread: 15 m.

Habit: Flattened, conical crown on tall, bare trunk.

Bark: Variable, usually dark reddish and scaly.

Foliage: Bluish-green needles in pairs growing on dwarf shoots. Needles are longer in young vigorous plants.

Inflorescence: Yellow male flowers at the base of the new shoots in May. Red globular female flowers at shoot tips.

Fruit: Grey-brown ovoid cones one year after pollination.

Growth rate: Moderately fast. Reaches 12 m in 20 years.

Tolerances: Polluted atmospheres and wet, clay soils.

Planting: 1 m high plants are best, but can be transplanted up to 5 m high.

Culture: Well-drained slightly acid soils.

OTHER FORMS

P.s. 'Aurea'—unusual yellowish foliage.

P.s. 'Fastigiata'—rare form with narrow habit.

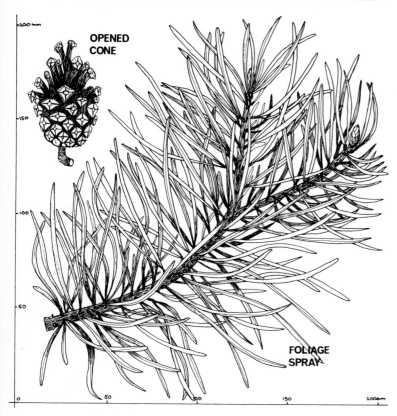

OPENED CONE

FOLIAGE SPRAY

Pinus contorta latifolia
The Lodgepole Pine, faster growing than the Scots and is useful for planting in difficult moorland sites.

438

Pinus nigra maritima

Corsican Pine

Widely distributed over South and East Europe it is one of the forms of the Black Pine. Commonly planted on heaths, clay and peat soils it is fast growing and is a valuable timber producer.

DESIGN USE

As it can withstand severe drought when fully established it is a useful tree for fixing sand-dunes and planting in other coastal situations. In less polluted areas it is an interesting tree for planting as a specimen or groups in parks, open spaces and gardens. Its evergreen habit gives it interest all the year round, and the dark foliage stands out well against paler leaved trees. Particularly useful as a shelter tree on exposed sites.

DETAIL INFORMATION

Height: 35 m.
Spread: 15 m.
Habit: Open, columnar crown with flat top.
Bark: Dark grey and flaking. Heavily ridged in older trees.
Foliage: Grey-green needles in pairs. Distinct twisting, particularly in younger trees.
Inflorescence: Yellow-green male flowers and reddish ovoid female flowers in June.
Fruit: Pointed ovoid cones, shiny brown when ripe.
Growth rate: Slow, reaching 10 m in 20 years.
Tolerances: Very alkaline, or wet, heavy soils.
Planting: 1 m high plants are best, but can be transplanted up to 5 m.
Culture: Most well-drained soils.

OTHER FORMS

P.n.—the Austrian Pine with an irregular, untidy habit.
P.n. caramanica—the Crimean Pine. A rather uncommon vigorous form.

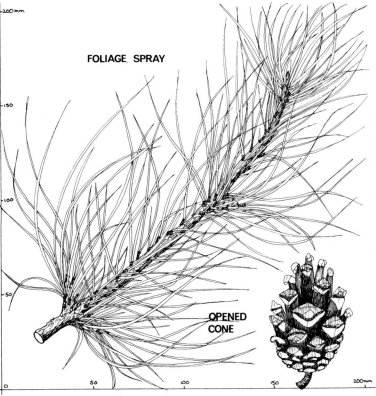

FOLIAGE SPRAY

OPENED CONE

Pinus uncinata
Syn. *P. mugo rostrata*, the Mountain Pine. A spreading form which can be treated as a shrub.

439

Platanus × hispanica

London Plane

A hardy, deciduous tree with a rapid rate of growth forming a large round head. Thought to be a hybrid of *P. occidentalis* and *P. orientalis* and first recorded in Oxford in 1663. The plane has been London's principal tree since the 18th century.

DESIGN USE

The large and bold green leaves and dappled trunk are of particular design merit. Because of its tolerance to polluted atmospheres it is invaluable for planting in industrial areas, and as a street tree it is able to withstand hard pruning and compacted soils. Its hardiness and resistance to cold winds make it useful for seaside planting and other cold exposed sites. The globular seed heads hang on the tree all winter.

DETAIL INFORMATION

Height: 30 m.

Spread: 25 m.

Habit: Wide-spreading, rounded open crown.

Bark: Tan, flaking off in winter to reveal creamy-brown patches.

Foliage: Large palmate, mid-green, sycamore-like leaves, borne alternately on stems.

Inflorescence: Separate male and female flowers in spherical clusters in April.

Fruit: Pendulous, globular seed heads, turning brown in September.

Growth rate: Fast reaching 12 m in 20 years.

Tolerances: Cold, exposed sites and very dry soils.

Planting: All sizes up to semi-mature.

Culture: All types of deep, well-drained soils.

OTHER FORMS

P. × hispanica 'Suttneri'—a rare form with attractive white variegated leaves.

Reaches 23 × 3·5 m

FLOWER

FRUIT

Platanus orientalis
Larger than *P. × hispanica* with short, broad trunk and rounded head. A long-lived tree.

440

Populus alba

White Poplar

An introduced, deciduous tree, naturalized in S.E. England. Of medium stature it produces an abundance of sucker growth making it unsuitable for planting near buildings. A very attractive white-foliaged tree which can be pruned to produce a shapely form.

DESIGN USE
Excellent for coastal planting where it can help to reduce soil erosion by forming thickets. Useful for shelterbelts and windbreaks in open, exposed situations. In urban parks and open spaces it is a good ornamental tree when planted in groups, particularly near water. On clay soils it should be planted well away from buildings to avoid structural damage from soil shrinkage by the roots.

DETAIL INFORMATION
Height: 21 m.
Spread: 13 m.
Habit: Dense, rounded crown with slightly drooping branches.
Bark: Grey-green, becoming creamy-white and pitted.
Foliage: Grey-green oval leaves with white downy undersides. White downy buds, shoots and petioles.
Inflorescence: Catkins appear before leaves in March. Grey and red male, and green female catkins.
Fruit: Fruit capsules contain small, fluffy seeds.
Growth rate: Fast. Reaches 13 m in 20 years.
Tolerances: Very acid soils.
Planting: Up to semi-mature size.
Culture: Most soils, tolerates chalk and dryness.

OTHER FORMS
P.a. 'Pyramidalis'—pyramidal habit with less suckering.
P.a. 'Richardii'—yellowish leaves.

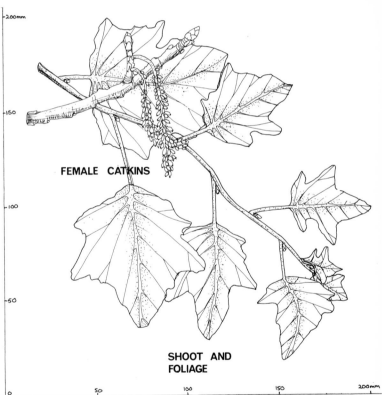

FEMALE CATKINS

SHOOT AND FOLIAGE

Populus canescens
The grey Poplar, with greyish-green downy leaves and dark grey bark. A good ornamental tree reaching 35 × 6 m.

441

Populus 'Serotina'

Black Italian Poplar

Believed to have originated in Italy in 1755, it is a late-leafing hybrid from the crossing between *P. nigra* and *P. deltoides*. Widely planted in Europe and America as a timber producer and for screening purposes. As a clone it is propagated vegetatively and only in the male form.

DESIGN USE

At its best as a screening tree for tall buildings and factories in rural situations. It is resistant to polluted atmospheres so it is therefore good for industrial town, parks and open spaces, where it can form interesting specimens. Because of its fast growth it is useful where an instant effect is required. Attractive reddish-brown early leaves.

DETAIL INFORMATION

Height: 40 m.
Spread: 20 m.
Habit: Irregular one-sided crown with open curving branches.
Bark: Grey, deeply fissured with prominent ridges.
Foliage: Triangular-ovate, grey-green leaves emerge in May, a reddish-brown colour.
Inflorescence: Conspicuous red male catkins open in April.
Fruit: No fruit. Male form only.
Growth rate: Fast. Reaches 22 m in 20 years.
Tolerances: Very acid soils.
Planting: Up to semi-mature size.
Culture: Grows equally well in moist or well-drained soils.

OTHER FORMS

P. 'S. Aurea'—Golden Poplar. Rich yellow leaves and pyramidal habit.

SHOOT AND FOLIAGE

MALE CATKINS

Populus tremula—Aspen. Open crown and attractive greyish-green leaves that turn a beautiful yellow in autumn.

442

Prunus avium

Wild Cherry

A flowering native tree common all over Britain particularly in woodlands over chalk soils. It is a medium-sized, fast growing tree, planted mainly for its beautiful display of white spring blossom. It can also be used as a stock for grafting of cultivated and ornamental cherries. The seeds are widely dispersed by birds.

DESIGN USE
An outstanding ornamental tree it has all the flowering qualities of cherry together with an attractive, natural form. The bark is a lovely shiny metallic-brown, and in autumn the foliage turns a bright yellow and red. Good for urban or rural planting in parks, open spaces and as a street tree. For maximum flowering effect plant in groups or lines.

DETAIL INFORMATION
Height: 28 m.
Spread: 18 m.
Habit: Dense, broad crown with upward spreading branches.
Bark: Smooth greyish-brown, peeling in bands with age.
Foliage: Elliptical, serrated leaves with reddish petioles 30 mm long. Red glands at leaf base.
Inflorescence: Bunches of white flowers in early May. Very profuse.
Fruit: Edible blackish-red fruits with black stone. June.
Growth rate: Moderately fast. 15 m in 20 years.
Tolerances: Wet, acid soils.
Planting: Up to semi-mature tree size.
Culture: Deep well-drained soils.

OTHER FORMS
P.a. 'Plena'—a profusion of double white, long-lasting flowers in May.

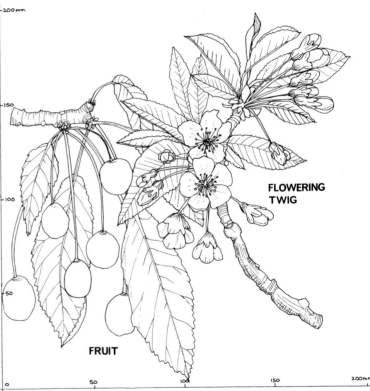

FLOWERING TWIG

FRUIT

Prunus padus—Bird Cherry. Smaller than *P. avium* White fragrant flowers in May and black fruit.

443

Quercus ilex

Holm Oak

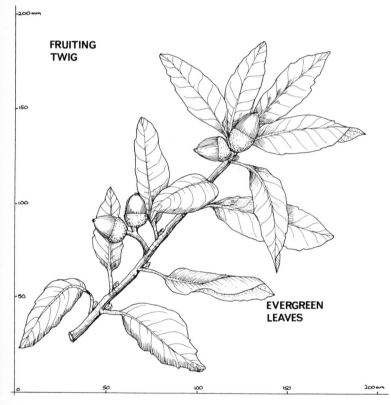

A large evergreen tree first introduced into Britain during the 16th century. An excellent tree for coastal planting, where it can naturalize. It is broad and dense and is one of the best of evergreen trees in terms of mature form and round the year interest.

DESIGN USE

Its resistance to salt spray and wind makes it a suitable tree for coastal shelterbelts and windbreaks. An impressive sight when used as an avenue tree, but is very slow growing and can only be planted when very small. Could be interplanted with faster growing trees which are removed when it has become established. Can also be treated as a large shrub as the foliage withstands clipping. As a specimen it requires space to develop.

DETAIL INFORMATION

Height: 28 m.
Spread: 28 m.
Habit: Broad domed, densely-leaved crown.
Bark: Black and rugged, divided into squares.
Foliage: Oval, dark green shiny leaves. Leathery texture with pale, hairy under-surfaces.
Inflorescence: Yellow male catkins, green-grey female catkins open in June.
Fruit: Light green acorns require 2 years to ripen.
Growth rate: Slow. Reaches 4 m in 20 years.
Tolerances: Will not tolerate cold, wet soils.
Planting: Young plants 1 m high only.
Culture: Slightly acid, well-drained soils. Sun or shade.

OTHER FORMS

Q.i. 'Fordii'—lanceolate leaves.
Q.i. 'Laurifolia'—long lanceolate shiny leaves.
Q.i. 'Rotundifolia'—round leaves, edible acorns.

FRUITING TWIG

EVERGREEN LEAVES

Quercus petraea—Sessile Oak.
Taller of the native oaks with dark green, thick leaves and clusters of acorns.

444

Quercus robur

Pendunculate Oak

A native, lowland oak growing as a dominant tree on clay soils. It is a tall spreading tree which can reach considerable girth dimensions and age. Some specimens have been recorded as being over 400 years old. Valuable as a timber producer.

DESIGN USE

A good tree for parkland and woodland it can be planted as a specimen in small groups or in an avenue. A mature specimen can present an impressive sight with its rugged form. Because of the light, open crown, other plants can be grown successfully underneath. Not suitable for tight, urban situations as it is extremely deep rooted and requires space to develop to its fullest extent.

DETAIL INFORMATION

Height: 35 m.
Spread: 36 m.
Habit: Spreading, domed crown with few large branches.
Bark: Grey, fissured bark, smooth when young.
Foliage: Pinnately, lobed, glabrous dark green leaves.
Inflorescence: Male catkins open in May. Female flowers from leaf axils of annual shoots.
Fruit: Whitish-green acorns in pairs, becoming brown.
Growth rate: Moderate. Reaches 12 m in 20 years.
Tolerances: Poor sandy soils.
Planting: Up to semi-mature size.
Culture: Deep moist loams.

OTHER FORMS

Q.r. 'Concordia'—Golden Oak. Greenish-yellow leaves. Uncommon tree.
Q.r. 'Fastigiata'—the Cypress Oak. Upright habit, good for restricted sites.

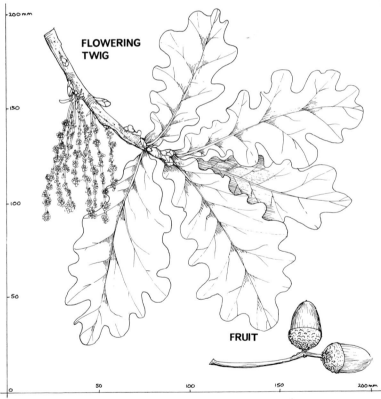

FLOWERING TWIG

FRUIT

Quercus cerris — Turkey Oak.
Upright crown with dark bark and rough, green leaves. Mossy acorn cups.

445

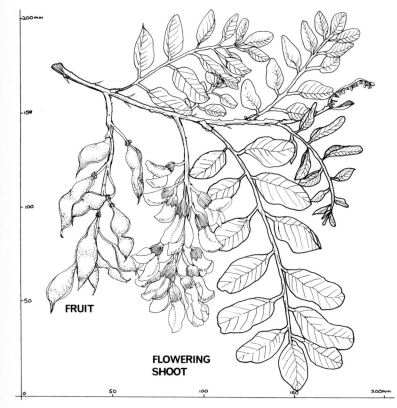

Robinia pseudoacacia

False Acacia

A deciduous tree first introduced into Europe from N. America by Jean Robin, a French botanist, in the 17th century. It is an excellent ornamental, town tree and on sandy soil it spreads naturally by root-suckers.

DESIGN USE

A very hardy, smoke resistant tree, which combined with its open light foliage and habit makes it good for planting in confined urban situations. It has shallow roots and prefers a well-drained soil and therefore does well planted in paved courtyards or as a street tree. It has very attractive bright-green foliage and a profusion of white, fragrant flowers.

DETAIL INFORMATION

Height: 25 m.

Spread: 16 m.

Habit: Open, domed crown with irregular, twisting branches.

Bark: Smooth and brown, becoming deeply fissured with age.

Foliage: Pinnate, compound leaves with oval leaflets. Bright green upper surfaces, bluish-green on under surfaces.

Inflorescence: White, fragrant pea flowers in drooping, dense racemes. 100–200 mm long in June.

Fruit: Dark brown oblong pods in bunches. Ripening in autumn.

Growth rate: Fast. Reaches 13 m in 20 years.

Tolerances: Cold exposed positions and wet soils.

Planting: Any size up to 8 m high.

Culture: Light well-drained soils in full sun.

OTHER FORMS

R.p. 'Bessoniana'—dense, compact habit.

R.p. 'Fastigiata'—columnar habit. Spineless.

R.p. 'Frisia'—golden foliage. Orange in autumn.

FRUIT

FLOWERING SHOOT

R. pseudoacacia in winter. Twisted, fluted trunk with brittle, rough branches. Dark red shoot and small winter buds.

446

Salix alba

White Willow

Common as a native waterside tree in S. England and the Midlands. Often pollarded for the production of shoots for basket making. There are several varieties of white willow which are planted solely for their timber, which is light, tough and pliable.

DESIGN USE

A large, beautiful, fast-growing tree it is useful for group planting on damp sites. A good tree for instant effect because it can be planted thickly as whips, which will quickly establish themselves. Its slender arching stems and foliage can be coppiced to produce an attractive screen or windbreak, particularly with the coloured stem varieties.

DETAIL INFORMATION

Height: 25 m.
Spread: 16 m.
Habit: Tall, conical crown with ascending branches.
Bark: Dark grey and ridged.
Foliage: Lanceolate serrated leaves 80 mm long. Silky blue-grey and white underneath.
Inflorescence: Yellow male catkins and green female catkins on stalks in May.
Fruit: Fluffy white seed dispersed by the wind.
Growth rate: Very fast. Reaches 22 m in 20 years.
Tolerances: Very dry, poor soils.
Planting: From whips to semi-mature size.
Culture: Prefers moist soils.

OTHER FORMS

S.a. 'Chermesina'—orange-red stems in winter.
S.a. 'Caerulea'—Cricket-bat Willow. Purple stems. Wood used for cricket bats.
S.a. 'Sericea'—striking silver-white leaves.

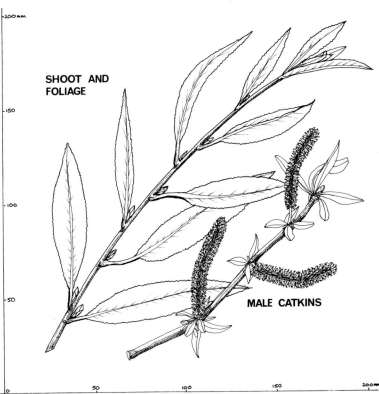

SHOOT AND FOLIAGE

MALE CATKINS

Salix fragilis in winter. The Crack Willow with heavy, twisted branches. Often pollarded, it has orange shoots in spring.

447

Salix × chrysocoma

Weeping Willow

An introduced, deciduous tree (often mistakenly called *S. babylonica* which is the uncommon Chinese Weeping Willow of the willow-pattern fame). Mature specimen trees are a spectacular sight with the golden-yellow young branches in winter.

DESIGN USE

Weeping Willow is usually associated with lakes and rivers where its superb winter colour can look its best reflected on the water surface. Makes a good specimen tree for waterside planting in urban and rural situations and provides colour and interest when there is little else around. Gives an instant effect when planted. Requires space to develop.

DETAIL INFORMATION

Height: 23 m.

Spread: 21 m.

Habit: Broad-domed crown with curved, pendulous branches.

Bark: Shallow-ridged, grey-brown in colour.

Foliage: Yellowish-green lanceolate leaves with silky white hairs underneath. Yellow autumn foliage.

Inflorescence: Yellow male catkins 80 mm long in April.

Usually male only clone.

Fruit: No fruit.

Growth rate: Very fast.

Tolerances: Poor sandy soils in exposed positions.

Planting: Trees up to 8 m high.

Culture: Prefers moist soils, but does well in dry or damp situations.

OTHER FORMS

No other forms available although *S. purpurea* 'Pendula', the American Weeping Willow, is similar but with a smaller habit and purple bark.

SHOOT AND FOLIAGE

Salix matsudana 'Tortuosa'. The Contorted Willow with sinuous stems and shoots, curled leaves, and semi-pendulous habit.

448

Sorbus aria

Whitebeam

A small deciduous tree, native to parts of England on chalk and limestone. Commonly planted in gardens and streets, it is a hardy attractive tree with its beautiful white underleaves. It has several cultivars that are an improvement on the basic form, with bigger leaves and fruit.

DESIGN USE

Because of its upright habit and resistance to wind and pollution it is particularly valuable as a street tree or in restricted urban places such as around buildings. Also good for seaside planting and shelterbelts. The most attractive feature of this tree is the foliage, which is quite spectacular when ruffled by the wind in massed planting. For the maximum effect plant in groups or lines 4 m apart.

DETAIL INFORMATION

Height: 12 m.

Spread: 9 m.

Habit: Upright, pyramidal habit with radiating branches.

Bark: Smooth and grey when young, becomes ridged with age.

Foliage: Simple toothed ovate leaves, silver in spring turning bright green with grey, downy underneath. Yellow in autumn.

Inflorescence: White flowers in half-umbellate heads, 15 mm across, are heavily scented and appear in May–June.

Fruit: Ovoid, dark red berries ripen in September.

Growth rate: Moderate. Reaches 10 m in 20 years.

Tolerances: Will not tolerate cold, water-logged soils.

Planting: Transplants up to semi-mature size.

Culture: Any well-drained soils, particularly chalk.

OTHER FORMS

S.a. 'Chrysophylla'—yellow upper leaf surfaces.

S.a. 'Decaisneana'—large, glossy leaves and large berries.

S.a. 'Lutescens'—yellowish green leaves.

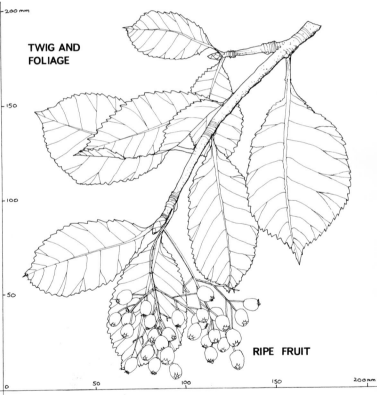

TWIG AND FOLIAGE

RIPE FRUIT

Sorbus aucuparia—Rowan. Small hardy tree with pinnate-compound leaves and berries that are particularly attractive to birds.

449

Tilia × europaea

Common Lime

A large deciduous tree, believed to be a natural hybrid between *T. platyphyllos* and *T. cordata*. Found as a cultivated tree all over Britain in parks, gardens and at roadsides. As a street tree it is often pollarded with ugly results. Not a good town tree because it has many bad characteristics.

DESIGN USE

Because of sticky 'honey dew' on the leaves Common Lime is not suitable for planting in and around car parks or, as a street tree. Planting in urban situations is restricted to parks and open spaces where it can form magnificent specimens. Very effective for group and avenue planting in rural or country parks where its vast proportions, in terms of scale, can best be appreciated.

DETAIL INFORMATION

Height: 40 m.

Spread: 20 m.

Habit: Tall, billowing domed crown with large branches.

Bark: Smooth grey, becoming fissured with age.

Foliage: Heart-shaped, toothed, pale green leaves 60–100 mm long. Green, glabrous petiole.

Inflorescence: Bunches of yellowish-white flowers with bracted stalk in July. Rich in nectar.

Fruit: Round, grey 'nut' holding single seed. Ripens in September.

Growth rate: Moderately fast. Reaches 10 m in 20 years.

Tolerances: Does not like wet-acid or poor-dry soils.

Planting: Any size up to semi-mature.

Culture: Deep, moist soils preferred.

OTHER FORMS

No other forms but a similar species is *T. platyphyllos* SCOP., the Large-Leafed Lime, which is more shapely than *T. × europaea*.

FLOWERING SHOOT

FRUIT

Tilia cordata
Native Small-Leafed Lime with dark shiny green leaves and cracked dark grey bark. Suffers from 'honey-dew'.

450

Ulmus procera

English Elm

Once abundant all over England in well-drained soils, mainly as a result of hedgerow planting it is now largely disappearing from our landscapes because of the ravages of Dutch Elm Disease. Often replaced with the more resistant *U. × hollandica* hybrids such as 'Commelin'.

DESIGN USE

A stately tree, whose magnificent form typifies the English landscape. Not suitable for urban situations since they are known to shed large branches without warning. Also their large, spreading form requires space to develop. The fast suckering shoots from the parent tree roots makes it a suitable tree for naturalizing in rural situations. Very hardy against frost and wind.

DETAIL INFORMATION

Height: 35 m.

Spread: 20 m.

Habit: Tall, billowing domed crown with few branches.

Bark: Dark brown and deeply furrowed.

Foliage: Oval, dark green leaves with rough, hairy upper surfaces and bright gold autumn colour. Varying in size and shape.

Inflorescence: Red tufts of stamens on shoots during March. Very profuse.

Fruit: Small, winged fruits with seed enclosed in membrane.

Growth rate: Fast when young, reaching 12 m in 20 years.

Tolerances: Waterlogged, cold soils.

Planting: Available up to semi-mature size.

Culture: Well-drained deep soils.

OTHER FORMS

U.p. 'Louis van Houtte'—upright, golden-leafed form.

U.p. 'Variegata'—white variegated foliage.

U.p. 'Viminalis'—narrow upright form.

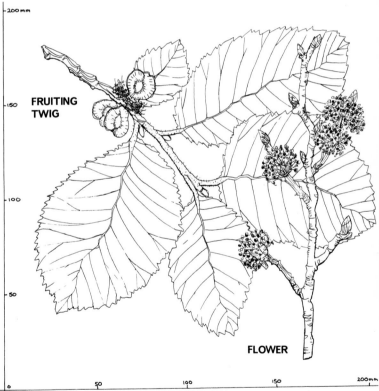

FRUITING TWIG

FLOWER

Ulmus glabra—The Wych Elm.
Large tree with dark green leaves. Several attractive forms available such as the weeping 'Pendula'

451

GENERAL INDEX

452